BEHAVING
Managing yourself and others

BEHAVING
Managing yourself and others

Baden Eunson
B.A.(Hons.), Dip.Ed., M.Env.Sci.
Lecturer in Communication
Box Hill College of TAFE

McGRAW-HILL BOOK COMPANY Sydney

New York St Louis San Francisco Auckland Bogotá
Caracas Hamburg Lisbon London Madrid Mexico Milan
Montreal New Delhi Oklahoma City Paris San Juan
São Paulo Singapore Tokyo Toronto

A52022

_____

National Library of Australia
Cataloguing-in-Publication data:
  Eunson, Baden.
    Behaving : managing yourself and others.

    Includes index.
    ISBN 0 07 452022 9.

    1. Organizational behavior. 2. Human behavior. 3.
    Personnel management. I. Title.

  658.3

_____

Produced in Australia by McGraw-Hill Book Company Australia Pty Limited
    4 Barcoo Street, Roseville, NSW 2069
Typeset in Australia by G.T. Setters Pty Limited
Printed in Singapore by Kyodo Printing Co (S'pore) Pte Ltd

Sponsoring Editor: Isabel Hogan
Production Editor: Daphne Rawling
Designer: George Sirett
Cover Illustrator: Michael Leunig
Technical Illustrator: Colin Bardill
Illustrator: Fabian Micali

for Annette

Contents

Preface

THIS book deals with some aspects of human behaviour, both inside and outside of organisations. Each of us relates differently to different organisations, acting in our various roles—employee, employer, client, opponent, and so on.

It's important to improve our understanding of human behaviour in such settings, for a number of reasons. First, even though the technical *content* of what we do—being employed, not being employed, being an engineer, clerk, process worker, manager, tinker, tailor, soldier, sailor—is different from what others do, we all have one thing in common, crashingly obvious though that is: we all have to deal with people. Our perceptions of others and the ways in which we communicate with others is central to our lives. Even someone who has chosen a life of total solitude (if such a thing is possible nowadays) is making a powerful statement about his or her ability, or inability, to get on with others.

Second, organisations are not simply bricks and mortar, products and processes; they are comprised of people as well. In fact, it is not uncommon for organisations to spend 70, 80, 90 per cent or more of their budgets on paying for people. Sadly, it is also not uncommon for organisations to ignore this fact totally, and for managers to continue to devote 80 per cent of their attention to the 20 per cent non-human factor.

The truth is dawning in many organisations that human resources are the key to productivity and satisfaction. This truth is also dawning at the national and international level as well, where time and again nations poor in physical resources but with highly developed human resources outperform nations which are rich in physical resources but are also restrained by underdeveloped human resources.

In an age which increasingly glorifies the machine and denigrates the human, it is important to point out these truths.

This book is about managing yourself and others. "Self-management" here is understood in two senses: at the personal level, we can better manage ourselves by learning more about managing stress and time, about being more assertive, about understanding the games we and others play, about understanding how we communicate without words, about what motivates us.

At the organisational level, there appears to be a long-term shift in power occurring, from the top of hierarchies to further down such hierarchies. This trend expresses itself variously as increased participation in decision-making, industrial democracy, making jobs more meaningful and satisfying, and so on.

This is a fascinating and at times frustrating thing to watch and experience, and whether the trend will continue, stop or reverse, no one can say. What can be said is that the clear line that separates those who manage from those who are managed, those who control from those who are controlled, is becoming blurred. Self-management skills are thus becoming important at the organisational level, as well as at the personal level; indeed, the two types of skills are merely two sides of the one coin.

This book draws upon research and analysis in various fields, predominantly those of organisational analysis, organisational behaviour, management and human relations. There is much in these fields that is enlightening, culturally unbiased, scientifically valid and liberating; there is also much which is none of these things. Much of the work in this area tends to place the values and needs of formally constituted management over and above those of other groups, such as labour and the community, and projects American values and needs on to all cultures. This book is an attempt to neutralise such distortions, and to discriminate between the worthwhile and the non-worthwhile in these important areas in the study of human behaviour.

This book was originally designed for use by students of individual behaviour, organisational behaviour and communication skills in TAFE Colleges, Colleges of Advanced Education and Universities. It can however be read with interest and profit by anyone—we are all students of human behaviour.

I would like to thank Margaret Patrickson, Roger Fry, Jenny Beaumont, Gay Storey, Deane Wells and Annette Carruthers for reading the manuscript. Thanks are also due to Gil Teague, Stephen Ives, Stuart Laurence, Isabel Hogan from McGraw-Hill, and Daphne Rawling, for much patience and perceptive criticism. Thanks also to Michael Leunig for the cover illustration.

Acknowledgments

Grateful acknowledgment is made to the following for permission to reproduce material:

Statistics Group of the Legislative Research Service, Parliament House, Canberra, for "Five Sector Analysis", from Jones, Barry, *Sleepers, Wake! Technology and the Future of Work* (Oxford University Press, Melbourne, 1983); Methuen London Ltd, 11 New Fetter Lane, London

EC4P 4EE, United Kingdom, for quote from Townsend, Sue, *The Secret Diary of Adrian Mole, Age 13 3/4*, (1985), and for quote from Python, Monty, *Life of Brian* (1979); Faber and Faber, 3 Queens Square, London, WC1N 3AL, United Kingdom, for quote from Eliot, T.S., "The Rock", *Collected Poems, 1909–1962* (1962), and quote from Ian Dury, *Hard Lines: New Poetry and Prose (1983)*.

I would also like to thank my students, not only for their general contributions to my own learning, but also for the specific input into Tables 9.3 and 9.4.

Work: The emerging context of organisational behaviour

What does the experience of work mean to human beings? What is it that distinguishes work from non-work, and are these distinctions static and eternal?

What will work and non-work be like in 10, 100 or 1000 years from now? To a considerable extent, the answer to this lies in finding out what work was like 10, 100 or 1000 years in our past.

In Chapter 1 (Work and the future) we attempt just this by considering traditional values of work and non-work, and also considering the ways in which work in different sectors—such as primary, secondary and tertiary sectors—has changed up until now. Several models which consider how such historical trends might continue or alter are examined. A number of technological and human checkpoints are identified, and some futures are described using the scenario technique.

1

Work and the future

The real danger is not that computers
will begin to think like men, but that
men will begin to think like
computers.
Sydney J. Harris

If there is technological advance
without social advance, there is, almost
automatically, an increase in human
misery.
Michael Harrington

Let us be grateful to Adam our
benefactor. He cut us out of the
"blessing" of idleness and won for us
the "curse" of labour.
Mark Twain

Pessimists have already begun to worry
about what is going to replace
automation.
Laurence J. Peter

To be able to fill leisure intelligently is
the last product of civilisation.
Arnold Toynbee

What is the future of work? Is
unemployment here to stay? Are
computers and robots forces for good
or for evil? Will future society be a
utopia where the work is done by
machines and most of us lead lives of
unending leisure, or a dystopia where
most of the work is done by machines
and most of us lead lives of poverty-
stricken unemployment while the
machine-owners lead lives of luxurious
leisure behind the walls of armed
compounds? Are these the only two
alternatives? Will the workforce of
tomorrow participate more, or less, in
decision-making? Will work organisations be large in scale or small?

All of these questions are asked
often and loudly by people today. The
changes that society is passing through
seem to be unique, without precedent.
Many people seem to be suffering from
"future shock", or the shock delivered
by a society where history seems to be
speeding up, bombarding us with a
bewildering array of sociological,
psychological, economic, political and
scientific changes.

Work: Future and past

Other chapters in this book will
examine a variety of ideas that impact
upon our working and personal lives—
motivation, non-verbal communication, assertiveness, decision-making
and problem-solving, organisational
design, and so on. All these concepts,
however, need to be seen within a
wider context. We need to ask basic
questions, such as: What is the point
of understanding the motivation to

work, if there is not going to be any work? What is the point of using time-management techniques to maximise efficiency, when our future world might be one of voluntary or compulsory leisure, where the whole point is to *not* get things done?

No mass society in history has ever had to face these problems. The only social classes that have ever had to face them have been leisure classes, nobilities, ultra-wealthy middle and upper classes. The models they present to us of people coping with dramatic changes in lifestyle are sometimes encouraging and inspiring, sometimes discouraging and depressing.

Many people have many ideas about what is happening to us today. Yet is is obvious that, in order to understand the present, we need to understand the past, and also to try and peer into the future. There is, predictably, much confusion and disagreement about what the future holds for us but, interestingly, there is also much disagreement about what actually did happen in the past which gave rise to our present circumstances. Let's have a brief look at the past (or pasts) that made us what we are today.

Work and life
Traditional patterns

Ten thousand years ago, the vast majority of people were nomads, moving from place to place, never settling down. People survived by hunting wild animals and gathering wild plants and seeds. Around 8000 BC, people began to domesticate wild animals and wild plants, raising herds of cattle, sheep and other animals, and fields of crops such as wheat, rice and barley. Obviously, such domestication could only take place if people remained in the one spot; towns and cities thus developed. Men and women developed new tools and technologies—wheeled transport, sailing vessels, mining and metallurgy, fabric manufacture, writing, irrigation, animal and plant husbandry. Historians refer to this phase as the *agricultural revolution*, or agricultural–pastoral revolution.

This revolution, Toynbee suggests, meant that humanity was no longer just a parasite upon nature but in fact became a partner with nature (Toynbee 1972). People no longer depended upon the vagaries of animal migrations and random distributions of plants, but instead began to produce food instead of simply gathering it. Producing meant planning, having foresight and self-control, planning harvests and slaughters far in the future and forgoing the impulse to live for the day.

Subsistence, surplus, specialists. . .

Whereas previously families and hunting bands lived at the subsistence level, gathering only enough for their immediate needs, now it was possible to increase food production dramatically so that surpluses were available. Such surpluses meant that specialised workers, producing goods and services that were not for immediate consumption, could be employed and fed. Such workers were, for example, metallurgists making swords and ploughshares, and irrigation workers reclaiming lands from rivers in Sumer and Egypt. While the metallurgists were something of a professional elite, however, the irrigation workers were little better than slave labour, compelled to work by the absolute monarchs and god-kings of the times.

The agricultural revolution appeared to rise in the Middle East and thence spread out to other parts of the globe, although as much controversy surrounds this as other questions of historical geography, such as where did humanity first appear.

The agricultural revolution was called a revolution because it was a process which radically transformed the way human beings lived. It took thousands of years for the new technologies and value systems of that revolution to penetrate to all parts of the globe. In fact, to some extent this revolution is still occurring: there are still hunter-gatherer nomadic cultures in some parts of the world, and most such cultures are becoming less nomadic.

For thousands of years, no similar revolutionary processes occurred.

The industrial revolution

Then, in the late 1700s in England and in Europe, a second wave of technological breakthroughs began to transform society. Agriculture was transformed as new inventions, particularly in textiles, led to dramatic increases in productivity. Most labour in the textile industry was of the "cottage industry" type: families would process and spin cotton within their homes, giving finished and semi-finished products to larger manufacturers (note that *manufacturer* simply means "maker-by-hand").

New technologies, however, made it more cost-effective to have workers centralised rather than decentralised, working with big machines rather than small ones such as spinning wheels and looms. Thus manufactories or factories sprang up, and workers—male and female, adult and child—now had to leave home each day to go to another place to work, not in order to produce food, clothing and shelter, but to earn money to buy food, clothing and shelter from others. Many crafts began to disappear as poorer quality, but much cheaper, goods began to emerge from the factories. Many families were broken up as adults and children were compelled by law or necessity to seek work where they could find it.

The machines multiply—but not without resistance

Agriculture became more automated, with new inventions making sowing of seed and reaping of crops less dependent upon vast numbers of semi-skilled employees. Substantial unemployment caused by such trends, together with the loss of common lands to enclosure by large private landowners, meant that many rural people had to seek work in the new city factories. Thus cities grew enormously in population. The new urban proletariat, with nothing but their labour to sell, worked in sometimes quite appalling conditions in factories which were described by the English poet William Blake as "dark satanic mills".

From 1811 to 1813, many English craftsmen in the textile industry rioted, smashing up the machinery that was putting many of them out of work. The *Luddites*, as they came to be called, were seen by many as romantic Robin Hoods, harassing the wealthy owners of the new labour-displacing technology. The Luddites were brutally suppressed with shootings, hangings and transportation. Since then, "Luddite" has become a byword for a person who is opposed to the introduction of new technology. Whether Luddites and neo-Luddites are villains, standing in the way of benign progress, or heroes, defending human dignity against the incursions of the machine, is still not clear.

Not one, but many industrial revolutions

Landes (1984) identifies four major features of the industrial revolution:

1. the substitution of inanimate for animal sources of power (in particular, the introduction of steam power fuelled by coal);
2. substitution of machines for human skills and strength;
3. invention of new methods for transforming matter (iron, steel, industrial chemicals); and
4. the organisation of work in large, centrally powered units (factories, forges, mills) that made possible the more immediate supervision of the production process and a more efficient division of labour.

Some historians have in fact called this period the first industrial revolution. The *second industrial revolution* is a term used to refer to a second period of technological innovation in the late nineteenth century (the internal combustion engine, the automobile, petroleum products, electrical power, the telegraph, the phonograph, photography, the telephone, chemical engineering). The *third industrial revolution* is a term used to refer to a still later period, from the middle of the twentieth century on, when atomic power, computers, electronics and space exploration were introduced. Whatever terminology is used, it is obvious that the rate of historical change is accelerating. Thus, whereas the agricultural–pastoral revolution took thousands of years to spread across the globe, the industrial revolution (or revolutions) took a few centuries (or decades) to effect similar changes.

Much of the economic growth of the industrialising countries in Europe, the USA and elsewhere depended upon the supply of cheap raw materials from "underdeveloped" countries, which led to the rise of *colonialism*. Today, countries which were formerly colonised by European powers are for the most part intent on following the European/American model of industrialisation. Much debate has occurred in the past few years, however, as to whether all countries can industrialise; this depends upon much higher levels of economic growth, and some observers see global *limits to growth*, in terms of apparently diminishing resource and energy supplies, combined with rising levels of pollution and population.

The changing mix of work

A useful way of understanding such changes is to consider how industries can usefully be broken down into at least three sectors. The first or primary industry sector is concerned with extracting goods from nature: mining, agriculture, fishing. The second, secondary or manufacturing sector, is concerned with processing the raw materials extracted by primary industry: steel and iron manufacture, automobile production, chemicals, food processing, and so on. The third, tertiary or service sector, is concerned with the provision of services rather than goods: banking, insurance, education, medicine, welfare, religion, government, and so on. Some basic pie charts show, in a relatively crude way, how the nature of work has changed in most Western societies over the centuries (Fig. 1.1). The experience has been different for all societies, but one pattern remains constant: The majority of the workforce is employed initially in primary industry, but then various forces, particularly automation and new technology, conspire to reduce levels of employment without reducing output.

In the second phase, the majority of the workforce is employed in secondary industries, but again, various forces, particularly automation and

time

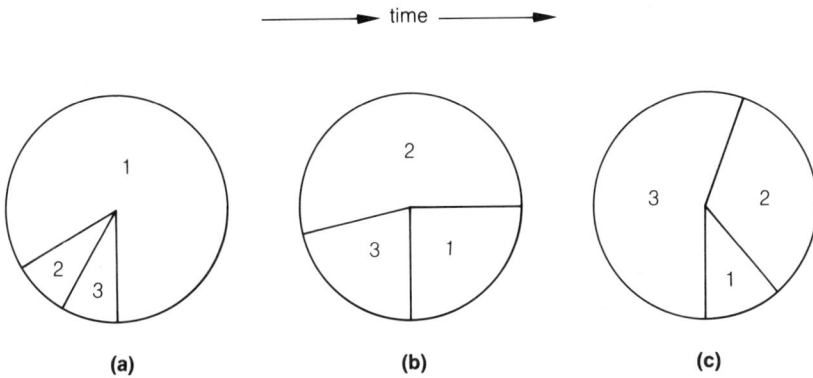

(a)   (b)   (c)

Fig. 1.1 *Changing patterns of work: Proportions of labour force in various industries (a) agricultural society, (b) manufacturing society, (c) services society. 1 primary sector, 2 secondary sector, 3 tertiary sector*

new technology, conspire to reduce levels of employment without reducing output.

Most Western societies, including Australia, are now in the third phase. Whether the same trend will be repeated is a matter of controversy. We will shortly consider a number of models which attempt to predict the future based upon these historical trends. Before we do this, however, let us turn our attention from the hardware of technology to the "softer" areas of human values and attitudes. How did they change through the various social revolutions?

Traditional values

Jones (1983) notes that work for the ancient Greeks and the Jews of the Old Testament was something quite distasteful. Indeed, in the first book of the Bible, Genesis, Adam and Eve are punished by God for eating the fruit of the tree of knowledge: the punishment for Eve was to bear children and to be subservient to Adam, and the punishment for Adam was to work:

> In the sweat of thy face shalt thou eat bread, till thou return unto the ground; for out if it wast thou taken: for dust thou art, and unto dust shalt thou return.

Adam and Eve were then thrown out of Eden, or Paradise, where all their material needs were catered for by the lush environment, where they could lead lives of permanent leisure and where they were immortal. Thus, for their sins, Adam and Eve—and therefore, in the Judaeo–Christian tradition, all people—were punished by sexual reproduction, patriarchal sex roles, work and death.

The Greeks too had a myth of human defiance of divine will and subsequent divine punishment. Zeus created Pandora, the first woman, and gave her a box which she was not to open. She did, and all mankind's ills were released, one of them being work. Greek leisured elites regarded manual work as degrading, fit only for the large slave class which through their labours supported the elite. Aristotle perceived the distastefulness of enslaving the many so that a few could concentrate on the finer things of life, but felt that slavery was inevitable, unless mechanical slaves could be created, for example, by making the statues of Daedalus, a great craftsman, move and perform labours. Harrington (1966) and Jones (1983) note that Aristotle's fantasy was probably the first scenario of an automated and robot world where human labour was unnecessary because machines were the slaves. Greek mythology and ideology did not, however, totally support the idea of an elite always consuming and lacking economic self-discipline: planning, thrift and saving rather than consuming were enshrined in Aesop's fable of the ant and the grasshopper. In the fable, the spendthrift grasshopper makes merry before the winter, while the sober, industrious ant lays up food; the ant later gives food to the starving and half-frozen grasshopper, with of course a sermon on the virtues of preparing for the future by planning in the present.

Jam today or jam tomorrow? The work ethic
Planning, saving and investing rather than consuming, having to choose between "jam today or jam tomorrow", all of these strategies are bound up with the central problem of economics—how to survive. Survival is probably enhanced by the development of certain skills and attitudes: self-denial, thrift, punctuality, foresight, sobriety. All cultures, eastern and western, have endorsed these values. Some cultures more than others have taken a stern view of other skills and attitudes: leisure-seeking, pleasure-seeking, self-indulgence, emotional release rather than constraint, conspicuous consumption.

Some sociologists have suggested that the Protestant religions were particularly negative towards pleasure-seeking and particularly positive towards self-denial, thrift, and so on. Some have suggested that this so-called *Protestant work ethic* was in fact the driving force of capitalism in various Western economies, particularly from the seventeenth century onwards. Protestant thinkers such as Calvin argued that work was not merely a sign of divine punishment, or even simply a boring price we had to pay for survival, but actually a means by which religious salvation could be achieved. People who worked hard, saved much, did not indulge their sensual appetites much or at all, were more esteemed by God. Salvation was possible not merely through faith—belief in God—but through works—the things people actually achieved materially in this life. Thus work takes on a spiritual, a psychological significance. Leisure, on the other hand, was often associated with the Devil—consider the old maxim, "an idle mind is the devil's playground". People who were extreme believers in such a work ethic would obviously feel guilty about leisure and virtuous about working continuously.

Such a work ethic was or is not the sole preserve of white European, American and Oceanic Protestants. Many cultures—in particular, the Chinese, the Japanese and the Jewish—have similar ethics, and capitalism was flourishing in parts of Catholic Europe well before the rise of Protestantism. Nevertheless, the ideology of holy thrift and holy profit-making did seem to be associated with the rise to economic and political power of Protestant states such as England, Germany and the Netherlands. When the aptly named Puritans left England for America, they took the work ethic with them, and this, together with the abundant natural resources of North America, seems to have produced even more economic and political power.

Thus, human values and attitudes reinforced the dramatic gains in productivity afforded by the technological breakthroughs of the first, and subsequent, industrial revolutions.

Jones' model

Figure 1.1 shows the manner in which economies change: the primary, then the secondary, and finally the tertiary sector of the economy employs the majority of workers. Waves of new technology usually lead to automation of work processes, and such automation tends to reduce the need for human workers while keeping constant or increasing productivity levels. Such changes have dramatic impacts upon the non-working population as well as on those working. Jones (1983) thinks that it is more useful to separate the work force into five sectors, rather than three. These are:

1. *Primary* Extractive industries: agriculture, forestry, fishing, mining, quarrying, oil extraction, biomass (growing crops such as sugar for liquid fuels). *The production of basic materials.*
2. *Secondary* Manufacturing and construction: manufacture of cars, television sets, carpets, refrigerators, tyres, ice-cream, breakfast cereals, beer, cigarettes; construction of houses, schools, office buildings, bridges and roads. *The process by which basic materials are converted into a finished product.*
3. *Tertiary* Tangible economic services: moving people, maintaining their bodies and hardware, heating and cooling them, provision of goods and services not based on information transfer or similar to home-based employment. *The processing of transfer of matter and/or energy; "hard" or tangible services.*
4. *Quaternary* Information processing: teaching, office work, research, public service, all forms of communication and the media, films, theatre, photography, posts and telecommunications, book publishing, printing, banking, insurance, real estate, administration, museums and libraries, creative arts, architecture, designing, music, data processing, computer software, ticket-selling, law, accountancy, psychology, social work, psychiatry, advertising, management, science, trade unions, the church, parliaments. *The processing of symbols and symbolic objects; "soft" or intangible services.*
5. *Quinary* Domestic and quasi-domestic servicing and/or making: care of children and the aged, home nursing, house care and maintenance, food preparation, washing and cleaning; home-based crafts (pottery, enamelling, jewellery), hobbies (producing eggs, vegetables, flowers), collecting of and trading in paintings, books, stamps; hotels, motels, restaurants, nurseries, creches, old people's homes, invalid day care, gardening, lawn-mowing, care of pets, house-cleaning, laundry and dry cleaning, minor house repairs, prostitution. *The provision of domestic services (generally unpaid), professional services similar to domestic work, charitable work, hobby-based occupations.* (Jones 1983)

The Australian labour force in the period 1891–1981, in terms of this five-sector approach, is shown in Figure 1.2. The interconnectedness and relative size of each of these five sectors can be seen in the way bread is created, marketed and consumed (Fig. 1.3).

The decline of the *primary* sector is the most dramatic trend in Figure 1.2. Many of Australia's primary industries are quite efficient by world standards, but much of that efficiency has been achieved by automation, which increases the capital-intensive nature of work and reduces the labour-intensive nature. Thus, while increased wealth might be generated by a "minerals boom", there may not be dramatic increases in employment in mining.

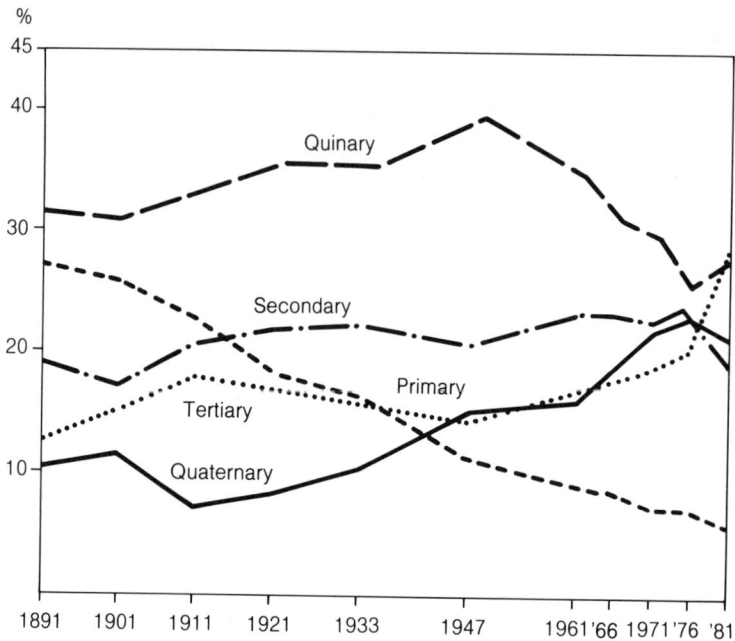

Fig. 1.2 *Five-sector analysis of the Australian labour force, 1891–1981* (JONES 1983, P.61. REPRODUCED WITH PERMISSION)

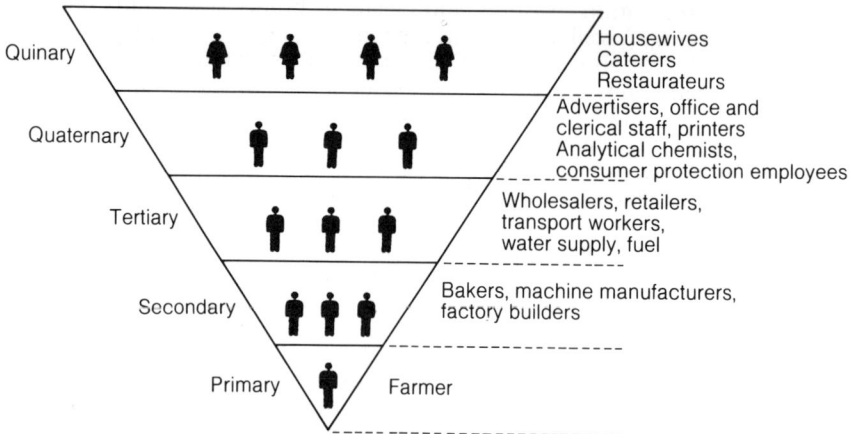

Fig. 1.3 *Creation, marketing and consumption of bread in Jones' five-sector model* (JONES 1983, P.54. REPRODUCED WITH PERMISSION)

The *secondary, or manufacturing, sector* is reasonably steady, unlike the experience in the United States and Europe, where automation has done to secondary industry what it had begun to do earlier to primary industry. Employment levels have been kept relatively high in Australia largely due to economic protection, whereby more capital-intensive products from other countries have been excluded by tariffs. How much longer we can keep this up is open to conjecture, although decreases in employment here are notable from the early 1970s onwards. Feingold (1984) notes that 28 per cent of Americans employed were in manufacturing in 1980, but he expected this to decline to 11 per cent in 2000 and to 3 per cent in 2030. Will we see similar declines here?

Jones argues that many *tertiary* craft skills—repair of television sets, radios, watches—will decline, because new manufacturing methods make it cheaper and/or simpler to replace them. He sees the most likely areas of expansion in the tertiary area as being domestic tourism, leisure and sport.

The *quaternary* sector is already beginning to feel the bite of computer technology, as Figure 1.2 shows. The printing industry has been revolutionised—or decimated, depending upon your point of view—by new technology. Areas long thought immune to automation, such as banking and insurance, are trying to come to terms with automatic teller machines (ATMs) and electronic fund transfer (EFT), and it is not yet clear whether these technologies will destroy or create jobs. The computer industry is growing dramatically, but Jones estimates that, for every job created by the computer industry, two will be eliminated elsewhere. Such trends are not confined to the borders of Australia: Jones suggests that, as so much high technology comes from the United States, jobs created there in telecommunications, computers, defence and aerospace may in fact displace labour elsewhere.

The notion of the *quinary sector* is relevant because economists are beginning to see that unpaid domestic work is in fact a crucial part of any economy and society. Women were strongly represented in industry at the turn of the century, but there was a trend from 1911 to 1947 of women returning to the home. The dramatic increase in women working in World War II is not shown because census data was not gathered in wartime. 1947 was the beginning of the "baby boom", when population increased substantially. Women returned to the formal workplace throughout the 1950s, 1960s and early 1970s, but there seems to be a reversal of this trend from the late 1970s onwards. Also included in quinary employment are such areas as child care and fast foods, although Jones is negative about the latter, seeing this area as offering largely "dead-end" jobs with low pay and few career prospects.

The future and futures: A matter of choice?

According to Jones, the future of work is not a matter of chance: there are many potential futures, and society chooses one option according to dominant values. Jones fears that divisions in society might become greater than they are now, with society being divided into the "information rich" and the "information poor": our life-chances increasingly depend upon information (skills, training, education), but not all of us have equal access to such information. A society increasingly dependent upon high technology will require more skills from its citizens and workers. "Australia's future economic and social growth will depend on increasing rates of educational participation at the higher levels" (Jones 1983, p.165). New technology is "de-skilling" workers but, generally speaking, it is the poorer rather than the wealthier who are being de-skilled. New technology—computers, robots, artificial intelligence—may not only pose a threat to some workers but to the human race, Jones warns. We ask these technologies to be our slaves, but the two qualities demanded of a slave—intelligence and subservience—are not compatible when taken to extremes. This is a "Frankenstein robots taking over" scenario and, while a gloomy one, is not necessarily an unrealistic one, unless conscious human choices are made to the contrary.

Toffler's model

Toffler (1970, 1980, 1984, 1985) approaches the past, present and future of work and life in a different manner. Part of his analysis concerns what he calls sector A and sector B of an economy. Sector A is that part of an economy where people "prosume", that is, they consume what they produce, or are self-sufficient. Goods and services are produced for use, rather than exchanged through a market. Sector B, on the other hand, is the sector where people produce goods and services for exchange, rather than use. They are paid to produce, and they use this money payment to purchase goods and services produced by others, that is, their roles as consumers and producers are quite separate (Kotler 1986).

Before the agricultural–pastoral revolution, and for a good deal after, the dominant mode of economic organisation was sector A. Particularly with the advent of the industrial revolution, sector B, the market sector, became more dominant, squeezing out sector A. But sector A never entirely went away, and in fact Toffler suggests that it is undergoing a resurgence.

This interplay of sectors A and B is linked with what Toffler calls the "waves" of historical change. The first wave is basically the agricultural–pastoral revolution, the second wave is basically the industrial revolution, and the third wave of change is what is happening at present, all the more difficult to define because we are inside it.

The rough proportions of sectors A and B are shown in Figure 1.4.

The sector A/sector B idea is fairly crude, and applies most directly to advanced industrial economies. However, as this advanced industrial economy is the model most less developed countries seem to aspire to, Toffler's ideas might have global relevance. The basic differences between sectors A and B are seen in Table 1.1. Most of us are more familiar with sector B, and that is as it should be, given that the market economy is still dominant.

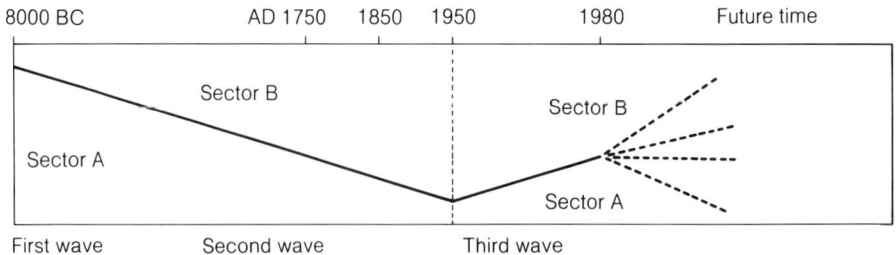

Fig. 1.4 *Sector A and sector B: Their proportions over time* (ADAPTED FROM TOFFLER 1980)

Table 1.1 Characteristics of Toffler's sector A/sector B model of society

	Sector A economy	*Sector B economy*
Nature of economy	invisible economy unpaid work production for use pre-, trans-market (subsistence, barter, black economy, etc.)	visible economy paid work production for exchange market
Work role specialisation (sexual)	low men and women share work; both prosumers (producers + consumers)	high stereotyped separate roles: men = producers women = consumers
Work role specialisation (general)	low creative—"jazz improvisers" many generalists, jacks-of- all-trades—revolt of the clients	high uncreative—"classical musicians" super-, over-specialisation many professions, monopoly on skill entry, credentials
Nature of skills base	self-help groups, networking DIY ethic, self-service economy	official channels
Type of production	customised, de-massified production emphasis on uniqueness outside-in design	mass production emphasis on uniformity inside-out design
Scale of operations	appropriate scale (big or small can be beautiful)	big is beautiful
Locus of workplace	decentralised workplace, e.g. electronic cottage flexiplace + flexitimes	centralised, structured workplace, e.g. factory, office uniplace, unitimes
Work-related values (general)	pre-, post-economic pre-, post-economistic motivation people are valued for what they do self-reliance	economic economistic motivation people are valued for what they own
Work-related values (hand:head)	headwork and handwork integrated, re-integrated	headwork (intellectual work) glorified handwork denigrated
Relationship of work and leisure	work and leisure blur into each other people prefer to do hobbies, work for barter, part-time work	work and leisure quite separate

Source: Adapted from Toffler (1980).

The sectors are different in terms of the *nature of the economy.* Sector B is the visible economy. Production is for exchange, and workers are paid wages. Sector A, prior to the arrival of the market, was a subsistence economy: production was for use. Later on, with the rise of trade, people bartered or exchanged goods and services, without the benefit of a medium such as money. As there was no money, there was no payment of wages. With the rise of the money system, the invisible or black economy began to take on large proportions: this meant not only a "black" market where forbidden or scarce items were sold at high prices, but also a system where many payments for goods and services were made in cash in order to avoid taxation. Barter also re-emerged, in new forms: for example, a dentist might give an electrician free dental work in return for free electrical work.

Further differences are obvious in the *specialisation of work roles* in the two sectors. There is low role specialisation in sector A. Anthropological studies have shown that nomadic tribes had some sex role specialisation— men left the camp to hunt, while women stayed closer to camp with children and foraged—but there was considerable equality between the sexes (Leakey 1981). Men and women were "prosumers"—they consumed what they produced. In sector B work role specialisation was high. Sexual equality suffered, with women marooned in the nuclear family while men went off to work in factories and mines (in fact, of course, many women and children also worked in industrial workplaces). Men became stereotyped as producers ("breadwinners") while women became stereotyped as consumers ("dependent spouses").

In sector B, this high role specialisation also meant that specialist professions emerged, and possibly *over-specialisation* occurred. Professions claimed a monopoly on skills, and many set up rigid entry criteria based on credentials. Much of this activity was healthy: trade guilds and trade unions were set up in this way, for instance. There can be too much of a good thing, of course, and many professions began to operate not entirely in the public interest (as George Bernard Shaw observed, all professions are a conspiracy against the layman). As roles became specialised, it became more difficult to get things done through informal contacts: as the sociologist Weber noted, as bureaucracies or organisations became bigger and more modern, routinised ways of doing things, of using *official channels*, became more the norm (see Chapter 13).

In the early, pre-industrial sector A, there were many generalists, or jacks and jills of all trades: everyone in the village could do a bit of hunting, cooking, story-telling and child-minding. In the post-industrial sector A, says Toffler, we are seeing a re-emergence of this pattern. Many clients of professionals are in revolt, either because they cannot pay the fees any more, or because they are dissatisfied with the goods and services sold by the professionals, or simply because they like doing things for themselves. The apparently trivial *do-it-yourself (DIY) movement* is having impacts upon the livelihood of professional mechanics, painters, doctors and solicitors, as people take up "hobbies" and become very serious about becoming more self-sufficient. The DIY trend is also encouraged by proprietors of banks and petrol stations, who make the customer the worker, and thus externalise labour costs (which can also be a discreet euphemism for putting people out of work).

Self-help groups in fields as diverse as alcoholism, schizophrenia, obesity, compulsive gambling and phobias are proving that mutual aid shared by non-professionals can be as effective, if not more effective, than professional help.

Official channels, notoriously clogged at the best of times, have not served people well, so the sector A shifts in roles are helped instead by *networking*—informal and formal groups, bulletin boards, stories and advertisements in local papers, specialist publications, computer conferencing and electronic bulletin boards.

Networking is nothing new; "old boy networks" have always existed, usually with the effect of excluding the non-elite from the spoils of a particular organisation. What is new is that newly vocal groups, traditionally from the non-elite (women, ethnic groups, non-professionals) are now using such tactics.

The *types of production* characteristic of the two sectors are also quite different. One of the most obvious aspects of the market system was the uniformity of goods and services produced via mass production. The lack of choice was taken as given: as Henry Ford said of his Model T Ford, "you can have it in any colour, so long as it's black". Mass production meant economies of scale—goods and services could be made more cheaply as volume went up, but this could only be done by presuming that all consumers' tastes and needs were the same, which of course they weren't. Goods and services were designed "inside-out", that is, firms created goods and services according to what planners inside firms thought the consumer wanted, without actually asking the consumer if this were the case.

Before the market system arose, most goods and services were created by craftsmen, on a small-batch or one-off basis. Toffler sees a resurgence today of this type of manufacture in the market as well as the non-market sector. Computer-aided design and computer-aided manufacturing (CAD–CAM) are growing in importance, and such techniques mean that a customer can order more options or modifications in a good or a service, in much the same way as a consumer asks for a particular combination of fillings in a sandwich or asks for a set of options on a car. Thus a consumer might ask a home computer connected to telephone lines to order a garment of particular dimensions, colours, cut, fabric, trim and price from a garment factory which has more computers and laser cutters than people in it. This style of manufacture does not need high volume to keep costs down. Consumers might pay extra for unique products, or they may not.

Cottage industries of craftsmen and women, working in garment-making, jewellery-making, insurance, portrait-painting, architecture, might also be able to provide unique, "de-massified" (i.e. not mass-produced) goods and services.

"Participation" is the catch-cry in many organisations throughout society, and consumers are now beginning to participate in the design of computers, refrigerators and other artefacts. This may be done through a panel of consumers, or market research, or by asking client groups in industry what they really want. This is "outside-in" design, where customisation becomes the rule, not the exception, where the customer has access to real and non-trivial options.

Closely allied to the types of production in each sector is the idea of the *scale of operations* in each sector. In sector B, "big is beautiful" was the catch-cry. Build a bigger assembly line for bigger profits and more efficiency; build a bigger skyscraper to house more people; have a bigger field of one variety of crop to maximise agricultural production; and so on. From the 1960s onwards, some people began to observe that big was not always beautiful. The bigger assembly line often left workers feeling alienated and dehumanised, and the volume of output could not be flexibly tailored to market fluctuations. The big skyscraper actually changed the climate around it, setting up high winds, it made people feel dwarfed and alienated, and fire ladders could only reach up the first ten storeys of the glass and steel monsters. Crop monocultures meant that one group of insect pests could wipe out the whole crop, so increased pesticides, as well as fertilisers, were needed to keep the crops alive and produce grains that were often nutritionally sub-standard. Schumacher (1974) coined the phrase "small is beautiful", alluding to the fact that there were *dis*-economies of scale as well as economies. People began to re-think their approaches to industry, organisation, agriculture, and their personal lives. To a certain extent, the small-is-beautiful movement went too far, decrying bigness in all things; bigness, however, can be quite appropriate. As Schumacher himself said, if he had lived in a world of small organisations, he would have written a book entitled "Big is Beautiful". Within the third wave of historical change, Toffler suggests, appropriate scale—small *or* big can be beautiful—is the way to go (see Chapter 13).

The *locus or place of the workplace* is also different in the two sectors. In the market sector, there is only one place to work, and that is within the centralised factory or office. Apart from shift-work, there is no flexibility of time available for the workers. By contrast, in sector A, workplaces were historically decentralised, in small cottage industries for the most part. Toffler sees a partial return to working at home using electronic technology to link a smaller centralised workplace with many decentralised "electronic cottages". People might be able to work at computer terminals in a home office. Both within this electronic cottage mode and within more conventional workplaces, more options are opening up for people to work at times which best suit their needs—flexitime, flexiweek, fleximonth, flexiyear, sabbaticals, job-sharing, and so on (see Chapter 12).

General work-related values differ between the two sectors. Within sector B, economics is the sole concern, and it is presumed that people have only an economic motivation—their sole concern is money, and piecework incentive schemes are the best way to structure work. This materialism transfers to the non-working hours of people's existence, and material possessions are presumed to be an index of a person's worth; people are valued for what they own. In sector A, other motives as well as money are apparent. As Toffler observes, many managers in the market sector lament what they see as the decline of the work ethic, but the same de-motivated workers are highly motivated outside the workplace, doing home repairs, growing their own vegetables, attending political meetings, and so on. People may still be valued partially according to how much money they make, but they will also be valued for what they can *do*. Are they versatile rather than over-specialised? Are they self-sufficient? Can they cook, do household repairs? and so on.

Such trends are seen in the *work-related values of hand and head*. The market sector, as it developed after the industrial revolution, saw the glorification of intellectual or head work, particularly as the service sector became dominant in the second half of the twentieth century. Those who "couldn't use their heads and were good with their hands", the "hewers of wood and the drawers of water", as well as tradesmen and women, were ascribed low prestige compared to the "professions" of law, medicine, architecture, teaching and management. The service professions deal with symbols and abstractions rather than concrete things, and Toffler suggests that this can have an alienating effect: people in air-conditioned offices have been cut off from the smells and feelings of the down-to-earth world. In sector A, people again seek this tactile involvement with reality, so that accountants take up weaving and house repairs and computer analysts take up pottery and gardening. Tradespeople, looked down upon by those in the "professions", gain new prestige, as the artificial separation of hand and head skills is removed.[1]

Finally, the *relationship of work and leisure* is different between the two sectors. Within sector B, work and leisure are quite separate. Work, usually seen as being horrible, is the meal ticket one must get to enjoy "real life"— leisure at home. Within sector A, these roles are by no means as clear. Here, work and leisure blur into one another. People may work from home, and work and leisure may be experienced in layers throughout the day (this, of course, would not be to everyone's liking). People's preference for doing hobbies, part-time work and barter work may lessen their dependence upon the market sector.

Toffler is not suggesting that the market sector, B, is going to go away; he is suggesting that it is going to be substantially modified by sector A, and in fact is already being substantially modified.

As the third wave of historical change continues, the sharp divisions between sectors A and B will weaken, as overlaps between columns in Table 1.1 suggest. Toffler's model of the future of life and work seems more optimistic than that of Jones, and indeed the third wave/sector A–sector B/prosumer model could be seen to be unrealistically optimistic and with an all-too-tidy happy ending to our problems.

Checkpoints for the future

We now have a good overview of the past, and of how we got to where we are today. The models of Jones and Toffler give us some insights into where we might be heading in the future. In planning for the future, or in planning to choose among multiple futures, we need to keep in mind a large and at times bewildering array of facts, trends, suggestions and phenomena. Some of these checkpoints for the future concern us only as individuals; others concern us as group members, organisational members, citizens of nation-states, and citizens of the planet.

Global resources

There is considerable disagreement about whether this planet has declining, static or expanding resources. Some people are extreme pessimists, seeing the planet as having too few resources and too little food, together with too much pollution and too many people; this, the pessimists argue, is a recipe for catastrophe, promising unparalleled death and suffering via starvation, poisoning and wars between resource-rich and resource-poor nations. Extreme optimists see pollution and population being well under control, now or in the immediate future, and perceive resources and food as being virtually limitless, whether seen solely from the point of view of mankind restricted to this planet, or mankind spreading out into the vast and bountiful reaches of space. Between these two extremes, there is a continuum of optimism to pessimism (Kahn *et al.* 1976). The view that we have about these

---

[1] Naisbett (1984) suggests that each further incursion of "high tech" into our lives—computerisation, glass, chrome and plastic environments and furniture, and so on—makes us feel more alienated. We thus seek out more "high touch" experiences—nature walks, surfing, pottery, antique furniture, soft comfortable furniture and clothing, etc.

matters strongly influence economic activity: Will we have high growth, no growth or contraction (negative growth)? Should we concentrate on quantitative factors, such as gross national product per capita, or should we concentrate on more intangible, qualitative measures, like the levels of happiness and well-being in society?

War

We have always been concerned with war, but in the past few years the level of concern about global war, particularly nuclear war, has risen. New and unlovely techniques of destruction—chemical, biological, electronic warfare, terrorism—are becoming more widespread. Rosow (1979) sees such concerns as leading to people becoming more demotivated in their jobs, not planning too far ahead, becoming more hedonistic and narcissistic as they realise they could be dead tomorrow or, indeed, in the next second.

Technology: Liberator or destroyer?

The history of mankind, as we have seen, is a history of technological changes which make certain jobs obsolete and give rise to new jobs. There has always been concern that a point would be reached where there would be no new jobs. The Luddites' response in nineteenth-century Britain was to try and destroy their machines. They, rather than the machines, were destroyed, but there are many who believe that the Luddites were either right or simply ahead of their time. Mead (1983), in an analysis of responses to technological change in Australia, found that employer groups tended to be happier with the prospect of new technology, while employee groups were more pessimistic. Critics such as Jones (1983) have argued that new technologies often lead to the deskilling of workers and to unemployment, but others such as Gruen (1980) disagree, pointing out that, since World War II, unskilled work has been decreasing in the economy, and that while Australia's unemployment rose dramatically in the 1970s, its use of industrial robots and computers was quite low relative to comparable countries.

There is a famous story about automation and unemployment that goes to the heart of the issue. As the story has it, Henry Ford, the American automobile manufacturer, once showed a totally automated assembly line to Walter Reuther, an American unionist. Ford, no lover of unions, said triumphantly, "There! Where does that leave your workers now?" Reuther replied, "Very clever, Mr Ford, but who is going to buy your automobiles?" Whether the story is true or not is immaterial. What is important is that the story demonstrates a paradox: There is some short-term gain in employers replacing people with machines, but there is no long-term advantage unless the unemployed are paid an unemployment benefit far above the subsistence level; increases in quantity and reductions in price on the supply side are no good unless there is an effective aggregate demand in an economy. The key question is "who gets what?" Who gets the increased profits from the superior efficiency of the machines? If it is only the machine-owners, who become incredibly wealthy while the unemployed become incredibly poor by comparison, then commentators like Jones feel that we will have civil war in our society, a literally violent war between the haves and the have-nots. Or as an Australian politician put it, more coloquially, the rich won't be able to ignore the poor because the poor won't just stop at kicking in Porsche doors.

If we solve these problems, then machines can liberate people from the drudgery of work. Machines can then be the statues of Daedalus, the mechanical slaves that allow the masses to live like the nobility. Everyone will belong to the leisure class. For some people, this will be heaven, but for others, it will be hell. Many people are fearful of what they would do if they did not have to work. Freud (1931) felt that work was a useful way of repressing the potentially uncontrollable instincts of sexual pleasure-seeking and aggression that he saw as being the basis of human personality; take away work, and society might collapse into decadence.

Probably the most sinister aspect of technology is that it may not only replace people in the workplace but that it may replace people, period. Science fiction is full of stories of robots taking over, making humans their pets, or their food, or simply destroying them. As the field of artificial intelligence continues to develop apace, the distinction between servile, non-thinking robots and computers and dominant, thinking humans seems to be shrinking. We will soon have machines which (who?) will be able to converse in spoken language, machines which will be able to reason, machines which can make other machines, and biots or biological robots—machines genetically engineered from organic matter. These, like all technology, can promise utopia or dystopia, heaven or hell. It all depends how we manage them, and it all depends on how much time we have left while we are still in control.[2]

High tech versus Low tech: Where the new jobs will be

The utopia (or dystopia) of robot slaves and permanent leisure for humans is still a long way away. Many new jobs will emerge in the next few decades. But will all these jobs be glamorous "high-tech" jobs, such as computers, robots, biotechnology, space manufacturing, and so on? A United States survey showed that the highest growth in demand for jobs in the 1980–90 period would be in decidedly low-tech jobs, jobs that require a minimum of skills, such as secretaries, nurses' aides, janitors, sales clerks, cashiers, nurses, truck drivers, fast food workers, clerks and waiters (*Time*, 30 May 1983). Possibly only 6 per cent of new jobs created in the 1984–95 period will be in high-tech jobs; even in glamorous industries such as electronics, many organisations have only 15 per cent skilled workers, the rest being unskilled clerical workers (Wilmoth 1984). Automation will continue to have an impact upon primary and secondary industries, but it will also have an impact upon tertiary industries such as banking and insurance. Whether this systematic disemploying will be greater or less than the creation of new jobs is a matter of intense controversy. With an increasing rate of social change, it will perhaps become normal for people to hold several major and quite different jobs throughout their life. In Table 1.2 you might see one or some of your next jobs. When you think about how strange many of them are, try to cast your mind back to, say, the mid-1930s, and imagine how strange to the people of that time would seems jobs such as plastics engineer, computer programmer, TV repairman, aerobics instructor, rock musician.

---

[2] An extremely pessimistic view is that of Wesley (1974):

It is the machine that pollutes the air, water, and earth. It is the machine that is making so many species of carbon-based life extinct. It is the machines of war that threaten mankind. Thus, for man to take action he would have to control the machines; but this he cannot do. The machine is now the more dominant species; it cannot be controlled. Machines will not go away, and their biomass will continue to increase . . . a rough guess would be about one hundred years to complete machine autonomy and perhaps two hundred years for human survival . . . The next few years may see some successes in (the) fight for a better environment and life for humans, but in the long run it appears hopeless (p.37).

Table 1.2 Occupational titles of the future

Here is a list of job titles that might appear in a Dictionary of Occupational Titles *of the future:*

Aquaculturist
Armed courier
Artificial intelligence technician
Arts manager
Asteroid/lunar miner
Astronaut
Battery technician
Benefits analyst
Biomedical technician
Bionic medical technician
Cable television auditor
Cable television salesperson
CAD/CAM technician
Career consultant
CAT scan technician
Certified alcoholism counsellor
Certified financial planner
Child advocate
Colour consultant
Communications engineer
Community ecologist
Community psychologist
Computer:
    analyst
    camp counsellor/owner
    designer
    graphics specialist
    lawyer
    microprocessor technologist
    programmer (software writer)
    sales trainee
    security specialist
    service technician
Contract administrator
Cosmetic surgeon
Cryologist technician
Cultural historian
Cyborg technician
Dance therapist
Dialysis technologist
Divorce mediator
EDP auditor
Electronic mail technician
Energy auditor
Ethicist
Executive rehabilitative counsellor
Exercise technician
Exotic welder
Family mediator/therapist
Fibre-optics technician
Financial analyst
Financial consultant
Forecaster

Forensic scientist
Fusion engineer
Genetic biochemist
Genetic counsellor
Genetic engineer technician
Geriatric nurse
Graphoanalyst
Hazardous waste technician
Health physicist
Hearing physiologist
Hibernation specialist
Home health aide
Horticulture therapy assistant
Hotline counsellor
House- and pet-sitter
Housing rehabilitation technician
Image consultant
Indoor air quality specialist
Information broker
Information research scientist
Issues manager
Job developer
Laser medicine practitioner
Laser technician
Leisure counsellor
Licensed psychiatric technician
Market development specialist
Massage therapist
Materials utilisation technician
Medical diagnostic imaging technician
Medical sonographer technician
Microbial geneticist
Microbiological mining technician
Mineral economist
Myotherapist
Naprapath
Neutrino astronomer
Nuclear fuel specialist
Nuclear fuel technician
Nuclear medicine technologist
Nuclear reactor technician
Nurse-midwife
Ocean hotel manager
Ombudsman
Oncology nutritionist
Orthotist
Paraprofessional
Peripheral equipment operator
PET scan technician
Physician's assistant
Planetary engineer
Plant therapist
Plastics engineer

Table 1.2 Occupational titles of the future (*continued*)

Pollution botanist	Solar energy consultant
Power plant inspector	Solar energy research scientist
Protein geometrician	Solar engineer
Radiation ecologist	Space botanist
Recombinant DNA technologist	Space mechanic
Relocation counsellor	Sports law specialist
Retirement counsellor	Sports psychologist
Robot:	Strategic planner
engineer	Systems analyst
salesperson	Tape librarian
scientist	Telecommunications systems designer
technician (industrial)	Thanatologist
trainer	Transplant coordinator
Security engineer	Treasure hunter
Selenologist (lunar astronomer)	Underwater archaeologist
Shrimp–trout fish farmer	Underwater culture technician
Shyness consultant	Volcanologist
Software club director	Waste manager
Software talent agent	Water quality specialist
Soil conservationist	Wellness consultant

Source: Feingold (1984), p.13. Reproduced with permission.

Technology, work and human behaviour

What then will the future be like? Will it hurt, or will it be fun, or will it be neither? Some attempts, more or less fanciful, at attempting to predict the future, are given in Box 1.A and Box 1.B.

If we are spared genocidal wars and genocidal robots, the future might be a very interesting place to be. Be it high tech, low tech, or middle tech, one thing will remain constant: people. If you are an engineer, a clerk, a soldier, a houseperson, an astronaut, a scientist, an explorer in voluntary or compulsory leisure, what you do is different to what most other people do; yet you will always have to cope with and communicate with people, just as other people have. We cannot simply shrug this off, and say that a job or activity is only the content, the technical routine. Unless we understand the process as well as the content, the human factors as well as the technical factors, we will get nowhere. Indeed, there are millions of people getting nowhere every day, in their jobs and personal lives, because other people are an unfathomable mystery to them.

You may find that parts of or all of this book can help to rectify this. Irrespective of the job or activity, everyone has to cope with stress, scarce time, making decisions, getting motivated, becoming assertive, understanding the games people play (off the sports field), and body language; they need to understand what goes on in groups and organisations; they need to know why jobs are like they are and what they could be; they need to know about leading and following, and whether leading and following are still relevant.

In short, they need to know why people behave the way they do. If you can begin to grasp such mysteries, then your personal vision of work and the future will become much clearer to you.

Summary

We can begin to understand the future of work by looking at the past. Changes in work patterns and society on the planet seem to have followed a pattern whereby first primary, then secondary, then tertiary industry is transformed by mechanisation. This was most notable in the industrial revolution which took place in Britain and Europe in the eighteenth century. New technologies destroyed many jobs and created new ones, and contributed to major social changes, such as shifts of populations from country to city areas.

Commitment and motivation to work in most cultures was underpinned by strong work ethics, which tended to glorify work as a means or as an end in itself.

Jones extends the basic primary–secondary–tertiary model of work to include quaternary and quinary sectors. Jones emphasises that humans need to choose between multiple futures, ensuring that we avoid a society where technology is venerated for its own sake and social divisions are widened rather than lessened.

Toffler distinguishes between two sectors in all economies, sector A (prosumption) and sector B (market exchange). Since the industrial revolution, sector B has tended to squeeze out sector A, but Toffler detects a re-emergence of sector A in today's and tomorrow's societies, with widespread and largely benign consequences.

Checkpoints for our understanding and potential control of the future are: global resources, war, technology: liberator or destroyer? and high tech or low tech: where the new jobs will be.

The factor common to all forms of work—past, present and future—remains the human factor, and such skills, interpersonal and organisational, as we can gain will help us in work and non-work situations.

Several views of the future, more or less fanciful, are given.

BOX 1.A: Australia in 2009—heaven or hell?

Here are two scenarios about the future, one optimistic (scenario A), and one pessimistic (scenario B). Which is most likely: A? B? Neither?

Scenario A

People pursue the good life at home and at work in many ways. Indeed, "work" has disappeared for many who choose to accept a living wage ($16 000 in 1986 dollars) and pursue a variety of leisure pursuits, the products of which they may exchange for money or barter for other goods and services. Depending upon which statistician you listen to, cultural goods and services—predominantly arts and crafts—are the biggest or the third biggest industry in the nation.

Governments claim that they really have no choice but to pay high amounts for what used to be called "the dole", because if people doing leisure work were paid low amounts, the levels of aggregate demand in the economy would decline, and so in turn would most economic activity. High levels of spending keep the wheels turning around.

For those still in the conventional workforce, the average work week is now 25 hours a week. "Average" is having less meaning, however, because people work in a variety of ways: flexiday, flexiweek, fleximonth, flexiyear and flexidecade. Shiftwork is popular with some, not so popular with others: over 60 per cent of private and public enterprises run 24 hours a day, seven days a week.

Over 30 per cent of the workforce do not work "at work", but at home, in electronic cottages connected to central workplaces by computers, satellites, telephone wires and television cables. Of the teleworkers, 26 per cent are working via satellite for overseas organisations. Eight per cent of the nation's gross product is generated by teleworkers in other countries. International agreements regulate such international trade in service labour, with advanced countries wealthy enough to tolerate lower intranational employment levels and perceptive enough to see international teleworking as the best possible form of international aid. National boundaries are beginning to blur, and a long-term decline in nationalism may be just what this planet needs.

Teleworking has led to a renewal of family and neighbourhood values which have not been seen since before the second war back in the twentieth century. Robots and automation have been very beneficial to our society: the slavery of machines has meant the liberation of human beings from virtually all dirty and dangerous jobs. No human job can be replaced by automatic means unless social and economic surpluses generated by the automatic process can be eventually channelled back to individual human workers (and non-workers).

The large-scale development of space has done much to transform the world of the 1980s and early 1990s, once described as "a nuclear-fuelled pressure cooker". Many mineral and energy resources have been discovered in space, and many pollution-intensive industries are now located in space colonies between the Earth and the Moon, thus reducing pollution levels. Most nations now feel that there are infinite resources for everyone, and major conflict seems unlikely.

Wealth is not defined purely in quantitative but in qualitative terms as well. People pursue materialistic and anti-materialistic lifetstyles side by side, using high technology and low technology alike to achieve their ends.

All in all, we've never been happier.

Scenario B

This country is a pretty grim place, a divided society of haves and have-nots. Unemployment levels are at 60 per cent, with the dole being a little over $3000 per year in 1986 dollars. Millions of people live in slums in what used to be the central city areas. Dozens suicide from broken skyscraper windows every day, or are killed in random gang violence, or simply overdose on the drugs which are provided cheaply or free from government drug shops ("a drugged population is a debugged population", as one politician once put it).

Most service or tertiary sector jobs are now handled by automated systems or by teleworkers, who work from home via computers. Even many teleworkers are under threat from far cheaper teleworkers in Asia, who work via satellite links. Most teleworkers live in guarded compounds, where private police hold off the periodic attacks of mobs and gangs from the Job Liberation Front (indeed, being a security guard is a prized job, what with private police outnumbering public police three to one).

In the same compounds, or in still wealthier ones, are the elite of automated factory and office owners, systems analysts and programmers, inventors, technocrats and politicians who have benefited most from this asymmetrical society, wherein the information rich get richer and the information poor get poorer.

Other tertiary sector workers work in low-pay, dead-end jobs in fast foods, drugs, burials, and computer and machine maintenance. Those jobs for humans left in primary and secondary industry are boring and demeaning machine-minding jobs, and there is no guarantee how long it will be before robot-supervisors will take over those jobs.

Automation, computerisation, robots and biots (genetically engineered organic materials shaped into stationary or mobile robots and computers) advance relentlessly into the workforce, enriching their owners and impoverishing the people they replace. Because people's purchasing power declines as a result, this has triggered much economic instability, and we now have a curious mixture of depression and minor boom, with government holding the whole precarious show together, but not daring to give more dole money out for fear of losing our international and domestic markets to countries with lower wage structures.

Some religious and politicial groups have sprung up, proclaiming Robot Liberation and Robot Rights, or seeing robots and computers as the next evolutionary step, with humans expiring on the scrap-heap of history and natural selection.

Others are more aggressive: splinter groups of the Job Liberation Front, such as the Likely Ludds and the Regressives, have invented chemical and electronic bombs which they are using to sabotage and destroy robots, biots and computers. NEMESIS, the seventh-generation computer used by the Justice Department, has recommended that such criminals be executed or transported to slave-labour camps at the mines on the Moon.

There has been a worrying upsurge of industrial and domestic accidents, deaths where humans have been attacked by robots and automated systems which have inexplicably gone haywire.

The gloom here is more than matched by events overseas. There was the Food War of 1996–97 between India and Pakistan, where chemical and biological weapons killed over 7 million, and up to 28 million were crippled. In 1998, when the Mafia threatened New York with a 10 kiloton atom bomb unless 5 billion dollars were handed over, something went wrong with the handling of the bomb (no one knows to this day what actually *did* go wrong) and it detonated, killing over 800 000 people and injuring and irradiating 2.3 million more.

When 1999 came to an end, many religious prophets predicted the end of the world on 31 December. It didn't happen, but the way things are going now, I think they may only have been 10 years out.

Box 1.B: You, your job and 2009: Some predictions by Phil Ruthven, Futures Consultant

THE year 2009 will see Australia with a population of about 29 million and a workforce totalling 12.5 million — some statistics which suggest there are many newcomers due to enter our life and work as a nation.

The growth is strong but the changes are startling: 53 per cent of that total population has either not yet been born or migrated to this country: and two-thirds of that workforce have not entered it yet because they are not born, still too young or have not yet migrated here.

The year 2009 may seem a long way off, but 25 years is not such a long time. It has already been more than that (28 years) since television was introduced to Australia.

Measuring the distance we have come is one way of getting some perspective on the future. A look forward to the year 2009 takes on some more sense if we first look backwards over the same number of years, back to 1959.

A quarter of a century ago, manufacturing reached its zenith and contributed 29 per cent of the nation's economic output. Now it has only 18 per cent of that total and can be expected to drop to 15 per cent by the year 2009.

While we had a passion for making things then, we were not so good at mining. In 1959, the mining industry hit bottom and contributed its lowest-ever share

(1.7 per cent) of our total economy. These days that figure is about 6 per cent and that will almost double over the next quarter of a century.

In 1959 the average family was spending 60 per cent of its household income on retail goods (cars, food, clothing and so on). By 2009, the average family will be spending only about a third of its income this way, with other services such as health, education and tourism using up the money saved.

Those statistics indicate some of the ways we have changed as a society, but we need go no further than the computer as a symbol of the shift we have made in a dramatic quarter of a century.

The year 1959 was still the dawn of the computer age. Very few businesses could then have foreseen that they might need a computer 25 years later, far less have terminals on a lot of desks and the fun side of them — video games — in so many of their employees' homes.

It would have been equally hard to have foreseen the changes in people's hopes and expectations. This is not so surprising, because our society in 1959 was enthusiastic about its recovery from one of the most extraordinarily difficult periods in modern history.

A string of events across half a century had limited the future for

Australians: the recession of the 1890s, the Boer War, World War I, the Great Depression of the 1930s and then World War II.

Few had lived through the whole series, of course, but there was still a very high proportion of society which — until the 1950s — had never really had a chance to catch its breath. Indeed, between the 1890s and the end of World War II, there had been no real increase in personal wealth.

So, by 1959, Australians had begun to enjoy one of their longest peacetime periods (despite the limited impact of the Korean War) in many decades, and the aspirations grew to match the possibilities.

While older people took the chance to catch up with things they had been denied, the younger ones had no direct experience that would curtail their expectations about the future.

In 1959 there was no real restriction on the means of fulfilling the hopes — work. Unemployment was virtually unheard of, and a rash of new graduates in the workforce were quite confident they would soon be earning the fantastic sum of £40 ($80) a week.

The huge demand for people in the manufacturing sector — for engineers, chemists and accountants — and the rapid growth of clerical jobs meant demand often outstripped supply, and that made job aspirations in 1959 almost unrecognisable when compared with those earlier in the century.

For one thing, many parents vigorously encouraged their children to set their sights on professional careers, as doctors and lawyers, so that they would be safely in good jobs should another depression ever hit the country.

For another, there was an end to the itinerant work which had dominated so much of Australia's history, for sheep shearers, fruit pickers and other casuals. By 1959, most entrants to the workforce saw themselves taking on permanent, full time positions and with the prospect of staying in the one location.

1984–2009: What's in store?

Looking at the changes which made the year 1959 what it was, and the developments since then, it would be unrealistic to imagine that the extent of the changes we face in the next 25 years will be any less.

In some cases the pendulum may well swing back a little. The return of the itinerant worker, though in a new guise, could be part of that, as those looking for work may have to go north to the new projects starting in the hitherto undeveloped areas of the nation.

Other workers will need a different kind of mobility. In the wake of the disintegration of the 9-to-5, Monday-to-Friday working week, employees can expect more and more flexibility in their hours and days of work. Other industries will follow the round-the-clock pattern already set by industries such as oil refining, emergency services, motels and international stockbroking.

Moreover, the types of industries and occupations with which we are now familiar are in for profound changes, with some careers all but disappearing in the same way that the hoopers who used to make wooden barrels are virtually extinct.

Parents, teachers and advisers will need to think again about the sorts of careers they recommend to young people. The future is less safe for lawyers, printers, many clerical workers and a whole host of production process workers than it was back in 1959.

A useful guide to their counsel is a look at the industries that will decline. Manufacturing is one: it used to provide about 30 per cent of all Australian jobs, now it is on the way down to 10 per cent and will probably be only 15 per cent by the year 2009.

Agriculture is another. It will grow strongly as an industry but will become more and more mechanised — a process that is likely to halve the number of jobs it currently offers.

The finance industry, easily the most exciting and changeable industry of this decade, will also continue to shed workers with more inroads being made by automatic tellers, electronic banking and the reduction in the clerical and middle management duties for so long associated with banking and finance.

Mining will be a very strong growth industry. Its present contribution of 6 per cent of our total economic output will probably rise to 11 per cent, but technology is making that possible and mining's share of the national workforce will see only a small rise, from 2 per cent to about 4 per cent.

The industries that will be offering most of the new jobs are construction, health, education, leisure, tourism, information and domestic services.

Construction will be a growth sector of the workforce, especially in the north, where big mining and agricultural projects will need the whole social infrastructure of roads, bridges, houses, schools, dams and so on.

Health and education will grow as we can afford better health and adjust to the ideal of life-long education, while domestic and personal services will grow at an equally spectacular rate as households go on surrendering the jobs they have been doing themselves.

Communications and information will continue to explode as industries and employers, as our lives are more and more shaped by our access to data bases, electronic shopping and more sophisticated links with our friends and relatives.

Those are the industries, but what will the jobs be? It can be a frightening question, and experts have warned us that half the jobs that will be employing people in the year 2000 have not been defined properly yet.

A sense of caution is well-founded if we look back, again, and realise that some jobs we now take pretty much for granted (computer operators, transplant specialists, many electronic engineering positions and merchant bankers, for example) were not properly established 25 years ago in 1959.

(Source: *The Age*, 6 October 1984. Reproduced with permission.)

Questions for discussion

1. Were the Luddites right?
2. Evaluate Jones' model of change, *or* Toffler's model, *or* compare the two.
3. Write two differing scenarios of the future.

References

Best, Fred (1984). "Technology and the Changing World of Work", *The Futurist*, April.

Feingold, S. Norman (1984). "Emerging Careers: Occupations for Post-Industrial Society", *The Futurist*, February.

Freud, Sigmund (1931). *The Future of an Illusion*. (Hogarth Press, London).

Gruen, F.H. (1980). "The Economic Perspective", in Wilkes, J. (ed.), *The Future of Work*. (George Allen & Unwin: Sydney).

Handy, Charles (1984). *The Future of Work*. (Basil Blackwell: Oxford).

Harrington, Michael (1966). *The Accidental Century.* (Penguin: Harmondsworth).
Jones, Barry (1983). *Sleepers, Wake! Technology and the Future of Work*, 2nd edn. (Oxford University Press: Melbourne).
        (1984). Interview, *Australian Playboy*, March.
Kahn, Herman *et al.* (1976). *The Next 200 Years: A Scenario for America and the World.* (William Morrow: New York).
Kotler, Phillip (1986). "Prosumers: A New Type of Consumer", *The Futurist*, September–October.
Landes, Davis S. (1984). "Economic History Since 1500", *The New Encyclopaedia Brittanica*, 15th edn. (Encyclopaedia Brittanica, Inc.: Chicago), Macropaedia, vol. 6.
Lansbury, R.D. (1983). "Human Resources and the Future for Work", *Human Resource Management Australia*, August.
Leakey, Richard. (1981). *The Making of Mankind.* (Sphere: London).
Mead, Margaret (1983). "The Effects of Technology: A Guide to the Literature", *Work and People*, vol. 9, no. 3.
Naisbett, John (1984). *Megatrends.* (Fawcett: New York).
Rosow, Jerome M. (1980). "Personnel Policies for the 1980s", in Sheppard, C. Stewart and Carroll, Donald C., *Working in the Twenty-First Century.* (John Wiley and Sons: New York).
Saul, Peter (1983). "The New Workforce: Directions for Change", *Work and People*, vol. 9, no. 3.
Schumacher, E. (1974). *Small is Beautiful: A Study of Economics as if People Mattered.* (Harper and Row: New York).
Toffler, Alvin (1970). *Future Shock.* (Pan, London).
        (1980). *The Third Wave.* (Pan: London).
        (1984). *Previews and Premises.* (Pan: London).
        (1985). *The Adaptive Corporation.* (Pan: London).
        (1987). "Riding a Wave of Change", *The Age*, Friday, 9 January 1987, p.9.
Toynbee, Arnold (1972). *A Study of History.* (Oxford University Press: Oxord).
Wesley, James Paul (1974). *Ecophysics: The Application of Physics to Ecology.* (Charles C. Thomas: Illinois).
Wilmoth, Peter (1984). "A Future that Works", *The Age*, Monday, 17 September 1984, p.11.

Films/Videos

Megatrends (Training Media Services).
Move Over, Mate, Parts 1 and 2 (Amalgamated Metals Foundry and Shipwrights Union).

Part B

Causes of behaviour

Why do people work? We all have to survive, but the "survival explanation" does not explain why some people work more than others, or less than others, or indeed why some people continue to work even when their survival does not depend upon their working.

In attempting to understand such basic behaviour patterns, we will explore two major approaches. In Chapter 2 (Motivation) we will examine drives, needs, philosophies and expectations. Particular attention will be given to our values and perceptions about money, and to what extent it motivates us. Cultural differences in motivational patterns will also be looked at.

All of these are internal behaviour patterns: no one has ever seen a drive, a need, a philosophy, and so on. Some social scientists see this as being a crucial weakness, and instead propose a more external model of behaviour, based upon observable verbal and non-verbal events. In Chapter 3 (Learning and Behaviour Modification), we explore this more external approach, wherein behaviour is explained as a consequence of such outcomes as rewards and punishments, and the timing of such outcomes.

It may be that external behaviours and internal behaviours are merely two sides of the one coin, and that to a considerable extent the approaches outlined in these two chapters are as complementary as they are competitive.

Motivation

We know nothing about motivation. All we can do is write books about it.
Peter Drucker

Hell is full of the talented, and Heaven is full of the energetic.
St Jane Francis de Chantal

If at first you don't succeed, try, try again. Then quit. No use being a damn fool about it.
W.C. Fields

Who are the men who do things? The husbands of the shrew and the drunkard, the men with the thorn in the flesh.
George Bernard Shaw

If you pay peanuts, you get monkeys.
Sir James Goldsmith

The fundamental thing behind *all* motivation and activity is the constant struggle against annihilation and against death.
Woody Allen

WHAT motivates you? What makes you run? What makes you tick? Would you work three times as hard if you were paid three times more, or wouldn't it matter? If you won a million dollars tomorrow, would you quit work? If you were offered a high salary, would you work as a lighthouse keeper? If you were to become or are presently unemployed, what values about work, striving and leisure would you adopt? If, as some futurists would have it, work will be obsolete for most people in a few decades due to automation, what will be your values about work, striving and leisure when life is a seven-day weekend?

All of these questions go to the heart of understanding what motivation is. If we can see what goes on inside people —if we can see their drives, needs, expectations and perceptions—then we can see what it is that motivates them. This looking inside people is made more complex if we consider that some behaviour may as well be unconscious as conscious.[1] Also, behaviourist psychologists such as B.F. Skinner have argued that it is nonsensical to talk about such "internal" things as needs, drives, and so on, because no one has ever seen such things, let alone "a motive" or someone's "motivation". We must, say the behaviourists, only concentrate upon behaviour that can be

---

[1] Sigmund Freud and Eric Berne were great believers in people being motivated by unconscious drives and behaviour—see Transactional Analysis, or Games People Play chapter. Dichter (1964) also takes a Freudian or psychoanalytic approach to why people buy cars, furs, cigars, coffee and other goods and services, i.e. he considers what motivates consumers. Packard (1979) discusses attempts at motivating people in sport and work situations by hypnosis, i.e. by placing motivations directly into the unconscious mind.

measured, that is, *external* behaviour. Behaviourist theories of changing people's behaviour on the job and in other circumstances (in effect, theories about motivating people) are considered in Chapter 3, which should be seen as complementary to this chapter. Can we motivate others, or must people motivate themselves? Can we de-motivate others, or ourselves? What does it mean to be demotivated? Is the department in which you work demotivated? Check Box 2.A to see.

To get the big picture on motivation, we must go back to the turn of this century to consider the first modern theories of motivation.

Classic motivation: Frederick Taylor and scientific management

Frederick Taylor (1856–1915) developed ideas about work organisation, ideas which he later labelled "scientific management".[2] He analysed workflow to determine what were the most effective ways of getting a job done. Certain processes he refined are now part of organisations throughout the world—job description, planned flows of work, systematic stock control, detailed unit cost accounting—while others, such as time and motion study and individual piecework incentives, are still controversial (Kelly 1982).

Up until the late nineteenth century, a large measure of control in factories rested with skilled tradesmen and foremen who acted often as entrepreneurs, managing raw materials and labour for owners, many of whom did not get involved in the daily routine of production. The rise of a separate managerial class, members of which did not necessarily own stock in the organisation but were separate from and superior to workers, took place when industry began to grow in scale and become concerned with national markets, long-term investments and cost accounting (Hirschhorn 1984).

Taylor, an engineer, was very critical of American managers generally, feeling that they were too sloppy and unsystematic and also too unassertive in taking control from workers—an essential move if real productivity gains were to be achieved:

> The gain from these slide rules is far greater than that of all the other improvements combined, because it accomplishes the original objects, for which in 1880 the experiments were started, i.e. that of taking the control of the machine shop out of the hands of the many workmen, and placing it completely in the hands of management thus superseding "rule of thumb" by scientific control. (QUOTED IN KELLY 1982, P.15)

Knowledge of who controls an organisation, and who gets what in terms of profits and wages, is central to an understanding of any organisation. Taylor was not welcomed with open arms by all managers and owners, however, because he felt that productivity gains accruing from application of scientific management techniques should be shared to a certain extent by paying workers higher wages (Drucker 1981).

Taylor described one of the approaches of scientific management thus:

1. Find, say, ten to fifteen different men (preferably in as many separate establishments and different parts of the country) who are especially skilful in doing the particular work to be analysed.
2. Study the exact series of elementary operations or motions which each of these men uses in doing the work which is being investigated, as well as the implements each man uses.

---

[2] Taylor's ideas are also considered in Chapters 12, 13 and 14.

3. Study with a stop-watch the time required to make each of these elementary movements and then select the quickest way of doing each element of the work.
4. Eliminate all false movements, slow movements, and useless movements.
5. After doing away with all unnecessary movements, collect into one series the quickest and best movements as well as the best implements. (TAYLOR 1947, PP.117–18)

BOX 2.A: Demotivation and your department

Are there signs of demotivation in your department? Check your situation against the symptoms in the following checklist.

	Yes	No
1. People spend a lot of time gossiping cynically about the organisation.	✓	
2. Sometimes it seems to you as if each day brings widespread petty complaints and grievances.	✓	
3. People frequently make sarcastic comments about the organisation and its management.	✓	
4. There has been a drop-off in employee suggestions for better operation of the department.	✓	
5. You often hear comments such as "All you can do is hang in" or "The name of the game is survival".		✓
6. There is a pronounced "them vs. us" tone when employees talk about higher management.	✓	
7. There are many covert conversations among employees from which you are conspicuously excluded.		✓
8. Employees say with disturbing frequency, "What's the point in killing yourself?"		✓
9. There is an increase in absenteeism, especially among employees who formerly had exemplary work attendance records.		✓
10. While employees will carry out your instructions, they are noticeably reluctant to offer to take on responsibility.	✓	
11. People who have demonstrated a high ability to work well now seem to turn in assignments that are minimally acceptable in quality or quantity.	✓	
12. Employees regularly label management policies and decisions as unfair.	✓	
13. There is a disturbing trend towards procrastination and missing deadlines.	✓	
14. People seem to you to be bored and generally fatigued.	✓	
15. Your departmental employees seem to have developed strong cliques.	✓	
16. Employees who used to be ambitious now seem cynical about their chances to get ahead in the organisation.	✓	

	Yes	No
17. Employees whom you always viewed as reliable now openly display resentment when asked to take on extra work.	✓	
18. Employees seem to you to give up quickly when engaged in a demanding or complex task and seek help from you.	✓	
19. Organisational rules are scorned and ignored.		✓
20. Lateness has increased generally among your employees.	✓	
21. Employees spend organisational time doing personal tasks or making personal telephone calls.	✓	
22. There is a frequency in unexplained absences from offices, desks or workstations.		✓
23. There is disproportionate complaining about wages and salaries.	✓	
24. There is widespread grumbling about working conditions.	✓	
25. Equipment is not taken care of properly.		✓
26. Employees are reluctant to stay after hours even to finish work that could be completed in a short time.	✓	
27. People do not seem to listen carefully when you give instructions.		✓
28. Employees spend inordinate amounts of time doing relatively simple tasks.	✓	
29. Employees make frequent references to how well off their friends and acquaintances are in other organisations.	✓	
30. Employees complain loudly and frequently that too many objectives come down from higher management for them to meet.	✓	
31. Employees complain that higher management sets conflicting priorities that make it difficult for them to work effectively.	✓	
32. You often have to follow up your assignments of tasks and responsibilities to make sure they are done correctly and on time.		✓
33. Many employees seem unwilling to pitch in and help co-workers.		✓
34. There is a neglect of routine chores.	✓	
35. Employees frequently rationalise sloppiness and errors.	✓	
36. There are frequent and widespread comments made about what employees consider errors by higher management.	✓	
37. There are frequent, belittling comments made about the capability of higher management.	✓	
38. In meetings with representatives of higher management employees often sit silently but become active in after-the-meeting meetings among themselves.	✓	

		Yes	No
39.	Some employees complain bitterly about what they regard as preferential treatment given to others.	___	✓
40.	Some employees complain frequently that other employees in the department are not carrying their share of the load.	___	✓
41.	You sense that one or more employees have become informal leaders in the department in covert opposition to your authority.	___	✓
42.	As you make rounds of your department, you are struck by the widespread socialising you see.	✓	___
43.	There are frequent comments by employees that reveal their suspicion that management is out to manipulate or take advantage of them.	✓	___
44.	There is a rise in mistakes and incompleteness even in routine work that employees have always performed well.	___	✓
45.	Employees seem reluctant to discuss their long-range plans with you.	___	✓
46.	There is inordinate resistance to and grumbling about even minor changes.	✓	___
47.	Employees appear to need frequent monitoring by you in order to apply themselves to their work.	___	✓
48.	You find yourself often giving pep talks to employees to energise them to do their work.	✓	___
49.	There has been an increase in unpredictable delays and snafus.	✓	___
50.	Employees who formerly seemed easygoing and relaxed now display frequent tension and irritability.	___	✓

While every person in a work situation will experience such demotivation symptoms from time to time, Quick (1985) suggests that if more than ten of these symptoms apply to most employees most of the time, then the department is headed for trouble.

Source: Quick (1985), pp.45–9. Reproduced with permission.

Money as a motivator

Such a time-and-motion study produced the "one new method" which was meant to be the acme of efficiency. Taylor, an engineer, also did extensive analysis of workflow and layout of factories and their machinery. Combining his engineering of humans with his engineering of factory environments, he was able sometimes to achieve spectacular increases in productivity. Thus, at the Bethlehem Steel Plant, Taylor trained a worker pseudonymously known as Schmidt to improve the efficiency of his task—loading steel ingots—by almost 370 per cent.[3] Taylor refined the notion of *piecework incentives*, that

---

[3] Or so Taylor claimed. Lee (1980) alleges that many of Taylor's results were fixed, i.e. Taylor lied about results.

is, getting more money per unit work achieved, and Schmidt received a 61 per cent increase in wages. As Dowling and Sayles observe,

> ... scientific management saw the worker, at least the hourly employee, as essentially a passive economic man with strong muscles and a weak mind only capable of absorbing the simple routines of mass-producing technology—and, incidentally, a person willing to accept a 61 per cent increase in wages for a 362 per cent increase in productivity. (DOWLING AND SAYLES 1979)

Taylor separated planning from execution, head-work from hand-work, labour from management, staff personnel from line personnel. His methods are still used widely today, particularly by engineering-minded managements, and are especially useful when computers and automated systems are being programmed to replace human labour. Taylor's recommendations for remuneration (or lack of remuneration) of Schmidt the labourer goes to the heart of the debate that still rages today: if people can be motivated to produce more, who gets what? Who gets the additional surpluses generated —labour, management, the owners, the government? Taylor, who worked mainly with batch-type production setups, and Henry Ford, who helped perfect the assembly line, both aimed for higher productivity and thus higher profits, but also for higher wages for workers—to this extent they were atypical of their time and ahead of their time. The key questions that still hang over their achievements are: were wage increases commensurate with profit increases? and did re-engineering of workflow have a negative effect upon workers?

Taylor was considerate enough of the *physical* needs of the workmen: jobs should be engineered so that a man did not have to work at a "pace which would be injurious to his health". However, to perform a specialised task with relentless monotony, Taylor advised that the average worker "should be so stupid and phlegmatic that he more nearly resembles, in his mental make-up, the ox than any other type" (Taylor 1947).

The *psychological* needs of the worker, then, were given very short shrift. Boredom, frustration and alienation experienced on such jobs were (and are) the basis of criticisms that the Taylor system was "dehumanising".

Taylor and his followers often saw the worker behaving as modern economists still do—as *homo economicus*, a being motivated by rational economic self-interest, weighing up individual profits and losses, and then acting accordingly. Later critics of Taylor have suggested that he did not understand the true pattern of human motivation, that he over-concentrated on individual piecework and neglected group dynamics and such "non-rational" group phenomena as output reduction (see below for discussion of Mayo and the Hawthorne experiments). Yet, as Kelly (1982) points out, Taylor was well aware of the effectiveness of work groups as opposed to individual workers, and he was well aware of groups holding down output (or "soldiering"). But Taylor was very suspicious of the countervailing pressure of unions and organised work groups, and felt that the best way to undercut such organisation was to appeal to the individual worker through piecework incentives. Taylor envisaged a "cooperative partnership" of labour and management, wherein labour unions would disappear entirely. Thus he established the central tenet of American management ideology which persists to this day.

Taylorism: Dead, but refusing to lie down

It is fashionable to dismiss Taylorism or "scientific management" as the barbaric pre-history of the workplace, the ideology of the bad old days before work became humanised by more compassionate management. This fashionable belief is quite wrong.

Taylorist ideas on work design are still at the core of most industries today, both in factories where blue collars are worn and in offices where white collars are worn (Cooley 1977). Their impetus has been weakened to a certain extent because:

1. The level of education has risen remarkably, so that foremen and workers now possess a high standard of technological literacy, and are less likely to be "ox-like".
2. The standard of living has likewise risen remarkably, thereby minimising the motivating stimulus of piecework.
3. Industrial unionism has emerged as a major force and has required managers to bargain collectively on many matters which were previously solved by unilateral (and often arbitrary) action (Juran 1974).
4. The interdependence of work roles does not permit a ready identification of individual effort (Katz and Kahn 1978).
5. Even if individual effort could always be clearly identified, the individual worker may be locked into a pace of work set by his or her colleagues "upstream".
6. Behavioural scientists have attempted to prove that such job design is not only inhumane, but inefficient, because it does not take account of certain psychological needs of the worker. Such scientists allege that workers compensate for dehumanisation by absenteeism, high turn-over, vandalism and "unjustified" industrial action. Their recommendation? Break down barriers between planners and executors: give some decision-making to workers and therefore "humanise the work-place" and improve the "quality of work life".

Nevertheless, despite these trends, Taylorism remains, as Juran (1974) notes:

American managers have a considerable investment in the Taylor system, and they cannot dismantle it easily since it is deeply rooted and has shaped much of the existing cultural patterns of managers and technical specialists... Many of the specialised planners (e.g. industrial engineers, quality control engineers) exhibit a vested interest in the status quo.

The same point is made—with more political fervour—by Frenkel (1977) and Braverman (1974):

The continuity of Taylorism is bound up with the past successes of American industry as governed by the principle of worker subordination to production for profit. A rising and relatively high standard of living has legitimated an economistic orientation by workers and a production-marketing perspective by top corporate management. In this way, staff managers such as those responsible for personnel and industrial relations have been relegated to less powerful positions in the corporate hierarchy. And it is precisely those people who specialise in "the human side of enterprise". They are most committed to humanising the workplace, yet they lack the power to effect such change. As Braverman so aptly puts it: "Taylorism dominates the world of production; the practitioners of 'human relations' and 'industrial psychology' are the maintenance crew for the human machinery."

While these remarks pertain specifically to America, they are roughly true for most industrialised countries, including communist countries such as Russia: Lenin and other early revolutionaries were keen students of Taylor's writings and implemented many of his ideas (Jones 1983).

We need to be careful when talking about Taylor and "Taylorism", of course. It is too much of a cliché to characterise Taylor the man as an inhuman genius who destroyed the souls of millions in factories and "dark satanic mills". Taylor was quite concerned about workers getting higher wages, and this in fact made him unpopular with many managers. Many people who applied his ideas did not wish to reward higher productivity with higher wages. Perhaps, just as Marx once said "I am not a Marxist", in ironic reference to others who had taken and twisted his ideas, Taylor might have said "I am not a Taylorist".

The human relations movement: Elton Mayo and the Hawthorne studies

Scientific management and its practitioners achieved some amazing increases in productivity by perceiving workers as being motivated primarily by economic wants. But man does not live by bread alone, and scientific management began to decline in prestige, as opposed to actual influence, with the rise of the so-called "human relations" movement of the 1930s. This school drew many new insights about work behaviour from a series of experiments conducted at the Western Electric factory in Hawthorne, Illinois, from 1924 to 1932. The chief researcher in these studies was Elton Mayo, an Australian psychiatrist who worked as a sociologist at the Harvard Business School.

Originally, the experiment was couched in scientific management terms: Would manipulation of variables such as illumination, temperature, humidity, rest pauses, hours of work, variety of tasks and monetary incentives and style of supervision cause productivity to rise? (Mayo 1953). The major experiment began in 1927 when a test group of five girls assembling telephone relays was subjected to all these variables over two years, at the end of which period output had risen by 30 per cent. The five girls, removed from the vast factory floor where other workers were, developed closer personal relationships with themselves and with their supervisors.'

Mayo and his associates hypothesised four explanations for the rise in output:

1. changes in the character and the physical context of the work task
2. reduction of fatigue and monotony consequent upon introduction of rest pauses and reduced hours of work
3. change in the payment system
4. changes in supervision with consequent social changes in group relations

A scientific management analysis of the problem would have emphasised the first three hypothesis as the correct ones, yet Mayo and his associates finished up plumping for the fourth one.

Hypothesis 1 was rejected out of hand because in a preliminary experiment, a test group worked under changed lighting conditions, and improved its output—but unfortunately, so did the control group working under unchanged conditions.

Hypothesis 2 was rejected because even though output increased when rest pauses were increased and hours were cut, output still remained high when original conditions were returned (although there is some confusion about this: Carey (1967) asserts that output *did* drop upon return to normal hours).

This left hypotheses 3 and 4 as the potential explanations. Accordingly, two experiments were set up: one testing the power of incentive wages to motivate, the other testing a new, more democratic and relaxed method of supervision.

The output of the incentive wages group went up 13 per cent almost immediately, but their peers outside the experiment complained about the test group's higher wages. The experiment was discontinued after nine weeks, whereupon the test group's output dropped 16 per cent. Mayo and his associates did not conclude that money motivates, however; they attributed the test group's performance to their psychological need to outdo the performance of other test groups in previous experiments.

This left the group working under changed conditions of supervision. Over a fourteen-month period, output rose about 14 per cent, and then went into decline. The experiment was discontinued in 1932 due to the Western Electric company laying off staff—the Depression had struck.

Behavioural pressures within the work group

Other experiments were conducted prior to 1932. A large-scale interviewing program took place, attempting to probe the psychological profiles of staff. A small-scale experiment took place within another test group, where close observation revealed that group behaviour can sometimes lead to actions that scientific management would be at a loss to explain. Some of these group *norms* or unofficial rules were:

1. the group did not perform to its maximum ability, but rather restricted output;
2. there were two informal groups or cliques in the room, and individual behaviour was partially dictated by the norms of the groups;
3. to be accepted by the group, one had to observe informal rules such as not doing too much work, not doing too little work, and never telling a superior anything that might be detrimental to an associate. (HODGETTS 1980, P.91)

In America, such unofficial rules meant that someone working too hard was a "ratebuster"; someone working too little would be a "goldbricker"; in Australia, one doesn't "dob on your mates"; if you do, you are "frozen out" or "sent to Coventry" (see also Chapter 11).

Such rules, while puzzling to psychological researchers, and infuriating to managements, do make some sense. If output goes up dramatically, management may renegotiate downwards wage-per-unit-output levels, or lay off "unnecessary" staff, or both. Not telling tales outside the group is a standard, and most effective, dynamic of groups as diverse as criminal gangs and cabinets of politicians.

Such unofficial rules binding together the work groups at Hawthorne were a revelation to Mayo. When combined with the findings of how styles of supervision or leadership seemed to affect output crucially, such phenomena implied that scientific management's model of economic man was not the whole picture.

As a result of the Hawthorne studies, behavioural scientists began to look more closely at factors such as group dynamics, leadership and employee counselling, trying to ascertain what impacts they might have upon productivity. One of the most interesting outcomes of the experiment was the spelling out of what came to be called the *Hawthorne effect*: the novelty or interest of a new situation will lead to positive results, at least in the short term. Thus, with the initial lighting experiments, both the test group and the control group increased productivity. It may be, Mayo posited, that both groups were so interested and excited about being in an experiment that they tried harder anyway.

The human relations approach: Defended and attacked

The influence of the "human relations" school of management, drawing scientific credibility from Hawthorne and other studies, increased. The president of the American Management Association said in 1946 that

> American business is taking concrete steps to ensure that its management in all echelons . . . is thoroughly conversant with intelligent and enlightened human relations policies. . . Top executives are stating flatly that knowledge of human relations is one of the most important, if not the prime requisite, to management at all levels. (QUOTED IN CAREY 1980, P.24)

This is a far cry from Taylor prescribing an "ox-like" temperament for the ideal worker and, undoubtedly, a long-term trend towards humanisation of the workplace and improvement of the quality of work life was begun at this time.

Nevertheless, a cloud hangs over the motives of the proponents of these "new" motivators drawn from psychology rather than economics. Carey, for example, has attacked the Hawthorne studies as being scientifically worthless, and probably an instance of falsification of facts. Thus, while Mayo and his associates discounted money as a motivator, Carey says the facts prove otherwise: the best results in output came from the group motivated by money incentives (Carey 1967).

Peter Drucker, doyen of American management consultants, made the following sweeping statement in 1950:

> The human relations policies which American management has been buying wholesale in the past ten years have been a conspicuous waste and failure. In my opinion . . . most of us in management . . . have instituted them as a means of busting the unions. That has been the main theme of these programs. They are based on the belief that if you have good employee relations the unions will wither on the vine. (QUOTED IN CAREY 1976, P.165)

Spillane says much the same thing, saying that the development of the human relations school came as a godsend to American and other management confronted with an increasing union militancy and labour surplus in the 1930s (Spillane 1981).

This is a lot of mud being thrown, and probably a good deal of it will stick. It may be that much of the Hawthorne studies' methods and conclusions are shaky, and it may be that many unscrupulous managers have used the prestige of the study to persuade employees that they really don't want more money, but better human relations instead. Nevertheless, certain outcomes of Hawthorne, such as new perceptions of the attitudes and values of managers and workers, are intriguing in what they suggest. Insofar as they are true, they provide a salutary corrective to the powerful thrust of Taylorism.

Maslow's hierarchy of needs: Becoming self-actualised

Abraham Maslow (1908–70) began to develop a theory of human motivation in the early 1940s that has since proved to be very influential. He argued that humans have needs, which can best be understood as levels in a hierarchy or ladder of sequence (Fig. 2.1). Humans share instincts, physiological needs (for food, water, sex, etc.) and safety needs (self-protection) with insects and animals. We presume that we alone experience the upper three needs: love or belonging or social need, esteem, and self-actualisation (development of psychological potential).

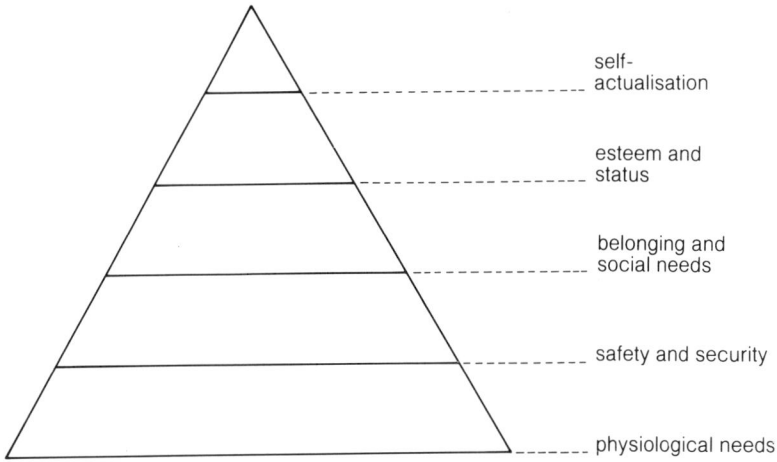

Fig. 2.1 *Hierarchy of behaviour* (MASLOW 1943)

If we define instinct as behaviour not acquired through learning, we see that the five levels of this hierarchy of behaviour have a crucial learning component. A newborn human body will not emerge from its mother's womb and instinctively begin foraging for food; it needs quite a few years' support from a culture before it can begin to do that. The child's socialisation into its culture will teach it some basic lessons about priorities in life, such as, one attends to one's basic needs before attending to higher needs ("grub first, then ethics", as the German playwright Bertolt Brecht put it).

By arranging human behaviours in a hierarchy, Maslow developed his theory of what motivates us, which can be put quite simply as *a satisfied need no longer motivates*. Once we have met our needs for food and sleep, we can relax and enjoy some leisure. The opposite pattern sometimes occurs, but not often. We may be motivated to find food when we are hungry, but once that need is satisfied, the motivation is not so strong. The strength of the motivation will return, but for the moment we are sated, and hence our attention wanders to, we are motivated by, other things.

The point about the return of hunger is noteworthy. Not only do needs recur, it is possible that needs can be partially satisfied and partially unsatisfied at the same time, as Maslow pointed out:

> In actual fact, most members of our society who are normal are partly satisfied in all their basic needs and partly unsatisfied in all their basic needs at the same time. A more realistic description of the hierarchy would be in terms of decreasing percentage of satisfaction as we go up the hierarchy. . . For instance, if I may assign arbitrary figures . . . it is as if the average citizen is satisfied perhaps 85 per cent in his physiological needs, 70 per cent in his safety needs, 50 per cent in his (social) needs, 40 per cent in his self-esteem needs, and 10 per cent in his self-actualisation needs. (MASLOW 1943, P.342)

By arranging needs in a hierarchy, Maslow not only created a model of motivation, but also a model of psychological growth—once we have reached a certain level, we are ready to explore our potential at the next level.

Let's now have a more detailed look at the five levels of human behaviour, and see how they help to explain the motivation to work.

Physiological needs

"I will die fairly quickly without. . ." is a good way to generate a list of basic physiological needs. Thus, we see food, drink, sleep, shelter and clothing probably come in here, and, while we personally may not die without sex, the species (prior to the advent of total genetic engineering) will, so we include sex as well.

Because Maslow never totally adapted his "pure" model of motivation to the "applied" area of work motivation, it is not clear where money fits in, but it probably fits most comfortably into this first basic level.

The physical environment in which we work has been given increasing attention in the past few decades (although the initial impetus lay with Taylor and the scientific managers). Lighting, heating, air-conditioning, cafeterias, toilet and cleaning facilities all impact upon these needs. So too do such arrangements as shiftwork and flexitime.

Sexual needs often come into focus when people work in remote locations such as deserts, arctic zones or space, or are in institutions such as prisons, the armed forces and boarding schools.

In China and Japan, calisthenics are considered to be a crucial part of the working day, while an increasing number of organisations in Western countries make gymnasium, running and aerobic facilities available to staff because of imputed linkages between fitness and productivity.

Medical care is made available in some organisations, and an increasing number of occupations are seen to have deleterious effects upon health. Health hazards which traditionally were tolerated as necessary evils (such as black lung disease in coal mining) are being questioned more seriously, while new occupational diseases (such as repetition strain injury or tenosynovitis in typists' wrists and eyestrain resulting from video display terminals) are causing concern. Hunt notes that strong physiological needs are typically found in process workers and manual workers, and in some physical fitness occupations (Hunt 1979, p.129).

Safety, security and structure needs

We all have needs to ensure that we are relatively safe and secure—and a good thing, too. We can become locked into this level of functioning, however. Maslow felt that the majority of people were unable to move much beyond this level (Maslow 1970).

There is obviously an overlap between safety needs and physiological needs: safety needs phenomena such as health regulations and workers' compensation legislation obviously are designed to ameliorate physiological hazards.

A person working in a relatively hazardous job for the money may change his job if he marries and starts a family. A person may resign from a job because there is too little structure—the rules are not spelled out, the job profile changes continually. A salesperson becomes stressed by the pressure of living off her commissions, and requests a transfer to a salaried job in administration. An engineering lecturer at a university toys with the idea of becoming a freelance consultant on a full-time basis, but decides to stick with teaching. All these people show high safety, security and structure needs— they choose one path rather than another because they wish to minimise risk more than anything.

Other people may have reduced safety needs. It is notorious that people in their late teens and early twenties, particularly males, feel the necessity to demonstrate their courage and daring, particularly in automobiles; as a result, the mortality levels in this group are disproportionately high. Many people are bored with the security of modern life, and take up high-risk pastimes such as mountain-climbing, sky-diving and car-racing. A middle-aged executive may horrify his peers by dropping out of "the rat-race" to live on a commune, choosing a life of self-reliance without the safety-net of superannuation, insurance, fringe benefits, etc.

Social factors can affect this need considerably. People who survived the 1930s depression may strike younger people as being over-cautious; the older people may, following the fable of Aesop, see themselves as the prudent ants, ready for whatever hardships the future holds, and the younger people as improvident grasshoppers. People born after World War II have benefited from relative affluence, and may have lower safety and security needs. People with high needs have traditionally gone into "safe" jobs such as banking, insurance, teaching and public service. Although traditionally immune from automation-induced unemployment, such areas are now not immune, and hence such people may develop still higher needs for security. Students of the 1970s and 1980s may seem less adventurous and critical than students of the 1960s, but this difference in behaviour may be due to the fact that the 1960s were boom times, whereas the 1970s and 1980s have been substantially harder.[4]

Social needs: Love and belonging

Dowling and Sayles (1978) discuss a survey done in Michigan where 401 workers were asked if they would continue working if they inherited enough money to live comfortably: 80 per cent said they would. They were not in it just for the money: the work environment was a social environment which provided emotional as well as financial satisfactions.

Many people do not experience a strong social need. They can work quite happily by themselves, and may in fact choose a job which has minimal contact with other people. Still others may loathe work in general, seeing it only as a "meal-ticket" which makes "real life'—their life away from the job—economically possible. Such people may be non-committal about the "strokes" they receive on the job, preferring the "strokes" they get from family and friends.

Hunt suggests that some 60 per cent of the workforce may often be quite content to stay at the bottom of work hierarchies, more satisfied with relationships than "self-actualisation". Such relationship-motivated people are different from self-actualisation-motivated people:

> They are not motivated by the same goals, and we should stop making assumptions about their ambitions, hopes, and even their needs. Man has a long history of projecting his own goal profile onto every other man. But what is success? Who gets the best deal—the highly successful executive, locked into his office on his own, or the chap on the factory floor, working, playing and drinking with his mates? (HUNT 1979, P.131)

Esteem needs

According to Maslow's model, once a person has satisfied physiological, security and social needs, she will only be motivated by the two higher needs—esteem and self-actualisation. Esteem is basically tied up with our

---

[4] Note the relationship between need for structure and power drive in Chapter 10.

self-image: Have we made it in life? Do we have the symbols of prestige and status we have craved? Have we reached a position of power to make things happen? Has our achievement been recognised by others, that is, is our self-esteem matched by the esteem given by others?

The first three needs act almost as a platform upon which we can achieve or, if you like, a nest from which we can take our first faltering swoops before we fly free. Rewards and punishments shape our behaviour and thus our self-esteem; if we succeed at school, if our parents are continually supportive of us and speak glowingly of our initial small achievements, we develop a healthy and confident self-image. A pattern of winning becomes apparent, and we say with Eleanor Roosevelt, "No one can make you feel inferior without your consent".

If an opposite pattern of defeat and punishment shapes us, we develop a poor self-image: We are not worthy of our own self-respect, so how can we engender respect from others?

Thus the successful person—and we must be careful of our criteria of "success", as Hunt has pointed out—begins to realise his or her esteem needs. For a business executive, esteem might be gratified by being given a higher credit rating and a lease on a luxury sports car. For a novelist, barely subsisting on a few thousand dollars a year, it might be the publication of a novel and a few favourable reviews. For a research scientist, it might be favourable comments in a professional journal on an experiment of hers. For a housewife acting as a charity worker, it might be a photograph in the local paper and some telephone calls from like-minded people working in the same area. For a shearer, it might mean being honoured with the title "gun shearer" by his peers in a country pub. For a criminal after performing a particularly violent murder, it might be a wink and a nod from a mob boss. All of these people have had an elevation in status, have demonstrated that they are more than just a journeyman in their chosen area of competence.

Some researchers have tried to expand Maslow's concept of esteem by talking of "independence" and "power" (Zoll 1974; Hunt 1979). These two latter concepts are much the same, because Zoll speaks of the prime constituent of independence being "the authority to get things done", that is, power. Many organisational theorists seem to be embarrassed by the concept of power—they seem to think it is in bad taste. This is particularly unfortunate when discussing the issue of motivation, because it is one of the central motives of human behaviour.

Self-actualisation

Self-actualisation is a rare behaviour: it is basically about making dreams come true, of being all that you can be. This is a very fuzzy definition, and betrays the simultaneous strength and weakness of this mystical enlightenment that awaits us at the top of Maslow's pyramid: for a self-actualiser may be a person, like a saint, whom we wish to emulate, but like a saint, does not give a clear idea *how* we can emulate his or her behaviour. Even Maslow's definition of self-actualisation is not terribly clear, or at least prescriptive:

> (Self-actualisation) may be loosely described as the full use and exploitation of talents, capacities, potentialities, etc. Such people seem to be fulfilling themselves and to be doing the best that they are capable of doing, reminding us of Nietzsche's exhortation "Become what thou art". They are people who have developed, or are developing to the full stature of what they are capable. (MASLOW 1970, P.26)

Yet self-actualisers often do not fit well into organisations, where conformity, rather than questing after truth for its own sake, may be the most desired personality attribute. Indeed, Hunt has suggested that self-actualisers may not make very good bosses, because they expect too much from others, don't explain adequately just what it is they want, and remain loners. Self-actualisers tend to prefer working alone or in small groups, and have high creative needs; they might be found working as film directors, writers, architects, artists, research academics, sportspeople, systems analysts, financial analysts, consultants, entrepreneurs, managing directors or politicians.

Pessimistically, there may only be room for a few self-actualisers anywhere; optimistically, this may not be such a bad thing:

> Organisations only absorb a small number of people with very strong goals for self-actualisation, because of their search for novelty and change, their intolerance of mistakes, their "flighty" shifts from one job to another, and their aversion to formal controls. Yet they are the innovators, the creators . . . (the self-actualiser) is the artist, poet, entrepreneur, research scientist, long-distance runner. He is alone, and that may be the price of self-fulfilment, and the danger in our mania with goal-directed behaviour. We may be producing a society of high-achieving loners, for whom interpersonal relationships are temporary and blatantly secondary in importance. (HUNT 1979, P.138)

Maslow's hierarchy of needs: Does it work?

Research attempting to prove or disprove the existence of Maslow's hierarchy of needs has not produced strong conclusions either way—if anything, the evidence is slightly against it being a true and predictive model of human behaviour (Dunphy and Dick 1981; Lee 1980).

You no doubt could conceive of instances where your behaviour would not always follow the hierarchical pattern suggested by Maslow; for example, you might place self-actualisation ahead of belongingness or even safety and security. Some, like Yankelovich (1981), argue that Maslow's idealising of self-actualisation or self-fulfilment has been *too* influential—it has produced the "Me Generation", a generation of people who use psychology as a religion and selfishly ignore others in their quest for perfect self-development.

In spite of these criticisms, the model is probably quite useful if we see it as a way of attaching priorities to the values we impose on the world (rather than as a precise measure of "needs" that mysteriously live within us). As such, it is useful for analysing needs in different situations, such as:

- the needs of different people on the one job;
- the needs of the one person throughout that person's life-cycle (see e.g. Hunt 1979);
- the ideal profile of needs for a worker in a particular job;
- the changing needs structure of a society at different stages of development (see e.g. Davis 1981, and below);
- the different needs structures of different cultures and groups (see e.g. Nevis 1983, for a comparison of American and Chinese needs profiles).

Davis has come up with hypothetical figures of the needs and structures of the United States' labour force in 1935 and 1995 (Fig. 2.2). Do you agree with his analysis? You may disagree with the shape of the profiles he has constructed, but if you feel you could draw more accurate profiles, then the

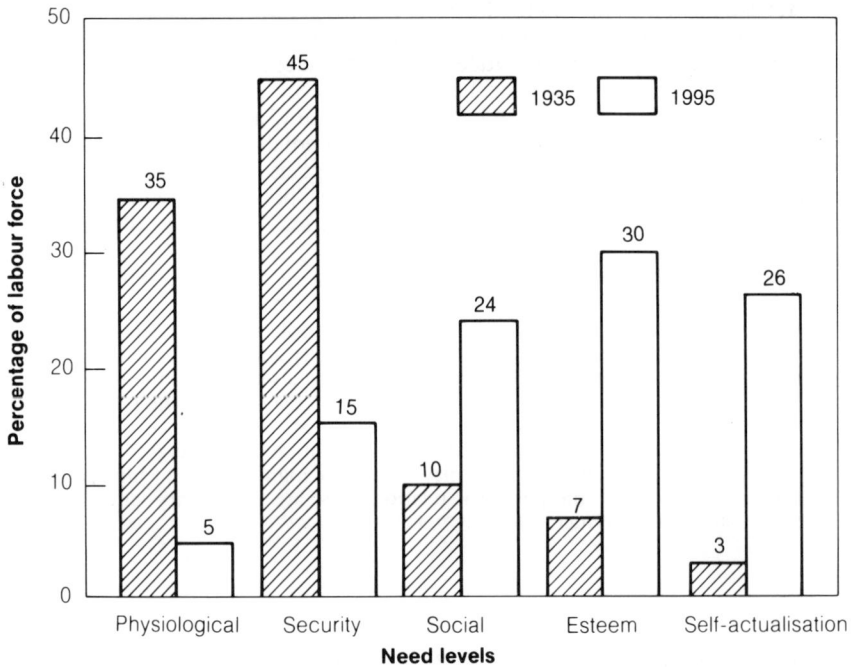

Fig. 2.2 *Possible changes in distribution of dominant needs in the US labour force, 1935–95* (DAVIS 1981, P.51. REPRODUCED WITH PERMISSION)

profile idea—and hence Maslow's hierarchy of needs—has some usefulness for you.[5]

Herzberg: The two-factor theory

The model of motivation developed by Herzberg (1968, 1976) can be seen to be a refinement of Maslow's model, albeit with significant differences. Fred Herzberg worked with several hundred engineers and accountants in Pittsburgh, USA, in the mid-1950s. In trying to find out what made them tick, or in fact what motivated them, he and his associates asked them:

> Think of a time when you felt exceptionally good or exceptionally bad about your job, either your present job or any other job you have had. This can be either the "long-range" or the "short-range" kind of situation, as I have described it. Tell me what happened. (QUOTED IN LUTHANS 1981, P.181)

In analysing the results of the experiment, Herzberg claimed that there were two separate factors involved in job-related behaviour. These he termed *motivators* and *hygiene* or *maintenance* factors (Table 2.1).

---

[5] Alderfer (1972) has collapsed Maslow's five needs into three: Existence needs (= Maslow's physiological and safety needs); Relatedness needs (= Maslow's safety, social, and some of the esteem needs); and Growth needs (= Maslow's self-actualisation and some of the esteem needs). Alderfer believes that these needs are active simultaneously, rather than sequentially or hierarchically. Milton, Entrekin and Stening (1983) report that some research suggests that Alderfer's model of behaviour is more useful than Maslow's, but that it is still early days in research and much work needs to be done and more data is needed.

Table 2.1 Herzberg's two-factor theory of motivation

Hygiene factors (extrinsic to job)	Motivators (intrinsic to job)
Pay	Achievement
Supervision	Recognition
Job security	Work itself
Status	Responsibility
Company policy, administration	Advancement

Herzberg called the "hygiene factors" just that because they were like preventive medicine—hygiene could prevent disease, but it did not do much for actually developing health. If these factors are not acknowledged in work situations, Herzberg claims, people will not work hard. But even if they are acknowledged, they will not motivate people; they will only prevent dissatisfaction.

If money, security, status, supervision and company policy will not motivate people, or at least will not motivate them well, what will? Herzberg suggests that the real motivation lies within the nature of the job itself, and whatever opportunities lie therein for recognition, responsibility and advancement. He suggests that these opportunities can be expanded through

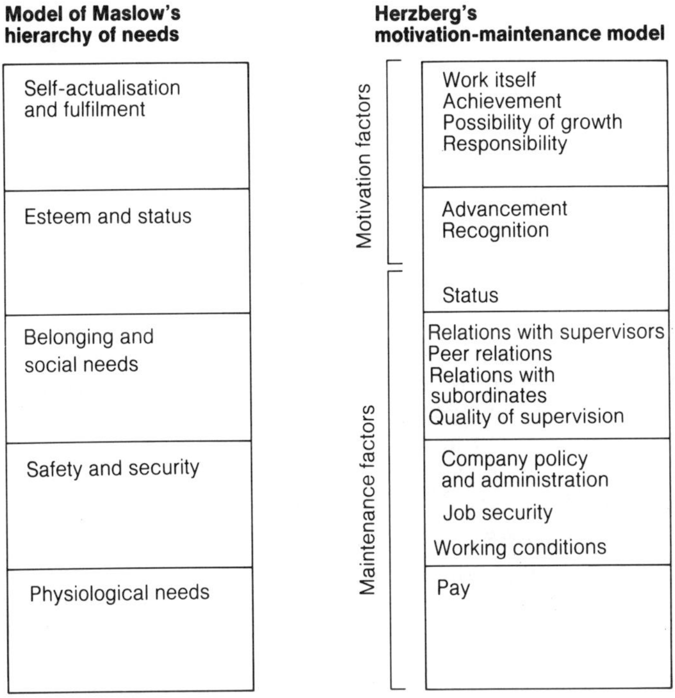

Fig. 2.3 *A comparison of Maslow's and Herzberg's models of motivation* (DAVIS 1981. REPRODUCED WITH PERMISSION)

what is termed *job enrichment*, wherein jobs are re-designed to incorporate motivators. Thus, a person could be given a complete natural unit of work (module, division, area, etc.) which would motivate through giving responsibility, achievement and recognition (see Chapter 12 for an analysis of job enrichment programs and philosophy).[6]

There are obvious similarities here to Maslow's model of motivation, with an emphasis upon psychological growth needs as being superior to more basic needs. It is useful to compare the two graphically (Fig. 2.3).

It is interesting to note that Maslow and Hunt combine recognition, esteem and status into the one category, whereas Herzberg feels that status is not a motivator.

Herzberg evaluated

How useful is Herzberg's model? Johnston and Bavin (1973) report some corroboration of Herzberg's findings, and Herzberg's more recent work (1976) contains claims that the theory has stood the test of time and hence is a genuinely predictive model of human behaviour. There are problems with the model, however. The "critical incident" interviewing method is quite subjective (i.e. it is difficult to compare the reports of interviews conducted by multiple interviewers). Also, simply because one is unhappy about something, such as pay or status, does not mean that one is not motivated by such things. . . [7] Money may not bring happiness, as the old joke has it, but it can certainly give you a more comfortable form of misery.

Davis (1981) also points out that when the Herzberg method is used to ask people what is good about a job, their egos lead them to report things that *they* have done, attributing bad facets of jobs—such as style of supervision— to others.

Spillane (1981) criticises Herzberg for characterising some workers' pre-occupation with money as being neurotic and, in some cases, being signs of mental illness. Spillane points out that many jobs are unlikely to be enriched, and for many workers to be pre-occupied with, or motivated by, money is not at all neurotic—in fact it is perfectly sane and rational.

Carey has been as critical of the two-factor theory as he has of the Hawthorne studies, and has noted some interesting inconsistencies in Herzberg's behaviour: Herzberg has been very well paid for his public appearances where he discusses the unimportance of money, but when questioned on this, Herzberg remarked, "But, hell, I believe in hygiene factors" (quoted in Carey 1976). As Carey remarks, "One is driven to the conclusion that Herzberg is either a comic artist, or an exploiter of the *comédie humaine* of some genius" (Carey 1976, p.165).

Theory X and theory Y: McGregor's view of motives and values

McGregor (1960) distinguished between two world-views and/or managerial styles, called theory X and theory Y (Table 2.2). Close examination of these theories shows that Taylorist scientific management is very close to theory X,

---

[6] Myers (1970) adopted Herzberg's theory to produce a variation of "goal-setting" job design and motivation (see Chapter 12).

[7] This is one of the criticisms advanced by expectancy theorists of motivation: they argue that the notion of "happy workers being productive workers" is a fallacy.

Table 2.2 Theory X and theory Y

Theory X	Theory Y
People by nature:	*People by nature:*
• dislike work; they are lazy, and try to avoid it as much as possible	• like work, and will seek it out
• need to be controlled and motivated by others, using rewards and punishments	• can control and motivate themselves
• dislike responsibility	• like responsibility
• dislike achievement	• like achievement
• cannot be trusted	• can be trusted
• never change	• can change
• are gullible and are easily manipulated	• are perceptive and not easily manipulated
• are self-centred and do not care about organisational goals	• want their organisation to succeed

Source: Adapted from McGregor (1960).

while theory Y ideas are present more in the Hawthorne studies and the theories of Maslow and Herzberg. Thus, theory X sees man as *homo economicus*, a creature motivated only by material rewards like money, preferably in a piecework situation. Theory X also has it that man does not really like to work, that work is as seen by the traditional Judaeo–Christian ethic, a punishment from God ("in the sweat of thy face shalt thou eat bread. . ." Genesis, 3.19). A theory X exponent such as Taylor might say that a theory Y exponent, with a vastly more optimistic and humanistic view-point, is naive in believing that workers can be motivated by the work itself, and are capable of responsibility and making their own decisions.

Yet it is not only idealistic academics trying to humanise the workplace who swear by theory Y: Robert Townsend, former chief executive officer of Avis car rentals claims that, by using theory Y, he was able to turn around a thirteen-year run of losses into record profits. When entering his job, he was advised to get rid of most of the existing staff, because it was presumed that they were incompetent. Townsend stuck with virtually all of the old staff, and turned them into a winning team:

> The only excuse for organisation is to maximise the chance that each (employee), working with others, will get for growth in his job. You can't motivate people. That door is locked from the inside. You *can* create a climate in which most of your people will motivate themselves to help the company reach its objectives. Like it or not, the only practical act is to adopt theory Y assumptions and get going. (TOWNSEND 1984, P.109)

Theory Y, says Townsend, can win real wars as well as market shares:

> Theory Y is the explanation for Ho Chi Minh's unbelievable twenty-five year survival against the mighty blasts of theory X monsters of three nations. . . (p.141)

How? Because (as Townsend tells it) North Vietnamese generals eschewed status displays which would separate them from private soldiers, and lived and fought alongside their men in the field. Thus, as Townsend sees it, motivation is merely another word for morale.

Theory X/theory Y has become a convenient shorthand way of noting people's philosophical differences about work and human attitudes to work. Troubles begin to arise, however, when people look at the motivation models of McGregor, Maslow and Herzberg and perceive them as *teleological* models, that is, as models of inevitable upward historical evolution, as stories with happy endings: We once were only concerned with lower level needs, hygiene factors and theory X, but now we are moving towards a utopia where we will only be concerned with higher level needs, motivators and theory Y.[8]

Rose (1975) has noted that the human relations orientation of theory Y, the Hawthorne studies, Maslow and Herzberg, has come under much attack of late. Left-wing critics claim to detect pro-management bias, antagonism towards trade unions, and advocacy of psychological manipulation to convince workers that they do not really want more money. Right-wing critics have attacked human relations theories of the workplace because they see such theories undermining the belief of management in the validity of individualism and competitiveness and the desirability and utility of money as a motivator.

In spite of these criticisms (and a good deal of them are valid), the usefulness of theory X/theory Y in the final analysis is that it reminds us of the difference between human beings. At the specific level, it reminds us that people bring certain needs to any work environment, and that those needs are often based upon wider philosophical assumptions about human nature:

- man is responsible/man is not responsible
- man is basically lazy/man responds to a challenge
- human nature never changes/man's potential for growth is unlimited
- people only work for the money/other things are more important

Often these views are not articulated, and the day-to-day running of organisations can often conceal the fact that many disputes are less about particular issues and more about general beliefs. McGregor's theory X/theory Y is a convenient way of identifying such beliefs, and filling in the context of specific issues. Theologians have been arguing about free will versus predestination, original sin versus human redeemability, for millenia; theory X/theory Y is merely one of the latest forms of this (so far) unsettled debate.[9]

McClelland: Power, achievement and affiliation

It is useful to distinguish between *micromotivation* (dealing with individual behaviour, needs and drives) and *macromotivation* (dealing with the behaviour, needs and drives of the culture, group or nation-state the individual is in). In this chapter, we are looking primarily at micromotivation, but macromotivation cannot be overlooked. Is it true, for example, that some nations seem to be more motivated to work than others? To what extent do matters of national policy, such as progressive income tax, impact upon individual motivations to work harder and make more money? (Davis 1981).

---

[8] Although Drucker notes that Maslow, for example, was aware of the distance to Utopia. After working at a Southern Californian company in the early 1960s, Maslow realised the practical problems of achieving theory Y and self-actualisation:

> He [Maslow] sharply criticised me [Drucker] and McGregor for "inhumanity" to the weak, the vulnerable, the damaged, who are unable to take on the responsibility and self-discipline which theory Y demands. Even the strong and healthy, Maslow concluded, need the security of order and direction; and the weak need protection against the burden of responsibility. The world is not, Maslow concluded, peopled by adults. It has its full share of the permanently immature. . . .
>
> Maslow—who until his death a few years later, remained a strong advocate of theory Y—concluded that it is not enough to remove restraints. One has to *replace* the security of theory X and the certainty it gives by another but different structure of security and certainty. There is need to provide by different means what commands and penalties do under theory X. Theory Y, in other words, has to go far beyond theory X. It cannot simply be substituted for it. (DRUCKER 1974 P233).

[9] Hilmer (1985) has analysed Australians' attitudes to work in terms of our earliest colonial experience of conscripted convicts and voluntary freeman labour. He believes that modern managers and workers have too much of a "conscript" and not enough of a "volunteer' mind-set. Obviously, "conscription" is similar to theory X and "volunteerism" is similar to theory Y.

One writer who has seriously considered macro- as well as micro-motivation is David McClelland (1961). He has attempted to define motivation in terms of three factors:

1. the need for achievement (abbreviated to nAch)
2. the need for power (nPow)
3. the need for affiliation, or social interaction (nAff).

nAch: The need for achievement

The need for *achievement*, or nAch, was measured by McClelland in a number of ways. People whose attitudes and needs were being measured were shown illustrations of people and situations and asked to tell stories about what was happening. A high nAch person would describe problem-solving situations. In group problem-solving situations, high nAch people will tend to choose to work with specialist problem-solvers whom they do not know rather than with friends, who may not be specialist problem-solvers (a high nAff person would make the opposite decision).

McClelland has also performed content analyses of popular literature of various nations (songs, stories in children's storybooks), looking for expressions of achievement, power and affiliation. Thus he says Indian textbooks often express spiritual themes and the vanity of earthly wealth, whereas Chinese textbooks stress individual striving to fulfil material goals. From this, McClelland concludes,

> It should not come as a surprise, therefore, if a nation like China tended in the long run to outproduce a nation like India, which appears to be more fatalistic. (P.15)

He also claims there has been a large decline in British nAch, as reflected in such sources, and this helps to explain Britain's long-term decline in this century.

Entrepreneurial attitudes learned in childhood would manifest themselves in such economic indicators as the amount of coal a society burned, the kilowatt-hours of electricity used, or the extent of foreign trade.

High nAchs typically are business people, often in sales or small business. They like to achieve, and they achieve in situations where there is close feedback on their performance. For such reasons, they often dislike gambling, because the skill component is so low. In many respects they almost caricature the person driven by the Protestant work ethic: introspective, demonstrating virtue by their self-discipline and success. They may not understand people who are more gregarious and have a higher nAff, and they may suspect high nPow people.

Horner has argued that sexist socialisation in our societies means that women often do not have as high nAch as men, and may in fact have learned to manifest a need to fail (Lazerson 1975). In a study of Australian small business operators, it is claimed that operators with higher than normal nAch have experienced more business success (Morris and Fargher 1981).

McClelland has some interesting observations upon nAchs' personal qualities:

> Some psychologists think that because I've done so much work on nAch I must like the kind of people who have strong need for achievement. I don't. I find them bores. They are not artistically sensitive. They're entrepreneurs, kind of driven—always trying to improve themselves and find a shorter route to the office or a faster way of reading their mail. (QUOTED IN LUTHANS 1981)

Thus, from one point of view, the high nAch is a cultural hero, making things happen; from another point of view, she is a bore, a workaholic and possibly self-destructing through self-administered stress.

nAff: The need for affiliation

"Good chaps make bad bosses" is a way of saying that people with high nAff—a high desire to be liked—may not be able to operate well in a position of power (McClelland and Burnham 1976). Because the high nAff prefers unskilled friends to skilled strangers in solving problems, problems may not be solved very well. The high nAff may be most uncomfortable being promoted over his network of friends/buddies/mates, and his difficulty in giving orders may be matched by the difficulty his new subordinates will have in accepting them. Such a well-meaning high nAff boss may confuse others with unclear instructions, and may in turn be manipulated by subordinates who play upon the high nAff's guilt with responses such as:

"Who do you think *you* are to push me around?"

"You've really sold us out now you're hobnobbing with the bigwigs, eh?"

Let us not be too stern and puritanical in dismissing the high nAff, however. Affiliative rituals can be very profitable in the real world: the socially skilled person operating through wide networks of working breakfasts, lunches and dinners, barbecues, clubs, pubs, service organisations, and so on, may be a very successful person. The most successful people may participate in and enjoy cohesive rituals such as discussion of football, wines, music, or whatever is the central non-job preoccupation of his work peers. The critical discussion or agreement may be transacted on the golf course or squash court or in the sauna. In a stratified, class-conscious society, social skills and graces may be an automatic entrée to certain corridors of power, just as to be without such skills and graces may exclude one from the corridors.

Western business people may be extremely impatient with social rituals in other countries (such as drinking tea or sake in Japan). Western high nAchs with low nAff may be disastrously unsuccessful if they do not see other rituals as being central, and not peripheral, to commerce and other transactions.

nPow: The need for power

The power motive is often ignored by analysts of organisational behaviour, and McClelland achieved a breakthrough in looking at power as a legitimate force and need. People with high nPow needs are superficially similar to people with high nAch needs, because both get things done in this world. However the high nPow person may be more concerned with the politics of getting things done, may be more blatantly manipulative, and may not be as concerned with improving work performance.

McClelland has argued that there are "two faces of power", that of *personal* power and *social* power. Social power has a positive connotation, personal power has a negative connotation. McClelland argues that Americans' historical experience of overthrowing British monarchical rule has made them extremely distrustful of power residing with one person: thus Americans tend to distrust politicians in the public arena, and people think twice about openly displaying pursuit of power within organisations. This "anti-leadership vaccine" running through the veins of American society is seen by McClelland as being counter-productive, because it means hard decisions will never be taken—possibly because the collective nAff is too high.

Given that Australians have a similar suspicion of authority, similar patterns of motivation and demotivation might well be in place here[10] (for further analysis of power, see Chapter 10).

Davis (1981) and others have linked power with the notion of *control* or *competence*. One's power is the extent to which one controls one's environment, and competence in one, several or many skills or behaviours may well be a crucial motivator. Thus, a person running a small business, with access to all information about what is being made, sold and handled at his fingertips (i.e. instant feedback on operations), may well be more motivated than a person working on an assembly line performing a small function—that person's effort obviously adds up to a finished product, but it is a mystery just *how* it adds up. (See Chapters 7 and 12 for discussions of experiences of control over work flow. Note also the "locus of control" idea in Chapter 6.)

Putting McClelland's theories to work

McClelland originally began his study of human motivation believing that people's motivational patterns were unchangeable, but he began to suspect that this might not be so:

> Initially, we had real doubts as to whether we could succeed (in training people to change their motivation), partly because like most American psychologists we had been strongly influenced by the psychoanalytic view that basic motives are laid down in childhood and cannot really be changed later, and partly because many studies of intensive psychotherapy and counselling had shown minor, if any, long-term personality effects. On the other hand, we were encouraged by the non-professionals: those enthusiasts like Dale Carnegie, communist ideologues or church missionaries, who felt that they could change adults and in fact seemed to be doing so. (MCCLELLAND 1967, P.16)

Accordingly, McClelland and his associates set up workshops in various countries with the expressed intent of teaching people to develop high nAch. This proved to be extraordinarily difficult, given that nAch is embedded in a matrix of cultural, religious, socio-economic, lifestyle and child-rearing factors. There has been some success in lifting nAch of entrepreneurs and salesmen, particularly where those individuals have had a fair amount of control over their own activities ("success" being measured by lifts in output, sales, etc). Nevertheless, as Lee (1980) points out, this target group where some successes have been scored with training *already have high nAch*—that is why they are entrepreneurs and salesmen.

> Both McClelland's wide ranging measurements of the motive to achieve and his attempts to alter it offer further support that the personality is a fairly stable structure. Such needs as the need for achievement, need for power, and the need for affiliation appear more clearly rooted in childhood than before McClelland's work began in the late 1940s. The development of these needs, moreover, depends upon socio-economic, ethnic, and child-rearing factors. Although many of those with high needs for achievement may respond to specialised training, this response will largely be a function of opportunities for expansion of entre-preneurial-like behaviour. . . Skeptical old-line managers who have resisted behavioural model-building on an intuitive basis as being oversimplified and restrictive can take heart. All the behaviour model-builders seem to be adding dimensions in the contingency style of "it (almost) all depends". (LEE 1980, P.88)

---

[10] Those making bid for power should take note of one of McClelland's findings. In a 20-year follow-up of Harvard graduates who had scored high on the need for power, 58 per cent had high blood pressure or had died of heart failure. (GUEST 1984, P.21)

Expectancy theory
Vroom's approach
Vroom has criticised most of the foregoing models of motivation because not only is the experimental evidence for them ambiguous, but they assume a fair amount of "irrationality" on the part of workers, and they are oriented towards a series of past behaviours, rather than future behaviours (Vroom 1964).

Any person working in any job is motivated by a series of well-thought-out calculations about the future. Merely, says Vroom, because I want something, like a promotion or incentive payments, does not guarantee that I will get it. My wants are controlled by my evaluation of *how likely* such an outcome is. If I am a research worker at the Antarctic, I may have an overpowering desire to sit in the sun naked and get a tan. Reality, however, does not coincide with my dreams.

Vroom terms my wants or preferences for a particular outcome my *valence*. The strength of my belief that my behaviour will produce certain outcomes—that is, my estimate of my probability of success—is my *expectancy*. My motivation can thus be quantified:

$$\text{motivation} = \text{valence} \times \text{expectancy}$$

Thus, in the Antarctic example, my motivation to go outside can be calculated as

$$\begin{array}{ccccc} \text{valence (want)} & \times & \text{expectancy} & = & \text{motivation} \\ 1.0 & & 0.001 & & 0.001 \end{array}$$

More realistically, another example might be: John and Joan work in the computing department of a large organisation. A position arises in the department for a project leader. The job profile calls for someone with experience in advanced statistics and operations research. John wants the money and prestige of this position rather badly—he is highly ambitious and his wife is about to have their second child, and he could use the extra money. He does not, however, have the relevant experience. Joan has the appropriate qualifications for the position, but was thinking about leaving the organisation for another job. This position interests her, but she will not strive desperately for it. The motivations of the two people can be thus computed:

$$\text{John's motivation:} \quad V(0.9) \times E(0.2) = 0.18$$
$$\text{Joan's motivation:} \quad V(0.4) \times E(0.8) = 0.32$$

Thus, even though John wants the job more than Joan, expectancy theory leads us to believe that Joan is in fact more "motivated". What would be the position of a third person, with lower valence than John (say, 0.6) and lower expectancy than Joan (say, 0.7)?

Porter and Lawler's approach
Porter and Lawler (1968) have refined this model of motivation still further. Their model (Fig. 2.4), while apparently over-complex for such an apparently simple thing as predicting motivation, is relatively straightforward. Boxes 1, 2 and 3 are the basic Vroom model, although Porter and Lawler substitute "effort" for "motivation". *But effort does not equal performance.* A person may simply not have the requisite abilities or traits (either through hereditary or educational deficiencies), and the person may misperceive her role and hence perform badly. Further, as Luthans and Kreitner note,

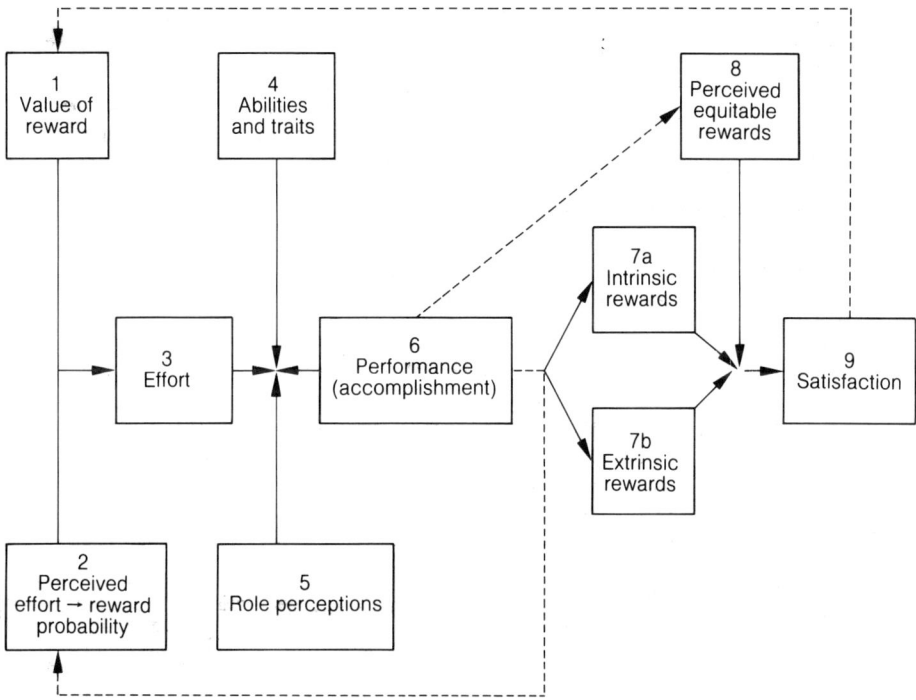

Fig. 2.4 *The Porter-Lawler motivation model* (PORTER AND LAWLER 1968, P.165.
REPRODUCED WITH PERMISSION)

> (the) Porter and Lawler (model) reverse(s) the traditional human-relations
> assumption that satisfaction causes performance. The model shows that perform-
> ance, if equitably rewarded, will lead to satisfaction. (LUTHANS AND KREITNER 1975,
> P.10)

Porter and Lawler see people being affected by intrinsic and extrinsic rewards
(respectively, motivators and hygienes in Herzberg's system), and the
equitableness of the system is also crucial (i.e. to what extent does a person
perceive that rewards are fairly matched to the demands of the job?).[11]

Expectancy theory helps us to see that merely wanting something is a
necessary, but not sufficient, condition for making something happen. The
advantage of such systems models as the Porter–Lawler one is that they
encourage us to see reality in systems terms, that is, not so much in A-causes-
B terms as A-causes-B-which-causes-C-which-in-some-cases-causes-A terms.
This is particularly useful when we are trying to explain job satisfaction, and
whether it motivates or not.

Factors such as expectancy and role perception heighten the need for
clear lines of communication in an organisation. If objectives are not clear,
and if job roles are not spelled out, then people will simply have less
powerful motivation (see, for example, the discussion of management by
objectives in Chapter 12). This clarity of communication must also carry over
to motivation by incentives:

---

[11] For a discussion of equity theories of motivation, see e.g. Milton, Entrekin and Stening (1984), Luthans (1981).

Since expectancy depends entirely upon the employee's view of the connection between effort and outcome, often a simple straightforward incentive is more motivating than a complex one. The complex one may involve so much uncertainty that the employee may not sufficiently connect effort with outcome. The simple incentive, on the other hand, offers a practical course of action that the employee can picture and understand: therefore it carries a higher expectancy. (DAVIS 1981, P.161)[12]

The last word on motivation?

Expectancy theory is sometimes referred to as *process* theory, to distinguish it from the *content* models of Taylor, Mayo, Maslow, Herzberg, Alderfer, McGregor and McClelland. Content models are concerned with innate needs and drives which energise behaviour, whereas process models allegedly are different because they concentrate on the variables that motivate and how these interrelate with one another. This, however, may be a distinction without a difference, or at least a difference of degree masquerading as a difference of kind. Burrell and Morgan (1980) note that expectancy theory, positing as it does a rational, literally calculative worker and manager, is in fact a return to the economistic model of human behaviour espoused by Taylor in his scientific management theories. To the extent that expectancy theory is an *over*-rational view of man, perhaps it is a reaction to the *a*rational theories which began with the Hawthorne studies of Mayo, as a reaction in turn to the mechanistic sterility of scientific management.

Does expectancy theory work? It is probably too early to judge as yet, for the research, particularly on the Porter–Lawler model, is inconclusive (Luthans 1981). The Porter–Lawler model is often difficult for managers and workers to understand, also. Many academics wring their hands at the way many in the workforce accept the Maslow and Herzberg models of human behaviour as being scientifically verified (they are not); yet probably the major reason why they are accepted as holy writ is that they are easy to understand, whereas systems models such as the Porter–Lawler look like a flowchart escaped from the data processing department.

Vroom's model is much less forbidding, and has a certain elegant simplicity about it; in fact, it is similar to models still used by economists in predicting micro- and macro-consumption behaviour. Yet the mathematical precision has been attacked by Lee (1980) and others as "nonsense" and "ridiculousness", because (says Lee) it invests a fairly trivial concept with a load of spurious equations which mean nothing. Do people really make such precise calculations about their actions? Vroom's model also neglects unconscious motivation, says Lee. Herzberg, sulking in the wings while the new prima donna of expectancy theory holds centre stage, dismisses the theory disparagingly as "tautology" (Herzberg 1976).

Money as a motivator

There have been many changes between scientific management and expectancy theory, but perhaps, as the French put it, the more it changes, the

---

[12] Davis' remarks point up similarities between expectancy theory and reinforcement theories discussed in Chapter 3. Note also the remarks of Stoner, Collins and Yetton (1985):

    ... both reinforcement theory and expectancy theory suggest that rewards should be tied closely to behaviour and that rewards should be frequent. In order to apply the implications of these approaches, managers must be able to set specific individual goals, tie rewards to individual behaviour and treat people fairly and equitably. This is not an easy task in complex organisations where, for example, much of the work is highly interdependent, where it is difficult to consistently observe employees, and where there may be rapid changes in goals, available resources, and external constraints. (P.539) more it stays the same. This is certainly true of the vexed question of whether money motivates or not. In Herzberg's terms, the key question remains: which is the more important, internal factors (such as job satisfaction), or external factors (such as money)? Particularly since the rise of Maslow and Herzberg, money has received something of a bad press:

> Maslow, Herzberg and the like, to their continuing credit, introduced us to the important idea that money is not the only motivator of human behaviour. Unfortunately, in the ensuing speculation about the relative impact of various "motivators" which was sparked by their theories (and they are, after all, theories, and not laws, in spite of the vigour with which they have been marketed as noble truths by their more zealous proponents) monetary reward has become cast in our minds as somewhere down the list in importance, and perhaps even off the list of motivators altogether. (PIAMONTE 1979, P.598)

Piamonte then goes on to give a behaviourist critique of existing incentive pay schemes, and why they do not motivate (they are not contingent, etc., see Chapter 3). He suggests that if incentive pay is contingent—if the employee can see immediate and concrete rewards, flowing from a clear view of where her effort fits into the big picture—then money becomes the best motivator.[13]

This is an uncomfortable proposition for some—it seems to herald the return of piecework, which is not only redolent of nineteenth-century sweatshops, but definitely a theory X creature. Yet monetary incentives, such as performance margins, and non-monetary incentives, such as "packages" of non- or partly taxable benefits, seem to be becoming more fashionable (see e.g. Globerson 1985). In the public sector, where bottom lines of profit are not clear or even existent, experiments are under way to provide performance margins for top performers (cf. the Victorian Public Service experience, Cullen 1984).

Even within communist countries such as Yugoslavia, Russia and China, incentives, not to mention retention of profits in privately owned industrial and agricultural enterprises, seem to be becoming surprisingly widespread (Juran 1974; Katz and Kahn 1978).

Incentives pro and con

A survey conducted by Fotiades in 1977 revealed that Australian employers and unions had mixed feelings about incentives (Table 2.3). Nevertheless, for the employers, advantages cited for incentive schemes outweighed the disadvantages, and although a majority of unions covered in the survey were against incentives, most of the anti-incentive unions had members receiving incentives (Fotiades 1979). Although it is obvious that incentives motivate in a wide variety of settings, Lee (1980) notes that when an organisation implements an incentive plan, changes are made in organisational and job design which probably should have been made long ago, and hence data from research on incentives is often methodologically "contaminated", at least in the short run.[14]

---

[13] Cf. Davis' discussion of incentives in terms of behaviour modification, expectancy theory, and equity theory (Davis 1981).

[14] Changes such as more accurate standards being established, improvements in tooling, equipment and work layout being undertaken, provision of more accurate feedback on output and wastage to supervisors and employees, and so on (Lee 1980, p.145).

Table 2.3 Attitudes towards incentive pay schemes

	Advantages	*Disadvantages*
Perceived by management	1. increased output 2. increased company profit 3. decreased absenteeism 4. increased quality 5. decreased labour turnover	1. lack of cooperation from employees 2. unfair discrimination against some employees 3. increase in industrial unrest 4. too much pressure on employees 5. high cost 6. difficult to administer 7. high taxation for employees acts as a disincentive
Perceived by unions	1. greater earnings 2. gives some control over jobs and wages 3. may lead to higher productivity, and perhaps to more jobs	1. difficult to measure, thus leads to disputes 2. can create disruptive competition 3. staff may take "short cuts" which lead to safety and quality problems 4. incentives are over-award payments, and thus may keep awards down 5. if productivity rises, staff may be fired 6. preoccupation with incentives may distract from gaining better working conditions 7. incentive wages can vary greatly—may drop dangerously 8. taxation may eat up gains 9. low achievers may feel inadequate, especially in group schemes—perceived as the "weak link" 10. health/stress risk of hitting maximum all the time

Source: Adapted from Fotiades (1979), pp.21–5.

Lee also notes that one of the disadvantages of incentive payments (as perceived by labour), the phenomenon of workers working themselves out of a job by increasing output, has to be addressed by managements contemplating installing an incentive system; if guarantees are given that people will not be punished for success, then management and labour will benefit from incentive systems.

Seen in this light, Lee suggests, restriction of output by workers, described as a social (i.e. economically "non-rational") factor by the Hawthorne researchers, was in fact an economic (i.e. rational) factor, whereby workers deliberately sub-maximised their performance to ensure further employment for all (Lee 1980).

Davis (1981) distinguishes between three types of incentive schemes: profit sharing; production sharing; and individual incentives.

Profit-sharing is very much a group phenomenon, wherein all employees identify their own interests with that of their organisation, as opposed to standard incentive schemes, which are aimed more at individuals (Davis 1981).

> Basic pay rates, performance pay increases, and most incentive systems recognise individual differences, while profit-sharing recognises mutual interests. . . . Greater institutional teamwork tends to develop. (DAVIS 1981)

Davis suggests that profit-sharing works better for organisations with a high growth pattern, and not so well for industries in decline with low profit margins and intense competition. He also suggests that such schemes work better for those already high up in the hierarchy, that is, executives rather than operating workers, because those higher on the pyramid have a clearer view of the relationship of their effort (input) to the end product (output). This of course is a job and organisational design problem.[15]

Production sharing is similar to profit-sharing: production-sharing schemes (or Scanlon plans) give rewards to the larger working group according to improvements in labour costs.

Individual incentives obviously appeal to the individual worker's self-interest, and it depends very much upon the nature of the work being performed as to whether individual, group and organisational interests coincide.

Sub-maximising behaviour

Can money make people work to their maximum all the time? Brown cites his experience studying piecework systems at British institutions such as Vauxhall and Lever Brothers, where it was found that workers would not always try to maximise their effort to maximise their pay envelope:

> . . . each individual has his own norm of pace of work and application to work and . . . given a reasonable physical environment, a level of work reasonably consistent with his capacity and a regular level of pay consistent with such work, he will produce, on average, that quantity of work which is his own optimum contribution. He can spurt for quite short periods in emergency but he cannot keep it up. (BROWN 1971, P.91)

Do people then optimise—or sub-maximise—rather than maximise? There may be a large variety of reasons why people do not hit their maximum, either intermittently or all the time, when incentives are there for maximising. Some of these reasons are:

1. a work-group may protect a "weak link" by setting a low norm;
2. individuals or groups may not want to set an above-average standard because they may become the standard, without commensurate pay rises; Davis (1981) tells of some salesmen who held back because they thought their quota might be raised in the following year and/or their territory split up; Mandel (1971) records similar behaviour in Russian factories, where some managers and workers are on incentives;

---

[15] An extension of profit-sharing is share or stock ownership, where employees are offered part-ownership of the organisation. Wildly divergent organisational, economic and, ultimately, political outcomes have been predicted for such plans. Ronald Reagan, later to become United States president, spoke of employee stock ownership plans (ESOPs) in these terms in 1975:

> . . . Each individual employee winds up owning stock in the company directly proportionate to his salary or wage level and he has a vested interest in the company's ability to prosper and to increase earnings.
>
> An ever-increasing number of citizens would thus have two sources if income—a pay cheque and a share of the profits. Could there be a better answer to the stupidity of Karl Marx than millions of workers individually sharing in the ownership of the means of production? (QUOTED IN FRISCH 1982, PP93–4)

Yet similar plans have been introduced in Sweden as a trade-off against wage increases in economically hard times, and some have denounced this as galloping socialism (Kuttner 1983). See Chapter 14.

3. following from (2), there is a chance that if productivity goes up, people will be laid off rather than have new positions created for them or new marketing campaigns initiated to sell additional product, that is, they may work themselves out of a job;
4. workers may deliberately work slowly if being observed by productivity experts (industrial engineers, time-and-motion study people, consultants), thus any recommendations from the experts which might make life more uncomfortable will be predicated on a false minimum;
5. rates may slip; anyone working on a job long enough may see ways to improve that job's efficiency, often quite dramatically—but if this is communicated to management, the productiviy gains might not be shared, the minimum rate may rise, life may get harder, and people may get laid off; thus the improvements may not be communicated (Davis 1981).

Added to these considerations are most of the factors listed under disadvantages of incentives, in particular those related to stress, safety and taxation. This is not to say that "malingering" workers are the sole cause of sub-maximising behaviour in the world. Management may be indulging in an even more elaborate pattern of sub-maximising behaviour, such as restrictive trade practices, cartelisation, administered prices, vertical and horizontal integration of production, lobbying for quota and tariff protection, and so on. What peer-group pressures would a doctor or a lawyer be under if he began to maximise his behaviour according to free market conditions, and began advertising and cutting prices?

It has to be borne in mind that much, if not most, of the theory in motivation research and allied areas of organisational behaviour is conducted from the point of view of management. When extreme terms like "neurotic" and "irrational" are used, they are usually used to describe workers, not management. Thus management is seen to be "normal" while workers are seen to be "deviant". This is not only methodologically unscientific (particularly when, as is often the case, management is footing the bill for the research), but at a more basic level, flagrantly unfair and biased.

Quasi-money, black money, trips and time

It was mentioned earlier that the success of any micromotivation program, such as incentives for individuals and groups, depends upon such macro-motivation practices as taxation policies of governments. Does it make sense to try harder and get more money if "it all goes in tax anyway"? There is a good deal of truth in this argument. While money flowing from the private purse to the public purse is supposed to benefit us all with greater provision of public goods and services (defence, education, medical care, etc.), many of us dislike "working for the government". Thus, with many executive positions advertised every week, the key motivator offered is not the salary but the *package*, which is salary, plus a range of non-taxable or only partly taxable extras such as low interest loans, free public school education for children, cars, perhaps a company house, subscriptions to clubs, credit cards, and so on. Such "lurks and perks" occur throughout a wide range of jobs, blue collar and white, including free or subsidised meals and free or subsidised transport.[16] It is a mistake to refer to such motivators as "non-monetary"—if the taxation system were different, the recipients would

---

[16] This of course may change with fringe benefits taxation introduced in 1986.

probably be glad to have the cash-in-hand equivalent. It is more appropriate to refer to packages and lurks and perks as *quasi-money*.

Governments of all political colours despair over the dramatic growth of the *"black economy"*, where goods and services are paid for in cash, so the transaction will not come under the taxman's scrutiny, or else paid for in barter terms: a dentist may do some dental work free or at reduced rates for a plumber in return for free or reduced-rate plumbing services. Machovec and Smith (1982) have pointed to the black economy phenomenon as proving that money is still the great motivator: it is spurious, they argue, to say that the work ethic is dying and people are choosing increased leisure in preference to long working hours;[17] it is more correct to say that people are fleeing from taxable work rather than work *per se*.

There are sometimes other reasons for using non- or quasi-monetary incentives—trips, merchandise and exotica such as access to company-owned time-sharing holiday resorts. One reason is that these really *are non-monetary incentives*, are in fact better than cold hard cash over or under the counter:

> Cash is not as motivating as travel or merchandise because it tends to be used for unexciting but demanding purposes such as paying the house rates, rather than for a holiday or some desired luxury item. When a program offers only merchandise or travel, recipients can take their awards guilt-free. (*RYDGE'S*, APRIL 1980)

Traditionally, such incentives have gone to such workers as salesmen and dealers, where output can be measured precisely. Increasingly, such deals are being offered by office and factory workers as incentives to lower costs, absenteeism and accidents, and improved productivity and quality control. There are still problems with such schemes; insofar that if they are to be effective, they must be specifically and closely linked in space and time to good performance if they are to motivate (according to expectancy and behaviour modification theorists). This problem is compounded by the fact that, within modern organisations, roles often overlap, and it is difficult to isolate the output of individuals, and sometimes even departments.

This is often a problem with large organisations selling services rather than goods, and is a particular problem in the public services, where alienation caused by (unnecessarily) amorphous job and organisational designs is often high. Managers usually do not have discretionary funds to offer incentives, and may have to fall back upon such measures as overtime or time off in lieu (which, given an initial premise that workload seems to be hard to measure, may well be counter-productive).

The motivators: Dare to be great!

McClelland was quoted earlier as saying that he and his colleagues were encouraged to develop theories of motivation and run training sessions in achievement motivation because of the success of "non-professionals" such as Dale Carnegie, communist ideologues or church missionaries. One might ask, if these "non-professionals" were successful, what is it they would have to do to be professional? Nevertheless, the point is well taken. "Communist ideologues", church missionaries, politicians, sporting coaches, salesmen, dictators, advertising agents, and so on, have proven most adept at changing people's behaviour, or "re-motivating" them. The eighteenth-century British

---

[17] See discussion on the work ethic and the leisure ethic in Chapter 1.

writer, Samuel Johnson, said, "Go into the street, and give one man a lecture on morality, and another a shilling, and see which will respect you most." Yet today there are many quite highly paid secular preachers of sermons on motivation who claim to be able to fire up the enthusiasm of individuals and organisations, and most of them seem to rate money as a relatively unimportant motivator (although one could perhaps compare their personal attitudes to motivation to those of Herzberg). Thus Ron Barrassi, a Melbourne football coach who also teaches motivation to such organisations as IBM, Kellogg, Kodak, Mayne Nickless, the National Bank, Qantas, Heinz, Golden Fleece, GM-H, Chrysler, Shell and AMP at $1000 a session, tells players on and off the field to be wary of "mental weakness":

> Nearly everything that goes wrong with your life is your fault. I believe that. And even if it's not true, you're still better off to believe that it is true, and work on it. (QUOTED IN POWERS 1979, P.96)

What motivates us? Pride, esteem, a sense of importance, and achievement based upon hard work rather than merely resting on the laurels of such abilities as we are born with, says Barrassi. Lee Saxon, a Melbourne hypnotist who has also turned to the motivation area, rates recognition as being the prime motivating force in our lives. You must also have goals, says Saxon, an overriding goal, an intermediate goal and a present goal. "Everyone wants something," says Barrassi. "If you don't want anything at all, nothing will motivate you." Terry Fearnley, a Sydney football coach and former sales manager, sees money motivation as the chicken which comes after the egg of attitude motivation:

> People who worry about money first are not going to make it. If you are successful you are usually well-paid. The sort of pride and determination needed at the top level aren't born out of money. (QUOTED IN *RYDGE'S*, AUGUST 1977, P.28)

The problem is, of course, no one has yet solved the problem of the chicken or the egg—money or determination, which comes first?

How effective are such motivators? Do they really get people fired up so that individuals, and the organisations paying for the motivator, become more driven and transcend their limitations? Can a sports-style "get out there and kill 'em" speech really work in a placid, air-conditioned clerical environment? Are "motivational" films and videos showing athletes conquering difficult situations (winning yacht races, climbing mountains) relevant to workers on an assembly line?

It certainly seems unlikely that organisations would continue to pay out large sums of money to motivation "superstars" if they did not do some good. Much of what the experts say is obvious, but the obvious is rarely obvious until the question is put. Thus it is useful to stress planning of goals, and it is useful to consider what Maslow would call "higher-level needs", such as the need for recognition. Yet doubts still persist about people staying motivated long after the expensive course has finished. As a Melbourne executive remarked of such a course,

> I question that you can push people at that pace for more than 12 months. You can do it but you destroy them. It's only the commando types that get through. (QUOTED IN *THE AGE*, 10 MAY 1980, P.3)

And what of the sport–work analogy? Is it valid? There are certainly some similarities. There is a need for training and preparation; the coordination and communication, the teamwork, that is needed in group or team sports has analogues in the world of work. But perhaps the dissimilarities are greater still (Table 2.4).

Table 2.4 Dissimilarities of sport and work situations

In sport situations	*In work situations*
• goals are clear, discrete	• goals are not always clear
• time-frame is limited	• time-frame is sometimes open-ended, multiple
• rules are known	• rules can be official and unofficial
• stable information environment—future is reasonably predictable	• turbulent information environment—future is not always predictable
• physical effort is crucial	• increasingly, mental effort only or mainly
• aggression is channelled	• overt aggression is usually inappropriate

Motivation and cultural differences

Most of the theories that have been considered in this chapter have been American in origin. The question needs to be asked: Are these theories valid outside America? Certainly, to the extent that most of the theories considered have crucial, sometimes fatal flaws, a further question can be asked as to whether the theories are all that relevant *inside* America. Hofstede (1980, 1981) proposes that many American theories of motivation, leadership and organisation design are simply inappropriate outside the United States. He attributes this to cultural arrogance, the arrogance of a superpower which has conducted cultural imperialism upon other countries by exporting various management and human relations theories. The recent fascination of Americans with Japanese theories of management, Hofstede suggests, is in fact an indicator of America's relative economic decline in a world moving away from bipolar dominance (dominated by the United States and the Soviet Union) to multipolar interconnection:

> The way Americans look to Japan these days closely resembles the way the French, British and Germans used to look to America thirty years ago. What the Japanese are doing with American ideas resembles what the Americans were doing earlier with European ideas. In several respects, history repeats itself. Disregard of other cultures is a luxury only the strong can afford. It is understandable that Americans regret their country's loss of economic power, but the consequent increase in cultural awareness represents an intellectual and spiritual gain. And as far as management theories go, cultural relativism is an idea whose time has come. (HOFSTEDE 1981, P.68)

Commenting upon Hofstede's critique, Hunt (1981) notes that, while American motivation theories have been valid to a certain extent in *all* cultures, they are by no means universally valid:

> Where the motivation theories came unstuck outside the American culture was when the writers (Douglas McGregor, Rensis Likert, Maslow, McClelland, Chris Argyris) proposed relationships between the common dimensions. Relationships between dimensions reflect culturally specific values. For example, a set of relationships suggested between the needs in Maslow's hierarchy of needs failed to hold outside the American culture and indeed had difficulty in holding even within that culture... Self-actualisation (whatever that is) is not the dominant "high" motive in Southeast Asia. (P.57–8)

Hunt concurs in Hofstede's view that the Americentric view of management and human relations put out by various motivation gurus is a sign of American arrogance and studied ignorance of other cultures:

This preoccupation with one culture, including the assumption that it is "right", has gained more strength from the current neo-human-relations movement, which has lost all the coyness of the movement in the 1950s and is being dumped increasingly around the world as multinationals attempt to win hearts and minds to the American way of doing business. Hence the Japanese executive (for whom privacy is paramount) is asked to let it all hang out in a "sharing laboratory" conducted by the American training manager of his multinational. In Japan he has little choice but to agree. (HUNT 1981, P.61)

Hofstede proposed as an alternative model to American theories a theory of behaviour which has four main dimensions of behaviour in organisations: power distance, masculinity/femininity, certainty/uncertainty, and individualism/collectivism. He based this theory on one of the largest behavioural surveys ever mounted: 116 000 people working for the same organisation (IBM) in almost 40 countries. Hofstede claims to have come up with quite significant differences in behaviour in the various countries. His research is considered to be one of the most influential non-American pieces of research ever carried out.

However, there may be a fatal methodological flaw in his work, insofar as he surveyed many people in many countries but all nevertheless belonging to the one organisation (complete with its own culture, its own way of doing things, a homogeneous training system, control system, etc.) (Hunt 1981). American theories of motivation and other aspects of organisational behaviour may not then be totally relevant to cultures such as Australia, while non-American theories may also be inappropriate.[18]

"I'd rather be sailing": Motivation and demotivation in the lucky country

Two American observers of Australia, Kahn and Pepper (1980), have identified three major tendencies within Australian culture that militate against high achievement, and one factor that conduces to high achievement:

1. *"No worries"/"she'll be right" attitude.* This attitude is more than just fatalism or a reliance on God's will—it is based upon a deeply felt belief that one can ignore the consequences of past actions, knowing that things will turn up trumps in the lucky country.[19]

---

[18]   Nothing differentiates the Australian character from the American so much as attitudes towards work. An Australian becomes aware at a very early age that work is a national joke.
  People who work hard are as likely to attract suspicion as praise, while a whole folk-lore surrounds the "bludger".
  In the United States, by comparison, work is a way of life, even a religion . . . The long hours at the office, the stuffed briefcase lugged home each evening, the pressures and the overtime to meet the critical deadline, the president who puts in two hours each morning before anyone else arrives, are characteristic patterns of American working life . . ." (HAUPT 19⁻⁻, P.⁻)

[19] Cf. Caldwell's remarks on fatalism, gambling as an expression of such fatalism, and peer-group conformity as demotivators in Australia:
  I wish now to speculate why Australians have a predilection for gambling and why the form of gambling is marked by heavy reliance on chance and so little on skill.
  In such a discussion some reference must be made to the nature of the Australian character and the value system—especially mateship, egalitarianism and fatalism. Numerous writers . . . have discussed the mateship ethos, part of which stipulates that a man must stick with his mates through thick and thin. One consequence of this ethos has been that Australians have displayed ambiguity about social and career mobility. If a person seeks promotion, it may necessitate "leaving one's mates". Taft and Walker state that the main bar to upward mobility in the working class is probably the lack of motivation which results from the high degree of class identification. Many Australians have not sought identity and success in the job or career, but in leisure. As Hancock has said, "a great deal of the spontaneous energy of Australians is spent in the pursuit of pleasure"—especially in sport and gambling. (CALDWELL 19⁻4, P.291)

2. *Mateship and egalitarianism.* Everyone is equal, and perhaps this has the negative effect of dragging down high achievers—"cutting down the tall poppies". If high achievers are to survive, they must always be modest about their success lest the "knockers" try to denigrate them.

3. *"Protect-my-corner" attitude.* "I'm all right, Jack" type selfishness means that collective welfare is often sacrificed. This is expressed, for example, in lightning strikes (particularly in transport), economic protectionism, foreign policy isolationism.

4. *Striving attitude.* Australia's current fairly high standard of living has been achieved by more than simply good luck. Many Australians want to achieve, from wine-makers who market their product aggressively overseas to migrants who have two jobs, to sports stars, musicians, film-makers, writers and artists who have achieved world renown.

These four factors, suggest Kahn and Pepper, are significant variations upon the Protestant work ethic found in similar cultures (see Chapter 1). Australians, however, according to these American observers, do have problems with a national sense of motivation: we are "prematurely post-industrial", that is, we are beginning to relax and develop a culture based on leisure decades sooner than we can economically afford such a lifestyle. The bumper sticker reading "I'd rather be sailing" sums this up.[20]

Kahn and Pepper, and Haupt and Caldwell, are saying, then, some fairly serious things about the state of macro- and micro-motivation in Australia. At worst, we appear to be lazy, conformist, fatalistic, too scared to excel and too ready to play the grasshopper rather than the ant—leading to a vaguely defined but potentially catastrophic historical demise.

What really motivates people?

Sundry theories on why we work or do not work have been examined in this chapter. Serious allegations of some motivation researchers "cooking the books"—fixing the facts to come up with unsubstantiated conclusions (in particular, conclusions along the lines that money is not a motivator)—have been noted. Motivation research perhaps boils down to whether money is important or not, and to what extent other, non-monetary factors are crucial to producing "striving behaviour".

Certainly, motivation understood as being an attitude or a value may not be enough. Other, more tangible factors may interact with it and even exceed it in importance. This is shown clearly in Sutermeister's model of factors which affect job performance and productivity (Fig. 2.5). Productivity is determined primarily by technological development and raw materials interacting with the job performance of employees. This performance is not simply determined by motivation, however, but by ability. As we proceed through other layers of the organisational universe, we see that there are many other factors, official and unofficial, predictable and unpredictable, that determine the way in which an individual will behave (note that the relative sizes of the various segments of the model, insofar as size expresses relative importance, will be different for each individual in any organisation).

---

[20] The end of the work ethic has been proclaimed in many other countries, of course—and some people would say "and a good thing, too" (see Chapter 1). Machovec and Smith are dubious about all of this "decline of the work ethic/motivation" argument. They suggest that the black or cash economy, so big in most countries, shows that people are not trading off less work for more leisure—they are working just as hard, if not harder; they merely wish to avoid the demotivating clutches of the taxman. (Machovec and Smith 1982)

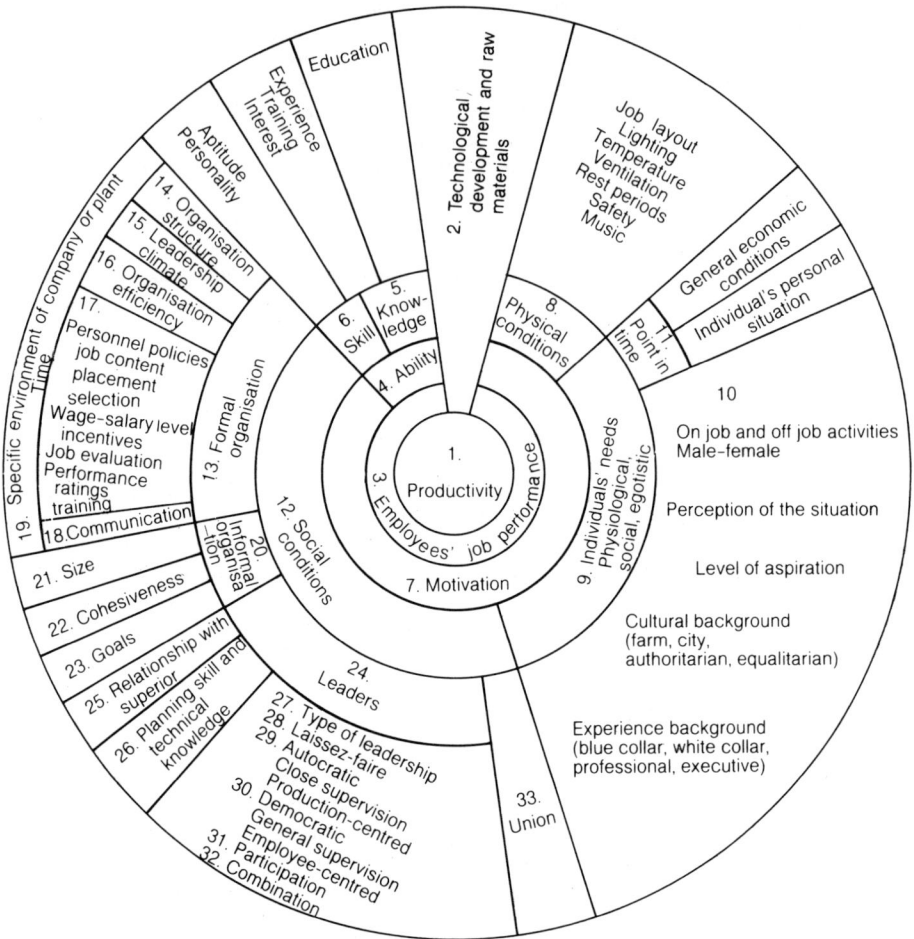

Fig. 2.5 *Major factors affecting employee job performance and productivity*
(SUTERMEISTER 1969. REPRODUCED WITH PERMISSION)

Just as patriotism is not enough to win a war, so motivation is not enough to lift productivity in an organisation or to ensure that a sporting team will win.[21] You can no more "motivate" someone than you can "volunteer" them. People have to volunteer themselves, because volunteering is voluntary (although some motivations, e.g. addictions, compulsive obsessions, are to some degree involuntary).

---

[21] Becker, for example, using the theories of Herzberg and Maslow, has written a book for South African managers entitled *Motivating Black Workers* (Becker 1970). To describe the "lack of motivation" of black workers as being due to lower level needs not being satisfied seems to be an almost ludicrously (if not obscenely) superficial way of analysing human behaviour.

Everybody is motivated by something. As Quick (1985) has said: "The answer to the question, 'What do you do with unmotivated employees?' is, 'You bury them.' The only unmotivated people are dead ones." If people aren't motivated by work, they might be motivated by leisure. Their real life might begin once they leave the place where they earn their meal-ticket. "Motivation" simply means what is important to you. Even if you are a nihilist, saying that nothing is important to you, it is still important to you (i.e. you are motivated by knowing) that others know that you don't care.

Even then, when we know what motivates people, or at least what satisfies people, can we presume that people with high job satisfaction will be productive? Sutermeister and the expectancy theorists tell us no, that is not the whole picture. People can be miserable, yet productive; satisfied, yet unproductive. It is a cliché that many artists (painters, musicians, etc.) did their best work when immersed in squalor and pain, yet became puerile and hackneyed when wealth and fame arrived. This is not an apology for the moral uplift of squalor and pain, it is merely to point out that the *satisfaction = productivity* equation is too crude.[22]

We have seen that much motivation research has downplayed the importance of money, classifying it as a hygiene factor, a theory X creature, and so on. In many respects, much motivation theory still seems to be in a state of extreme reaction to Taylorism. Scientific management engineered machines and people in the same way, it seemed, alienating workers by forgetting about the human side of enterprise. However, in arguing against the concept of the worker as *homo economicus*, many human-relations-oriented writers went to the other extreme and called workers "irrational".[23] Human relations theorists who have argued that people do not really care for money and instead are motivated by "higher level psychological needs" have been attacked by both the political left and the political right: the left claims that such beliefs play into the hands of management (who are only too happy to hold down wages and "bust unions" (Drucker)), while the right claims that such beliefs undermine the profit motive and incentive (Rose 1975).

---

[22] Spillane (1980) points out the results of many "job satisfaction" surveys are potentially biased. Many questions ("Are you satisfied with your present job?" "Do you have the impression you are doing something useful?") often get a positive response merely because employees are resigned and fatalistic about their current position. Other questions which relate less to present circumstances and more to future circumstances ("Do you get enough information about your career prospects?" "Is the person affected by a change of job sometimes the last one to know about it?") tend to get more negative (i.e. dissatisfied) responses. People may be resigned to the present (the "I can stand it" syndrome), but they want the future to hold more hope. Yet, suggests, Spillane, it is the first set of questions and their responses that motivation researchers dwell on. The proof of the pudding—the proof that dissatisfaction is widespread, in spite of what surveys "reveal"—is shown by undiminishing or increasing levels of absenteeism, strikes, industrial unrest, and lower productivity. Spillane notes:

> . . . it could also be argued that some of those who report dissatisfaction with their jobs are motivated to change their unsatisfactory environments. This determination to create better work conditions is not necessarily a reflection of neurotic behaviour (as suggested by Herzberg) but could be viewed as mature, creative behaviour. Similarly, some employees who report satisfaction may be demonstrating an alienated acceptance of the inevitable rather than reflecting the self-actualised human being. (p44)

[23] Drucker has suggested that much human-relations-type management theory is a form of "psychological despotism" or control through psychological manipulation. Theory Y thus may be worse than the theory X many believe it will naturally replace:

> The work relationship has to be based on mutual respect. Psychological despotism is basically contemptuous—far more contemptuous than the traditional theory X. It does not assume that people are lazy and resist work, but it assumes that the manager is healthy while everyone else is sick. It assumes that the manager is strong while everyone else is weak. It assumes that the manager knows while everyone else is ignorant. It assumes that the manager is right, whereas everyone else is stupid. These are the assumptions of foolish arrogance.
>
> Above all, the manager-psychologist will undermine his own authority. There is, to be sure, need for psychological insight, help, counsel. There is a need for the healer of souls and the comforter of the afflicted. But the relationship of healer and patient and that of superior to subordinate are different relationships and mutually exclusive. (DRUCKER 1974, PP243-5)

Money then is important.[24] But this is not to say that non-monetary factors such as higher psychological needs are unimportant. The problem is usually put as a choice: *either* money *or* satisfaction. But the choice is a fake one. It is true we do not live by bread alone, but we will be very dead without bread. Why either/or? Why not both/and? The practicalities of just how this is done, is best left to other chapters, in particular, Chapters 12, 13 and 14.

Summary

Frederick Taylor based his scientific management theories upon money as a motivator. He was aware of psychological factors such as work group cohesion and output reduction, but chose to undermine such phenomena by individual piece-rates. A distinction may need to be drawn between Taylor and Taylorism, between the founder of scientific management and his followers.

Elton Mayo and his associates de-emphasised the role of money as a motivator in their Hawthorne studies. They saw "non-rational" factors such as group norms to be powerful forces in determining individual and group work behaviour. The impact of the Hawthorne studies led to emphasis being given by managements to human relations in the workplace, although their motives for doing so have been questioned.

Abraham Maslow arranged human motivations in a hierarchy, proceeding from physiological needs to self-actualisation. Once a need is satisfied, it no longer motivates.

Frederick Herzberg drew a distinction between hygiene factors which were extrinsic to a job (pay, supervision, etc.) and motivators which were intrinsic to a job (achievement, recognition, etc.). Motivators motivate, hygiene factors do not.

Douglas McGregor drew a distinction between two different philosophies of work—theory X and theory Y. Our philosophies determine what motivates us.

David McClelland saw people as being motivated by needs for affiliation, achievement and power.

Victor Vroom, Lyman Porter and Edward Lawler prefer to emphasise the rational expectations people have as being their prime source of motivation.

Motivation as a technique of exhortation, as with sport, has considerable limitations. The cultural backgrounds of Americans and Australians can help to explain different motivational patterns. Productivity is not only determined by attitudes or motivations—non-attitudinal factors are important and often predominant. The choice between money *or* job satisfaction may be a false choice.

---

[24] Even though, as Spillane notes, people sometimes rank money as not being of primary importance in questionnaire surveys. But there may be reasons for this that are not immediately apparent:

Blue collar employees often rank satisfaction with remuneration about fourth or fifth on a list of ten factors behind such factors as supervision and working relationships. Influenced by the human relations fad since Hawthorne, many researchers concluded that money was less important to factory workers than were solid interpersonal relationships. Such a conservative philosophy found great appeal in management circles and industrial psychology was set on a track from which it has only recently departed. Industrial relations scholars and trade union officials were quick to point out that a plausible interpretation of the surprisingly low ranking of remuneration reflects the expectations in the economic *status quo* and are beyond the everyday scope of employees and are often invested in periodic legalistic arbitration far removed in space and time from the factory. (SPILLANE 1980, P46)

Traditional reticence and taboos—'never discuss three things—sex, religion and money'—also influence people's behaviour in expressing opinions in surveys.

Questions for discussion

1. Scientific management saw workers as rational beings, motivated only by self-interest. Is this an unrealistic perception of all people?
2. In what way did the findings of the Hawthorne experiments alter the thrust of scientific management?
3. Construct your own hierarchy of needs, paying particular attention to self-actualisation. Compare your hierarchy with those constructed by others. Do you have any needs which would be permanently unsatisfied?
4. What is the difference between extrinsic and intrinsic factors of motivation? Is one set of factors more powerful than the other?
5. Which is the more correct view of human nature—theory X or theory Y? Can you think of a "theory Z" which would present a third view?
6. Do people need the same mix of power, achievement and affiliation motivation to succeed in all jobs?
7. "Expectancy theory is just scientific management in newer jargon." Is it?
8. How hard will people work for money? What things would you do, and not do, if the price was right?
9. Can exhortation make people work harder?
10. Are there real differences in the motivation to work in different cultures? How can we best explain these differences?

References

Alderfer, Clayton P. (1972). *Existence, Relatedness, and Growth.* (Free Press: New York).

Becker, H. (1970). *Motivating Black Workers.* (McGraw-Hill: Johannesburg).

Braverman, H. (1975). *Labour and Monopoly Capital.* (Monthly Review Press: New York).

Brown, Wilfred (1971). *Piecework Abandoned: The Effect of Wage Incentive Systems on Managerial Authority.* (Heinemann: London).

Burrell, Gibson and Morgan, Gareth (1980). *Sociological Paradigms and Organizational Analysis.* (Heinemann: London).

Caldwell, Geoffrey (1974). "The Gambling Australian", in *Social Change in Australia: Readings in Sociology* (ed. Donald D. Edgar). (Cheshire: Melbourne).

Carey, Alex (1967). "The Hawthorne Studies: A Radical Criticism", *American Sociological Review*, vol. 32, no. 3 (June).

(1976). "Industrial Psychology and Sociology in Australia", in *The Professions in Australia: A Critical Appraisal* (ed. P. Boreham, et al.). (University of Queensland Press: St Lucia, Queensland).

(1977). "The Lysenko Syndrome in Western Social Science", *Australian Psychologist*, vol. 12, no. 1 (March).

(1980). "Worker Motivation: Social Science, Propaganda, and Democracy", in *Work and Inequality: Ideology and Control in the Capitalist Labour Process* (ed. P. Boreham and Geoff Dow). (Macmillan: Melbourne).

Cooley, Michael J.E. (1977). "Taylor in the Office", in *Humanizing the Workplace: New Proposals and Perspectives* (ed. Richard N. Otway). (Croom Helm: London).

Cullen, R.B. (1984). *Guidelines for Performance Assessment and Performance Pay for Members of the Senior Executive Service* (mimeo). (Victorian Public Service Board: Melbourne).

Davis, Keith (1981). *Human Behaviour at Work: Organizational Behaviour*, 6th edn. (McGraw-Hill: New York).

DiCaprio, Nicholas S. (1974). *Personality Theories: Guides to Living.* (W.B. Saunders: Philadelphia).

Dichter, E. (1964). *Handbook of Consumer Motivations.* (McGraw-Hill: New York).

Dowling, William F. and Sayles, Leonard R. (1978). *How Managers Motivate: The Imperatives of Supervision.* (McGraw-Hill: New York).

Drucker, Peter F. (1974). *Management: Tasks, Responsibilities, Practices.* (Heinemann: London).
　　(1981). "The Coming Rediscovery of Scientific Management", in *Towards the Next Economics and Other Essays.* (Harper and Row: New York).

Dunphy, Dexter C. and Dick, Robert (1981). *Organizational Change by Choice.* (McGraw-Hill: Sydney).

The Economist (1970), "Does Your Job Bore You or Does Professor Herzberg?" 6 June.

Fotiades, Peter (1979). "A Two-Sided Look at Incentives", *Work and People*, vol. 5, no. 1.

Frenkel, Stephen J. (1977). *Workplace Reform in Britain and the United States: An Essay in the Dialectics of Power and Knowledge.* (Dept. of Industrial Relations: Univ. of NSW).

Frisch, Robert. A. (1982). *ESOP for the 80's.* (Farnsworth Publishing Company: New York).

Globerson, S. (1985). *Performance Criteria and Incentive Systems.* (Elsevier: Amsterdam).

Guest, David (1984). "What's New in . . . Motivation", *Personnel Management*, May.

Haupt, Robert (1977). "Americans: Friends, but not Mates", *Financial Review*, 14 June.

Herzberg, Frederick (1968). "One More Time: How Do You Motivate Employees?" *Harvard Business Review*, Jan.–Feb.
　　(1976). *The Managerial Choice.* (Richard D. Irwin: Illinois).
　　(1979). "New Perspectives on the Will to Work", *Personnel Administrator*, December.

Hilmer, Frederick G. (1985). *When the Luck Runs Out: The Future for Australians at Work.* (Harper and Row: Sydney).

Hirschhorn, Larry (1984). *Work and Technology in a Postindustrial Age.* (MIT Press: Cambridge, Mass.).

Hodgetts, Richard M. (1980). *Modern Human Relations.* (Dryden Press: Illinois).

Hofstede, Geert (1980). *Culture's Consequences.* (Sage Publications: San Francisco).
　　(1981). "Do American Theories Apply Abroad? A Reply to Goodstein and Hunt", *Organizational Dynamics*, Summer.

Hunt, John (1979). *Managing People at Work.* (McGraw-Hill: London).
　　(1981). "Applying American Behavioural Science: Some Cross-Cultural Problems", *Organizational Dynamics*, Summer.

Johnston, Ruth and Bavin, Ronald A. (1973). "Herzberg and Job Satisfaction", *Personnel Practice Bulletin*, vol. 29, no. 2, June.

Jones, Barry O. (1983). *Sleepers, Wake! Technology and the Future of Work*, 2nd edn. (Oxford University Press: Melbourne).

Juran, J.M. (1974). "Motivation", in *Quality Control Handbook*, 3rd edn. (McGraw-Hill: New York).

Kahn, Herman and Pepper, Thomas (1980). *Will She Be Right? The Future of Australia.* (University of Queensland Press: St Lucia, Qld).

Katz, Daniel and Kahn, R.C. (1978). *The Social Psychology of Organizations,* 2nd edn. (John Wiley: New York).

Kelly, John E. (1982). *Scientific Management, Job Redesign, and Work Performance.* (Academic Press: New York).

Kuttner, Bob (1983). "Making the Welfare State Work", *National Times,* 11–17 November.

Lazerson, Arlyne (ed.) (1975). *Psychology Today: An Introduction,* 4th edn. (CRM/Random House: New York).

Lee, James A. (1980). *The Gold and the Garbage in Management Theories and Prescriptions.* (Ohio University Press: Athens, Ohio).

Luthans, Fred (1981). *Organizational Behaviour,* 3rd edn. (McGraw-Hill: New York).

Luthans, Fred and Kreitner, Robert (1975). *Organizational Behaviour Modification.* (Scott Foresman: Illinois).

McClelland, David D. (1961). *The Achieving Society.* (Van Nostrand: Princeton, NJ).

(1967). "The Urge to Achieve", *New Society,* 16 February.

McClelland, David and Burnham, David (1976). "Why Good Chaps Make Bad Bosses", *Psychology Today* (UK edition), vol. 2, no. 2.

McGregor, Douglas (1960). *The Human Side of Enterprise.* (McGraw-Hill: New York).

Machovec, Frank M. and Smith, Howard R. (1982). "Fear Makes the World Go 'Round: The 'Dark' Side of Management", *Management Review,* January.

Mandel, Ernest (1971). *Marxist Economic Theory.* (Merlin Press: London).

Maslow, Abraham (1943). "A Theory of Human Motivation", *Psychological Review,* July.

(1970). *Motivation and Personality,* 2nd edn. (Harper and Row: New York).

Mayo, Elton (1953). *The Human Problems of an Industrial Civilization.* (Macmillan: New York).

Milton, Charles A., Entrekin, Lanny and Stening, Bruce R. (1983). *Organizational Behaviour in Australia.* (Prentice-Hall: Sydney).

Morris, J.L. and Fargher, K. (1981). "Achievement Drives and Creativity as Correlates of Success in a Small Business", *Australian Journal of Psychology,* vol. 26.

Myers, M. Scott (1970). *Every Employee a Manager.* (McGraw-Hill: New York).

Nevis, Edwin C. (1983). "Cultural Assumptions and Productivity: The United States and China", *Sloan Management Review,* Spring.

Packard, Vance (1979). *The People Shapers.* (Pan: London).

Piamonte, John S. (1979). "In Praise of Monetary Motivation", *Personnel Journal,* September.

Porter, Lyman W. and Lawler, Edward D. (1968). *Managerial Attitudes and Performance.* (Richard D. Irwin: Illinois).

Powers, John (1979). "The Motivators", *Australian Playboy,* October.

Quick, Thomas L. (1985). *The Manager's Motivation Desk Book.* (John Wiley and Sons: New York).

Rose, Michael (1975). *Industrial Behaviour.* (Penguin: Harmondsworth).

Rosen, Corey, Klein, Katherine J. and Young, Karen M. (1986). "When Employees Share the Profits/Employee Ownership: It's the Money that Counts", *Psychology Today,* January.

Rydge's Magazine (1976). "How to Motivate in Hard Times", March.

(1977). "The Winning Formula: High Level Motivation", August.

(1979). "Package More Important than Pay", October.

(1981). "The Motivating Power of Incentive Tools", March.

Skinner, B.F. (1953). *Science and Human Behaviour.* (Free Press: Massachusetts).
Spillane, R.M. (1980). "Job Satisfaction—Anticipation or Resignation?", *Human Resource Management Australia*, Autumn.
    (1981). "Intrinsic and Extrinsic Job Satisfaction and Labour Turnover", in Ainsworth, W.M. and Willis, Q.K. (eds), *Australian Organizational Behaviour: Readings.* (Macmillan: Melbourne).
Stoner, James A., Collins, Roger R. and Yetton, Phillip W. (1985). *Management in Australia.* (Prentice-Hall: Sydney).
Sutermeister, Robert A. (1969). *People and Productivity*, 2nd edn. (McGraw-Hill: New York).
Taylor, Frederick (1947). *Scientific Management.* (Harper: New York).
Townsend, Robert (1984). *Further Up the Organization.* (Alfred A. Knopf: New York).
Vroom, Victor H. (1964). *Work and Motivation.* (Wiley: New York).
Yankelovich, Daniel (1981). "Maslowism: The Biggest Trap of All", *Psychology Today*, April.
Zoll, Allen A. III (1974). *Explorations in Managing.* (Addison-Wesley: Massachusetts).

Films/Video

Motivation—Myth and Realities (Training Media Services).
Theory X and Theory Y, Parts 1 and 2 (Power Human Resources).
The Will to Win (Ron Barrassi) (Seven Dimensions).
The People Factor: The Hawthorne Studies for Today's Managers (Power Human Resources).
Maslow's Hierarchy of Needs (Power Human Resources).

3

Learning and behaviour modification

For behaviour, men learn it, as they take diseases, one of another.
Francis Bacon

Society attacks early, when the individual is helpless.
B.F. Skinner

They constantly try to escape
From the darkness outside and within
By dreaming of systems so perfect that no one will need to be good.
T.S. Eliot

Behaviourism has substituted for the erstwhile anthropomorphic view of the rat a ratomorphic view of man.
Arthur Koestler

Behavioural psychology is the science of pulling habits out of rats.
Douglas Busch

WHAT motivates you? What is the relationship of your personality to the way in which you are motivated? In Chapter 2, personality, motives, needs, drives (both conscious and unconscious) and expectancies were examined. Expectancies—our logical expectations of our environment—are a crucial part of a motivation/job design theory known as *goal setting*, which is examined in Chapter 12. The locus of control of individuals, understood as the extent to which we perceive we are or are not in control of our environment, is considered in Chapter 6.

To many social scientists, such things as personality, motives, expectancies, needs, drives and perceptions of control are self-evident. Social scientists who style themselves *behaviourists* are not so sure. Behaviourists such as B.F. Skinner see such things as being mentalistic, that is, they are presumed to take place within our heads; no one has ever seen or felt a motive or drive. It is, say behaviourists, foolish to concentrate on such cognitive or internal states; what really counts is behaviour which can be measured, and thus which is external to "the mind", such as verbal and non-verbal behaviour and action in general. Behaviour, behaviourists assert, is totally or almost totally learned from the environment, so we must look to learning processes to understand human behaviour.

Cognitive psychologists, on the other hand, sometimes argue that drives, needs and motives can be measured—

for example, by observing behaviour, constructing type and trait personality theories to explain that behaviour, and then creating instruments (e.g. a questionnaire) that will reveal inner personality characteristics. This controversy is important in many fields, not least of which is the field of organisational behaviour. Behaviourists proposing a system called *behaviour modification* claim that an external or learning model of organisational behaviour does away with the problem of speculating about whether a person is motivated or not; the key question is their performance, which can be seen and measured, and to what extent this performance can be changed. Luthans (1981) and others have begun to advocate an approach wherein methods of applying behaviour modification to organisations are seen not as an alternative to the internal models, but rather as complementary to those internal models. Let us now examine some of the basics of learning and behaviour modification theories.

Classic conditioning: Pavlov and conditioned reflexes

The Russian physiologist, Ivan Pavlov, conducted a series of experiments on dogs in the 1880s which came to have profound consequences for psychology as well as physiology. Pavlov noted that dogs began to salivate merely at the sight of food. In an experiment, bells were rung when food was presented. After this had happened a number of times, it was possible for Pavlov to trigger salivation in the dogs merely by ringing a bell, with no food actually present. Pavlov thus was able to induce or condition a reflex action—salivating—by the stimuli the dogs were exposed to. In classic conditioning terms, what happened was this:

> *Phase 1 Before conditioning:*
> An unconditioned stimulus (UCS)—meat—
>
> > caused
>
> an unconditioned response (UCR)—salivation
> At this stage, ringing a bell produced no effect at all, i.e. it was a neutral stimulus (NS).
>
> *Phase 2 After conditioning:*
> Now, a conditioned stimulus (CS)—bell ringing—
>
> > caused
>
> a conditioned response (CR)—salivation (no food present).

Classic conditioning can help to explain such things as phobias, fears experienced by adults as a result of conditioned responses caused by early traumas. Classic conditioning is concerned primarily with reflexive or automatic or involuntary behaviour. Of course, what is involuntary and what is not is very much a matter for conjecture. Newer methods of psychological and physical self-management, such as biofeedback, mean that people can now begin to control processes such as heartbeat, blood pressure, brain waves and muscular tension (Hellriegel, Slocum and Woodman, 1983; see also Chapter 7).

The dynamics of classic conditioning are those of stimuli affecting responses, S → R. This is one of the key differences between classic conditioning and a later, probably more comprehensive, behaviourist

Table 3.1 Differences between classic conditioning and operant conditioning

Classic conditioning	Operant conditioning
1. A change in the stimulus (UCS to CS) will elicit a particular response.	1. One particular response out of many possible ones occurs in a given stimulus situation. Stimulus situation serves as a cue, that is, it does not elicit the response but serves as a cue for a person to emit the response. Critical aspect is what happens as a consequence of the response.
2. Strength and frequency of behaviours are mainly determined by the frequency of the eliciting stimulus (environmental event that *precedes* the behaviour).	2. Strength and frequency of behaviours are mainly determined by the consequences (the environmental events that *follow* the behaviour).
3. UCS, serving as a reward, is presented every time.	3. Reward will occur only if the organism performs the correct response. The organism must operate on the environment in order to receive a reward. Response is instrumental in obtaining the reward.

Source: Adapted from Luthans (1981), p.237.

approach known as *operant conditioning*, which is more concerned with the opposite process of responses affecting stimuli, R → S.

Operant conditioning: Skinner and consequences

Operant conditioning as described by B.F. Skinner and others is not so much concerned with reflex actions as the actions of organisms, such as people, operating upon their environment. The operant conditioning behaviourist imitates the behaviour of natural selection or evolution, waiting for an animal or person to behave in a certain way in response (R) to the environment, and then reinforces the behaviour with a stimulus (S).[1] This means that *behaviour is a function of its consequences*. In other words, our behaviour (or units of behaviour, known as "behaviours") is strengthened, maintained or weakened by its consequences. Basic differences between classic conditioning and operant conditioning are given in Tables 3.1 and 3.2.

---

[1] Much data used by psychologists, behaviourist psychologists in particular, has been generated using animal populations, such as rats and pigeons. In order to "shape" the behaviour of pigeons (see "Shaping", p.79) Skinner had to wait for the bird to make a certain move that he wished to reinforce, and then reinforce it. A man of infinite patience, he thus played the role of the Great Natural Selector in the Sky:

Both phylogenetic (racial) and ontogenetic (individual) contingencies may seem to "build purpose into" an organism. It has been said that one of the achievements of cybernetics has been to demonstrate that machines show purpose. But we must look to the construction of the machine, as we look to the phylogeny and ontogeny of behaviour, to account for the fact that an ongoing system acts as if it had purpose.
Another apparent characteristic in common is "adaptation". Both kinds of contingencies change the organism so that it adjusts to its environment in the sense of behaving in it more effectively. With respect to phylogenetic contingencies, that is what is meant by natural selection. With respect to ontogeny, it is what is meant by operant conditioning. Successful responses are selected in both cases, and the result is adaptation. But the processes of selection are very different, and we cannot tell from the mere fact that behaviour is adaptive which kind of process has been responsible for it. (SKINNER 1969, P.194)

Table 3.2 Examples of classic and operant conditioning

	Classic connection	
	(S) Stimulus ─────────▶	(R) Response
The individual is:	stuck by a pin tapped below the kneecap shocked by electric current surprised by a loud sound	flinches lower leg flexes jumps/screams jumps/screams
	Operant connection	
	(R) Response ─────────▶	(S) Stimulus
The individual:	works talks to others enters a restaurant enters a library works hard	is paid meets more people obtains food finds a book receives praise and a promotion

Source: Luthans (1981), p.238. Reproduced with permission.

A way of visualising the relationship between behaviour and consequences is the A-B-C model (Fig. 3.1). In this model, the stimulus or antecedent is what occurs before behaviour happens, while the consequence is what happens after the behaviour occurs. Such antecedent–behaviour–consequence sequences occur many times each day for all of us. Proponents of behaviour modification argue that it is possible to change behaviour by controlling antecedents, but in particular by controlling consequences. This control can take the form of strengthening, maintaining or weakening such consequences. To understand how this might happen, consider the positive and negative consequences given in detail in Table 3.3.

Behaviour is a function of consequences, and four ways in which behaviour can be changed are:
1. by positive reinforcement;
2. by negative reinforcement;
3. by punishment;
4. by extinction.

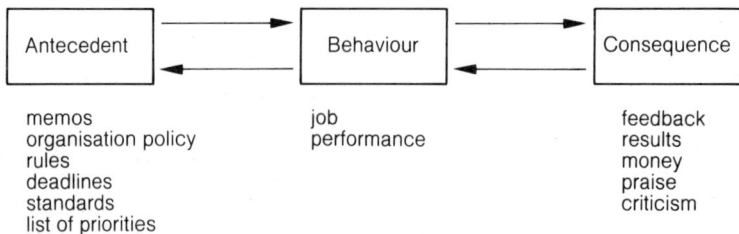

Fig. 3.1 *The A-B-C model of behaviour* (ADAPTED FROM BROWN 1982, P.11)

Table 3.3 Positive and negative consequences

	Positive consequences	*Negative consequences*
Material	pay increase bonus promotion better office privileges job rotation	pay cut higher tax demotion reprimand removal of privileges no job rotation dismissal
Verbal	"Good job." "You're terrific."	"Lousy job." "You're useless." Silence.
Non-verbal	smile pat on back attention	frown push head shake

Behaviour is positively reinforced when positive consequences are applied or accepted. Behaviour is negatively reinforced when negative consequences are withheld or avoided. Behaviour is punished when negative consequences are applied or accepted. Behaviour is extinguished when positive consequences are withheld.

Let us have a closer look at reinforcement, punishment and extinction.

Positive reinforcement

Positive reinforcement is a strategy of "accentuate the positive" in order to "eliminate the negative". If a person does a number of things wrong and one thing right, it may feel good to come down on the person like a ton of bricks and punish them, but it may not change their behaviour. By complimenting the person on her lone success and/or giving monetary or other recognition, that successful behaviour may be strengthened and hence will be more likely to occur. One often hears around an organisation the following refrain: "We do great work here 99 per cent of the time, and they don't notice or give a damn. When we make a 1 per cent mistake, they yell blue murder!" If positive reinforcement is made contingent upon good behaviour (i.e. is seen to be causally linked to good behaviour, and thus the reinforcement comes rapidly and not six months later) then the good behaviour becomes more likely. Behaviour is a function of its consequences. First behaviours to be reinforced can sometimes appear quite trivial, but they could well include:

- the person doing it right one time in a hundred
- the person asking a question about how to do it
- the person offering a solution that couldn't possibly work
- the person recognising that she has made a mistake (O'Brien and Dickinson 1982).

The trick is, then, to catch people doing something right, and then let them know about it (Blanchard and Johnson 1983). Feedback about performance, particularly positive feedback, is a powerful way to change people's behaviour.

Other types of positive reinforcement might be the positive consequences listed in Table 3.3, plus things like trophies, commendations, appliances for the home, after-work parties, paid-up insurance policies, recognition in the house newspaper, and use of company recreation facilities

(Luthans 1981). Many of these rewards, of course, when applied by managers in organisations trying a policy of positive reinforcement, may appear as arrant bribery and as comically manipulative ("jumping for jellybeans"). If administered rapidly and continuously, the effects of these rewards will wear off—satiation will set in. The timing or scheduling of these rewards thus becomes a critical consideration (see below).

Negative reinforcement

Negative reinforcement means *increasing* the frequency of a behaviour by withdrawing a condition in a contingent manner. If, for example, a worker works harder simply to prevent a supervisor nagging about poor perform-ance, and the supervisor then remains silent, then the worker has been negatively reinforced (Luthans and Kreitner 1975). Negative reinforcement should not be confused with punishment: negative reinforcement increases frequency of behaviour, while punishment decreases frequency. As Luthans remarks:

> . . . negative reinforcement is actually a type of "blackmail" control of behaviour; the person behaves in a certain way in order not to be punished. Most organisations today control participants in this manner. People come to work in order not to be fired and look busy when the supervisor walks by in order not to be punished. Under positive control, the person behaves in a certain way in order to receive the desired consequence. Under positive control people would come to work in order to be recognised for making a contribution to their department's goal of perfect attendance or would keep busy whether the supervisor was around or not in order to receive incentive pay or because they get self-reinforcement from doing a good job. (LUTHANS 1981, P.279)

Punishment

Punishment occurs when an unfavourable consequence is made contingent upon a behaviour, and that behaviour decreases in frequency. Punishment has been extremely popular in most cultures throughout history. Phrases like "vengeance is mine", "revenge is sweet", "an eye for an eye", all attest to this. Punishment as a doctrine crucially affects sub-populations, such as children, students, prisoners, drivers, as well as the entire population. Behaviourists often argue that punishment is not so much immoral as inefficient—it doesn't work terribly well. Thus, while it may achieve short-run changes, it may elicit strong emotional reactions which prevent people from getting on with the matter in hand. When the punisher is not physically around, "the mice will play". The punisher will have difficulty in administering positive reinforce-ment in future situations (i.e. role conflict in the eyes of those being reinforced); punishment can inhibit more general behaviour such as creativity and flexibility. Also, while punishment diminishes one behaviour, it does not reinforce a substitute, more desirable behaviour.

Punishment is also not always perceived as punishment, and may in fact be a form of concealed positive reinforcement, that is, instead of causing a behaviour to be less frequent it causes the behaviour to be more frequent. If a teacher punishes a student by reprimanding him in public, and the student's peer group thinks that such reprimands are amusing and a sign of glamorous non-conformity, then the "punishment" will not punish at all. A Florida sheriff noted that putting young toughs in jail on bread and water had this counter-productive effect; he shifted the punishment diet to baby food, which proved to be really punishing in that it was very unglamorous, and produced an improvement in overall behaviour (Connellan 1978). A parent may punish a child with verbal and/or physical violence, thinking that the child will not behave that way again. However, if punishment is the only way a child can get attention, then the behaviour will increase, not decrease.[2] Concomitantly, the parent may try bribery: if the child stops misbehaving, she will give him a biscuit. Misbehaviour increases in the following days and, indeed, in the following years and decades. Who is being positively reinforced, and for what? Who is being punished, and for what? Who is controlling whom?

Punishment can be effective, however, if the following points are observed (Schermerhorn, Hunt and Osborn 1982; Hellriegel, Slocum and Woodman 1983):

1. Tell the person what he or she has done wrong, in specific terms.
2. Tell the person what is right, that is, positively reinforce correct behaviour.
3. The punishment should follow soon after the undesirable behaviour, and not left until later, that is, make it contingent.
4. Follow the maxim, "punish in private, praise in public".
5. Be fair: make the punishment fit the transgression.

Extinction

You can tell extinction has occurred, because nothing happens, or nothing happens any longer. A door-to-door salesman will call a certain number of times, but if no one is at home (i.e. his behaviour is not reinforced) then he will not call again—his behaviour will have been extinguished. If a crying child or complaining employee are simply ignored, and their behaviour ceases, then extinction has occurred. A group may reinforce an individual's disruptive behaviour by laughing; if the group ceases to laugh, then the disruptive behaviour may be extinguished. A manager through insensitivity may fail to positively reinforce competent performance of a worker, and that excellence may be extinguished (Hellriegel, Slocum and Woodman 1983).

Extinction as a matter of deliberate policy is not all that easy. Connellan (1978) notes that, "when a previously reinforced behaviour is no longer reinforced (extinction), the amount of that behaviour temporarily goes up". Thus if one attempts to extinguish the office clown's joke-telling behaviour by ignoring him, or if one attempts to extinguish a child's crying behaviour by ignoring it, there will be a last-ditch stand from both child and clown—or perhaps escalation of hostilities is a better way of putting it.

Shaping

As we have seen, behaviour modification sees human behaviour as a repertoire of learned behaviours which have been positively or negatively reinforced, extinguished or punished. Figure 3.2 is a useful model for

---

[2] Compare reinforcement and punishment with the transactional analysis concept of "strokes" as the fundamental unit of human interaction. In TA terms, if the child cannot get a positive stroke (positive reinforcement), then it will settle for a negative stroke (punishment) rather than be ignored. As George Bernard Shaw put it, "The worst sin towards our fellow creatures is not to hate them but to be indifferent to them." Purist behaviourists, of course, would not be pleased to see similarities between their discipline and such a mentalistic area as TA, depending as it does not merely upon "hypothetical" consciousness but a "worse than hypothetical" unconscious.

Consequence of Contingently	Reward (something desirable)	Noxious stimuli (something aversive and undesirable)
Applied	POSITIVE REINFORCEMENT (Behaviour increases)	PUNISHMENT (Behaviour decreases)
Withheld	EXTINCTION (Behaviour decreases)	NEGATIVE REINFORCEMENT (Behaviour increases)

Fig. 3.2 *Behaviour modification: Four basic mechanisms* (LUTHANS 1981, P.251. REPRODUCED WITH PERMISSION)

understanding the dynamics of these four behavioural mechanisms. Shaping is simply a systematic way of using these four mechanisms as behavioural strategies in controlling a person's behaviour. Positive reinforcement is usually considered to be the most effective of the four strategies. Shaping is basically breaking complex tasks down into smaller tasks, and then reinforcing a person when she has completed each small task.[3]

Conditioning plus modelling: Bandura

Bandura (1977) and others have accepted the learning model of behaviour given by the principles of behaviour modification, but have attempted to expand upon it. Bandura, for example, is less deterministic than Skinner about human behaviour, arguing that man's cognitive powers give him much more free will in determining his actions. Thus, while Skinnerian behaviourism could be represented thus:

environment ⟶ behaviour

Bandura's model of behaviour is represented by Figure 3.3. All three factors influence each other, or reciprocally determine each other. Society teaches the individual lessons which are not strictly within the Skinnerian framework. Culture, family and other institutions transmit information about the

[3] An amusing, and perhaps faintly disturbing example of shaping is given by Lefrancois (1975):

Early in the semester, my (psychology) class had been introduced to Skinner, operant conditioning, and shaping. Immediately thereafter, (myself and five other students) decided that they would become "head-nodders"—head-nodders are very reinforcing for professors. To begin with, these head-nodders decided that they would reinforce pacing behaviour by nodding at the professor's wisdom as he paced. Within four lectures, he paced incessantly as he lectured. The experimenters then decided to extinguish this behaviour and to reinforce lecturing from one corner instead. This too was accomplished easily and rapidly. The next step was to condition lecturing from another corner. Once this had been done, the experimenters attempted to reinforce what they called "spaces between words". Every time the professor paused, he was to be smiled and nodded at. This part of the conditioning procedure was never particularly successful, perhaps because the instructor spoke too fast. In addition, he probably assumed that the reinforcement was for what he had just said, and therefore hastened on to what he would say next. In any case, he never knew as he paced up and down before the class that he was a walking example of one of his lectures. (PP60-1).

If you are a student, you might consider doing this yourself. Your consideration should, of course, encompass the central question of behaviour modification: is it ethical?

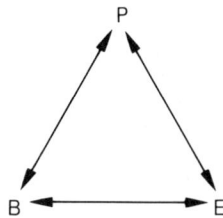

B = Behaviour
E = Environment
P = Cognitive and other internal events that can affect
    perceptions and actions

Fig. 3.3 *Bandura's model of reciprocal determinism* (HJELLE AND ZIEGLER 1981, P.240)

past so that we can learn to anticipate the future. Behaviour is also *modelled* for us, so that we learn by imitation:

> Although behaviour can be shaped into new patterns to some extent by rewarding and punishing consequences, learning would be exceedingly laborious and hazardous if it proceeded solely on this basis. . . It is difficult to imagine a socialisation process in which the language, mores, vocational activities, familial customs and educational, religious and political practices of a culture are taught to each new member by selective reinforcement of fortuitous behaviours, without benefits of models who exemplify the cultural patterns in their own behaviour. Most of the behaviours that people display are learned either deliberately or inadvertently, through the influence of example. (BANDURA 1976, P.5)

Some of Bandura's research on modelling behaviour has suggested that violent behaviour portrayed in television programs can act as a model for children watching (Bandura 1977). Modelling is really *vicarious* reinforcement, punishment and extinction. Thus modelling can be understood simply as imitation. Advertising hopes to change our behaviour by presenting beautiful, high-status people in fantasy situations using certain commodities. We assume the beauty and the status are causally related to the commodity, and we thus imitate this modelled behaviour and buy a bottle of Fizzrott or the new 500 horsepower Machogorilla coupe. In organisations, similar training principles are used. A demonstrator can show how to load a computer program or complete a sale, breaking the process down into discrete steps, and positively reinforcing the learners at each step. Like the preceding intervention strategies, modelling is something we have been doing all our lives anyway.

Schedules of reinforcement

We now know *what* some learning theories can contribute to an understanding of organisational and personal behaviour. It is now essential to know *when* they are to be used. Reinforcements are timed or scheduled according to two major categories—continuous and partial (or intermittent).

Continuous reinforcement

Continuous reinforcement occurs after each time a behaviour occurs. It is quite useful for new and/or weak behaviours, but after a while satiation may set in and it will lose its power. Consider the positive consequences of Table 3.2, and also the positive reinforcers discussed under "Positive reinforcement". How long might it be before satiation sets in with various rewards? Consider walking into an area where you know many people. If you liked all of them (are positively reinforced by them), you may not grow tired of greeting them all one by one. If you see them many times throughout the day, however, you would not greet them on subsequent occasions as you would on the first.

Intermittent reinforcement

With your greetings of colleagues and friends, you would change the greeting or acknowledgment each time. You would have rationed out or scheduled your interaction with them to an intermittent basis. Intermittent reinforcement schedules are of four types:

1. *Fixed ratio.* Reinforcement occurs on a fixed ratio when a fixed number of responses are emitted. Piece-rate incentive systems are an example of this—for each item of work produced, I get a pre-set sum of money.
2. *Variable ratio.* Reinforcement occurs here when a variable number of correct responses are emitted. If employees become eligible for a ticket in a lottery if they are not absent or late, they are being reinforced on a variable ratio. If an employee leaves his office or factory and goes to his club to play poker machines, he is again receiving variable ratio reinforcement:

   > The common slot machine serves as a testimony of the tremendous power that intermittent schedules of reinforcement have on behaviour. Its potential of a payoff on the next lever-pull promotes coin-insertion and lever-pulling responses. The gambling devices pay off after a varying number of lever pulls and thus reinforce lever-pulling on a variable schedule ratio. (LUTHANS AND KREITNER 1975, P.52)

3. *Fixed interval.* Here, reinforcement occurs simply because an interval of time has elapsed. Thus, I get paid every week, fortnight or month, barring really deviant behaviour on my part. Similarly, I will get a gold watch when I retire. This interval is not considered to be a powerful reinforcer in all circumstances, because it is not contingent upon immediate or recent performance.
4. *Variable interval.* This is reinforcement at random times. A supervisor might "take a prowl" through her department but, just to keep them on their toes, does not follow a predictable routine. She may, however, be adhering to an average monthly figure of taking her walks.

Table 3.4 summarises the various reinforcement schedules.[4]

---

[4] Various authorities disagree on terminology and concepts: thus, while Davis defines piece-rate work as a continuous schedule phenomenon, Luthans (1981) defines it as an intermittent fixed ratio phenomenon.

Table 3.4 Types of reinforcement schedules

Reinforcement schedule	Example
1 *Continuous.* Reinforcement accompanying each correct behaviour	A piece rate of 10 cents is paid for each acceptable piece produced.
2 *Partial.* Reinforcement following only some of the correct behaviours	
(a) *Time intervals*	
• *Fixed interval.* Reinforcement after a certain period of time	A paycheque arrives every two weeks.
• *Variable interval.* Reinforcement after a variety of time periods	The safety department makes safety checks of every department four times a year on a random basis.
(b) *Ratio*	
• *Fixed ratio.* Reinforcement after a certain number of correct responses	Sales employees are given a bonus after every fifth automobile sold.
• *Variable ratio.* Reinforcement after a variable number of correct responses	There is a lottery for employees who have not been absent during the week.

Source: Davis (1981), p.73. Reproduced with permission.

Applying behaviour modification principles to organisations

Luthans and Kreitner (1975) and Luthans (1981) have developed a model from the ideas of Skinner and Bandura that applies behaviour modification to organisations (Fig. 3.4). Let us see how the model works, by working through each step.

Identification of performance-related behavioural events: Pinpointing

If any behaviour is going to be modified, then it must be possible to identify and measure each behaviour. The key questions to be asked are: (a) can it be seen? and (b) can it be measured? (Luthans (1981)). We sometimes think we know just what is wrong, or at least what needs to be changed in a particular situation, but often our language and perceptions are dangerously vague—we confuse attitudes, values and prejudices with behaviours. In other words, we label behaviour rather than pinpoint behaviour, and this isn't good enough. Table 3.5 shows the differences between labelling a person's behaviour and pinpointing that behaviour. Only when it has been pinpointed can proper analysis begin.

Measurement of behaviour

Once targeted behaviours have been identified (lateness, customer relations, safety, production output, reporting, control of receiving and shipping cost, control of scrap rates, etc.) then it is essential to get data on such behaviour. First, the behaviour must be specifically described and quantified. What is

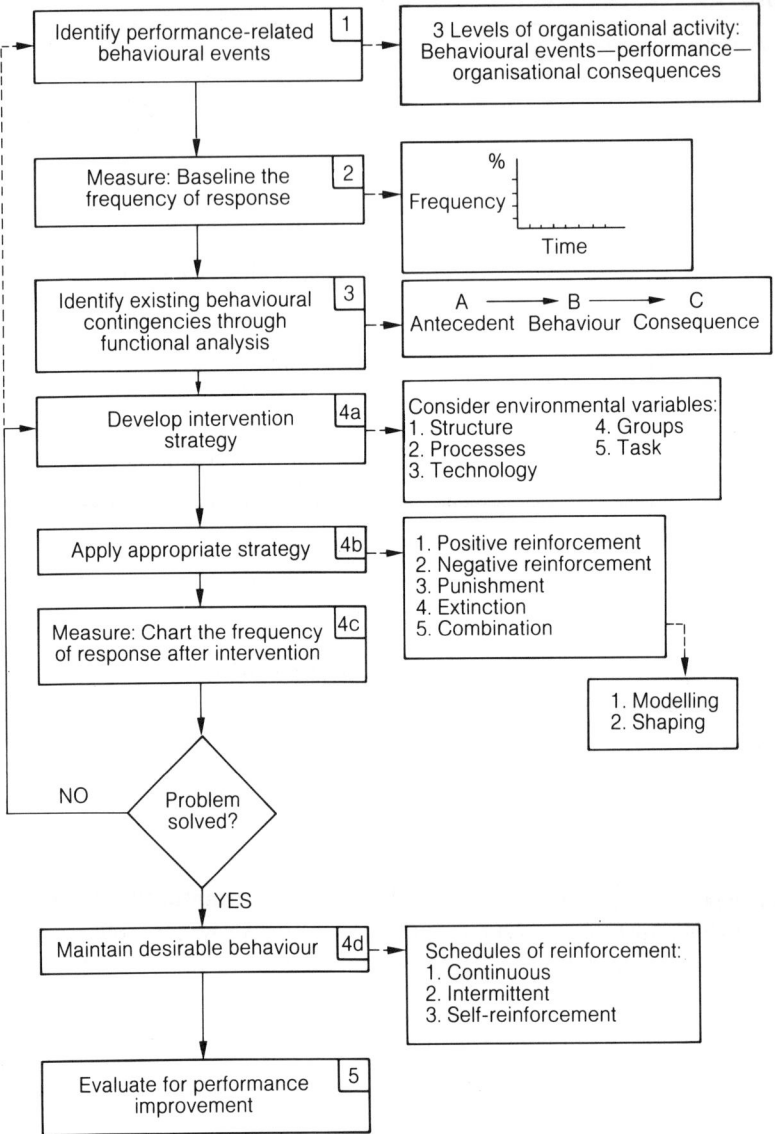

Fig. 3.4 *Steps in organisational behaviour modification* (LUTHANS AND KREITNER 1974. REPRINTED BY PERMISSION OF THE PUBLISHER. © 1974 BY AMACOM, A DIVISION OF AMERICAN MANAGEMENT ASSOCIATIONS, NEW YORK. ALL RIGHTS RESERVED.)

Table 3.5 Labelling versus pinpointing behaviour

Examples of labelling behaviour	*Examples of pinpointing behaviour*
"Steve. . ."	"Steve. . ."
1. is disagreeable.	1. argues and complains.
2. is unmotivated.	2. is late and extends coffee breaks.
3. is stubborn.	3. refuses to acknowledge lateness and argues about it.
4. is aggressive.	4. calls proposals stupid or dumb.
5. is a disruptive influence.	5. makes jokes and is sarcastic.
6. is insubordinate.	6. breaks company rules, e.g. about smoking, parking, etc.
7. has poor perceptual ability.	7. switches overhead transparencies around.
8. doesn't think rationally.	8. does not organise presentations and reports.
9. is immature.	9. uses cute phrases and jokes.
10. has poor reasoning power.	10. mixes up the sequence on reports and forgets to ask crucial questions.
11. lacks drive.	11. refuses to participate in company training programs.

Source: Brown (1982), p.28. Reproduced with permission.

meant by "lateness", for example? Then data needs to be recorded to find out what the true picture is, before any type of behaviour modification intervention is attempted. This may reveal that the problem is a real one, but it also may reveal that the problem is only a perceived one—there may not really be a problem with lateness, or bad customer relations, and so on.

If there is still a problem, then such initial, pre-intervention data gives a baseline of data. Once data has been recorded on a tally-sheet, it can be charted on graph paper, with frequency of behaviour (e.g. in percentage terms) on one axis and time on the other axis (Fig. 3.5). After the intervention, modified behaviour can be charted, giving a "before-and-after" impression of whether the intervention has been successful.

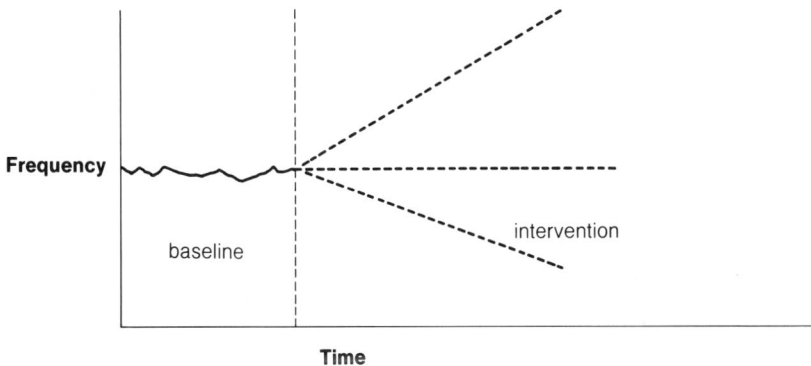

Fig. 3.5 *Charting target behaviours*

Functional analysis: The A-B-C model

We have seen earlier it is useful to see the connections between antecedents of behaviour, the behaviour itself, and the consequences of the behaviour (Fig. 3.1). Once behaviour has been pinpointed, measured and charted, it is necessary to ask what were the preconditions of the behaviour and, more importantly, what were the consequences? For example, what are the consequences of excellent performance and mediocre performance? Is excellence positively reinforced, is mediocrity punished or extinguished? It may be that excellence is extinguished because no one notices it; or excellence may be punished if some decide that excellence is more trouble than it's worth: for example, group members may decide that an individual is working too hard, or a manager feels that an employee shows her up by outstanding work. If mediocrity, excellence and blithering incompetence all call forth the same response—apathy—then there will tend to be a lot of blithering incompetence, because blithering incompetence is usually so much easier than mediocrity, and almost certainly easier than excellence. In other words, behaviour is a function of its consequences.

Develop intervention strategy

This strategy needs to take account of certain preconditions or environmental variables before conditioning and modelling are applied. These conditions are:

1. state of equipment—in good shape, or out of date, poorly maintained?
2. standards of performance required—are they unrealistically high?
3. are behaviours to be changed related to performance? If not, then perhaps there is more labelling than pinpointing going on (see below).
4. is training of workers adequate?
5. type of organisational structure—is the structure centralised and formal, decentralised and informal? Centralised/formal structure will need tightly designed contingencies, decentralised/informal structures will need less tightness.
6. processes of decision-making, communication and control.
7. technology: machinery, knowledge, procedures and techniques (cf. points 1 and 4). How does technology predetermine the environment?
8. group dynamics: might psychological behaviour of groups be relevant? e.g. might piecework strategies be undermined by a group holding down the norm of behaviour to protect a member?
9. task: does the task itself conduce to an organisational behaviour modification procedure? e.g. can all behaviours be observed and measured?

Apply appropriate strategy

Now it is possible to develop an appropriate strategy based upon positive reinforcement, negative reinforcement, punishment, extinction, or a combination of some or all of these factors. Shaping and modelling may also be crucial parts of the strategy.

In applying positive reinforcement (or, for that matter, extinction), it is useful to know what specifically reinforces the behaviour of an individual. A reinforcer survey questionnaire is shown in Figure 3.6, and such a form may be useful in getting hard data.

1. In my free time my favourite activity is _____

_____

2. My favourite evening entertainment is _____

_____

3. I would really like to visit _____

_____

4. My favourite hobby is _____

_____

5. Something that I really want to buy is _____

_____

6. If I had $10 to spend on myself right now I would _____

_____

7. If I had $100 to spend on myself right now I would _____

_____

8. My job would be more rewarding if _____

_____

9. If my manager would _____
   I would enjoy working here.

10. I would work harder if _____

_____

11. The place I most like to shop is _____

_____

Fig. 3.6 *A sample reinforcer survey questionnaire* (ADAPTED FROM MILLER 1978, P.149)

Determine whether problem is solved

Following standard flowchart structure (Fig. 3.4), we see that if the problem is not solved, we should go back to the beginning of the process. If the problem is solved, we should proceed to the next phase.

Maintain desirable behaviour

Desirable behaviour is maintained by determining which would be the most appropriate schedule of reinforcement—continuous, intermittent, or self-reinforcement (see below).

Evaluation for performance improvement

Because behaviour modification interventions depend upon pinpointed behaviour and hard data recorded and charted, evaluation is not too difficult. Has behaviour changed? Has performance changed? Can the intervention process be changed still further, modifying reinforcers or schedules of reinforcement?

Behaviour modification: Spreading the word

Behaviour modification in organisations, organisational behaviour modification, or OB mod., has been in use in the private and public sectors particularly since the early 1970s. Most of the intervention programs have been American. Perhaps the most famous intervention was at Emery Air Freight. Measurement of baseline data on small packages being packed efficiently and shipped in large containers showed that this was happening only about 45 per cent of the time, as opposed to the 90 per cent which management believed to be the case. Upon a program of providing feedback on performance and giving verbal and non-verbal recognition (compliments, touching) to workers, performance seemed to improve dramatically, improving to 95 per cent in one day in some areas (Davis 1981).

Other interventions, noted by Brown (1982), include:

* Improving performance in a fast-food restaurant. Observation showed that two behaviours, smiling at and talking with customers, needed improvement. Workers were trained to smile at least four times when with customers, and smiling rates increased from 41.2 per cent to 67.3 per cent. Workers earned a five-minute break each hour for talking with at least five customers.
* Reducing elevator use. The intervention was to discourage elevator use, in order to save energy, and encourage people to use stairs. Using feedback (displaying charts showing current and previous week energy use) did not change behaviour, but slowing down the elevator door-closing mechanism (from 10 seconds to 26 seconds) did.
* Improving safety in a bakery. Training was given, and visual feedback was given by charting safety performance and displaying this. Supervisors also gave verbal feedback, recognising workers when they observed safety procedures. One department went from performing 70 per cent of items safely to 95.8 per cent.

Behaviour modification in organisations has been popularised by the *One Minute Manager* books by Blanchard, Johnson and Lorber (Blanchard and Johnson 1983; Blanchard and Lorber 1984). These use cognitive, that is, non-behaviourist, notions like goal-setting, but also use behaviourist tools such as praisings (positive reinforcement) and reprimands (punishment), A-B-C analysis, and so on. Johnson has used the goal-setting/praising/reprimand sequence in books aimed at mothers and fathers bringing up children (Johnson 1983*a*, 1983*b*).

Self-management through behaviour modification

Behaviour modification has been used extensively in therapeutic situations with retarded people, people with psychological phobias, and so on. Bandura and others have begun to emphasise the possibility of individuals using behaviourist principles to modify their own behaviour—to lose weight, to cut down smoking, to improve time management skills, to improve one's speed in handling a particular task (Bandura 1977; Goldfried and Merbaum 1973; Martin and Poland 1980; Luthans 1981). The methods used are similar: quantifying behaviour, establishing a baseline frequency, charting one's progress on a graph or diary. Rewards and punishments are administered by the person, not by someone else. An attempt by a student to improve his study habits, with the cooperation of his roommate, is shown in Figure 3.7.

SELF-CONTRACT

Date: *15 September 1980*
Self: *Jack Wilson*
Other: *Mike Thompson*

Goal: *To improve my study habits*

Agreement

Self: *I agree to go to the designated area in the college library at 6.00 p.m. on five evenings per week and to devote my time there exclusively to studying.*

Others: *Mike Thompson (my roommate) agrees to praise me whenever he observes me doing this and criticise me whenever I do not.*

Consequences

Provided by Self (if contract is kept) *If I stick to the above agreement, I will reward myself with a pizza every Wednesday evening and a movie on the weekend.*
(if contract is broken) *If I do not keep the above agreement during a particular week, I will shine both pairs of my roommate's shoes on Wednesday evening instead of having a pizza, and I will not go to a movie that weekend.*

Provided by Other: (if contract is kept) *Mike will (1) praise me for systematically studying in the library, and (2) shine my shoes each week that I keep the contract.*
(if contract is broken) *For each week that I fail to keep the contract, Mike is authorised to (1) criticise me, (2) insist that I shine his shoes, (3) eat pizza and make derogatory remarks while watching me shine his shoes, and (4) refuse to lend me his car on the weekend.*

Signed *Jack Wilson*

15 October 1980   *Mike Thompson*
Review Date   Witness

Fig. 3.7 *Self-contract for study habit improvement* (HJELLE AND ZIEGLER 1981, P.272)

Do you think you could control one or several of your own behaviours through such a system?

Does it work and is it nasty?

Behaviour modification has its own language which, as you may have experienced, is difficult to master. Indeed, learning about learning theories such as these can be arduous. Critics claim that the language of behaviourism is stilted and bloodless, and this, they claim, is no accident. Behaviourism, to its critics, is an anti-human and dangerously manipulative system, a system in which a rat pushing a lever to get food and a poet reciting poetry to an audience that has ceased clapping are both described in the phrase "the organism was reinforced to emit a response, a response shaped by previous contingent reinforcements". In other words, behaviourism seems to take away the dignity of being human, and imposes a mechanistic view of human functioning upon us. The cognitive psychologist, Locke, who has developed an extensive model of goal-setting behaviour (see Chapter 12) expresses this type of criticism:

> Skinner has long argued that resorting to mentalistic concepts tends to pre-maturely cut off the search for the real causes of behaviour. While this may be true if the mentalistic concepts are pseudo-scientific, semi-mystical concepts like Freud's "id", the opposite is the case if the mentalistic concepts are clearly definable and verifiable through introspection. It is empty behaviourist concepts like "reinforcement" which delude investigators into thinking they understand the organism's behaviour, and thus cut off the search for the real causes, i.e. those characteristics of the organism, including its mental contents and processes, which explain why it reacted as it did in response to, or in the absence of, the so-called reinforcements. (LOCKE 1979, P.205)

This leads Locke to make telling points against behaviourist analyses of job interventions which depend upon statements such as "feedback auto-matically reinforced the behaviour which preceded it". As Locke points out, this is absurd if taken literally—if feedback *as such* automatically reinforced previous behaviour, people would never change since the feedback would reinforce whatever they did previously (and the would-be reinforcer might wait from now until doomsday for "the organism" to do something right).

Who will control the controllers?

There are ethical problems with, for example, gathering data on the perform-ance of someone, not to mention planning and executing modifications upon their behaviour. Further, there is the problem of honesty in human communi-cation that behaviourism entails. Spontaneous human behaviour such as smiling, complimenting, and so on, becomes all part of the behaviourist equation. Thus, a character in a case study written by Luthans (1981) says,

> This contingent reinforcement approach really works. Before, the goody-goody people up in personnel were always trying to tell us to understand and be nice to our workers (i.e. the human relations motivation approach). Frankly, I couldn't buy that. In the first place, I don't think that there is anybody who can really *understand* my people, let alone me. More important, though, is that under this approach I am only nice *contingently*—contingent upon good performance. That makes a lot of sense, and my evaluation proves that it works. (P.302)

This is repellent to many people, and smacks of manipulating people by twisting emotions.[5] Skinner argues that there is no way that we can *not* control each other—it is happening all the time—so why not make it effective control.

There is, potentially, a lot of authoritarianism built into behaviour modification. It presumes that the controllers of behaviour, the shapers, the modellers, the reinforcers and punishers, have the same degree of control as the experimenting human in a psychology laboratory dealing with organisms such as rats and pigeons. This, to say the least, is problematic. As Andre and Ward point out in *The 59-Second Employee*, their response to the popular *One Minute Manager* books, employees can counter-control, can manage up, because employees control rewards and praisings that managers crave (being on time, doing the job without much supervision, giving the manager high scores on the annual personnel survey) and also control punishments the manager fears (interrupting, playing stupid and forcing the boss to do the work, griping to their boss's boss, etc.) (Andre and Ward 1984).[6]

Nevertheless, the power of management to buy material reinforcers (such as colour TVs for the attendance lottery, bonus payments, piece rates, etc.) is great, and some managers may come to believe that they can buy people's behaviour (although the hidden message of some early behaviour modification programs seemed to be that people's behaviour could be bought with a pat on the back and a smile). The ultimate power of management, of course, is to punish with dismissal.

Problems of practicality

Behaviour modification techniques, particularly as they pertain to punishment, make much of distinguishing a person's *behaviour* from the person herself. To some, this is bad logic, if not schizophrenic perception: a person *is* one's behaviour, rather than being separate from it.[7]

Behaviour modification's insistence upon looking only at behaviour which can be quantified is, on the one hand, refreshing—it asks us to be precise about human behaviour—but it is also limiting. As De Bono says about traditional and scientific logical problem-solving,

---

[5] Cf. Villere's remarks on conditional and unconditional strokes (see Chapter 5).

We want to make it clear that *unconditional positive* strokes are useful in organisations only when used in conjunction with *conditional positive* strokes. *Only* giving good strokes to people, whether they are productive or not (unconditional positive strokes), will soon lead to the downfall of the business or organization. On the other hand, *only* giving positive strokes when an employee is productive (conditional positive strokes) or when you want to get something out of them can lead workers to feel that they are being exploited or manipulated. The impression will be accurate. (VILLERE 1981)

Cf. also the example of behaviour modification given earlier of fast food employees being "shaped" to smile and talk more. Note the discussion on smiling as "emotional labour" in service industries in Chapter 4.

[6] Authoritarianism can be obvious or subtle. Is it coincidental that Johnson reinforces sex-role stereotypes by looking at (1) one-minute reprimands, (2) one-minute praisings (3) one-minute goal-settings in *The One-Minute Father*, but in *The One-Minute Mother* uses the sequence: (1) one-minute goal-settings, (2) one-minute praisings and (3) one-minute reprimands? (Johnson 1983*a*, 1983*b*).

[7] The problematic distinction between a person and that person's behaviour is parodied by Andre and Ward: Dave's one-minute manager has just given him a one-minute praising:

When he (Mr Ketchum, Dave's boss) paused, Dave said, "Why thank you Mr Ketchum. It's very kind of you to say so."

"Not at all, Dave, you deserve it. Or rather, your behaviour deserves it. Or rather . . . well, you know what I mean." And he touched him lightly on the shoulder and walked off, looking perplexed, as he sometimes did.

Thinking back on it, Dave confessed to mixed feelings: "I felt, well, OK about it. But not great. Not super-motivated. More than a little embarrassed, actually. Mr Ketchum followed the rules, all right. Hey they say they've tried this out on pigeons and rats and little kids and it worked on them. Maybe there's something wrong with me." (ANDRE AND WARD 1984, PP14–15).

(there is a) danger . . . that you tackle only that part of the situation that can be tackled with precision and ignore the rest as if it did not happen. (DE BONO 1974)[8]

Western Airlines in the United States finally gave up on a behaviour modification plan it was trying to implement because it was too hard to identify quantifiable behaviours. One manager said, "how do you quantify what a flight attendant does?" (Davis 1981). Behaviourists will often retort, usually in unison with proponents of such approaches as "management by objectives", that "you haven't tried hard enough; it's a sign of sloppy management that job profiles can't be written, objectives stated, and behaviour patterns analysed and quantified". There is some truth in this counter-claim. It is reassuring to many of us to say that systems don't work, chaos does. We are happy with chaos, with muddling through, and systems such as behaviour modification threaten us with the demand to get organised.

Flowing from this, Lee (1980) asserts that much of the improvements alleged to have occurred in workplaces because of behaviour modification interventions are not so much due to the rigamarole of reinforcements and scheduling, but merely to the performing of a performance audit, which is what managers should have been doing in the first place. That is, once employees knew what they were meant to be doing, and once managers knew how badly they themselves were performing, miracles happened. This type of methodological contamination of research results also helps to explain results from a number of more cognitively based motivation and job re-design experiments (see Chapters 2 and 12).

Past and its future

There are similarities between OB mod. and Taylorism or scientific management, which is discussed in Chapter 2. Both systems see man as being rationally motivated in the sense that money motivates; it is possible to break work up into pieces and paying for those pieces is an excellent way of getting work done. In the late 1960s and early 1970s, there was a tendency to sell OB mod. as a system where you could reinforce by just smiling (contingently, of course). Since then, there has been a swing back to seeing money as the great reinforcer/motivator, and this has had substantial implications for the motivation debate (Feeney 1981; Piamonte 1979). Carpenter (1974) has even gone so far as to say that, in a totally Skinnerian world, jobs which reinforce through their own intrinsic satisfaction (e.g. executive decision-makers) should receive low reinforcement in wages (i.e. low wages) and jobs which have little intrinsic satisfaction and/or were onerous (e.g. rubbish collecting) should receive high reinforcement in wages (i.e. high wages).

---

8 Behaviourist ideas have also been applied in clinical settings, where, for example, psychological phobias are treated, and in educational settings, where principles of reinforcement-based learning have been applied to programmed learning approaches such as teaching machines, computer-based self-paced learning programs, and programmed learning textbooks. Weekes (1978) notes that behaviour modification techniques are sometimes quite successful with specific phobias (fear of heights, spiders, etc.), but with less specific phobias, such as agoraphobia (fear of open places, literally, but usually also fear of confining situations, such as queues, meetings, lifts, and so on), less success is observed. Similarly, programmed learning has had a fair amount of success in areas where mastery of facts and techniques is paramount (e.g. using a machine, maths and sciences), but has had less success where values and discussion of those values are more important (e.g. the humanities and arts). Thus, in clinical and educational situations, as well as organisational and personal situations, behaviourism is not terribly good when confronted with phenomena that are difficult to quantify and isolate as a single variable, phenomena that manifest differences of kind rather than of degree—in defiance of E.L. Thorndike's classic behaviourist dictum: "Everything that exists, exists in some degree, and can therefore be measured."

The issues of potential manipulation, the difficulty of quantifying behaviour, and various methodological issues continue to dog behaviour modification. Yet some who remain opposed to it on philosophical and/or technical grounds concede that the approach has some beneficial aspects; for example, pinpointing rather than labelling behaviour as an aid to communication, or the antecedents–behaviour–consequence (A-B-C) model as a tool for analysing what happens in appraisal systems.

As was pointed out at the beginning of this chapter, the contents of Chapters 2 and 3 have been kept separate because of disagreements among social scientists about the true nature of consciousness and behaviour: Is behaviour that which can only be observed externally, or does behaviour emanate from our mind, our consciousness, and hence is partly invisible? It's up to you to decide how valid the distinction is, or if the debate is a worthwhile one. Whether motivation and learning are totally separate things, or whether they are merely two sides of the one coin, they are both powerful tools for understanding human behaviour.

Summary

Behaviourists argue that behaviour cannot be explained by things which may or may not occur in the mind: personality, needs, drives, motives, expectancies and perceptions of control. We can only describe and predict behaviour which can be seen and measured, and this behaviour is learned, rather than inherited; thus, to understand human behaviour, say behaviourists, we must study how we learn.

A distinction is drawn between classic conditioning and operant conditioning. Classic conditioning, as demonstrated in Pavlov's experiments in conditioning reflexes in dogs, is concerned with the way in which stimuli affect responses. Operant conditioning, by contrast, is concerned with the way people operate upon their environment, or the way in which responses affect stimuli and the way in which behaviour is a function of its consequences.

Behaviour can be understood as being preceded by antecedents and followed by consequences (the A-B-C model). Behaviour can be controlled by positive reinforcement, negative reinforcement, punishment, extinction, shaping and modelling. Reinforcement can be scheduled on continuous or intermittent bases.

Applying behaviour modification to organisations entails pinpointing rather than labelling behaviour, measuring and charting behaviour, applying the A-B-C model, controlling for environmental variables, applying strategies such as reinforcement, maintaining desirable behaviour through appropriate scheduling, and evaluating performance. Behaviour modification has become a popular technique for changing behaviour at the interpersonal and organisational level. While many assert its efficiency, many others criticise it for methodological lapses, impracticality and its being potentially coercive and unethical.

Questions for discussion

1. Explain the differences and similarities in the behaviourist and cognitive approaches to human behaviour.
2. What is the difference between classic conditioning and operant conditioning?

3. Apply the A-B-C model to two personal and two professional situations you are familiar with.
4. Write a role-play in which people use at least three behaviour control strategies (positive reinforcement, negative reinforcement, extinction, punishment, shaping, modelling).
5. Analyse two work situations in terms of continuous and intermittent schedules of reinforcement. What would happen under different schedules?
6. Use pinpointing and behaviour measurement and charting in analysing a personal or professional situation.
7. What criticisms have been made of behaviour modification? Are they justified.

References

Andre, Rae and Ward, Peter D. (1984). *The 59-Second Employee: How to Stay One Second Ahead of Your One-Minute Manager.* (Panther: London).

Athanasou, J.A. and Murphy, G.C. (1981). "Absenteeism and Behaviour Modification: A Review", *Human Resource Management in Australia*, Autumn.

Bandura, Albert (1976). "Social Learning Theory", in J.T. Spence, R.C. Carson and J.W. Thibaut, *Behavioural Approaches to Therapy.* (General Learning Press: Morristown, NJ).

——— (1977). *Social-Learning Theory.* (Prentice-Hall: New Jersey).

Berthold, Howard C. (1982). "Transitional Contingency Contracting and the Premack Principle in Business", in O'Brien *et al.* (1982).

Blanchard, Kenneth and Johnson, Spencer (1983). *The One Minute Manager.* (William Morrow and Company, Inc: New York).

Blanchard, Kenneth and Lorber, Robert (1984). *Putting the One Minute Manager to Work.* (Fontana: London).

Brown, Paul L. (1982). *Managing Behaviour on the Job.* (Wiley: New York).

Carpenter, Finlay (1974). *A Skinner Primer.* (Free Press: Massachusetts).

Connellan, Thomas K. (1978). *How to Improve Human Performance: Behaviourism in Business and Industry.* (Harper and Row: New York).

Davis, Keith (1981). *Human Behaviour at Work: Organizational Behaviour.* (McGraw-Hill: New York).

De Bono, Edward (1974). *PO: Beyond Yes and No.* (Penguin: Harmondsworth).

Feeney, Edward J. (1981). "Getting More Out of Your Employees", *INC. Magazine*, November.

Goldfried, M. and Merbaum, M. (1973). *Behaviour Change Though Self-Control.* (Holt, Rinehart and Winston: New York).

Hellriegel, Don, Slocum, John W., Jr. and Woodman, Richard W. (1983). *Organizational Behaviour*, 3rd edn. (West Publishing: St Paul).

Hjelle, Larry A. and Ziegler, Daniel J. (1981). *Personality Theories: Basic Assumptions, Research and Applications.* (McGraw-Hill: New York).

Johnson, Spencer (1983a). *The One Minute Mother.* (William Morrow and Company: New York).

——— (1983b). *The One Minute Father.* (William Morrow and Company: New York).

Komacki, J., Blood, M.R. and Holder, D. (1980). "Fostering Friendliness in a Fast Food Franchise", *Journal of Organizational Behaviour Management*, vol. 2, pp.151–64.

Lee, James A. (1980). *The Gold and the Garbage in Management Theories and Prescriptions.* (Ohio University Press: Athens, Ohio).

Le Francois, Guy R. (1975). Psychology for Teaching: *A Bear Always/Usually Faces the Front*, 2nd edn. (Wadsworth: Belmont, Calif.).

Locke, Edwin A. (1979). "The Myths of Behaviour Mod. in Organizations", in Steers, Richard M. and Porter, Lyman W. *Motivation and Work Behaviour*, 2nd edn. (McGraw-Hill: Tokyo).

Luthans, Fred. (1981). *Organizational Behaviour*, 3rd edn. (McGraw-Hill: New York).

Luthans, Fred and Kreitner, Robert (1974). "The Management of Behavioural Contingencies", *Personnel*, July/August, p.13.

(1975). *Organizational Behaviour Modification*. (Scott Foresman: Illinois).

Martin, R. and Poland, E. (1980). *Learning to Change: A Self-Management Approach to Adjustment*. (McGraw-Hill: New York).

Miller, Lawrence M. (1978). *Behaviour Management: The New Science of Managing People at Work*. (Wiley: New York).

O'Brien, Richard and Dickinson, Alyce M. (1982). "Introduction to Industrial Behaviour Modification", in O'Brien, Richard *et al.* (eds). *Industrial Behaviour Modification: A Management Handbook*. (Pergamon: New York).

Piamonte, John S. (1979). "In Praise of Monetary Motivation", *Personnel Journal*, September.

Schermerhorn, John R., Hunt, James, G. and Osborn, Richard N. (1982). *Managing Organizational Behaviour*. (Wiley: New York).

Skinner, B.F. (1953). *Science and Human Behaviour*. (Macmillan: New York).

(1969). *Contingencies of Reinforcement: A Theoretical Analysis*. (Appleton-Century-Crofts: New York).

(1975). Interview with Elizabeth Hall, *Psychology Today* (UK edition), vol. 1, no. 6, September.

Van Houten, R., Nau, P.A. and Merrigan, M. (1981). "Reducing Elevator Energy Use: A Comparison of Posted Feedback and Reduced Elevator Convenience", *Journal of Applied Behaviour Analysis*, vol. 14, pp.377–87.

Villere, Maurice F. (1981). *Transactional Analysis at Work*. (Prentice-Hall: New Jersey).

Weekes, Claire (1978). *Simple Effective Treatment of Agoraphobia*. (Angus and Robertson: Sydney).

Films/Videos

Behaviour Modelling (Training Media Services).
One Minute Manager (Training Media Services).
Discipline without Punishment (Video Channel).
Business, Behaviourism and the Bottom Line (Video Channel).
The Power of Positive Reinforcement (Video Channel).
You Can Lead a Horse to Water (Training Media Services).
Who Did What to Whom? (Power Human Resources).

Part C

Communication processes

If life were a play, we might think that the total reality of that play were to be found in the script, in the literal words on the page. We might also believe that all characters in the play saw with total clarity the motivations of themselves and others, and that communication was always easy and clear, and hardly ever broke down, and when it did, such breakdowns were mysterious and inexplicable.

We might think all these things— and we would be wrong.

The chapters in this section deal with communication processes that are often more non-verbal than verbal and often more unconsciously motivated than consciously so.

In Chapter 4 (Non-verbal communication) we find that we communicate in many ways apart from words—by the physical structure of the body, by facial expressions, gesture, posture, touching, and so on. In Chapter 5 (Transactional analysis, or the games people play) and Chapter 6 (Assertiveness) we find that most human communication can be understood in terms of personality patterns that are identifiable and thus to a certain extent predictable and controllable. Transactional analysis lets us see individuals as having multiple or partial or fractional personalities, and when we communicate with others we interact with other multi-faceted individuals via many channels, not few or one. Unless we understand such interactions, the experience of communicating is often hurtful and confusing, locking people into playing destructive mind-games and into mutilating roles, rendering them incapable of expressing liking and honesty.

Assertiveness is more specifically concerned with the dominance and submission aspects of communication. Within such aspects, we see that much human behaviour can be analysed into four styles (assertive, aggressive, passive, manipulative) which can inhibit or facilitate understanding between people.

4

Non-verbal communication

Watch out for that man when he laughs and his stomach doesn't move.
Chinese proverb

Manners are especially the need of the plain. The pretty can get away with anything.
Evelyn Waugh

President Lincoln turned down an applicant for a job and gave as his reason: "I don't like his face." One of his members of cabinet indicated that he did not think this was a sufficient and satisfactory explanation. Lincoln disagreed: "Every man over forty is responsible for his face."
Clifton Fadiman and Carl Van Doren

What you are thunders so loud I can't hear what you say.
Ralph Waldo Emerson

Experience tells you that the man who looks you straight in the eye, particularly if he adds a firm handshake, is hiding something.
Clifton Fadiman

NOWADAYS, most of us are familiar with the idea of "body language". Our gestures, postures, eye contact, and so on, are meant to reveal our "real" inner nature. If such body language actually exists, then not only can we learn more about ourselves, we can learn more about others. Obviously, this means that others can also learn more about us—perhaps more than we want them to know. Consequently, body language appears to be a black art which allows knowledgeable people to manipulate and control others not so knowledgeable—a form of thought control, if you like. Certainly much of the body language literature which has flooded onto the scene in the last decade or so has made such claims of control. But is it really true? Judge for yourself after reading this chapter. If you conclude that body language is not all that it's cracked up to be, then you can set your mind at ease—and straighten out the ideas of friends and associates who claim to be able to read your body language. If you conclude that body language is a real and powerful phenomenon, then you will have gained new knowledge which you can use in a number of ways—not least among which is self-defence.[1]

The terms "body language" and "non-verbal communication" are often used interchangeably, but they are not the same thing. Body language is the narrower of the two concepts, and

---

[1] Note also the validity or otherwise of non-verbal communication concepts in Chapters 3, 5 and 6.

embraces phenomena such as gesture, posture, eye contact, facial expression, and so on; non-verbal communication is the wider of the two concepts, including all body language but also including body structure, clothing and adornment, speech inflection and volume, grooming, various other extensions of ourselves such as cars, rooms, furniture, and also our sense of time and the way this sense shapes our behaviour. A model of these different aspects of non-verbal communication (NVC) appears in Figure 4.1. Body language embraces zones 3 (gesture), 4 (posture), 5 (orientation), 6 (touching) and parts of 9 (personal space/territory) and 2 (head, voice, eyes, facial expression, smell). Note here that taste and hearing have been excluded from zone 2 (head, etc.). Malandro and Barker (1983) do include taste as a form of NVC, but it is not included here because it is presumed that—to the best of our knowledge so far—we do not communicate with taste, we merely passively experience (as with hearing). Note also that the sense of touching is treated separately from other senses, and treated separately from gestures.

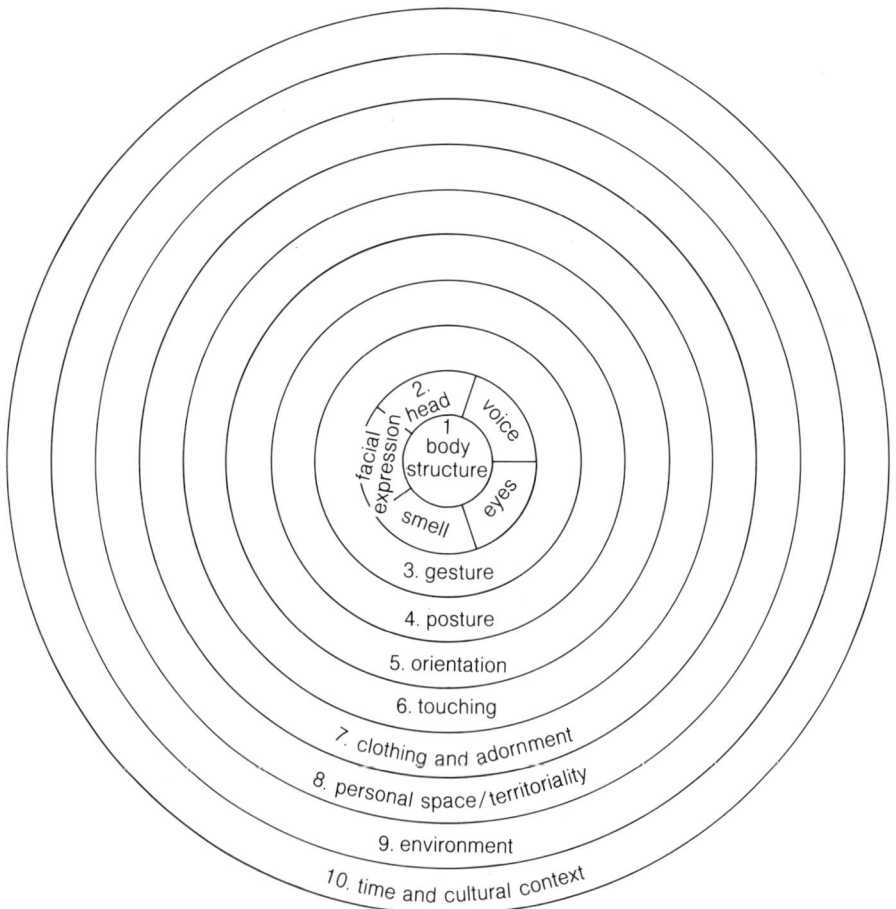

Fig. 4.1 *A model of non-verbal communication, from the structure of our innermost self to our relationships with others and the outside world*

Gestures here are understood as emphatic and/or descriptive movements of limbs that do not involve touching of others (although they may involve self-touching). Orientation—the angle at which we face people—is treated separately from both posture and personal space. Non-verbal communication usually occurs across several or all zones simultaneously—it is not confined to tidy little categories.

Body structure

A number of scientists, generalising from animal behaviour to human behaviour, have suggested that much human anatomy has evolved in particular ways to communicate various behaviours, in particular aggression or dominance and sexuality. Guthrie (1976) suggests that many of the bodily characteristics we associate with extremely dominant males—broad shoulders, wide, protuberant chin, heavy eyebrows and pronounced cheek-bones—have evolved as threat devices. The combination of these character-istics, particularly when seen on tall, heavily muscled males, presents a very threatening sight even in these relatively civilised times. Guthrie argues that these features were *adaptive*, that is, they enhanced the prospects of survival for those proto-humans who possessed them, and thus were genetically transmitted and socially venerated. It may be, for example, that beards evolved, not so much to keep the male face warm, as to extend the dominant effect of the chin. Eibl-Eibesfeldt (1972) suggests that the "tingling up and down the spine" we feel in threat situations may be a remnant from when proto-humans were able, like dogs and other animals today, to raise hackles of fur on the shoulders in order to create a larger, more threatening prospect to enemies. Nowadays, males try to recreate this dominance effect with epaulettes on uniforms, shoulder-padding, and so on. We speak of people having a "weak chin", or a non-dominant chin, meaning we impute weakness of character to that person. Super-heroes in comics and cartoons of course have super-dominant jaws. Even though teeth were not and are not a major aggressive tool for our species, we still give a ferocious lip/tooth display when threatened.

Guthrie and Morris (1977, 1985) suggest that similar evolutionary mechanisms shape our sexual anatomy, particularly female sexual anatomy. When pre-humans walked on all fours, males sexually penetrated females from behind. When *Homo erectus* began to walk erect, the visual sexual stimulus of the female buttocks framing the genitalia was no longer readily available to males, and thus—the theory runs—females' breasts began to mimic or genitally echo the buttocks by becoming much larger than was necessary for the primary function of breasts, lactation and suckling of young. Breasts thus took on erotic or sexually cueing functions as well as nurturing functions. Breasts on other primates are much smaller, and lips on other primates function quite well without being everted or slightly turned inside-out as ours are. Pursuing the genital echo theory still further, Guthrie and Morris argue that the reddish lips of the female (made even redder with cultural amplifiers such as lipstick) imitate the labia or outer sexual organs of the female (*labia* in fact is the Latin word for lips). Lips also become redder and more swollen during sexual arousal.[2]

---

[2] "The fact that males also possess visible lips need not be an objection. Males also possess nipples, but this does not mean that nipples are not primarily female." (MORRIS 1977, P.239).

BOX 4.A: Non-verbal communication in communicators lacking words

How is it possible to communicate without words, or verbal communication? To some, the concept itself is almost as absurd as "non-air breathing" or "non-water swimming". But while man is the only species with a verbal language (or the only species that we know of at present), obviously other species communicate all the time without the benefit of words. Consider the NVC of the average household dog, for example. Messent (1979) has noted that dogs have quite a rich language of communication (see illustration). The posture of the back, the display of ears and teeth in particular, are crucial indicators for other dogs and other species in attempting to understand the animal's behaviour.

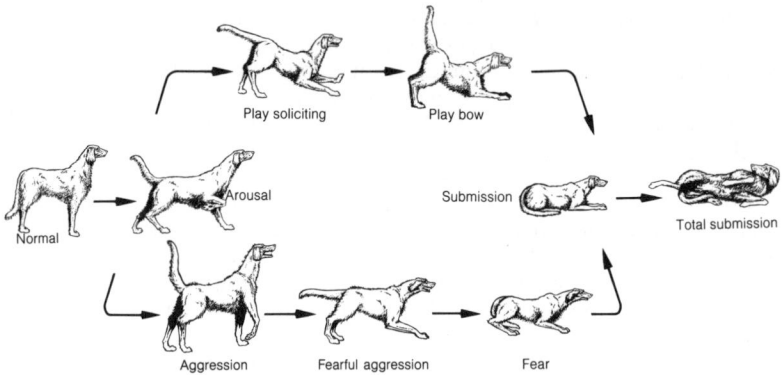

The dog's expressive body language (MESSENT 1979, P.36)

Behaviour here is defined by two poles—aggression and submission—and this polarity is critical to the understanding of much animal and human non-verbal communication.

Irrespective of the validity of these ideas, the notion that anatomical features are more than just accidents, are in fact mirrors of behavioural patterns, is a long-lived one. Up until last century, students of physiognomy claimed that body features revealed character, and much of early criminology was taken up with trying to identify "criminal features". Phrenology, or reading character through bumps on the head, palmistry, or reading fates in the patterns on hands, and other activities are by no means totally dead even in today's culture.

Vaughan (1982) claims that it is possible to detect personality characteristics such as possessiveness, tolerance/intolerance, patience, ability or inability to handle money, introversion/extroversion, and even psychotic tendencies, simply by examining features such as eyes, eyelids, brows, lips, foreheads, hairlines, and so on. Sheldon (1954) argued that body shape and temperament were integrally linked. He divided body types into three main somatotypes (*soma* = Greek "body"): endomorphs, mesomorphs and ectomorphs. Endomorphs are oval or pear-shaped people, mesomorphs are muscular, compact people, and ectomorphs are thin, fragile people. Endomorphs, so the theory runs, are generally happy and cheerful, sociable, emotional and relaxed. Mesomorphs are dominant, enterprising, don't like to lose, and have low guilt levels. Ectomorphs are shy, tense, awkward, indoor types (Sheldon 1954; Malandro and Barker 1983; Vaughan 1982). Both physically and behaviourally, people can be either one of these extreme types or a combination of several types.

We are all aware of physical differences between people, but you will have to evaluate for yourself the idea that physique and behaviour are so closely linked.

Head, facial expression, eyes, voice, smell

Moving out from zone 1 in Figure 4.1, body structure, we come to a system of more variable non-verbal behaviour, located on and around the head and face area.

Head movements

Charles Darwin, in his pioneering work on non-verbal communication (Darwin 1872), suggested interesting explanations for the two most basic head nods, those for yes and no. The "no" gesture (horizontally) he suggests derives from the suckling infant, having had her fill, moving her head away from the nipple in the easiest direction, that is, side to side. The "yes" signal may be a relic gesture of the bow of submission and deference.

The "yes" nod is an important form of feedback in conversation. Watch a group of people talking: if they are in fundamental agreement, you will notice a lot of head-nodding taking place. These head nods are not pronounced and are quite subtle; most of us in fact are not even aware of them. Try an experiment with a friend in this regard: as she is talking, keep your head quite still. The chances are your friend will become uneasy for reasons she is not sure of, because subtle head-nods are approvals and permissions to continue, just as "uh-huh", "hmm-hmm" and other "friendly grunts" are vocal reinforcers of what we are saying. Feedback in our transactions with others is a very subtle thing—we may not know it exists until it is not there. Try another experiment with a friend: when having a telephone conversation, resist the urge to give "friendly grunts" as well as other verbal reinforcers. If you were standing face to face, such lack of auditory feedback may not be a problem if there were visual feedback, but on the telephone this deathly silence may provoke an uneasy "are you still there?" from your friend.

Facial expression

Dominance and submission are also tied up with facial expressions. Darwin noted in 1872 that, among apes, the loser in a competition opens his mouth, lifting his lips upwards. Humans would call this a smile. Henley (1977) argues that in our culture, dominant people rarely smile, but are smiled at; rarely look at subordinates, but are looked at often by subordinates; and touch subordinates more often than subordinates touch them. She notes that this dominance–submission behaviour is a powerful non-verbal aspect of sexism.

Women are expected to smile more than men; in a conversation between a man and a woman, a woman will probably smile more and nod more, giving the feedback of being "a good listener", no doubt. Plasticity and openness of expression are associated with immature, subordinate people, whereas control of expression which masks emotions is usually associated with dominance.[3]

One of the most common and clichéd aspects of this dominance–submission behaviour is that employees laugh at the boss's jokes more than vice versa; the dominant initiates the joke-telling, the subordinates propitiate or appease the dominant with massive feedback. To the extent that smiles usually accompany the word "yes", that makes them yes-men. Control is thus linked to self-control. Whether this degree of self-control is psychologically healthy or not remains to be seen.

Hochschild (1983), in her study of airline stewardesses/hostesses and other service industy workers in the United States, argues that smiling has become "emotional labour", and that labour is exploited by managements who insist that workers must always smile and never get angry, even with abusive and violent clients. This tendency will get worse, she suggests, as we move from an industrial to a service economy, and people behind counters in fast-food shops, banks, department stores, as well as in aeroplanes, will be required to "engineer their emotions".

Eye behaviour

Eye contact conveys different meanings in different cultures. In white, Anglo-Saxon culture, a steady direct gaze is usually read as meaning honesty—a "shifty-eyed" person who refuses to "look you in the eye" is simply not to be trusted. Yet this is not the case for all cultures. In many instances of human (and animal) interaction, the direct gaze of a dominant individual is usually not matched by subordinates; instead, subordinates avert their gaze, or at least blink first and/or more often. Thus, as Henley (1977) and Fast (1971) note, in some cultures, such as the Japanese, Puerto Rican, Mexican-American, Black American and West African, aversion of gaze is not indicative of "shifty" character but in fact of respect.

Breaking and re-establishing eye-contact is a subtle tool in the non-verbal communication of white Anglo-Saxons, particularly when verbal communication is taking place. Thus Argyle (1983) notes that in conversations, particularly in groups, the person speaking may break eye contact with one or several people when speaking, re-establishing gaze only when ready to "yield" to the other person.

Eyes: The portals of the soul
The physical structure of the eye also communicates, although most of us are unaware of this. Hess (1975) has shown that the dilation (growing larger) and constriction (growing smaller) of the pupil can give indications of our own

---

[3] Henley further notes:

Writers on organisational behaviour make a distinction in their works between "the managerial elite's logic of efficiency" and "the workers' logic of sentiment". Needless to say, this ideology has worked to support the exclusion of women from management, and no doubt many unassimilated men of ethnic background, as "temperamentally unfit". The wooden countenance, though it shares nothing with friends, also gives away no secrets to enemies. This control of facial expression is one form of overall information control, which in turn is an important factor in authority: "Knowledge is power." Compare the controlled aura of the professional or VIP (doctor, corporation head, judge) with the more variable demeanour of ordinary people, particularly children, working class people, women, and persons of "ethnic" background. . . (HENLEY 1977, PP172-3).

true feelings about things. Thus, as a general rule, the more positive we feel about something or someone, the larger our pupils become; the more negative we feel about something or someone, the smaller our pupils become. In one of his experiments, Hess showed two photographs of females to male subjects, asking them to choose the more attractive one. The photographs were in fact exactly the same, except that one copy had been altered: the female's pupils had been enlarged with ink. Most people chose the lady with the "bedroom eyes" rather than the "beady little eyes". Morris (1977) tells of how Chinese gem traders in days of yore used to watch the pupil dilation of prospective customers when displaying gems—if they were really interested (and hence willing to pay a high price) their pupils would dilate. Modern advertisers and market researchers have tried to exploit the same unconscious mechanism when pre-testing a product or commercial before a preview audience. The pupil also dilates when we are in darker surroundings. Thus expansion means, at the most basic level, that we are taking in more visual information.

This openness or receptivity to the environment is well expressed in the eyes, "the portals of the soul". The large eyes and pupils of infants trigger off nurturing responses in adults. Women's eye makeup often helps to amplify the sexual signals of submissiveness and receptivity (particularly if the eyes are blue and the hair is blond, as with newborn children). We raise our eyebrows at things or people that prove interesting or shocking. This particular behaviour is notable when we greet someone and give them the automatic "eyebrow flash" or raised eyebrows of salutation (Scheflen 1976).

Voice

Non-verbal communication is also present when we are communciating verbally, adding to the meaning conveyed as surely as the melody adds meaning to the lyric of a song. Argyle (1975) calls this aspect of NVC non-linguistic aspects of speech, and includes under this heading loudness, emphasis, pitch, timing, speed, voice quality (e.g. breathing, resonance), as well as class, race and cultural indicators. Consider the variations in one passage from Shakespeare read by ten different actors, for instance, or even the one passage played by one actor on ten different occasions. Guthrie observes that we tend to use a lower pitch in our voice when talking to strangers (as a sign of dominance or threatening when confronted with the unknown), while we use a higher pitch with friends (Guthrie 1976). Consider the pitch of our "telephone voice" when answering the phone, and the way it changes when we recognise a friend on the other end. These speech patternings are not constant among all cultures, as we might expect after seeing cultural variations in other aspects of NVC. Hall notes that in the Arab world, loud voices mean strength rather than aggressiveness, while soft voices mean weakness, at least among equals.

> Personal status modulates voice tone, however, even in the Arab society. The Saudi Arabian shows respect to his superior—to a Sheik, say—by lowering his voice and mumbling. The affluent American may also be addressed in this fashion, making almost impossible an already difficult situation. Since in American culture one unconsciously "asks" another to raise his voice by raising his own, the American speaks louder. This lowers the Arab's tone more and increases the mumbles. This triggers a shouting response from the American—which cues the Arab into a frightened "I'm not being respectful enough" tone well below audibility. (EDWARD HALL AND WILLIAM WHYTE, IN BURGOON AND SAINE 1978, P.158)

Closely related to pitch is inflection. We usually upwardly inflect at the end of a question, to cue a response. Compare the way you would say "I am going down the street" to "Are you going down the street?" Some of the more civilised countries in the world even use the ¿ symbol before a question in print (still retaining the conventional ? at the end of the question) to alert the reader to the appropriate inflection. But upward inflection can be overdone: if a person continually upwardly inflects at the end of sentences (and indeed within sentences) then we might infer that the person is insecure, not certain of what is being said, and perhaps submissive. Narelle ("You're not wrong, Narelle") in the *Naked Vicar* television series had this infuriating mannerism, together with the equally infuriating "ya know?". Lack of inflection can indicate monotony or self-control. Perhaps the laconic, impassive demeanour of the outback dweller can be heard in regional variations of inflection (or lack of it), such as the uninflected "eh?" at the end of some Queenslanders' sentences.

Smell

It seems absurd to think that we can actively communicate with, as opposed to being passively aware of, smell. Yet, as W.S. Cain notes,

> If man does not communicate via chemical secretion, he is an exception to a very general rule. Other primates employ odourous secretions to mark territory, assert dominance, repel rivals, and attract mates. Perhaps the human primate's ability to verbalise his feelings reduced the need to communicate via olfaction. (QUOTED IN MALANDRO AND BARKER 1983, P.321)

Yet we do seem to have some basic modes of communicating via smell. Helen Keller, that pioneer of the dignity and ability of blind people, claimed she could identify people by smell (Young 1984), and indeed, some blind people claim they can detect by olfaction or smell whether a person is blonde, redhead or brunette (Malandro and Barker). Folk wisdom is rich in tales of dogs, horses and other animals being able to recognise humans by smell, and also of being able to recognise (and act upon) the "smells" of fear and confidence.

Animals communicate via smell by releasing pheromones, substances that by turn attract sexually, change oestral cycles and mark out territory. It is unclear whether there are human pheromones, although pheromone-type behaviour may be caused by the apocrine sweat glands: these glands, having a different structure to the normal eccrine sweat glands (which cool the body by evaporation), are located on the hairier parts of the body (armpits, chest and genitalia) and operate only after puberty and before menopause. These apocrine glands, which combine with bacteria to produce body odour, may mark out our personal space and/or territory, but the puberty/menopause factor suggests a sexual attractant phenomenon (Young 1984; Guthrie 1976). Sweaty is sexy? Not for many people. But we must remember that the cultural inventions of the past few thousand years include clothes and artificial indoor environments (not to mention perfume and plumbing). Eibl-Eibesfeldt has observed courting rituals among some cultures wherein young males wear handkerchiefs in their armpits before a dance, then take out the handkerchiefs and waft them beneath the noses of female admirers (Eibl-Eibesfeldt 1972).

Smell stimulates the memory dramatically, and it can stimulate sexually through perfumes, but for the most part smell seems to have taken on negative connotations. Darwin (1872) argued that our facial expressions of contempt, disgust, hauteur ("turning one's nose up at . . .") had a physical basis, in that our pre-human ancestors soon learned the hard way that certain substances with certain smells could kill or injure, and that henceforward it was adaptive to wrinkle the nose, turn the head, reject with open palms, and walk away from such substances. We have many smell taboos in our culture today—bad breath, smelly feet, smelly underarms and crotches—and so we deodorise, wash, disinfect and depilate ourselves and our environment, sometimes to the extent of doing damage (e.g. by drying out our skin). There are, of course, enormous cultural variations in this: whereas white Anglo-Saxons (Australians, British, New Zealanders, Americans, etc.) have taboos on smelling breath and thus on short distances between people, some Arab peoples stand quite close to others, preferring to smell the breath of the person they are talking to (Hall 1976*a*).

Gestures

The videophone has not yet been invented, yet how many times have you gestured when talking on the telephone. The person on the other end of the line receives the verbal part of our communication, but cannot see the gestures and postures in our non-verbal channel of communication. Obviously, gesturing fulfils a useful communication need. For deaf and dumb people, people of different cultures meeting for the first time, professional mimes, and party-goers playing charades it is the only means of communication.

Darwin analysed many gestures, arguing that certain "relic gestures" are still in our non-verbal vocabulary, even though we have forgotten their original meaning. He suggested that the salute was a relic gesture dating from the time when warriors wore protective headgear and, after combat, the loser was the first to remove his helmet in a gesture of submission (cf. his analysis of handshakes, p.113).

The most basic cluster of gestures seem to be hand-to-head or hand-to-mouth. Touching and scratching in this area is usually the accompaniment to emotions such as fear, nervousness, confusion, and deliberation.[4] When children are insecure, they suck their thumbs, a surrogate for the real or artificial nipple that provided such solace in infancy. Insecure oral behaviour in adults is quite similar—nail-biting, knuckle-biting, chewing of pens and spectacle arms. Nervous people tend to smoke more, drink more and eat more. Smokers, particularly cigar-smokers and pipe-smokers, seem to get as much tactile pleasure out of smoking as they do from the taste.

Lying and evaluation

This retreat to the mouth is also part of the explanation for the behaviour of people who are uncertain or are deliberately lying. Try this experiment. Deliberately tell several lies to people (preferably lies without hurtful implications or repercussions). You may find that your facial skin becomes itchy when you are telling the lies, and you may scratch your cheek, rub your nose, pull your earlobe, or scratch your eyelid. Although not always the case, these apparently random gestures are seen by most body language specialists as indicating that the truth is not being told (e.g. Pease 1981; Nierenberg and Calero 1971).

---

[4] For more on self-touching, see Morris's discussion of jaw support, chin support, hair clasp, cheek support, mouth touch, temple support, arm-crossing, leg-crossing, masturbation, etc. (MORRIS 19⁻⁻ 102-05).

People also touch the face when evaluating something. The most common form of this gesture is the chin-stroke. Guthrie, ever the socio-biologist, argues that this is a relic gesture of beard-stroking, which in turn is a relic gesture of touching the mother's long hair in times of stress. As females do not have beards, what gestures might indicate that they are appraising something?

The barrier cross

One of the most common gestures we perform many times a day is what Morris (1977) calls the barrier cross or barrier signal. When we are entering a physical area we are not familar with, most people will, in some way, cross their body with an arm: by touching a cufflink, by adjusting a purse, by pushing hair away from the face, by scratching part of the body. A good place to observe barrier behaviour is at some type of a large threshold, like a railway station entrance or the doorway to a frequently used room. Not everyone does it, but a large proportion of people do. You may in fact do it yourself, and possibly dozens of times each day, even within your own home. Morris and Guthrie speculate that the barrier cross is a relic gesture of self-protection when entering a strange environment (like a stone-age cave, perhaps?). The ritual crossing of the body used in some religions may have some distant connection with the barrier cross.

Anticipation, closure, despair, self-control, confidence, pomposity

We gesture with our limbs to indicate other internal emotional states. Thus, we rub our hands with anticipation, but this gesture is closely related to the "dusting-off" gesture of hand-clapping we use as a terminal gesture—"there, that task's done". We wring our hands with despair, perhaps to release some of the nervous energy, perhaps as a prelude to spreading our hands palms upwards to appeal to someone else. When we are in need of self-control, we may grasp another part of the body, the hand or forearm. When we feel grandly confident, we may sit back in our chairs and place our hands behind our heads (possibly accompanying this with the territorial gesture of putting our feet on the table). When we are quietly confident, or possibly pompously superior, we steeple (put our two sets of fingers together at the tips, forming a structure similar to a church steeple). When we are feeling arrogantly confident, or provocative, we may hang our thumbs from our pockets, or loop our thumbs under our belts. Our hands may go to our hips, the ready-for-a-fight gesture.

Leg gestures

We send out messages with our nether limbs, the legs, as well. Ankles crossed or locked may indicate stress, particularly when combined with crossed arms or wrist or arm-gripping. The impatient person may not only drum her fingers, but may also swing a crossed leg. Police interrogators versed in NVC often watch for rapid and/or expansive crossing of legs when critical questions are asked—it may mean that the leg-crosser is unsure or is in fact lying. The tense person may jiggle one or two legs up and down when sitting. The person with a poor self-image usually tilts the angle of her feet inward rather than straight ahead or outward. The arrogant person may strut about, the dejected person may do a stand-up version of the foetal slump (see "Posture", p.109), the active thinker may walk about with hands on hips, the pre-occupied thinker may walk with hands behind back and head bowed.

The arrogant person may turn a chair around and straddle it. Pease (1981) suggests that this is because the backrest of the chair acts as a barrier which protects the straddler, but the chair-straddle also has a sexual component—to a considerable extent it is a crotch or genital display, a notable form of male-to-male aggression in the animal world (Guthrie 1976). To a certain extent, the thumbs under the belt gesture is sexually threatening in a similar way. Would a female straddle a chair? This raises the whole issue of modesty in dress, the concealment or exposure of the genitals for sexual or aggressive reasons, and the cultural differences in male and female clothing—what is revealed and what is concealed. What powerful taboos lie behind females crossing and uncrossing their legs, the curious invention of the sidesaddle, the male executives turning apoplectic at the sight of a woman in trousers (or a male in a muu-muu)? Sexual taboos, of course (see "Clothing and adornment", p.116).

Courtship gestures

When people become sexually interested in one another, they deploy a number of gestures to check that their appearance is most favourable. They groom or preen themselves by smoothing their hair back, or down, or out (with females particularly displaying their palm), checking their clothing (men adjust their ties, women might rearrange a collar or cuff) and so on (Nierenberg and Calero 1971).

Posture

Bodily posture also conveys a rich complexity of meanings. Schoolchildren are admonished to "stand up straight, there", while army recruits may be told the same thing. Why is it so important to stand up straight? There are no compelling medical reasons for standing up straight—indeed, the backbone is naturally curved, and keeping it rigid for a prolonged period can in fact inflict damage. No, standing up straight conveys the non-verbal message that we are "at attention", that we are paying respect, that we are disciplined and self-controlled. An orthopaedic surgeon has suggested that you can tell which classes in a school are interesting—they're the ones where the students are sitting up straight. Alternatively, in boring classes the students are slumped over (Campbell 1977).

We also slouch over when we are depressed. We go into "foetal closure", that is, we move into the curled-up position which was natural at the most secure time in our life—when we were still in the womb. Consequently, when stressed you might hear someone say "I wish I could just roll up into a ball and die".

Height, dominance, compensation and over-compensation

Guthrie suggests that height connotes power—the taller you are, the more authority you seem to have. Arguing from animal behaviour, he notes that in the resolution of conflict, the victor always stands up straight in a dominance display, while the loser lowers his body in submission. This may be the origin of the bow and the curtsey, Morris (1977) suggests. In threat situations, many animals raise their hackles, specific tufts of hair and skin that give the effect of increasing height and enlarging the body outline. As was seen on page 101, humans still appear to have physical and behavioural remnants of this threat and counter-threat mechanism.

We also stick out our chests as a threat display, and females may deliberately protrude their breasts in a display of sexuality to males (and possibly a threat display to other females). This leads us to another aspect of posture, that of compensation or over-compensation. Freud spoke of compensation as an ego defence mechanism, whereby a person perceived a weakness in himself and attempted to obviate this by exaggerating the offending characteristic or its opposite. Thus adolescent girls sometimes have slumped posture because they are embarrassed or confused by their maturing breasts. Similar over-compensation sometimes happens with people who are tall, and who slump over, the stereotyped image of the round-shouldered, gangly adolescent. At the other extreme, many short people over-compensate by stretching themselves up to their full height, and then some. Known in pop psychology as the "Napoleon complex", people with such a complex allegedly are more aggressive and overbearing than most. Over-compensation then is concerned with trying to look "normal", by disguising one's identity by postural distortion.

Postural echo and "catching" NVC

Another subtle aspect of postural NVC is what is known as "postural echo", or mimicking or mirroring. We often imitate the behaviour which is modelled for us by others in childhood, but this process does not stop with childhood. Modelling is a basic mechanism for learning many behaviours (see Chapter 3). Just as a child might learn to imitate the strut or slouch of a parent, we sometimes mirror the postures, gestures, verbal inflections of others. Who are these others? Sometimes they are people we like, and sometimes they are people we dislike, or at least are strongly influenced by. Thus, two close friends may sit opposite each other on a couch, mirroring each other's posture, gestures and expression. The same may happen with a group of subordinates standing with their superior: they may mirror his sergeant-major posture, his shrugging and arm-crossing gestures, his chin-stroking, and so on. This imitative process may be deliberate, that is, conscious, or it may be unconscious. We have all had the experience of "catching" a yawn from someone else; how many other non-verbal behaviours do we "catch" from others, how many do we give to others?

Lowen (1977) has used Freudian or psychoanalytic categories to classify NVC (the oral posture, the phallic–narcissistic posture). Dunkell (1977) has claimed that we also assume significant postures when we are asleep when we are, by definition, not conscious or not totally conscious. We assume several positions in our "body language of the night", says Dunkell, but we usually have a dominant position which non-verbally reveals our true state of mind. Thus people who assume the foetal position are usually insecure, as are those who assume the "mummy" position (wrapping themselves up in the bedclothes). The prone sleepers, Dunkell suggests,

> show a similar compulsion to regulate the events of their waking lives; they do not like the unexpected and organise their lives to avoid it. They are always on time for appointments, and they are neat, exact and fussy about details. (DUNKELL 1977, P.54)

Do you agree with Dunkell's analysis? More interestingly, how would you go about proving or disproving his ideas?

Orientation

Moving on from posture, we next look at orientation (which may or may not be different in kind or degree from posture). Orientation means the angle at which we stand to other people. Mehrabian (1971) and Fast (1977) have argued that if we are interested in communicating with a person we stand with the front plane of our body parallel to the other person. The less interested we are, the more the angle between us opens up. Thus if you are stuck with a person you consider boring at a party, you may find that you maintain a fair amount of eye contact with that person, but your body may be pointing away to a more interesting conversation or person in another part of the room. The evidence here, as in much of the NVC research, is, however, ambiguous. Thus if we see two people standing or sitting side by side, both facing the same direction, making little or no eye contact, does this mean that they dislike each other intensely? Or might it not be that they are such intimates that they can dispense with a lot of normal non-verbal communication, and are in fact "mirroring" each other (see "Posture", p.109).

Despite the ambiguities, orientation is a powerful aspect of NVC, especially when combined with personal space. American and Vietnamese negotiators met in Paris in 1968 to reach a settlement of a war, yet they argued for days over the procedural, symbolic matter of the shape of the negotiating table before they proceeded to the substantive matters of war and peace. Yet they were not being frivolous. "The head of the table" usually means that the person at the narrow end of a rectangular table is the boss. King Arthur had a round table made to defuse the squabbling of his knights over the symbolic position of the seating—if the table were round, then all were equally placed. (As legend has it, the gesture was futile: an informal power/status system sprang up, based upon the nearness to or distance from the King.) Nierenberg and Calero (1971) argue that the positioning around a table of buyer and seller, negotiator and negotiator, lover and lover, is crucial to whatever is taking place verbally. The next time someone tries to convince you of something, ask yourself "What's her angle?"—verbally and non-verbally.

BOX 4.B: Sherlock Holmes reads Dr Watson's body language

Finding that Holmes was too absorbed for conversation I had tossed aside the barren paper and, leaning back in my chair, I fell into a brown study. Suddenly my companion's voice broke in upon my thoughts.

"You are right, Watson," said he. "It does seem a most preposterous way of settling a dispute."

"Most preposterous!" I exclaimed, and then suddenly realising how he had echoed the inmost thought of my soul, I sat up in my chair and stared at him in blank amazement.

"What is this, Holmes?" I cried. "This is beyond anything which I could have imagined."

He laughed heartily at my perplexity.

"You remember," said he, "that some little time ago when I read you the passage in one of Poe's sketches in which a close reasoner follows the unspoken thoughts of his companion, you were inclined to treat the matter as a mere *tour-de-force* of the author. On my remarking that I was constantly in the habit of doing the same thing you expressed incredulity."

"Oh, no!"

"Perhaps not with your tongue, my dear Watson, but certainly with your eyebrows. So when I saw you throw down your paper and enter upon a train of thought, I was very happy to have the opportunity of reading it off, and eventually of breaking into it, as a proof that I had been in rapport with you."

But I was still far from satisfied. "In the example which you read to me," said I, "the reasoner drew his conclusions from the actions of the man whom he observed. If I remember right, he stumbled over a heap of stones, looked up at the stars, and so on. But I have been seated quietly in my chair, and what clues can I have given you?"

"You do yourself an injustice. The features are given to man as the means by which he shall express his emotions, and yours are faithful servants."

"Do you mean to say that you read my train of thoughts from my features?"

"Your features, and especially your eyes. Perhaps you cannot yourself recall how your reverie commenced?"

"No, I cannot."

"Then I will tell you. After throwing down your paper, which was the action which drew my attention to you, you sat for half a minute with a vacant expression. Then your eyes fixed themselves upon your newly framed picture of General Gordon, and I saw by the alteration in your face that a train of thought had been started. But it did not lead very far. Your eyes flashed across to the unframed portrait of Henry Ward Beecher which stands upon the top of your books. You then glanced up at the wall, and of course your meaning was obvious. You were thinking that if the portrait were framed, it would just cover that bare space and correspond with Gordon's picture over there."

"You have followed me wonderfully!" I exclaimed.

"So far I could hardly have gone astray. But now your thoughts went back to Beecher, and you looked hard across as if you were studying the character in his features. Then your eyes ceased to pucker, but you continued to look across, and your face was thoughtful. You were recalling the incidents of Beecher's career. I was well aware that you could not do this without thinking of the mission which he undertook on behalf of the North at the time of the Civil War, for I remember your expressing your passionate indignation at the way in which he was received by the more turbulent of our people. You felt so strongly about it, that I knew you could not think of Beecher without thinking of that also. When a moment later I saw your eyes wander away from the picture, I suspected that your mind had now turned to the Civil War, and when I observed that your lips set, your eyes sparkled, and your hands clenched, I was positive that you were indeed thinking of the gallantry which was shown by both sides in that desperate struggle. But then, again, your face grew sadder; you shook your head. You were dwelling upon the sadness and horror and useless waste of life. Your hand stole towards your old wound and a smile quivered on your lips, which showed me that the ridiculous side of this method of settling international questions had forced itself upon your mind. At this point I agreed with you that it was preposterous, and was glad to find that all my deductions had been correct."

"Absolutely!" said I. "And now that you have explained it, I confess that I am as amazed as before."

"It was very superficial, my dear Watson, I assure you."

Source: Doyle, Sir Arthur Conan, "The Adventures of the Cardboard Box", in *The Memoirs of Sherlock Holmes*, in *The Sherlock Holmes Illustrated Omnibus* (Book Club Associates, London, 1979. By arrangement with John Murray (Publishers) Ltd/Jonathan Cape Limited), pp.17–18. Reproduced by permission.

Touching

Touching of one person by another occurs, says Morris (1977) when the attraction process of the bonding between two people overcomes the natural inclination of each individual to defend his personal space. We can touch and not touch, according to what is a taboo zone on the other person's body and what is not taboo. Taboo zones are usually sexual and/or religious in origin, and Morris suggests that, the more people leave behind tribal/rural living and begin to live in cities, the more taboos there are, because the need for privacy becomes greater in the human zoos that are cities.

Conway suggests that there are strong taboos or at least inhibitions on touching in the Australian family, particularly where males are concerned (Conway 1978). Violence might occur as easily as affectionate touching, and indeed violence might be, in a misbegotten way, an attempt at touching, or relieving touch starvation. Berne (1983) has noted that infants denied normal touching (e.g. in orphanages) often develop serious physical health problems: this may be because humans have biologically programmed *stimulus hunger*, i.e. we need a certain amount of touching to stay physically and psychologically healthy.[5]

The origin of touching behaviour is not always clear. Darwin thought that the handshake was another "relic gesture", going back to the time when, if two strangers wished to parley and guarantee that neither would attempt to harm the other, they would grasp each other's right hand or forearm, thus preventing either from drawing swords or clubs (a custom which undoubtedly contributed to the suspicion of left-handers in most cultures throughout recorded history).

Morris (1977) distinguishes many different types of touching behaviour, among which are:

1. The hand-shake. Correctly or otherwise, people make judgments about the character of people with "cold-fish" or "knuckle-crusher" handshakes. Expression of strong feeling is helped by using the two-handed shake.
2. The body guide. This gesture is where one person guides or points another person in a particular direction, usually by putting a hand on the other's back. Dominant people do this to subordinate people, hosts do it to guests: it is a demonstration of power, control and ownership or territory.
3. The pat. Pats can demonstrate greeting, congratulations, comfort, love and friendship. Patting another adult person can imply a quasi-parental, or dominance, relationship.
4. The arm-link. When used by old or infirm people, this act can show physical dependence. When used by younger or healthier people, it shows emotional linkage, and some dominance may be expressed. Used by non-homosexual males in some cultures when conversing.
5. The shoulder embrace. Basically a masculine act. Because males are usually taller than females, this is a way of showing affection without inhibiting movement. Often used as a male–male tie-sign, or linking gesture.
6. The full embrace. Performed often by young lovers, and less often by other adults, as a sexual expression or as a "break-and-remake" tie-sign (farewells and reunions). Also appears in modified form when people dance, or when sportsmen and women rejoice over scoring a point, or when people greet and farewell each other in less intense situations, such as parties (where bodies, especially the lower bodies, hardly make contact).
7. Hand-in-hand (touching). Used to support and lead infants and children, used by adults to express intimacy that is more equal than that expressed by, say, the arm-link.

---

[5] Related to stimulus-hunger is the concept of *recognition-hunger*, the need for psychological or social "strokes" analogous to physical stroking. See Chapter 5.

BOX 4.C: How well can you read non-verbal communication?

Here are illustrations of nine pairs of people. Observe various aspects of their NVC (gestures, eye contact, posture, personal space, etc.) and then try and match the behaviour descriptions in List 2 with the pairs' identifying letter in List 1.

List 1   List 2
A   nervousness/suspicion
B   acceptance/courtship
C   readiness
D   boredom/confidence
E   cooperation/acceptance
F   openness
G   reassurance/evaluation
H   secretiveness
I   defensiveness

(answers on page 118)

D

E

F

G

H

I

Source: Nierenberg, Gerard I., and Calero, Henry H. (1971), pp.159, 160, 163. Reproduced with permission.

8. The waist embrace. When a person's embrace shifts from the "friendly shoulder" to the "amorous waist", sexual intimacy is suggested.
9. The kiss. The kiss seems to have its origins in mothers premasticating food for their children and then transferring it mouth to mouth. This still occurs in some cultures. Kisses can represent sexual passion, or social greeting (e.g. the mutual cheek kiss), or they can connote dominance and submission (e.g. kissing the top of the head/forehead/nose-tip, and the hand kiss).
10. The hand-to-head. Suggests intimacy, because of the sensitive and vulnerable nature of the head: we will not be too alarmed if a stranger touches our arm, but we will be alarmed if he touches our head.
11. The head-to-head. Usually used by lovers to exclude the world.
12. The caress. Using the hand, nose, tongue or foot to caress someone else shows emotional and usually sexual intimacy.
13. The body-support. Used by parents with children who are tired or ill or simply small. Used by adults to demonstrate real or symbolic dominance (e.g. carrying the bride across the threshold). Also used in a purely functional way when adults are ill or drunk.
14. The mock attack. When friends or lovers perform mock-aggressive actions upon us (shoulder-punching, hair-ruffling, etc.) we accept them as expressions of affection.

There are many other ways in which we can be touched in non-taboo ways in our society—by the professional touchers, for example (masseurs, manicurists, hairdressers, doctors, priests, dentists, etc.). We can also be touched in crowd situations, such as at sporting occasions and in mobs (Canetti 1973). If individuals are touch-starved, they may seek out such professional and public touching often (Montagu 1971).

Clothing and adornment

As was mentioned earlier, body language and non-verbal communication are not the same thing. Whether valid or not, we often make inferences about people's behaviour from the type of car they drive and the house they live in, their clothing, grooming, whether they have a tattoo, and a range of other seemingly meaningless phenomena. Let us see whether there are clear messages, clear NVC, coming from our clothing and adornment. "Clothing" is an apparently straightforward term, but what is meant by "adornment"? Adornment here means various social inventions which have been produced by different cultures to emit messages of attractiveness and/or dominance, among which are: makeup, tattoos, wigs, shaving, not shaving, jewellery, medals, circumcision, ear-piercing, foot-binding, plastic surgery, and suntans, to name but a few.

Clothing and adornment communicate non-verbally by performing one, two or all of three functions:
1. protection;
2. definition of sex roles (in terms of modesty/immodesty and dominance/submission);
3. definition of social roles (in terms of status and group identification).

Protection

Our soft bodies obviously need protection in a variety of hostile environments—under water, on mountain tops, in space, in blast foundries, in genetic engineering laboratories, in places where it is too hot, or too cold. Morris (1977) argues that primitive man probably went naked, and probably lived in Africa. When the race began to disperse to harsher climes, man adapted by inventing clothing. Darwin entertained similar ideas, but was baffled by the inhabitants of Tierra del Fuego, who went naked even when the snow was falling in those high latitudes. Morris notes that modern man, able to control his domestic environment almost totally by artificial heating and cooling, *could* go naked, but in fact does not. Obviously, the purely protective function of clothing is not the full explanation for why we wear clothes. Horn and Gurel (1981) point out that people often undergo considerable discomfort, and sometimes pain, in following the dictates of fashion or certain initiation rites. Nevertheless, the same writers point out that clothing can perform the function of psychological protection as well as physical protection. The native protecting his genitals from the evil eye by wearing a loincloth and the executive wearing his "lucky" tie are both seeking psychological protection from their garments.

Definition of sex roles

Why would you not go naked in an air-conditioned flat? Because you would probably be embarrassed. Such embarrassment flows from clothing and adornment's second function, that of defining sex roles. The Bible has described how, when Adam and Eve ate of the fruit of the tree of knowledge, they realised they were naked. God was angry that they were aware of this fact, and expelled them from the Garden of Eden, with fig-leaves covering their genitals. If one reads the Bible allegorically, one sees that "eating of the fruit of the tree of knowledge" is in fact the discovery of sexual intercourse, so that sex becomes associated with shame and the first clothes—fig-leaf aprons—were designed to cover that shame and introduce the concept of modesty. Morris, putting the evolutionist viewpoint, sees modesty as a necessity to "turn off" the sexual signals of genital display. This was not a problem when we walked on all fours and females were only in oestrus or heat for a specific period of the year. But when we stood up straight and oestrus became a year-round thing, it became necessary—if civilisations were to be built—to distract ourselves into less enjoyable but economically and culturally more substantial activities. Hence, clothes were a modesty device. On this, at least, evolutionists and fundamentalists agree. Certainly, modesty and decency are protected by clothing. The typist who wears a see-through blouse and the male clerk who wears skin-tight jeans with no underpants will probably be made aware that they are engaging in inappropriate sexual displays—inappropriate, at least, to the workplace. But just what constitutes "modesty" varies enormously in time and place. While in our culture, the sexual organs must be concealed (or appear to be concealed), in other cultures it is the mouth, the face, or the thighs (Horn and Gurel 1981). In Victorian times, modesty was in such fine fettle that the curved legs of grand pianos were sometimes draped with pantaloons lest their voluptuous curves excite the baser emotions of courting couples, while to even mention such obscene words as "limbs" might well cause a few swoons in the parlour. Yet, even in the Victorian era, all was not what it appeared to be. Female attire was based upon the hourglass figure, with over-accentuation of the breasts and buttocks with contraptions such as corsets and bustles (Glynn 1982). Clothing perhaps is more about *im*modesty than modesty, if the truth be known:

> It now appears that sexual attraction, rather than repulsion, has long served as one of the major purposes of clothing as decoration. It fulfils our instinctual desire for the equivalent of the luxurious plumage of the male bird—to populate the species. In many primitive societies, where little dress is worn, the genitalia are not only protected but accentuated. Australian Aboriginal women perform a lascivious dance wearing an apron of floating feathers. The Victorians may have been so prim that Mrs Trollope was horrified to see a young lady embroidering a petticoat in the presence of a young gentleman, but the fact was that perhaps never in the history of Western dress had the inviting curves of the female breast and buttocks been more exaggerated in dress. (BATTERBURY AND BATTERBURY 1982, P.11)

Submission and dominance in male and female clothing

Sexual provocation and allure are then a crucial part of our clothing and adornment. It was noted earlier that a lot of facial NVC is bound up with male dominance and female submission, and this accounted for much sexist behaviour. But what is "sexist" and what is "biologically natural"? Certainly, much clothing and adornment phenomena are well explained by male dominance and female submission. If the stereotype cave-dwellers of our past are composed of muscular male hunters and soft, passive females who stay at base and gather plants while nurturing children, to what extent do we imitate them? It is today's males who wear shoulder pads and epaulettes to amplify the signal of strong shoulders. It is today's women who depilate their skin, wear makeup and stockings, to amplify the signals of infantile smoothness of skin. Think of the colour and texture of typically male and female clothing. Whose clothes (and, for that matter, skins) are usually darker? Whose clothes are coarser, whose are smoother? In conventional Western society, we expect to see a businessman wearing a soberly dark suit (showing he is a respectable and dependable breadwinner) accompanying his wife wearing a pale silk and satin dress and not vice versa. Dichter (1964) even goes so far as to say that the stone age and the modern age are one when it comes to the question of women's furs: furs (at least prior to the advent of animal liberation) connote a hunting trophy, the ultimate gift from a successful—economically and biologically—male.

Generally speaking, stereotyped female clothing is less practical than its male counterpart, reinforcing messages about social roles. To a certain extent, there have been tendencies towards androgyny or unisex in recent years. One thinks of modern Western youths, male and female, wearing long hair, T-shirts and jeans, as well as Chinese men and women wearing loose cotton "Mao" suits. The female executive in our society walks a very thin line between being "too female", that is, either sexually provocative and/or submissive, or "too male", that is, wearing a suit and tie. She usually has to compromise by wearing a tailored dress and coat, and a blouse that usually has some type of gathering or tie at the neck, mimicking the male tie. Kilts and kaftans aside, the message about the maleness of trousers and the femaleness of dresses is deeply embedded in our culture. On this point, there is curious agreement of sorts between the chauvinist male executive—who flies into a rage at a woman in a trouser suit, and tells his friends that *he* wears the pants in his household—and the radical feminist, who sees dresses as a symbol of sexual oppression (because the female is thus always sexually "available").[6]

Definition of social roles

The third function that clothing and adornment perform is that of defining social roles, in terms of status and group identification. Traditionally, there has been one main determinant of high status: does the person have to work, or is he a creature of leisure? The more leisure one has, the more one can conspicuously consume, showing that one does not have to work. Chinese mandarins proved this by growing very long fingernails. European noblemen proved this by first wearing ruff collars, and then draw-strings linking the collar, thus concealing any proletarian, sweaty cultural messages about chest hair. These draw-strings then evolved into that wonderfully useless thing, the tie, the presence or absence of which still provokes powerful social reactions (Guthrie 1976).

Time was, working class women were notable for their tan, which showed that they laboured in the fields all day, while ladies of leisure affected parasols and face powder (with rouge, to show symbolic good health). Nowadays, of course, to have a tan is an indicator that one is of the leisure class, and thus it is a high status, not low status symbol.

Morris (1977) notes how most male fashions have come from sports, that is, those activities indulged in by the high-status leisure class. Thus, the top hat and tails was originally a hunting outfit, while shooting tweeds evolved into the lounge suit. It goes without saying that the hunting and shooting of the leisure class was not functional, the pursuit of subsistence nutrition, but a ritualised, hypertrophied way of "playing at work".[7]

This playing at work behaviour is also seen in the recent fashion of the cowboy look, or denim jeans and jackets with boots. Originally such outfits were totally utilitarian, the most practical thing to wear when working on the range or the outback. If one is leisured, however, one's pre-faded jeans may well be emblazoned with a famous designer's name and have only recently been dry-cleaned. Guthrie notes how recent fashions have been plundered from popular sports: the polo or T-shirt, tennis shoes, surfer shorts, riding boots, gridiron football jerseys with three-quarter sleeves, baseball caps, tennis or cheerleader miniskirts, yachting bell-bottoms and safari bush jackets. The tracksuit seems currently to be evolving from a utilitarian garment seen only in sporting situations (to keep athletes warm and absorb perspiration) to a less practically coloured and textured garment seen in the streets and supermarkets. Perhaps the velour tracksuit/jumpsuit/ski-suit is the formal wear of tomorrow.

---

[6] Similarly, some women see makeup and long hair as sex-role stereotypes connoting child-like submissiveness, and modify their appearance accordingly.

[7] As Oscar Wilde described foxhunting: "the unspeakable in pursuit of the uneatable".

Table 4.1 Clothing and adornment phenomena

Kilt	Wedding costumes	Lace gloves
Kaftan	Plainclothes police	Yarmulka
Low neckline (decolletage)	Plainclothes priests	Tiara
Ruff collar	Long (Isadora) scarves	Pearls and twinset
Cufflinks	Long fingernails	Culottes
Veil	Coloured tennis outfits	Streaking
High heels	Bustle	Elbow patches
Elevator shoes	Removal of hair (female)	Sporran
Trench coat	Chest wigs (male)	Moustaches
Codpiece	Punk safety-pin through	Black lipstick
Tattoos	nose, ear	Red eyeshadow
Hair transplants	Long underwear	Briefcase
Facelifts	Perfume for women/	Rings—
Judges' wigs	deodorant for men	friendship
Mini-skirt	Tracksuits/jumpsuits	eternity
Maxi-skirt	Bathing costumes—on and	Fashions in the field
Muff	off beach	Sidesaddle
Welder's goggles	Bathing costumes and high	Glasses—
Sunglasses—	heels in beauty contests	granny
mirrored	Aerobics outfits—	aviator
tinted	leotards for women	horn-rimmed
Skinhead haircut	shorts, T-shirts for men	Black mesh stockings
Long hair on men	Padded bra	Feather boa
Short hair on women	Leather jeans	Hot pants
Platform shoes	Choker	Lip gloss
Contact lenses	Garters	Cigarettes
Red socks	Old school ties	Chewing gum
School uniforms	Spats	Shoulder pads in
Medals	Chaps	dresses
Gold chain, open neck on	Cravat	
male	Warpaint	

Identification

Clothing and adornment also perform the social role of identifying us with particular groups. Thus, we may see uniforms in the armed forces, factories, hospitals, and take-away food restaurants. But who is to say that the modern executive in his conservative suit, collar and tie is not wearing a uniform? And who is to say that the members of the skinhead gang, jeering at the uniformed school children, are not also wearing a uniform: a certain brand of jeans, a certain brand of boots, a certain style of shirt, a certain hairstyle, tattoos of a particular kind (not to mention a particular style of talking, gesturing, posture, and so on). Groups, be they neighbourhood gangs or nation-states, have powerful ways of enforcing conformity and punishing deviance, and norms of clothing and adornment NVC are part of their powerful tool-kit.

You might like to ponder further on such NVC. Consider for example, the clothing and adornment phenomena listed in Table 4.1. What functions do they perform?

Personal space and territoriality

How close can people get to you before you become uncomfortable? Obviously, it will depend upon the person—friend, associate, lover, enemy. Hall (1966) notes that we define space around our body in zones: the intimate, the personal, the social-consultive, and the public (Fig. 4.2). Note that the

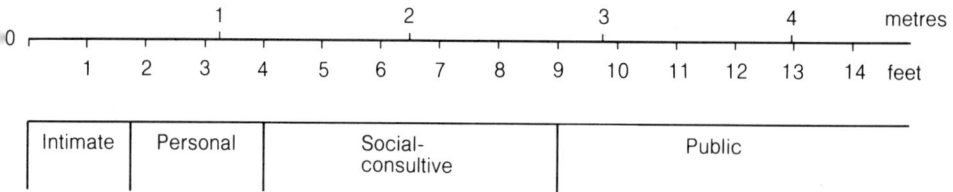

Fig. 4.2 *Personal space zones for a middle-class North American of North European heritage* (ADAPTED FROM HALL 1966)

space zones here are appropriate for a certain socio-economic class and ethnic group, and inappropriate for other classes and groups. We shall examine the implications of this shortly.

It would be appropriate use of personal space to talk to a close friend or lover within the intimate zone, and similarly appropriate use of space to address a small group safely situated in the public zone. Should these situations be reversed, of course, we would feel confused and uncomfortable. Animal behaviourists have studied the *territoriality* behaviour of animals, wherein animals stake out pieces of territory and announce their ownership of such territory by threat displays and chemical communication such as urination (Lorenz 1966; Morris 1977). Thus, when you move into a new neighbourhood in a twentieth-century city, one of the first things the family dog does is to inspect the local streets, sniffing for deposits of urine left by other dogs, to determine who owns what territory in the neighbourhood. While we do not announce our territorial ownership in such a basic way, we have a range of more subtle territorial markers—the beach umbrella, the lunch bag left on the table, the coat on the footpath left in a queue, the poster on the dormitory wall, the gang slogan sprayed on the wall, the bumper stickers on cars telling other drivers in a humorous and/or obscene way to keep their distance, the fences and gardens around our suburban homes, and so on.[8]

Spatial behaviour: Sitting and queueing

Morris (1977) notes that spatial behaviour can be seen quite clearly when a number of people enter a hitherto unoccupied space, such as waiting rooms, cinemas, public toilets, aeroplanes, trains and buses. The first person to enter such a space will probably sit at the end of a row or edge of a space. The second person will not sit at the other end of the row or the opposite edge of the space but at a point about half-way between these points. The next person will sit approximately between these two people, and so on.

Similar spacing behaviour can be seen in queues: although queues are usually public phenomena, commonsense dictates that they should be reasonably compact. Yet people still maintain their "bubble" of personal space around them, not getting too close to others. A queue-jumper is an invader of territory, and often meets with hostility. Queues as devices for rationing access are not to be found in all cultures, however. An Australian or American attempting to queue orderly for a bus in some Middle Eastern countries might be surprised, not to say horrified, to find that queueing is

---

[8] Burgoon and Saine (1978) distinguish between *personal space* (characterised by indivisibility and flexibility, and based on psychological needs) and *territoriality* (characterised by tangibility and inflexibility, and based on survival needs).

simply not an accepted custom, and access to the resource of the bus is gained by a free-for-all push and shove. There are, as we shall see, marked dissimilarities in the way in which different cultures communicate non-verbally as well as verbally.

Communication cut-off: The downtown effect

A queue in an enclosed area means that people have to invade each other's intimate spatial zone. Intimacy implies extremely personal, usually sexual, interaction, and as queues rarely turn into orgies, people develop defence mechanisms to indicate that even though they are very close physically to other people, the situation is non-intimate and quite temporary. Thus they cut off all eye contact with others, and make their faces as expressionless as possible. This effect can also be seen in crowded lifts, trains, buses, and other situations where people are arbitrarily and artificially thrown together. Attempting to strike up a conversation in a lift or train with a total stranger pressed up against you usually provokes embarrassment or anger or both. Again, this does not hold true for all cultures. Guthrie (1976) calls this the "downtown effect", because it is so often seen in city crowds. But he notes that the downtown effect also occurs among animals who are placed in crowded zoo pens—they, too, become more withdrawn, less expansive in their gestures, more impassive in facial expression, and they avoid eye contact more.

Invasion and defence of territory

As was mentioned in the discussion of smell as a form of non-verbal communication, white Anglo-Saxons such as Australians and Americans have strong taboos on giving off bodily smells and of smelling other people's bodies, whereas some Arabs prefer to breathe on others and smell the other person's breath (Hall 1976a). Obviously, smell will have a powerful effect upon different people's perceptions of what is appropriate and inappropriate personal space or territory. Peoples of some cultures (e.g. Southern European, Arab, Jewish/Israeli) may stand much closer to others than is considered appropriate by people of other cultures (British, Americans, etc.). There may also be significant differences in terms of other aspects of non-verbal communication, such as gestures, eye contact, voice, and so on. Much misunderstanding and bad communication can happen when people from different cultures get together and do not understand the non-verbal rules operating: Anglo-Saxons may regard Mediterraneans as pushy, or even making sexual overtures, whereas Mediterraneans may see Anglo-Saxons as remote and cold. At a social gathering, two people from different cultures may play a game of advance and retreat, dance a dance of lead and follow all around the room, without being consciously aware of what is going on.

Pease (1981) argues that rural Australians have a larger personal distance bubble than city-dwellers, and city slickers (e.g. tractor salesmen) invade this territory at their peril. Many country people feel quite claustrophobic in "the big smoke"—as the song goes, "don't fence me in". Many city-dwellers, by contrast, sometimes find the wide open spaces of the country oppressive—they are, in fact, mildly agoraphobic (fearful of open spaces).

Writers such as Korda (1975) have suggested that personal-space invasion can be a handy negotiation tactic: take the client to lunch, use the table as a chessboard, encircle him with salt and pepper shakers, your cigarette lighter, the bottles of wine that you have bought, and so on.

Territoriality at the macro level

Ardrey (1966) has suggested that territorial behaviour is so deeply rooted in our genetic makeup that it not only accounts for interpersonal quarrels, but for wars as well. Hitler certainly was not the first politician to use the alibi of *lebensraum* (living room, room to expand) to initiate military conquest of other people's territory. If the population of the planet continues to expand, with consequently less territory for each individual to feel safe in, does this mean that aggression must increase, that territorial conflict is inevitable? The territoriality plus population growth equals war equation is by no means a proven one. Thus, cities with very high population densities such as London and Amsterdam have very low per capita crime rates compared, for example, to some sparsely populated American states (Argyle 1975; Insel and Lindgren 1978). Merely because n rats in a box co-exist peacefully, but $n + 1$ rats begin to squabble and fight, doesn't mean that crowded but civilised human beings will behave in the same way—or does it?

Environment

We are greatly influenced by our environment—rooms, furniture, buildings, cars, cities, countryside, colour, temperature, lighting, sound—and we take great pains to try and control such factors. To the extent that we control our environment (and perhaps to the extent that we don't control it), our environment is an expression of ourselves. On that fact hangs the livelihood of interior designers, architects, town planners, furniture and car salespeople, and many more. To a certain extent, our environment is just a larger edition of our clothing and adornment. As Winston Churchill said, "We shape our buildings, and later they shape us."

Colour is a critical determinant of environment. What colours make you feel tranquil or frantic? Could you sleep in a black or purple room? Would you be happier if a dentist's rooms were decorated in bright red or light blue? An American football coach ensured that his team rested at half-time in rooms painted blue, but last-minute pep-talks were always conducted in a smaller room painted with brighter colours.

Space is important, as we have just seen with personal space and territoriality. Henley (1977) notes that we feel awed in courtrooms, churches and government buildings, as we are meant to: the large spaces are way beyond human scale, and we feel dwarfed by the larger purposes apparent in such places. Open plan offices seem very democratic and friendly, but, suggests, Henley, they make it much easier for workers to be supervised; power and dominance are conveyed by presiding over other people in open spaces, or in having a private space, or best of all, having a spacious private space (e.g. a suite instead of an office).

As we have seen height also connotes power, and height with space connotes a lot of power. Judges at their benches, priests at their altar, police sergeants at their desks, executives on the upper floors of buildings, parents towering over children—all of these situations exude power.

Dominance is conveyed through various other environmental cues (Morris 1977; Mehrabian 1980; Henley 1977).

1. The telephone display—having more telephones on one's desk than is functionally necessary, including private lines (and having subordinates perform the manual labour of dialling such telephones).

2. The briefcase display—the more dominant you are, the less bulky is your briefcase (because important people only carry the few important papers). Supreme dominants of course have their papers carried for them, that is, they have no briefcase.
3. Office seating—dominants arrange it so that their seat is higher than their guests'/subordinates', thus reinforcing height dominance.
4. Expansive and convenient home architecture.
5. The servant/subordinate display—others dance attendance on the dominant. Important here is the chauffeur: a chauffeur demonstrates that you are powerful to have a large and powerful car, but you are also so powerful that you do not have the manual work of driving (these dominance signals become confused when energy shortages mean that big cars are frowned upon, and democratic traditions lead to a resentment of the master–servant relationship inherent in professional driving; cf. the informal but powerful social tradition in Australia of passengers riding next to taxi drivers in the front seat).
6. Availability of luxury objects (cars, stereos, swimming pools, and other mechanical and electronic gadgets) which are designed to minimise effort and tension and to maximise aesthetic appearance, comfort, efficiency and relaxation.
7. Freedom from routine and controlled order—low-status people, such as students, prisoners and soldiers, are regimented into rows and ranks, whether stationary or moving (or rather, being moved). Women are also more confined than men—in the home, in the kitchen, in the typists' pool. Women are often confined because the city streets are alleged not to be safe, but when Israeli male policy-makers proposed a curfew for women because of the danger of street attack, a female policy-maker, Golda Meir, pointed out the obvious fact that the streets are safe when women walk them alone and therefore it made more sense to have a curfew on men.

What of the environments of the future? Will our future world be like the visions of some film-makers—glass, chrome, plastic, steel, a high-tech heaven (or hell, depending upon your point of view)? Naisbett (1984) thinks not; he suggests that for every *high-tech* modification of our environment, a balancing *high-touch* re-modification emerges. Thus the high-tech and minimalist furniture of the 1970s (glistening, skeletal surfaces, cold to the touch) has not achieved dominance, but has touched off new interest in furniture and environments which feature soft colours, such as pastels, and cosiness, plumpness and the unconstructed look. Similar trends have hospitals trying to look more homelike (carpets, wood surfacing, indirect lighting), and even country music as a response to electronic music.

Time and cultural context

Just as the way we use space is an important part of non-verbal communication, so too is the way we use time. There are enormous differences in the way people from different cultures use time—in the way we do or do not keep appointments, in the way the trains do or do not run on time, and so on. Hall (1976*b*) has attempted to combine time-use behaviour with other aspects of non-verbal communication. He divides the cultures of the world into *high context* and *low context* cultures. High context cultures, such as China, Japan, Middle Eastern countries, most South American countries, and most Southern European countries:

1. define personality more in terms of the group than the individual;
2. tend to have a high sensory involvement, that is, have much less pronounced interpersonal space defences, tend to initiate and receive more bodily contact when talking;
3. are "polychronic", that is, have a sense of different "times" which is quite different from the monochronic time of low context cultures, which is characterised by punctuality, tight scheduling, and so on.

Low context cultures are more individualistic than group-oriented, and their non-verbal communication is characterised by large boundaries of personal space, little touching, and so on.

Hall argues that communication in high context cultures depends less upon words than context; the very opposite of low context cultures:

> ... in some cultures, messages are explicit; the words carry most of the information. In other cultures, such as China or Japan or the Arab cultures, less information is contained in the verbal part of the message, since more is in the context. That's why American businessmen often complain that their Japanese counterparts never get to the point. The Japanese wouldn't dream of spelling the whole thing out ... in general, high-context cultures can get by with less of the legal paperwork that is deemed essential in America. A man's word is his bond and you need not spell out the details to make him behave. . .
>
> (The German-Swiss) are low-context, falling somewhere near the bottom of the scale. Next, the Germans, then the Scandinavians, as we move up. These cultures are all lower in context than the US. Above Americans come the French, the English, the Italians, the Spanish, the Greeks, and the Arabs. In other words, as you move from Northern to Southern Europe, you will find that people move towards more involvement with each other. (HALL 1976*b*)

There is a case for saying that cultures such as Australia and America were not always low context, that in earlier, simpler times, group solidarity was more important than individual freedom, we were less obsessed by time, and were more open and less "downtown" in our non-verbal communication. To a considerable extent, there is a case for saying that rural areas in these countries are today more high context than urban areas.[9] Nevertheless, today these cultures are recognisably low context, and many misunderstandings arise when people from different cultures with differing levels of context meet.[10]

---

[9] Hall's anthropological ideas of high context and low context have a lot in common with the sociologist's ideas of *gemeinschaft* (community) and *gesellschaft* (society). Gemeinschaft groupings are "blood is thicker than water" type groups—kinship groups, village communities, ethnic groups, religious communities, guilds. *Gesellschaft* groups are those which engage people only in one, functional role: the business organisation, the sporting club, the political branch meeting. Gemeinschaft roughly equates with high context, gesellschaft roughly equates with low context. Which is the better lifestyle, as defined by these concepts: the high context/gemeinschaft atmosphere of the country town, where the pace of living is easy and community spirit and emotional support are high, or the low context/gesellschaft city, where wage-slaves huddle together in places where they don't know their neighbours, the pace of living is dominated by time urgency, and everyone feels alienated, believing in nothing? Or perhaps the reverse is true: country towns are boring and parochial, where everyone knows everyone else's business and privacy is non-existent, while cities are dynamic, exciting places, where individuals can revel in their anonymity and freedom? For further discussion on gemeinschaft and gesellschaft see, for example, Nisbet (1970).

[10] Hall has used the notion of high/low context to lambast popularised treatments of "body language" of the "how to succeed in business and become popular with the opposite sex" variety:

> ... When body signals are not seen in context, their meaning can only be distorted. The popularisers of body language take a low-context, manipulative, exploitative view of high-context situations. When I speak of silent language, I mean more than body language. I refer to the totality of behaviour as well as the products of behaviour—time, space, materials, everything. (HALL 1976*a*).

BOX 4.D: Non-verbal communication and understanding other cultures

By observing the behaviour of people in other cultures, we can not only understand those cultures better, but we also get insights into what is usually too obvious to notice—our own culture's non-verbal behaviour.

Behaviour	Arabs	Japanese
Posture	Squat cross-legged, squat to urinate.	Bowing important as greeting: higher the status of person, the shallower the bow.
Gaze	Direct gaze very important in conversation. Dislike of sun-glasses. Not facing directly is impolite.	Much aversion of eye contact—look at neck rather than face. High-status persons looked at less.
Spatial behaviour	Talk standing closer together, at more direct angle than Westerners. Little personal privacy at home but plenty of free space.	Traditional rules that young people should walk behind parents, wives behind husbands. Not much privacy in home.
Touch/body contact	Males touch each other a lot in public (hold hands, embrace, kiss hands, face or beard on special occasions). Females not touched in public at all.	Very little contact in public, not even hand-shaking. Much touching in private (bathing together, sleeping in same room) but with few sexual overtones.
Expression of emotions	Emotions normally under control, but often violent public displays of joy, hostility or sorrow (tears, screaming, clothes-tearing).	Emotions should not be shown in public, especially negative emotions, like sorrow, anger.
Clothes	Arabs keep themselves well-covered; women are particularly subject to strong conventions of modesty (must only have eyes showing in public).	Almost all occupational groups have special uniforms, e.g. students, gangsters (dark glasses), as well as police, etc. Company badges show status in firm.
Interpersonal attitudes	Polite conversation often stereotyped, attitudes conveyed mainly by tone of voice and other NV signals. Status, honour important; shame more important than guilt. Flattery often used.	Hierarchical relations very important, established by bowing, tone of voice, etc. Outsiders treated with much more reserve than members of family or work group.

Behaviour	Arabs	Japanese
Ritual	Much stereotyped behaviour at meals (unwanted food needs to be rejected thrice). Buying and selling involve lengthy bargaining.	Correct use of subtle, restrained NVC is vital in traditional ceremonies such as tea ceremonies, flower arrangement, etc.

(*Source:* Adapted from Argyle 1975, pp.87–94.)

Summary

Non-verbal communication can be presented in terms of a ten-zone circular model, proceeding from the physical structure of the body out to our relationships with others and the outside world. The concept "body language" refers to only some of these zones, whereas the concept "non-verbal communication" refers to all zones.

Evolutionary theorists have suggested that the very structure of our bodies communicates messages of dominance/submission and sexual attractiveness. Other theorists have tried to analyse behaviour in terms of physical features such as head and facial features and physique.

Head movements (e.g. nodding), facial expression (e.g. smiling), eye contact, voice patterning and even bodily smell can communicate much about internal states of mind.

Arm and leg gestures can tell us much about a person's truthfulness, their experience of stress in particular environments, and their experiencing despair, self-control, and so on. Posture can reveal much about dominance and anxiety, whether we are sitting, standing or lying. The angle at which people face each other, or orientation, can reveal much about people's like or dislike for others. Touching, whether gentle or violent, reveals much about more intimate aspects of communication, and seems to be an expression of deeply felt needs.

Clothing and adornment communicate non-verbally by performing one, two or all of three functions: protection, definition of sex roles, and definition of social roles.

Personal space and territoriality reveal much about the needs of humans and animals for closeness or distance from others. Cultural differences are sometimes great here, and can often lead to misunderstandings among people of different cultures who do not understand others' greater or lesser needs for space.

Environmental factors, such as colour, space, height, possessions, and artefacts also communicate much about ourselves and others.

Finally, the way different cultures and individuals use time seems to be a significant mode of communication, both in itself and in its relationships with other aspects of non-verbal communication.

Questions for discussion

1. Consider the model of non-verbal communication in Figure 4.1. Devise an alternative model (e.g. by combining touching with gesture, eliminating time and cultural context, etc.).

2. Using the ten categories of Figure 4.1, analyse the ways in which dominance and submission are expressed in human relationships.
3. Compare and contrast two different areas of non-verbal communication.
4. Interview persons from at least two cultures other than your own on various aspects of non-verbal communication (e.g. gesture, eye contact, time use, etc.). Write a brief report on the basis of these interviews.
5. Take an extract from an existing play/screenplay, or write a brief scene or two yourself. Rewrite the passage twice, giving ample non-verbal directions for actors, so that the two versions will give differing impressions of characters, plot, etc.

References

Ardrey, Robert (1966). *The Territorial Imperative.* (Collins: London).
Argyle, Michael (1975) *Bodily Communication* (Methuen: London).
    (1983). *The Psychology of Interpersonal Behaviour.* (Penguin: Harmondsworth).
Barker, Larry A. (1978). *Communication.* (Prentice-Hall: New Jersey).
Baron, Robert A. *et al.* (1980). *Psychology: Understanding Behaviour*, 2nd edn. (Holt, Rinehart and Winston: New York).
Batterbury, Michael and Batterbury, Ariane (1982). *Fashion: The Mirror of History.* (Greenwich House: New York).
Berne, Eric (1983). *Games People Play: The Psychology of Human Relationships.* (Penguin: Harmondsworth).
Birdwhistell, Ray (1970). *Kinesics and Context.* (University of Pennsylvania Press: Philadelphia).
Brain, Robert (1978). *Rites Black and White.* (Penguin: Ringwood).
Burgoon, J.K. and Saine, Thomas (1978). *The Unspoken Dialogue: An Introduction to Non-Verbal Communication.* (Houghton Mifflin: Boston).
Campbell, Frank (1977). "Straighten Up There!", *The (Melbourne) Herald* 9 July.
Canetti, Elias (1973). *Crowds and Power.* (Penguin: Harmondsworth).
Conway, Ronald (1978). *Land of the Long Weekend.* (Sun Books: Melbourne).
Darwin, Charles (1872). *The Expression of Emotion in Man and Animals.* (John Murray: London).
Dichter, Ernst (1964). *Handbook of Consumer Motivations.* (McGraw-Hill: New York).
Dunkell, Samuel (1977). *Sleep Positions: The Night Language of the Body.* (William Morrow: New York).
Eibl-Eibesfeldt, I. (1972). *Love and Hate: The Natural History of Behaviour Patterns.* (Holt, Rinehart and Winston: New York).
Fast, Julius (1971). *Body Language.* (Pocket Books: New York).
    (1977). *The Body Language of Sex, Power and Aggression.* (Evans: New York).
Glynn, Prudence (1982). *Skin to Skin: Eroticism in Dress.* (Allen and Unwin: London).
Goffman, Erving (1976). *Frame Analysis.* (Penguin: Harmondsworth).
Guthrie, R. Dale (1976). *Body Hot Spots: The Anatomy of Human Social Organs and Behaviour.* (Van Nostrand Reinhold: New York).

Hall, Edward T. (1966). *The Hidden Dimension.* (Doubleday: New York).
(1973). *The Silent Language.* (Doubleday: New York).
(1976a). "How Cultures Collide", *Psychology Today*, July.
(1976b). *Beyond Culture.* (Doubleday: New York).
(1979). "Learning the Arabs' Silent Language", *Psychology Today*, August.
Henley, Nancy M. (1977). *Body Politics: Power, Sex and Non-Verbal Communication.* (Prentice-Hall: New Jersey).
Hess, Eckhard (1975). *The Tell-Tale Eye.* (Van Nostrand Reinhold: New York).
Hewes, G. (1957). "The Anthropology of Posture", *Scientific American*, January.
Hochschild, Arlie Russell (1983). *The Managed Heart: Commercialization of Human Feeling.* (University of California Press: California).
Horn, Marilyn and Gurel, Lois (1981). *The Second Skin.* (Houghton Mifflin: Boston).
Insel, Paul M. and Lindgren, Henry Clay (1978). *Too Close for Comfort: The Psychology of Crowding.* (Prentice-Hall: New Jersey).
Kanter, Rosabeth May (1975). "Women and the Structure of Organizations: Explorations in Theory and Behaviour", *Sociological Inquiry*, no. 2-3.
Knapp, M.L. (1972). *Nonverbal Communication in Human Interaction.* (Holt, Rinehart and Winston: New York).
Korda, Michael (1975). *Power! How to Get It, How to Use It.* (Random House: New York).
Lamb, Warren and Watson, Elizabeth (1979). *Body Code: The Meaning in Movement.* (Routledge and Kegan Paul: London).
Levine, Robert and Wolff, Ellen (1985). "Social Time: The Heartbeat of Culture", *Psychology Today*, March.
Lorenz, Konrad (1966). *On Aggression.* (Metheun: London).
Lowen, Alexander (1977). *The Language of the Body.* (Collier: New York).
Lurie, Alison (1981). *The Language of Clothes.* (Random House: New York).
Malandro, Loretta A. and Barker, Larry (1983). *Nonverbal Communication.* (Addison-Wesley: Reading, Mass.)
Mehrabian, A. (1971). *Silent Messages.* (Wadsworth: California).
(1980). *Basic Dimensions for a General Psychological Theory.* (Oelgeschlager, Gunn and Hain: Cambridge, Mass.)
Messent, Peter (1979). *Understanding Your Dog.* (Quarto Books: London).
Montagu, Ashley (1971). *Touching: The Human Significance of the Skin.* (Harper and Row: New York).
Molcho, Samy (1985). *Body Speech.* (Sun Books: South Melbourne).
Morris, Desmond (1979). *Intimate Behaviour.* (Triad/Panther: London).
(1977). *Manwatching: A Field Guide to Human Behaviour.* (Triad/Panther: London).
(1979). *Gestures: Their Origin and Distribution.* (Jonathan Cape: London).
(1985). *Bodywatching: A Field Guide to the Human Species.* (Jonathan Cape: London).
Morris, K.T. and Cinnamon, K.M. (1975). *A Handbook of Non-Verbal Group Exercises.* (CMA Publishing: Kansas City).
Naisbett, John (1984). *Megatrends: Ten New Directions Transforming Our Lives.* (Warner Books: New York).
Nierenberg, G.I. and Calero, H.H. (1971). *How to Read a Person Like a Book.* (Hawthorne Books: New York).
Nisbet, Robert (1970). *The Social Bond: An Introduction to the Study of Society.* (Knopf: New York).
Pease, Alan (1981). *Body Language: How to Read Other People's Thoughts by their Gestures.* (Camel Publishing: Sydney).

Scheflen, A.E. (1976). *Body Language and the Social order.* (Anchor: New York).

Scheflen, Albert E. and Ashcraft, Norman (1976). *Human Territories: How We Behave in Space–Time.* (Prentice-Hall: New Jersey).

Sheldon, W.H. (1954). *Atlas of Man: A Guide for Somatotyping the Adult Male at All Ages.* (Harper and Brothers: New York).

Vaughan, Bruce L. (1982). *Body Talk: Understanding the Secret Language of the Body. (Argus Communications: Dallas, Texas).*

Young, Stephen (1984). *"Are we Led by the Nose?", New Scientist, 20–27* December.

Films/Videos

Communication: The Non-Verbal Agenda (Video Channel).
Body Business (Training Media Services).
Body Language, Parts 1 and 2 (Alan Pease), (Power Human Resources).

5

Transactional analysis, or the games people play

TRANSACTIONAL analysis (TA) is a system of analysing and understanding human relationships first developed by an American psychiatrist, Eric Berne. Drawing upon the theories of the psychoanalyst, Sigmund Freud, and others, he produced a model of human behaviour that avoided the technical jargon of Freudian psychoanalysis.

Transactional analysis has proceeded from humble beginnings in the 1950s to the status of being one of the most popular, if not *the* most popular, approaches to understanding ourselves and others. Critics have argued that, in trying to avoid one set of jargon, practitioners of TA have merely set up another. Criticism has also been made of TA for being "too American"—a charge that means different things to different people. As with all the theories advanced in this book, you will have to be the final judge of worth.

Freud's model of behaviour

Freud's approach to human behaviour was to emphasise human sexuality. He believed that, for the most part, human personality was laid down in the first six years of life, and that our personalities developed according to the way reality was reflected through different parts of the body.

The first stage of development, from birth to about one year or to the end of the weaning phase, was the *oral* stage of development. In this stage, the infant tests the environment by putting things in its mouth, and derives most pleasure and security from being fed from breast or bottle. In later life, people may retreat to the mouth when insecure, for example, by biting nails, biting pens, sucking thumbs or fingers, compulsively eating, drinking, smoking, talking, rubbing the lips or chin, stroking moustaches or beards, and so on.

Once weaned, the next major life-task for the infant to perform is to be toilet-trained. In this stage, the *anal* stage, the infant learns that to please or displease its parents it must control its bowels. In the anal-expulsive sub-stage, the child may express aggression by voiding its bowels; in the anal-retentive sub-stage, the child may try to earn the love and regard of its parents (or indeed, may try to provoke the concern of parents) by retaining its bodily wastes.

The third phase is known as the *genital* or *phallic* stage. After having learned to control its body, the child now begins to become a more normal member of the family community. Freud argued that at the third stage (between the fourth and six years), the child actually experiences sexual urges: male children sexually desire their mother, and wish to get rid of or kill their father, while female children desire their father and wish to get rid of *their* rival, their mother. Freud named these behaviour patterns the Oedipus complex (for male children) and the Electra complex (for female children), after Greek myths where similar patterns occurred. When the child realises, said Freud, that a sexual relationship with its parent is impossible, it loses most of its sexual impulses and enters a period called *latency*, which lasts until the onset of puberty, at which time sexuality re-enters the child's life and sexual desires can be focused upon more attainable partners.

It is possible, said Freud, to become *fixated* or "trapped" in one particular stage: thus, adults with an anal-expulsive fixation might be aggressive and untidy, while adults with an anal-retentive fixation might be super-tidy, stingy (and, indeed, constipated).

Freud believed that women had a fundamental disadvantage compared to men: female children perceived that they did not have a penis, and thus somehow felt that they had been punished with castration (castration complex) and envied males for their apparent superiority (penis envy).

What are we to make of these ideas? Many have criticised these parts of Freud's theory because of its strong—some would say wildly exaggerated—emphasis upon sexuality, and because of the assertion that much if not most of the adult personality is determined by experiences in the first few years of life. Yet, while the followers of Freud constitute only one of many schools of thought in the social sciences, his ideas have been widely influential.

Freud's model of the mind and human coping

Freud also argued that our personalities, determined by our first few years' experience, could be understood in terms of a three-part model of the mind. When we are born, we are not very rational; we are, said Freud, largely tools of our two dominant instincts, sex and aggression.[1] This instinctual basis

[1] Freud was so horrified by the destruction he saw in World War I (1914–18) that he began to feel that mere aggression was not an adequate explanation of such super-destructive behaviour. Accordingly, he modified his theory to suggest that we are driven by two instincts: eros or sexual reproduction (thus ensuring the continuity of the species) and thanatos, or death, the longing to return to the inanimate matter that existed before life evolved. The battle of the death instinct and the life instinct was thus part of us, just as the battle between the superego and the id. Aggression towards others was seen as shifting self-destructive energy away from ourselves. Whenever we hurt ourselves, say Freudians, these events are not "accidents" or unmotivated behaviour—they are subsconsciously motivated by our own self-destructive instincts.

remains with us all our life, and Freud called this part of our personality the *id* (Latin = "it"). It is only later that we develop the two other parts of our mental structure, the *ego* and the *superego*. The ego is our rational self, the developing sense of our individuality, separate from our parents and the rest of the world. The superego is that part of us which we learn from our parents or parent-surrogates, the conscience which tells us what is right and proper.

The ego is the conscious part of our mental being; the id and the superego are largely unconscious. Many of our problems are caused by the conflicts that rage between the id (motivated by sexual desire, the pursuit of pure pleasure, and the aggressive impulse) and the superego (the judging, often judgmental and punishing conscience which is a remnant of parental do's and don'ts). Our rational self—the ego—then has to cope with the tug of war between id and superego, but we also have to cope with outside reality.

Freud and his followers posited a series of *ego defence mechanisms* which we use to cope with all these stresses. Many of these mechanisms are not terribly healthy, but they often ensure psychological survival of a type. Some of these mechanisms are:

1. *Repression.* If an event is too threatening, we may simply repress or push away the perception of the event. Thus we may "forget" that we had a dentist's appointment.

2. *Denial* is similar to repression, only it is more conscious. We may deny that something is going to happen by resorting to escapism or procrastination.

3. *Rationalisation.* This in turn is similar to denial: it simply means making up reasons for doing things that we know we shouldn't do. We may say "everyone does it", or we may do something "unthinkingly" and make up reasons for doing it later on.

4. *Fantasy* is when we cannot cope with the danger or boredom of reality and so we escape to a fantasy world where we are much stronger, wittier, more intelligent, more fashionable than we really are. We daydream, like Walter Mitty, and may even prefer the dream to the reality. One of the most common forms of this is being beaten in an argument, and then having a "what I should have said was. . ." fantasy, in which we win the argument. Such fantasies can be useful if we learn from them, but we must be able to turn off the fantasy and then act in reality.

5. *Projection.* If we have failed in something, or if we unconsciously experience feelings we do not wish to acknowledge consciously, we may claim to see blame or blameworthy behaviour in others. Thus a person whose self-image is that of a peaceful person, but who in fact harbours strong aggressive impulses, may pretend to see, or see and magnify, aggression in others. Thus we are quickest at seeing and condemning our own faults in others.

6. *Displacement* is similar to projection, except that we are sometimes consciously aware of our own shortcomings, and the transfer of energy to others is sometimes physical as well as verbal. Thus, a man may have been verbally attacked by his boss at work; rather than retaliate directly, the man may verbally attack his wife (who may then attack their son, who attacks their daugher, who attacks their dog, who attacks their cat, who attacks the mice, who, in a state of shock, leave and set up house in the boss's home, keeping him up all night, thus causing him to be in a bad mood the next day. . .). Objects like

squash balls, golf balls and tin cans are often the targets of displacement activities as well. Displacement, then, is about bullying, about not picking on someone your own size, to vent your frustrations.

7. *Identification* is primarily about mirroring others in order to determine what you believe in. This identification may take the form of imitation of verbal and non-verbal behaviour, badges, T-shirts, bumper-stickers, uniforms, etc.

8. *Introjection* is a more extreme form of identification, and the opposite of projection. When we can't beat 'em, we may join them, often with a vengeance. Religious and political true believers who make a strong conversion to the other side (when the other side is totally dominant) would be examples of this. The superego is largely formed by the introjection of parental values and prejudices.

9. *Compensation* is trying to change one's behaviour so that one will more closely resemble others, and thus gain acceptance. Some non-verbal examples of compensation would be tall people stooping and short people standing extremely rigid or being very argumentative (projecting aggression onto others—the "Napoleon complex").

10. *Regression* is retreating to an earlier form of personality functioning. Examples might be executives playing football at lunchtime ("just like when we were kids!"), an adult throwing a tantrum, an adult becoming orally insecure when threatened.

11. *Reaction formation.* As with projection, we can have feelings which we, or our rational conscious selves, find unacceptable; rather than project these feelings onto others, however, with reaction formation we go to the other extreme within ourselves. This reversal is not always successful: as DiCaprio (1974) suggests, a man who unconsciously dislikes his wife may consciously try to please her, by buying her presents, but he may get her things she does not want (candy when she is on a diet, flowers that remind her of funerals, etc.).

12. *Undoing.* This is basically doing penance for sins which others aren't aware of. Thus, if a woman has a dream in which she kills her lover, she may buy him a present.

13. *Sublimation.* This is a more socially acceptable form of displacement. Desires, often of a sexual nature, are transferred to a more public and desirable mode of activity. Examples might be a female nurse who never married and cares for her patients as if they were her children, and also cares for a pet poodle as if it were an infant, or a man who has lost his children, and dedicates himself to working with scouts or wayward boys (DiCaprio 1974).

Freud used the ego defence mechanisms, together with his ego–superego–id model of the mind, and the developmental model of personality, to practice *psychoanalysis*. This entailed his working with people with psychological problems, often by getting them to relax (on the couch so beloved of cartoonists) and discuss their waking experiences and their dreams (which Freud believed revealed, albeit through symbols, the workings of the unconscious mind). For Freud, much of our behaviour was motivated by unconscious drives, and we were not as much in control of ourselves as we might like to think.

Freud and Berne

Berne's transactional analysis bears some strong similarities to Freud's psychoanalysis. While Freud separated the individual consciousness into

Freud	Berne
Mental states	*Ego states*
superego	Parent
ego	Adult
id	Child
Ego defence mechanisms	*Games, life positions, etc.*
repression	Kick Me
denial	Rapo
sublimation	I'm OK, You're Not OK
. . . etc	. . . etc

Fig. 5.1 *Freud and Berne: Some basic ideas*

three parts, using the Latin terms superego, ego and id, Berne made a similar distinction, using the English words parent, adult, child (Fig. 5.1). Freud's analysis pertained to individuals in therapy situations, and later he even psychoanalysed whole cultures and religions. Berne's analysis emphasised the dynamic nature of relationships in the real world, where people are linked not only by economic transactions, but behavioural transactions as well. Some of these transactions Berne saw as being "games"—games which were often quite hurtful, but were nevertheless tools many people used to make some kind of twisted sense of their reality. Berne gave names to these games that were in plain English, and were often quite whimsical—Why Don't You . . . Yes But, Rapo, and Kick Me, for example. There are many paths up the one mountain, and Freud's ego defence mechanisms and Berne's games are similar to tools of analysis used by other schools of thought, for example, the styles of distorted thinking described by practitioners of rational emotional therapy (RET) (see Chapter 7, see also Dougherty 1976).

Ego states
Ego states are the component parts of our personality. Berne in his later work came to extend the Freudian three-part model into a five-part model:
1. nurturing parent
2. punishing parent
3. adult
4. natural child
5. adapted child

The verbal and non-verbal characteristics of each of these ego states are shown in Table 5.1. We can literally "be" in any or some or all of these ego states throughout the day; in fact, in some circumstances we could switch to all five ego states within a few minutes. Remember, the ego states do not correspond to chronological ages: thus, a 60-year-old can behave like a petulant child, while a 7-year-old can take care of a 3-year-old sibling like a caring parent.

Where do ego states come from? Working in the psychoanalytic tradition, Berne argues that we acquire ego states from the experiences we have in the first few years of life. In fact, the idea of ego states first came to Berne when he was treating a 25-year-old lawyer, who said "But I am not really a lawyer. I'm just a little boy" (Wallechinsky and Wallace 1978).

Table 5.1 Behavioural clues indicating which psychological state is at work

Divisions or basic norms	Nurturing parent	Punishing parent	Adult ego state	Natural child	Adaptive child
Voice tones	Solicitous, comforting, caring, soothing.	Condescending, criticising, putting down or accusing, taut, insistent, tongue-clicking, sighing.	Matter-of-fact, even, calm.	Rising, high-pitched, usually noisy.	Whining, shrieking with rage, begging, contrite, supplicating.
Vocabulary clues	What's wrong? Are you OK? Can I help? Don't worry. Everything will be OK.	Shocking. Nonsense. Lazy. Poor thing. Everyone knows that. You should never. The only way. I can't understand why in the world you would ever. It is extremely important. Do it. You never.	How? What? When? Where? Why? Who? What's the probability? Is it probable? Is it possible? In what way? I speak only for myself and not others.	I'm mad at you. Hey, great. I wish. I dunno. Gee, crazy. Rats. Wow.	It always happens to me. I guess I'm just unlucky. I never seem to win at anything. That's not fair. Everybody else does it. Come on, let's. I won't.
Physical postures	Open arms protecting from a fall or hurt, pat on back, arm around shoulder.	Stroking chin, puffed up, super correct, very proper. Superior attitudes: talking behind hand, throwing hands in air.	Relaxed, attentive, eye contact, listening with openness, squared-up posture. Adult listening is identified with continual movement of face, eyes, and body.	Playful, excited, running, dancing, jumping up and down, head cocked.	Withdrawn and retreating, beat down, overburdened, self-conscious, teasing, agitated, tantrum behaviour.
Facial expressions	Concerned, supportive, encouraging, warm, happy.	Frowns, worried or disapproving looks, taut lips, jutting chin, stern gaze.	Alert eyes, paying close attention.	Excitement, surprise, body tense, mouth open.	Downcast eyes, quivering lip or chin, tic, pouting, whining, moist eyes, red face.
Gestures	Reaching for, hugging, holding, protecting and shielding from harm.	Pointing index finger or pencil, tapping foot, arms folded across chest, hands on hips, striking table with fist, shaking fist.	Leaning forward in chair, eye-to-eye contact, listening with openness.	Laughter, limbs moving freely, playful.	Wringing hands, withdrawing into corner, raising hand for permission, stooped shoulders, hung head.
General	Support and concern.	Closure to new data, automatic judgments based on archaic material.	Data gathering, sensitivity, openness, and thinking.	Aroused feelings suggesting that the child has been hooked.	Complaining and expectation-meeting, or withdrawing and expectation-avoiding.

Source: Reprinted, by permission of the publisher, from *T.A. and the Manager* by Dudley Bennett, pp.26-27 © 1976/78 by AMACOM, a division of American Management Association, New York. All rights reserved.

Thus our (upper-case) Parent ego state comes from our (lower case) parents, logically enough, or from significant adults who assume a parental or semi-parental role. There may be genetic influences upon our behaviour; certainly, there are strong environmental factors, particularly as parents model a whole series of behaviours for us at our most impressionable age. We learn that the universe of experience is structured around rewards and punishments. When our parents reward us, they are nurturing, they encourage and support us. When our parents punish us, they blame, restrict and judge.

When we are very young, we obviously do not have spoken and written language, and thus we learn about others non-verbally. Non-verbal modes of communication remain extremely important for us throughout our lives, not only because of the way in which non-verbal communication reinforces verbal communication but also because of the way in which non-verbal communication contradicts or conflicts with verbal communication (for an extremely detailed analysis of non-verbal communication in transactional analysis, see Steere 1982). Thus, we may "inherit" many of the postures, gestures and expressions of our parents, as well as the attitudes and values that such behaviours convey.

Our Child ego state, naturally enough, comes from our own childhood experience. Berne subdivided the Child ego state into two parts—that of the Natural Child and that of the Adapted Child. The Natural Child is just that, the style of behaviour children have naturally before social conditioning constrains them to change. Spontaneity, intuition, curiosity and truthfulness are the characteristics of this condition. However, experience may teach children to conceal their true feelings and/or get what they want through emotional manipulation. The feelings of self-love and love for others of the Natural Child may be replaced by the feelings of self-hate and hate and fear of others of the Adapted/Adaptive Child.

Our Adult ego state begins to develop when we have a clear sense of our identity, needs, values and behaviours as being significantly different from others, specifically our parents. When we begin to understand and manipulate our environment in a rational and systematic way, then our Adult ego state is forming.

When do the ego states specifically form? Berne believed that the Child came first, specifically the Natural Child. This would accord with Freud's model of personality, when our first component of personality, the Id (i.e. the instinctual infrastructure of sexual and aggressive drives) comes first. Other TA specialists, such as Harris, disagree with Berne on this, suggesting that the positive feelings of self-worth ("I'm OK") of the Natural Child are not as important in infancy as the negative feelings of self-worth ("I'm Not OK") of the Adapted Child—mainly because small, powerless children feel so overwhelmed by huge, powerful adults (see "I'm OK—You're OK", p.155). Harris and Berne both agree, however, that the Child ego state comes first, irrespective of subdivisions. The Parent ego state develops next, as we take into ourselves (or introject, as Freud would say) the nurturing and punishing behaviours of our parents. The Adult ego state begins to form around about the age of 10 months, as we begin to test and control our environment (i.e. we begin to hypothesise "If I do this, that will happen" and then test the hypothesis).

Does everyone have the same mix of ego states within them? No. We all have had unique experiences in our childhood, we all have learned different

BOX 5.A: Ego states

What ego states do you think are represented by the following?

1. Would you like me to drive you to work?
   (concerned expression, arm around shoulder of person being asked)
2. I don't have enough information to make a decision on that.
   (direct gaze, open hands)
3. Come on, let's pinch some fruit from Johnson's orchard. Everyone else does. You're not chicken, are you?
   (conspiratorial wink, tilted head)
4. It's not fair!
   (quivering lip, slumped over)
5. It's so typical that you would do this! You must never do it again!
   (shaking head, pointing finger)
6. Isn't it great just lying here in the sunshine, without a worry?
   (shining eyes, laughter)
7. No thanks, I never drink, especially at orgies. I would like to talk to you about your insurance cover, however. . .
   (direct gaze, open hands)
8. He may be a mass-murderer, but he's still my boy, and I'll hide him.
   (concerned expression, hugging person being spoken to)

things. We may have had more negative experiences than positive, or vice versa. We may have developed our ego states earlier or later than others.

Is one ego state preferable to another? Generally speaking, the Punishing Parent ego state and the Adapted Child ego state are not very lovable ones, nor very effective. They may be useful in some circumstances, however. The Natural Child ego state may be a fine one to be in when we are at a party or making love, but it may be a quite inappropriate one at a funeral or in combat. The Adult ego state will be a very useful one to have in a work situation, but a person continually in an Adult state may be a bore, unable, for example, to have a good time (use his Child) at the office party.

Individuals have ego states, but it is also useful to picture groups, organisations and nations as having ego states as well. We can see differences between individuals, groups, etc., by sketching pie-charts or other graphic tools to show the proportions of ego states (see Box 5.C).

Strokes: What you stroke is what you get

Now that we have a clear basic idea of what the TA model of personality is, it is necessary to find out how these personalities communicate with each other. In TA, the most basic unit of communication is known as a *stroke*. If I say "hello" to you in the morning, that's a stroke. If I touch you with affection, that's a stroke. If I yell abuse at you, that's a stroke. If I hit you, that's a stroke. The only time I might not stroke you is when I ignore you totally. TA theorists say that, so great is the human hunger for strokes, we will do almost anything to avoid being ignored, of being denied strokes. Thus, a child, ignored by its mother, may deliberately create such a commotion that

BOX 5.B: Five chairs exercise

To better acquaint yourself with the ego states within you, try this exercise. First, get six chairs. Arrange them in the following manner (if chairs are unavailable, use cushions, or paper sheets on the floor).

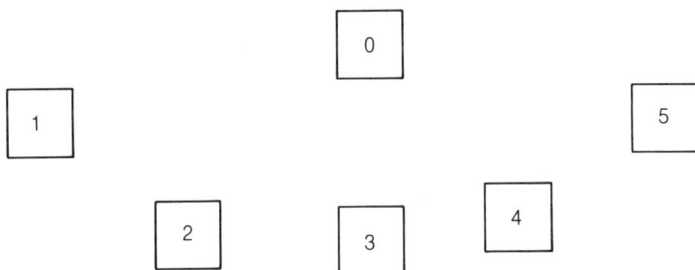

```
                    ┌─────┐
                    │  0  │
                    └─────┘
┌─────┐                              ┌─────┐
│  1  │                              │  5  │
└─────┘                              └─────┘
        ┌─────┐   ┌─────┐  ┌─────┐
        │  2  │   │     │  │  4  │
        └─────┘   │  3  │  └─────┘
                  └─────┘
```

The sixth chair (O = Other) is occupied by a friend, co-worker or relative. Discuss a topic with that person with which you are both familiar. As you feel yourself changing from one ego state to another, shift chairs. Discuss the transitions. Did they help or hinder problem-solving? Did you favour some and neglect others? Was the choice of chairs affected by the other person? Would it have been different with another person?

Variation 1

Only five chairs and yourself are needed. Pick a topic and role-play the different ego states, spending an equal amount of time in each chair to see how each state feels. Which is the most "natural" for you?

Variation 2

Five chairs plus five people plus more people in an audience needed. Five people sit in chairs, facing audience. They each carry large identifying cards (CP = Critical Parent, etc.). They discuss an issue. Anyone from the audience can replace anyone in a particular chair at any time.

Variation 3

Ten chairs, plus two people. Chairs in a circle. Both people discuss an issue. Each person changes ego states as the mood takes them. (This variation is very useful for understanding the Transactions and Games sections later).

(Adapted from Villeré (1981))

BOX 5.C: Ego-states charts

Two hypothetical charts are shown.

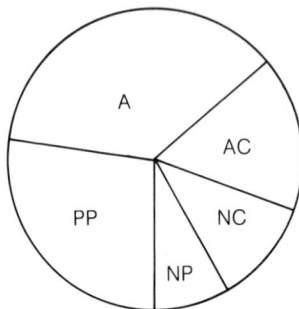

Person A

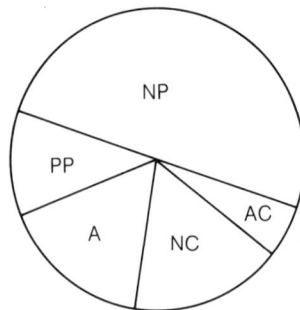

Person B

Complete charts for the following:
1. Formal work group
2. Informal work group
3. Prison
4. Twentieth century school
5. Eighteenth century school
6. Where you work (have worked/would like to work)
7. Twentieth century Australia
8. Eighteenth century Australia
9. Modern Russia
10. Modern America

You may find it useful to have another person (friend/colleague/relative) do the same exercise and compare results and perceptions.

the mother, in rage and annoyance, gives the kid a good whack. The child cries as a result, but the child has *not been ignored*, and that's the main thing.

Stroking, then, is simply *paying attention* to someone. There are different kinds of strokes. For example, a stroke may be *positive* or *negative*. A positive stroke is something you will like, a negative stroke is something you won't like. Saying hello and touching affectionately would be positive strokes for most, while abuse and violence would be negative strokes for most. TA practitioners sometimes describe positive and negative strokes in more colloquial language: cold pricklies (negative strokes) and warm fuzzies (positive strokes).[2]

Jongeward and Seyer (1978) point out that in small organisations, strokes, especially positive ones, are given all the time. Thus people have feedback on what they are doing and thus also motivation remains reasonably high. Yet

---

[2] Halfway between a positive and a negative stroke is a *mixed* stroke, e.g. "That was pretty good—for a woman", "Not bad—for an old man".

as organisations grow, so often do formality and structure, and thus the strokes get fewer, people become demotivated and alienated—"nobody cares, nobody seems to know who's in control anymore". Interestingly, Jongeward and Seyer note that such an environment can lead to a dramatic rise in inefficiency, for reasons that are surprisingly similar to our child who cries and throws a tantrum merely to get noticed. People need strokes, and if they cannot get warm fuzzies, then they will settle for cold pricklies (rather than be ignored). Thus people may unconsciously start doing things wrong, merely to get attention; the routine suddenly becomes shot through with crises, and only heroic efforts will save the day. If people get strokes, positive or negative, for crisis management rather than smooth, uneventful management, then of course there will be a miraculous rise in crises (see Chapter 8). Thus, as TA specialists often put it, *what you stroke is what you get*, or, as a behaviourist might put it, what you reinforce becomes more likely (see Chapter 3 for discussion of reinforcement theory).

Paradoxically then, punishing someone, or giving out negative strokes or cold pricklies, can serve to maintain, rather than get rid of, the very behaviour the punisher doesn't like. The incompetent clerk or manager learns, just like the tantrum-throwing child or criminal, that if one continues to be deviant, one is noticed—attention is paid.

What is the solution to this quandary? The TA practitioners are at one with the behaviourists here: positively stroke or positively reinforce competence, rather than waste time in negatively stroking or punishing incompetence—accentuate the positive in order to eliminate the negative. This, of course, is easier said than done. Giving out positive and negative strokes is not as simple as it seems. Most cultures teach us that we should discount or play down any positive strokes given to us or by us, and magnify or play up negative strokes given to us or by us. Thus, if someone compliments you on an achievement, what is your response likely to be? "Thank you very much, I've worked hard to get this" or "Oh, it was nothing really . . . I must have been lucky"? Very few of us are assertive enough to give an answer similar to the first one, because people might think we are egotistical—or so we think (Wagner 1981). Most of us are hypocritical about the way we stroke and are stroked (there are obvious similarities here between TA and assertiveness training; see Chapter 6).

We can stroke others, but we can also stroke ourselves. Accepting a compliment with good grace is one way we can stroke ourselves. But there are bad or harmful ways of stroking ourselves. So great is people's hunger for strokes—being paid attention—that if strokes from others are not forthcoming, we may stroke ourselves in negative ways—smoking, drinking too much, eating too much, going on spending binges, and so on (Wagner 1981).

Just as strokes can be verbal or non-verbal, positive or negative, so too they can be *conditional* or *unconditional*. Strokes which are unconditional relate to the person's unchangeable characteristics—they are strokes for being. Strokes which are conditional relate to the person's behaviour—they are strokes for doing (Wagner 1981). Examples of these would be:

Positive unconditional:	"I love you." "I really admire tall people."
Positive conditional:	"You went well this time." "You look good today."
Negative conditional:	"That tie doesn't suit you." "You mucked that one up."
Negative unconditional:	"I hate you." "I loathe tall people like you."

Villere (1981) suggests that running organisations is basically all about administering conditional negative and positive strokes. If you continually administer unconditional negative and positive strokes, there is nothing that the other person needs to do—he is either an angel or a devil. Obviously, such a conditional/unconditional approach to stroking applies off the job as much as on. By encouraging competence and discouraging incompetence, it is possible to change people—co-workers, children, friends, criminals. Of course, changing human behaviour may not be possible. TA, behaviourism and many other psychological theories are reasonably optimistic about human nature. A pessimist might say, however, that it is a false distinction to separate behaviour from self, being from doing—that in fact what we do is what we are, and no amount of stroking or reinforcing or whatever will change that. This question of optimism versus pessimism regarding human nature will be taken up again in the "I'm OK, You're OK" section (p.155).

Transactions: The mechanics of communication

If strokes are the fundamental units of social action, then an exchange of strokes constitutes a *transaction*, which is the fundamental unit of social intercourse (Berne 1983). There are three types of transaction we can have with others—complementary, crossed and ulterior. A *complementary* trans-action occurs when one person sends a message or stimulus (S) from one ego state to an ego state of another person, and gets an expected response (R). Here, lines of communication are open, and this type of transaction or interchange can continue indefinitely. Some examples of this are shown in Figure 5.2.

Crossed transactions occur when a stroke is given one way and the response is unexpected: the lines of communication are not parallel, and conflict or misunderstanding usually ensues. Some examples of crossed transactions appear in Figure 5.3.

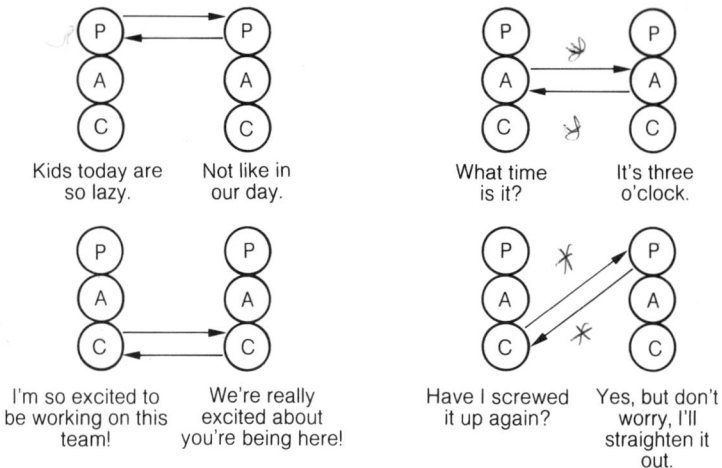

Kids today are so lazy.   Not like in our day.

What time is it?   It's three o'clock.

I'm so excited to be working on this team!   We're really excited about you're being here!

Have I screwed it up again?   Yes, but don't worry, I'll straighten it out.

Fig. 5.2 *Complementary transactions*

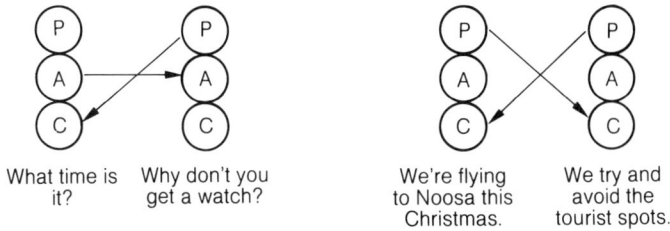

What time is it?	Why don't you get a watch?

We're flying to Noosa this Christmas.	We try and avoid the tourist spots.

Fig 5.3 *Crossed transactions*

Ulterior transactions occur when there is a difference between the social and psychological levels of meaning, that is, when we say one thing and mean another, conveying hidden or ulterior meanings. Thus, we distinguish between the social or apparent stimulus (SS) and the psychological or ulterior stimulus (PS) and the social or apparent response (SR) and the psychological or ulterior response (PR) (see Fig. 5.4).

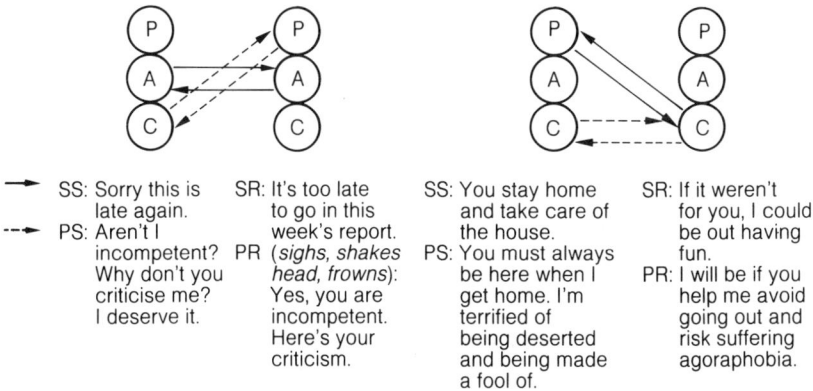

SS: Sorry this is late again.
PS: Aren't I incompetent? Why don't you criticise me? I deserve it.

SR: It's too late to go in this week's report.
PR (*sighs, shakes head, frowns*): Yes, you are incompetent. Here's your criticism.

SS: You stay home and take care of the house.
PS: You must always be here when I get home. I'm terrified of being deserted and being made a fool of.

SR: If it weren't for you, I could be out having fun.
PR: I will be if you help me avoid going out and risk suffering agoraphobia.

Fig 5.4 *Ulterior transactions* (ADAPTED FROM BERNE 1983)

Notice that the transactions at the social and psychological levels are complementary.

Often, the psychological or ulterior level of communication is expressed by non-verbal communication that is at odds or is not congruent with the verbal level of communication. To understand this, try role-playing the ulterior transactions in Table 5.2.

Table 5.2

Social (verbal) meaning)	Psychological (non-verbal) meaning
Can you show me how to do this?	I'm interested in you sexually.
Let's have lunch.	Let's not have lunch.
Isn't that an interesting book?	I like you, let's be friends.
What is your opinion of. . .?	Who cares what your opinion is?

Transactions then are the key to communication, or lack of communication, in work and non-work situations.[3]

Games people play

Berne and other transactional analysis specialists argue that people often play hurtful psychological games with each other. A game is basically an ulterior transaction: a complementary transaction on the social level, accompanied by a complementary transaction on the psychological level. Some of these games appear below.

Why don't you . . . yes, but. . .

Someone asks for advice, initiating an Adult–Adult transaction on the social level. When others supply advice/answers/solutions, the WDY–YB player answers "Yes, but. . .", that is, she doesn't really want answers, she merely wants to demonstrate that other people are fools (much as a querulous child might keep up a barrage of "Daddy, why is the sky blue?" type questions until Daddy loses his temper).

I'm only trying to help you

The game player may offer advice to others, but the advice is probably not very good. The other person continually fails because of the bad advice, and returns for more. This means that the player knows that at least one person depends upon him, even though the player may simultaneously despise the other person for being so incompetent.

Blemish

The player nit-picks and criticises other people, totally neglecting the good things and achievements of the other person. The player says that her criticisms are constructive, but they are in fact always destructive.

Harried

The player believes that everyone else is incompetent or immature, and that it is the player's divine mission to do everyone's work for them. Because the player starts off with the basic belief in everyone else's incompetence, he never gives others the benefit of the doubt or indeed even trains others up to a level of competence. The player thus proves his own indispensability (everyone must now give him positive strokes), and often destroys his health in the process.

Kick me

The player gets negative strokes from being incompetent (remember, if people cannot get positive strokes, they will settle for negative strokes). The player may deliberately provoke other people with increasingly outrageous displays of incompetence, triggering an outburst of verbal violence towards

---

[3] Cf. Bennett's analysis of organisational autocracy and democracy:

Since Parent–Child is the primary transaction of our institutions, we populate society with people lacking a strong sense of personal integrity and of responsibility for others and their group. Social products of our society are more comfortable being either dependent or rebellious. The family, religion, school, military and business are all authority-obedient systems. . . This is why advocates of industrial democracy often discover that the majority of workers when given full responsibility for their work site look to others for answers. In order to build responsible work teams, companies will have to undo the work of the public schools that taught individuals to be dependent rather than independent. (BENNETT 1978, PP67–8).

the player from the other person. The player then wails, "Why does this always happen to me?"—an all too rhetorical question.

Schlemiel

While the purpose of the Kick Me player is to get punished, the purpose of the Schlemiel player is to get forgiveness. The Schlemiel may infuriate others with displays of clumsiness, sloppiness and general life-incompetence, but this outrage dissolves into indulgent forgiveness as the Schlemiel turns on the "ain't I cute and how could you yell at me?" non-verbals. Many humans, and also pets, excel at this.

Corner

The player sets someone else up so that the person is damned if she does and damned if she doesn't. Corner players ask, "Have you stopped beating your wife?" type questions (of course the correct answer to such a question is "At what?").

Now I've got you, you son of a bitch (NIGYSOB)

The NIGYSOB player also sets people up, although in situations where there is a correct answer or way of doing things, but the player has conveniently neglected to tell others the requisite minimum information, so that they must inevitably fail. When this happens, the NIGYSOB player can deliver a sanctimonious "you really are totally useless" barrage to the other person.

Rapo

This was originally applied by Berne only to women (just as Harried was only applied to housewives). This is not only sexist, but too narrow an application of an illuminating model of behaviour. Rapo is basically enticing someone into a situation, sexual or non-sexual, with come-ons and provocativeness, and when the other player indicates a desire for greater involvement, the Rapo player can self-righteously say "what kind of a girl/boy/accountant/burglar, etc. do you think I am?" Such a set-up game obviously has much in common with NIGYSOB and Corner.

Wooden leg

Many people have handicaps, both real and imagined; either by individual effort, or with help from others, many can transcend those handicaps. Some, however, choose to use the real or imagined handicap as an excuse, to gain sympathy and pardon inaction—"what do you expect of someone with a wooden leg/wrong sex/wrong race, etc.?" Berne notes that Wooden Leg is often played in legal situations, where people may (not always without justification) try to avoid legal consequences of their actions by making an insanity plea ("what do you expect from someone not in control of themselves?") or an ideological plea ("what do you expect from someone who lives in a society like ours?"). Hypochondriacs are also great players of Wooden Leg. The obverse of Wooden Leg is a game called Rickshaw—"if they only had (rickshaws) (duckbill platypuses) (girls who spoke ancient Egyptian) around this town, I would never have got into this mess."

Courtroom

Courtroom is most commonly seen when two or more children appeal to a parent or parents to settle a dispute, placing the parent(s) in the role of a judge in a courtroom: "She did this to me!" "No, he did this to me!" Husbands and wives may play courtroom with a family friend or relative, or employees may play it with a supervisor, or unions and management may play it with arbitrators, and so on. This is not to trivialise or denigrate real conflict; real conflict over substantive issues occurs all the time. With Courtroom, as with all games, it is wise however to apply this rough rule: if the transaction occurs once without a satisfactory resolution, then that's just too bad; if it occurs twice, then that's a coincidence; if it occurs three or more times, over minutes or decades, you are wise to suspect that a game is being played. Courtroom players are often projecting their own guilt on to others, or simply attacking first, hoping that some mud will stick and that they will be able to shout down the innocent or less guilty party. Like the child who throws a tantrum in order not to be ignored, Courtroom players are basically saying to the third party: "We're fighting, why don't you come and break us up (and thus not ignore us)?"

Debtor

Debtor is an extremely common game. Basically, it entails running up lots of debts—mortgages, time payments, credit cards—in a pattern of behaviour that is very similar to that of compulsive gambling (see Cops and Robbers, below). Berne notes that taking on massive debts, usually by a young male entering marriage, is a rite of passage in societies as diverse as New Guinea and America; the celebration occurs, however, when the person takes on the debts, rather than when they are repaid.

We all need necessities, by definition, but we all want luxuries, and we are subjected to massive pressure by advertisers to ensure that we consume to and often beyond the best of our ability. We sometimes go on spending binges because we are stroke-deprived, but often also because we like the thrill of the chase, the combat between creditors playing "try and get away with it" and debtors playing "try and collect". Also, there may be the consolation of being trapped into a victim role in life ("if it weren't for the debts") which simplifies life experience and means that the player doesn't have to be responsible for changing her circumstances (see "If it weren't for you", below). Financial counsellors working with "Creditaholics'" playing Debtor often have a great deal of difficulty in changing the behaviour of game players, because the counsellors are not aware that a game is being played; they feel that it is enough to offer rational advice (of course, if such counsellors are aware of irrational or a-rational game-playing, and persist with purely "rational" advice, they may themselves be playing "I'm only trying to help you").

Cops and Robbers

Berne distinguishes between professional criminals (whose Adult wants to win and make money, and never moves unless the crime is a sure thing) and amateurs (whose Child secretly wants to lose, and thus confirm the status of victim). The amateur playing Cops and Robbers is basically saying to the world, "see if you can catch me"; when the C&R player inevitably botches it, he consoles himself with typical victim self-talk, such as "I almost got away with it" and "I've always been a loser". The C&R burglar, for example, rather than just getting the goods, indulges in gratuitous acts of vandalism, leaving bodily secretions and excretions on clothes, in beds and baths, etc. This is particularly notable with that sad deviant of our times, the teenage burglar with a drug habit to support (see "Alcoholic/Addict" below).

The professional bank robber may take great pains to avoid violence, preferring the calculated risk of gaol rather than being injured or killed; the C&R player, on the other hand, is spoiling for a fight. Similar self-destructive behaviour—"proving" that life is unfair, that you can't win—is often seen with other "clumsy" criminals, playing variations on C&R—"Auditors and Robbers" (embezzlers), "Customs and Robbers" (smugglers), "Shops and Robbers" (shopstealers), "Great Men and Nobodies" (assassins).

The professional gambler knows that the house (and Adult percentage players) always win in the long run; the compulsive gambler, like the C&R player, often plays from an Adapted Child position of self-hate ("this is a mug's game"), and even when she wins, cannot make the rational Adult decision to get out, but will continue to gamble until ("tragically") her "luck" changes and she loses the lot (and possibly more than the lot).

One of the main motivations for playing games is simply to avoid boredom in one's life, and the tacky glamour of various deviant lifestyles, where the victim's dream comes true (failure is success), is a powerful motivator for many people.

Alcoholic/Addict

The person addicted to alcohol and/or drugs is also playing a victim game. The player is basically saying to society, "See how bad I've been; see if you can stop me". There are a number of persecutors available, particularly where drugs are involved, to confirm the player's role of a glamorous deviant. Rescuers are also plentiful, people who are "only trying to help", particularly as society gives increasing sanction to the idea of alcoholism as an organic disease. While this idea of alcoholism as a disease is not proven, the widespread notion that it has been proven gives the alcoholic a chance to play Wooden Leg ("What else can you expect from someone who's sick?" "Hand me my medicine, please."). Real and not-so-real perceptions of the stresses we all live under (the threat of war, pollution, crime, etc.) often give permission for the drug addicts to cop the Ideological Plea ("What can you expect from someone who lives in a society like this?").

Like Schlemiel, where the pleasure of making a mess is surpassed by the pleasure of obtaining forgiveness, the Alcoholic/Addict player is in it not so much for the pleasure of the bender or hit (which in fact is often not at all pleasurable) but for the pleasure/pain of being forgiven by relatives, social workers, psychiatrists, etc. The Alcoholic/Addict player also derives pleasure from indulging in pastimes with fellow Addicts/Alcoholics ("I was more adventurous, I had a whisky with an egg and rat's blood/speedball of heroin and cocaine." "You think *that's* a hangover/bad trip/flashback, well, let me tell you about...."). Such pastimes—"Mine is bigger than yours" and "Technique"—are played by all of us in different situations, but usually not to such self-destructive effect as when played by the Alcoholic/Addict player ("See, I'm killing myself—why don't you try and stop me—and prove that I'm a tragic hero and you're a sucker—or persecute me—and prove that I'm a tragic hero and you're a villain."). As with all game playing, the Alcoholic/Addict is willing to step up the stakes so high merely to achieve recognition—stroke me negatively if you must (abuse, assault, dismissal, imprisonment, contempt, slow-motion murder) but *never* ignore me.

If it weren't for you

The dynamics of IIWFY are shown in the second ulterior transaction diagram in Figure 5.4. At the social level, a domineering husband tells his wife that she must stay home and take care of the house, while the rebellious wife counters this by saying, "If it weren't for you, I could be out having fun". At the psychological level, however, things are quite different. The dominant husband is in fact terrified of being alone, while the last thing the wife really wants to do is go out and have fun. "If it weren't for you" is just the propaganda of the willing slave, who is terrified of freedom. Berne suggests that people choose their partners in life and work because those partners will satisfy deep-felt needs. Thus, the IIWFY player here has deliberately chosen a tyrant for a husband. If either or both players here called the other's bluff, then the game would collapse—possibly into a healthier, game-free relationship, possibly into a disastrous denouement. The IIWFY player takes a victim role, and consoles herself with a rich fantasy life (for example, after losing an argument, which is often, such a person might fantasise "What I should have said was...).

Permission

This is the opposite of IIWFY, and it is similar also to "Why don't you ... yes but". The Permission player appears to seek information from others in a rational way, that is, is initiating an Adult–Adult transaction. What the player really wants however is a Child–Parent transaction, wherein permission is given to do something. The Permission player may in the process deliberately distort the nature of the alternatives:

> "Gee, I just don't know what to do, Doris. That hunky new supervisor wants me to work back tonight, and I think it's more than just professional interest. I suppose I really should say no, and go home and cook another meal for boring old George."

Doris, if she is not aware of the game, or if she is also consciously playing the game (but does not want to break it) may suggest that the Permission-seeker in fact stay back—she may even become an accomplice, and telephone George on the player's behalf. If things work out fine with the supervisor, the player is happy because a solution has been given and she has put it into practice (thus, she is not playing WDY-YB)—and her conscience (Punishing Parent) is assuaged, because another person has given permission. If things do not work out however, with the supervisor and/or husband, Doris might be abused by the player for giving bad advice. Thus, the player's position, as with most game-playing, is I win—You lose, irrespective of the outcome. A variation on Permission is when the player gives, rather than seeks permission, even though this permission is not explicit. If a king is having trouble with an archbishop, and rhetorically declaims "will no one rid me of this meddlesome priest?", then his courtiers will correctly decode the game message: kill the archbishop, and if caught, you're on your own; kill the archbishop, not get caught, and subtly reveal this to the king without actually admitting responsibility, and be rewarded.

Gee, you're wonderful, professor

GYWP is also known as Groupie. A person in a less powerful position (student, patient, interviewer, fan, subordinate) may pay compliments to a person in a more powerful position (teacher, doctor/therapist, interviewee, actor/musician/artist, supervisor). If the flattery is done well (or if the more powerful person is simply massively egocentric and insensitive), then the less powerful person gets on closer, sometimes more intimate terms. Once the GYWP player has proven to himself that the other person is merely mortal and/or has used the person to advance his interests, his adulation will cease. The player may then move on to other more powerful people. This is similar to WDY-YB, except that here flattery, rather than questioning, is used in a Child–Parent transaction that proves that all dominant people (i.e. parent-surrogates) are fools, after all.

Let's you and him fight
The LYAHF player basically sets up two other people to fight, and then sits back to watch the fireworks. The player is often a skilled manipulator of the rumour mill or grapevine, ensuring that innuendo and scuttlebutt motivates the two suckers. This is important, because the player will be able to disclaim all responsibility for causing conflict. If open prompting of the two suckers is unavoidable, the player, if confronted and accused of maliciousness, slips straight into a game of "I'm only trying to help". Seductresses (and seducers), journalists and children excel at this one.

Uproar
This game has much in common with Courtroom, and can in fact lead to that other game. On the surface, Uproar seems to be an Adult–Adult question and answer session, but as tempers flare and both parties storm out of the room, it is obvious that this in fact is not the case. Uproar is played by two players spoiling for a fight, and often the game becomes ritualised and occurs over months or years.

Ain't it awful
AIA is a game played by most of us, at least in its milder form. In its Parent–Parent form, it may take the form of a "Nowadays" game:
    Jimmy (age 9): Gee, but these kids are spoiled nowadays! When we were younger, we didn't have computer games to play with.
    Jenny (age 8):   Yeah, these kids don't know what it's like to go without.
In its Adult–Adult form, AIA may take the form of detailed discussions of medical problems, where the players try to outdo each other with demonstrations of My Pain is Greater than Yours, all the time demonstrating of course that life is terrible and that we have no choice but to tragically endure.

    In its Child–Child form, AIA is usually played with the catch-cry "Look what they're doing to us now!" This is faintly paranoid, as "they"—the government, top management on the 23rd floor, the Russians, the Satanists, the stars, fate, the railways, etc.—are seen to be totally in control. This is convenient, because it means that AIA players do not have to be solution-oriented—there is *no* solution, the game-players would have us believe.

Psychiatry
Psychiatry as a game (as opposed to the profession) is used by game-players to control others. It is an occupational hazard of studying theories of behaviour, such as transactional analysis. A little learning can be a dangerous thing, and the Psychiatry player may start to tell others that they should control their Punishing Parents, or that they are playing games such as Blemish or Alcoholic (or that their body language gives them away, or that they are displaying type A stress symptoms, etc., etc.). Rather than using this

information to help others, or suggesting that others see professional therapists rather than amateurs, the Psychiatry player blinds others with pseudo-science. The game has a lot in common with I'm Only Trying to Help You. (The truly skilled Psychiatry player, of course, will get in first with accusing others of playing Psychiatry before being accused of this herself.)

Happy to help

Most of the games discussed in TA are harmful; a few, however, are not so harmful, and Happy To Help is one of these. The HTH player helps others— gives money, advice, boosts people's careers, and so on. If games are notable for their ulterior transactions, what is ulterior here? Usually, the player feels guilt about previous actions, and tries to expiate this guilt by helping others (cf. the ego defence mechanism of Undoing). As Berne notes, the enemies of the HTH player attack their motives and minimise their actions while the player's friends are grateful for their actions and minimise their motives.

Games, then, are basically ulterior transactions. There are many more games that people play, and if you wish to study further, try reading Berne (1983), and Ernst (1974).

Many people find diagrammatic expositions of games easier to understand than verbal descriptions. Try and identify the games shown in Box 5.D. You may find it useful to diagram some other games discussed here, and possibly some games you are aware of that are *not* discussed here. Remember, non-verbal communication is often as important, and sometimes more important, than verbal communication, especially with ulterior transactions.

Games and roles: The drama triangle

How do people use games? Do they always stick with one or two, or do they vary them, playing some at work and some at non-work, playing some one minute/month/decade and playing others another minute/month/decade? Other transactional analysis concepts, such as time structuring, life positions and scripts, are useful for putting game-playing in context. Of more immediate relevance, however, is the concept of the Drama Triangle, or the Persecutor–Rescuer–Victim (PRV) Triangle, which shows how people adapt and change roles in their transactions with others, and how these roles affect game-playing.

Karpman (1968) suggests that game-players are, at any time, playing one of three roles: that of a persecutor, that of a rescuer, or that of a victim. Although it is conceivable that one person can play a game by herself (but between ego states), it is much more usual for a person to play with another person. Thus a persecutor needs a victim, and so does a rescuer. A rescuer may try and control a persecutor who is persecuting a victim. As surely as a masochist (a lover of pain) and a sadist (a person who loves giving pain) need each other, so too do role-players. Role-players may in fact switch roles continually, moving around the drama triangle (Fig. 5.5). An example of such switching of roles might be the following trialogue:

Daughter (as persecutor of Father): Why won't you let me go to the concert? Don't tell me you can't afford it again! God, it's so embarrassing, living with Mr Cheap!

Father (as victim): Gee, I'm sorry honey, but I *am* broke. I just don't seem to be able to give you things that your girlfriends get.

BOX 5.D: Identify these games

Analyse these games in terms of
Social stimulus (SS)
Social response (SR)
Psychological stimulus (PS)
Psychological response (PR)

A: Coming for lunch, B?
B: No, you go with the others. Someone's got to finish this work off (*sighs*).

A: Got that report, B?
B: Oh, yes, it's around here somewhere . . .
A: Is this it? With the coffee stains everywhere? You always muck things up, don't you?

A (*shouting*):
   Where have you been?
B: Out! Leave me alone!
A: Who have you been out with?
B: None of your business! (*Exits, slams door*)
A: These damn kids! (*Exits, slams door*)

A: You've mucked this up!
B: Why are you so hostile? Are you hostile to everyone?
A: Yeah, I'm damned hostile whenever anyone loses money due to incompetence!
B: Perhaps you see me as a father figure, and you have to rebel against me? Your body language shows that you're not quite sure of what you're saying.

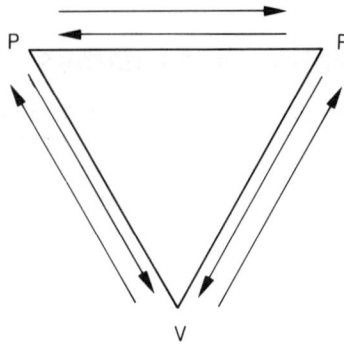

Fig 5.5 *The drama triangle*

Mother (rescues Father, persecutes daughter):	How dare you speak to your father like that! We've broken our backs for you! The only reason I'm working is to pay for *your* education and for the house extensions so *you* won't feel so cramped! Get to your room, madam!
Daughter (in room, as victim):	It's just not fair! They send me to a posh school, but won't let me socialise with my friends. Everyone at school laughs at me 'cause I just stay at home! Why does this always happen to me?
Father (as rescuer to Daughter):	Now don't tell your mother, but here's twenty dollars. Let's call it an advance on your pocket money. It's only money, after all.
Father (returning to Mother as persecutor):	Mary, I think you came down on that girl too hard. She just wants to have fun, and she's only young once.
Mother (as victim):	Well, I can't do anything right, can I? I was only trying to help you. I suppose I'm just a failure as a mother and a wife.
Daughter (reappearing, now as rescuer of Mother and persecutor of Father):	Hey Dad, give it a rest, mum's just a lot more tired than you are, that's all.

(Adapted from Jongeward and James 1978)

Games can be understood in terms of roles. Table 5.3 shows how the games mentioned in this chapter can be understood in terms of Persecutor, Rescuer and Victim roles. Classification of games into one of these three roles is by no means watertight. Thus a Kick Me or Schlemiel player, in order to get a persecuting response from someone else, may be positively persecutory in the way they relentlessly provoke others; a Rescuer playing I'm Only Trying to Help may in fact be playing a Persecutor role by continually feeding her victim wrong information; the Psychiatry player may come on as a

Table 5.3 Games as drama triangle roles

Persecutor	Rescuer	Victim
Why Don't You . . . Yes But	I'm Only Trying to Help You	Harried
Psychiatry Blemish	Happy to Help	Kick me
Corner		Schlemiel
Now I've Got You, You Son		Wooden Leg
of a Bitch (NIGYSOB)		Debtor
Rapo		Cops and Robbers
Courtroom		Alcoholic/Addict
If It Weren't For You		Permission
Gee You're Wonderful,		Ain't It Awful
Professor		
Let's You and Him Fight		

Rescuer; the Why Don't You . . . Yes But. . . player may initially project the appearance of a Victim; and so on. Determination of the actual role being played often depends upon non-verbal factors, such as gesture and posture, inflection and phrasing: thus, the Mother's final Victim lines in the family squabble on page 152 could well be read sarcastically, giving the lines a Persecutor feeling.

Time-structuring

Do people play games twenty-four hours a day, or is there something else to life? Berne suggested that in the time between birth and death, we hunger for strokes and also for structure. Structuring our time means that we will avoid boredom, the experience of which is as bad as being ignored. In TA, time is seen as being structured in six different ways.

Withdrawal

Withdrawing is temporarily choosing to be ignored, temporarily choosing to not receive strokes from others. We might do this by daydreaming, watching television or films, sleeping, "tuning out" of a conflict or a boring situation, simply being alone, and so on. This can be healthy (for example, having a daydream while a boring speaker drones on) or it can be unhealthy (for example, when a person withdraws almost permanently, leading a figuratively or literally autistic life).

Rituals

Rituals are safe, predictable and socially sanctioned complementary trans-actions that have a formal or stereotyped aspect to them. The following are rituals: ceremonies, etiquette, church services, parades, or simply exchanging "Hi, how are you?" type greetings. Rituals vary enormously from culture to culture, and sub-culture to sub-culture.

Pastimes

Pastimes are similar to rituals, except that they tend to be more informal and it is often difficult to tell when a pastime has ended. People indulge in pastimes when they gossip and chat about the weather, politics, fashion, inflation, sports. Games like Ain't It Awful can also be seen as a pastime, as the transactions may be simply complementary, rather than ulterior. They may only be ulterior to the extent that, while discussing a phenomenon or problem, such as kids today, the weather, or a political scandal, pastimers have no intention of actually doing anything about such things, and will promptly withdraw strokes from anyone who is insensitive enough to suggest that action be taken.

Activities

We structure time with activity when we work, devote ourselves to hobbies or sports, or perform duties and chores; that is, when we direct our energies to external reality and we are interested in achieving tangible results. While activities are obviously the most practically useful method of time structuring, there can be too much of a good thing here, as when a workaholic cannot bear to have fun or share intimacy or even be alone (this of course verges on game-playing).

Games

A game is "an ongoing series of complementary ulterior transactions which can lead to a well-defined, predictable outcome" (Berne). As we have seen, most game-playing is quite destructive. Games are best understood as occurring halfway between pastimes and intimacy. They are usually transmitted through cultures, specifically through families. Games, Berne felt, were largely unavoidable, therefore it is best to try and concentrate attention upon good games (such as Happy to Help), where the social contribution flowing from the games outweighs the complexity of the motivations of the game-player. This pessimism about the inevitability of games is not shared by all proponents of TA.

Intimacy

Intimacy is basically sharing thoughts and feelings with others to the maximum, game-free extent. It is the most rewarding, but also the most risky way of structuring time. Intimacy can be physical or verbal, but it can be unpleasant or pleasant. Intimacy might be sharing a confidence, silently comforting someone, sex, an emotional showdown, a display of trust, smiling at a stranger in the audience at a moving point in a play. Intimacy, together with spontaneity and awareness, can lead to increased *autonomy*, which basically means being aware of the degree of social programming that can pre-determine your life, and then transcending that programming to lead a life that minimises game-playing and maximises intimacy.

We all have different mixes of time structuring in our lives.[4] Two different people might structure their lives as shown in Figure 5.6.

How do you structure your life? How does someone you know structure theirs? How would you *like* to structure your life? Sketch your own pie charts to depict these states.

---

[4] Ways of time-structuring are not mutually exclusive. Thus, Woollams and Brown point out that a woman may *withdraw* from her husband in order to avoid his complaining and busy herself by washing the dishes (*activity*), while another person might attend a religious service (*ritual*) in order to maintain a guilt *racket* or *game* (WOOLLAMS AND BROWN 1979, P.89).

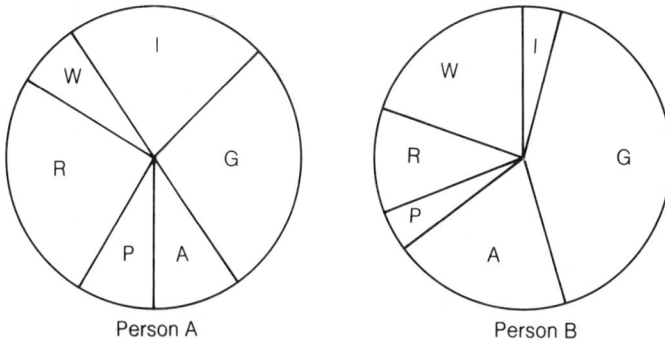

Fig **5.6** *Two different approaches to time structuring*

Life positions: I'm OK, you're OK

The ways in which we choose to structure time depends upon two other concepts known as *life positions* and *scripts*. Life positions and scripts are just two ways of looking at the same thing—the programming that we all receive in the first few years of our life and the extent to which that programming pre-determines the mix of happiness and unhappiness in the rest of our lives. There are four basic life positions that people adopt. These are positions or philosophies that tell us what we think of ourselves and what we think of others. The positions are:

1. *I'm OK, you're OK (I+Y+)*. People who have this attitude have a basically healthy self-concept. They are happy with their strengths and weaknesses, without being either complacent or egocentric. They are self-critical and wish to grow and change, but their self-criticism is not so extreme as to be paralysing, and thus counter-productive. They relate in a similar way to others, respecting the individuality of others, as well as others' rights to disagree and behave differently. The I'm OK, You're OK person is a problem-solver, not a game-player, and works with others to achieve goals that could not be achieved by individuals acting alone.

2. *I'm OK, you're not OK (I+Y−)*. People who have this attitude feel basically superior towards others. They loathe others for not being like themselves, and suspect anyone who in turn seems to be superior to them. There is more than a touch of the paranoid about I+Y− people. Such people may slip into Persecutor roles, but may also play Rescuer (you poor incompetent, let me solve your problems for you), and even play a type of Victim game, such as Harried or Cops and Robbers.

3. *I'm not OK, you're OK (I−Y+)*. People who hold this attitude feel basically inferior towards others. Everyone else is more competent, articulate and worthy of praise. The I−Y+ person often is depressed, fearful and guilty, and often plays Victim games like Kick Me and Schlemiel.

4. *I'm not OK, you're not OK (I−Y−)*. Whereas the I−Y+ person at least feels that other people can make it, the I−Y− person sees no hope at all. All is futility, you might as well give up. People with this position often end up in institutions and may commit acts of extreme violence towards others and themselves.

Table 5.4 How life position influences employee behaviour

AN EMPLOYEE → ... when his life position is:	Communicates	Accepts delegation	Develops	Handles disagreement	Solves problems	Spends time	Is moved to act	Feels toward others
I'm OK—You're OK	Openly	Readily	Independently, learns willingly.	By seeking clarification and mutual resolution.	By consulting others, trusting himself.	Taking necessary action and producing.	On assignment or initiative.	Equal
I'm Not OK—You're OK	Defensively Self-deprecatingly	Timidly	Slowly. Needs reassurance and coaching.	By perceiving differences in opinion as evidence of his inadequacy.	By relying almost completely on others.	Brooding or over-compensating in constant activity.	By praise or admonition.	Inferior
I'm OK—You're Not OK	Defensively Aggressively	By procrastinating, bickering, and bargaining	With difficulty. Learning is blocked.	By placing blame on others.	By unilaterally rejecting others' ideas.	Boasting, provoking others, playing persecutor.	When forced; may demand official instructions.	Superior
I'm Not OK—You're Not OK	Hostilely Abruptly	By trying to beg off, delegating upward. Unwillingly accepts responsibility	With difficulty. Withdraws and repeats errors.	By escalating the conflict; involving a third party.	By succumbing to problems.	Withdrawing; playing a variety of games.	By reprimands or threats.	Despondent, alienated

Source: Reprinted, by permission of the publisher, from *Transactional Analysis on the Job* by Charles Albano, *Communicating with Subordinates*, edited by Thomasine Rendero, p.29, © 1974 by AMACOM, a division of American Management Associations, New York. All rights reserved.

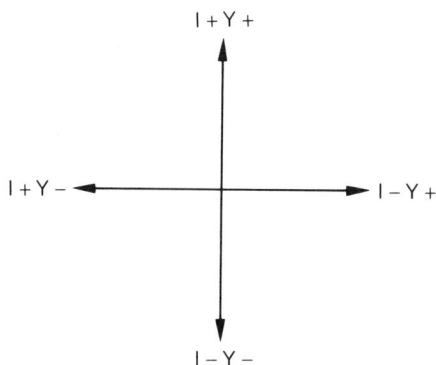

Fig 5.7 *Map of life positions*

Table 5.4 shows how life positions can influence the behaviour of people on the job. We choose these life positions, as we choose our scripts, in the first few years of life. This time of our life is of course "pre-rational"—our Adult ego state has not yet formed, and our view of the world is often distorted. It's as if we turned over the driving of the car to a three-year-old child—not a very wise thing to do. Yet the life positions chosen by people at such a pre-responsible age to a large extent determine how we go through life. Irrational, unfair, but that's the way it is, or at least that is what transactional analysis specialists say it is. To continue the driving metaphor, it is useful to consider the four positions as compass directions on a map (Fig. 5.7). We tend to proceed in the one direction, perhaps veering away from an extreme point now, perhaps making side journeys,[5] but fundamentally moving in the one direction.

Are we born feeling I+Y+, or do we feel something else? There is controversy within the TA camp on this issue. Berne felt that we are born princes, and get turned into frogs, that is, our initial life position is I+Y+. Harris disagrees with Berne, suggesting that our initial life position is I−Y+. Harris suggests that is so because, as newborns, we are terribly vulnerable, and feel weak and inferior to the giants moving about us. Harris' position is criticised by pro-Berne writers who dismiss Harris' view as the "original sin" view.

Whatever our first position is, TA theorists of all persuasions are fairly optimistic about our being able to move towards the most desirable position—I'm OK, you're OK.

Scripts

When we are young, we have ideas about what we want to be when we grow up. As the life positions concept suggests, however, we sometimes develop general, and often negative and self-destructive, ideas about ourselves and the world. If we are "programmed", where does the programming come from?

---

[5] Thus a person might relate to his spouse in an I+Y− way, with his boss in an I−Y− way and with his peer group in an I+Y+ way.

It comes from the culture we are born into, our family, our teachers and mentors, from the myths of fairy tales, religious mythology, media heroes, sporting heroes, peer groups, and so on. We learn from these role models what it is to be human, and what reality is. If all the world is a stage, as Shakespeare suggests, then we each play multiple roles on that stage. TA uses this theatrical metaphor to develop the idea of scripts. If our life position is I+Y+, then we are game-free, and we are script-free. If, however, our life position is I−Y+, I+Y− or I−Y−, we play games and act out scripts. Scripts are, if you like, patterns of games (and are thus similar to the persecutor-rescuer–victim roles). You might think of games as tactics, and scripts as strategies, in the game of life (tactics and strategies that are not, needless to say, very healthy). If "when I grow up I want to be. . ." is our career plan, then "my script is. . ." is our *life plan*, but a plan that means our self-image is a cliché, a stereotype, shackled to the past and denying our true potential.

The Pygmalion effect

Is programming really that powerful? Surely we have some resources to ensure that our personalities are not totally moulded by others when we are too helpless to change their dominance? We probably do have personal resources, but they do not greatly modify programming. The images and expectations held of us by others, no matter how irrational or undesirable, are powerful shapers of our personalities. Consider for example the so-called Pygmalion effect. Pygamlion was a Greek sculptor who so loved a statue he carved that it came to life. This effect has been noted in experiments when teachers are (wrongly) informed of the character and potential of a group of students—"these students are stupid", "this group is really bright". The groups of students involved are in fact of largely equal ability, within and among groups. At the end of a period of teaching, however (say, a year), distinct differences are notable: the "stupid" group really is behaving stupidly, the "bright" group is turning in top performance. What has happened? The teachers, like Pygmalion the sculptor, have changed the behaviour of the students according to the teachers' unconscious perceptions: "these ones are stupid, therefore I will teach them in this way, letting them know verbally and non-verbally that my expectations for them are low"; "these ones are bright, therefore. . ." In other words, the situation becomes a self-fulfilling prophecy. This Pygmalion effect has been noted not only in educational situations, but work situations as well (Jongeward and Seyer 1978).

Messages from others shape our personalities

We get a series of messages from our culture, our sub-cultures, our families, our friends, the media, and so on. They are not always spelled out clearly, but are rather strong for all that. Some examples would be:

Winning is the only thing that counts.
You're just like your father.
With your gift of the gab, you could be a lawyer.
The Lord made you female to have children.
We Irish (Jews, Italians, etc.) have always been known for good deeds (good fighters, brains, etc.)
You Irish (Jews, Italians, etc.) have always been drunkards (wastrels, cowards, etc.).
Play around, but don't marry that kind.

You'll never amount to anything.
And they all lived happily ever after.
Why can't you be good with your hands, like your brother?
Men in this family don't cry.
Real men don't eat quiche.
Real men smoke Neanderthal Cigars.
Play with this doll, and stay away from those dirty little girls.
If your mother doesn't buy you this, you won't be popular.

Not all of these messages are unhealthy, of course, but we take them all in, without discriminating or filtering. At an early age, we don't have any standards or criteria by which we can reject and accept things. When we are getting our programming—most of which is a parent-to-child transaction at this early stage—we learn a series of do's and don'ts. This series helps to develop our own Parent ego state, our ethical norms. So long as these do's and don'ts emanate from our Nurturing Parent later in life, we do not have much to fear. If however, they emanate from the Punishing Parent, then we are in trouble. Some "do" messages are:

1. *Do be perfect*. Strive for impossible goals and pursue them in an obsessive, self-defeating way. Punish yourself when you inevitably fail with the motto "you should do better".

2. *Do hurry up*. Always be on the move, someone will catch you being idle, and an idle mind is the devil's playground. Squirm, jump, interrupt, sleep faster, punish yourself with the motto "You'll never get it done".

3. *Do try hard*. Attempt everything, never relax, be a chip off the old block, make us proud, never be lazy, you're not working unless you're moving, ulcers and wrinkles are medals in the battle of life; punish yourself with the motto "you've got to try".

4. *Do be strong*. Show no mercy—they won't, the show must go on, triumph is spelled "try" with "umph" added, laughing on the outside but crying on the inside, don't care, know that they can't make you care; punish yourself with the motto "you can't let them know you're weak".

5. *Do please me*. Serve others totally, you owe us everything, never think of yourself, prove you love me, when I say "jump", say "how high?"; punish yourself with the mottoes "you're not good enough" and "make others feel good".

Some "don't" messages are:

1. *Don't exist/don't be*. Here, the message, verbal and/or non-verbal, is "I wish you'd never been born". This message will occur in the first year of life unless its opposite is given. The person learns what rejection is, and carries it all her life. The child may be physically abused or psychologically teased. Instead of learning optimism and trust, the person learns pessimism and mistrust. Wagner (1981) suggests that people with this "don't" message may become self-destructive, for example excessive eating, drinking, smoking, reckless driving, engaging in dangerous work or leisure activities, picking the "wrong" people to confront or fight; when things go too well, such a person may feel nervous until he can make things go wrong again. The person decides at a painfully early age that "Maybe it's OK if I survive, if I don't really live".

2. *Don't feel.* The message here is don't feel sensations, don't feel emotions. The infant wants to explore all senses—sight, hearing, taste, touch, smell, and whatever other senses there are. The infant may, however, be punished for exploring her environment and her body, learning that the full range of sensations are sinful. She may also learn not to express feelings such as being angry, being sad, being glad or being afraid. Thus the Natural Child ego state gets eaten away and replaced by the managed emotions of the Adapted Child. The child's parents may make it a habit never to show emotion to each other in front of children: the child thus gets the idea that all adults are cool, thinking beings, and thus the child grows up to imitate this (thus scripts and games are passed from generation to generation). "Don't feel" thus leads to the crushing loneliness of "don't get close".

3. *Don't think.* If children are not playing the game of "why is the sky blue?" (let's ask so many questions it drives them nuts), then questioning is a healthy activity: the child learns about her environment, and her Adult ego state is developed. If parents punish such questioning, however, not taking the time to explain processes and concepts, the child may learn it is no use asking about reality, that's just the way it is. Women traditionally have been scripted not to think (women's intuition; women feel, not think; woman driver). Steiner (1971) suggests that alcoholics and addicts follow a "don't think" injunction, getting stoned so that they won't have to analyse things rationally.

4. *Don't be you.* Children may get messages from their parents and culture that all is not well: you're the wrong sex, you remind me of your no-good father, why don't you look like your father's side of the family?, you Neanderthals aren't as racially pure as we Cro-Magnons, you're so skinny, you walk funny, how dare you think differently to us, just do it the way we show you, who cares what you think? People who don't recover from this type of programming, Wagner suggests, may spend the rest of their life sensing that they are in the wrong body, the wrong relationship, the wrong profession, and constantly seek out (and change) gurus, role models, memberships, labels, bumper stickers, hairstyles, clothing—anything to give a sense of identity.

5. *Don't be a child.* Telling children to "grow up!" and "act your age!" can be useful cues for them to give up inappropriate immature behaviour. But we are only young once, and children should be allowed to be children, advice which is lost on parents who ram this injunction down the throat of their child (usually the eldest child—you must be a substitute parent and help us). People who receive this "don't" find it very hard to have fun without massive guilt feelings—to indulge their Natural Child. They are often workaholics, and try to make leisure either non-existent or else very hard work.

6. *Don't grow up.* This programming is often given to the youngest child in the family. The child is loved for being cute, is regarded as a pet, and hence parents have a vested interest in keeping the child an infant (doing everything for her, not preparing her for adult behaviour, such as sex and moving out).

7. *Don't succeed.* Children and employees often learn that, to get strokes, you should fail, because then someone will show you how to do it (i.e. if you do it right, they will take it for granted). This "don't" is really just another way of saying "do be perfect".

All of these do's and don'ts can add up to a script, or harmful life plan. Our script might be a melodrama, in which we are hero or heroine, or where we wait for a hero or heroine to save us; a tragedy, in which we are losers, victims of a fatal flaw; a slapstick comedy, in which we play the buffoon; a situation comedy, in which we play clichés like the henpecked husband, the dizzy blonde, the punk son, the rebellious daughter; a fairy tale, in which we play Mother Hubbard, the Little Red Engine Who Tried, the Big Bad Wolf, Prince Charming; a fable, in which we play the Ant or the Grasshopper, the Boy Who Cried Wolf, the Tortoise or the Hare; a comic book in which we play Superman or Dagwood; a religious myth, in which we play Jesus or Judas. All these images, of course, can be as helpful in defining our identity as they can be harmful in confusing our identity; the key question is, do they help or hinder us in becoming game-free, autonomous and achieving the I+Y+ life position? To a large extent, this depends upon whether the do's and don'ts of our childhood programming were balanced, and preferably out-weighed, by opposing don'ts and do's—*do* feel, *do* think, *don't* think you always have to try and please me, etc.

Putting it all together

If you've made it this far, congratulations. Grasping the gist of TA means learning many terms and concepts (TA's critics, as we shall soon see, say that there are too many terms and concepts). You may find it useful to use a graphic model which integrates most of what we have covered so far. First, there were ego states—the three states of Parent, Adult and Child—which makes up the basis of an individual's personality (Fig. 5.8(a)).

We communicate with others by exchanging strokes, which can be verbal or non-verbal, positive or negative or mixed, conditional or unconditional. This stroke exchange is called a transaction. Hence the study of communication is called "transactional analysis" (Fig. 5.8(b)).

Whether we transact in a complementary, crossed or ulterior way depends on how we structure our time—in withdrawal, ritual, pastimes, activities, games or intimacy. Games can also be understood in terms of three roles—Persecutor, Rescuer and Victim (Fig. 5.8(c)).

How we structure time depends upon our life position and, if we have a script, the type of script we have (Fig. 5.8(d)).

This Chinese-box model is rather clumsy, and inadequate in a number of ways (for example, why not put ego states logically *prior* to life positions?). Nevertheless, it may help to conceptualise and integrate TA.

How can you use TA?

The avowed aim of TA specialists is to help people lead happier and healthier lives. That's not a bad aim, and the techniques they recommend are[6]:

1. Give and accept positive strokes rather than negative strokes.
2. Work with your Natural Child, Adult and Nurturing Parent; give up using your Adapted Child and Punishing Parent.
3. Stop playing games—refuse to play the complementary hand, give an unexpected response.
4. Don't put others down—accept that they are OK.
5. Don't put yourself down—accept that you are OK.

---

[6] Adapted from Jongeward (1976), Jongeward and James (1978).

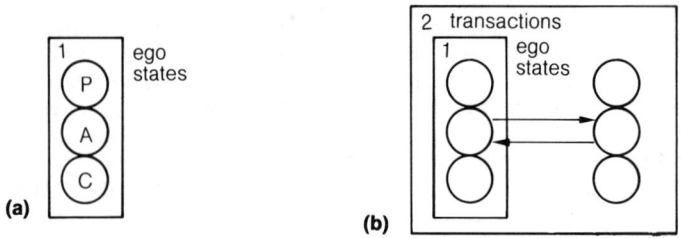

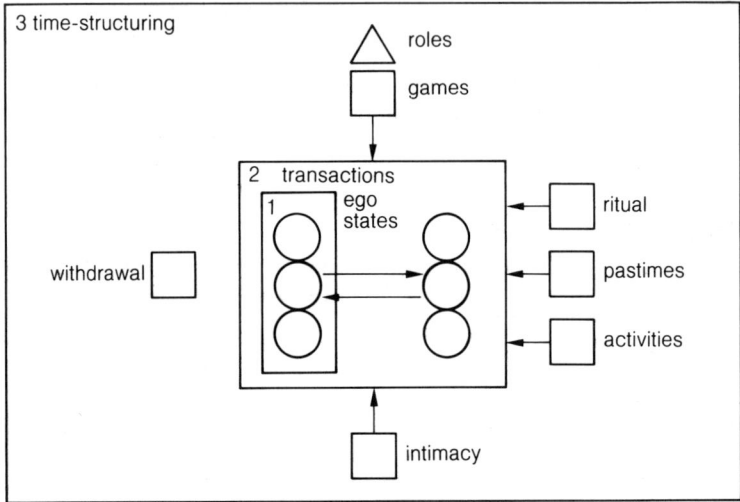

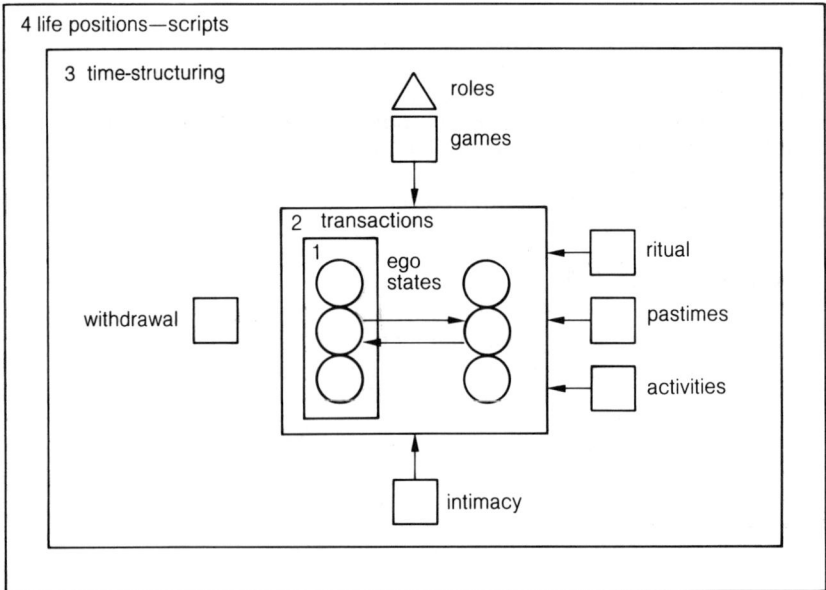

Fig 5.8 *A model of TA*

6. Invest more time in intimacy, activities and fun.
7. Stop playing Rescuer—helping those who don't need help.
8. Stop playing Persecutor—criticising those who don't need it.
9. Stop playing Victim—acting helpless or dependent when you are quite capable of standing on your own two feet.

Transactional analysis: Not entirely OK?

TA is not without its critics—indeed, you might be one of them. The main criticisms of TA are as follows:

1. TA is too slick, too laden with jargon.

This is a paradox, because Eric Berne, in developing TA, wanted a system of psychotherapy that was not saddled with Freudian psychoanalytic jargon. He wanted plain English terms, that were slightly whimsical and lots of fun (i.e. that tickled the Child). TA has been contributed to by many, all of whom have contributed terms and concepts; indeed, many of these terms and concepts have not been covered here, not only for reasons of space, but also to avoid information overload.[7] Thus, many people find TA too gimmicky and confusing, rather than clear.

2. TA is over-optimistic

TA, to many, is like a fairy tale with a happy ending, a toy for happy idiots unaware of the more tragic areas of life. TA practitioners like Berne and Steiner were and are all too aware of the darker side of human nature; it is true, however, that some of TA's popularisers have tried to sanitise and oversimplify.

3. TA is "too American"

This is rather tricky: it is in fact an unconditional negative stroke. Certainly, Americans have churned out some dreadful and banal pop psychology in the past twenty years; but "Americans" are not a monolithic group—pop psychology, or at least the worst kind, gets as unkind a reception inside America as outside it. Certainly, there seem to be American traditions of confessing one's psychological problems in a free and extroverted way that do not travel well to other cultures, where a greater premium is placed upon self-control and little discussion of personal problems (e.g. Australia, Britain). Nevertheless, much of TA is colloquial Freud, yet few people criticise TA for being "too German" (or "too Austrian").

4. TA is manipulative

TA devotees sometimes play the game of Psychiatry using TA terms to tell other people what is wrong with them. Steiner (1974) in particular is critical of the way many people have "ripped off" TA concepts so that salesmen can manipulate clients, employees of banks, airlines and race tracks can "switch troublesome customers into a better ego state", and so on. This, of course, is the age-old story: technique is ripped out of philosophy, and used for ends not entertained in the philosophy. Steiner notes:

> . . . transactional analysis was invented for use as a contractual therapeutic technique. Berne was very suspicious and antagonistic to one-sided situations

---

[7] Terms not discussed here include: stamps, contamination, little professor, rackets, discounting, redecisions, sweatshirts, electrode, pig parent, earshotting.

where one person held all the cards . . . its one-sided use as a tool for behaviour control is an abuse of its potency, similar to slipping a customer a sedative in a coke so that he'll buy a used car. . . (P.12)

5. *TA is just another prop for the status quo*

Rosen, criticising the "psychobabble" of much pop psychology, points out that many psychological theories merely seem to adjust the person to the status quo of society, and that TA is guilty of this as well:

> (people who use TA) aspire to be the Adult who can honestly say "I'm OK, You're OK", as if the only desired outcome of emotional growth should be blanket tolerance towards oneself and others, and not also an increased suspicion of appearances. . . By objectifying mature or rational behaviour as the Adult with its "I'm OK, You're OK" mentality, TA is suggesting that all problems may be solved on the personal level; what the world needs, TA implies, is just more grown-ups who do not challenge the existing order. (ROSEN 1977, P.167)

6. *TA is inconsistent on whether we have free will or not*

TA has a very strong determinist (i.e. anti-free will) bias, which it takes from Freudian psychoanalysis: our personalities are laid down in the first few years of life. Psychoanalysis says that there is not much we can do about this, but TA says that we can, that is, it switches to free will. The only difficulty is that TA then goes to the other extreme: we are presumed to control everything (thus we "choose" game-playing work and marital partners). This not only confuses conscious and unconscious decision-making, but looks like a super-game, a super-Psychiatry if you like: while TA is left looking OK, we are left feeling not OK.

How valid are these criticisms? Only you can answer that. TA OK or not OK? It's up to you.

Summary

Transactional analysis is a method of understanding communication between people in terms of differing parts of our personalities. It is useful to note the development of TA from the original ideas of Freud. Freud argued that the personality developed in the first few years of life, and was divided into three areas—the superego, ego and id. The ego, our conscious self, copes with stressful realities by using various defence mechanisms, some of which may be unconscious in their operation.

Berne developed his model of personality around the Parent, Adult and Child ego states. We can tell whatever ego state a person is in because of the verbal and non-verbal behaviour appropriate to each state. We communicate with other people by giving strokes, which can be verbal or non-verbal, positive, negative or mixed, and conditional or unconditional. Exchange of strokes by two people is the basic transaction of human communication, and transactions can be complementary, crossed or ulterior, and occur at the social or psychological level.

A particular type of ulterior transaction is the game. There are many of these, and most of them are harmful. Games and bad communication can also be understood by the three roles of the drama triangle: persecutor, rescuer and victim.

Games are one of six different ways of structuring time: withdrawal, rituals, pastimes, activities, games and intimacy. The ways in which we structure our time depends upon our life positions and scripts. There are four life positions (I'm OK, You're OK; I'm OK, You're not OK; I'm not OK, You're OK; I'm not OK, You're not OK). Scripts are unconsciously acquired life-plans, often destructive, based upon messages given to us by others.

TA has been criticised for various reasons, including the suggestion that it is slick, manipulative and over-optimistic.

Questions for discussion

1. Write a role-play in which two people each use five or more ego defence mechanisms (e.g. one person asks another to go out on a date, one person argues with a workmate over low productivity in their department).
2. Try this variation on the five chairs exercise (p.139). Write NP (Nurturing Parent), PP (Punishing Parent), A (Adult), NC (Natural Child), AC (Adaptive Child) on five pieces of paper. Put these in a hat or other receptacle.

    Another person sits opposite, able to draw from but not see into the receptacle. Decide on an issue for discussion (e.g. children today have no respect for their elders, there is too much violence and sex on television). The other person draws a slip of paper every 30–60 seconds. Whatever ego state is on the slip, you must role-play it, discussing the issue. Replace the slips each time and do this for 8–12 rounds. Does the sequence affect the flow of ideas and opinions?
3. Think of as many mixed strokes as you can. What effect do mixed strokes have upon people?
4. Devise another ten ulterior transactions where there is a conflict between verbal and non-verbal messages.
5. Write a role-play in which you string together as many games as you can. If you can identify new games, that is, ones not identified here, so much the better.
6. Write a role-play in which you string together as many Persecutor–Rescuer–Victim switches as possible.
7. Analyse a play, TV soap opera, novel, etc. and estimate how time is structured within that fictional world. Construct a six-part pie-chart, and compare it with analyses made of the same work by others.
8. Write a monologue in which one person shifts through all four life positions. Pay attention (e.g. by using video, mirror) to the non-verbal behaviour appropriate to each position. Topics for the monologue might be: preparing for a job interview, rehearsing conversation for a dinner party.
9. What type of "do" and "don't" messages were given to you when younger which have shaped your behaviour in later life?
10. "TA is nothing more than slick, manipulative, dangerous psycho-babble." Discuss.

References

Albano, Charles (1974). *Transactional Analysis on the Job/ Communicating with Subordinates* (ed.) Rendero, Thomasine. (Amacom: New York).
Appignanensi, F. and Zarato, O. (1979). *Freud for Beginners.* (Writers and Readers Press: London).

Barnes, Graham (1979). *Transactional Analysis After Eric Berne: Three Schools of Thought.* (Houghton Mifflin: New York).
Bennett, Dudley (1976). *T.A. and the Manager.* (Amacom: New York).
Berne, Eric (1964). *The Structure and Dynamics of Organizations and Groups.* (Free Press: New York).
    (1983). *Games People Play.* (Penguin: Harmondsworth).
DiCaprio, J. (1974). *Personality Theories.* (Free Press: New York).
Dougherty, Denis (1976). "Rational Behaviour Therapy and T.A.", *Transactional Analysis Journal*, October.
Ernst, Ken (1974). *Games Students Play.* (Celestial Arts: Los Angeles).
Fine, Marvin J. and Poggio, John P. (1977). "Behavioural Attributes of the Life Positions", *Transactional Analysis Journal*, October.
Freed, Alvin (1976). *T.A. for Teens (And Other Important People).* (Jalmar: Los Angeles).
Fromm, Eric (1982). *Greatness and Limitations of Freud's Thought.* (Abacus: London).
Harris, Thomas (1978). *I'm OK, You're OK.* (Pan: London).
Harris, Thomas and Harris, Amy Bjork (1985). *Staying OK.* (Harper and Row: New York).
James, Muriel (1975). *The OK Boss.* (Addison-Wesley: Reading, Mass.).
James, Muriel and Jongeward, Dorothy (1975). *The People Book: Transactional Analysis for Students.* (Addison-Wesley: Reading, Mass.)
James, Muriel and Savary, Louis (1977). *A New Self: Self Therapy with Transactional Analysis.* (Addison-Wesley: Reading, Mass.).
Jongeward, Dorothy (1976). *Everybody Wins: Transactional Analysis Applied to Organizations.* (Addison-Wesley: Reading, Mass.).
Jongeward, Dorothy and James, Muriel (1978). *Winning with People: Group Exercises in Transactional Analysis.* (Addison-Wesley: Reading, Mass.).
Jongeward, Dorothy and Seyer, Phillip (1978). *Choosing Success: Transactional Analysis on the Job.* (Wiley: New York).
Rosen, R.D. (1977). *Psychobabble: Fast Talk and Quick Cure in the Era of Feeling.* (Athenaeum: New York).
Steere, David A. (1982). *Bodily Expressions in Psychotherapy.* (Brunner/Mazel: New York).
Steiner, Claude (1971). *Games Alcoholics Play.* (Grove Press: New York).
    (1974). *Scripts People Live.* (Bantam: New York).
Villere, Maurice F. (1981). *Transactional Analysis at Work.* (Prentice-Hall: New Jersey).
Wagner, Abe (1981). *The Transactional Manager: How to Solve People Problems with Transactional Analysis.* (Prentice-Hall: New Jersey).
Woollams, Stan and Brown, Michael (1979). *T.A.—The Total Handbook of Transactional Analysis.* (Prentice-Hall: New Jersey).
Woollams, S., Brown, M. and Huige, K. (1976). *Transactional Analysis in Brief.* (Huron Valley Institute: Ann Arbour, Michigan).
Wallechinsky, David and Wallace, Irving (1978). *The People's Almanac #2.* (Bantam: New York).

Films/Video

Transactional Analysis (Video Channel).
I Understand, You Understand (Training Media Services, Power Human Resources).
Games Customers and Customer Service People Play (Power Human Resources).

6

Assertiveness

HOW can we become more assertive with others? Is assertion the
same as aggression? How can we best
explain aggression? What is it that determines which person will prove to be
dominant and which will prove to be
submissive? Does a person have to be
angry or emotionally involved to inflict
pain upon another person? How can we
best cope with persons who are aggressive, or are totally submissive, or are just
plain manipulative? In this chapter, we
will examine these questions and
attempt to find some answers to them.

The nature of aggression

Sometimes people begin analysing an
argument by saying "let us define our
terms". Sometimes it is useful not only
to define terms, but to look at the
original meaning of those terms, to look
at the etymology, or origin, of words.
Thus, Lindgren (1969) notes that the
Latin root *hos* (stranger) has given rise to
many disparate English words, such as
"hospitality", "host", "hostage" and
"hostility". Hence, "our treatment of
the stranger depends on how we perceive him: if we see him as a threat, we
are hostile, but if not, we greet him with
hospitality". Much aggression that we
direct towards others, therefore, may be
simply due to the fact that we do not
immediately understand or recognise a
person not from the in-group, the in-
race, the in-organisation, the in-religion,
and so on. This behaviour may have
been adaptive in the times when people
were scarce, and it made sense not to
trust immediately others who wanted
to share your cave or your sabre-tooth

tiger steak. Does this mean then that aggression is a genetically programmed behaviour, or do we learn it?

The hereditary explanation

Is aggression instinctive? Freud felt that the two great instincts which drove human nature were the sexual instinct and the aggressive instinct. He later modified this to the dual instincts of life force (eros) and death force (thanatos). To a large extent, Freud believed that we had to displace this self-destructive instinct to others, or else we would hurt ourselves (have "accidents") or kill ourselves. This displaced force was, of course, aggression.[1]

The notion that aggression is an instinct, and not learned, has been given a lot of force by two fairly new sciences, ethology and sociobiology. Both disciplines are still quite controversial, but have nevertheless produced some interesting data on animal behaviour, particularly in regard to aggression. Ardrey (1968), Lorenz (1966) and Wilson (1975) have pointed out that aggression in animals can be understood in terms of mechanisms of social control, such as territoriality and rank order. Animals need a certain amount of territory or space: *territorial behaviour* seems to be based upon carrying capacity of a particular area, that is, the extent to which a particular physical environment can comfortably support a given number of an animal population. If the carrying capacity is exceeded, there is an excess of population, and therefore competition for scarce resources, such as food. Such competition may take the form of aggressive rituals.

What implications does this have for densely packed populations of animals or humans? What insight does territoriality give us into human behaviour such as possession of private property, the desire for privacy, or the desire to have a "bubble of personal space" which non-intimate others penetrate at their peril (see Chapter 4)? Drawing analogies from animal to human behaviour can be tricky, of course. Thus, while throwing another rat into a box of rats may precipitate violent and fatal conflict, that does not necessarily mean that areas of human habitation with high densities (such as London or Amsterdam) will automatically have higher crime rates than areas of low density (such as the American mid-west).

What of the social mechanism of *rank order*? Hierarchy appears to be an extremely widespread—some would say universal—means of social control in the animal kingdom. Pecking orders are notable among some species of birds: the most dominant in a group pecks the next most dominant, who, rather than retaliating in kind, proceeds to peck the next lowest ranking animal. This continues until the lowliest animal is reached, and this animal is often attacked by many others. The survival of the fittest? Only the strong survive? Possibly. But what implications can we draw from this for human social inventions, such as socio-economic class, group exclusion of deviants, and so on? How slickly can we generalise in the quest to show that "aggression is biologically programmed"?

The environmental explanation

For someone who believes we have little or no instincts, genetics cannot be an adequate explanation of behaviour. Behavioural environmentalists believe that behaviour is learned—we pick it up from the environment. For many of

---

[1] See Chapter 5.

the philosophers of the French Enlightenment movement of the eighteenth century, at pains to rebut the traditional religious dogmas of man being tainted with original sin, man was a *tabula rasa*, or blank tablet or stone, upon which nature or the world wrote: change what was written, and you would change "human nature". Some modern psychologists, particularly behaviourists such as Skinner, continue this tradition of believing that behaviour is learned, not inherited (see Chapter 3). Thus, if aggression can be learned, for example, by having aggressive behaviour modelled on television by cartoon characters or soap opera heroes and villains, then it can also be unlearned, by exposing individuals to less violent modelled behaviour.

Which explanation do you find more convincing: aggression is part of our biological program, or aggression is a bad habit we learn which we can unlearn? We may not be able to give a final explanation to aggression just yet—indeed, we may never be able to solve the environment/heredity dilemma. Certainly, we need to take other models of behaviour into account. Consider, for example, whether it is possible for a person to be aggressive towards another person without experiencing any strong emotions such as hatred or anger.

Aggression and obedience

In 1962, Adolf Eichmann, the Nazi war criminal, stood trial for war crimes in Jerusalem. A Jewish intellectual, Hannah Arendt, speculated upon the nature of Eichmann's crime—complicity in the destruction of millions of Jews in World War II—and concluded that it was too simple to believe that Eichmann was sub-human or insane, and that "ordinary people" could not commit similarly horrific crimes. Arendt thought that Eichmann manifested the banality or commonplaceness of evil, and something which is common is, by definition, shared by all (an observation which brought her much criticism in the Jewish community).

Stanley Milgram, an American social psychologist, devised an experiment to see whether evil was banal, to see whether ordinary people could be trapped into a social situation where they would be asked to inflict pain upon others: would they resist the suggestion, or would they, like countless Nazi war criminals, find themselves in a situation where they too were "only following orders"? Milgram offered to pay volunteers for taking part in what was ostensibly a learning experiment at Yale University. On entering the laboratory, a volunteer would meet another person who appeared to be a volunteer, and the experimenter, a serious-looking man wearing a lab coat and carrying a clipboard. The experimenter announced to the two volunteers that the experiment was to study learning in adult humans, and was specifically concerned with whether punishment would help people remember things. A ballot was drawn to determine which volunteer would be the learner, and which would be the teacher. The learner was then taken to an adjoining room, and strapped into a chair with electrodes connected to his skin. The teacher was seated at a panel of switches, which were labelled from 15 volts to 450 volts in 15 volt increments. The teacher read a long list of word pairs ("blue...day", "fat...neck"). When this list was completed, the teacher was to read the first half of the word pairs ("blue...", "fat...."). If the learner remembered the pairs, then nothing would happen; if the learner forgot, however, the teacher was required to give him a shock: first 15 volts, then 30 volts for the second mistake, and so on, up until 450 volts.

But all was not as it appeared:

> The "teacher" is a genuinely naive subject who has come to the laboratory to participate in an experiment. The learner, or victim, is an actor who actually receives no shock at all. The point of the experiment is to see how far a person will proceed in a concrete and measurable situation in which he is ordered to inflict increasing pain on a protesting victim. At what point will the subject refuse to obey the experimenter? (MILGRAM 1974, P.19)

The learner in the next room would protest increasingly loudly as the "voltage" rose, and in fact there was no response from the learner after 300 volts. If the teacher showed hesitation or a desire to check the condition of the learner, the experimenter would simply say, "the experiment has to continue". This was the second version of the experiment. There were four versions in one series, and the results were as shown in Table 6.1.

Thus, the more physically involved was the teacher with the actual process of inflicting pain, the more likely such a person was to defy the official authority of the experimenter. Nevertheless, the number of people who will obey authority to perform quite horrifying acts is, if the Milgram experiments are any indication of the general behaviour of Americans, startlingly high. (Wesley Kilham performed one version of the experiment upon Australians and got an even *higher* obedience response (Dale 1974).) Although he received much criticism from the social science community for the ethics of the experiment, Milgram claimed that the experiment produced a number of important and disturbing conclusions. Three of these are:

1. It is possible for people to inflict punishment upon, that is, be aggressive towards, other people without experiencing emotions of anger or hostility towards those people. Thus, while one has to be psyched up to stick a bayonet through an enemy's stomach, being so psyched up would interfere with the performance of a bombardier or rocket launcher—the outcome, however, would not only be the same but infinitely more destructive.
2. Common decent people, placed in a situation where they are required to inflict punishment on others, may obey much more readily than we think; such people will then rationalise their behaviour by saying that they were not personally responsible, they were only doing what they were told. Such a rationale was continually invoked by Nazi war criminals on trial at Nuremberg after World War II. To attempt to

Table 6.1 Responses in Milgram's obedience experiment

Experiment version	Percentage of subjects who defied experimenter's orders (refused to continue)
1. Teacher cannot see or hear victim in another room.	30
2. Teacher can hear victim in another room.	37.5
3. Teacher is in same room as victim.	60
4. Teacher in same room as victim; required to force victim's hand onto shock plate.	70

Source: Adapted from Milgram (1974).

prevent such behaviour occurring again, the United Nations developed concepts which have been enshrined in the Geneva Accords, which state that a soldier in battle is morally responsible for his own decisions, and has the right to disobey orders that violate human rights, for example, the order to perform mass murder upon civilians. This is a very tricky area for the soldier: where is the line drawn between following one's conscience, and disobeying an order under fire (usually punishable by summary execution)?

3. Consequently, it is meaningful to distinguish between two psychological types of people: those who will always follow orders, or simply see themselves as an agent of the will of others (*agentic* personalities), and those who will, when their conscience is challenged, defy authority and act independently of such authority (*autonomous* personalities). It is interesting to speculate whether modern political and educational systems encourage the growth of autonomous or agentic behaviour.

Locus of control

A model of behaviour similar to Milgram's agentic/autonomous model is Rotter's notion of locus of control (Rotter 1954, Rotter and Hochreich 1975, Pareek 1982). Rotter developed a learning theory which distinguished between people who are *internals* and people who are *externals*: internals believe that they control their own reinforcements, and thus behaviour, while externals believe that outside forces control the way they are reinforced, and hence their behaviour (for more on the idea of reinforcement, see Chapter 3). Thus if a child is encouraged to believe that individual actions can change circumstances, he will grow up with a quite different outlook to someone who has been encouraged to believe that the individual cannot do much at all. The difference between externals and internals can be seen in the types of beliefs extreme types of each might hold (Table 6.2).

Internals tend to be more conscientious in using seat belts, getting inoculations, engaging in exercise, losing weight, avoiding alcoholism and practising birth control. They tend, however, to be not very sympathetic to others in trouble, believing that people make their own trouble and thus deserve it: thus internals are much less likely than externals to offer sympathy, help or financial aid (Baron, Byrne and Kantowitz 1980) (see Box 6.A). Obviously, Rotter's internals would have a lot in common with Milgram's

Table 6.2 Expectancies of internals and externals

	Internal	External
Specific expectancies	1. Practice will improve tennis skills.	1. You're either born with athletic ability or you're not.
	2. Cigarettes cause lung cancer.	2. Nobody knows for sure what causes lung cancer.
	3. Grades depend on how hard you study.	3. Grades depend on the biases of a teacher.
	4. You do well on a job if you work hard.	4. You do well on a job if your boss likes you.

Source: Adapted from Baron, Byrne and Kantowitz (1980).

BOX 6.A: Internal and external control

Consider the following statements. Use the statement number and either a simple cross or an extended line to indicate where on the continuum of external/internal control you would locate each statement, e.g. statement 16 is probably an extreme internal position, whereas statement 2 is a much more external position.

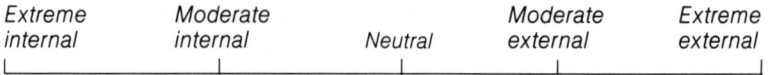

Extreme internal	Moderate internal	Neutral	Moderate external	Extreme external

1. I am the master of my fate: I am the captain of my soul.
2. There's no point in fighting the system—it's rigged against you.
3. I'm going to work my way up to the top because I believe in myself.
4. The rich get richer and the poor get poorer.
5. Spiritually, I believe that my salvation or otherwise depends upon what good deeds I do here and now.
6. Spiritually, I believe that my salvation or otherwise is pre-determined, so it doesn't really matter what I do.
7. I'm joining a political party to work with others to change things.
8. To win races, I have to train very hard—but I always carry my rabbit's foot chain for luck anyway.
9. I'm so frustrated, I'm going to make my mark by shooting someone important.
10. She got to the top by sheer will power.
11. She got to the top because she came from the right class, religion, race, and social clique.
12. I'm almost broke, but if I gamble everything I've got I might get lucky.
13. What's the point in giving up smoking? You're going to die anyway.
14. Behaviour is determined totally by hereditary influences.
15. Behaviour is determined totally by environmental influences.
16. The fate of the world depends upon me.
17. The harder I work, the luckier I get.

autonomouses, and externals would have a lot in common with agentics[2] (see also the connection between internal/external orientation and power drive in Chapter 10). Note also the rational–emotional therapy styles of distorted thinking known as fallacy of internal control and fallacy of external control (see Chapter 7).

---

[2] O'Brien and Kabanoff (1981) report that Australians are more external than Americans, females are more external than males, and older people (24+) are more internal than younger people. Occupations, ranging from most internal to most external, are: rural, administrative/executive, transport/communication, professional, trades, services and clerical.

Stress and behaviour

To a considerable extent, hereditary or biological factors have an impact upon the way we behave in social situations. Thus, the degree to which we are aggressive or submissive, agentic or autonomous, or internally or externally controlled, is strongly influenced by the way we behave under stress. We can have stress which is unpleasant in quality, and stress which is pleasant; we can have too great a quantity of stress, and too small a quantity. A critical response is what is called the *fight-or-flight response* (see Chapter 7). In primaeval times, we reacted to physical threats, such as marauding animals, by either fighting or running away. Our bodies became adapted to either or both of these responses in various ways: changes in heartbeat, pulse, breathing rate, alertness and hyperalertness, etc. To use the aggressive–passive model of behaviour: when we are aggressive, we adopt the fight response (attacking, waving fists, baring teeth, talking loudly and yelling, glaring eyes, threat displays such as hands on hips), and when we are passive, we adopt the flight response (retreating, imploring gestures with hands, mumbling and whining, averted eyes, submission displays such as bowing).

Aggression, passivity, manipulativeness, assertiveness

All this talk of aggression and passivity and fight-or-flight response may suggest to some that all human transactions seem to be rather brutal and animalistic in nature. Is this necessarily so? Not at all. We can think of another style of behaviour, such as manipulativeness, which is not strictly aggression or passivity. Manipulative people are the ones who continually flatter others, while perhaps simultaneously stabbing them in the back. Manipulativeness is not a lovely form of human behaviour, but it exists and, for the purpose of analysis, it is sufficient to note here that it is not aggression or passivity. It seems to partake of both those states, and in fact may be called the passive–aggressive style.

Another style which is neither passive nor aggressive is the assertive style. Assertiveness has many definitions, although one which will suffice is: "getting what you want from others without infringing upon others' rights". This of course is easier said than done, but specialists in assertiveness training (AT) claim that it is possible to relate to others in ways that do not involve destructive behaviour, such as the dominance of aggressors, the under-handedness of manipulators, or the capitulation of passives. Further clarification is needed to separate these four styles of behaving. Yet perhaps it is true to say that, while most of us have a clear idea of what is meant by aggression, passivity and manipulation, we are not terribly clear on what is specifically meant by assertion. To the extent that this uncertainty exists, that is a rather damning statement about our culture and our interpersonal relationships.

Before comparing these four styles of behaviour, then, we need a clearer idea of what assertiveness is. Box 6.B contains a matrix of assertive behaviours. If you fill out this matrix, you will have a much better idea of what assertive (and non-assertive) behaviour actually is.

BOX 6.B: Assertion self-assessment matrix

Down the left-hand side of the matrix (pp.176–7), we have a series of assertive behaviours. These are grouped under three major headings: Expressing positive feelings, Self-affirmation and Expressing negative feelings.

Expressing positive feelings

Giving compliments. Within our culture, we don't often pay compliments to others. It's sad, but we often feel that people who pay compliments are manipulatives—they don't really mean it, they're only trying to flatter us. When was the last time you gave an unprompted compliment, without an ulterior motive?

Receiving compliments. Perhaps people are even more threatened by getting compliments than giving them. Many, after having a compliment paid to them, say something like, "It was nothing", "I was just lucky" or "That's what I'm paid for". Any attempt to avoid this ritual of self-denigration and instead say something like, "Thank you, I've worked hard at succeeding on this", is often interpreted as being a dangerous and contemptible display of ego. Yet if the "Thank you . . ." type phrase is said without obvious arrogance, why shouldn't we be able to say it?

Make requests, e.g. ask for favours, help, etc. Much assertive behaviour is about communicating with others, about building bridges between people instead of walls. Wall-building—withholding the self, all of us remaining on lonely little islands—is reinforced by being incapable of paying or receiving compliments, and also by being incapable of making requests. Many interpret making a request as being a sign of weakness: why do you need help? *I* don't. This is very destructive behaviour, and almost certainly very inefficient: no one can be master of all trades, and if we attempt to demonstrate our universal mastery, we almost certainly will botch things up. Making requests, therefore, is not only more emotionally gratifying, it is more efficient.

Expressing liking, love and affection. If people experience trouble with the first three behaviours, they will almost certainly experience agonies over this one. To express such feelings is to be very open, and therefore to take risks by sharing feelings. Many people's defences—their emotional walls—are so rigid and thick that it is almost impossible for them to do this. Perhaps they have had negative experiences in this area, either in their personal or professional lives. Without trying to be trite, and to trivialise the real pain they did and do feel, it may be that if they conducted their personal and professional lives in a more assertive way—free of the mind-games of aggression, passivity and manipulation—then this behaviour would not be so risky.

Initiate and maintain conversation. A lonely person sitting at home brooding on the question, "How do you *meet* new people?" and a clerk in an office thinking to herself, "I really need a raise in salary, but I don't know how to ask", are both deficient in this behaviour: they don't know how to strike up a conversation, and keep it going. Many people believe that you either have "the gift of the gab" or you don't. This is not so. This behaviour, like all the others listed here, can be studied, rehearsed, put into practice and improved upon.

Self-affirmation

Stand up for your legitimate rights. Someone changes your behaviour; you say, "but it's not fair!"; nevertheless, you do nothing to restore your old behaviour or change their behaviour. Almost certainly, you have just had your legitimate rights trampled over. If this does not happen to you, then you have no problems with this behaviour.

Refuse requests. Manuel Smith, in his book *When I Say No, I Feel Guilty* (Smith 1975), points out that many of us are manipulated into granting requests because our self-talk, our internal monologue of our behaviour, runs like this: "When I say 'No' I feel guilty, but if I say 'Yes' I'll hate myself". Such manipulative requests from others may range from a boss trying to get you to work overtime when you don't want to, to someone trying to bluff or ingratiate you into a sexual encounter. To be able to say "no" in a firm, polite, inoffensive but effective manner is an extraordinarily helpful skill, which seems to desert many of us at crucial times: we usually respond aggressively ("No! How many times. . ."), passively ("Oh, all right, if that's what you want. . .), or manipulatively ("Gee, I'd love to help, but I've got to sit with my sick elephant that night. . ").

Express personal opinions, including disagreement. Silence betokens consent, and if we want a quiet and low stress life, we will be silent. If we want to be honest, however, we have to cope with the stress of speaking out, often in the face of considerable group and/or cultural pressure. Many of us are not up to this, or at least not for all of the time.

Expressing negative feelings

Express justified annoyance and displeasure. Assertiveness is not, as some think, concerned with bottling up negative emotions and always putting on a pleasant face. It must be possible to express harsher feelings in a reasonably controlled way, without lapsing into an uncontrollable outburst. We need to have the skill of criticising with tact (remember, a good definition of tact is "making a point without making an enemy").

Expressing justified anger. It has to be possible for us to express extreme feelings without, for example, resorting to symbolic and physical violence. Aggressive people express anger in this way, and, interestingly, so do passive people, or at least sometimes: the worm turning can be a healthy sight, but if years of bitterness and rage explode, one had better hope that no lethal weapons are lying about.

Across the top of the matrix, we have the names of various persons we interact with. We may respond in the same manner to all of these persons, irrespective of the situation of time and place, or we may vary our responses, according to the person and/or according to the situation.

Scoring the matrix

The matrix can be used to determine your assertive (and unassertive) behaviours. It can also be used to analyse your patterns of stress, as it relates to your assertive/unassertive behaviour.

Step 1

In reading the matrix, use the following question with each row and column heading:

(The creators of this matrix, Galassi and Galassi, suggest that it is usually inappropriate to express liking, love, affection to authority figures and business contacts. If you agree, simply colour in those particular cells.)

Behaviours	Friends of the same sex	Friends of the opposite sex	Intimate relations, e.g. spouse, boyfriend, girlfriend	Parents, in-laws, and other family members	Children	Authority figures, e.g. bosses, professors, doctors	Business contacts e.g. sales-persons, waiters	Co-workers, colleagues, and sub-ordinates
Expressing positive feelings Give compliments								
Receive compliments								
Make requests, e.g. ask for favours, help, etc.								
Express liking, love, and affection								

Behaviours	Friends of the same sex	Friends of the opposite sex	Intimate relations, e.g. spouse, boyfriend, girlfriend	Parents, in-laws, and other family members	Children	Authority figures, e.g. bosses, professors, doctors	Business contacts e.g. sales-persons, waiters	Co-workers colleagues, and sub-ordinates
Initiate and maintain conversations								
Self-affirmation Stand up for your legitimate rights								
Refuse requests								
Express personal opinions including disagreement								
Expressing negative feelings Express justified annoyance and displeasure								
Express justified anger								

Source: Galassi, Merna Dee, and Galassi, John P. *Assert Yourself! How to be Your Own Person* (Human Sciences Press, New York, 1977), p.9. Reproduced with permission.

Do I (*row heading*) to/from/of/with (*column heading*) when it is appropriate?
For example, if you begin with the upper left-hand cell, you would form the following question:
Do I *give compliments* to *friends of the same sex* when it is appropriate?

Step 2
In scoring the matrix cells, use the following symbols:
usually (U)
sometimes (S)
rarely (R)

Step 3
After completing the matrix, check each column and row. Do you have more than three (S) or (R) responses? *If you do, it may be that you have an assertiveness problem with that person or that behaviour.*

Step 4
To evaluate your stress responses, it is useful to reconsider each person/behaviour cell, and consider whether you experience stress in such situations. (See "Stress symptoms" in Chapter 7.) Stress, if not creatively channelled, may cause you to react in a variety of aggressive, passive or manipulative ways. Record stress reactions with a "yes" or "no", or with a tick or cross.

Step 5
As with step 3, check each column and row to see whether a pattern of difficulty with a particular person or behaviour is emerging.

Figure 6.1 is a model of how these four styles of behaviour may relate to one another. Aggression and passivity are extreme poles of behaviour, perhaps most clearly denoted by fight-or-flight behaviour. Manipulative behaviour is neither aggression nor passivity. The manipulative person would perhaps like to be aggressive, but does not have the resources or motivation

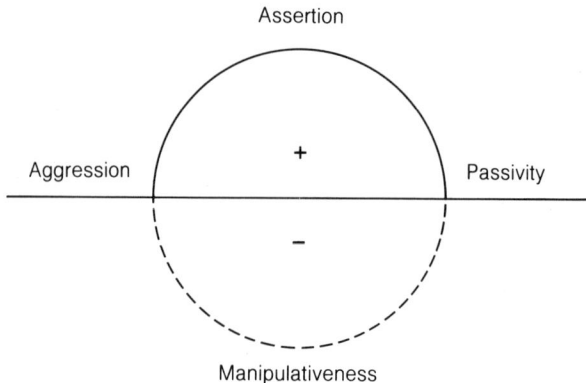

Fig 6.1 *A model of behaviour*

to be so. By the same token, the manipulative does not continually get steam-rollered by reality, as is usually the case with passive people. Indeed, the manipulative often gets her way, albeit by sneaky means. Because manipulation has a negative connotation, the lower hemisphere of Figure 6.1 has a negative sign. Because it is usually covert behaviour—beneath the surface—it is shown by broken lines.

Assertion also partakes of qualities of aggression and passivity, although the synthesis is a more positive, constructive and "other-regarding" one. Because of this, the assertive upper hemisphere of Figure 6.1 is given a positive sign.

Let us now analyse these four styles. We need to consider the general behaviour of the four styles, as well as their specific verbal and non-verbal behaviour. We need to keep in mind that people (including ourselves) often combine styles, and that people (including ourselves) may display a style in one situation but not in another.

The aggressive style

As we have seen, it is still a matter of some controversy as to whether human beings are "naturally" aggressive. In comparing different styles of behaviour, our concern should be to find out to what extent people can change their behaviour once they are made aware of it.

Is aggression a "boo" concept or a "hurrah" concept? Certainly in the 1960s, when the ethology and sociobiology scholars and popularisers began to examine the question of "genetic" aggression, aggression was seen as a "boo" concept—something that had outlived its usefulness in a world where nuclear weapons had made obsolete the concept of combat as a solution to problems. Yet to a certain extent, aggression has today made a partial comeback, being used with a wide variety of "hurrah" connotations. The media is full of reference to "aggressive marketing strategies" and "aggressive political campaigns". Macho (and womacho) posturings get a lot of kudos in a lot of areas. Perhaps global recession and hard times have produced a new type of radical selfishness and I'm-all right-Jack head-kicking.

Frankly opportunistic books such as Ringerman's *Winning through Intimidation* and *Looking Out For Number One* perhaps capture the spirit of the age. Critics of assertiveness training, such as Eglash (1980), are not surprised at the new trendiness of aggression: they see it as the dark side of assertiveness, something which had to emerge into the daylight sooner or later (see below p.197).

General behaviour

The aggressive person may be high or low in status in groups and organisations. Aggressives are apparently totally self-assured, aware of their own perfection and all too painfully aware of other, mere mortals' imperfection (see Table 6.3). They treat others as things to be used and then discarded. They often punish and are extremely critical. For many aggressives, however, this is just an act: many aggressives are really very insecure, feeling that they have to kill or be killed. The world is a rough place, but it isn't often as rough as all that. Aggression is often like revenge—sweet in the short term, but often counter-productive in the long run. Thus, because the aggressive has a self-image of being perfect and infallible, she cannot afford to make mistakes and, of course, does not dare delegate. This leads not only to a very lonely life, but a very stressful one.

Table 6.3 Four styles of behaviour

Style—Aggressive

General behaviour	• wishes to dominate, humiliate • wishes to win at all costs—often very insecure • believes in her own perfection, indispensability, superiority to others • doesn't trust, delegate • often over-reacts—then feels guilty • self-righteous, patronising • punitive, critical • sees others as objects to be used • makes enemies—creates own enemies (overt, covert opposition)
Verbal cues	• talks loud, fast • abuse, obscenities • interrupts others, completes sentences for them • tsk, tsk, tsk • "I" statements • "You must/should/ought . . ." • "You always/never. . ." • explains badly: either impatiently, aggressively ("surely you've got it now!") or condescendingly, patronisingly, over-deliberately, as if speaking to a child or intellectually handicapped person (learner's inevitable failure confirms her belief that everyone else is incompetent and her belief that "kindness" doesn't work) • opinions expressed as facts; requests expressed as instructions or threats
Non-verbal cues	
Eyes	• glaring—tries to stare down • rolls eyes in disgust • looks down nose • breaks eye contact to interrupt, freeze out
Facial expression	• eyebrows raised in mock amazement, disbelief • frown • bared teeth • clenched teeth • jutting jaw • flared nostrils
Posture	• rigid • relaxed while others are tense • walks fast • arms crossed—unapproachable • invades others' personal space
Gestures	• hands on hips • clenched fist • pounds fist into palm • points finger • shakes head as if other person isn't to be believed • snorts, exhales loudly and martyr-like, whistles in mock wonder • impatient tapping of feet, drumming of fingers • steepling • hands behind head • feet on desk

Table 6.3 Four styles of behaviour *(continued)*

Style—Passive	
General behaviour	• abdicates authority/gives decisions to others to avoid responsibility (then resents others making decisions) • has decisions hijacked by others—plays doomed martyr • helplessness—feels a victim of life's cruel game • broods, stews on others' aggression • complains, doesn't act • gets "nerves" in meetings, public situations • avoids conflict at all costs • has difficulty in accepting positive feedback • plays dumb and confused, and thus becomes a burden to others • "shyness"
Verbal cues	• stumbles over words—"um . . . ah . . ." • uses continuers—"sort of . . . like . . . you know . . . and that . . . and them . . ." • mumbles—needs to repeat words • overpolite • "why does this always happen to me?" • few "I" statements • avoids saying "no" • breathy, little girl, "baby doll" voice (you musn't attack me, I'm too weak) • "I should have. . ." • "If only. . ." • "This is probably stupid, but. . ." • "I'll do it . . . you go home" • upwardly inflects often (seeking approval) • monotone • whinging, whining • silence • trails off sentences—expects to be interrupted • sighs
Non-verbal cues Eyes	• evasive eye contact; often downcast • rapid blinking • tears
Facial expression	• eyebrows raised—questioning, pleading • weak smile; smiling at everyone, even when angry—propitiation • blank expression—mask of pain • super-mobile expression (cf. children, slaves, social inferiors) • nods continually • sullen sulk • rapid biting, wetting of lips • rapid swallowing, blushing
Posture	• slumped over—foetal slouch, infantile rocking • rigid
Gestures	• wrings hands • covers mouth with hands—oral insecurity • self-touching • toes clenched, fingers clenched • feet turned inward

Table 6.3 Four styles of behaviour *(continued)*

Style—Passive

Non-verbal cues
Gestures

- arms crossed—protective
- shuffles feet
- fidgets with objects
- sighs often

Style—Passive–aggressive (manipulative)

General behaviour

- wants power without responsibility
- over-politicised—always tries to get her own way through connections, name-dropping, mutual back-scratching, secret networks
- bitchiness, backstabbing, character assassination, rumour-mongering, innuendoes
- seduction, manipulation
- flattering, while undermining
- sabotage—procrastination, habitual lateness, forgetting
- feigned innocence
- feigned stupidity—slow learner
- womanly wiles, coyness, archness
- plays hard to get
- plays on guilt
- emotional blackmail
- intellectualisation—disclaims emotional involvement
- sees others as objects to be used

Verbal cues

- "I'll wrap him/her around my little finger. . ."
- seductive come-on
- undue emphasis on words—"Who, *me*? Oh *NO! Never!*"
- sarcasm
- hostile kidding
- silent treatment

Non-verbal cues
Eyes

- rolling eyes
- over-elaborate winking
- raised eyebrows—wide-eyed puzzlement, wounded innocence when accused
- not establishing eye contact when trying to get something from someone
- tears

Facial expression

- pursing of lips
- fawning expression
- facetious expression
- conspiratorial expression

Posture

- huddling conspiratorially
- body oriented away from "uninteresting", "uninfluential" people—even when speaking to them

Gestures

- sighing with exasperation
- yawning
- drumming fingers, tapping toes—impatience
- hand in front of mouth when talking
- steepling

Table 6.3 Four styles of behaviour *(continued)*

Style—Assertive	
General behaviour	• takes appropriate action towards getting what she wants, without denying the right of others • negotiates, evaluates • trusts, delegates • deals with power and power politics openly • proactive—is solution-oriented • consistent • acknowledges and respects others' feelings, including fear, anger • takes risks with expressing her own feelings—models behaviour for others • claims right to make mistakes • claims right to be non-assertive • feels good about herself now and later • non-verbal and verbal behaviour congruent
Verbal cues	• "I choose to. . ." • "Let's look at what alternatives we have. . ." • When, where, who, how, what • no "shoulds", "oughts" • "tell me something good" • "tell me the good news and the bad news" • says no when it can't be done—doesn't feel guilty • distinction drawn between fact and opinion • constructive criticism, without blame or assumptions • appropriately firm, warm tone • expressive, emphasising key words

Non-verbal cues
  Eyes
  Facial expression
 	
  Posture
 	
  Gestures
	
	• direct—not staring
	• attentive
	• congruent with what is being expressed
	• relaxed
	• open
	• open hand movements (showing honesty; inviting others to speak)
	• establishes appropriate body contact with others

Source: Adapted from Bloom, Coburn and Pearlman (1975), Jakubowski and Lange (1978), Burley-Allen (1983), Alberti and Emmons (1978), McNeilage and Adams (1982), Kelley (1979), Beck and Beck (1982), Phelps and Austin (1975).

Because the aggressive thus cuts herself off from the normal verbal and non-verbal cues and feedback that would normally let her know that she was going over the top, she often over-reacts, and then feels guilty about it. Perhaps most self-defeating of all, the aggressive calls forth (quite justifiably) hostility from others: this either leads to overt opposition from others assertive or aggressive enough to stand up to her or, even worse, covert opposition from passive and manipulative people. Not everyone hates an aggressive, of course: agentic people, to use Milgram's terminology, the fearers of freedom, the adorers of brute force, will always be around to play the groupie ministering to the aggressive's raging and fragile ego.

Verbal cues

The aggressive uses words and the withholding of words to demonstrate her dominance. She talks loud and fast, and often interrupts others and completes their sentences for them. The aggressive is thus a close relative of the stress-prone type A person (see Chapter 7).

The aggressive can shift from a torrent of abuse and obscenities to the patronising and punitive "tsk, tsk, tsk" (often accompanied by the non-verbal cues of breaking eye contact, rolling of eyes, and shaking of head). The aggressive, like the assertive, is given to "I" statements, but with the aggressive this smacks more of the raging egocentricity of a small child or a minor and grouchy god rather than the mature demonstration of responsibility.

The aggressive uses punitive and judgmental phrases, peppered with inflexible absolutes: "You must/should/ought/always/never. . ." Thus the aggressive does not leave any leeway for rational negotiation. For the aggressive, negotiation means losing, which is unthinkable. The notion of discretion being the better part of valour, or flying when fighting is useless, is not on for the (highly maladaptive) aggressive. This inflexibility is also seen when the aggressive needs to express opinions and requests, but can only bear to issue "facts" and instructions or threats. The aggressive can, either through genuine good intentions or malign game-playing, seem to communicate directly, for example, in giving instructions on how to do something. The explanation however is usually useless: either it is given in an impatient and aggressive manner (punctuated with helpful phrases such as "Surely you see it now? Why, the greatest idiot could see that. . .") or else in a condescending and patronisingly over-deliberate fashion, as if speaking to a child or an intellectually handicapped person. This shows that the aggressive is really only at home in relationships where roles are clearly spelt out, with major differentials of power between roles (with the aggressive, of course, having more rather than less power). The person being "shown exactly how to do it" of course doesn't get it, thus confirming the aggressive's belief that the rest of the world is incompetent, and showing "kindness" just doesn't pay.

Non-verbal cues

The aggressive delights in childish things, such as the childhood game of staring your opponent down (with the loser blinking first). She may also roll her eyes in disgust, or look down her nose haughtily to indicate the disgust she feels for others. She is very good at interrupting others, and facilitates this by breaking eye contact with the person currently speaking: it is difficult to regain the floor once someone has interrupted you, usually by speaking more loudly and looking away from you. This breaking of eye contact may also be used as a general tactic to freeze people out; it is usual for people of high status to be looked at more often by others than they look at others, so that the aggressive attempts to boost her status by so doing.

The aggressive will also use raised eyebrows to convey mock amazement and disbelief. Sarcasm is an important verbal weapon here. She may also attempt to intimidate others with a range of threat signals that would not be out of place in the combat rituals of primate animals: frowns, clenched teeth, bared teeth, jutting or protruberant jaw, and flared nostrils.

Her posture is often rigid and controlled (although some non-verbal theorists have suggested that, in egalitarian societies such as America and Australia, it may be poor taste to flaunt high status too obviously; thus high status people may exert power by appearing relaxed while subordinates remain alert and tense). The aggressive may walk fast (thus showing she is a busy and important person), and may march into other people's personal space to assert dominance. To demonstrate self-control and total unapproach-ability, she often folds her arms, particularly in conflict situations (and isn't that all the time for the aggressive?).

Her hands may go to her hips in a readiness/combat stance, or this may signify disapproval (particularly if accompanied by drumming fingers and tapping feet). She may perform mock combat gestures such as clenching her fists and shaking them, or pounding her fist into her palm. The verbal harangues of the "you should/never. . ." variety are often accompanied by the pointing finger. Her talent for pantomime is revealed by shaking her head in an exaggerated way when listening to others talking. Like a steam engine, she may snort, or whistle in mock wonder, or exhale loudly, to indicate how much she is being martyred by incompetent others.

She may convey pomposity and territorial dominance by steepling, putting her hands behind her head, and placing her feet on the desk. Much of this book attempts to break down sexist stereotyping by often referring to people in general as "she" and "her". Nevertheless, the average reader would consider most of the verbal and non-verbal behaviours of the aggressive type as being more typical of males than females. Phelps and Austin (1975) go so far as to say that women have been oppressed by men, and all oppressed classes throughout history usually only have a choice of being passive or manipulative, not aggressive or assertive. Does this mean that all passives, and in particular, manipulatives, are female? Far from it.

The passive style

The passive is an agentic person in Milgram's terms, an external in Rotter's terms. The agentic person of course lacks autonomy—independence of thought—and defines her role as that of an agent of others, ready to obey and follow, thankful that other, "natural" leaders are there to give orders. The external personality feels totally controlled by circumstances and people— her fate is predetermined, and free will has nothing to do with reality.

Is passivity a natural thing, the normal behaviour of many people in a Darwinian world of winners and losers? Or is it a socially learned behaviour, which, having once been learned, can be unlearned? Zimbardo *et al.* (1975) argue that shyness, a critical component of passivity, is in fact socially and culturally learned. Comparing American and Japanese societies, they speculate that shyness occurs because both societies over-emphasise competition, individual success and personal responsibility for failure. Thus, those who are not aggressive extroverts are forced by social pressure into its opposite—shyness, introversion—because the culture does not easily allow a middle point between the extremes.

Zimbardo and his co-workers speculate that shyness may even have been eliminated in China because communist ideology encourages the social skills of group interaction and articulateness (in contrast to more traditional values which emphasised docility and modesty before others of higher classes, especially among females). Shyness is then seen to be merely social programming, the personal prison that cultural values may create. To the extent that Zimbardo *et al.* are right, shyness and passivity have more to do with environmental than hereditary factors.

General behaviour

The passive is rarely happy being a passive. More so than the other three types—aggressive, manipulative and assertive—the passive is often torn apart by self-hatred and regret. Thus, the passive avoids responsibility by abdicating authority and giving decisions to others to make; she then often resents others for making those decisions. This can lead to decisions being permanently taken by others ("hijacked") because others presume (correctly) that she won't act or won't act in time or won't act adequately. She may complain about such injustices, but of course she won't act: she will brood and stew on the injustice of it all. Alternatively, the passive may go to the other extreme, overcommitting herself, masochistically taking on everything aggressives and manipulatives want to offload (and then some). She will, of course, fail—disastrously and publicly. Secretly, she may fancy the tacky melodrama of this "doomed martyr" behaviour.

Any stress makes the passive go to water. Thus she gets "nerves" in meetings or any type of public situation. She avoids conflict at any cost. She flies, even when she could fight and win (just as the aggressive fights, even when she really should fly on some occasions). Although she cannot handle criticism, she endures it. Paradoxically, she cannot handle positive feedback either: compliments imply competence, and it is her whole life-myth that she is incompetent. Thus she often plays dumb and confused, and becomes a burden to others. In transactional analysis terms, she plays "Kick Me", confounding the nurturing guidance of others and provoking them into abusing and disowning her (thereby re-proving her incompetence and removing the stress of trying and risking success). She is the victim, the murderee, looking for the punishment she knows she so richly deserves.

Verbal cues

The extremely poor self-image and lack of confidence of the passive is evident in the period between opening her mouth and saying anything of significance. She often stumbles and mumbles her words, and overuses the continuer phrases most people use: "sort of . . . like . . . you know . . . and that . . . and them. . .". In contrast to the rudeness of the aggressive, the passive is painfully polite. She uses few "I" statements, because that would imply that she knew her own mind. She avoids saying "no", and thus becomes hopelessly overcommitted to fulfilling the needs, dependencies and power-trips of others. If she is driven to the extreme of playing the doomed martyr, we may hear her say things like, "Oh all right . . . I'll do it . . . you go home . . . I'll work back late . . . it's the best time for getting things done, really. . ." When she inevitably fails, she will have many excuses, or even worse, say that she has no excuse (i.e. please kick me).

Her language is shot through with self-putdowns, hindsight and victim-type mentality: "I should have . . . if only . . . this is probably stupid, but . . . why does this always happen to me?" Females may deliberately adopt as a life-strategy the sexist ploy of using a breathy, little girl, "baby doll" type verbal delivery, which again amplifies the signal of passivity.

The passive upwardly inflects quite often, thus showing a never-ending need for reassuring feedback and approval. She may whinge and whine ("ain't it awful?"), but may retreat to the social autism of silence, or at least speak in a dispirited and bitter monotone, varied only by despairing downward inflections and much sighing. She may trail off her sentences, never tidily completing them on a neutral inflection, because she expects to be interrupted. Her expectations are usually met.

Non-verbal cues

The passive finds the world terrifying and unfair, so it is no wonder that she literally does not want to face it. Consequently, her eye contact with others is evasive, and her eyes are often averted altogether. When stressed, which is most of the time, she blinks quite rapidly. Her eyebrows are often raised in questioning and/or pleading situations, and this usually matches the verbal upward inflections. She often has a weak smile on her face, to propitiate others, who seem to be permanently angry at her. We smile to propitiate and appease others, but the passive overdoes it, to the point of doing something quite bizarre and self-mutilating: she smiles even when angry at others "laughing through the tears" ("I'm *really* angry at you!"). Most of us, when confronted with a dissonance between verbal and non-verbal behaviour, usually accept the non-verbal signal, so this exercise in suppressed rage is quite counter-productive.

The passive's smile is part of her whole facial expression, which is often super-mobile or super-plastic, that is, shows positive emotions so exaggerated as to be caricatures. As mentioned before, non-verbal communication is often about submission and dominance, and generally speaking, dominants do not smile and do not look at others, while subordinates smile at and look at dominants. Compare, for example, children versus parents, slaves and servants versus masters, and social inferiors versus social superiors. The passive's hyper-alert features thus betray that she is the child, the slave, the servant, the inferior. This super-feedback to others is also conveyed through constant nodding to others, to madly signal approval (with the unrequited hope that this will be reciprocated). Paradoxically, this expression can also shift to a blank expression, a mask of pain, which usually accompanies the social autism of the silent treatment. Like the autistic, the passive is giving notice here that she is shutting down all or most transactions with the cruel world, and that she is emotionally on strike. This may sometimes appear as a sullen, sulking expression, particularly when she is brooding on the injustice of it all.

Because she is stressed so continually, she often exhibits stress symptoms such as rapid biting and wetting of her lips, rapid swallowing, and blushing. With her posture also, the passive can shift from one extreme to another. She may slump over into a foetal slouch, or rock back and forth like a stressed and/or tantrum-displaying child. Alternatively, she may go quite rigid when in her autistic persona.

Her *gestures* also reveal much about her. She often wrings her hands, a classic gesture of despair. Her hands are often near her mouth, to provide the quick emotional hit of oral gratification—nail-biting, knuckle-gnawing, cigarette smoking, and so on. She may touch herself continuously, stroking, patting, touching, not so much as an auto-erotic display but as an exercise in existential reassurance—yes, I'm still all here.

Her fingers and toes may be clenched, particularly in conflict situations or where she feels she has made a fool of herself. Her feet may be turned inward, which can often mean a lack of self-confidence. So great may be her need to discharge the anxiety within her that she may constantly fidget with ornaments such as rings and watches, and objects such as pens (a more civilised culture, of course, would give her permission to toy with worry beads or similar adult pacifiers). This nervousness—the restless energy that will never be released in action—is also shown in "jumpy" legs, jiggling up and down, and tapping feet, engines eternally in neutral, or reverse. The passive may also shuffle her feet when beaten, a type of non-verbal mumbling. Because life is so tough, she often sighs with her body, as well as with her mouth and nose.

The passive–aggressive or manipulative style

The manipulative combines elements of the passive and aggressive styles. Some manipulatives would secretly like to be aggressives, some are happy, or not unhappy, the way they are. As mentioned before, Phelps and Austin (1975) argue that women have never been allowed the behavioural option of aggression (except perhaps towards others still lower in the social pecking order), and hence have had to make do with being manipulative. Many men, however, are just as manipulative as those women whose style is manipulation, just as men can be as vain, irrational and weak as the most stereotyped of women.

General behaviour

The manipulative primarily wants power without responsibility. She sees the world, however, not just in a political way, but an over-political way: she is always trying to get her way through connections, name-dropping, mutual back-scratching and secret networks. When these don't work, she gets nastier: she uses bitchiness, backstabbing, character assassination, rumour-mongering and innuendoes. She is the compleat Machiavellian, and would certainly qualify as a high mach (see Chapter 10).

She seduces (sometimes literally), she manipulates, she flatters others while simultaneously undermining them. Female manipulatives will have no qualms about using sexist tactics such as "womanly wiles", coyness and archness. The manipulative often plays hard to get, in semi-sexual or non-sexual situations, even when such tactics are unnecessary except to demonstrate her own influence to herself.

To protect herself against manipulation, the manipulative often feigns innocence. To protect herself, to irritate others, or to ingratiate herself with others, she may feign stupidity, so that others will have to spend time with her showing her how it's done. She may exploit others' guilt feelings, and emotionally blackmail others in a wide variety of situations. Her own emotions are all too closely under control: she sees others as objects to be used, and she intellectualises away any misgivings she may have about such callousness ("the end justifies the means").

Verbal cues

The manipulative may use phrases (never, of course, in public) such as "I'll wrap him/her around my little finger". Just as she over-politicises everything, so she over-sexualises everything, using semi-sexual and sexual come-ons to get her way (indeed, for the manipulative, sex may be just another extension of politics and politics just another extension of sex).

From behind a civilised mask, she mocks others with frequent undue emphasis on phrases: "Who, *me*? Oh no! Never!" This is particularly true when she is gossiping, which is often. She has a vicious tongue, often using sarcasm to devastating effect, often with a bitterness which is truly twisted and frightening.

Just as the passive may mix up verbal and non-verbal signals by smiling when angry, the manipulative attacks through humour, using hostile kidding (if challenged, she retreats and retorts, "can't you take a joke? I was only kidding"). Alternatively, she is a past mistress of the silent treatment, freezing people out who are on to her game or people who are non-influential and not worth wasting time on, or people who are potential or actual competition.

Non-verbal cues
The manipulative uses eyes to good effect. She will roll her eyes to indicate disapproval. She rarely does this overtly to the person disapproved of, but rather does it covertly to others, implicating them in the conspiracy of ridicule. Another conspiratorial cue is over-elaborate, stagey winking. When accused of being what she is, she will use eyebrows to great effect, feigning wide-eyed puzzlement and wounded innocence. Her manipulation is sometimes so obvious, she will not even look directly at someone when trying to get something from them (cf. body orientation).

She often purses her lips, not so much prissily but in a judgmental way. When she is playing the sycophant, the yes-lady, the crawler, she has a fawning expression on her face to accompany her flattering patter. When she is letting rip her formidable powers of sarcasm, she has a facetious expression on her face (eyebrows up, eyes rolling, mouth in a moue or pout). When conspiring, she looks suitably conspiratorial: furtive, darting eyes, lowered voice, body huddled, usually non-verbally "mirroring" the posture of her conspirator. Alternatively, her body may be oriented away from people she considers "uninteresting" and/or "uninfluential", even when speaking to such people—an amazing display of rudeness and egomania.

The manipulative may have a whole series of quite theatrical gestures that reveal her unlovely character: sighing loudly with exasperation, yawning to indicate how boring everyone else is, expressing her impatience with others by drumming her fingers and tapping her toes, talking conspiratorially with her hand in front of her mouth, and arranging her fingers in that gesture of pompousness, the steeple.

The manipulative, then, is not a very pleasant person; how good it is to be able to recognise manipulatives by their verbal and non-verbal behaviour! But it may not be as simple as that. The truly skilled manipulative, the superstar of slyness, may well be aware of this repertoire of behaviours, and may take great pains to ensure that she has *none* of them. Remember, it is only the really skilled liars who can look you sincerely in the eye and lie. In the worst of all possible worlds, manipulatives would study assertive behaviour (because it is usually the most effective) and mimic it.

The assertive style
The assertive person is as notable for what verbal and non-verbal behaviours she *doesn't* have as well as for what she does have (note, for example, the number of non-verbal behaviours the four styles have, Table 6.3).

General behaviour
The assertive person tries to avoid I win/you lose situations. She takes appropriate action towards getting what she wants, but ensuring that getting what *she* wants does not deny the rights of others. She tries not to play games with others: she negotiates, using compromise (i.e. she doesn't always win,

but she doesn't lose). She evaluates impartially, trying to accept others and their ideas on their own merits. She is relaxed and competent enough to be able to trust others, and thus delegates much of her work. She is not naive about political processes: she deals with power and politics openly, unlike the crafty manipulative, the pushy aggressive, and the anxious and gullible passive.

The other three styles are often *re*active, reacting to crises with recriminations, second-guessing and blaming. The assertive tends to be more *pro*active —seeing crises as symptoms rather than causes, and concentrating on solutions, what we are going to do, rather than on what we should have done (see Chapter 8).

The assertive person is not ethereal and saint-like, without feelings and fallibility—quite the reverse. She acknowledges and respects others' feelings, including their fear and their anger; she also takes risks with expressing her own feelings, and tries to act as a model of behaviour for others. She claims the right, not the privilege, to make mistakes. She thus avoids the massive stress that aggressives, who must always appear infallible and thus never delegate, are under. Because she anticipates mistakes, and will not be crushed when they happen, she can take risks with change and innovation, like all good evolutionary successes do. Interestingly, she also claims the right to be *non*-assertive. In a world infested with manipulatives, passives and aggressives, it can be wearing being an assertive, because assertion is such a violation of the status quo. Consequently, even the assertive person needs to lapse every now and then into another behaviour style.

The assertive person tends to be consistent in her behaviour, and does not experience guilt feelings about things she has said and done, or has not said and done—unlike the aggressive, passive, and manipulative. Of all the four behaviour types, the assertive alone has non-verbal and verbal behaviour which is congruent: in other words, there is no contradiction between her words and her action.

Verbal cues

In Milgram's terms, the assertive person is autonomous, not agentic. She makes decisions independently of the need to win approval from or dominate others. Consequently, she is given to statements such as "I choose to. . ." Because she is so proactive or solution-oriented, she is continually examining alternatives. She asks fact-finding questions (when, where, how, why, who, what). She avoids the "shoulds" and the "oughts" of the punishing aggressive and the self-punishing passive.

Because she is proactive and a problem-solver, she wants others to be proactive and problem-solvers. She may nudge this behaviour along by saying to them, "tell me something good" and "tell me the bad news and the good news". She knows that it is essential that others know they can tell her bad news—mistakes, fiascoes, accidents—because if she punishes honesty (shoot the bearer of bad news) then she will get dishonesty from then on. But she also wants them to see, not in an idiotic Pollyannaish way, of course, that there are good aspects of most situations, that many problems are opportunities, and that relentless negativity is counter-productive.

When something cannot be done, the assertive person simply says no—to pushy bosses, manipulative lovers, wheedling and only apparently helpless relatives—and doesn't feel guilty about it. Unlike the aggressive, the assertive draws a clear distinction between fact and opinion. When the assertive criticises, it is a constructive process, not a destructive one characterised by blaming and unwarranted assumptions. The assertive uses an appropriately firm and warm tone when speaking, emphasising key words to clarify rather than manipulate or patronise.

Non-verbal cues

The assertive person maintains direct, not staring eye contact with others, which conveys openness and trust. Her face shows attentiveness to others, and her general expression is congruent with what is being expressed. Her posture is relaxed and open, in contrast to the complicated and stressful gyrations of the manipulative, the passive and the aggressive. She opens her hands when speaking to indicate honesty, and when she has finished speaking, the palms remain open to cue others into giving the opinions she values highly. She demonstrates trust and empathy by touching others, according to their role and need for personal space and privacy.

Becoming assertive

Most people (not all) would say that the assertive style was superior to, and preferable to, the aggressive, passive and manipulative styles. If we prefer assertion, and want to be more assertive, how can we do it? We can learn to adopt the general behaviour and the specific verbal and non-verbal behaviour of the assertive style. We can learn to recognise the tactics of the aggressives, passives and manipulatives, by learning to recognise their general behaviour and specific verbal and non-verbal behaviours. There are other tools of control and counter-control that assertive people and would-be assertive people can learn, however. Let's look at these now.

Verbal skills

1. *Broken record* is the skill of calmly repeating what you want, over and over again, just like a broken record. If you know you can depend upon Broken Record, you do not have to psych yourself up for a dialogue with someone else, and you can also calmly sidestep irrelevant logic and baiting from the other person.
2. *Fogging* is the skill of calmly acknowledging that criticism of you may well be justified. Your antagonist, instead of lashing out and hitting something solid, thus lashes out but finds no resistance, as if they were trying to punch fog. Fogging helps to separate personalities from problems.
3. *Free information* is the skill of giving and recognising basic factual information that can help conversation beyond the basic "what do you think of the weather" type lines.
4. *Self-disclosure* is the skill of revealing positive and negative aspects of yourself to others. The next step on from free information.
5. *Negative inquiry* is the skill of actively seeking constructive criticism from others. This will provide you with useful information and/or exhaust the manipulative/aggressive ploys of others.
6. *Positive inquiry* is the skill of actively seeking information from others about what solutions they see to their problems. This will provide you with useful information and/or exhaust the manipulative/passive ploys of others.
7. *Workable compromise* is the skill of proposing a negotiated solution to a conflict that will satisfy both parties, without sacrificing the self-respect of either party.

These specific tools can be of great help in coping assertively with a wide variety of situations.[3] Let us look at three situations in personal and professional situations involving aggressive, manipulative and passive behaviour, to see how such tools can be used.

Dialogue 1: Jane gets a prescription for a contraceptive pill from her family doctor

Jane Richards' doctor is Doctor John Russell. The doctor is an old friend of Jane's family, and in fact delivered Jane at birth. Jane is used to calling him "Uncle John". She has always been regarded by her friends and family as a shy girl, in need of protection from a dangerous world. Jane is fed up with this image, and wants to develop more assertive relationships with others. She has a boyfriend, and wants to start a sexual relationship with him. She will be eighteen in several months.

Doctor: Hi Janie, How's mum and dad?
Jane: They're fine. *So am I.* (Free information)
Doctor: Well then, what can we do for you, pet?
Jane: (plucking up her courage): I would like a prescription for a contraceptive pill.
Doctor: Surely you can't be serious? That's absurd!
Jane: *I can understand how you might feel that way, but I would like a prescription.* (Self-disclosure, Broken record)
Doctor: But how old are you, girl, what, fifteen, sixteen . . .
Jane: *I'll be eighteen in 10 weeks, and I would like that prescription. (Free information, Broken record)*
Doctor: But lassie, you're so young for your age, you know so little of the world. Why, it was only a few years ago that I delivered you . . .
Jane: *What you say may well be true, but I still want the prescription.* (Fogging, Broken record)
Doctor: Of course, many girls like you *say* that they want the pill, but they really don't. Look, I've got other patients who have been waiting for an hour. Why don't you come back later on, or tomorrow, with your mother, and we'll talk about it? (attribution of ignorance: you don't really know what you want. Guilt induction—you're holding up others)
Jane: *I appreciate that other people have needs, but so do I. I would like you to fill out that prescription.* (Fogging, Broken record)
Doctor: But some pills have nasty side effects. You don't want to get sick just because you want to play around with some boy, do you? (guilt induction)
Jane: *No, I don't want to get sick. I have faith in your ability to prescribe the least harmful one, and my research tells me that this is still the safest method of contraception. Please write the prescription for me.* (Self-disclosure, Broken record)

---

[3] Smith (1975) also includes the skill of negative assertion: "A skill that teaches acceptance of your errors and faults (without having to apologise) by strongly and sympathetically agreeing with hostile or constructive criticism of your negative qualities." This is a useful skill, but initially many people confuse it with fogging and negative inquiry.

Smith does not use positive inquiry, but I feel that this is useful, particularly in dealing with passive people.

Doctor: Look, if you won't bring your parents in, perhaps you should talk to Dr Johnstone. She's filling in while Dr Renfrew's away. She's a woman, and she can explain these things better than I can.

Jane: *Will she give me a prescription?* (Broken record)

Doctor: No, of course not! (anger to throw her off balance). Well, I can't say. . . (hasty retreat)

Jane: *If she gives me a prescription, can I get a renewal from you?* (Workable compromise)

Doctor: Look Jane, your parents won't forgive me!

Jane: I'll tell my parents about it when the mood is right. I'll take full responsibility.

Doctor: But how can I be sure of that? Your parents will still blame me! I can't let you do it.

Jane: *I understand how you feel,* but *I still want that prescription. I will have told them by the time I need another prescription, and I'll tell you how it went.* (Self-disclosure, Broken record, Workable compromise)

Doctor: But they'll blame me.

Jane: I'll tell them that the prescription was not a favour from a friend but a transaction between a professional and an adult client. *If you feel that you can't see things like that, that's fine—I respect your feelings. Perhaps I should consult someone else.* (Self-disclosure, Workable compromise)

Doctor: Ye Gods, Jane, you're not the sweet little thing I used to know. The way you're talking, you've become hard as nails. You sound like you're a thousand years old. (guilt induction, anger display)

Jane: *You may be right. Perhaps I have had to toughen up, and I'm sorry if I've gone to the other extreme. Nevertheless, I still want a prescription.* (Fogging, Self-disclosure, Broken record)

Doctor: All right, Jane, but please promise me you'll tell them first, in a level-headed way, like you are now, and not let them find out about it, one way or another.

Jane: *I promise* (takes prescription). Thanks, Uncle. (Workable compromise)

Doctor: Drop that "uncle" crap. You'd better call me John from now on.

Dialogue 2: Janine copes with an incompetent subordinate

Janine: Ah, Rick, we need estimates on the Snowfoam job. I'd like it on my desk by 10 o'clock tomorrow, right? (puts papers on Rick's desk)

Rick: Tomorrow. . . (looks through papers) . . . whew . . . don't know, mate . . . it's a tall order . . . I could work back, I suppose (sighs) . . . or take it home. . .

Janine: It's been a long time since we were at school, Rick. No one expects you do to homework. *Just re-schedule the Adelaide stuff, if they don't buy it, give them my number—they owe me one. Ten o'clock tomorrow, OK?* (Workable compromise, Broken record)

Rick: Look, I'd really like to help you, you know that . . . but . . . well
. . . just between you and me and the gatepost, everyone
knows that I'm a screw-up artist . . . it's a wonder I wasn't
rolled years ago, actually . . . I'll probably let you down . . .
anyway, that's your speciality, this stuff, isn't it? (flattery, attempt
at upward delegation).

Janine: *I appreciate that you see a risk in doing it, and I'm sure you will
appreciate that I'm taking a risk in wanting you to do it. I won't
hit you with a sermon or lay a guilt trip on you,* but *both of us
know that you didn't screw up on that Rotex job. Do you see
any similarities between that job and this one?* (Self-disclosure,
Positive inquiry)

Rick: Well . . . I was lucky with Rotex, I reckon . . . let's see . . . oh,
yeah . . . the Tasmanian data file . . . um . . . God, I've
forgotten how to calculate *that* . . . um . . . oh hell, look, it's
not fair! I've got all these jobs to do for Mary and Ralph. I said
I'd do them a favour. You don't want me to muck them around,
do you? Jeez, I dunno . . . (sighs) (anger display, guilt
induction)

Janine: They often dump their work on you, don't they? Until you get
paid their salaries as well, I suggest you learn to say "no" to
them. *Would you like me to re-schedule their work, or will you
speak to them?* (Positive inquiry)

Rick: Gee, they'll be burned off . . . (scrabbles through diary) Well . . .
if you wouldn't mind . . . but I suppose I should fight my own
battles . . . God, they'll have my guts for garters! . . . those
bastards are always ripping me off, you know! Still, when you
look at it from their point of view . . .

Janine: Come on Rick, life's too short *(flips coin) Call it.* (Workable
compromise)

Rick: Um . . . uh . . . ah, heads, it's you.

Janine: No, it's you. See? Just tell them your own work has to take
priority. *If they squawk, send them to me. I'll make a point of
working with their supervisor this afternoon, and he'll be very
interested in their delegation technique.* (Workable compromise)

Rick: Gee, thanks . . . that'll get them off my back, for this week at
least . . .

Janine: No, Rick, off your back permanently. If they try it again, play it
by the book. Don't be indispensable, you won't get promoted
(they both laugh). *Now, with Snowfoam, how many estimates do
we need to get a full picture? How many variables do you think
there are?* (Positive inquiry)

Rick: Well, um . . . I suppose if it's like Rotex . . . yes, it's similar in
lots of ways . . . we need to know about retailers' mark-ups . . .
and road transport costs . . . I suppose three or four estimates
. . . does that sound right?

Janine: Sounds fine. Make it four, to be on the safe side. *Can you do
me a memo by 10 tomorrow, giving four estimates, in writing
and on a graph, with your recommendations for priority?*
(Broken record, Positive inquiry)

Rick: 10 . . . jeez . . . um . . . yeah, well, I suppose if Ralph and
Mary are off my back I can do it . . .

Janine: Fine. *I'll see you at 10 tomorrow,* we'll have coffee and discuss
it. *Ring me at 3 today to tell me how it's going, OK?* (Broken
record, Positive inquiry)

Rick: OK.

Dialogue 3: Joe copes with correcting one of his mistakes

Brenda: (throws report down on Joe's desk): What do you mean by handing in rubbish like this?

Joe: Ah, the Holocube report. *Yes, it's not up to our usual standards*—we didn't get the specs until the day before the deadline. Would you like. . . (Self-disclosure)

Brenda: Well, you've got a barefaced cheek, admitting you fouled up!

Joe: *I can understand how you feel,* but *it's probably better that I didn't muck you around by lying.* (Self-disclosure, Workable compromise)

Brenda: Well, it's just not good enough!

Joe: *I agree, it's not. Now that we have the specs, would you like me to re-do it and get it to you before tomorrow's meeting?* (Fogging, Workable compromise)

Brenda: Forget it, it's probably too damn late for the meeting.

Joe: *I'm sure you feel upset,* but *should I get it to you before tomorrow?* (Self-disclosure, Broken record)

Brenda: It's too late, and besides, the footnotes are all wrong.

Joe: *I don't understand, can you tell me how you want them done?* (Negative inquiry)

Brenda: It's an American system, you wouldn't understand.

Joe: *Can you tell me some more about it?* I'll re-format the whole thing on my word-processor. (Negative inquiry)

Brenda: Don't come on all assertive with me, boyo! You're not going to knock the wind out of my sails! I've got a right to be angry!

Joe: *I agree, and I am partly at fault. Would you like me to leave you alone? Would you like another assistant here?* (Fogging, Self-disclosure, Negative inquiry)

Brenda: No . . . we've got a bloody report to do, haven't we? God knows why, but we do seem to turn out good product. Hang on . . . who was it who gave you the specs late? I should know.

Joe: *I agree you should know.* . . (Fogging)

Brenda: Don't fog me around! Who was it?

Joe: Well actually it was you—you left them at the pub on Thursday, and a waitress gave them to me on Friday.

Brenda: Hmmph . . . I suppose you think you're pretty good, eh?

Joe *(turns on loudest printer):* Sorry Brenda, this printer is so loud. Have you got the title page there? (Workable compromise)

Exercises

You may find it useful to *rehearse* (*role-play*) these verbal skills before going in to an actual encounter with someone. Observe the people around you, noting their general behaviour, their verbal and non-verbal behaviour. To what extent do they fit comfortably into the aggressive/passive/manipulative/ assertive model? To what extent do they combine aspects of different behavioural styles? Once you are clear on these points, write and rehearse some dialogues, preferably with someone else. It helps to switch roles, putting you in the place of the passive, manipulative or aggressive (or indeed, assertive) who is giving you trouble. Perhaps you may even see that their behaviour towards you is not devoid of rhyme or reason.

It helps greatly to have a video system to give you feedback on your and your colleague's performance. The poor man's video—a mirror—is better than nothing, but it will not give you the detached (and replayable and re-analyseable) viewpoint of the video. This is important in analysing your verbal behaviour, and particularly important in analysing your non-verbal behaviour: are your "non-verbals" congruent with your "verbals"? Is your body contradicting your mouth? Are the words comic but the music tragic, or vice versa?

To build your confidence, role-play some of the following situations:
1. You admit you are wrong.
2. You ask for information you need from professionals.
3. You ask for a raise.
4. You reject the sexual advances of someone of the opposite sex.
5. You reject the sexual advances of someone of the same sex.
6. You tell a person you like/love him/her.
7. You end an unsatisfactory relationship.
8. You tell a person who has called you are too busy to talk.
9. You ask people in a theatre to stop talking.
10. You send back unacceptable food in a restaurant.
11. You refuse to contribute to a worthy cause.

(adapted from Kelly 1977)

It is also useful to *visualise* other, atypical behaviour in relation to people you have problems with. Visualise how you would like your aggressive, passive or manipulative associate to sound. If you are greatly daunted by authority figures, imagine such figures in atypical surroundings: doing the dishes, playing with children, as a child, sitting on the toilet, at a barbecue, sick, dead, in reversed roles.

Schwimmer (1979) suggests it is useful to further build up your confidence by constructing a *risk-list*, and then beginning to take those risks in the real world. You might try the following:
1. Asking to share a taxi with a stranger on a rainy day.
2. Asking a fellow passenger not to smoke.
3. Telling someone that they have offensive breath/body odour.
4. Remonstrating with a queue-jumper.
5. Asking a shop attendant to give you change for a $50 note, without buying anything.

Limitations of assertiveness

Assertiveness training (AT) seems to many people to be a totally effective way of learning to communicate with other people. But are there any drawbacks to it? As with any other idea, we must be ready to criticise, and there is certainly a good deal to criticise in AT, not only at the technical level (*do* the techniques work?), but at the ethical level (*should* the techniques work?) and at the social level (what happens if everyone starts getting assertive?).

It is likely that AT does not work with extreme passives, aggressives and manipulatives. Schwimmer (1979) suggests that there is only one assertive technique that works on a true tyrant—walk away for good (if that option is open to you). McNeilage and Adams (1982) argue that the true manipulative is totally bad news; there is nothing you can do with the extreme type, because such a person has simply forgotten what it is like to conduct open communications with anyone else. Similarly, with the extreme passive, it is difficult to wean them away from their agentic behaviour. You yourself must also beware of becoming trapped into destructive game-playing, such as—to use TA terminology—Why Don't You—Yes But (WDYYB) and I'm Only Trying to Help You (IOTTHY) (see Chapter 5). All three extreme types are sociopaths, and all three will be secretly delighted if yet another assertive missionary-type comes to impale herself on their ancient defence systems.

Smith (1975) notes that AT techniques will also not work in some particular situations, no matter how skilled you are. Two of these situations are *legal situations*, and situations when you are *physically threatened*. It makes no sense to try Broken Record on a judge in a courtroom—you know what the outcome must be.[4] There is also no point in trying Broken Record or Fogging on a criminal who is threatening you with a gun or a knife. The movie myth of the super-practical dowager who tells a gunman not to be silly and hits him with her umbrella is just that—a myth.

There is also the charge which can be laid upon the AT philosophy that it is fundamentally naive. AT, like TA (transactional analysis), RET (rational–emotional therapy), and many other products of American humanistic psychology, seems fundamentally committed to a mode of communication between people that depends upon total honesty. But is it always wise to be honest? Schwimmer, for example, suggests that "those who climb the ladder of success do so by being fair, forthright and sincere" (Schwimmer 1979). Is this always the case? McNeilage and Adams acknowledge that politics is a part of any situation, professional or personal, and the truly assertive is a political operator when called upon to be so. Alberti and Emmons (1978) assert that it is all right to choose deliberately not to be assertive in a number of situations. These deviations from honesty-is-the-best-policy are, however, rare within the AT literature.

Eglash (1980), in his idiosyncratic but perceptive critique, puts the opposite view: that AT is not naive, but in fact is super-slick, manipulative and quite nasty. He calls AT *RT*: Refusal Training. He suggests that AT is the perfect philosophy for the selfish "Me Generation", a philosophy which teaches people to refuse and reject other people's advice, apologies, criticisms, humour, genuine inquiries about our lives, their requests for help, and their offers of help. AT, he says, encourages heroic and mutilating self-sufficiency and isolation, and discourages a more natural and humane method of communication which acknowledges the interdependence of people.

He also notes how yet another allegedly humanistic psychological technique (AT) becomes, when applied to work settings, yet another tool of the powerful, a tool for the managers rather than the managed. Thus he notes that virtually all treatments of assertive supervision presume that faults lie with employees, rather than supervisors and/or company policy and procedure (or even that the fault lies with no one).

Perhaps most damning for Eglash is that he sees AT denying us expression of our most natural and healthy emotions—aggression, anxiety, fear and guilt. This unnatural suppression, he suggests, is in fact stress-prone type A behaviour (see Chapter 7).

Finally, there is the problem, or at least the puzzle, of what happens if everyone becomes assertive. Virtually all AT books and articles are produced by psychologists, and as such are usually concerned only with relationships between individuals in small groups, or micro-behaviour, rather than macro-behaviour at the social level. Perhaps we are already seeing macro-assertiveness with the plethora of special interest groups which have recently become

---

[4] You can, of course, be more assertive in legal situations by knowing your rights: see, for example, Bennett (1983).

active—environmentalists, feminists, racial groups, consumer groups, anti-war groups, education groups, pro- and anti-abortion groups, and so on. Radical and liberal political scientists are reasonably comfortable with this type of pressure group/single-interest group behaviour, seeing it as a long overdue expression of alternative points of view and also as a counterweight to the traditional pressure groups of business, the military, the churches, and other professional groups. Conservative political scientists are not so sure. They argue that political systems can only accommodate a narrow spectrum of views and interests, and the new groups threaten the whole system with overload: political systems, they say, are about compromise and coalitions, and single-interest groups by definition are not very interested in compromise and coalitions.

Finally, there is the question of whether macro-assertion is possible, given our biological heritage. As discussed earlier, the extreme hereditarian viewpoint would have it that humanity is driven by powerful genetically ingrained behaviours of aggression and submission. AT, as we have seen, is a very environmentalist philosophy—it places great faith in people's ability to *learn* new behaviours, rather than be controlled by dark forces, in our ability to steer a middle course between aggression and submission (but away from manipulation).

Summary

Assertiveness can be defined as getting what you want from others without infringing upon others' rights. Assertiveness training is a series of techniques and philosophies for assertively dealing with aggressive, passive and manipulative (and, of course, assertive) people.

A good way to understand types of behaviour is to examine the hereditary and environmental causes of aggression. Is aggression genetic, or do we learn it from our environment? How does this explain dominant and submissive behaviour in animals and humans? The answers are not clear.

Milgram suggests that agentic people can be forced to be aggressive towards others, whereas autonomous people cannot be forced. A similar model of behaviour is that of Rotter, who distinguishes between internal people, who believe that they control their own behaviour, and external people, who believe their behaviour is controlled by others.

Our being dominant or submissive, autonomous or agentic, internal or external, is partly determined by our response to stress, which in turn is partly hereditary and partly a learned phenomenon.

Four styles of behaviour—assertiveness, aggression, passivity and manipulation—can be identified by unique verbal and non-verbal behaviours.

Assertive behaviour can be learned by practising verbal skills, such as Broken Record and Fogging. Rehearsal, role-playing, visualisation and working through a risk-list can also help.

Assertiveness training has been criticised on various grounds, including the notions that it leads to selfish behaviour, it ignores genetic predispositions to aggression and passivity, and so on.

Questions for discussion

1. Is aggression genetically programmed, or is it environmentally learned?

2. How can we best encourage autonomous behaviour (in Milgram's sense)?
3. Is it better to be an internal personality rather than an external personality?
4. To what extent might stress determine whether we behave assertively or otherwise?
5. Construct a role-play in which a person is, by turns, aggressive, passive, assertive and manipulative, in different situations (e.g. different telephone conversations, walking through four different work areas, dealing with four different children). How does it feel, shifting behaviour so much? Are such changes realistic?
6. Construct alternative outcomes for dialogues 1, 2 and 3 (pp.192–5), for example, write dialogue 1 so that the doctor assertively refuses to help Jane.
7. Devise your own rehearsal role-plays, visualisations and risk-lists.
8. Under what circumstances could assertiveness skills be used to hurt others?

References

Alberti, R. and Emmons, M. (1978). *Your Perfect Right.* (Impact: New York).
Ardrey, Robert (1968). *The Territorial Imperative.* (Pan: London).
Baron, Robert A., Byrne, Donn and Kantowitz, E.A. (1980). *Psychology: Understanding Behaviour,* 2nd edn. (Holt, Rinehart and Winston: New York).
Beck, Ken and Beck, Kate (1982). *Assertiveness at Work: A Practical Guide to Handling Awkward Situations.* (McGraw Hill: London).
Bennett, John (1983). *Your Rights.* (Victorian Council for Civil Liberties: Melbourne).
Bloom, Lynn, Coburn, Karen and Pearlman, B. (1975). *The New Assertive Woman.* (Delacorte: New York).
Bower, Sharon Anthony and Bower, Gordon H. (1978). *Asserting Yourself: A Practice Guide for Positive Change.* (Addison-Wesley: Reading, Mass.).
Burley-Allen, Madelyn (1983). *Managing Assertively: How to Improve Your People Skills.* (Wiley: New York).
Cohen, Herb (1982). *You Can Negotiate Anything.* (Dell: New York).
Dale, David (1974). "Taking Orders", *The National Times,* 3–7 June.
Eglash, Albert (1980). *The Case Against Assertiveness Training.* (Quest Press: California).
Galassi, Meerna Dee and Galassi, John P. (1977). *Assert Yourself! How to be Your Own Person.* (Human Sciences Press: New York).
Jakubowski, Patricia and Lange, Arthur J. (1978). *The Assertive Option: Your Rights and Responsibilities.* (Research Press: Champaign, Ill.).
Kelley, Alison (1977). *Assertion: A Trainer's Guide.* (University Associates: San Diego, Calif.).
Lindgren, Henry (1969). *An Introduction to Social Psychology.* (John Wiley: New York).
Lorenz, Konrad (1966). *On Aggression.* (Methuen: London).
McNeilage, Linda A. and Adams, Kathleen A. (1982). *Assertiveness at Work: How to Increase Your Personal Power on the Job.* (Prentice-Hall: New Jersey).
Milgram, Stanley (1974). *Obedience to Authority.* (Tavistock: London).
O'Brien, G.E. and Kabanoff, B. (1981). "Australian Norms and Factor Analysis of Rotter's Internal–External Control Scale", *Australian Psychologist,* vol. 16, no. 2.

Pareek, Udai (1982). "Internal and External Control", *The 1982 Annual Handbook for Group Facilitators* (ed. John Pfeiffer and Leonard B. Goodstein). (University Associates: San Diego, Calif.).

Phelps, Stanlee and Austin, Nancy (1975). *The Assertive Woman.* (Impact Press: California).

Ringerman, Robert (1976). *Looking Out for Number One.* (Bantam: New York). (1978). *Winning Through Intimidation.* (Circus: Melbourne).

Rotter, J.B. (1954). *Social Learning and Clinical Psychology.* (Prentice-Hall: New Jersey).

Rotter, J.B. and Hochreich, D.J. (1975). *Personality.* (Scott Foresman).

Schwimmer, Laurence D. (1979). *How to Ask for a Raise Without Getting Fired and Other Assertive Techniques.* (Bantam: New York).

Smith, Manuel J. (1975). *When I Say No, I Feel Guilty.* (Bantam: New York).

Wilson, Edward D. (1975). *Sociobiology: The New Synthesis.* (M.I.T. Press: Mass.).

Zimbardo, Phillip, Norwood, Robert, and Pilkonis, Paul (1975). "Shackles of Shyness", *Psychology Today* (UK Edition), September.

Films/Videos

When I Say No, I Feel Guilty (Power Human Resources).
Conflict Management (Training Media Services).
Managing Conflict (Power Human Resources).

Part D

Self-management skills

Decisions, problems, stress, time—so often, these things are totally managed for us, by others. Regaining control over these things, managing ourselves, would be a good thing, but to what extent can this occur? Removing all external control of our lives is impossible, and probably undesirable (indeed, to the extent that we increase control over our own lives, to a similar extent we increase control over others).

Nevertheless, we can and should get more control over the decisions, problems, stress and time in our lives. Indeed, there are substantial overlaps between these apparently disparate areas.

Making decisions and solving problems, managing stress and time are all concerned with setting priorities. In a universe of infinite possibilities and all-too-finite resources, we need to be able to plan and sequence and make trade-offs.

Study and mastery of these areas can also teach us to be more proactive and less reactive. If we are always simply reacting to a series of apparently random events and pressures, we become exhausted and quite ineffective; we need to proact, to anticipate, to not only behave more effectively in the face of events and pressures, but to change the very nature of those events and pressures.

Finally, we need to understand that such self-management skills are not simply a kit of objective techniques; we need to understand that they have a large subjective component of personality factors and apparently non-rational behaviour patterns. To attempt to manage time, manage stress, solve problems and make decisions in purely technical, operational ways without taking into account the human factor is to miss the point of self-management.

In Chapter 7 (Stress management) we consider techniques such as meditation, biofeedback, and life-event stressors analysis, as well as personality types and rational–emotive therapy. In Chapter 8 (Time management) we consider meetings, paperwork and planning and priority-setting, as well as the behavioural aspects of pro-crastination and crisis management. In Chapter 9 (Decision-making and problem-solving) we consider lateral thinking scenarios and critical path method, as well as learning styles and Murphy's Law.

7

Stress management

The time to relax is when you don't
have time for it.
Sydney J. Harris

Work done with anxiety about results
is far inferior to work done without
such anxiety, in the calm of self-
surrender. Seek refuge in the
knowledge of Brahman. They who
work selfishly for results are
miserable. . .
(The wise man) puts aside desire,
Offering the act to Brahman.
The lotus leaf rests unwetted on water;
He rests on action, untouched by
action.
Bhagavad-Gita, II,V

Keep cool: it will all be as one a
hundred years hence.
Ralph Waldo Emerson

Eat a live toad the first thing in the
morning and nothing worse will
happen to you the rest of the day.
Paul Dickson

Today we seem to hear more and
more about "stress", "burnout",
"pressure", "coping" and "anxiety".
Stress is sometimes referred to as the
modern epidemic—a widespread condition that makes life extremely unpleasant, and a pathological disease that
needs to be cured. Our use of the
concept "stress" is similar to our use of
the concept "crisis". We almost automatically think of a crisis as being a
negative, harmful thing, but if you look
in a dictionary, you will see that crisis is
not negative but neutral in meaning—a
crisis can be a critical event with a good
or bad outcome.

So with stress. An incurable optimist
might say, "there are no problems in
this world—only challenges". But
whether life events are problems or
challenges, they all cause stress—the
challenges as much as the problems.
Look at a photograph of two people
being reunited after a long separation.
What do their faces show, pleasure or
pain? Sometimes it is difficult to tell.
And many of the bodily reactions of
pleasure are the bodily reactions associated with pain.

Selye (1983) has developed a model
of stress that helps clarify the multi-
dimensional nature of stress (Fig. 7.1).
We can have stress that is good in
quality (*eustress*, from Greek "eu") or
bad in quality (*distress*), or high in
quantity (*hyperstress*) or low in
quantity (*hypostress*).

Our experience of stress, from time
to time and from situation to situation,
is a unique combination of qualitative
and quantitative factors. If Selye's model

Overstress
(hyperstress)

Good stress ——————— STRESS ——————— Bad stress
(eustress)   (distress)

Understress
(hypostress)

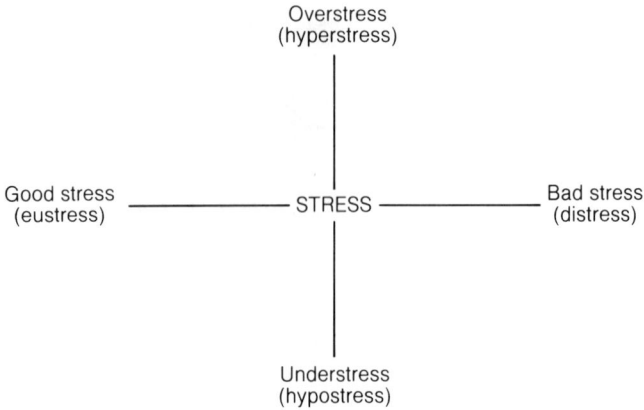

Fig 7.1 *Selye's model of stress* (SELYE 1983, P.18. REPRODUCED WITH PERMISSION)

is reconceptualised as a map, and we think of stress dimensions as being points of the compass, or better still as latitude and longitude, we should be able to mark a point or a line which shows what type of stress we are experiencing. Thus, a eustress reaction might occur if we are reunited with someone, and a distress reaction might occur if we are being separated. Eustress might occur when we win a race or have an orgasm or our side wins; distress might occur if we lose a race, are deprived of sex, or our side loses. In all circumstances, we might cry, cry out, touch ourselves and others, and be extremely agitated.

We are overstressed or hyperstressed when we are too "psyched up" to perform well, when we are overstimulated; we are understressed or hypostressed when we are bored, listless, underchallenged, understimulated. Our stress is sometimes best mapped as a dynamic line or curve rather than as a static point. The work of police officers, and soldiers in war, for example, is often characterised as 95 per cent boredom and 5 per cent terror: while most work activity is routine and dull (hypostressing), parts of the routine can be hyperstressing (shifting from shuffling papers to conducting a car pursuit of armed criminals, sitting in a dugout waiting, and then running across a field firing a weapon). In fact, violent shifts across Selye's "stress map" can in themselves be stressful.

Stress can be deferred in time: some people only become ill on their holidays, because of guilt they may feel about being sick on the job. A variation occurs when people undertake classes in, for example, relaxation techniques to better manage their stress, but paradoxically find themselves flooded with the stored-up stress of years of suffering and, in the short term, at least, find themselves more stressed than usual.

To better understand the multi-dimensional aspects of stress, you may find it useful to draw on Figure 7.1 the points or lines appropriate to these stress experiences:

1. speaking in public, and then receiving warm applause
2. speaking in public, and receiving boos and catcalls
3. reunion
4. torture
5. birth
6. boredom
7. gambling
8. sexual experiences
9. winning a footrace, fighting nausea
10. retirement
11. retirement, followed by a mild heart attack
12. unemployment
13. addiction (drugs, gambling)
14. procrastinating, then panicking on finishing a job
15. working on an assembly line
16. working in an executive position

You might find it useful to compare your mapping of these experiences with the mappings of other people. You may find significant differences in what others experience as various degrees of eustress, distress, hyperstress and hypostress. Such differences in individual responses to the same events are a critical factor in our understanding of stress and its management (see below).

Selye suggests that we should try to strike a balance between hypostress and hyperstress, while also trying to maximise eustress and minimise distress. This, of course, is easier said than done.

Stress: A sequence model

What actually causes stress? Do our environments filter or magnify stress? Do different individuals experience the same reaction to the same stressors? What type of physical and psychological reactions do people actually undergo when stressors are applied to them? Finally, what techniques and philosophies can we use to minimise such reactions and symptoms, and can we in fact prevent such symptoms and reactions from occurring in the first place?

Let's use a five-stage sequence model (Fig. 7.2) to understand what actually happens when someone says, "I feel stressed". Box 1 of the model is the objective events that may happen to us and/or that we may cause to happen to us. The environments in which we find ourselves—for example, our work environments—may filter or magnify the pressures which flow from such events (Box 2). But not all of us respond to objective events and objective environments in the same way, and thus we must take account of subjective or individual responses (Box 3). Only then can we see what symptoms of stress will actually be experienced (Box 4), and what stress management strategies will be appropriate (Box 5). Let's see how the model works in detail.

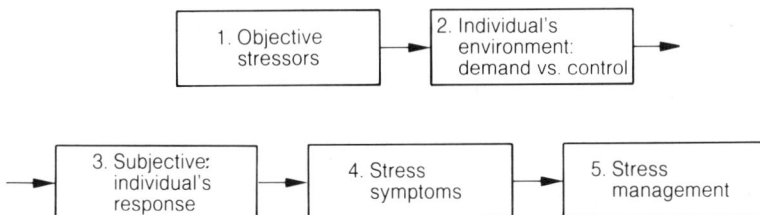

Fig 7.2 *A sequence model of stress*

Table 7.1 Life event stressors

Life event	Mean value
1. Death of spouse	100
2. Divorce	73
3. Marital separation	65
4. Detention in gaol or other institution	63
5. Death of a close family member	63
6. Major personal injury or illness	53
7. Marriage	50
8. Being fired from work	47
9. Marital reconciliation	45
10. Retirement from work	45
11. Major change in health or behaviour of a family member	44
12. Pregnancy	40
13. Sexual difficulties	39
14. Gaining a new family member (e.g. through birth, adoption, oldster moving in, etc.)	39
15. Major business readjustment (e.g. merger, reorganisation, bankruptcy, etc.)	39
16. Major change in financial state (e.g. a lot worse off or a lot better off than usual)	38
17. Death of a close friend	37
18. Changing to a different line of work	36
19. Major change in the number of arguments with mate (e.g. either a lot more or a lot less than usual regarding child-rearing, personal habits, etc.)	35
20. Taking on a mortgage or loan for a major purchase (e.g. for a home, business, etc.)	31
21. Foreclosure on a mortgage or loan	30
22. Major changes in responsibilities at work (e.g. promotion, demotion, lateral transfer)	29
23. Son or daughter leaving home (e.g. marriage, attending college)	29
24. In-law troubles	29
25. Outstanding personal achievement	28
26. Spouse beginning or ceasing work outside the home	26
27. Beginning or ceasing formal schooling	26
28. Major change in living conditions (e.g. building a new home, remodelling, deterioration of home or neighbourhood)	25
29. Revision of personal habits (dress, manners, association, etc.)	24
30. Troubles with the boss	23
31. Major change in working hours or conditions	20
32. Change in residence	20
33. Change in a new school	20
34. Major change in usual type and/or amount of recreation	19
35. Major change in church activities (e.g. a lot more or a lot less than usual)	19
36. Major change in social activities (e.g. clubs, dancing, movies, visiting, etc.)	18
37. Taking on a mortgage or loan (e.g. for a car, TV, freezer, etc.)	17
38. Major change in sleeping habits (a lot more or a lot less sleep, or change in part of day when asleep)	16
39. Major change in number of family get-togethers (e.g. a lot more or a lot less than usual)	15
40. Major change in eating habits (a lot more or a lot less food intake, or very different meal hours or surroundings)	15
41. Vacation	13
42. Christmas	12
43. Minor violations of the law (e.g. traffic tickets, jaywalking, disturbing the peace, etc.)	11

Source: Holmes and Rahe (1967), p.216. Reproduced with permission.

Objective stressors

Table 7.1 contains a list of stressors, mainly hyperstressing and distressing, but also to a lesser extent eustressing and hypostressing (for most people). The compilers of this social readjustment rating scale, Holmes and Rahe, studied more than five thousand people over a 25-year period, and found that, generally speaking, the higher an individual's life change unit (LCU) score, accumulated in one year (death of spouse = 100 points, minor violations of the law = 11 points), the greater was their chance of becoming ill (Table 7.2).

Change, however, can be an indicator not a predictor of illness (Gmelch 1982). Before we can say that a score of over 300 points in one year will mean physical or psychological illness, we have to remember a number of things:

- 21 per cent of Holmes/Rahe's sample scoring over 300 life-change units in one year did not get sick
- measurement error might have occurred (via selective memory, either for purposes of denial or for illness justification)
- genetic influences may exist
- personal perceptions as to what is truly stressful may exist
- differences in ability to cope may exist (GMELCH 1982).

After we have taken these factors into account, however, the life event stressors list is a useful tool for quantifying stress *potential* (even though we may assign different quantities to the stressors). Before we can jump from Box 1 (objective stressors) to Box 4 (stress symptoms) in our stress sequence model (Fig. 7.1) however, we need to examine the environments that people live and work in, and also we need to look at the similar and differing responses of different individuals to stress.

The individual's environment: Demand versus control

Can environments filter or magnify the impact of stressors? Karasek (1981) has developed a model which not only takes into account demands made upon people in job situations but also takes into account the amount of control or discretion given to those people in job situations (Fig. 7.3):

Examples of different types of jobs would be:

- low control/low demand *passive jobs*:
  Unskilled, semi-skilled, watchmen, attendants, clerks
- high control/low demand *low stress jobs*:
  Some professional, managerial, teaching jobs
- high control/high demand *active jobs*:
  Professional, managerial
- low control/high demand *high stress jobs*:
  Unskilled, semi-skilled, production-line operators, bus drivers, VDU operators, telephonists

(LANSBURY AND SPILLANE 1983)

Table 7.2 Stressors and their impact upon health

Life change unit (LCU) score in one year	Type of life change	Percentage of people becoming ill in following year
150–199	mild	37
200–299	moderate	50
300 +	extreme	79

Source: Adapted from Holmes and Rahe (1967).

Job demands

Low   High   Unresolved
                           strain
                                    A

Job decision latitude   Low   PASSIVE   HIGH STRAIN
(control over   JOB   JOB
job-related decisions)
                         High   LOW STRAIN   ACTIVE
                                JOB   JOB
                                                    B

                                            Activity
                                            level
Diagonal A = disproportionate levels of job demand and job discretion
Diagonal B = matched levels of job demand and job discretion

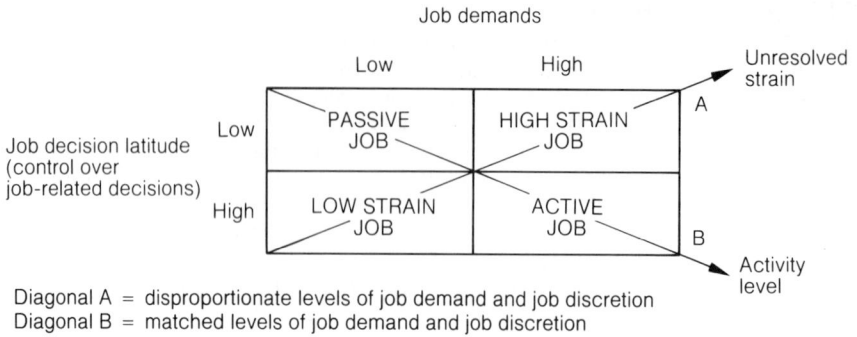

Fig 7.3 *Karasek's job strain model* (KARASEK 1981, P.78. REPRODUCED WITH PERMISSION)

One of the conventional wisdoms of stress on the job is that managers have the greatest stress, while other workers, for example assembly-line operators, have the least stress. Karasek acknowledges that many managers and professionals have high *demands* placed upon them, but they also have a fair amount of *control* over those demands, or in the ways in which they can respond to those demands. In other words, increased responsibility usually means increased power to handle those responsibilities. In contrast, many workers with high demands placed upon them have little control over those demands or the way in which they can respond to those demands; these would include people whose work routine gives them little freedom to move physically or to alter circumstances, such as assembly-line operators. It was this group which Karasek found experienced the highest levels of stress (manifested as exhaustion, depression, etc).

Thus, Karasek asserts, the most stressed people on jobs are those in high demand/low control jobs; the next most stressed are those in high demand/high control jobs; the next most stressed in low demand/high control jobs; and the least stressed of all in low demand/low control jobs.

Karasek found also that jobs socialised people into behaviour patterns displayed off the job. Thus, people in low demand/low control (passive) jobs were also very passive in their leisure pursuits (reading, window shopping, spectator sports), while more active people had more active leisure pursuits; that is, there is little evidence that deficiencies in the work environment are compensated for by choice of leisure. On the other hand, workers in high stress (high demand/low control) jobs seemed to express a protest by being involved in mass political action.

Karasek sees wide-ranging implications from this research for job and organisational design:

... alternative organisational structures with wider participation in decision-making would be optimal from the perspective of both the individual worker and the organisation as a whole.

This implication is in direct contradiction to very early "job design" strategies, such as those proposed by Frederick Taylor. Thus it is not surprising that Taylor's strategies met with severe opposition from workers and have recently been regarded as a major source of feelings of job dissatisfaction and job "meaningless-ness". Taylor advocated increasing output pressure on the worker while simultaneously drastically reducing his decision latitude. In the "bargain" the worker was to get a higher wage, but the magnitude of the unanticipated negative consequences in terms of workers' mental strain and motivation were rarely discussed (or apparently even ascertained). (KARASEK 1981, PP.89–90)[1]

Of course, it may be too simple to say that increased control over working conditions will reduce stress for all workers. Some workers may become stressed by being asked to participate more, rather than less, in decision-making. It may be that some workers are perfectly happy with "boring and monotonous" jobs and fear any type of "job redesign" or "job enrichment" like the plague (see Chapters 12 and 13).

Thus in looking at the way objective life events may stress individuals, we have to look at objective factors such as job design in the work environment, and also at subjective factors, such as individuals' needs and personalities. Let us pursue this last point further.

Subjective responses to stress

It is a truism to say that we are all different, but we need to know how differing individuals will respond to the same life events and the same work/non-work environments.

Behaviour and physical health: Are you type A, B or C?

It may be that there are stress-prone personality types. The so-called "type A" personality, for example, would answer "yes" to all or most of the questions in Table 7.3. Early research in the 1960s seems to show a correlation between such behaviour patterns as the pure or extreme type A personality and the prevalence of coronary heart disease. Type A (coronary-prone) people live lives that are characterised by

... extremes of competitiveness, striving for achievement, aggressiveness, haste, impatience, restlessness, hyperalertness, explosiveness of speech, tenseness of facial musculature, and feelings of being under pressure of time and under the challenge of responsibility ... people having this particular behaviour pattern were so often deeply involved and committed to their work that other aspects of their life were relatively neglected. (COOPER AND MARSHALL 1978, P.104)

Most people have a bit of type A within them. Very few people are pure type A but, by the same token, very few people are pure type B (totally relaxed, disinterested, satisfied). On the continuum at the bottom of Table 7.3, most of us would fall into the A_2–B_2 range.

There is a fair amount of proof for the "extreme type A = heart problems" equation; although Selye has his doubts, and thinks that it may be more correct to say that people are either "racehorses" (who thrive on stress) or "turtles" (who can't handle much pressure at all) (Selye 1978).

Type As may make things harder for themselves by deliberately choosing high-stress jobs precisely because of type A traits (impatience, ambition, competitiveness, aggressiveness). There are many names for type A people: workaholic, the "Harried" player in transactional analysis, and so on. Ellis has a delightfully obscene name for type A behaviour—*mustabatory* behaviour, that is, behaviour that is compulsive and that demonstrates wrong priorities:

- perfectionism, dire need for success and approval (tyranny of the "shoulds")
- the dire need for considerateness and justice
- the dire need for immediate and constant gratification and ease (ELLIS 1978, P.46)

---

[1] See also Tacy (1982).

Table 7.3 Type A and type B personality checklist

Answer the following questions by indicating what *most often* applies to you:

Yes	No	
_____	_____	1. Do you feel compelled to do most things in a hurry?
_____	_____	2. Are you usually the first one through during a meal?
_____	_____	3. Is it difficult for you to relax, even for a few hours?
_____	_____	4. Do you hate to wait in line at a restaurant, bank or store?
_____	_____	5. Do you frequently try to do several things at the same time?
_____	_____	6. Are you generally dissatisfied with what you have accomplished in life?
_____	_____	7. Do you enjoy competition and feel you always have to win?
_____	_____	8. When other people speak slowly do you find yourself trying to rush them along by finishing the sentence for them?
_____	_____	9. Do you become impatient when someone does the job slowly?
_____	_____	10. When engaged in conversation do you usually feel compelled to tell others about your own interests?
_____	_____	11. Do you become irritated when something is not done exactly right?
_____	_____	12. Do you rush through your tasks to get them done as quickly as possible?
_____	_____	13. Do you feel you are constantly under pressure to get more done?
_____	_____	14. In the past few years, have you taken less than your allotted vacation time?
_____	_____	15. While listening to other people, do you usually find your mind wandering to other tasks and subjects?
_____	_____	16. When you meet aggressive people, do you usually feel compelled to compete with them?
_____	_____	17. Do you tend to talk fast?
_____	_____	18. Are you too busy with your job to have time for hobbies and outside activities?
_____	_____	19. Do you seek and need recognition from your boss and peers?
_____	_____	20. Do you take pride in working best "under pressure"?

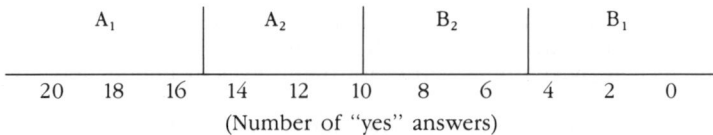

A_1	A_2	B_2	B_1

20	18	16	14	12	10	8	6	4	2	0

(Number of "yes" answers)

Source: Gmelch (1982), pp.99–100. Reproduced with permission.

Does the type A person really exist? Should we sneer at the workaholic? The answers are not simple. Workaholics may simply have wretched families, their work may be more interesting than golf or video games and, as Freud said, in defence of guilt, the world was built on repression (and therein may lie our undoing as we move into the "leisure economy/nobility for the masses" system of the future). Also, as transactional analysis approaches to the workaholic game of "Harried" bear out, if someone else is playing the complementary hand of "Kick Me", then perhaps "Harried" becomes "Objective Harried", that is, everyone else really *is* too incompetent to get it done. Is the solution to this situation heroic behaviour, which we can all admire, or self-destructive messianic behaviour, which we can all sneer at? Or is the solution more simple: heroes should delegate to and train more villains, so that heroes can lose some of the pleasure of heroism and the villains can lose some of the pain of villainy?

Other ways in which type As can kick their behaviour and its consequences include:

- drive in the slow lane—drive with patience
- choose long queues to wait in—wait with patience
- smile and laugh more
- talk slowly and less emphatically, interrupt less
- spend time physically relaxing
- do not take on additional tasks without at least reducing the current ones
- establish life-goals—use time management to plan short-, medium- and long-term goals—avoid hyperactivity, activity for its own sake
- learn to accept ambiguity—remember that a successful life is always un-finished—only a corpse is completely finished!

(ADAPTED FROM FRIEDMAN AND ROSENMAN (1974); SMITH (N.D.))

If the type A–type B model is true, does this mean that, in order to avoid stress-triggered disease, we should all become totally unaggressive and accept whatever the world tries to do to us? In other words, in the language of Chapter 6, should we become passives in order to avoid aggressive-induced heart attacks? The answer is no: if we did, we would be misunderstanding the nature of stress and personality, we would fail to balance out type A and type B behaviour, and we would run the risk of going past type B behaviour to something which may be much worse: type C (for cancer) behaviour. Although research is still in its early phases here, there is a strong suggestion developing that a behaviour pattern of suppressing expression of emotions, particularly suppressing emotions such as legitimate anger, may help to induce certain types of cancer (Wood 1985; Spillane 1985).[2]

Locus of control and stress

Another way of looking at the differences between individuals' personalities is to consider the concept of locus of control. People who are classified as *internals* perceive that they have control over their environment, whereas *externals* perceive that they have little control (as a result, externals usually believe more in luck and fate) (see Chapter 6). A study of owner-managers reacting to flood damage of property showed that internally oriented managers responded to the disaster in a more task-oriented way and with less

---

[2]   (Women studied by researchers and found to have malignant breast cancer) "may well be reluctant to appear in any way socially unacceptable" and such an explanation certainly fits with a description a therapist once used to describe her clients to me. "Cancer patients," she said, "are awfully nice." Others have gone much further in trying to explain why patients with cancer seem to suppress their emotions. Some psychoanalysts trace it back to an early home life in which as children they had to learn to suppress their own emotional outlets for fear of losing their parents' affection. The analysts sum it up with statements like "cancer patients have never learned to express their cries for help". At a more practical level is the observation that cancer patients often have a history of traumatic life events, particularly losses of important relationships, which lead to feelings of helplessless and depression. There is now an expanding literature on how such a sense of loss may increase the secretion of corticosteroids, hormones produced by the adrenal glands which, in turn, suppress either the production or the activity of those white blood cells whose normal role is to seek out and destroy developing cancer cells. The whole subject has been given a name—psychoimmunology—but it is still in its infancy and is a minefield of conflicting results. (WOOD 1985, P.14).

See also Maier and Laudenslager (1985).

stress, whereas more externally oriented managers responded with anger, hostility and greater anxiety (Quick and Quick 1984).

Internals are not always less prone to stress, however: in situations in which they perceive they really do have little or no control, they may be more stressed than externals.

Stress symptoms

After having considered the interplay of life-event stressors, the environment in which individuals find themselves, and the personalities of individuals, we can begin to better understand why some people do or do not manifest certain symptoms of stress.

A list of stress symptoms appears in Table 7.4. A good deal of these symptoms are part of what is known as the *fight-or-flight response*. This response is a series of behaviours that is part of our genetic inheritance. The response was invaluable for our early human ancestors, because it enabled them to fight a threat or run away from it. Whether they fought or flew largely depended upon whether they could meet the threat and defeat it—for example, a wild animal. Our caveman ancestor might experience the following reactions:

- increased heartbeat
- high adrenalin levels
- increased perspiration
- muscular tension—increased blood flow to muscles
- pupils dilate
- drop in skin surface temperature
- increased clotting of blood
- hair stands on end

These responses ensured that the body was in a high state of readiness, to fight, or to run away and fight another day. The "tingle up and down the spine" when danger threatens meant that hair on shoulders would raise slightly as a threat device (see Chapter 4). Blood would clot, the better to staunch bleeding if the skin was ruptured. Increased perspiration would cool down the body, ensuring that overheating would not occur at higher levels of operating. Blood would flow to the muscles, away from the digestive tract (thus sometimes triggering loss of control of the bowels—which, if nothing else, would mean that our caveman could run away faster once his weight had lessened). Pupils would dilate to take in more visual information so that responses to threats could be quicker . . . and so on.

These responses worked extremely well for meeting physical threats. Like our blink and startle reflexes, these reponses were *adaptive*—they kept our ancestors alive, and thus ensured that we would exist, and also stay alive. But what happens if you are required to speak in public in two hours' time, before a large audience? Such a situation is far removed from a sabre-tooth tiger appearing 100 metres away. Yet our bodies (or more accurately, our minds) react to such a socially challenging situation as if it were a physical threat. We begin to experience the fight-or-flight response, and usually this is a distress experience. The actor with butterflies in the stomach (i.e. nausea), the perspiring politician at the press conference, the student who continually leaves the examination hall to go to the toilet, the white-knuckled and wide-eyed interviewee, are all experiencing the *maladaptive* fight-or-flight response—there is no physical threat, only a social or symbolic one. Yet

Table 7.4 Stress symptoms

1 Headaches	31 Worrying or stewing about things
2 Nervousness or shakiness inside	32 Feeling no interest in things
3 Being unable to get rid of bad thoughts or ideas	33 Feeling fearful
4 Faintness or dizziness	34 Your feelings being easily hurt
5 Loss of sexual interest or pleasure	35 Having to ask others what you should do
6 Feeling critical of others	36 Feeling others do not understand you or are unsympathetic
7 Bad dreams	37 Feeling that people are unfriendly or dislike you
8 Difficulty in speaking when you are excited	38 Having to do things very slowly in order to be sure you were doing them right
9 Trouble remembering things	39 Heart pounding or racing
10 Worried about sloppiness or carelessness	40 Nausea or upset stomach
11 Feeling easily annoyed or irritated	41 Feeling inferior to others
12 Pains in the heart or chest	42 Soreness of your muscles
13 Itching	43 Loose bowel movements
14 Feeling low in energy or slowed down	44 Difficulty in falling asleep or staying asleep
15 Thoughts of ending your life	45 Having to check and double-check what you do
16 Sweating	46 Difficulty making decisions
17 Trembling	47 Wanting to be alone
18 Feeling confused	48 Trouble getting your breath
19 Poor appetite	49 Hot or cold spells
20 Crying easily	50 Having to avoid certain things, places or activities because they frighten you
21 Feeling shy or uneasy with the opposite sex	51 Your mind going blank
22 A feeling of being trapped or caught	52 Numbness or tingling in parts of your body
23 Suddenly scared for no reason	53 A lump in your throat
24 Temper outbursts you could not control	54 Feeling hopeless about the future
25 Constipation	55 Trouble concentrating
26 Blaming yourself for things	56 Weakness in parts of your body
27 Pains in the lower part of your back	57 Feeling tense or keyed up
28 Feeling blocked or stymied in getting things done	58 Heavy feeling in your arms or legs
29 Feeling lonely	
30 Feeling blue	

Source: Manuso, J. (1980). Reproduced with permission.

bodily evolution has not advanced as fast as historical evolution, and consequently we experience stress. Yet while a socially maladaptive response may be educated out of us (e.g. the conditioned reflex foot action of a driver used to depressing a clutch in a manual as opposed to an automatic car), biologically maladaptive responses are much more difficult to control.[3]

The fight-or-flight response is triggered by the sympathetic nervous system, which ensures that stress hormones such as adrenalin reach all areas

---

[3]   . . . human reaction to stress is an example of maladaptation. What is essentially a protective and life-saving mechanism has turned around on itself and become a damaging one. The most striking example of this is probably the increase in platelets in the blood in response to stress. The very mechanism that in primitive man decreased the risk of bleeding to death often plays an entirely opposite role in the 1980s executive. By thickening the blood there is a greatly increased chance of producing a clot to block already partly furred-up heart or brain vessels, thereby producing a coronary or a stroke. (SEDGEWICK 1983, P.17)

of the body within eight seconds. When threats diminish, or at least the
individual's rational or not-so-rational perceptions are that the threat has
diminished, the parasympathetic nervous system comes into operation,
shutting down or reversing the changes triggered by the sympathetic system.

> The sympathetic and parasympathetic branches of your nervous system thus
> operate in a see-saw fashion, first escalating and then de-escalating your body as
> the situation demands. . .
> From the neurological standpoint, the nervous, chronically tense, over-
> reactive person has lost the ability to mobilise his parasympathetic nervous system
> fully. (ALBRECHT 1979, P.58)

Stress management

In Figure 7.2 we saw how objective life-event stressors combine with
objective environments and subjective individual responses to lead to the
presence (or indeed the absence) of stress symptoms. How can we reduce
such symptoms in the short run, and ensure that they are under control or
do not reappear in the long run? Let's have a look at a range of stress
management strategies that can achieve this aim, but only after seeing what
stress management is *not*.

Ineffective coping strategies

Albrecht (1979) suggests that people often try to cope with stress by using a
series of drug-using and game-playing tactics:

1. drinking liquor
2. frequent or heavy eating, especially sweet foods
3. smoking
4. drinking coffee, colas, or other high-caffeine drinks
5. using marijuana, heavy drugs, or mind-altering pills
6. using prescription drugs such as tranquillisers and pain pills
7. using patent medicines to suppress specific symptoms
8. using sleeping pills
9. withdrawing psychologically; mechanising one's behaviour; self-
destructive behaviours (crime; going crazy; suicide)
10. lashing out at others; displacing anxiety and anger on to other people

In the long run, most of these are useless, or worse than useless; in the short
run, they can provide some temporary relief.

Role analysis

Let's now look at real methods of stress control, beginning with one that
draws upon social–psychological analysis of the roles we play in everyday life
(Palmer 1981; Quick and Quick 1984). Palmer sees the *roles* people play as
being the critical determinants of stress. Throughout the day a person might
play multiple roles—spouse, parent, child, relative, friend, enemy,
subordinate, supervisor, team member, expert, naif, insider, outsider,
conformer, deviant, religious devotee, football supporter, member of an
ethnic group, member of a sex, member of a class, member of an age-group,
member of a political party, member of a service club, and so on. Palmer
argues that stress arises through these roles in ten different ways:

1. *Conflict within a role* This occurs most usually when a role is defined
in terms of obligations to two or more groups, and it is impossible to
satisfy both. A classic instance of this type of stress is that of a foreman
or supervisor. Promotion to the job may initially be seen as a success,

but a forelady's former peers may accuse her of "selling out to the bosses". Her superiors in turn may suspect her of forsaking management imperatives for the sake of solidarity with her former peers. "It is ultimately a no-win, 'damned if you do and damned if you don't' situation for the individual." (Palmer 1981)

2. *Conflict between two or more of a person's roles* This is quite similar to (1), except the stressed person has two clearly defined roles, both of which demand 100 per cent of time. The most obvious instance of this situation would be a working mother. Even in these so-called liberated days, many women finish one job in the afternoon to go home to their second job, that of the homemaker. In trying to satisfy many needs, both psychological and economic, the working mother experiences fatigue and guilt, both stressful feelings.

3. *Conflict between the roles of two persons* In the best of all possible worlds, all persons' roles would be clearly delineated—all would have clear and unambiguous specifications written down, these would dovetail perfectly, and they would never change from now unto eternity. Unfortunately, this is rarely so. There is an almost necessary conflict built into the roles of husband and wife, supervisor and subordinate, driver and back-seat driver—the prescribed versus the perceived versus the performed role: "A person does not marry his or her in-laws, but they become role partners and the relations with the role partners form a role set that is associated with the status of husband or wife." (Broom and Selznick 1977). This role overlap within the extended family is a useful mode of stressful role overlap—conflict—in a variety of settings.

4. *Role over-demand* This occurs, for example, when people bite off more than they can chew, or where the role expands with time, outstripping the role-holder's ability, or where the responsibilities of the role far outweigh the power disposed by the role.

5. *Undemanding roles* Quite the opposite to role over-demand is underdemand or under-challenge in a role. An example of role under-demand would be a boring assembly-line job, or a job in an inefficient bureaucracy:

> Many workers in bureaucracy are required to do only routine tasks that present little challenge, little opportunity to use their abilities. Bureaucracies usually have built-in controls that discourage and punish attempts to increase the demands of work roles. Rate busters are penalised and ostracised. Those who suggest innovative procedures are ignored or shunted aside. The essence of bureaucracy, coercing individuals to act out narrow role demands—regardless of individual differences and needs—is preserved. (PALMER 1981)

6. *Restrictive roles* These have much in common with undemanding roles. Restrictive roles lock people into a routine, stunting any potential growth. There is more information available about what one cannot do than what one can do. A person may rebel against this, or conform, becoming so dependent upon an authoritarian structure of rules that she cannot cope if that structure is taken away. Prisoners, some homemakers and some bureaucrats fit into this category. Rebellion and liberation both bring stress.

7. *New roles* Taking on new roles is stressful to the extent that one is not adequately prepared for them; but can one ever be adequately prepared for new roles such as spouse, parent, supervisor, and so on?

8. *Role loss* If a role gives a person a feeling of identity, then a loss of
that role will probably have stressful impact. To get divorced, to break
up a relationship, to suffer a bereavement, to retire, to lose one's job—
all of these are sudden role losses which can cause very high stress.

9. *Role rejection* When aspiring to a new role, there are no guarantees
that a person will succeed, particularly in highly competitive circumstances. Failure to get a job that you have just interviewed for, failure
to persuade a loved one to marry you, and so on, are stressful
experiences. The question you have to ask yourself is: "why am I not
good enough?"

10. *Role encroachment*

> Encroachment refers to the attempts, or what we believe to be the
> attempts, of others to take over part or all of one or more of our roles. . .
> The wife-mother may experience severe annoyance when her mother-in-
> law, or her own mother, attempts to take over the running of the home and
> the guidance of the children . . . The corporate vice-president is likely to
> fight with tooth and nail if someone tries to move in on his "territory",
> meaning his rights and responsibilities. When the "new member of the
> club"—the new worker in the office, for example—tries to tell the old-
> timers how to do this or that, he or she is likely to be squelched very
> quickly. (PALMER 1981)

These ten *causes* of role stress, Palmer suggests, call forth one, several or all
of eight *responses* to stress. These are:

1. *Aggression* People sometimes handle the stress of roles by becoming
aggressive, usually by displacing feelings of frustration—aggression
towards the self—on to others.

2. *Self-destructive behaviour* This in the extreme form is suicide, but it
may also be over-working, over-eating, smoking, drinking, drug abuse.

3. *Distortion* If our roles are stressing us, it may be too painful to face
the truth, and hence we may rationalise that it is not our fault (when
it is), that it is the fault of others (when it isn't), and so on.

4. *Withdrawal* Under stress, we may physically flee the scene, either
never to return or simply to think things over for a few days, until the
crisis blows over; or we may psychologically flee into ourselves,
becoming more defensive, less communicative to the hurtful world.

5. *Compulsive conformity* Here, one conforms to the role. As the
inherent stresses of this situation emerge, or continue to get worse, one
becomes more compulsive, more ritualistic in behaving in order to
deny the stress. Thus one remains at one's post and insists upon using
the proper channels, one rearranges the deckchairs on the *Titanic*,
even when all evidence suggests that these courses of action are
counter-productive. The compulsive conformer is dangerously close
to meeting the definition of a fanatic: one who redoubles his efforts
after forgetting his original intention.

6. *Risk-taking* This may take several forms. The stressed person may see
no other way out but to risk everything on a long shot. Others may
take up dangerous sports or gambling not only for the excitement
inherent in winning but for the excitement of losing—perhaps losing
everything.

7. *Physical illness* This response to stress is perhaps the one we think of
first. Physical symptoms, such as the fight-or-flight response, and the
symptoms listed in Table 7.4, are the way some people meet role
stresses:

An important side effect of physical illness, of course, is that it may be sufficiently incapacitating to cause the person to be removed from the causes of role stress. Physical illness is generally a socially acceptable basis for setting aside many role responsibilities. Taking on the role of the sick person automatically precludes or suspends the carrying out of various other roles. (PALMER 1981)

8. *Coping innovatively* Roles tend to lock out innovative coping. By diagnosing causes and effects of role stress (see Table 7.5), we can see our way clear to changing roles or changing within existing roles. We may also grow to discriminate between distress and eustress, and seek out eustress situations—not only because coping with eustress is intrinsically worthwhile, but because it may help us to cope better with distress. The innovative coper says, I am the master of my fate, I am the captain of my role(s).

You may find it useful to compare Palmer's responses to role stress with the Freudian ego defence mechanisms (see Chapter 5; see also p.230). Compare them also with the rational emotional therapy (RET) styles of distorted thinking (p.227).

Do you have role stress? You may find it useful to analyse your roles (parent, spouse, lover, subordinate, superior, peer, team-member, church-member, relative, etc.) using the matrix in Table 7.5.

Relaxation techniques

Let's look at relaxation techniques as the first of our "physical" coping techniques. Relaxation techniques are useful in that they reunite us with our ape-selves, our minds and our bodies still trapped in the fight-or-flight response. Even though a sabre-tooth tiger is not about to walk into the kitchen or the office, your body and mind may be reacting as if it were. You would probably be surprised at the levels of muscular tension in your body, even in "relaxed" situations. Processes such as massage or biofeedback can demonstrate this dramatically. You may think that you are relaxed after self-medication with tranquillisers or alcohol or drugs, but you might be surprised to measure your heartbeat and pulse while under such medication.

Approaches to relaxation therapy (e.g. Meares 1976, 1980) tackle the most obvious symptom of stress, namely muscular tension. The standard approach is often something like: "tense your toes (breathe in) . . . now relax your toes (breathe out); tense your calves (breathe in) . . . now relax your calves (breathe out)" and so on. By moving up the body and relaxing different muscle groups, you can learn to relax, say the experts. Sparkes (1962) combines this approach with types of self-hypnosis and conditioning of responses. Thus he suggests that you think of a number when you relax progressively and, with practice, merely recalling this number will evoke the learned response of relaxation, even in stress situations. This approach, using hypnosis and behaviourism, is remarkably similar to meditation and yoga approaches which use a mantra chant (see p.220).

If you want to swim in rough waters, it's probably better to learn in calm waters, so in order to be able to use relaxation methods in real-life, stressful situations, you should practise in quiet areas. Take the phone off the hook, put a "Do Not Disturb" sign on the door, send the kids out to play or have a baby sitter in while you're at home, locate an unused room at work, sit on a toilet, drive your car to a deserted area and relax in the car, relax in a sauna, relax on the beach—wherever you can get some privacy, go there. It's sometimes better to relax on a hard surface than a soft surface; relaxing on

Table 7.5 Matrix of causes of and responses to stress

Causes of stress

Responses to stress	1 Conflict within a role	2 Conflict between two or more of a person's roles	3 Conflict between the roles of two persons	4 Role over-demand	5 Undemanding roles	6 Restrictive roles	7 New role	8 Role loss	9 Role encroachment	10 Role rejection
A. Aggression										
B. Self-destructive behaviour										
C. Distortion										
D. Withdrawal										
E. Compulsive conformity										
F. Risk-taking										
G. Physical illness										
H. Innovation										

Source: Adapted with permission from Palmer (1981), pp.154, 155, 157.

a soft bed may simply make you drowsy. If restful sleep is your aim, it's probably better to relax on a hard floor first, and then climb into bed and relax again. Be careful of flexing your neck and your back, particularly if you have problems in those areas. Remember, self-help is usually the best form of help, but that doesn't mean that you shouldn't spend a few dollars on discussing any stress management technique with a sympathetic doctor or therapist.

BOX 7.A: Managers and stress

Many people find promotion to managerial positions quite stressful. The role shift to a position of greater power and responsibility can be very pleasant, but often the workload increases. This is not a major problem in sub-managerial positions—services above and beyond the call of duty are usually rewarded with overtime and penalty payments. Yet the remuneration convention in executive positions is such that these variable payments are dispensed with. There are compensations in the total executive package of salary and other (non-taxable) benefits, of course, but many a new recruit to management has found that she has become just another executive slave, working 60 to 80 or more hours a week.

New skills are called for as well, sometimes causing role over-demand, as De Largy Healy and Lord note:

> When, for most, the tried and trusted skills which middle managers use to interpret policy—loyalty, technical knowledge, judgment, patience, good common sense—are not accompanied by the special package of constitutional and psychological attributes needed for coping at the entrepreneurial level, the threat to self-esteem is extreme. The attendant depression can be very real, deep and enduring. (DE LARGHY HEALY AND LORD 1980)

Cooper and Marshall (1978) see similar patterns in managers being unable to cope with ambiguity and change. The high structure of roles at lower levels is replaced by low structure and greater fluidity of roles at high levels. This turbulent environment usually calls for political skills and people skills rather than detailed command of technical processes, and those who cannot shift emphases away from task-oriented behaviour to people-oriented behaviour may experience stress (to a certain extent, this shift away from tasks is essential—no one can do all other tasks). Management in this sense is definitely getting things done through others.

Of course, we usually presume that when someone is promoted to a new position they will be competent in that position; but what happens if this is not the case? What happens, for example, if the dreaded Peter Principle is in operation ("In a hierarchy every employee tends to rise to his level of incompetence.")? Rix (1984) found this to be a significant stressor among Australian executives (stress compounded no doubt by the locking-in effect of Parkinson's fifth law, "expenditure rises to meet income").

Greater people-orientation may be a necessary but not sufficient cause of lower stress. One can be concerned with people, but in a paternalistic and punitive way. De Larghy Healy and Lord suggest that participative management styles can help to ameliorate the "main cause of organisational stress—poor communication". This is not to say that participation is an antidote to stress for all: it might be more stressful for a manager to run a participatory situation than an authoritarian situation, and it may also be stressful for an employee to "participate" when she just wants to be left alone.

One of the key factors usually associated with executive workload is promotion involving transfer to another city. Yet Rix (1984) and others have found these combined life-events to be extremely stressing, often to the point where the stresses undergone by executives and their families cause short-term and long-term health and performance problems that more than outweigh any alleged gain to the organisation accruing from the transfer.

Meditation, yoga

Meditation and yoga are not so much techniques as philosophies, religions. Practitioners of either approach would resent being mentioned in the same breath as the other. In many respects, meditation is less of a religio-ethical lifestyle approach to stress. Its practitioners would say that this is a good thing, while many yoga practitioners would say that this merely shows the superficiality of meditation.

Transcendental meditation or TM was a somewhat controversial mystical movement in the 1960s, but today is more widely accepted, and accepted by some as just another secular technique. The meditator learns techniques of regressing to other types of consciousness, usually by chanting a mantra or Sanskrit word. Relaxation is a by-product of this process, but is not the primary goal. Goleman (1976) argues that TM is different from other relaxation techniques in that the mind stays alert, and does not become drowsy. This combination of tranquillity and alertness is cultivated in some martial arts also.

Yoga uses meditation, exercises, diet, prayer, even sex, to transform consciousness—it depends on which school you are following. Properly considered, yoga is more of a religious commitment than meditation, and one would no more expect a quick fix of "stress management" from yoga than one would expect to be able to walk into a church of which one was not a member and make a confession of sins so that a nervous headache might go away. The ability of yogis to control physical stress-related behaviours (heartbeat, pulse, brainwaves) is by now fairly widely acknowledged. Sherman makes some interesting distinctions between Western psychology and yoga:

> Psychology believes in the material universe as the ultimate. Yoga says that while matter is real it is impermanent. Yoga therefore concentrates on spirit as its ultimate. Psychology strives for a strong, integrated ego as the means for attaining the ultimate. Yoga says that the ego is both a source and a manifestation of ignorance and is a hindrance towards real growth. The ego for Yoga is something to be overcome. Psychology measures health in terms of one's ability to work and produce. Yoga measures health in terms of one's control over one's personal complex and therefore one's level of awareness or development. Yoga stresses that each assertion of one's "self" (ego) is a step backward rather than a sign of proper functioning. (SHERMAN 1978)

BOX 7.B: Blue-collar industrial workers

Halfpenny (1980) argues that it is false to assume that stress occurs most at the top of organisations. In reality, he says, it is more likely to occur among low- or semi-skilled workers. Thus for example the suicide rate of professional/managerial personnel in Australia is 2.3/10 000, while it is 8.2/10 000 among industrial workers. Among those industrial jobs he designates "low stress", the accident rate is 4.8 per cent, while among "high stress" jobs it is 13.7 per cent. Some of the specific stressors given by Halfpenny are:

- boredom, job dissatisfaction;
- too much or too little work;
- too easy or too hard work;
- job uncertainty and the accompanying financial insecurity, particularly relevant in view of Australia's massive unemployment, our swing to capital-intensive resource industries, and technological change;
- responsibility for other people;
- lack of participation in decisions affecting the job;
- a need for concentration;
- lack of social support from fellow workers or supervisors;
- stress and uncertainty of piecework;
- migrants coping with language barriers and culture shock;
- women coping with two jobs—their paid job and the job of housewife;
- sexual harassment of women.

Tacy (1982) notes that non-management personnel are likely to be stressed because of their lack of control over their jobs (cf. Karasek's model, Fig. 7.3). She suggests that stress can be minimised by job redesign strategies that give more participation and control at the lower work levels, and also suggests that consultation of lower-level workers on the nature and amount of technological change will help to reduce stress.

Many of the concepts discussed in this book—ego defence mechanisms, self-actualisation, assertiveness, and so on—are obviously very self-oriented. What might an experienced practitioner of yoga say about them? There are many good books available on yoga, but it's probably better to discuss it with practitioners to see if it is for you.

Diet

Changes to diet and exercise are, for many people, the most practical way to approach reduction of stress. It is a conventional wisdom these days to say that many children are "hyperactive", largely due to the deleterious effect of chemical preservatives, pesticides, weedicides, rodenticides, colourings, and other additives in our food (Feingold 1976). While the "additives = hyperactivity" hypothesis is by no means an incontestable scientific truth, it stands to reason that much of what we eat and drink might have impacts upon our stress levels. This is not only in the chemical composition of what we put in our mouths, but in the psychological way we use food and drink to allay anxiety—"nervous eating", and so on.

There seems to be some connection between intake of refined sugar and loss of B-group vitamins, for example (Girdano and Everley 1979). The B-group vitamins seem to be important in helping us to control stress.[4] Yet there may be a vicious circle here: many people, when stressed, resort to nervous eating, particularly of sweet foods and beverages, such as chocolate or an extra teaspoonful of sugar in their drink. Obviously this will aggravate rather than alleviate the distress they feel because of the sugar/B-group vitamins interactions.

Caffeine is probably the most powerful foodstuff stressor we take into the body. The most obvious source of caffeine is coffee, but it is also to be found in tea, chocolate and cola drinks. We use caffeine like we use sugar—for a quick hit of energy and alertness. As with all such fixes, the initial impact weakens quickly, and we are often left feeling worse than before. The solution? Another quick hit. . . This, of course, is addictive behaviour. Many people in our society work not with their hands but with their brains, usually sitting behind desks or standing at counters. We placate our under-exercised bodies with a series of oral treats—coffee, candy, gum, cigarettes, pen-tops, fingernails, and so on. Of all these bribes for the body to keep still, coffee works the least well. It accelerates bodily processes, making us physically alert as well as mentally alert. Obviously, this makes us more restless, and our concentration spans narrow. Bored schoolchildren behave in much the same way with cola drinks, becoming similarly restless. We also expect them to hunch over desks for most of the day, quietly and immobilely concentrating. Nevertheless, given that the cultural game *is* hunching over desks, we would be appalled to see schoolchildren drinking colas and coffee at their desks all day long; why then do we see nothing wrong with adults doing the same? These effects are quite apart from the physiological effects, which are still not well understood (although it has been proved that the amount of caffeine in twenty straight cups constitutes a fatal dose!) (Girdano and Everley, 1979).

If we use caffeine as a quick way of getting some eustress, we use *alcohol* as a way of blunting the distress of modern society. This is not necessarily a bad thing. Gmelch (1982) posits that "moderate drinking" *reduces* stress, more so in fact that teetotalling. It's when we begin to use alcohol as a general anaesthetic that problems arise. Alcohol is well accepted as a reducer of stress—if someone were to enter a roomful of people and say "I need a stiff brandy to calm my nerves", most people would not be shocked, indeed would be more interested in finding out the cause of the trauma than the remedy proposed. Yet just as a three-hour boozy lunch wrecks anyone's chances of getting work done in the afternoon, so do other socially acceptable rituals significantly impair our abilities to cope with quite basic psychomotor tasks (such as driving), let alone more intellectually demanding tasks. Work underload (hypostress) can be as powerful a cause of alcohol dependency as work overload (hyperstress). Alcohol-related phenomena (absenteeism, accidents, poor performance) may be as noticeable on the assembly-line as it is in the boardroom. Will increasing leisure increase or decrease alcohol-related problems?

---

[4] See Cheraskin *et al.* (1976) for a discussion of the role of sugar and other refined carbohydrates in causing hypoglycemia, or low blood sugar (which allegedly can manifest itself in a range of physical and psychological symptoms, ranging from nausea to anxiety and depression). So-called *orthomolecular* medical practitioners and scientists, such as Cheraskin and Pfeiffer (1975), see diet as being integral to physical and psychological health; many mainstream medical practitioners and scientists remain unconvinced.

BOX 7.C: White-collar stress for public servants

McMullen (1980) sees stress in the Australian public service coming from numerous quarters. Government policy, for example, has led to the imposition of staff ceilings, and this in turn has led to job overload and increased anxiety about job security. As a result, hypertension as a ground for workers' compensation is increasing. Like supervisors who are "the meat in the sandwich" between workers and bosses, public servants who man counters of organisations such as Medicare have to take the brunt of public animosity towards changes in government policy. Like all public contact roles, this role is stressful in that it is hard to keep smiling when people want a piece of someone and, if there's no one else, *you're it*.

New technology can also be a stressor. Visual display unit (VDU) operators and microfiche operators have begun to report behavioural symptoms related to their work, such as headaches, difficulty in concentration, inability to watch television or carry on hobbies involving close work (e.g. sewing).

Palmer (1981) is, by contrast, more critical of the internal causes of stress in bureaucracies (undemanding and restrictive work roles, under-demand, compulsive conformity). A literal believer in Parkinson's First Law ("work expands to fill the amount of time available") would discount much of McMullen's analysis, arguing that bureaucrat-bashing is perhaps distressing for the bureaucrats but eustressing for society.

Salt is also over-represented in our diet. Sodium supplied by salt is essential in small quantities but, in larger quantities, it builds up in the body, causing more water to be retained, in turn triggering an increase in blood volume, which places more strain on the heart and arteries. This process can lead to raised blood pressure and hypertension (Haney and Boenisch 1982).

Fats, like salt, are a necessary part of our diet, but as with salt, most of us overdo it. Saturated fats (e.g. meat fats, whole milk, vegetable shortening, butter, etc.) contain much cholesterol which, when dumped into the bloodstream, accumulates on artery walls, slowly closing them off and making many people more prone to heart disease (especially those with type A tendencies) (Haney and Boenisch 1982; Gmelch 1982). Polyunsaturated fats (e.g. almonds, corn oil, fish, margarine, etc.) actually decrease blood cholesterol levels, although Meyer Friedman, who did much of the original work on the type A personality model, advocates minimising both saturated and polyunsaturated fats.

Exercise: The survival of the fittest

While approaches to stress such as yoga and meditation cater to the angel in man, approaches such as relaxation and exercise cater to the ape. The fight-or-flight responses within us are constant reminders of how our physical evolution has not kept pace with our social evolution. These responses are largely physical, even though the "threats" we meet today are largely non-physical, are more social and symbolic. Yet unless we relieve some of the physical tension inherent in these responses, we are stepping on the body's brake and accelerator at the same time—with dire consequences for the system. After an extremely stressful situation, some people find it useful to "let off steam" by playing squash or golf or going for a walk rather than going to the pub. In the long run, these people are doing more good for their system. Exercise can "cure" in this way, but it can also prevent extreme distress reactions. When your energy levels are low, you know how much more prey to stress you are. It stands to reason that if you establish a new norm of health considerably above your old one, you will have reserves of energy that you can call on in times of stress:

> Paradoxical as it may sound, you'll have more energy after exercise than you did before. Like any piece of fine machinery, your body works better when it's used regularly. (TUBESING 1981, P.91)

Are well-exercised people necessarily less stressed than others? Not at all. A classic type-A person may believe in a "work hard–play hard" approach to life, and deliberately choose highly competitive sports as recreation. This may not necessarily lead to a more relaxed musculature. Even then, relaxed muscles do not necessarily *cause* relaxation generally—all we can say is that there is a high correlation between relaxed muscles and general relaxation (cf. biofeedback, p.225).

Different approaches to stress management can either reinforce each other or work against each other. Albrecht (1979) has suggested that exercise, diet and relaxation techniques can mutually reinforce each other in a dramatically efficient way (Table 7.6).

Table 7.6 How exercise, diet and relaxation reinforce each other

This factor:	Enhances this factor: Relaxation	Exercise	Diet
Relaxation	Calmer attitude makes living more enjoyable; relaxation and recreation get higher priority.	Changes time priority; makes it easier to make time for exercise.	Reduces anxiety-related eating; increased body awareness and relaxation reduce over-eating at meals.
Exercise	Improved physical condition enables the body to consume stress chemicals; makes relaxation skills easier to learn and maintain.	Improved physical condition raises energy level; makes more exercise easier and enjoyable.	Regular exercise burns calories, promotes gradual weight loss, increases metabolic level, reduces appetite.
Diet	Reducing consumption of alcohol, tobacco, and caffeine makes parasympathetic relaxation response easier.	High-quality diet increases energy level; exercise becomes easier as weight decreases.	Good eating habits become easier to maintain over time.

Source: Albrecht (1979), p.227. Reproduced with permission.

Biofeedback: Let me hear your body talk

Biofeedback is a general name for a number of processes that measure and amplify certain behaviours so that an individual can learn to control those behaviours—to use the jargon of behaviourism, one can shape or modify one's behaviour (see Chapter 3). Stress can be easily and dramatically measured and displayed via a number of approaches. Four of these are:

1. *temperature:* skin temperature drops with high stress.
2. *galvanic skin response (GSR):* with an increase in stress, the electrical resistance of the skin drops.
3. *electroencephalograph (EEG):* brainwaves really do exist, and one wave in particular—the alpha wave—seems to increase with increased stress.
4. *electromyograph (EMG):* muscular tension increases with stress.

Machines are available which can take these behaviours and display them as a visible pattern on a screen or convert them into an audible signal. When the individual is hooked up to such a machine, she can—by a process of trial and error, of tensing and relaxing muscle groups—begin to gain some measure of control over her stress levels, i.e. she begins to get feedback over her own biology, and hence can control it (Shapiro 1981).

Biofeedback is thus an exciting technique, because it makes stress "real"—like an x-ray machine can make one's skeleton "real", like a microscope can make one's blood cells "real". Biofeedback goes even further, however; it can lead to an individual having enormous control of hitherto involuntary, automatic bodily functions. This, Brown suggests, quite changes the way we perceive "dis-ease" as being *either* physical illness *or* psychological illness:

> ... high levels of muscular tension are a common denominator in many psychosomatic diseases. The possibility, in fact the probability, that an illness is psychic in origin is so well known that it often comes to mind even in established physical illness. Yet psychic origin is almost totally ignored in medical treatment. The reverse is generally true of the psychiatrist or psychologist, who rarely follows physiological indicators in treatment. Biofeedback can help bridge this gap between the non-psychic treatment by medicine and the non-body treatment by traditional psychiatric methods (BROWN 1975, P.27)

Massage

So much of the fight-or-flight response is bound up with muscular tension: the body is in a state of arousal but, if the conflict is symbolic and verbal rather than physical, then there is no release. Exercise can release it, and so can massage.

Downing (1983) suggests that a masseur can detect unhealthy levels of body tension by looking for, among other things:

- shoulders which are too high, or hunched forward, or held rigidly back; one shoulder pulled up higher than another
- all or part of the face appearing pinched and tight
- the S-curve of the back (wideness in the top part of the "S" indicates tension in the shoulders, upper back; wideness in the lower part indicates tension in the pelvis and lower back).

BOX 7.D: Police—blue uniform stress

The critical problem for police officers, as Palmer notes, is that

> . . . Society wants police officers who seem to uphold the law at every turn but who really do so selectively, who close their eyes to some violations by certain individuals and prosecute others vigorously. Officers know, of course, that some politicians and some influential citizens take this view. However, they are likely to conceive of them as the unusual ones. Rarely do they comprehend that social values in general are thus. True, not all of us share in those values—but those are the prevailing ones. (PALMER 1981)

Palmer is speaking of the highly politicised environment of American police forces, where many officials are elected rather than appointed, but much of his general analysis holds true for Australian society. Police officers are the ambassadors of extremity, the translators of deviance for most of us—their appearance in our lives causes us stress, and this in turn causes stress for them. Thus police officers at a political demonstration may experience severe role conflict, particularly if they have to arrest people they agree with. Milte (1980) notes that the negative image of police work stresses police workers in other ways: police may not wear their uniforms home because they do not want their neighbours to know their profession, while their children may be branded "piglets" at school.

A considerable amount of work has been done into the "John Wayne syndrome" in police officers: the syndrome of toughness, of hyper-manliness, which not only ensures that police forces recruit a certain type of "public hero" personality but also ensures that police administrators are predisposed to look upon stressed police as "just weak—they shouldn't be in the police force" (Milte 1980). Are psychological defences such as these ultimately eustressing or distressing?

Police work also can switch quickly from understressing routine work to overstressing ultra-dangerous work, with far more danger than the common work role can encompass. The average worker, thinking of compensation arrangements, may think of mutilation and death as being remote contingencies, but a police officer may think of these as being less remote. Police workers, like nursing, ambulance, military and fire workers, are often under-educated and under-paid, yet we expect extraordinary performances from these people. The gap between their performance and our expectation is wide and widening, and causes stress. There is increasing evidence that such role-players in our society are less willing to be motivated by non-monetary needs. Can society expect to continue to trade upon the altruistic drives of people in such roles?

Massage, using oils (vegetable, mineral) or powders in preference to simple skin-to-skin contact (due to friction problems), is an enjoyable way of breaking down tension in the body. The shadier practitioners of massage have contributed to massage being seen as a sexual activity, and indeed, as Downing says, massage can be part of sexuality; massage can however be a non-sexual, but sensual, experience and a useful way to manage stress.

Rational–emotive therapy

So far, we have looked at a role approach to stress (the analysis of the tensions of the individual in her social context) and also various psychophysiological techniques and philosophies. Yet another approach is that of rational–emotive therapy. This approach has more in common with the role approach, while RET practitioners are openly cynical about approaches such as yoga, exercise, and so on:

> In recent years dozens of articles have been published exhorting managers to reduce their level of anxiety, worry less, think more positively and be less aggressive in their relationships with colleagues. Techniques which have been recommended to achieve these desirable goals include: relaxation therapy, yoga, meditation, exercise, hobbies, positive thinking, dietary therapy and many others. . . . (these techniques) are palliatives. They encourage people to *feel* better rather than to *get* better. (SPILLANE 1978, P.33)

For RET practitioners, it is not so much the effects of stress that need to be attacked as the causes, and these causes have more to do with attitudes and philosophies of individuals than anything else. They argue that we manufacture most anxieties by "negative self-talk", the word-games we play with ourselves at the conscious and pre-conscious levels. Consider, for example, the styles of distorted thinking in Tables 7.7 and 7.8. You may detect some similarities between these styles and the Freudian ego defence mechanisms and the transactional analysis "games" that have been considered elsewhere.

Thus a person may be prey to one or the other of the *control fallacies* (and, interestingly, may be subject to both at different times). If Joe feels externally controlled, he will feel that "they" run his life, he is an eternal victim, life is terrible and there is nothing he can do about it. If Joe feels internally controlled, he may feel that the world depends upon him, that he is totally indispensable, that he must be a superman continually rescuing others who are too incompetent to save themselves. Both perceptions are untrue of course, but they cause enormous strain for all that.

Josie may have an attack of the *shoulds*—she should always be right, she should always be totally competent, she should never make mistakes, she must be totally independent of others, she ought to be available to all people with their problems at all times, and so on. Ellis has labelled this "*must*abatory behaviour", because it is so sterile and obsessive (Ellis 1978).

John *personalises* everything—everyone else is better, faster, stronger than he is. If he is standing in a queue for concert tickets and, with five other people in the line before him, the attendant announces that all tickets have been sold, John says to himself: "why does this always happen to me"?

As with Freudian ego defence mechanisms and transactional analysis games, there is some overlap between differing distorted styles, and is quite possible that individuals use more than one style and that individuals use complementary styles when with partners and friends/enemies.

Spillane and other rational–emotive therapy writers argue that analysing and correcting distorted thinking are more efficient tools for managing stress than other approaches discussed above, because such therapies presuppose that stress is something external, which happens to us, and hence can be negated by something external—a therapy which solves stress for us. RET, by contrast, posits that stress is self-generated, by individuals using faulty logic. Critics have attacked RET on the grounds that it leads to a mechanistic, over-rational view of reality, although RET practitioners assert that this should not happen, that ideally RET will lead to a fuller, rather than a narrower emotional life (Ellis and Harper 1975).

Table 7.7 Some styles of distorted thinking

1. *Overgeneralisation*	You come to a general conclusion based on a single incident or piece of evidence. One bad experience means that whenever you are in a similar situation, you will repeat the bad experience. Cue words that indicate overgeneralisation are: all, every, never, always, everybody, nobody.
2. *Shoulds*	You have an absolute and unchangeable set of rules about the way people should behave. People who break the rules anger you and you feel guilty if you violate the rules. Cue words that indicate shoulds are: should, ought, must.
3. *Heaven's reward fallacy*	You expect all your sacrifice and self-denial to pay off, as if there were someone keeping score. You feel bitter when the reward doesn't come.
4. *Catastrophising*	You expect disaster. Any problem immediately becomes a major problem, for which there is no solution.
5. *Fallacy of change*	You expect that other people will change to suit you if you pressure them or cajole them enough. You need to change people because your hopes for happiness seem to depend entirely upon them.
6. *Personalisation*	You think that everything people do or say is some kind of reaction to you. You also compare yourself to others in a hyper-competitive way, trying to determine who's more talented, more intelligent, better-looking etc.
7. *Emotional reasoning*	You believe that what you feel must be true, automatically. If you *feel* stupid and boring, then you must *be* stupid and boring. Always believing your emotions is like believing everything you see in print.
8. *Fallacy of internal/ omnipotent control*	You feel responsible for everything and everyone around you. You are over-sensitive to the needs of people around you, you have an exaggerated belief in your power to fill those needs, and you have the expectation that you, and not they, are responsible for filling those needs.
9. *Fallacy of external control*	You see yourself as helpless, a victim of fate. All people are helpless, you more so than most. There is no point in striving for solutions because you can't win. The fact that, if your world-view is true, then others must have achieved some success in controlling you, is an annoying and ignorable detail.
10. *Being right*	You are always on trial to prove that your opinions and actions are correct. Being wrong is unthinkable, and you will go to any lengths to demonstrate your rightness.
11. *Mind reading*	You imagine that people feel the same way you do and react the same way you do (i.e. you project your behaviour on to others).

Source: Adapted from McKay, Davis and Fanning (1981).

Table 7.8 Rational–emotive therapy (RET) matching exercise

Using the definitions of styles of distorted thinking in Table 7.7, match up the words in the first column with the distorted styles in the second column.

1. All Ford drivers are the same. He'll never change.	Personalisation
2. She says in her letters that she likes me, but why would she like someone like me?	Shoulds
3. That's the second stomach ache I've had this month. I know it's cancer, but I don't want to know about it from some doctor.	Fallacy of internal control
4. But you heard what he said? "We've all got to work together as a team." That's a dig at me, you know.	Heaven's reward fallacy
5. I couldn't possibly take a vacation. How could my customers cope?	Overgeneralisation
6. What's the point? They'll get you in the end.	Catastrophising
7. You shouldn't be sick today or any day. You must learn that your place is here.	Being right
8. I feel depressed, life must be pointless.	Fallacy of external control
9. I built her a doll's house. Why won't she play in it?	Mind reading
10. How dare you suggest I'm wrong! Where's the proof, huh?	Fallacy of change
11. This department would collapse without me. Some day they'll see that, and then my supervisor will be sorry.	Emotional reasoning

Answers are on page 231.

Source: Adapted from McKay, Davis and Fanning (1981), pp.17–45.

BOX 7.E: Stress as future shock: Stressors in the "civilised environment"

Toffler (1970) has made much of the concept of "future shock", the stress or pressure that we feel as history seems to speed up. The increasing complexity and fragmentation of experience can disorient us. Our lifestyle is characterised by accelerating change, increased crowding, decreased stability and permanence, and *information overload* (information seen not only as the media but noise pollution, the information explosion, and so on). These are new pressures which are overlaid upon the pressures that previous generations have had. This can be seen most dramatically today when so-called "under-developed" cultures try to cope with "developed" cultures:

> There is evidence, for example, to suggest that the increasing neurotic symptomatology manifested by individuals who move from an African tribal milieu to a coastal city is at least in part due to the dramatic increase in the choices suddenly made available to them . . . Stanley Milgram, in his classic paper "The Experience of Living in Cities", has described urban life as consisting of "a continuous set of encounters with overload". (MADDISON 1977)

Ego defence mechanisms

Originally described by Freud, these include behaviour such as repression (forgetting uncomfortable truths), denial (simply refusing to believe that something is going to happen), and so on (see Chapter 5). Most of these mechanisms are not very effective long-term methods of coping with stress.

Job and organisational re-design

Box 2 of the stress sequence model in Figure 7.1 dealt with the individual's environment, particularly the control versus demands dimensions of jobs. It may be that one of the best methods of stress management is to look at the job and organisational designs that people work within and reconstruct them to be more in harmony with human needs (see Chapters 12, 13 and 14).

Time management

Time management, understood as setting priorities, establishing tradeoffs and avoiding compulsive behaviour patterns such as procrastination, crisis management and workaholism, can be a crucial part of managing stress (see Chapter 8).

Stress: The overview

If, then, stress is the new epidemic, which of the many approaches discussed in this chapter are the miracle cures and which are the snake oil treatments? To a considerable extent, the answer to this question will vary with each individual. If you have developed powers of intellectual analysis, role analysis and RET will instantly appeal as tools to control stress. If you feel that our contemporary lifestyle is over-materialistic and spiritually impoverished, yoga may well be the approach for you. Alternatively, it may be that what appeals to you may not necessarily be the best thing for you. Thus, fatty food "appeals to" overweight people more than lean food, and non-exercise "appeals to" unfit people—but that it not to say that improvements in diet and exercise would not be the best way to reduce such people's stress.

Possibly the healthiest thing about the whole phenomenon of stress is that it is now socially acceptable to discuss it as a normal phenomenon. Previously, many people believed that life was a rat-race, which you either survived or did not survive. Those who didn't survive were labelled "crazy", or had "nervous breakdowns", while those who did survive saw nothing remarkable in lifestyles that embraced little exercise, over-eating, self-medication through alcohol, tobacco, caffeine and pills, insomnia, ulcers, heart attacks, short concentration spans, aggression, submission to mutilating roles, psychologically and physically hazardous jobs, and distorted styles of thinking. Approaches to stress management let us see that

1. susceptibility to stress is not an either/or phenomenon, but rather a continuum, and
2. where we are on that continuum is largely up to ourselves to determine.

It's a good feeling to be able to say to yourself—and to others—"I am stressed", and not be too stressed by admitting that stress. It's a good feeling to be able to analyse the symptoms of stress that you are feeling, and know that there are techniques and philosophies of stress control available. It's a good feeling to know that there is eustress as well as distress, that stress can be enjoyable, and that the only beings totally free of stress are the dead.

Summary

Stress is not necessarily a negative concept. It can be seen as having four aspects: distress (unpleasant stress), eustress (pleasant stress), hyperstress (too much stress) and hypostress (not enough stress). Objective stressors such as various life-events can exert stress upon us, although not all of us will respond to such events in the same way. The environment of the individual, for example, a job, can influence the way stress is experienced, particularly the dimensions of control and demand in that environment.

Personality factors play a role in stress: so-called type A, type B and type C personalities may have specific outcomes for health, as may perceptions of internal and external control.

Stress symptoms are what we experience after the factors of life-events, environments and personalities are taken into account. A central factor in understanding symptoms is the biologically determined fight-or-flight response.

Various stress management techniques and philosophies are: ineffective coping strategies, role analysis, relaxation techniques, meditation, yoga, diet, exercise, biofeedback, massage, rational–emotive therapy, ego defence mechanisms, job and organisation redesign, and time management.

Questions for discussion

1. Generate as many examples as you can of eustress, distress, hyperstress and hypostress. Under what circumstances could some of these stress patterns be converted into their opposites?
2. Invent two or three fictional people, and speculate on how they would react to the life-event stressor list.
3. How do people experience stress on the job (in terms of demand and control factors)?
4. What symptoms of stress are there? Can you think of any not listed in this chapter? How might we use non-verbal communication as a way of detecting stress symptoms?
5. Compare two or three different stress management techniques and philosophies.

Answers to Table 7.8
1. Overgeneralisation
2. Mind reading
3. Catastrophising
4. Personalisation
5. Fallacy of internal control
6. Fallacy of external control
7. Shoulds
8. Emotional reasoning
9. Fallacy of change
10. Being right
11. Heaven's reward fallacy

References

Albrech, Karl (1979). *Stress and the Manager: Making it Work for You.* (Prentice-Hall: New Jersey).

Anonymous (1981). "Rate Your Managers—Are they Stayputs or Type A?" *Rydges*, May.

     (1979). "Program to Reduce Executive Stress". *Rydge's*, November.

Bartley, H.L. (ed.) (1980). *Stress at Work.* (Latrobe University: Melbourne)

Benson, Herbert (1986). *The Relaxation Response.* (Collins: London).

Bernstein, Douglas A. and Borkovec, Thomas D. (1973). *Professional Relaxation Training.* (Research Press: Illinois).

Bower, Sharon Anthony and Bower, Gordon. H. (1978). *Asserting Yourself.* (Addison-Wesley: Boston).

Broom, Leonard and Selznick, David, *Sociology: A Text with Adapted Readings,* 6th edn. (Harper and Row: New York).

Brown, Barbara (1975). "Bringing Body and Mind Together—Biofeedback", *Psychology Today* (UK), June.

Cheraskin, E., Ringsdorf, W.M. and Brecher, Arlene (1976). *Psychodietitics: Food as the Key to Emotional Health.* (Bantam: New York).

Coleman, Vernon (1978). *Stress Control: How to Cope with Anxiety.* (Pan: London).

Cooper, Cary L. and Marshall, Judi (1978). "Sources of Managerial and White Collar Stress", in Cooper and Payne (1978).

Cooper, Cary L. and Payne, Roy (eds) (1978). *Stress at Work.* (John Wiley: Chichester).

Cooper, Kenneth H. (1976). *Aerobics.* (Bantam Books: New York).

Curtis, John D. and Detert, Richard A. (1981). *How to Relax: A Holistic Approach to Stress Management.* (Mayfield: California).

De Larghy Healy, P. and Lord, D. (1980). "Management Perspectives", in Bartley (1980).

Downing, George (1983). *The Massage Book.* (Penguin: Harmondsworth).

Eifert, Georg H. (1984). "Cognitive Behaviour Therapy: A Critical Evaluation of its Theoretical–Empirical Bases and Therapeutic Efficacy", *Australian Psychologist*, vol. 19, no. 2, July.

Ellis, Albert (1978). "What People can do for Themselves to Cope with Stress", in Cooper and Payne (1978).

Ellis, Albert and Harper, Robert A. (1975). *A New Guide to Rational Living,* rev. edn. (Wilshire: California).

Feingold, Ben F. (1976). *Why Your Child is Hyperactive.* (Random House: New York).

Friedman, Meyer and Rosenman, Roy (1974). *Type A Behaviour and Your Heart.* (Fawcett: Connecticut).

Fuller, George D. (1976). *Biofeedback—Methods and Procedures in Clinical Practice.* (Biofeedback Institute of San Francisco).

Girdano, Daniel and Everley, George (1979). *Controlling Stress and Tension: A Holistic Approach.* (Prentice-Hall: New Jersey).

Gmelch, Walter H. (1982). *Beyond Stress to Effective Management.* (Wiley: New York).

Goleman, Daniel C. (1976). "A Mantra a Day Keeps the Tension Away", *Psychology Today* (UK edition), September.

Goodwin, Rowland (1976). *Stress at Work: A Study of a Growing Problem in Industry.* (Chester House: London).

Greenwood, James W. (1974). *Managing Executive Stress: A Systems Approach.* (John Wiley: New York).

Halfpenny, John (1980). "Stress at Work: A Trade Union Viewpoint", in Bartley (1980).

Haney, C. Michele and Boenisch, Edmond W. Jr. (1982). *Stressmap: Finding Your Pressure Points.* (Impact: California).

Holmes, T.H. and Rahe, R.H. (1967). "The Social Readjustment Rating Scale", *Journal of Psychosomatic Research*, vol. 11, pp.213–18.

Karasek, Robert Allen (1981). "Job Socialization and Job Strain: The Implications of Two Related Psychosocial Mechanisms for Job Design", in Gardell, B. and Johansson, G. *Working Life.* (John Wiley and Sons: Chichester).

Lansbury, Russell D. and Spillane, Robert (1983). *Organizational Behaviour: The Australian Context.* (Longman Cheshire: Melbourne).

McKay, Matthew, Davis, Martha and Fanning, Patrick (1981). *Thoughts and Feelings: The Art of Cognitive Stress Intervention.* (New Harbinger: California).

McMullen, V.B. (1980). "Stress in the Public Service Sector: The Effects of Technology", in Bartley (1980).

Maddison, David (1977). "Anxiety in Every Age", in Yogendra (1977).

Maier, Steven F. and Laudenslager, Mark (1985). "Stress and Health: Exploring the Links", *Psychology Today*, August.

Manuso, J. (1980). *Manage Your Stress*, CRM Multimedia Module. (McGraw-Hill: New York).

Meares, Ainslie (1976). *Relief Without Drugs.* (Fontana: London).
(1983). *The Wealth Within.* (Hill of Content: Melbourne).

Milte, K. (1980). "The Stress of Policing", in Bartley (1980).

Palmer, Stuart (1981). *Role Stress: How to Handle Everyday Tension.* (Prentice-Hall: New Jersey).

Pfeiffer, C.C. (1975). *Mental and Elemental Nutrients.* (Keats, Connecticut).

Poulton, E. Christopher (1978). "Blue Collar Stressors", in Cooper and Payne (1978).

Quick, James C. and Quick, Jonathan D. (1984). *Organizational Stress and Preventive Management.* (McGraw-Hill: New York).

Rix, Susan (1984). "The Deadly Dangers of Stress", *Australian Business*, 28 March.

Sedgewick, Hugh (1983). *Stress and Counterstress: Guidelines for Executives and High Achievers.* (Sun Books: Melbourne).

Selye, Hans (1976). *Stress Without Distress.* (Hodder and Stoughton: London).
(1978). "Interview", *Psychology Today*, March.
(1983). "The Stress Concept: Past, Present and Future", in *Stress Research* (ed. Cooper, Cary L.) (John Wiley and Sons: Chichester).

Shapiro, David (1981). "Biofeedback and Behavioural Medicine in Perspective", in Shapiro, David (ed.), *Biofeedback and Behavioural Medicine, 1979/80: Therapeutic Applications and Experimental Foundations.* (Aldine: New York).

Sherman, Robert (1978). "Yoga versus Psychology", in Yogendra (1977).

Smith, Deborah (no date). "Type A: A Time Bomb in your Chest", *National Times Health and Fitness.*

Sparkes, Laurance (1962). *Self-Hypnosis: A Conditioned-Response Technique.* (Wilshire: California).

Spillane, R.M. (1978). "Overcoming Anxiety: Relaxation is not Enough", *Human Resource Management Australia*, Winter 1978.
(1985). *Achieving Peak Performance.* (Harper and Row: Sydney).

Tacy, Lynne (1982). "Stress: Not a Management Monopoly", *Work and People*, vol. 8, no. 2.

Toffler, Alvin (1970). *Future Shock.* (Pan: London).

Tubesing, Donald A. (1981). *Kicking Your Stress Habits—A Do-It-Yourself Guide to Coping with Stress.* (Whole Person Associates: Minnesota).

Wood, Clive (1985). "The Healthy Neurotic", *New Scientist*, 7 February.

Yogendra, Shr Vijayadev (ed.) (1977). *Mind-Made Disease: Is Your Sickness Real?* (Yoga Education Centre/Helen Vale Foundation: Melbourne).

Films/Videos

Managing Stress (Video Channel).
Manage Your Stress (Video Channel).
Your Own Worse Enemy: Stress (Video Channel).
Manager Under Pressure (Power Human Resources).

8

Time management

Time is the scarcest resource and unless it is managed nothing else can be managed.

Peter Drucker

... "time management" is actually a misnomer. In the strict sense one does not manage time, for the minute hand is beyond our control. It moves relentlessly on. Time passes at a predetermined rate no matter what we do. It is a question not of managing the clock but of managing ourselves with respect to the clock.

R. Alec Mackenzie

Work smarter, not harder.

Anonymous

Everyone should have a granny, especially those who have no TV. Grannies are the only grown-ups who always have time.

English child, quoted by Annejet Campbell

How can we best manage our time? Is time a manageable commodity, or is it more accurate to say that time manages us? Most of us do have problems setting priorities, avoiding (with greater or lesser success) procrastination, trying to plan, trying to delegate, trying to manage telephone calls, mail, filing, meetings, trying to trade off the conflicting demands made upon us by our personal and professional commitments. But chaos sometimes has a pattern, and the type of problems you might experience managing your time are problems shared by many people. Consider, for example, the types of things that waste your time (Box 8.A). If, after analysing your time-wasters, you get other people to do a similar analysis, you will probably find more similarities than dissimilarities between your own experience and the experiences of others.

Time management has emerged in the past decade as a separate field of self-management skills, sharing much in common with decision-making and problem-solving and stress management. You may notice interesting overlaps between the chapters of those names in this book and this chapter. Much of the advice given out in time management books, articles, films, videos and seminars is useful, although not a small part of it verges on the silly and shonky. The difficulty is that what some people consider useful, some consider silly and shonky, and vice versa. You may perceive that many of the "rules" of time management given here have significant exceptions, and the exceptions may disprove the rules. You may find however that at the end of this chapter you have a useful residue of concepts and tools that can help you to manage your personal and professional lives with greater efficiency and effectiveness.

BOX 8.A: Time wasters

	Big problem for me	Often a problem	Seldom a problem
Planning			
1. Not setting goals	____	____	____
2. No daily plan	____	____	____
3. Priorities unclear or changing	____	____	____
4. Leaving tasks unfinished	____	____	____
5. "Fire fighting" or crisis management	____	____	____
6. No self-imposed deadlines	____	____	____
7. Attempting too much—unrealistic time estimates	____	____	____
Organising			
8. Personal disorganisation/cluttered desk	____	____	____
9. Duplication of effort	____	____	____
10. Confused responsibility and authority	____	____	____
11. Multiple bosses	____	____	____
Directing			
12. Doing it myself	____	____	____
13. Involved in routine details	____	____	____
14. Ineffective delegation	____	____	____
15. Lack of motivation	____	____	____
16. Not managing conflict	____	____	____
17. Not coping with change	____	____	____
Controlling			
18. Telephone interruptions	____	____	____
19. Drop-in visitors	____	____	____
20. Lack of self-discipline	____	____	____
21. Too many interests	____	____	____
22. Mistakes/ineffective performance	____	____	____
23. Inability to say "no"	____	____	____
24. No standards, progress reports	____	____	____
25. Incomplete information	____	____	____
Communicating			
26. Meetings	____	____	____
27. Under-/unclear/over-communicating	____	____	____
28. Failure to listen	____	____	____
29. Socialising	____	____	____

	Big problem for me	Often a problem	Seldom a problem
Decision-making			
30. Snap decisions	____	____	____
31. Indecision/procrastination	____	____	____
32. Wanting all the facts	____	____	____
33. Decision by committee	____	____	____
34. Perfectionism	____	____	____
For homemakers only			
35. Poor planning of errands and shopping	____	____	____
36. Not planning meals ahead	____	____	____
37. Doing jobs other family members could do	____	____	____
38. Family appointments (doctor, music lessons, etc.)	____	____	____
39. Children's interruptions	____	____	____
40. Chauffeuring children	____	____	____
41. Inability to say "no" to volunteer requests	____	____	____
42. Looking for family's misplaced items	____	____	____
43. Perfectionism	____	____	____
Others			

Source: Ferner, Jack D. (1980), pp.33–35. Reproduced with permission.

Interruptions

Life is made up of interruptions, as W.S. Gilbert wrote in *Patience*. Or at least it seems to be. Procrastination (which we will get around to in a few pages) seems to be different from interruptions: we are willing to take the blame for procrastination, but interruptions seem quite objective, external, "out there"—matters over which we have no control. But is this in fact the case? Consider the types of things in Box 8.A which you felt were time wasters. Some are externally caused, but some are caused by ourselves (Table 8.1).

Table 8.1 External and internal causes of interruptions

External causes	Internal causes
Phone calls	Lack of self-discipline
Drop-in visitors	Failure to delegate
Crisis-prone environment	Cluttered desk
Overcurious/overcontrolling/insecure boss	Procrastination
	Ego (only *I* can answer their questions)
Lack of secretary/assistant	Fear of offending (if I don't answer my phone)
Overdependent/untrained staff	
Inadequate phone system	Desire to appear available (call me, drop in, any time)
Physical location (next to front door/ vending machine/rest rooms)	Being interruption-prone: insecurity, short attention span, dislike for your work

Source: Adapted from Ferner (1980), Mackenzie and Waldo (1981).

Some people may be accident-prone, but might some people also be interruption-prone? For example, we sometimes speak of children as being hyperactive, but what about hyperactive adults? These are the people fuelled with adrenalin and caffeine, who find it impossible to sit still and work with concentration upon one particular task.[1] They might pace up and down ("it helps me to think"), they may do the grand tour of the office or factory[2] just to see what's happening (possibly interrupting many people on the way). They are in effect *interrupting themselves* by doing this, because they never quite get around to doing just one thing. When they do eventually return to the task, they have to spend more time re-familiarising themselves with the particulars. The time taken to begin the task, then re-familiarise oneself with the task (possibly several or many times), and then complete the task, is usually greater than the time it would have taken to complete the task in the one sequence. Self-interruption is a variation on procrastination, and it is a self-destructive form of game-playing we could well do without.

Other internal causes of interruptions, such as not wishing to offend people and wanting to appear available and accessible at all times, are often due to a nasty speech impediment—the inability to say the word "no". Yet we cannot not say no: if you've avoided saying no to an interrupter, either on the telephone or face to face, you have already said no to your own work.[3]

One form of "internal" interruption is procrastination, while one form of "external" interruption is being in a crisis-prone environment. Yet many crises are self-started—the line between external and internal causes is not hard and fast. Also, being crisis-prone and procrastinating are often merely two sides of the one coin.

Procrastination

Procrastination, or putting things off, is not always a bad thing. Thomas Jefferson said delay was preferable to error. Problems can sometimes benefit with age, like wine. Politicians and bureaucrats are fond of saying that a particular problem could benefit from "benign neglect". And of course, there is the famous anecdote of Napoleon stuffing letters, documents and other paraphernalia of state into a drawer, and not looking at them until several months had passed—whereupon he found that most of the problems had solved themselves.

Nevertheless, procrastination is the thief of time for most of us. Why then do we procrastinate? Some of the causes are:[4]

1. conflict avoidance—we do not wish to confront people, data, paperwork that is threatening

---

[1] This behaviour has much in common with the type A personality; see Chapter 7.

[2] Walking around without gratuitously interrupting may of course have positive payoffs—in fact, some management gurus see the Japanese technique of "management by walking around" as helping, not hindering productivity.

[3] This, of course, is unassertive behaviour. See Chaper 6.

[4] Some more humorous, but nonetheless accurate explanations are:
The laws of procrastination
1. Procrastination shortens the job and places the responsibility for its termination on someone else (the authority who imposed the deadline).
2. It reduces anxiety by reducing the expected quality of the project from the best of all possible efforts to the best that can be expected given the limited time.
3. Status is gained in the eyes of others, and in one's own eyes, because it is assumed that the importance of the work justifies the stress.
4. Avoidance of interruptions including the assignment of other duties can be achieved, so that the obviously stressed worker can concentrate on the single effort.
5. Procrastination avoids boredom; one never has the feeling that there is nothing important to do.
6. It may eliminate the job if the need passes before the job can be done. (DICKSON 1981, P.175)

2. fear of success—some procrastinators may fear actually achieving something—delaying ensures failure
3. procrastination as a silent protest against others—your spouse, your boss, the electricity authority, the taxman (*Omega*, July/August 1983)

Knaus (1979) suggests that three types of mental diversions make us delay. These are:

1. *Manana*—we all know this game we play with ourselves: "I'll do it tomorrow . . . I *could* do it now, but I'll wait until inspiration strikes."
2. *Contingency manana*—the person playing this game says: "I'll do a substitute (or less important activity) before I do the relevant (or more important) activity." Now there are *two* things to procrastinate about! Thus, John will not marry Marsha until he has enough to buy a house outright, even though Marsha has offered to pay half the deposit.
3. *Catch-22*—with (1) and (2), at least there is a theoretical chance that they will happen, unlike the Catch-22. This is being played when a person makes action contingent upon impossible events: "I'll never be attractive to men/women unless I look like Farrah Fawcett/Robert Redford."

A case of distorted thinking

Contingency Manana and Catch-22 are expressions of what Ellis and Knaus (1977) call *must*abatory behaviour—a half-facetious word that means compulsive behaviour, driven by the unconscious demand "do it perfectly, or not at all". This is an example of what exponents of rational–emotional therapy (RET) call a style of distorted thinking; see Chapter 7.

There is nothing wrong with doing a job properly, of course—far from it. But the mustabatory person sees everything in black and white—"What's the point in starting?—I'll only make a botch of it." Not for them the Chinese maxim "the journey of a thousand miles starts with a single footstep". To

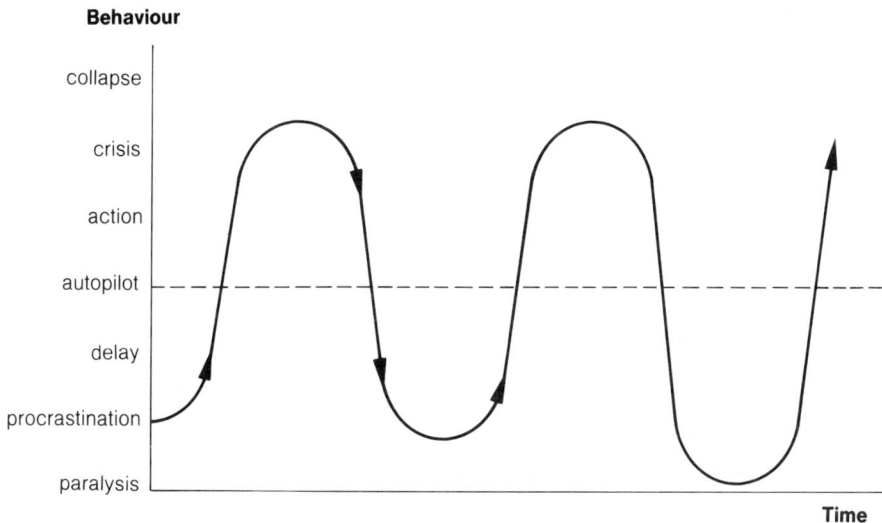

Fig 8.1 *A model of time-use behaviour*

Table 8.2 Demand terms and desire terms

Demand terms	Desire terms
ought	wish
should	want
must	prefer
expect	aspire
have to	hope
got to	trust
need	
necessary	
require	
imperative	
demand	

Source: Adapted from Ellis and Knaus (1977).

acknowledge such a philosophy would be to acknowledge that performing well is often an arduous and gradual process. If such a person has a *low frustration tolerance* (and she usually does) then she becomes locked in a game wherein one does not enter a race for the first time because there is no iron-clad guarantee that the first prize is automatic. Such a person's motto is "I cannot stand present pain for future gain", and clings to the infantile belief that she must always feel *happy* about whatever she is doing. Thus if the choice every night is between television and doing the dishes, then the dishes must always get low priority, or at least until those green things moving on last Wednesday's plates should really be taken care of. The life pattern of such a person must necessarily oscillate violently between procrastination and crisis management: nothing is done until nothing is done, and then extreme action is necessary (Fig. 8.1). Instead of being reasonable, or even reasonably inefficient, and keeping one's behaviour hovering around the *autopilot* level (where all problems are routine, and routine is no problem), occasionally moving down to *delay*, but then switching to *action*, the mustabatory person is trapped on a behavioural roller-coaster (which, if it goes too high, or too low, could have dire consequences).

Ellis and Knaus suggest that such compulsive behaviour can often be revealed in the very words we use. Thus, a mustabator will use *demand* terms rather than *desire* terms (Table 8.2). Demand terms are absolutist, perfectionist, and lock the user into a black and white universe, where everything is all or nothing (and for the procrastinator, it's usually nothing).

Desire terms, on the other hand, are more probabilistic, and show that the user of such terms is more willing to negotiate with reality than throw a tantrum.

Procrastination has to be justified to our own consciences, of course, and so we resort to what Knaus called *addictivities*—activities that are so seductive that they fill up our time and prevent us from achieving our original aims. Addictivities can be things like chain-smoking, over-eating, sleeping, talking on the telephone, watching more television/another video, doing too much housework, et cetera, ad nauseam.

Overcoming procrastination

The best solution to procrastination, like all time management problems, is setting priorities and making decisions according to those priorities. Other solutions might be applying what Bliss calls the *salami technique*: break jobs down into manageable slices or pieces, so they don't look quite so terrifying, and do them one piece or slice at a time. Make a list of the pieces and then make a neurotic's bargain with yourself—promise yourself you won't force yourself to do the whole thing, so long as you do one or two pieces now, and a few more pieces when you get some spare time in the next few days (Bliss 1977).

You might also consider setting up a *procrastination drawer or file* (Reynolds and Tramel 1979), so that you can put things off within a structure, hoping that some things will take care of themselves (or that the problems will "mature"). The whole noxious pile is there to look at in one spot when guilt becomes too much, and there may even be similarities between tasks procrastinated on, and a common thread or a quick-fix solution to some, most or all of them may miraculously disappear. Of course, when the procrastination drawer or file becomes more full than all the other drawers or files, then it is apparent that procrastination has become an end in itself rather than a means to an end.

You might also try *creative or alternative procrastination*. This means that if you have activity A (housework) to do, as well as prepare a report (activity B), procrastinate on activity A by doing activity B. When you become bored and/or tired of this, reverse the process.

One of the most familiar forms of procrastination is this type of rationalisation: "I'll do it (prepare the report, study for the exam) at the last possible minute, not because I'm procrastinating, but because I only function well under pressure." This is managing by crisis, and, as we saw in Figure 8.1, it is linked with procrastination.

Management by crisis

Often, today's crises are merely yesterday's soluble problems—the ones we never got around to solving. Consequently, we are locked into *reacting* rather than *proacting*, that is, our work manages us rather than vice versa. Crises might also be self-inflicted because they are fun. Zoll argues that one of the best tests of whether a workplace is efficient is whether it appears to be a dull place: if it's dull, it's efficient; if there is excitement everywhere, that probably means that it is crisis-prone (Zoll 1974). How absurd, you might say. People don't create their own crises—they've got better things to do. It goes without saying that they have got better things to do, but that doesn't necessarily mean that they are not manufacturing crises. How often have we heard, for example, the following ringing phrase: "This country/team/family/ organisation is only at its best in crisis." It certainly sounds romantic, glamorous and dramatic, but the drama is usually only melodrama. Consider the student who always ends up cramming for each exam, the writer "waiting for inspiration to descend", and the executive who has procrastinated badly on a report because "I only really get motivated by pressure". All three are in fact managing by crisis, and obviously are therefore not managing very well. Such individuals are usually locked into a self-fulfilling prophecy style of behaviour, just like the teams, nations, families and organisations who believe that they are only at their best in times of crisis. That is, because there are these beliefs about crises, pressure and heroic behaviour, there will tend to *be* more crises. Crises can certainly be fun: there is excitement, high emotions, dramatic action, fires real or metaphorical to be extinguished, and all of these can be extremely gratifying. People have been known to look back nostalgically upon wars, because life during a war is relatively simple—action is everything, crisis is the order of the day, only heroic efforts will be satisfactory, and often people who formerly lived and worked separately from others are thrown together in a warm, supercharged intimacy that bonds together the group under pressure.

If life is too dull in nations and organisations, people may decide to generate their own excitement, lighting fires (consciously or unconsciously) in order to put them out again. The excitement-starved person says, "Gosh, this looks like a job for Crisis Man/Woman!" and their day (or indeed their week or year) is filled. This style of coping has much in common with workaholic behaviour (see Chapter 7).

Crisis avoidance and planning

The root cause of crisis management is lack of planning. Why don't we plan? We cannot anticipate all contingencies, but we can be prepared for the likely and the unlikely. After all, even chance favours the prepared mind. Such active anticipation or pro-action can insulate us from being locked into a cycle of oscillation of reacting to the current crisis/not noticing the next crisis building up/reacting to the next crisis, and so on. Basically, time management is about planning and, in particular, the setting of priorities. There are a number of useful techniques for setting priorities which will be looked at soon. But why don't we plan? Usually the reason given is that we don't have time to plan. We would if we could, but we can't so we won't... This is a sure-fire recipe for managing by crisis, of course, and, as the folk wisdom has it, there's never time to do it right, but there's always time to do it over.

Possibly we don't want to sit down and plan because we might be horrified at just how complex the situation really is: we might be trying to get 300 hours of activity into a 168 hour week. And that might mean that we should trim some of the fat—social commitments, responsibilities for particular areas, addictivities, academic subjects, and so on. But this is a harsh reality for our self-image: I'm the Renaissance Man/Superwoman who can tackle anything—don't tell me I'm hopelessly overcommitted or inefficient. Let me deny in peace or a semblance of peace that crisis can be.

Yet overcommitment may be the harsh truth. Time management techniques may help you to live your current lifestyle in a more efficient way, but such techniques may also lead you to the inescapable conclusion that you are attempting more than the maximum (and almost certainly only achieving more or less the minimum), and that therefore your lifestyle has to change. If so, you probably need to share or delegate some tasks. But delegation is easier said than done.

Delegation

A manager asks a subordinate to take over a particular project. A mother asks her children to do the dishes while she is engaged on other tasks. Both the manager and the mother are delegating to others, and hence are getting more done than they otherwise would. A hackneyed but accurate definition of management is "getting things done through other people". Obviously, by this definition, we are all managers in the many different roles we play throughout out day.[5]

---

[5] See Chapter 10.

Many managers perceive delegation as abdication, or passing the buck, and so on. If they are not trained to see the wider effectiveness of work-sharing, many of the delegates—children doing the washing up, clerks answering letters—will also see delegation as buck-passing and abdication, a weakness, rather than a strength. Many others have so little faith in the competence of the people they should delegate to that they never delegate anything. How can these problems be overcome?

Consider, for example, the problem of the alleged incompetence of potential delegates:

"Yes, I know the kids are old enough to do their own washing and ironing, but they're just not responsible enough to do it correctly. . ."

"Never mind, you go home, I'll stay here and fix it . . . I don't know—if you want something done properly, do it yourself. . ."

Remarks like these indicate that the speakers have a very low view of the maturity of their subordinates. Subordinates, however, do not learn their tasks by telepathy or osmosis—they need to be trained. If the trainer (i.e. the manager) is competent, then the trainees should prove to be competent and hence people who can be safely entrusted with delegated jobs. But many managers believe that they do not have the time to train people, or at least assign it a very low priority. Consequently, they tend to supervise people very closely indeed, never giving responsiblity "because they'd only screw it up".

Upward delegation

You can always tell when a decision-maker holds such attitudes—she's the one with a queue of people outside her office door, all wanting approval for the most trivial tasks and processes. The decision-maker may feel slightly annoyed by such a queue ("they're such children, they probably need a blueprint to tie their shoes"), but at least she is certain she has not delegated important matters to incompetent people. But has she avoided delegation? Not really. It has yet to sink into her thick skull that in any organisation, once it exceeds a certain level of complexity, delegation *must* happen—if not *downwards*, then *upwards*.

In other words, if people are not taught to be mature and self-starting, they must necessarily remain in a dependent role. Thus, such dependent people must delegate tasks upwards—"this is too hard for us, let's give it to Superman/Superwoman". This means that the manager ends up doing everyone's job, including her own. How well she is doing all of these jobs is another matter, of course.

In such situations, the manager who may feel that she is the solution to the organisation's problems is in fact the biggest problem of all. She is the bottleneck in the decision-making process because she is over-controlling, suspicious rather than trusting, and perhaps punitive (the bottleneck is usually at the top of the bottle).

It is, of course, extremely hard to train people well. This is due not only to the time involved, but also due to the fact that, beyond a certain point, people have to act and, inevitably, to make their own mistakes. Watching fledgeling birds fly from the nests can be an extremely nerve-wracking experience. In many situations, it can also mean large and painful expenses. But at least mistakes indicate that someone stopped talking long enough to do something.

The indispensability trap

Part of the problem of managers having a low opinion of their subordinates is that such managers usually have a very high opinion of themselves. They are *indispensable*. No one is in fact indispensable, nor should they be ("don't be indispensable—you'll never get promoted"). An interesting test of whether a manager has been able to cultivate real maturity in her subordinates is this: when she walks out of work today, what will happen if she walks under a bus? Will the organisation continue on with only a few minor hiccups, or will it collapse? If it collapses, then the late lamented manager has been playing indispensability games. Almost certainly, she has not delegated, trained or trusted.

This Great Person game is very familiar in politics, both in totalitarian countries and in countries such as Australia. A Great Person survives, by hook or by crook, and reigns for a long time. But even Great Persons die, and so the problem of succession presents itself. Where are the Great Persons to succeed? Usually there are none, because anyone with talents similar to the Great Person was weeded out years ago, or else has left in disgust at continually being thwarted and patronised.

This leaves only mediocrities, but even mediocrities can perform well if they have been trained, if they have had tasks delegated to them, with all due power and responsibility. Such delegation, however, is by definition a partitioning of the Great Person's power (as the Great Person sees it), and that is precisely what she does not want to happen. Consequently, the Great Person will only be able to see gloom and destruction after she goes—*'après moi, le déluge"*. Countries that are unfortunate enough to experience this pattern of leadership usually have an unstable pattern of oscillation: Great Person dies, leaving mild chaos/succeeded by mediocrities who make chaos worse, paving way for/another Great Person to provide strong leadership and reverse chaos, etc.

Dispensing with indispensability

Thus, politicians who do not provide for successors have the same class of ego problem as does the mother who finds it hard to cut the apron-strings from her grown-up children, or the manager who doesn't trust her subordinates and consequently feels that she has to do everything herself. Their relationship to others is one of dominance/submission, and it is an extremely ineffective relationship. It is hard to say what they fear more: the incompetence of others, or the competence of others (and hence, by symmetry, their own incompetence).

So delegation is seen to be not a luxury but a necessity. A supervisor may feel, for example, that time is too short because of *external* events, such as mail, visitors and reading. But can some or all of these be delegated? If they can, but the supervisor does not want to relinquish part of her empire to mere subordinates, then the time management problem is an *internal* one.

Turla and Hawkins (1985) offer a number of practical suggestions for overcoming the poor or non-existent delegation techniques of others. When a boss is *under-delegating*, or procrastinating in delegating, write a proposed action plan in an "Unless I hear otherwise" memo ("Unless I hear otherwise, I propose to do the following things. . ."). This of course is contingent upon your having extracted clear guidelines as to what power you have to operate in a particular area. Attempt to overcome further procrastination and vagueness by rephrasing all discussions and instructions in your own words, so your boss understands what you understand the case to be. Ask for specific deadlines for each part of a major project (a modified salami technique).

When a boss is *over-delegating*, have a "to do" list made up of all activities you plan to achieve on a day or in a week, and ask your boss to decide what the new priorities should be. This reminds the boss that you have many demands on your time, and shifts the burden of responsibility for making decisions about priorities back to where it belongs (the boss), giving the boss a not-so-subtle reminder that the purpose of her staff is not to clean up the mess caused by her crisis management style.

When someone is attempting *reverse delegation* on you, suggest the problem can be jointly solved, but ask the would-be delegator to brainstorm two or three possible solutions, in writing, and *then* you'll discuss it. This again shifts responsibility back to where it belongs, will probably lead to less attempts at upward delegation, and train would-be upward delegators to be more independent.

Meetings

One of the greatest time-wasters for people in organisations is meetings. Group decision-making and problem-solving processes are considered in greater detail in Chapter 11, but it is useful to comment here on the ways in which meetings can be used to manage or mismanage time. Meetings, of course, certainly have a bad press: "Meetings are where minutes are kept and hours lost"; "A camel is a horse designed by a committee"; and so on. Certainly, meetings, particularly those held in a crisis atmosphere, can be spectacularly wasteful of people's time unless certain basic groundrules are followed. For example, consider the following points:

Is this meeting really necessary?
Is it crucial that a number of people be in one room at the one time? Might a conference telephone call, or a Confravision video hook-up, be preferable in terms of time and money? (Costs and benefits depend upon such things as salary per minute costs.)

Is the meeting simply the creature of a leader's over-delegation, that is, the leader cannot make a decision, and needs to have her hand held, or has the leader in fact already made her decision and merely wishes the group to rubber stamp it?

What would happen if the sacrosanct daily/weekly/monthly meeting *simply wasn't held*? What catastrophic events would befall the organisation? Disasters do occur, and such an experiment might be a dangerous one. But it is a cynical truth that meetings sometimes expand to fill the amount of agenda available, that is, in a slack period, people might manufacture issues simply to have something to talk about. A content analysis of the minutes of your past ten meetings might well bear this out.

Is the meeting well planned?
Is there a well planned agenda, giving background information on matters arising? Or is there a cryptically skeletal agenda, or no agenda at all? This situation usually leads to the leader continually presenting a surprise package of information or even worse, continually declaring battle stations to meet the latest crisis. If surprise packages are normally the order of the day, then the group is not pooling its resources—it is merely pooling its ignorance. The

meeting is not a meeting—it is merely a briefing session, a pre-meeting for the next meeting, when everyone can bring their information. It would have been more useful to stay at home in bed, and read the minutes of the meeting the following day. Surprise packages are usually associated with crisis management, for a number of reasons. The leader has probably procrastinated on agenda items: it is rare that most crises happen just a few minutes before the meeting—today's crises are yesterday's routine problems, after all. Such a set-up can only encourage passivity on the part of the assembled group—they are like viewers watching a newscast of dramatic, violent but mysteriously acausal events. When the leader asks for "any ideas?" the silence is deafening, or perhaps the noise is deafening as top-of-the-head solutions are desperately manufactured. Then it is usually time for someone to suggest that the group will have to "drop everything to get this under control", or other such heroic declarations.

Towards more effective meetings

It is useful to compute the salary per minute cost of a meeting. Thus, a meeting of ten people on an average salary of $20 000 has perhaps a salary/minute figure of:

40 hrs/wk × 48 weeks = 1920 hours
1920 × 60 = 115 200 minutes
$20 000 × 10 = $200 000
$200 000/115 200 = $1.73 per minute

Thus, a one-hour meeting is worth about $104 of their time, and so on. If they meet for ten hours a week in various groups, it goes to $1040. This exercise can be trivial, but it can also be unpleasantly enlightening. If C. Northcote Parkinson is right ("the amount of time spent on an agenda item is usually in inverse proportion to its importance"), then $70 of time may well be spent on an item involving a few dollars.

Time-limiting of agenda items can be a useful way of overcoming the Parkinson effect; it also helps to allocate priorities—just what *are* the most important items to consider?

Start on time and finish on time. Starting late means that you have penalised the virtuous and rewarded the sinful; consequently you will find that more of the virtuous will be sinful. Finishing on time also means that the group members can start their other activities—such as other meetings—on time.

You might also try tricks like mentioning lateness in the minutes, or fining people, or requesting that the latest person be responsible for having the minutes typed and distributed. Punitive approaches like these can backfire, of course.

Conduct some meetings standing up. Many otherwise lengthy meetings might suddenly become manageably short. Carried to extremes, such measures would be punitive and indicative of a time-obsessed mentality. Yet in moderation, they can act as an antidote to the over-socialising meeting, where people find it so pleasant to be with others that they don't particularly want to leave. Empathy may be an explicit objective of the meeting, of course—the meeting may be about creative brainstorming, or attempting to solve sensitive interpersonal communication problems. But for the common run of meetings, it is interesting to see how many people will linger if there are no chairs (or the time is fast approaching for lunch or knock-off time).

The next time you are considering having a meeting, or have been summoned to a meeting, consult the checklist in Box 8.B to see whether your time is going to be wasted. Of course, it is extremely hard to predict the way some meetings will turn out, so sometimes it is useful to do a post-mortem on a meeting, the better to ensure that the next meeting will be better. To perform such a post-mortem, have copies of the meeting evaluation form (Box 8.C) run off, have meeting members complete it and deliver it *anonymously*, and then collate the responses. The results might be illuminating—either as a ray of sunshine revealing a tranquil landscape of satisfaction and happiness, or as a lightning flash revealing scenes of horror.

BOX 8.B: Bad reasons for having a meeting: A checklist

1. *Habit.* We *always* have a meeting on this day at this time. Such assumptions should be tested by simply not having the traditional meeting, and seeing what happens. The same scrutiny should also be applied to committees whose origins are buried in the mists of time.
2. *Other departments have one.* If this is so, then this department should clarify its perceptions about whether meetings are objectively necessary, or whether they are seen merely as a status symbol a department should have (like a separate photocopier, tea urn, etc.), or whether meetings are seen as indications that Something Is Being Done (which may be concealing real work with window-dressing).
3. *Socialising.* Getting people together on the thinnest pretext may be all right on one or two occasions, particularly when there is a need for more than a few people to get to know one another. Then again, perhaps lunch might serve this purpose better. If meetings in the long term seem to achieve little except exchange of low-grade gossip (as opposed to high-grade, grapevine-approved gossip, of course!), then the meeting needs to be put out of its misery. (A hidden reason for socialising, of course, is that many people get lonely working by themselves.)
4. *Escape from real work.* Very similar to socialising. Meetings can look like work, but if they are merely circuses of ego-tripping, buck-passing, paper-pushing and back-seat driving, then it may be that people should go back to work.
5. *Passing the buck.* If someone doesn't want to be saddled with responsibility for something that is definitely theirs, they may try and dilute responsibility for it within a group. This is the sleazy side of participative decision-making. The decision-avoider may in fact later disown the decision coming out of the group, thus achieving all (manipulative) power with no responsibility (cf. *pseudo-participation*, below).
6. *It's another crisis, and we need a quick decision.* If this is so, there probably won't be an agenda, or ample notice for people to analyse the problem. Decision-making thus will probably be sloppy, ad hoc, temporary, and in fact decisions put off until further information is at hand. In other words, the meeting will have been a pre-meeting meeting, not a complete one. There must always be the flexibility to

call snap meetings, of course, but if the organisation is crisis-prone, then there will be too many of such meetings.

7. *Concealed reprimand and conflict avoidance.* The meeting-caller may not know how to discipline a few deviants in the wider group, and thus call the wider group together to give a lecture about various sins (late arrival, late submission of reports, unprofessional conduct, etc.). Net effect? The sinful think that everyone else had to be doing the same thing (and thus the sinful have no incentive to change their behaviour), while the virtuous have their morale shaken and time wasted.

8. *Provide an audience.* The meeting-caller may wish to "brainstorm", "bounce a few ideas of the wall"—but only her ideas, mind you. Ego-tripping like this can also be undertaken by individuals in the meeting who wish to inform everyone of all details of their pet projects.

9. *Pseudo-participation.* Authoritarian meeting-callers may conceal their true character by going through the motions of getting everyone's opinion, but in fact bulldozing through precisely what they want to get through.

(Adapted from Le Boeuf (1979), Reynolds and Tramel (1979), Fletcher (1984).)

BOX 8.C: Meeting evaluation form

	YES	NO
1. Was this meeting really necessary?	___	___
2. Could this meeting be abolished permanently?	___	___
3. Could this meeting be abolished temporarily, e.g. miss one day/week/month, etc?	___	___
4. Could this meeting have been postponed? If so, for how long?	___	___
5. Could this meeting have been conducted via technology, e.g. party telephone videoconference line (if so, circle one or both).	___	___
6. Could this have been a stand-up meeting?	___	___
7. Could the business of the meeting be better handled by one-to-one conversation	___	___
8. Could the business of the meeting be better handled in writing, e.g. memo?	___	___
9. Was there enough notice given?	___	___
10. Was the agenda (with supporting materials where necessary) supplied well in advance?	___	___
11. Was there enough detail on the agenda items to indicate problem causes, possible solutions, etc.?	___	___
12. Were agenda items time-limited?	___	___
13. Were start and finish times clearly spelled out?	___	___
14. Did any agenda items go over time?	___	___
15. Did meeting start and finish on time?	___	___
16. Was the place of the meeting appropriate? If not, how?	___	___

	YES	NO
17. Were appropriate aids (whiteboard, projectors, etc.) available? If not, what was missing?	____	____
18. Were there too many people present? If so, who should not have been here? Why?	____	____
19. Were there not enough people here? If so, who should have been here? Why?	____	____
20. Did the chairperson handle interruptions, distractions, well?		
21. Did the chairperson handle conflicts well?	____	____
22. Did the chairperson summarise key points for the group?	____	____
23. Did the chairperson seek out all points of view, even potentially unpopular ones (i.e. was groupthink avoided)?		
24. Were real decisions made?	____	____
25. Were deadlines set?	____	____
26. Does everyone know who is responsible for implementing decisions of the group?	____	____

(OPTIONAL)

	YES	NO
27. Were minutes of the previous meeting distributed within 48 hours of the meeting?	____	____
28. Were minutes of this meeting distributed within 48 hours?	____	____

29. Salary cost of meeting.
List meeting participants' names and approximate/inferred salaries.
Add salaries.
Divide to find hourly/minute salary of group.
Multiply to find out how much meeting costs.
e.g. 10 people
total salary (approx.) $270 000 per year

$$\frac{\$270\,000}{52\text{ weeks (excluding holidays)}} = \$5192/\text{week}$$

$$\frac{\$5192}{40\text{ hours}} = \$130/\text{hour}$$

Communications overload
Telephones

In his books *Future Shock* and *The Third Wave,* Alvin Toffler has noted that people today have to cope with an enormous amount of information. Information is not only data in print but also spoken information, information transmitted through the media, and so on. Compared to our grandparents, we have many more channels of information and the flow of information through those channels is much heavier; we live, Toffler says, in an age of *information overload*. The modern organisation cannot escape this trend: indeed, at times it seems to be drowning in information in paper files, microfilm, memos, letters, photocopies, reports, computer printouts and programs, telephone calls, periodicals, newspapers and books.

Reynolds and Tramel (1979) note that the telephone in particular is "the greatest nuisance among conveniences and the greatest convenience among nuisances". Certainly we are almost terrorised by the telephone. Its imperative ring demands that we acknowledge it, and it is a brave (or foolhardy) person who deliberately ignores it. One approach to controlling the telephone tyranny (and indeed to discourage people just dropping in to kill time) is to institute a *quiet hour* in the day. In this hour—for example from 9 to 10 in the morning—accept no incoming calls, except for emergencies (Fig. 8.2). This places telephonists, secretaries and assistants in a screening role, and often they have to be most diplomatic and articulate to explain to callers just what a quiet hour is. Alternatively, screening can be done by your peers and colleagues, the whole process being managed on a roster system. Once screeners are trained, callers usually adapt to the system, and the callers may in fact ponder on the idea of the quiet hour and institute it in their own organisations.

We should not be cowed by the imperative ring of the telephone. As Joseph Trickett has remarked:

> No one expects a physician or surgeon to answer the phone during an examination or operation. No jurist is expected to answer the phone while he is in court. No professor is expected to answer his phone when he is teaching a class. Why then should an important business executive be expected to be always "on tap" and available to his telephone? (QUOTED IN MACKENZIE 1972, P.96)

If your calls can be screened for you, the screener can promise a call-back at a time or times convenient to both parties. In calling back, you can group your calls, rather than spread them out through the day, and you can have all appropriate information (files, etc.) in front of you.

Technology can cut your telephone time considerably. An automatic answering machine can give pre-recorded messages about when you will be available (and if you want to be really sneaky, you can listen in to the incoming calls and screen as you go, taking those calls you want to). There are now available telephone/PABX systems that will automatically redial busy numbers and transfer incoming calls to your next destination. This latter facility can be of particular use even between extensions within the same organisation—we have all suffered the frustration of being endlessly transferred around various extensions, and sometimes being cut off.

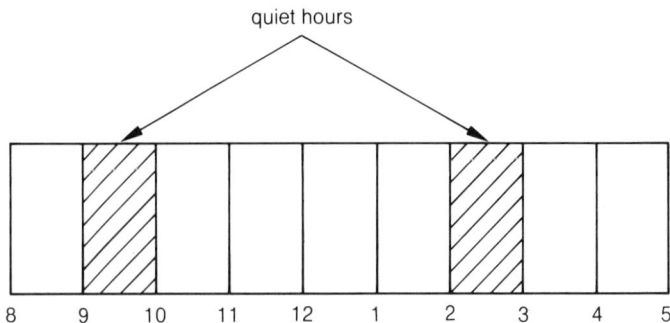

Fig 8.2 *Quiet hour zones in the daily schedule*

The paper war: Filing

The paper war can probably never be won, but at least it can be kept at the status of a cold war rather than a hot one. When handling paper, it is useful to remember that your desk is not a two-dimensional horizontal filing system. Just because you need to attend to something does not mean that it has to be permanently on display. This approach is about as rational as keeping your favourite records and books filed on the living room floor, or keeping crockery, cutlery, glasses and food ingredients permanently on the kitchen benches (a favourite, but not terribly effective, method of housekeeping for some).

The decks need to be cleared if you are to see the exact nature of the problem (objective fact) and also if you are not to become discouraged with the chaos of it all (subjective fact). Be flexible about this: preparing for the job may be done in such a systematic way that we are merely procrastinating in an ingenious way ("well, I'm ready now . . . but it's too late to start today"). If it's your turn to cook, others may be pleased by the kitchen's spotlessness, but they still want to know: *where's the food?*

Consequently, you should be able to file current matters without feeling that this means the stuff will be sunk without trace. If you do harbour such anxieties, it probably means that you know the grisly truth about your filing system—it's hopelessly disorganised. As was said before, a good test of whether authority was well delegated in an organisation was whether the organisation could function smoothly if the boss walked under a bus tomorrow. What would happen if you walked under a bus or, less dramatically, were ill and couldn't attend? Would it be possible for others to use your filing system, locate documents on your desk, and so on, without much bother? Would this be too embarrassing and humiliating to contemplate? Or perhaps your system is deliberately idiosyncratic, thus keeping nosy people out, and demonstrating your uniqueness and indispensability.

Creative destruction: Wastebasketry and purging

In relation to filing materials, another interesting question to ask yourself is: if a fire went through the place tomorrow, how disastrous would this be? Is the information stored in the system totally unique, irreplaceable? Or could it be located elsewhere without too much bother? This is certainly something to keep in mind when considering whether to file something or throw it away. A criticism of older people is that they often won't throw things away; they squirrel, they hoard, saying "you never know when it will come in handy". A criticism of the young is that they are too ready to throw too much away—a direct reflection of their consumption patterns in general. Nevertheless on this point the throw-away mentality has definitely got something going for it. Many time management experts recommend that we cultivate the art of *wastebasketry*, that is, being quite ruthless with what we keep and what we throw away. Keep in mind that if it is not irreplaceable—if it can be located in another building or library in the same city—then it won't be the end of the world if you throw it out. Mackenzie (1972) suggests that 80 to 99 per cent of files are *never* used after initial use. While that figure may be somewhat high for some people and some organisations, it would be interesting to do an inventory of your files.

An even more interesting process would be to purge the filing system periodically, in much the same way as you would purge your cupboards, attic and garage of rubbish. Reynolds and Tramel (1979) tell of an American organisation that has a "tear-up and throw-away day" on the first day of spring each year. Everyone comes in to the office wearing old clothes and thinking cruel and heartless thoughts. The files are then purged quite ruthlessly, resulting in a dramatic slimming of most files and the disappearance of many. A whole day? Isn't that wasteful? Probably not, when you consider the amount of time wasted by many people throughout the year trying to extract information from the system in a quick and easy manner.[6] Marks and Spencer, the large British retail chain, has long had a war on paperwork, getting rid of 26 million cards and sheets weighing 120 tons in one year (Bliss 1977). The criteria applied are: "Would our entire business collapse if we dispensed with this?" and "When in doubt, throw it out". Marks and Spencer management give a fair amount of leeway to clerical staff to make decisions of this nature: this not only means that the staff closest to the action can make appropriate decisions, but that further paperwork is reduced because management does not need a paper-intensive apparatus of control (reports, manuals, time cards, etc.). Apparently theory Y uses less paper than theory X (see Chapters 2, 12 and 13).

Obviously, certain documents are sacrosanct, in particular, legal documents such as contracts, etc. But generally, filing cabinets, those vertical graves, tend to expand to fill the amount of floor-space (and contain the amount of junk mail) available. Unless you and your colleagues are historians, you need files, not archives.

Microfilm, photocopy, printout: Solutions or problems?

There are technical solutions to the filing dilemma, such as microfilm systems. Sometimes these can be a two-edged sword, however. Many people are not content with reading microfilm, and either want or genuinely need hard copy. Consequently, photocopying tends to undergo exponential growth. Photocopy, like computer printout, is very convenient in the short run but very inconvenient in the long run—it has has to be filed if it is of permanent value. Many educationists rue the day that photocopiers were installed in educational libraries. Prior to this, students took notes in laborious longhand. After the introduction of photocopiers, student demand for the machines seemed to be insatiable. Many students, after spending a day slaving over a hot photocopier, take home a reassuringly thick wad of photocopy—only to never look at it. The psychological game played by such students goes something like this: "I have invested a lot of time getting this material—therefore I have 'worked' on it (besides, it'll come in handy some day...)" Similar games are played by people in organisations with photocopy and computer printout.

Paperwork: Do it now, do it then, don't do it?

To return to your desk. If it looks like a large papier mâché statue just before the water and glue are poured on, then you're fooling yourself. A desk is a desk, and a filing system is a filing system—don't confuse them. If you do want to have other projects near at hand, have a table or even a second desk nearby. Files and other materials can be laid out on this for when you need to work on them or when you are going to make telephone calls regarding them.

---

[6] 48 weeks × 5 days = 240 days; 8 hours/day × $\frac{1}{240}$ = $\frac{1}{30}$ = 2 minutes/day, i.e. if you save more than two minutes a day because of reorganisation, it's worth it.

Most of us are usually working on more than one thing at any given time. You can turn this to your advantage by shifting from project to project to inject some variety into the routine. After all, if you go stale on something, you're not giving it your best. Keep in mind that this is to increase variety rather than to legitimise procrastination. As was pointed out earlier, self-interruption is one of the most pernicious forms of procrastination, because of the amount of time we have to take to refamiliarise ourselves with just what it was we were working on. Reynolds and Tramel propose an interesting antidote to this type of game. *Next step slips* (Fig. 8.3) are attached to the various piles of work that you put aside. These act as a memory-refresher next time you pick up that piece of work. They cunningly propose that you

NEXT STEP

The next step is: ....

The next step is: ....

The next step is: ....

The next step is: ....

The next step is: ....

The next step is: ....

The next step is: ....

The next step is: ....

Time displacement
(in hours and minutes)

Date: ....   Time: ....

Date: ....   Time: ....

Date: ....   Time: ....

Date: ....   Time: ....

Date: ....   Time: ....

Date: ....   Time: ....

Date: ....   Time: ....

Date: ....   Time: ....

TOTAL TIME:

TASK/PROJECT: ....

Due Date: ....   Actual Completion Date: ....

Fig 8.3 *Next step slip* (REYNOLDS AND TRAMEL 1979, P.48. REPRODUCED WITH PERMISSION)

finish off a phase of the project so that the next step is an easy one—we are too inclined to procrastinate if we know that the next step is a hard one.

Keep in mind that a lot of paperwork is not as overwhelming as it first seems. Lakein (1973) says *do it now*, never handle a piece of paper more than once. Turla and Hawkins (1985) suggest a good way of monitoring your handling of paper is the *measles technique*: each time you handle a piece of paper, put a red ink-dot in the top right-hand corner; after a day or so, diagnose why certain pieces of paper have measles and some don't (are you procrastinating on some pieces, and if so, why?).

But what about, for instance, an incoming letter that requires a carefully thought-out and detailed response? Surely such things take a lot of time? Not necessarily. As Mackenzie observes:

> The most common cause of paperwork frustration is indecision. The average manager should be able to make an immediate decision on about 80 per cent of items in his "in" box. Typically he won't know a bit more about the subject tomorrow, or several days from now. The person who gets accustomed to making decisions right off the bat will find that they are as good as though he had put the issues aside for two or three days to think about them. And then he has to re-read them to recall what they are about. Two benefits arise from quick decisions. One is that you gain time—and in a competitive situation, time is critical. Second, you have more time to correct the occasional decision that was wrong. As you postpone a decision, you get to a point of irreversibility. When you finally make it, it's too late to change—and the risk of being wrong is enhanced. (MACKENZIE 1972, P.38)

Paperwork: Questions and answers

In handling paper coming in and going out, keep in mind a number of questions.

Am I the best person to handle this?

It may be that others have a more specific competence in this area than you, or they simply have more time at their disposal. Remember delegation isn't only a vertical process (superior to subordinate, subordinate to superior), it can also be a horizontal process—sharing work out among peers.

What shortcuts can be used?

Much incoming mail, apart from urgent matters, can be non-events. A telephone call, telegram or telex would have served the same purpose, and in a fraction of the time. We often hear of how the art of letter-writing, along with conversation, has died, and to a certain extent this is true: a letter that evokes calmness and authority rather than uncertainty and crisis-generated turbulence is a joy to behold. Yet the world *does* move faster these days, and when gauged against criteria such as cost (salary costs of writer, dictater/stenographer, typist, typing, redrafting, mailing, etc.) and the availability of alternatives (telephone, telex, telegram, facsimile transmission, etc.), many letters are seen to be unnecessary.

How to respond to incoming letters, good and bad? With bad or unnecessary ones, a simple, brutal tactic is to *ignore* them. Not exactly good manners, but efficient—why should someone else with apparently surplus time on their hands presume they have the right to take up your scarce time?

If a letter is called for, by all means go ahead and write it. If the letter deals with a common situation, have a copy put in a *form letters file*. Then, whenever the situation or a similar one recurs, you can cannibalise it and not waste time composing another masterpiece. The logical extension of form letters are *memory typewriters and word processors*. If you can scrawl on a letter "answer 6B" and give it to a typist driving a processor, it saves a lot of time. The recipient of the letter is also not insulted or annoyed at receiving an obviously "canned" letter of the junk-mail variety, where names and circumstances are all too clumsily dropped in.

A considerable time-saver is the *dictating machine*. If you have access to a secretary or a typing pool, tape dictation can improve the overall efficiency of yourself and the typist by several hundred per cent. There are a number of human problems here: many secretaries do not like dictating machines as they prefer the human contact of taking dictation. This feeling of alienation is even stronger in typing pools, where typists may never meet the owners of the voices playing through their headphones. In the case of individual secretaries, it might be pointed out that it is much quicker to use the automatic process rather than the human one, thus leaving the secretary more time for more enriching tasks. Interestingly, dictating to a secretary can often encourage imprecise communication on the part of the dictater: continual re-editing ("no, that's no good . . . how does this sound?") can lead to an increase in quality, but it can waste a lot of time.

The other human problem with dictating machines is that the dictater feels alienated also—it's too impersonal. This is a hang-up that should be overcome; the dictater should look upon this as just another skill in one-way communication—like leaving a clear message on a *telephone-answering machine*—that can enhance her total communication. To visualise a written response—particularly in terms of paragraphs, subheadings, and the like—forces the communicator to be clear and analytical, and can only carry over beneficially into her conversation or ability to speak in public.

Other substitutes for letters, particularly when other written materials are enclosed, are *business cards, "with compliments" slips*, and *memos*. Memos in particular can save time. If certain communication situations recur, a standard checklist memo with appropriate categories (see me/please read and discuss wth me/please handle this inquiry/please proofread) can be even more time-saving.

Memo-itis: How not to communicate

Memos can, however, waste time, particularly the memos Webster (1967) gives as examples of "memo-itis":

1. The memo to postpone work—a note saying you are going to act enables you to do nothing for a little longer with a clear conscience.
2. The memo to demonstrate efficiency (not effectiveness)—"Following my memo of the first of last month. . ." (the real message is "I know what it says; let's see if you can find your copy").
3. The militant memo—a tough-worded statement like "John, this situation can no longer be tolerated. It must be dealt with immediately!" (Often sent by a mild-mannered or insecure manager who is afraid to take a stand in person.)
4. The accusative memo designed "for the record". It's a "your fault" approach: if the recipient does answer it (which will take hours), the sender can always contest the answer; and if recipient doesn't answer, she has him "fixed" in the files!
5. The status-making memo "From the desk of . . ." might be more tasteful if simply "From. . ." in dignified but attractive type and paper. Desks don't send memos.

6. The "see-how-hard-I'm working" memo is penned by the insecure subordinate who wants to prove her worth by inundating the boss with paper. Of course, all the time required to write the memo subtracts from time she could be devoting to her work.
7. The "blind copy" memo in which a person writes ostensibly for one audience but is actually addressing the unseen, unlisted recipients of the blind copy.

Planning and priorities

Many people confuse action as an end in itself with action as a means to an end. But action needs to be planned, or else we fall into the trap of confusing *effectiveness* with *efficiency*. Efficiency is doing things right; effectiveness is doing the right things. Time management then is *not* about just doing things efficiently, because we might be doing the wrong things efficiently. We need to set goals, set priorities, because there are an infinite number of things to be done, but only a finite amount of time. Time is a scarcer commodity than we might think: as Drucker (1982) points out, there aren't really twenty-four hours in a day, only two—the two hours in the day you can wrest from routine to handle the important tasks.

Yet if you are managing by crisis, then you by definition are not planning. Managing by crisis is reacting; planning is proacting, anticipating, being prepared for other people's crises, but fortunately not your own. The most commonly heard complaint about planning is that the idea itself is fine, but "it's different here—things are simply so hectic that there isn't time to plan". Unfortunately, such alibis are just that—alibis. All systems—your work, your kitchen, your vehicle, your personal relationships, your health, your garden tools—left to themselves behave like all systems in the universe: they are prey to what scientists call the second law of thermodynamics, and they run down and get worse. Order is replaced by disorder or entropy. The only way permanence occurs is when negative entropy is created. In practical terms, this means that all systems need maintenance. If you "haven't got time" to exercise, then you will have lots of time on your hands when you get sick. If you "haven't got time" to clean up the kitchen, then you'll starve because the next meal can't be prepared. Josie Bloggs is so flat out working, she hasn't had a holiday in years—she "hasn't got time". Yet she knows she's only working at about 50 per cent of her peak performance. If she took the holiday, she would return refreshed and operate at 100 per cent, and be ahead of the game. In other words, maintenance of the systems of your life is not a luxury, it's a necessity. You cannot afford *not* to maintain them, and you cannot afford *not* to plan—they're very similar processes.

Fun is compulsory, planning is compulsory, and compulsoriness in everything else is optional.

Time logging and charting

Before you can plan, you need to analyse your own time-consumption patterns. You may have recognised some of your behaviour in this chapter, but you need to quantify this behaviour. One of the best means of doing this is keeping a time log and time chart. This means in effect keeping a numerical and visual diary of your activities. It's probably only necessary to keep a log and a chart for a week for your consumption patterns to emerge. You may say that you are perfectly aware of where your time goes, and that you don't

Fig 8.4 *Time priority matrix* (ADAPTED FROM BLISS 1977, PP. 11–14)

need such gimmicks. Perhaps so; and perhaps you shouldn't knock it until you've tried it.

As Peter Drucker says, memory is treacherous when we try to remember where our time goes. In constructing a time log, and in fact in any general planning of your time, it is useful to have a system of *priorities*. This is simply a matter of saying that some things are more important than others. You in fact already have a system of priorities in allocating your time, but you may not be aware of it, and you might not be very pleased with it if you did know about it.

A useful way of looking at priorities is by looking at a matrix system, such as that in Figure 8.4. Many things that we do are urgent, but are they necessarily important? Urgent matters are imperative, forcing us into instant action. This is all right for matters that are urgent *and* important, but when we attend to matters that are urgent and unimportant, it is usually to the detriment of matters that are important but not urgent. Important but not urgent matters left to themselves have a habit of building into problems and then crises. Consequently, many people give second priority to P3, and third—sometimes fourth—priority to P2. What are some examples of these priorities?

P1
- The bathtub is overflowing.
- Your presentation of sales figures is needed at the annual general meeting tomorrow.
- You are asked to help at the scene of an accident.

P2
- You are asked to prepare an analysis of the long-term prospects of your organisation—due in five months.
- You have exams at the end of the year.
- You should throw out old clothing and newspapers around the house.
- You should pay your parents a visit.
- You should keep up your piano practice.
- You should train people so you can delegate to them.
- You should make an appointment with your dentist for a check-up.
- Leisure.

P3
- You have to attend a class/meeting in a few minutes; it's notoriously boring, but attendance is mandatory.
- You have to feed the parking meter.
- You must get to the bank by four.
- People keep telephoning you about the position you advertised, but the job has been filled.

- The computer is down for the seventh time this year; five typists will have to do overtime to complete all invoices.

P4
- A three-hour lunch three times a week.
- Watching television
- "Just muckin' around". "Killin' time".

P1s are fairly obvious. P2s are fairly obvious too—isn't it interesting the number of "shoulds" that appear in the list? P2s of course are not urgent *now*, but they will probably become urgent *then*. If the system is not maintained, then terminal entropy sets in. P3s require a bit of explanation. Urgent matters are rarely unimportant. If you don't feed the parking meter, for example, there will be consequences. It's a matter of *relative* unimportance compared to P1s and P2s. Also, what may be unimportant to you may be important to others—that's why they want a piece of your time. But what about the computer and the typists? Surely that's important? Yes it is, but is it important that *you* handle it? Furthermore, *why* is the computer breaking down for the seventh time? If a problem recurs again and again, it gets fixed—that is, unless management by crisis is the rule of the day. If P2s focus our failure to avoid procrastination, P3s focus our dependence upon management by crisis, our inability to delegate, and our tendency to tolerate and invite interruption. P4s are interesting; for many people, they are, at least unofficially, the top priority. Bliss (1977) suggests a fifth category of "wasted time", to which he consigns television watching, but it may be tidier to put this under P4. Television watching can be very relaxing, of course, and therefore is perhaps legitimate leisure. In fact you may feel that it belongs in P2 with leisure. Before doing so, however, you may be interested to attempt a rough calculation of how much time *in your life* you have spent watching TV. For example, if you are 25 years old and have watched two hours of TV a day since, say, you were five, then that means you have spent the equivalent of a year and eight months of your life in front of the box—that's twenty months, 24 hours a day. Lakein, in his book *How to Get Control of Your Time and Your Life* (1983) identifies TV as one of the great time-wasters, and even suggests tactics for "weaning off" TV. You have to be the judge as to whether this is being obsessed by time management, but you may conclude that there is certainly room for improvement.

A blank time log, a blank time chart, and a sample completed time chart are shown in Box 8.D. Pick a typical week, and begin to record your activities on the log and chart. It may well be that you do not have a "typical" week; if so, take any two weeks and do logs for them. Make sure that you are not kidding yourself by saying that there is no such thing as a typical week—you may be being melodramatic about your uniqueness. You may be unique within a particular setting, but there are probably others in different settings or situations who are doing things similar to you. And if you are totally unique, well, here's your chance to demonstrate it by filling out a time log and showing how totally useless the idea is for someone as unique as yourself.

It's probably better not to tell anyone else you're doing a time log. Someone else may ensure your honesty and punctuality in filling it out every quarter of an hour, on the quarter hour, but this may also force you into behaving atypically. Don't make the mistake of deciding to fill out the log every few hours, or at the end of the day. Carry it with you in a diary or on a clip-board and be conscientious.

Once you have logged and charted your time behaviour, it's useful to see how your days pan out. If you want to construct yet another visual aid to

BOX 8.D: Time log and chart

At the foot of this page is the beginning of a time log. Using these headings, draw up such a log, allowing for a sub-total for each hour. The original made provision for eighteen hours in a day. You may need more, or less. Make enough copies to cover one week. Keep these copies together, and look after them.

You may take a few minutes each time to fill in the log, but consider this form-filling a temporary P1, i.e. a top priority.

Try and fill in the log each quarter of an hour. Note the time in the far left column (7.00 a.m., 7.15, 7.30 . . .), and briefly note a description of your activities. Work out whether an activity is a P1, P2, P3 or P4, and write in the approximate time in minutes in one of the far right columns.

Sub-total these each hour.

Once you have completed the day's activities, you may like to make a visual record of all this activity on a time-use chart (see p.260). Transfer the P1, P2, P3 and P4 sub-total figures to the chart: for example, if at 11 o'clock in the morning, you have in the hour 10 a.m.–11 a.m. spent 23 minutes on P1s, 16 minutes on P2s, 17 minutes on P3s and 14 minutes on P4s, go to the 11 o-clock line on the horizontal axis, and mark in the P1, P2, P3 and P4 figures according to the minute values on the vertical axis. After you have made these point marks for the entire day, join up the dots or marks to create P1, P2, P3 and P4 lines. The sample completed time chart on page 261 shows how this might look.

It is quite possible that P1s, P2s, P3s and P4s for any hour might add up to more than sixty minutes. You might be listening to the radio while you study or are preparing a meal; you might be doing some photocopying while thinking about a letter; and so on. Multiple time use can be a guide to creative use of time, but it may also be a symptom of overload.

Note the interplay of the four curves, noting in particular the rise of P3s, which may signal interruptions. Are there any systematic patterns over a weekly or daily cycle?

TIME LOG

	Urgent	Not urgent
Important	1	2
Not important	3	4

DAY: _____

DATE: _____

Time (quarter hours)	Brief description of activities	Approx. time in minutes			
		P1	P2	P3	P4
	sub-total				

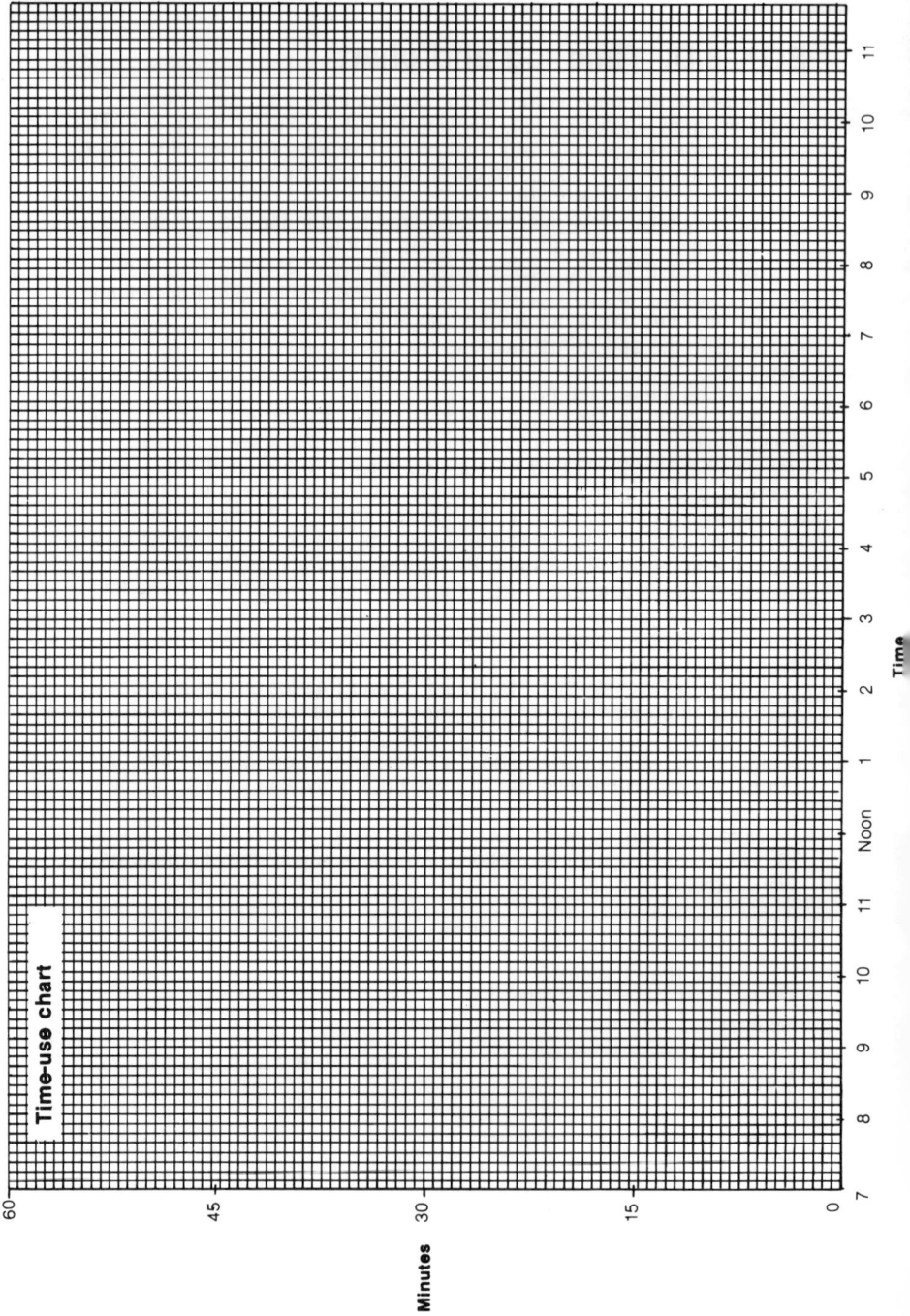

Time-use chart

Minutes

60

45

30

15

0

Time

7 8 9 10 11 Noon 11 1 2 3 4 5 6 7 8 9 10 11

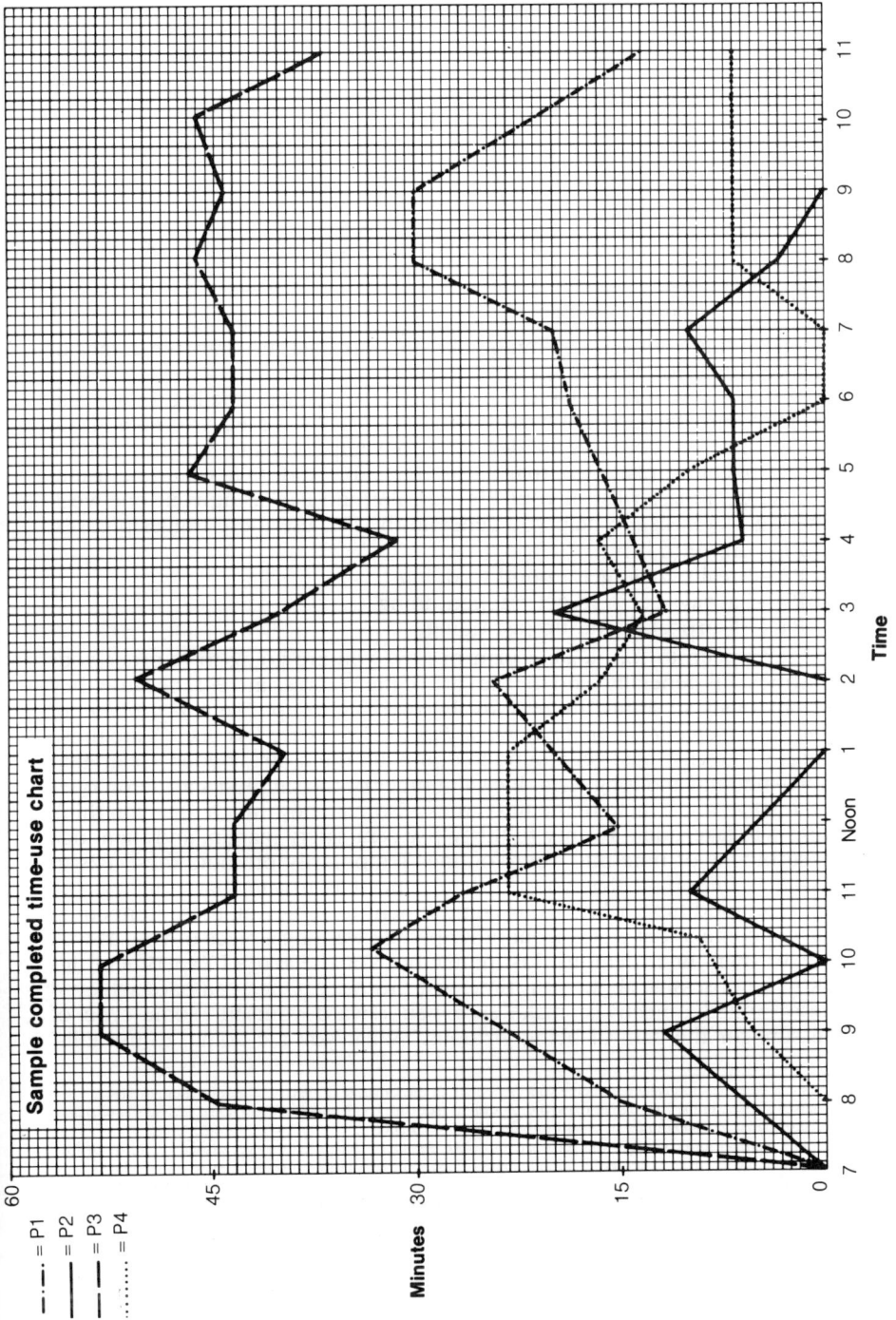

Sample completed time-use chart

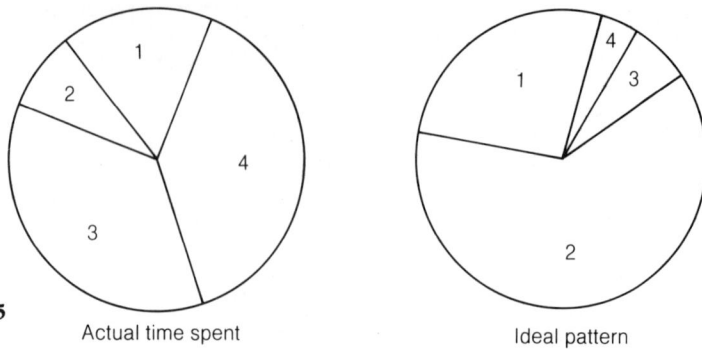

Fig 8.5

Actual time spent   Ideal pattern

understanding yourself, you might take the time data and draw pie graphs of time consumption (Fig. 8.5).

You may give a P3 or P4 to the activity of keeping a time log for a week. You may find after doing it however that it in fact was a P2 or even a P1. Of course, once you conceive an ideal time consumption pattern, then you have already begun to plan. See, that didn't hurt a bit, did it? It would be useful to make up a master list of your P1s, P2s, P3s and P4s, using your one-week time log as a basis. To help you generate the list, use these trigger phrases:

P1—I have to do. . .
P2—I really must get around to doing. . .
P3—I always seem to get trapped doing. . .
P4—I'll probably end up just doing. . .

You now need to formulate a plan of how you are going to re-order your priorities. P1s generally tend to take care of themselves, and P4s, because they are obviously so sinful, are reasonably easy to give up. *The real problem of time management is how to increase P2s and decrease P3s.* As P2s are those things you really must get around to doing, do them. Break your P2s up into short, medium and long-term. Pick a number of the simplest short-term ones and resolve to do them in the next week. Estimate how much time you think these will take, add a twenty to thirty per cent safety margin, and then lock those blocks of time into your routine. Temporarily promote these P2s to P1s—it is important that you do them, and it is *urgent* that you begin to cultivate good time habits. Your commitment to achieving these jumped-up P1s will come under attack from other people wanting a piece of you, as well as your own inner demons. Just remember, for the sake of experiment, it's OK to be obsessive about your time, just this once. Once you have achieved these limited objectives, make sure you reward yourself—some type of pleasure for the pain of being virtuous.[7] What you are doing, to use Ellis'

---

[7] This can be either positively reinforcing your behaviour, in the language of behaviour modification, or giving yourself strokes, in the language of transactional analysis (see Chapters 3 and 5). Transactional analysis's approach of stroking is, according to Scott, crucial for good time management:

As a manager (or co-worker), you get what you stroke. People produce what they get strokes for. It may be for getting the job done or it may be for only looking busy. Who gets more strokes—the secretary who looks busy all the time, or the one who really gets the work done? . . . If the people who stomp out emergency fires get more strokes than the effective planners who avoid constant crises, the organization can expect more fires. After all, the stroke salary is higher for firefighters than for planners. . . Most information about time management is rational. It is useful information but may not be followed. TA helps to clarify the emotional side of time management—the side that *really* motivates us. The kind and quality of strokes does much to influence how we use time. (SCOTT 1974, PP.76–9).

Thus, after achieving some time measurement goals, it is necessary to stroke the Child ego state with some fun or pleasure, and it is necessary to turn off the guilt/time urgency messages which come from the Parent ego state. Cf. also the notion of time-structuring in transactional analysis.

terms, is raising your frustration tolerance level; you are learning to stand a bit more present pain for future gain.

Priorities and goal-setting

Once you see that it is possible to achieve some simple short-term P2s, you begin to redefine your experience of the texture of time. You also begin to realise how deceptive that texture can be—as the old saying has it, days are long, years are short. The time frame for your short-term goals was a week. Why not allocate your goals into these time frames?

short term: one week
medium term: one month
long term: one year

You may feel that one year is too long a time frame to be practically useful. This may be the case, but it may also be that it is too *short* a time. Remember tactics are usually determined by strategy, and not vice versa. It's not very encouraging when you have been a very efficient secretary of the Flat Earth Society for twenty-four years and suddenly one day you notice that the horizon is curved. What has all the efficiency been useful for if you have not been effective?

Take the metaphor "time-frame" literally, and think of your goals as a series of Chinese boxes: the smallest goals fit inside the next largest, and so on. Where will you be in five years' time? Is that where you want to be or where others want you to be? What tactics will best serve this strategy? Performance of what tasks will cause your goals to materialise? There are very few occasions when we take this long-term perspective. Much of our social folklore tends to be against planning—consider, for example, the way most people approach New Year's resolutions with the expectation of failure rather than success. It's more convenient for us to shrug and say "life is what happens to you when you're busy making other plans" rather than "chance favours the prepared mind". The first statement embodies the attitude that Murphy's Law reigns supreme, that life is chaotic; the second embodies a similar attitude, but suggests that even chaos has a pattern.

Getting organised

In other words, "tomorrow we've got to get organised". Until we invent a time machine or a space craft that can go through a black hole into a different space–time continuum, we cannot manage *time*, we can only manage ourselves. The best place to start such management is a large stationery shop selling office and business systems: diaries, planning charts, index systems, and so on. These are pretty and useful toys for analysing and planning. Cheap and well-written time management books such as Ferner (1980), Mackenzie and Waldo (1981) and Reynolds and Tramel (1979) have many excellent models of tools such as:

- personal and professional goal analysis forms
- delegation planning guides
- procrastination records
- routing slips
- analytical memos
- analytical agenda item recommendation sheets
- checklists for efficient meetings, conference telephone calls
- project planning time lines

Decision-making and problem-solving methods such as critical path method (see Chapter 9) are also useful for structuring your time. Keep in mind, of course, that all of these approaches are terribly rational, and rationality, as opposed to rational analysis of irrationality, may not be the prime criterion for good time management: we have to keep in mind that such behaviour patterns as internal causes of interruptions, mustabatory behaviour, and out-of-kilter ego states may be more important in a time management program, at least in the initial stages.

Time management: Science or shonkiness?

Time management is becoming an increasingly trendy concept. Yet, as we have seen, it is little more than a grab-bag of self-management techniques drawn from fields as diverse as office administration and leadership. One could imagine in a world vastly more overcrowded than it is at present, a concept like "space management" might also emerge to better organise the use of the scarce resource of living space. Does time management help us to better use the scarce resource of time? Certainly, for almost every rule of time management given to us by the gurus of the field, there are significant qualifications. Thus, if one discourages drop-in visitors by adopting a closed-door policy, one may inadvertently become cut off from the informal communication structure—the grapevine—that *really* keeps the organisation going. If one stops calling regular meetings, one may remove the only forum available for less socially skilled people to raise matters or one may prevent any ad hoc brainstorming on issues. If one "does it now", what about the problems that could well have matured into solution via benign neglect, not to mention the problems that would have gone away or the new problems that might arise because of too much haste?

Harold Geneen was Chief Executive Officer and is now Chairman Emeritus of the American multinational giant ITT, by any standards a competent operator; he is curtly dismissive of many time management nostrums. He speaks derisively of the "clean-desk executive", arguing that, if you know what you are doing, you are probably doing many things at the one time, and the best place for the paperwork is not in the filing cabinets, but on your desk. Geneen rarely delegates, taking many calls personally, writing his own letters and speeches, and is not averse to drop-in visitors, believing that people will not deliberately try to waste his time. He suggests that the clean-desk executive who delegates is little better than a traffic-cop—earning much more than traffic cops do. He suggests that the tight time-structuring of meetings puts creativity in a straightjacket, and if the unexpected comes up, it should be developed thoroughly, even if the meeting goes over time; in fact, Geneen says he is always running late. The final sin of the clean-desk executive, says Geneen, is the mentality of

> ... an unwarranted self-confidence and complacency based upon the fallacious belief that your future will produce what you planned for. Don't you believe it.
> (GENEEN 1984, P.160)

Nevertheless, if, after all of these qualifications have been taken into account, time management still seems meaningful to you, then all is well. It may be only half-science, with the other half being shonkiness and charlatanism, but the fact that "time management" has become such a buzz-phrase in the past few years indicates that the potential of the concept, if not the actuality, corresponds to the real needs of many people. If time management helps people to plan their personal and professional lives more effectively, then the science probably outweighs the shonkiness—which at least is more than can be said for many of the other things which distract us in this frantic modern world.

Summary

Time management is a form of self-management, overlapping related areas such as stress management and decision-making and problem solving. Handling interruptions in our lives depends on our seeing that these can be caused externally, by other people and situations, and also can be caused internally, or by our own failings.

There are many things which waste our time, which can be subdivided into our life at home and our life at work (the latter area understood in terms of classical management areas such as planning, organising, directing, controlling, communicating, and decision-making). It is possible to analyse procrastination in terms of definable and reversible behaviour patterns, and it is useful to see procrastination as being linked directly to crisis management (reacting to reality rather than proacting upon reality).

Much time can be saved by delegating to others, by giving up the self-perception of indispensability. Care must be taken to avoid the traps of upward or reverse delegation, under-delegating and over-delegating. Meetings seem to waste the time of many, but if meetings are well planned, and time is handled well in them, or even if meetings are dispensed with altogether, then they need not be so wasteful of time.

Information overload stresses us all, and in organisations this information comes in the form of telephone conversations, paperwork, filing, microfilm, photocopy and printout. Techniques such as the quiet hour, wastebasketry and purging can help reduce information overload. The pressures of writing letters and memos can be reduced if we use short-cuts, technology and close examination of our purpose in writing. It is essential not to confuse efficiency (doing things right) with effectiveness (doing the right things): time management is more about effectiveness than efficiency.

In order to do this, we need to clarify our priorities and goals, in terms of urgency and importance. Priority matrixes, logs, charts and diagrams can help us to analyse our ideal and actual time-use patterns. The tenets of time management can help us to manage ourselves in more effective ways, but only if we understand exceptions to rules, and understand that planning for total control over our lives is not possible.

Questions for discussion

1. What is the relationship between external and internal causes of interruptions?
2. What are the most important and the least important causes of interruptions for you? How does this pattern compare with those of other people?
3. Write a role-play in which a person experiences different types of time use (collapse, crisis, action, autopilot, delay, procrastination, paralysis).
4. What should and what should not be delegated?
5. In what ways do meetings save and waste time?
6. What barriers might there be to wastebasketry and purging?

7. In what ways can written and spoken communication be stream-lined?
8. What might be the time priorities of differing people (an executive, a houseperson, an unemployed person, a typist, etc.)?
9. Make up a five-year plan (personal and/or professional) for yourself.
10. Do a for/against chart of the key concepts of time management (delegation, procrastination, handling paperwork, setting priorities, etc.).

References

Bliss, Edwin C. (1977). *Getting Things Done: The ABCs of Time Management.* (Macmillan: Melbourne).

Davidson, Jim (1978). *Effective Time Management: A Practical Workbook.* (Human Sciences Press: New York).

Dayton, Edward R. (1979). *Tools for Time Management: Christian Perspectives on Managing Priorities.* (Zondervan: Grand Rapids).

Dickson, Paul (1981). *The Official Explanations.* (Arrow Books: London).

Drucker, Peter. F. (1982). *The Effective Executive.* (Pan: London).

Douglas, Merrill (ed.) (1978). *Time Talk,* vol. 1, no. 1, January.

Ellis, Albert and Knaus, William J. (1977). *Overcoming Procrastination.* (New American Library: New York).

Fanning, Tony and Fanning, Robbie (1979). *Get it All Done and Still be Human.* (Ballantine Books: New York).

Ferner, Jack D. (1980). *Effective Time Management.* (John Wiley and Sons: New York).

Fletcher, Winston (1984). *Meetings, Meetings: How to Manipulate Them and Have More Fun.* (Michael Joseph: London).

Geneen, Harold with Moscow, Alvin (1984). *Managing.* (Doubleday and Co.: New York).

Greiff, Barrie and Munter, Preston K. (1980). *Tradeoffs: Executive, Family and Organizational Life.* (New American Library: New York).

Knaus, William J. (1979). *Do It Now: How to Stop Procrastinating.* (Prentice-Hall: New Jersey).

Lakein, Alan (1973). *How to Get Control of Your Time and Your Life.* (Signet: New York).

Le Boeuf, Michael (1979). *Working Smart: How to Accomplish More in Half the Time.* (Warner Books: New York).

McGrath, Joseph E. and Rotchford, Nancy L. (1983). "Time and Behaviour in Organizations", in *Research in Organisational Behaviour.* (JAI Press, Inc.: New York).

Mackenzie, R. Alec (1972). *The Time Trap—How to Get More Done in Less Time.* (McGraw-Hill: New York).

Mackenzie, R. Alex and Waldo, Kay Cronkite (1981). *About Time: A Woman's Guide to Time Management.* (McGraw-Hill: New York).

Omega Science Digest, July/August, 1983, "The I'll Do-It-Tomorrow Syndrome".

Reynolds, Kay and Tramel, Mary (1979). *Executive Time Management: How to Get 12 Hours' Work Done in 8 Hours.* (Prentice-Hall: New Jersey).

Schuler, Randall S. (1979). "Managing Stress Means Managing Time", *Personnel Journal,* December.

Scott, Dru (1974). "T.A. and Time Management", in Jongeward, Dorothy, *Everybody Wins: Transactional Analysis Applied to Organizations.* (Prentice-Hall: New Jersey).

Toffler, Alvin (1970). *Future Shock.* (Pan: London).
     (1980). *The Third Wave.* (Pan: London).

Turla, Peter and Hawkins, Kathleen L. (1985). *Time Management Made Easy.* (Panther: London).

Webster, Eric (1967). "Memo Mania", *Management Review*, September.

Zoll, Allan A. (1974). *Explorations in Managing.* (Addison-Wesley: Mass.).

Films/Videos

Tell My Wife I Won't be Home for Dinner (Training Media Services).

The Time Trap (Training Media Services, Power Human Resources).

Time is Money (Training Media Services).

Do It Now (Training Media Services, Power Human Resources).

No-Nonsense Delegation (Power Human Resources).

9

Decision-making and problem-solving

Nothing is so exhausting as indecision, and nothing so futile.
Bertrand Russell

We don't know who discovered water, but we're pretty sure it wasn't a fish.
Father John Collins, SJ

True genius resides in the capacity for evaluation of uncertain, hazardous and conflicting information.
Sir Winston Churchill

Unhappy the general who comes on to the field of battle with a system.
Napoleon

The easiest way to get into trouble is to be right at the wrong time.
W. Braude

Impelled by a state of mind which is destined not to last, we make our irrevocable decisions.
Marcel Proust

How can we learn to make better decisions and to solve problems more effectively? In this chapter, we shall consider various techniques and philosophies of problem-solving and decision-making, which may or may not be of help to you in answering this question.

"Problem-solving" and "decision-making" are terms which are often used interchangeably. They will be treated as different concepts in this chapter, "decision-making" being understood as a subset of the larger concept of "problem-solving".

"Problem-solving" is taken to mean the following process:

1. definition of problem
2. re-definition of problem
3. analysis of problem
4. generation of solutions
5. prioritising or ranking of solutions
6. sequencing of tasks and assignment of roles
7. execution or implementation
8. evaluation

"Decision-making" is taken to mean steps 5, 6 and 7 of this process (see Fig. 9.1).

We follow (or perhaps *should* follow) similar sequences of thought when we are diagnosing a medical complaint, buying a pizza, planning a wedding, divorce or murder, marketing a new invention, finding the meaning of life, or agonising over whether to get up early or late.

Let us look at these processes in greater detail, beginning with problem definition.

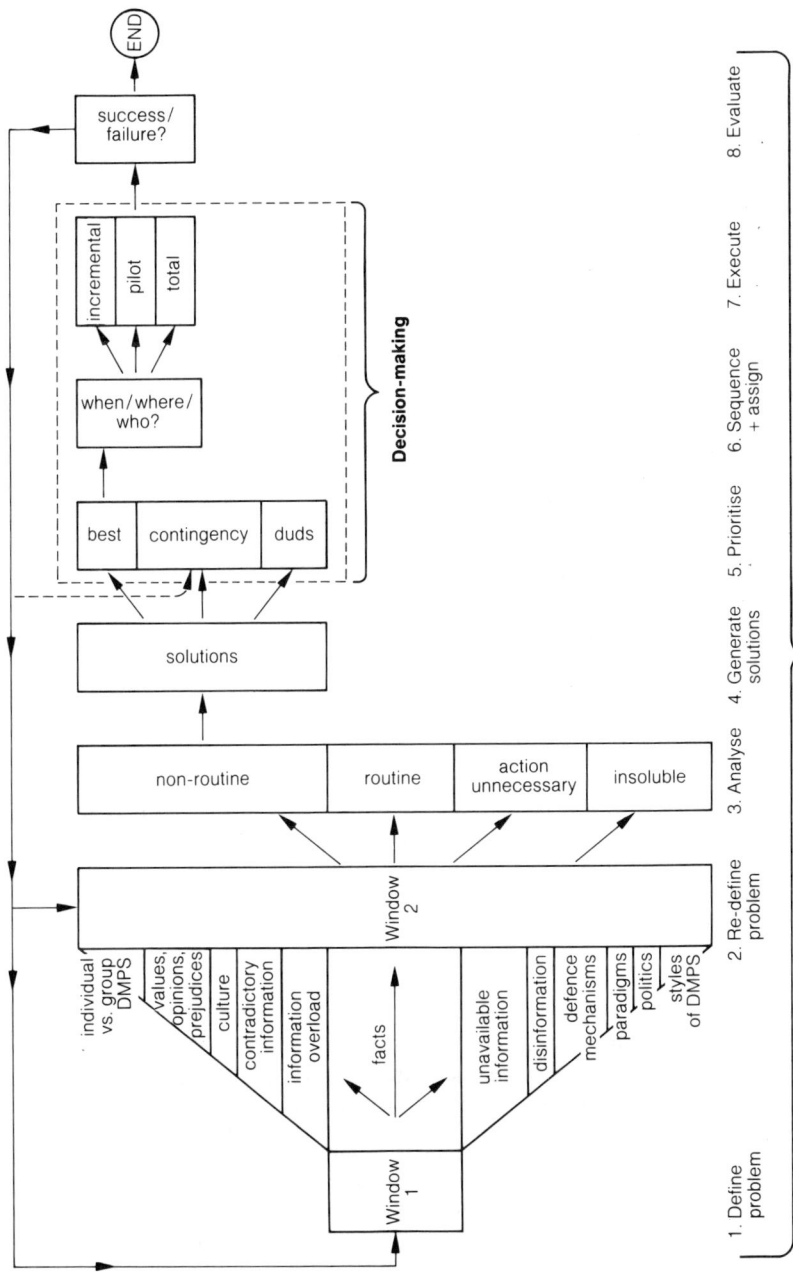

Fig 9.1 *A model of decision-making and problem-solving*

Decision-making

END

success/
failure?

incremental
pilot
total

when/where/
who?

best | contingency | duds

solutions

non-routine | routine | action unnecessary | insoluble

Window 2

individual vs. group DMPS
values, opinions, prejudices
culture
contradictory information
information overload

facts

unavailable information
disinformation
defence mechanisms
paradigms
politics
styles of DMPS

Window 1

Problem-solving

1. Define problem
2. Re-define problem
3. Analyse
4. Generate solutions
5. Prioritise
6. Sequence + assign
7. Execute
8. Evaluate

Definition of the problem

A problem well-defined is half-solved, or so the folk wisdom would have it. How do we define a problem? Some people often presume that defining a problem and finding a solution are much the same process. Some people often respond to a problem with, "get the facts". If they are more than normally paranoid, they may say, "get the facts before the facts get you".

Certainly, we cannot do without facts: they are the foundation upon which all problem-solving must build. However, even though facts are conventionally distinguished from opinions, it is sometimes a matter of opinion as to whether a fact is a fact or not. Thus, hundreds of years ago, it was a "fact" that the earth was flat. People sometimes betray their uncertainty about whether something is a fact or not by using the tautology "true facts"—what other kind should there be?

In perceiving a problem, then, many people concentrate their attention upon the facts, the whole facts, and nothing but the facts. But the facts may not be the whole truth. Let us presume that people who depend totally upon facts are perceiving a problem through window 1 in Figure 9.1. Window 1, however, is not as big as it needs to be. To get a proper perspective on a problem, we need to consider the broader view through window 2. To do this, we must re-define the problem.

Re-definition of the problem

Problem of the problem

Perhaps one of the critical weaknesses of concentrating upon facts alone is that one leaps in and concentrates on solutions instead of perhaps asking fundamental questions, such as, "does a problem really exist?" The problem may not really exist, or it may be someone else's problem: it may be transferable and/or able to be delegated (see Chapter 10). US President Richard Nixon was fond of quoting the management maxim, "there are no problems, only challenges/opportunities". Stoner (1980) has described this attitude as one of Pollyannaism, that is, unrealistic optimism. Irrespective of the validity of the maxim, it nevertheless shows how a change of perspective can re-define what was hitherto thought to be given, or "obvious".

Types of information

A basic question that needs to be asked about facts is, "how many?" One can have too many facts, and have the situation of *information overload*. It is probably better to have too much rather than not enough fact, because the only task involved with too much fact is to sift through the data and reject that which is irrelevant. This is sometimes easier said than done, however. The information explosion is prevalent in most fields of endeavour, and most people try to cope by becoming more specialised; consequently, it is more difficult to get the big picture in one field, let alone similar and dissimilar fields. Computer databases can open up vast areas of information, but unless you know exactly what to ask for, you are no better off. De Bono (1983) suggests that it is useful to know when to leave off throwing more *information* at a problem and begin searching for a new *idea*.

At the other extreme is too little information or *unavailable information*. It is obvious that there is a certain threshold of facts that needs to be surpassed before one can build theories about a problem.[1]

Also, it must be remembered that, to a certain extent, one *always* has imperfect or inadequate information. If one waits until all the information is in, one will never act. The longer the wait for information about a situation, the more likely it is that the situation will have changed anyway. If you keep waiting for the latest information, you will wait forever, because information —books, magazines, ticker tape, newspapers, videotext, gossip, a warning shout—is continuously being created. Waiting until all the information is in can be one of the more sophisticated forms of procrastination (see Chapter 8).[2]

Unavailable information and information overload are by no means mutually exclusive. It is quite possible, for example, to have too much of the wrong information and not enough of the right information: many a harassed researcher has gathered data to try and prove or disprove an hypothesis, only to find that she has gathered the wrong data, and that she should have collected data *after* she had formulated the hypotheses. It is also possible to have too much of the right information, if its very abundance makes certain parts of it unattainable.

There is also the problem of *contradictory information*, where the facts do not so much speak for themselves as squabble among themselves. At this point, there is much to be said for using what the mathematician A.N. Whitehead called "the greatest invention of twentieth century science": the suspended judgment, or deciding not to decide. If this cannot be done indefinitely, then it may be necessary to acknowledge that there may be *no* solution.

Finally, there is the concept of *disinformation*. Disinformation is false information deliberately planted to lead you astray. It may be in the form of a malicious rumour, leaked press releases, anonymous or pseudonymous documents, or good old-fashioned lies, followed by categorical denials that such lies were ever uttered.

Beyond the realm of facts, there are many other factors which can enlarge the definition of the problem. They are less "objective" and "rational", but nonetheless real for all that.

Opinions, prejudices and values

Peter Drucker (1982) observes that one should not get the facts first, but instead get *opinions* first, then facts. His reasoning behind this is that facts can be recruited to serve any point of view: it is very rarely that "the facts speak for themselves". Hence it makes sense to get people's opinions, prejudices and values out in the open as soon as possible. If this is not done, then vested interests and hidden agendas may operate to ensure that one, rather than another, conclusion flows from a body of facts. We aspire to disinterested evaluation and problem-solving, but not only is this rarely the

---

[1] The great Sherlock Holmes often cautioned Dr Watson against drawing conclusions from too little data; otherwise the investigator begins to twist facts to suit theories, instead of theories to suit facts (see, e.g. "a Scandal in Bohemia", *Adventures of Sherlock Holmes*, by Sir Arthur Conan Doyle).

[2] Time priorities are a crucial part of decision-making and problem-solving. Where might a time management tool like the urgent/important priority matrix of Chapter 8 be best integrated into Figure 9.1? Section 5, perhaps? A further important point to note regarding priorities and information is *cost*: What is the cost of the information? What is the cost of waiting for more information? What is the cost of not waiting?

case, it may not in fact be such a good thing: as Oscar Wilde remarked, "It is only about things that do not interest one that one can give a really unbiased opinion, which is no doubt the reason why an unbiased opinion is absolutely valueless".

Politics

The consideration of vested interests leads on to *political* considerations: are solutions to the problem politically viable? Politics can be the "macro-politics" of elected and non-elected politicians and bureaucrats, or it can be the "micropolitics" of normal interaction within organisations and groups (see Chapter 10). The sheer technical beauty of a solution may not be sufficient to ensure its implementation if such implementation were to damage the vested interests of various groups and constituencies. After listening to an idealistic and rational proponent of one viewpoint, an Australian macropolitician allegedly said, "Mate, you can have the logic . . . I'll take the numbers"; what was important was not so much the technical efficiency of the idea as the numbers, the way people would vote according to organised blocs of vested interests. Roskin (1975), Stoner (1980) and others have also pointed out that a decision's potential effectiveness depends upon two dimensions: the *quality* of the decision (which relates to technical efficiency, or objective or impersonal attributes), and the *acceptance* of the decision (which relates to political viability, or subjective attractiveness or desirability). The more people involved in the decision, the greater the need to consider the acceptance factors. Thus if a management elite makes a decision which will have considerable impact upon those who are to implement it, and if the non-elite were not consulted or at least considered, then the non-elite, usually acting as the informal organisation but also possibly as the formal counter institution of organised labour, may significantly modify or countermand the original decision.[3]

Culture

A still wider perspective on different perceptions of problems comes if we consider *cultural* differences between people. This, to say the least, is a vast topic, where hard data is as scarce as stereotype and prejudice are abundant. Differences may be quite broad and clear-cut. Thus, European and American business people who train native Africans in production work are often amazed when such workers quit after a few months and return to home villages. From the European point of view, the African is lazy and improvident, because he does not conform to the Western economic/rational model of behaviour: one works indefinitely, because one's wants are indefinite. From the African point of view, however, the worker who quit after a few months may be behaving more rationally than Westerners: the African worker may have left his community for a particular purpose—to earn cash to buy a motor-bike, or meet a bride-price—and once this cash has been accumulated, it makes sense to return home (Murphy 1979).

Differences between cultures are not always so clear, however: Haviland (1975) points out that a French farmer may have less in common with a

---

[3] Much of the management literature on the "quality/acceptance" problem seems to imply that quality has to be traded off against acceptance, i.e. the purity of an individual manager's idea may have to be degraded in order to placate less perceptive but more numerous others. This is not always the case: getting more people involved in problem-solving and decision-making may increase, rather than decrease, the quality of solutions and decisions. See Chapters 10, 11, 12, 13 and 14.

French factory worker than he does with a German farmer, that is, occupational and social statuses tend to cut across national boundaries.

Within organisations in different cultures, there must also be differences in values, perceptions, and "the way we do things". Hofstede (1980, 1981) and England (1978) have made notable contributions here (see Chapters 2 and 10).

Paradigms

Paradigms are patterns or models of thinking. We often think of any body of information ("physics", "cooking", "accountancy", "astrology") as being clearly understood by everyone, supported by facts, and undergoing only smooth and gradual change. Kuhn (1970, 1981) suggests that this is an illusion. With science, for example, the pattern of change is quite a violent and messy one, the sequence being *normal science—crisis—revolution—new normal science*. Normal science has certain paradigms, or ways of viewing the world. These paradigms are shared and defended by an in-group of researchers who support each other professionally via professional communications, refereeing one another for jobs, and generally taking in each other's intellectual washing. The cosy smugness of the in-group means that the paradigms or conventional wisdoms are rarely challenged by deviants or out-groups. Scientists thus suffer from "groupthink" just as much as any other group (see Chapter 11). Yet paradigms are their own undoing: precisely because so much energy is put into making paradigms precise, such paradigms expose anomalies, uncomfortable facts; these anomalies build up to an unbearable extent, triggering crisis, revolution and the arrival of a new paradigm. Thus, the Ptolemaic view of the universe (the Sun moves around the Earth) was supplanted by the Copernican (the Earth moves around the Sun), and the Newtonian view of space and time was supplanted by the Einsteinian. Thus science, rather than being a dignified, ordered arena where unemotional people dispassionately quest after absolute truths, is just like the rest of the world—an undignified, chaotic arena where people with pet theories and vested interests squabble with allies and enemies, a place of flux and at best relative truths. Drucker's words about facts and opinions are thus seen to have significance far beyond the management audience he addresses himself to (see p.271).

When attempting to solve problems in a particular area, therefore, it is essential to determine what are the paradigms or prevailing models of truth. Do these paradigms describe reality well, or are they less than effective in this task? If they are less than effective, then a *paradigm shift* may be under way. If this shift is happening, then "facts" will be contradictory, consensus will be impossible, and people will be very uncomfortable with the turbulent environment, yearning for the placid environment of yesterday when truth was pure and simple and the sacred paradigms were never challenged.

Of course, it may not be all that healthy to point out that a shift is under way or, even worse, that you have an inkling of what the new paradigm is: people have a way of making it uncomfortable for people who are right at the wrong time.

Psychological defence mechanisms

Mention was made in Chapter 5 of various ego defence mechanisms, first described by Freud (cf. the "psychological games" of the same chapter, and the rational–emotional therapy "styles of distorted thinking" in Chapter 7.) Such a-rational behaviour usually hinders efficient problem-solving. While all of them are relevant, it is useful to consider two mechanisms in particular, repression and rationalisation. Problem-solving is concerned with trying to make a better future, based upon our experience of the past. Yet if problem-solvers repress uncomfortable truths from the past, they may suffer: those who do not learn from history are condemned to repeat it. Rationalisation may also lead to hindsight, the view that present-day reality was inevitable, that past events *had* to happen in the way they did. But history is not as predictable as that: as Edmond and Jules de Goncourt observed, "History is a novel that did take place; a novel is a history that could take place". Using fictional techniques, such as scenario writing (see below), we can break out of the mental straitjacket of "facts" and "inevitability". There is no such thing as "the past", only "pasts" recorded by different people. There is no such thing as "the future", only "futures" which are determined by human actions. Only by believing this can problem-solvers rid themselves of hindsight into the past and reverse hindsight into the future. This is easier said than done, of course, because defence mechanisms are deeply rooted behaviours that protect us from uncomfortable truths, such as the notion that reality is not very predictable (and hence that things are out of control until we take control).

Styles of decision-making and problem-solving

It is commonly thought that, when confronted with problems and decisions, we are confronted with one variable (the problem/decision) and one constant (us, the community of problem-solvers/decision-makers). But is this necessarily so? What if we are also a variable? What if people approach problems and solutions in dramatically different ways? Do engineers and artists agree on how a thing is to be done? Do systems analysts and marketing people agree on how best to run an organisation?

Just as there are real differences between people in terms of opinions, values, organisational politics, cultures, paradigm perceptions and defence mechanisms, so there are differences in *styles* of decision-making and problem-solving. These differences are real, not trivial, and our ability to solve problems and make decisions is enhanced considerably if we are aware of what goes on inside the heads of others (particularly when we have to work with others in groups or teams). Some people might disagree with this, suggesting that it is only results that count, and results are determined by using the best *techniques* of decision-making and problem-solving. But what if *style determines technique*, that is, what if we are "programmed" by our perceptual patterns or even the very structure of our brains to select certain techniques rather than others? Alarming or fascinating as this may be, there may be some foundation in fact that this is so.

Physiology of the brain

Recent research on the evolution of the brain suggests that we still carry remnants of the "old" or "visceral" brain of our pre-human ancestors. Sagan (1979) suggests that the deepest part of this "old" brain is the "reptile" brain: similar in structure to the brains of reptiles, it is also similar in the behaviour it produces—unemotional and aggressive, without any discrimination of whether aggressive behaviour is appropriate. Suojanen (1980) suggests that pre-human and early human creatures were not very good at calm reflection, learning from experience, or detailed planning of future actions. As a result, the "old" brain within us tends to preserve older, maladaptive behaviour, such as being too concerned with the present, and not enough with the future, and also being too fond of quick fixes and reactive (as opposed to proactive) tactics whenever new situations or crises arise.

The "old" brain sits in the core of our skull. The "new" brain sits on top of this, taking up the larger volume within our skull. But this "new" brain is divided into two hemispheres, the left and the right. These two hemispheres, some research suggests, perform quite separate functions (Fig. 9.2). Physically, the left hemisphere controls the right side of the body, while the right hemisphere controls the left side of the body. Behaviourally, the left hemisphere tends to specialise in language, deduction, mathematics (or at least algebra), linearity, sequence and segmentation. The right hemisphere, by contrast, tends to specialise in artistic skills such as induction, intuition, and holistic or gestalt perception (seeing that wholes are often greater than the sum of their parts) (Agor 1983).

It may be that one hemisphere will be more dominant in one individual, whereas the other hemisphere will dominate another. Thus, their person-alities and styles of decision-making and problem-solving may be quite different. Conflicts may arise when a "left-hemisphere" person tries to interact with a "right-hemisphere" person. Congruence or cooperation may produce a synergistic style of approaching problems and decisions, where different strengths are combined, rather than different weaknesses and blind spots. It is perhaps easier to imagine conflict than congruence in such pairs as engineer/musician, economist/politician, and science teacher/humanities teacher.

Nugent (1981) argues that the left-hemisphere or rational style has tended to dominate in our society. Societies that build empires need quantitative and rational approaches to reality, although such approaches usually squeeze out qualitative and intuitive approaches, because they are not as "hard" and predictable. Good decision-making and problem-solving depends upon people understanding each other's different ways of seeing reality, and seeing that left-hemisphere perceptions and right-hemisphere perceptions are not competitive but complementary.

Mintzberg (1979) has suggested that, within organisations, the right-hemisphere style will be more effective within the upper levels of the hierarchy, where the "big picture" or overall view is needed to coordinate the activities of the lower levels. At those lower levels, the left-hemisphere

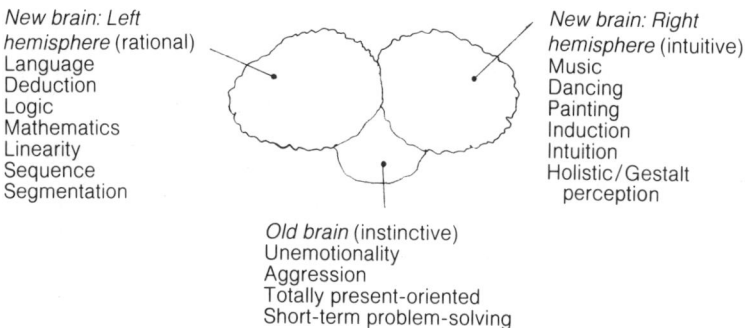

New brain: Left hemisphere (rational)
Language
Deduction
Logic
Mathematics
Linearity
Sequence
Segmentation

New brain: Right hemisphere (intuitive)
Music
Dancing
Painting
Induction
Intuition
Holistic/Gestalt perception

Old brain (instinctive)
Unemotionality
Aggression
Totally present-oriented
Short-term problem-solving

Fig 9.2 *A view of physiological and behavioural structure of the brain* (ADAPTED FROM SUOJANEN 1980, P.33)

style—rational, sequential, good with detail—may be the operative one (see also Agor 1983). This analysis, while superficially true, should not be taken too far, for fear of implying that a managocratic caste has a level of superior, indeed, biologically rooted, skills to which the common proles will never evolve. It is good to restore intuition to a basis of parity with rationality, but it is no good making it superior to rationality, so that "intuitive managers" do not need to justify proposed solutions and decisions except to say that they were arrived at "intuitively" and hence must be right. Levy (1985) has in fact suggested that the right brain/left brain idea has been too rapidly taken up by "pop psych" exponents. It has not been conclusively demonstrated that the brain halves are quite independent of each other, for example, and it is premature to talk of "right-hemisphere" and "left-hemisphere" people as if they were polar extremes, rather than being identifiable on a gradual continuum of behaviour.

Intelligence and creativity
What then of the concept of intelligence? Do "more" or "less" intelligent people make better or worse decisions? To answer this question, we need to be able to measure intelligence—which is easier said than done. Psychologists usually attempt to measure intelligence with intelligence quotient (IQ) tests. People perform differently on such tests, and this is often taken to imply that some people are better than others at solving problems (and making decisions). Thus Medcalf (1977) claims that IQ is closely correlated with occupation: the less your IQ score, the more likely you are to have an unskilled job, while the higher your IQ score, the more likely you are to have a professional job.

But to what extent is "intelligence" the same as "test performance"? For example, is intelligence inherited, and hence invariable? or to what extent can it be modified by education and coaching? Psychologists such as Eysenck (1977) have argued that intelligence is primarily hereditary, and hence largely averse to change. Wilson (1974), Whimby (1975) and Strenio (1981) take a more environmentalist position: they say that intelligence, *or at least performance on intelligence tests*, can be taught. (As Binet, a French pioneer of intelligence testing, once observed, intelligence tests measure how good a person is at completing intelligence tests.) If this is true, then it does not solve the problem of whether "intelligence" is primarily determined by hereditary or environmental factors, but it does cast doubt on placing total faith in IQ test results as a predictor of careers and problem-solving ability.

A further point to be considered is: is intelligence the same as creativity? Critics of IQ tests have pointed out that most test items are very precise, with one correct answer for each question or item (e.g. "What word can be made out of these jumbled letters?" "What do these numbers add up to?"). Yet, as the critics point out, reality is not often like that. There are several, sometimes many, solutions to the one problem. IQ tests, according to the critics, do a reasonable job of measuring *convergent* thinking, that is, problem-solving where there is only one solution. They do not, however, give a good measure of *divergent* thinking, that is, problem-solving where there are many solutions. Accordingly, attempts have been made to measure divergent thinking through so-called creativity tests, or creativity quotient (CQ) tests. Some items from such tests are: "Name as many uses as you can think of for a toothpick"; "Write as many meanings as you can for the words 'pitch' and 'sack'." (Hilgard, Hilgard and Atkinson 1979).

Whether CQ tests measure "creativity" is as problematic as whether IQ tests measure "intelligence". CQ tests are useful, however, insofar as they represent alternative models of problem-solving to the still highly influential IQ concept. Perhaps the most difficult CQ test item of all is how to score, and then rank, CQ test items.[4] Note also the similarity of convergent and divergent thinking with left-hemisphere and right-hemisphere thinking, respectively.

Kolb's model

Kolb's model of DMPS styles uses the distinction between convergent orientation and divergent orientation, as well as the familiar distinction between orientation towards people and orientation towards tasks or things (see Chapter 10) and the distinction between extroversion and introversion.[5]

Kolb approaches the problem from the viewpoint of *learning* styles but, to a considerable extent, learning is merely the other side of the coin in relation to decision-making and problem-solving (see Chapter 3). Kolb distinguishes four modes of learning:

1. *Concrete experience (CE)*. People who rely heavily on this mode rely heavily on feelings to make up their minds, rather than rely on theories. They prefer specific cases rather than generalities. They relate well to people rather than to symbols and things.
2. *Reflective observation (RO)*. People who rely heavily on this mode tend to be introverts who like to remain tentative and impartial when solving a problem. They are among life's watchers rather than doers.
3. *Abstract conceptualisation (AC)*. People who rely heavily on this mode rely heavily on logical thinking and rational evaluation. They prefer to get the big picture rather than become bogged down in specifics. They relate well to symbols and things rather than to people.
4. *Active experimentation (AE)*. People who rely heavily on this mode tend to be extroverts who like to jump into a problem, solving it by experimentation and action.

The combination of these modes of learning gives rise to four learning styles (see Fig. 9.3 and Tables 9.1, 9.2). These are:

1. *Diverger.* The diverger's dominant learning abilities are concrete experience (CE) and reflective observation (RO). Such persons tend to be emotional, preferring people to things or ideas, and are means-oriented. Such persons tend to have broad cultural interests, and specialise in the arts. Within organisations, divergers are found in areas such as counselling, personnel and organisational development. Divergers are very good at generating alternatives and identifying trends; they are comfortable with ambiguity. They are, however, often paralysed by too many alternatives, and they are not very good at single-solution problems.
2. *Assimilator.* The assimilator's dominant learning abilities are abstract conceptualisation (AC) and reflective observation (RO). Such people tend to be interested in abstract concepts rather than people (although they are not greatly interested in the applications of such concepts).

---

[4] Gardner (1983) goes further, distinguishing six "intelligences": language use, logical/mathematical ability, musical ability, visual/spatial skill, kinesthetic talent (e.g. dance), and emotional empathy.

[5] The psychologist Carl Jung distinguished between extroversion (concern with the outside world) and introversion (concern with self).

They reason inductively (from the specific to the general), and are means-oriented. Such people are usually found in the basic sciences and pure mathematics areas. In organisations they are usually found in research and planning departments. They are not unduly impressed by "facts". They are good at planning, getting "the big picture", and discovering underlying patterns or gestalts (the wholes rather than the sums of parts). They analyse alternatives. Precisely because their vision is so wide, however, they often can't see the wood for the trees, and may be impractical.

3. *Converger.* The converger's dominant learning abilities are abstract conceptualisation (AC) and active experimentation (AE). The converger solves problems deductively (reasoning from the general to the specific), and is ends-oriented. Such persons tend to be unemotional, preferring things and ideas to people. They tend to have narrow technical interests, and sometimes become engineers. They are very good at solving IQ-type problems: one solution per problem. They are also good at selecting from alternatives presented to them. Such people however are not very good in situations which involve the human element, or any ambiguity or messiness. They often reach solutions prematurely (because they do not like uncertainty) and they often over-emphasise quantitative, as opposed to qualitative, factors.

4. *Accommodator/executor.* The executor's dominant learning abilities are concrete experience (CE) and active experimentation (AE). Such people tend to be interested in people rather than things, and are ends-oriented. Such people usually come from (or go to) technical or business backgrounds. In organisations, they are often found in "action-oriented" jobs such as sales or marketing. Such people are very interested in doing things, taking risks, and getting involved in new experiences. They test alternatives under actual conditions. This very love of activity for its own sake can often lead, however, to a confusion of efficiency with effectiveness (they often get things done right, rather than do the right thing). They tend to manage by crisis for similar reasons. They mistrust theory too much, and they believe in "facts" too much.

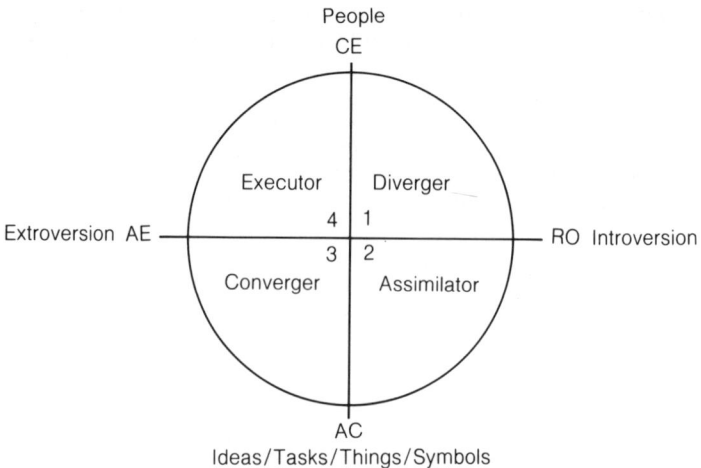

Fig 9.3

Table 9.1 Kolb's model of DMPS: Modes and styles

	Active experimentation (AE)		*Reflective observation (RO)*
Concrete experience (CE)	Executor		Diverger
		4	1
		3	2
Abstract conceptualisation (AC)	Converger		Assimilator

Source: Adapted from Kolb (1979), Carlsson *et al.* (1979) and Jervis (1983).

To a certain extent, we all have all four styles within us. Innate predisposition and/or our socialisation may lead to one or two being dominant, however. It may also be that we might use different styles in different situations: at a business meeting or around the dinner table, for instance. Birds of a feather flock together, and we might expect to find groups of like-minded decision-makers and problem-solvers in distinct occupational groupings as well (see Table 9.2). Thus, in a crude sense, DMPS style = destiny. Looking at Figure 9.3 and Table 9.1, we can see that it is useful to impose a clockwise pattern upon the four styles: (1) Diverger, (2) Assimilator, (3) Converger, and (4) Executor. Thus, for example, if four people, each with a separate dominant style, were solving a problem, it would make sense to solve the problem in such a sequence, allowing the person with the appropriate style to lead the group's activities in that phase, acting as group "expert".[6] As will be seen from Table 9.2, there are DMPS techniques appropriate for each style. Techniques, like styles, are neither right nor wrong, merely appropriate to the situation. Note that, to a large extent, *style determines selection of technique* (some of these techniques will be discussed later, p.282).

How valid is such a model? Similarly, how valid are the other models of styles of decision-making and problem-solving: left-right-old brain and intelligence versus creativity? This is a very difficult question or problem, but in a very real sense we don't have to have a definitive answer. It is sufficient to say that there *are* differences among individuals, and it makes more sense to acknowledge such differences than to suppress them. If we are aware of

---

[6] This is not (to complicate matters still further) a blanket endorsement of "experts". Kahn (1979) notes that many experts suffer from *educated incapacity*—the more expert (or at least the more educated) a person is, the less likely that person is to see a solution when it is not within the framework in which he or she was taught to think. In other words, when we get expertise, we get the blind spots of those who give us the expertise. Thus sometimes a gifted amateur can see what the professionals don't (or can't or won't) see; sometimes it is the wild-eyed deviant, the outsider, who triggers the paradigm shift that has been resisted by the establishment for so long. Thus, an electronics engineer may shake up the field of nutrition; a physicist may cause breakthroughs in economics; a poet may contribute insights into meteorology; experimental scientists may harass and shame doctors into accepting new techniques, such as smallpox vaccination and penicillin; a child may point out that the emperor is not wearing any clothes.

Experts may not only be fools, they may be knaves, i.e. they may be deliberately trying to mislead us: as George Bernard Shaw remarked, each profession is a conspiracy against the layman (see Chapter 10). Thus, for example, when a converger is holding the floor, the executor, diverger and assimilator should listen respectfully, but they should not be dominated by her. They must be allowed to ask embarrassingly naive questions, and expect thorough, jargon-free and non-patronising replies. Experts should be on tap, not on top. We are all experts and ignoramuses, in differing situations. Because the information explosion is so dramatic, no one person can hope to know everything about everything. Like it or not, everyone needs everyone else.

Table 9.2 Kolb's model of DMPS: Analysis of styles

Styles	Dominant learning abilities	Emphases	Strengths	Weaknesses	Favoured jobs, training	Favoured DMPS techniques
Diverger	Concrete experience (CE) Reflective observation (RO)	emotional people, not things means-oriented	views concrete situations from many perspectives generates alternatives identifies trends comfortable with ambiguity	paralysed by alternatives, overchoice not good at single solution problems	arts/humanities counsellor personnel organizational development human/social services	brainstorming MFCs lateral thinking intuition participation Delphi NGT
Assimilator	Abstract conceptualisation (AC) Reflective observation (RO)	interested in ideas, not people not interested in applications of ideas inductive means-oriented	Not overly impressed by "facts" goes for "big picture" discovers patterns, gestalts analyses alternatives	impractical can't see woods for trees	basic sciences pure maths planning and research	game theory model building scenarios paradigm shifting force-field analysis Delphi NGT
Converger	Abstract conceptualisation (AC) Active experimentation (AE)	unemotional things, not people deductive ends-oriented	"IQ test" problems—one answer per problem deciding choosing alternatives	misunderstands ambiguity, messiness, human element premature closure overemphasises quantitative	applied sciences engineering data processing/ systems analysis	experimenting decision trees/ CPM flowcharting
Accommodator/ Executor	Active experimentation (AE) Concrete experience (CE)	people, not things ends-oriented	goal-oriented doing things getting involved in new experiences risk-taker testing alternatives	confuses effectiveness with efficiency likes crises too much mistrust of theory over-reliance on "facts"	technical, business background sales, marketing	cost-benefit analysis satisficing muddling through rat cunning participation CPM

Source. Adapted from Kolb (1979), Carlsson *et al.* (1979).

such differences, we can put them to work by ensuring that individuals' strengths are maximised and their weaknesses or blind spots are minimised. When differing individuals work in groups, mutual understanding of each other's strengths can lead to that group being much more effective than it would otherwise be.[7]

Individual versus group decision-making

Finally, in looking at ways to re-define problems, attention should be paid to the problem of whether individuals or groups are better at solving problems and making decisions. Is it a case of too many cooks spoiling the broth, or of many hands making for light work? The issue is considered in depth in Chapter 11, where group techniques such as brainstorming, nominal group technique and Delphi are considered. (Note also the discussion on participation in Chapter 14 and the discussion of delegation and participation in Chapter 10).

Analysis of the problem

Once we have proceeded through phases one and two of the DMPS model, we are now aware of the facts, *plus* a range of other factors. In the light of all of these variables, we will be able to generate solutions. Before we can do this, however, we need to analyse just what kind of problem we have.

For example, the problem may be *insoluble,* This is a very unpopular thing to admit, yet it may be resorted to too quickly by people who haven't tried hard enough. It may be that many runs will have to be made through the model before we end up in this dead end, but at least if you know you are in a dead end, you can save energy. Many people consider political problems like the Middle East and Ireland to be insoluble problems; others regard them as being all too soluble. Many people regard the existence of God as being not provable and not disprovable; again, many would disagree.

It may be that *no action is necessary* at all. As the old saying goes, when it is not necessary to decide, it is necessary not to decide. Politicians and administrators are fond of talking about "benign neglect", or of leaving processes to themselves to get better spontaneously.

A further distinction can be drawn between action being unnecessary *at this time* versus action being unnecessary forever. It can, for example, be the very essence of wisdom to defer solving a problem by deciding to sleep on it or stew on it, or leave it and come back to it, or deliberately do something unconnected with it like exercising or getting drunk, leaving unconscious processes miraculously to produce new perspectives. These "hands off" approaches can obviously be very useful; the trick is also obviously knowing when to use and when not to use them. Problem-solvers using this approach permanently should also bear in mind that not acting can be done equally well by a well-paid human and a block of wood (cf. the maxim, when two people agree all the time, one of them is unnecessary).

Once it is presumed (at least for the moment) that problems are soluble and that action is necessary, we need to separate problems into those that are *programmed* or *routine* and those that are *non-programmed* or *non-routine* (Simon 1961). Routine problems can be solved by policies and procedures.

---

[7] Other useful models of styles of decision-making and problem-solving are: Jung's introversion/extroversion, thinking/feeling model (e.g. Hellriegel, Slocum and Woodman (1983), Hogan and Champagne (1980)) and Harrison and Bramson's synthesist/idealist/pragmatist/analyst/realist model (Harrison and Bramson (1983)).

Organisations cope with routine problems by using habit, clerical routines, standard operating procedures (SOPs), electronic data processing (EDP), and quantitative models. The situation is not so clear with non-programmed or non-routine problems: there are no clear guidelines, precedents, policies and procedures, and each problem has to be handled as a unique case, using DMPS techniques of the kind to be discussed shortly. Thus, in a very real sense, routine problems are not problems at all. They *were* problems long ago, when they arose as non-routine problems, but solutions were reached long ago, and these solutions have since become routine. Thus, learning to drive a car is a major problem, but once learned, is not a problem, or at least not a major one. If you have an accident and it is your fault, then driving, of course, is obviously a major problem. Thus, while it is useful to distinguish between routine and non-routine problems, it is a mistake to presume that these two categories are watertight. Non-routine problems can become routine, but routine problems can well become non-routine: a clerk infuriating her customers with sloppy telephone technique, a concentration camp guard "just following orders", an astronomer refusing to believe that the Earth goes round the Sun—all have an unjustified faith in the correctness of "routine".

Generally speaking, as people move up through hierarchies, they are presented with more and more non-routine problems. While routine constricts them to a certain extent, routine can liberate them also, as surely as it is liberating not to have to remind yourself to breathe every few seconds. This is just as well, because upper levels of hierarchies usually have to cope with more non-routine problems. In managing by exception such people often encounter more initial stress, but usually have more variety in their work (not to mention *power* to solve problems, which of course reduces stress: see Karasek's model of job design in Chapter 7). Of course, if the "future shock" and "turbulence" hypotheses are correct (see Chapters 1 and 13), then the world is increasingly unpredictable for all of us, no matter where we work and live.

If we are satisfied that the problem we have is a clear-cut unprogrammed or non-routine one, then we can proceed to the next phase of the DMPS model to generate solutions to that model.

Generation of solutions

Now we can begin to look at solutions. Here we need to be "divergent" in our thinking, generating the maximum number of approaches without unduly worrying about quality. We must in other words create, and be careful of making too many premature judgments about the intrinsic worth or otherwise of what we create. That comes later.

Morphological forced connections (MFCs)

This technique has a good deal in common with brainstorming and lateral thinking, particularly in that it requires people to let down their guard and allow their sense of fun and serendipitous adventure to prevail over their rational, "sensible" side. Basically, one thinks of a problem, usually an object to be redesigned. The attributes of the object are listed, and then alternatives for each of the attributes are sought. Generally speaking, the more "far out" the alternatives, the better. These alternatives are recorded in a grid (see Figs 9.4, 9.5). Runs are then made through the grid, connecting variables from different columns, to see whether a new and viable, or at least provocative

ATTRIBUTES	shape	base	rose	walls	tap	drainage	water
ALTERNATIVES	square	sponge	hose	glass	button	evaporation	steam
	circular	tile	jet	mirror	foot-lever	gutter	milk
	cylinder	gold	perforated walls	heated	cord	vacuum	bubbles
	room	concrete	perforated floor	soap	electric beam	thirsty dog	alcohol
	conical	grate	oscillating	sponge	voice-control	sponge	mud
	mushroom	mirror	massage	back-scratch	coin	fan	air

Fig 9.4 *Design a better shower*

and suggestive composite object appears. Most of the suggestions for a better shower or a better toilet in the figures are, of course, ridiculous, but some of the ideas generated are not so ridiculous. Of course, some "ridiculous" ideas may only appear to be so at first sight. Thus, if such nineteenth-century engineers had done an MFC exercise on road transport, some might have come up with such ridiculous ideas as replacing horses with engines, steering from behind a weatherproof window, and using rubber wheels. Van Gundy (1981) notes that this technique is useful in that it is systematic, and thus avoids trial-and-error approaches, and that its systematic patterning can not only be understood by most people, but can be easily adapted for computers to do more sophisticated run-throughs (particularly where more than two dimensions are involved). There are disadvantages, of course: its structured nature may inhibit freer spirits who want to make a radical break with the entire original concept, and the mechanical nature of the MFC model may mean that it is more suited to tidy, quantitative problems (such as product design and technological forecasting) rather than messy human problems (such as whether people should get a divorce, or whether God exists).

Lateral thinking

De Bono (1966, 1977, 1978, 1982a, 1982b, 1983) has developed an approach to problem-solving known as "lateral thinking" (LT). LT is basically an extended elaboration of the technique of brainstorming (see Chapter 11). Lateral thinking is unconventional thinking, which de Bono contrasts with conventional or vertical thinking (VT) (Table 9.3).

ATTRIBUTES	seat	bowl	cistern	paper	floor	water
ALTERNATIVES	vibrating	bucket	vacuum-suction	velvet	water-bed	quicksand
	armchair	garden	balloon	brushes	heated	bubbles
	hanging-straps	built-in bidet	laser	water-jet	built-in TV	milk
	squat-bar	grinder	fish-tank	grass	bar	cotton-wool
	lying down	fire	hand-basin	tongs	mirrors	vacuum-suction
	air-jets	laser beam	hot water	slaves' hands	footbath	alcohol
	upside down	centrifuge	rain-jar	sponges on conveyor belt	quicksand	kitty-litter

Fig 9.5 *Design a better toilet*

Table 9.3 Major differences between lateral and vertical thinking

Lateral thinking	Vertical thinking
1. Tries to follow new ways for looking at things; is concerned with change and movement.	1. Tries to find absolutes for judging relationships; is concerned with stability.
2. Avoids looking for what is "right" or "wrong". Tries to find what is different.	2. Seeks yes/no justification for each step. Tries to find what is "right".
3. Analyses ideas to determine how they might be used to generate new ideas.	3. Analyses ideas to determine why they do not work and need to be rejected.
4. Attempts to introduce discontinuity by making illogical jumps from one step to another.	4. Seeks continuity by proceeding logically from one step to another.
5. Welcomes chance intrusions of information to use in generating new ideas; considers the irrelevant.	5. Selectively chooses what to consider for generating ideas; rejects any information not considered to be relevant.
6. Progresses by avoiding the obvious.	6. Progresses using established patterns; considers the obvious.
7. Increases the odds that a solution will be found; avoids any guarantees.	7. Guarantees at least minimal success in finding a solution.

Source: Van Gundy (1981), p.236. Reproduced with permission.

Lateral thinking is a useful antidote to such conventional techniques as flowcharting and systems analysis, which depends upon a crude yes/no logic and the assumption that if a factor can't be quantified, it doesn't exist. De Bono compares vertical thinking to the traditional method of taking a photograph: the photographer plans lighting, seating, postures, expression, exposure, and then takes a shot. A modern photographer might not plan anything, merely expose many frames in different lights, with different expressions, and so on, selecting only *after* the film is developed; this is closer to lateral thinking. With vertical thinking, we know what we want before we proceed to get it; with lateral thinking, we may not know what we are looking for until we have found it.

Lateral thinking uses discontinuity and irrelevance to generate new ideas, all the while carefully avoiding the rigid (and mutilating) logic of vertical thinking. Sacrosanct assumptions might be challenged. Thus, if a government body is finding it is losing revenue on parking meters relative to the cost of parking inspectors, a vertical thinking (VT) solution would be to increase the parking rates. An LT solution, however, might be to question the very existence of the whole system. What are meters for? They are to ration space, and thus ensure a turnover of motorists. How can motorists be motivated to move on, without paying money? LT solution: abolish the parking meters and inspectors altogether, and make a law that anyone can park for as long as they like, so long as they leave their headlights on. Another example drawn from the motoring world: a motorist drives into a country lane and comes up behind a flock of slow-moving sheep. He cannot move around them. Is the motorist then condemned to a long wait until the road widens? Not if the shepherd uses LT, motions the driver to stop, turns the flock around, drives them around the car, and turns the sheep around again. Thus an LT solution would reverse our perceptions, concentrating on getting the sheep past the car rather than getting the car past the sheep.

Randomness and discontinuity can also be introduced by using the nonsense word PO. PO is an alternative to yes or no. De Bono derives it from words such as hyPOthesis, supPOse, POssible, and POetry. It can also stand for "provocative operation". PO is used with a random, apparently wild or ridiculous idea. Rather than say "yes" or "no" to such an idea, PO "protects" the idea and allows people to brainstorm. Thus, de Bono has used the provocation "PO cars should have square wheels" to generate ideas such as a bolt-on "square" wheel to be fixed to the normal wheel in mud, sand or snow, or special "braking wheels" for heavy vehicles which would normally be out of contact with the road surface but which would be forced down hydraulically should an emergency occur (de Bono 1982).

Always better than vertical thinking?

LT is not a permanent replacement for VT. Indeed, VT does well for about 95 per cent of the time, while LT should only be tried about 5 per cent of the time. Thus LT might generate new approaches, at which point VT takes over in the development of that idea. Similarly, VT might be fine for much of a problem, but then lead to a dead end, at which point LT takes over to rescue the problem. There is thus a strong connection between LT and VT on the one hand and convergent/divergent thinking and DMPS style models such as Kolb's.

Perhaps the greatest disadvantage of LT is that many people forget the 95/5 rule for VT/LT, and give LT much more prominence than is necessary.

As a consequence, some LT activity is characterised by gratuitous silliness and unredeemed impracticality. This of course can only call into disrepute the whole attempt to introduce play, spontaneity and randomness into problem-solving.

Yet LT has a number of advantages. De Bono uses LT to distinguish between *intelligence* and *thinking*; he appears to suggest that intelligence is inborn, while he is quite adamant that thinking is a skill that has to be learned. In fact, he argues that some highly intelligent and highly educated people are often poor thinkers, in that they unduly favour VT processes. This is a useful distinction.

LT is also useful in that it provides us with a buzz-word which can be used to protect evolving ideas from premature analysis. Just as PO can be used to avoid yes/no dualism, so the phrase, "Oh, I'm just lateral thinking (brainstorming, bouncing ideas of the wall, etc.)" can act as a constraint on the onslaught of vertical thinking. As de Bono suggests, "the need to be right all the time is the biggest bar there is to new ideas".

Scenarios

Scenarios are attempts at writing history in reverse. The technique was first developed in US think-tanks such as the Rand Corporation, where researchers such as Herman Kahn were working on, for example, the problem of predicting likely outcomes of nuclear war. Taking the term from the world of theatre and film—where it means a plot outline or script—scenario writers began to write fictitious accounts, based heavily on fact, of nuclear war, energy policy, business policy and transport policy. Scenarios are presumed to be written by hypothetical observers of events 5, 10, 50 or 1000 years from now. It is rare, however, to find just one scenario; in fact, the essence of the scenario technique is that there should be multiple scenarios, which start from the same or similar point but, with just a few differing variables added, arrive at substantively different outcomes. Consider for example the pessimistic and optimistic scenarios of Australia in 2009 in Chapter 1.

The scenario technique makes people aware of the interconnectedness of events, and makes speculation and brainstorming more possible. Scenarios can be overtaken by events all too easily of course; but it is the most banal and counter-productive hindsight to say that old scenarios are wrong because history didn't happen like that: history could have happened in many other ways. (Indeed, physicist John Gribbin (1974) has suggested that within space-time as we know it, an infinite range of events is happening in an infinite range of circumstances, and this "reality" is only a connected series of branch points through these infinities; somewhere else in space-time, the roof has just fallen in on "you" and killed you. . .) Indeed, to take the example of World War II, scholars are finding (now that 30- and 40-year old classified documents are being released) that the outcome of that conflict was not inevitably an Allied victory. In fact, there is hardly anything inevitable about the past or, for that matter, the future: there is no such thing as "the future", only "futures", and, to a lesser extent, there is no such thing as "the past", only "pasts" (depending upon which historian is consulted, which eye-witnesses to an accident are called, or which family member reminisces about old times).

Scenarios: Future schlock?

Scenarios are a good way of controlling hindsight and reverse hindsight. A scenario writer will usually construct "best case" and "worst case" scenarios, with possible variations in between. Scenarios can be "surprise-free", or predictable extrapolations of existing circumstances, or they can feature small or large variables of high or low probability. At their best, scenarios can provide fresh perspectives on past experience and future trends. Scenario writers can flex their imaginations, while bearing in mind de Bono's observation that the technique acknowledges that there are laws of organisation which ensure that trends coalesce into defined patterns, that while there can never be certainty about the future, there is also a limited number of possible event-patterns (de Bono 1983, p.112). At their worst, scenarios can degenerate into anarchy, where everyone writes totally far-out scenarios with all too predestined outcomes, and no one is willing to acknowledge the validity of other people's perspectives. In this case, scenarios are a case of what Kahn has called "future schlock" (Kahn 1979). Scenarios may also be misunderstood as being what the writer wants to happen or thinks will definitely happen; this is not necessarily the case.

Scenarios can be written about industries, countries and planets, but they can also be written about groups, families and individuals—either forward (future) scenarios or backwards (past) scenarios. You could, for example, write three scenarios of your life for the next ten years to help you make career or personal choices; you could go back years to a critical point in your life, and play "what if this had happened instead?"; or you could look forward to your death, and write epitaphs or obituaries for yourself.

Modelling, muddling and "Murphyologising"

The methods of solution generation so far proposed all embody one basic assumption: people can understand reality. To question such an assumption is rather a daring thing to do, and almost verges on the "some problems have no solutions" area. Three groups of thinkers, however, question whether mere humans are up to understanding the riddle of life, and their approaches have great significance for whatever types of solutions we want or can gain access to.

Perhaps the most "respectable" of these groups is that of the *modellers*. These are people who put trust in mathematical and symbolic models, usually generated by computers, rather than in a puny human brain (or any hemisphere or region thereof). Two modellers are Forrester (1971) and Meadows (1972), who have used complex mathematical models run through computers to analyse the dynamics of industries and cities as well as global trends of population, pollution, food and resources. Forrester argues that humans can only analyse part of a problem, because our brains are relatively simple and we thus depend greatly on intuition. Problems are usually large and complex systems, however, and such systems behave "counter-intuitively". We cannot see the second- and third-order effects, the feedbacks, that our initial efforts at solution generate.

Thus, a bus company may be losing money; the solution is proposed: raise fares; patronage falls off even further, thus causing greater money loss. Insect pests in Latin America and Africa are doused with DDT which instead kills the pests' natural predators, thus causing the pests to flourish. Economic growth, rather than eliminating global poverty and hunger, may aggravate these conditions by causing environmental decay and population explosion.

Only computers, says Forrester, can plot the interrelationships between hundreds of variables in complex systems; only computers, says Forrester, can avoid the workings of Forrester's First Law—"In any complex system, attack, however apparently intelligent, on a single element or a symptom generally leads to a deterioration of the system as a whole." Thus modellers or systems thinkers tend to try to generate solutions using quantitative methods of DMPS, such as systems analysis and operational research.

A second group that believes in our semi-incompetence is that of the *muddlers*. Muddlers, however, have no truck with computers, believing them to be part of the problem, rather than the solution. Systems analysis using computers implies large amounts of information being available, clear-cut goals and objectives, and detailed grand strategies—in short, rational and comprehensive planning. Muddlers don't plan, they just muddle through in a pragmatic and incremental or piece-by-piece way. They know that they can never get enough information,[8] that goals and objectives are rarely clear-cut, and that grand strategies are usually grand fantasies.

The muddler, says his champion, Lindblom (1972), is a problem-solver who is wrestling bravely with a universe that he is wise enough to know is too big for him. We have already considered the influence of such "irrational" factors as opinions, prejudices, arguments and politics upon DMPS processes. Generally speaking, modellers do not like to consider such factors, while muddlers wearily acknowledge them, and set about trying to build various rickety coalitions of forces in order to achieve small gains[9] (Forester 1984).

Golde (1976) suggests that it is possible to settle whether analytic reason (modelling) or muddling is the more appropriate strategy for any given situation. The key variables to consider are:

1. *People versus things.* Machines, materials and money can be more easily quantified, and hence controlled rationally. People, of course, are irrational, or at least a-rational much of the time. So, when dealing with people, muddle, don't model.

2. *Self versus others.* Remember, other people's problems are simple. That's because you are outside them, or at least more outside them, and can thus be objective. With yourself, however, you have to be necessarily more subjective, so muddle, don't model.

3. *Size and complexity.* If a problem is small to medium in size and complexity, model. If it is very big, forget it, it's too big—muddle.

4. *Knowledge.* Where there is too little or too much information—muddle.

5. *Certainty.* Certainty is merely another form of knowledge. Where there is a high uncertainty, muddle.

6. *Control.* Where you have high control over a situation, reason. Where you have low control, muddle.

7. *Degree of newness.* Newness in a situation means lack of knowledge. Thus, in a very new situation, muddle. Paradoxically, a lack of newness may also be bad news for reasoners, because lack of newness means tradition, and tradition is often hidebound and irrational.

---

[8] Muddlers and modellers agree on one thing concerning computers: GIGO, or garbage in = garbage out (i.e. the quality of the output is dependent upon the quality of data which is input). Modellers believe that it is possible to get semi-perfect information; muddlers believe that such things can never be.

[9] Cf. Lakoff's observation on the differing cognitive styles of diplomats and scientists:

Unlike a diplomat, who tends to think there are no solutions, but only steps towards a resolution of conflict, a scientist, is apt to believe that by the use of reason solutions can be identified, whether or not the parties to a particular conflict will accept them. (LAKOFF 1977, P.372).

BOX 9.A: Some laws of Murphyology

Why do things always (or, at least, often) go wrong? These humorous (but not necessarily untrue) "laws" of the universe may help to explain why more rational methods of problem-solving and decision-making do not always bring success to human ventures.

Murphy's Laws
1. If anything can go wrong, it will.
2. Nothing is ever as simple as it seems.
3. Everything takes longer than you expect.
4. If there is a possibility of several things going wrong, the one that will go wrong first will be the one that will do the most damage.
5. Left to themselves, all things go from bad to worse.
6. If you play with something long enough, you will surely break it.
7. If everything seems to be going well, you have obviously overlooked something.
8. If you see that there are four possible ways in which a procedure can go wrong, and circumvent these, then a fifth way, unprepared for, will promptly develop.
9. Nature always sides with the hidden flaw.
10. Mother Nature is a bitch.
11. It is impossible to make anything foolproof, because fools are so ingenious.
12. If a great deal of time has been expended seeking the answer to a problem with the only result being failure, the answer will be immediately obvious to the first unqualified person.

The Yulish additions to Murphy's Laws
1. Persons disagreeing with your facts are always emotional and employ faulty reasoning.
2. Enough research will tend to confirm your conclusions.
3. The more urgent the need for a decision, the less apparent becomes the identity of the decision-maker.
4. The more complex the idea or technology, the more simple-minded is its opposition.
5. Each profession talks to itself in its own unique language. Apparently there is no Rosetta Stone.

NASA Truisms
1. Research is reading two books that have never been read in order to write a third that will never be read.
2. A consultant is an ordinary person a long way from home.
3. Statistics are a highly logical and precise method for saying a half-truth inaccurately.

Sevareid's Law
The chief cause of problems is solutions.

Brien's First Law
At some time in the life-cycle of virtually every organisation, its ability to succeed in spite of itself runs out.

Pastore's Truths
1. Even paranoids have enemies.
2. This job is marginally better than daytime TV.

Parkinson's Laws
1. Work expands so as to fill the time available for its completion.
2. Expenditure rises to meet income.
3. Expansion means complexity, and complexity means decay.
4. Delay is the deadliest form of denial.
5. Successful research attracts the bigger grant which makes further research impossible.
6. The progress of science varies inversely with the number of journals published.
7. An enterprise employing more than 1000 people becomes a self-perpetuating empire, creating so much internal work that it no longer needs any contact with the outside world.

Peter's Laws
1. In every hierarchy, whether it be government or business, each employee tends to rise to his level of incompetence; every post tends to be filled by an employee incompetent to execute its duties.
2. Incompetence knows no barriers of time or place.
3. Work is accomplished by those employees who have not yet reached their level of incompetence.
4. If at first you don't succeed, try something else.
5. Internal consistency is valued more highly than efficiency.
6. The unexpected always happens.
7. An ounce of image is worth a pound of performance.

Phases of a project
1. Exultation.
2. Disenchantment.
3. Confusion.
4. Search for the guilty.
5. Punishment of the innocent.
6. Distinction for the uninvolved.

IBM Pollyanna Principle
Machines should work; people should think.

The Unspeakable Law
As soon as you mention something...
... if it's good, it goes away.
... if it's bad, it happens.

Sturgeon's Law
90 per cent of everything is crud.

The Golden Rule of Arts and Sciences
Whoever has the gold makes the rules.

Source: Bloch (1979, 1980), Dickson (1979, 1980), Gall (1979), Peter and Hull (1977).

The third group of people who do not have great faith in man's abilities to solve problems are the *Murphyologists*. These are, if you like, the disreputable cousins of the muddlers. Their view of the universe is pessimistic to the point of absurdity. Their leader is the mythical Murphy, whose first law is "anything that can go wrong, will go wrong". Numerous collections of "Laws" have appeared over the past few years, giving various other humorous and pessimistic views on the way the world actually is. But humour should always be taken seriously, because humour, emotion and other "deviant" qualities can give us insights that more serious and respectable approaches cannot. Some of the central beliefs of the Murphyologists are presented in Box 9.A.

For/against lists

The final "divergent" or options-generating skill we shall look at is the humble for/against list, or pro/con table (see also Chapters 12, 13 and 14). For/against lists provide a simple but stark means of reducing a problem to two dimensions, within which we can brainstorm as many factors as possible. We can then either accept all fors and againsts as being of equal weight, or weight each item differently and add up numerical totals for and against.

For example, presume that you, together with some other people, are contemplating moving to either of two cities. You would need to generate a list of factors (e.g. cost of relocation, climate, night-life, housing costs, journey to work, proximity to friends, etc.). Would you give all of these factors equal weight, or would you give more weight to some factors and less weight to others? Further, would the people you are planning the move with assign the same weight values as you? Weightings are measures of personal values, and values, to state the obvious, vary enormously between individuals. (Weighting, of course, is a ranking or prioritising activity, and therefore strictly belongs to the next section of our DMPS model, but let's not get too convergently pedantic about such things.)

Ranking/prioritisation of solutions

Step 5 (ranking or prioritisation of solutions), step 6 (sequencing and assignment) and step 7 (execution) of the larger problem-solving sequence (see p.269) are most directly concerned with decision-making. Thus, with step 5, once an abundance of solutions has been generated, it becomes necessary to sort through them and decide on some order of priority. In this phase, the divergent problem-solving skills give way to the convergent. Priorities are crucial. As de Bono points out, without priorities we look at the attractiveness of an alternative in itself; with priorities we look at its attractiveness to us (de Bono 1983).

Priorities can be allocated using various criteria, for example, time. Is time a scarce or an abundant resource? Time management tools like the urgent/important priority matrix can be of use here (see Chapter 8). Abundance or scarcity of other resources and information also has to be taken into account. If the degree of difficulty varies among options, is it adequate simply to plump for the easiest? And what happens if we give an option top priority and go with it, and it goes bad? Do we have a fall-back position from which we can try again, or have we put all our eggs in the one basket? In other words, is there a Plan B (or Plan C, or Plan Z), and if not, why not?

It is useful to separate options into three groups: *duds, contingencies* and *the best*. The duds are fairly simple. These are the outrageous ideas, or the superficially pretty ideas that really don't stand a chance. Of course, it would be silly to throw all duds *too* far away. Of the ones that do stand a chance, a distinction can or should be drawn between those that are final choices and those that could well have been final choices but did not make it this time. This latter group are not so much duds as contingencies, or alternatives, and should be kept ready if the best ideas turn out to be not so good. Distinguishing between duds, contingencies and the best is easier said than done. What methods do we have of making decisions? How satisfactory do decisions have to be?

Satisficing

Simon (1961) suggests that the problem-solving process has its own problems—inadequate information, resources, skills and time. In the real world, therefore, rationality as a process is bounded or limited, and optimising, or searching for optimal or best or perfect solutions, is a wild-goose chase. All we can hope for, says Simon, is to find satisfactory solutions: we cannot hope to optimise, only to "satisfice", that is, accept the first satisfactory solution.[10] This is a playing-safe strategy that may not be emotionally very satisfying but that usually proves to be statistically effective[11] (Forester 1984).

Sequencing and assignment

Once decisions have been made about *what* is to happen, decisions have to be made about *when* and *where* it is to happen and *who* is responsible for making it happen. Here, standard planning techniques such as critical path method (CPM) and program evaluation and review technique (PERT) come into their own. Both CPM and PERT are types of network analysis, wherein the relationships of multiple parts of a program or sequence are visually rendered. Table 9.4 and Figure 9.6 are examples of a CPM approach to planning the building of a custom-designed car. Table 9.4 shows the rough order in which the car is to be constructed (first column), the description of the specific processes to be undertaken, the immediate predecessors of each specific job (e.g. B must be completed before C, D, E, G, H and J can be commenced), and the time for each job. Figure 9.6 shows how this information is converted into a critical path method (CPM) chart. The critical path is the longest path through the network, in terms of time, and thus is the major factor in determining the total time for the project. Other paths, called *sub-critical* paths, may have slack time in them, and it might be possible to transfer personnel and/or resources from the shorter sub-critical paths to the long critical path, thereby shortening the time taken for the critical path and thus for the total project.

CPM and PERT are very good for providing a "time map" for different areas and personnel (here, designers, builders, managers, etc.) and thus facilitating communication and coordination. Bottlenecks and slack can be identified in advance, and overall resources can be most effectively maximised. CPM and PERT are not perfect, of course: they can be expensive,

---

[10] The "satisficing" concept is used in some simulation games, e.g. Moore (1978).
[11] Statistics, of course, depend on probability, and probability is probably true most of the time. New mathematical theories, such as catastrophe theory, nevertheless suggest that we cannot depend upon our sense of the probable (see e.g. Postle 1980).

Table 9.4 Sequence, predecessors and time requirements of car-building tasks

Job letter	Description	Immediate predecessors	Normal time (days)
A	Start		0
B	Design	A	8
C	Order special accessories	B	0.1
D	Build frame	B	1
E	Build doors	B	1
F	Attach axles, wheels, fuel tank	D	1
G	Build body shell	B	2
H	Build transmission and drivetrain	B	3
I	Fit doors to body shell	G, E	1
J	Build engine	B	4
K	Bench-test engine	J	2
L	Assemble chassis	F, H, K	1
M	Road-test chassis	L	0.5
N	Paint body	I	2
O	Install wiring	N	1
P	Install interior	N	1.5
Q	Accept delivery of special accessories	C	5
R	Mount body and accessories on chassis	M, O, P, Q	1
S	Road-test car	R	0.5
T	Attach exterior trim	S	1
U	Finish	T	0

Source: Stoner, Collins and Yetton (1985), p.243. Reproduced with permission.

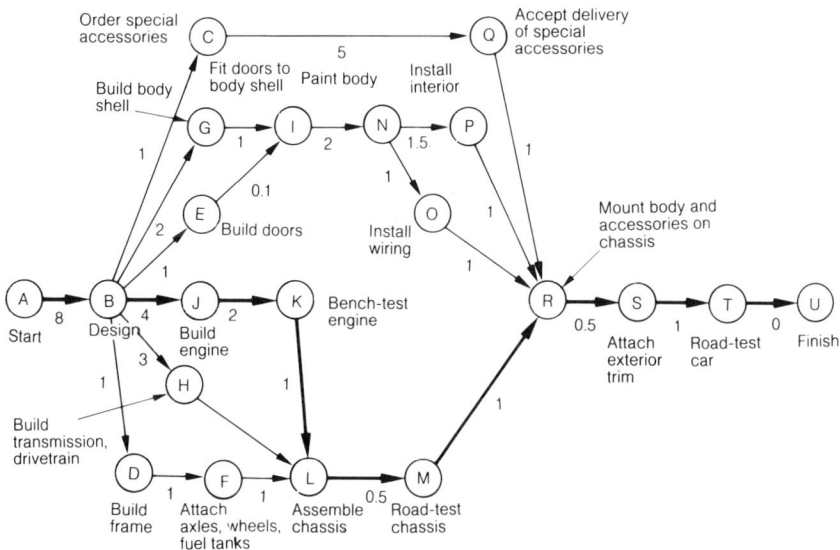

Fig 9.6 *CPM chart for building a custom-designed car* (STONER, COLLINS AND YETTON 1985, P.244. REPRODUCED WITH PERMISSION)

particularly in terms of computer time, and they can become the objects of obsession of particularly inflexible managers who refuse to modify the chart to meet the inevitable contingencies of reality—management–subordinate communication problems, raw material delivery problems, and so on. Like computer flowcharts, CPM and PERT are superb tools for simple, quantitative yes/no problems, but are relatively useless (and perhaps worse than useless) when confronted with more messy, PO (de Bono) problems (remember also that DMPS techniques are not only relevant and irrelevant to different *problems* but also to different *people* with different DMPS *styles*).

Rational techniques such as these then are ideal for determining *when* and *where*, but what about *who*? It is also crucial that if more than one person is involved (and for that matter, even if only one person is involved) then roles should be clearly defined. Who is responsible for what? How shall we know it is done? What mechanisms of feedback and accountability are built in to prevent failure and the inevitable chorus of "don't blame us!"/"Nobody told us!"? The most perfect solution in the world still needs people to carry it out, and our understanding of people's imperfections should be perfect if we want to succeed perfectly.

Execution

If we now know what, when, where and who, how about *how*? Phase 7, execution, tells us. Execution is simply going ahead and doing it. But how should we do it? Should we take a leaf out of the muddlers' book, and do it piece by piece, incrementally? The advantage of doing things piece by piece is that if disaster threatens, we have not risked all, and can pull back and cut our losses. *Incrementalism* of course is not good value when the situation is a "crash-through-or-crash" one, which requires a total effort or no effort at all. Cautious incrementalism is a method for proceeding from the known to the unknown, but it may not be much of a guide in proceeding from an unknown to another unknown. In other words, when we live in a turbulent rather than a placid environment, where change is the norm rather than the exception, incrementalism may mean hesitating and losing (Toffler 1985).

We could crash through or crash and commit our resources in a rational and comprehensive way. Folklore tells us that fortune favours the bold. Folklore unfortunately also tells us that we shouldn't put all our eggs in the one basket. Thus *total commitment* is a technique also fraught with problems. An execution technique half-way between incrementalism and total commitment is that of the *pilot* project or study. A pilot is a small-scale simulation of a large-scale endeavour but without the risks inherent in the large-scale endeavour. Pilot programs can be very useful, but not in all circumstances. Thus if the success of a total commitment depended upon economies of scale, then a pilot program would not reveal such economies, and might even distort them into diseconomies (Schulman 1980).

Obviously, decisions about how, when, where, who and what inter-penetrate to a considerable extent. Decisions about how, however, may be the most difficult to make precisely because they can be so final.

Evaluation

Has the solution worked? How do we know? Do bells ring? Are we dead? Is there a vague shuffling of red tape and the uninterrupted experience of boredom and ennui? For a Murphyologist, into which of the phases of a project does evaluation fall into (see Box 9.A)? As with assignment of roles, there have to be mechanisms of feedback and accountability to give us some kind of indication that something has happened to change the world (or perhaps deliberately not to change the world). We must know if we have succeeded. Whether we like success is another matter. As the cynics say, don't wish too hard for something, you might end up getting it. The cynics also say that all problems are caused by solutions to previous problems.

If we have failed, then we have to move back to earlier phases of the problem-solving model (Fig. 9.1). We may only have to go back to phase 5, to pick up a contingency plan. When such plans have been exhausted, we must of course return to phase 1 or phase 2. There is the chance we will end up in phase 3.1: problem insoluble. If that happens, at least we will have the cold comfort of knowing that there is no choice but to be there.

Summary

Decision-making and problem-solving can be seen as two distinct processes, with decision-making being a part of the larger problem-solving process. In making up our minds, it is essential to know that we cannot totally depend upon facts. We need to understand that there can be too much information, not enough information, contradictory information, and information that is deliberately distorted, or disinformation.

We need to be aware of the opinions, prejudices and values of those involved in the problem-solving process. We need to be aware of what political factors, or vested interests, are operating. We need to understand the cultural background of the problem and the solvers. We need to see whether paradigms or dominant models of reality are helping or hindering our perceptions. We need to know whether psychological defence mechanisms are distorting our perceptions in still other ways. We need to be aware that different people solve problems in different ways, and if we can take such differences into account, we will solve problems more rather than less effectively. And we need to be aware of the strengths and weaknesses of individual and group problem-solving. We need to know what type of problem we have before us in order to determine the method of solution (if indeed it can be solved).

We need to be aware of the strengths and weaknesses of various methods of generating solutions, such as morphological forced connections, lateral thinking, scenarios, computer modelling, Murphy's Law, and for/against lists.

We need to be aware of assigning priorities to solutions once generated, using methods such as "satisficing". Sequencing of solutions is crucial, so we need to be familiar with methods such as the critical path method. Task roles need to be assigned so that roles and responsibilities are clear. Execution of solutions through sequences can take place little by little, all at once, or in pilot form. Finally, we need to evaluate the solution to see whether it worked, to try again, or to determine whether we are happy with success.

Questions for discussion

1. Think of a familiar problem. Make up four lists, under the headings *information overload, unavailable information, contradictory information,* and *disinformation (real, suspected, potential)*. Which type of information is the biggest barrier to the problem's solution? Do this with several other problems.

2. Observe a conflict in the public or private arena (an argument between friends, an industrial dispute, etc.). What is the relationship between the facts of the case and the various opinions, prejudices and values and political factors in operation? Is there any consensus on just what are the facts?
3. List the paradigms of an area you are familiar with. Is there any evidence of paradigm shift taking place?
4. Analyse your own DMPS style in terms of right brain/left brain, convergent versus divergent thinking, or Kolb's learning styles. What areas of cooperation and conflict might arise if you were working or living with people with different styles?
5. Work with other people on making a list of insoluble problems. Is this an easy task, or is it an insoluble problem? Why/why not?
6. Using the morphological forced connections (MFC) model, design a better (a) aeroplane, (b) car, (c) living room.
7. Generate ideas from the following statements:
   (a) PO cups should have holes in them.
   (b) PO books should be burnt.
   (c) PO houses should be made of glass.
8. Write multiple scenarios (best case, worst case, medium case) for the following situations:
   (a) transport in 1995
   (b) robots and the workplace, 2005
   (c) genetic engineering in 2123.
9. What is the best way to repeal Murphy's Law?
10. Do a for/against list for any of the DMPS techniques you are familar with (including for/against lists).
11. Do a critical path method chart for
   (a) holding a dinner party
   (b) launching a new product
   (c) taking a vacation
12. List the various actual and planned activities of an organisation or group you are familiar with (household, workplace department, sporting team, etc.). Which activities are best executed
   (a) incrementally?
   (b) as a pilot?
   (c) as total commitments?

References

Agor, Weston, H. (1983). "Tomorrow's Intuitive Leaders", *The Futurist*, August.
Beyer, Janice M. (1981). "Ideologies, Values and Decision-Making in Organizations", in Nystrom, Paul C. and Starbuck, William H. (eds) *Handbook of Organizational Design, vol. 1, Remodeling Organizations and their Environments*. (Oxford University Press: New York).
Bloch, Arthur (1979a). *Murphy's Law—Why Things Go Wrong*. (Methuen: London).
    (1979b). *Murphy's Law, Book Two—More Reasons Why Things Go Wrong*. (Methuen: London).
Carlsson, Barbara, *et al.* (1979). "R and D Organizations and Learning Systems", in Kolb, D. *et al.* (eds) *Organizational Psychology: Readings*, 3rd edn. (Prentice-Hall: New Jersey).

De Bono, Edward (1986). *PO—Beyond Yes and No.* (Penguin: Harmondsworth).
    (1977). *Practical Thinking.* (Penguin: Harmondsworth).
    (1978). *The Use of Lateral Thinking.* (Penguin: Harmondsworth).
    (1982a). *Lateral Thinking for Managers—A Handbook.* (Penguin: Harmondsworth).
    (1982b). *De Bono's Thinking Course.* (BBC: London).
    (1983). *An Atlas of Management Thought.* (Penguin: Harmondsworth).
Dickson, Paul (1979). *The Official Rules.* (Delacorte Press: New York).
    (1981). *The Official Explanations.* (Arrow Books: London).
Drucker, Peter (1982). *The Effective Executive.* (Pan: London).
England, George W. (1978). "Managers and their Value Systems: A Five-Country Comparative Study", *Columbia Journal of World Business*, Summer.
Eysenck, Hans (1977). *Know Your Own I.Q.* (Penguin: Harmondsworth).
Forester, John (1984). "Bounded Rationality and the Politics of Muddling Through", *Public Administration Review*, January/February.
Forrester, Jay (1971). *World Dynamics.* (Wright-Allen Press: Massachusetts).
Gall, John S. (1979). *Systemantics: How Systems Work, and Especially How They Fail.* (Fontana: London).
Gardner, Howard (1983). *Frames of Mind: The Theory of Multiple Intelligences.* (Basic Books: New York).
Gilmour, Peter (1978). *Moving Goods and People: Transport in Australia.* (Penguin: Harmondsworth).
Gold, Roger A. (1976). *Muddling Through: The Art of Properly Unbusinesslike Management.* (Amacom: New York).
Gribbin, John (1979). *Time Warps.* (Dent: London).
Harrison, Allen F. and Bramson, Robert M. (1983). *Styles of Thinking: Strategies for Asking Questions, Making Decisions and Solving Problems.* (Anchor/Doubleday: New York).
Haviland, William (1975). *Cultural Anthropology.* (Holt, Rinehart and Winston: New York).
Hellriegel, Don, Slocum, John W. and Woodman, Richard W. (1983). *Organizational Behaviour*, 3rd edn. (Harcourt, Brace, Jovanovich: New York).
Hilgard, E.P., Hilgard, J. and Atkinson, A. (1979). *Psychology: An Introduction*, 7th edn. (Harcourt, Brace, Jovanovich: New York).
Hofstede, Geert (1980). *Culture's Consequences.* (Sage: Los Angeles).
    (1981). "Do American Theories Apply Abroad? A Reply to Goodstein and Hunt", *Organizational Dynamics*, Summer.
Hogan, R. Craig and Champagne, David W. (1980). "Personal Style Inventory", in Pfeiffer, J. William and Jones, John E., *The Annual Handbook for Group Facilitators, 1980.* (University Associates: La Jolla, Calif.).
Jervis, Paul (1983) "Analyzing Decision Behaviour: Learning Models and Learning Styles as Decision Aids", *Personnel Review*, vol. 12, no. 2.
Kahn, Herman (1979). *World Economic Development.* (Croom Helm: London).
    (1984). *Thinking About the Unthinkable in the 1980s.* (Simon and Schuster: New York).
Kahn, H. and Pepper, Thomas (1980). *Will She Be Right?—The Future of Australia.* (University of Queensland Press: St Lucia).
Kolb, David, Rubin, Irwin and McIntyre, James (1979). *Organizational Psychology: Readings*, 3rd edn. (Prentice-Hall: New Jersey).
Kuhn, T.S. (1970). *The Structure of Scientific Revolutions.* (Chicago University Press: Chicago).
    (1981). "A Function for Thought Experiments", in Hacking, Ian (ed), *Scientific Revolutions.* (Oxford University Press: Oxford).

Lakoff, Sanford A. (1977). "Scientists, Technologists, and Political Power", in Spigel-Rosing, I. and De Solla Price, D. (eds), *Science, Technology and Society.* (Sage: California).

Levy, Jerre (1985). "Right Brain, Left Brain: Fact and Fiction", *Psychology Today,* May.

Lindblom, Charles E. (1972). "The Science of 'Muddling Through' ", in Thompson, J. (ed.), *Politics, Policy and Natural Resources.* (Free Press: Mass.).

Meadows, Donella, *et al.* (1972). *The Limits to Growth.* (Universe: New York).

Medcalf, William (1977). *Understanding People in Business: Human Relations in Australian Management.* (Sun: Melbourne).

Mintzberg, Henry (1979). "Planning on the Left Side and Managing on the Right", in Kolb *et al.* (1979).

Moore, B. (1979). *Australian Management Games.* (University of NSW: Kensington).

Murphy, Robert F. (1979). *An Overture to Social Anthropology.* (Prentice-Hall: New Jersey).

Nugent, Patrick S. (1981). "Management and Modes of Thought", *Organizational Dynamics,* Spring.

Peter, Lawrence J. and Hull, Raymond (1967). *The Peter Principle.* (Pan: London).

Postle, Dennis (1980). *Catastrophe Theory: Predict and Control Personal Disasters.* (Fontana: London).

Rawlinson, J. Geoffrey (1981). *Creative Thinking and Brainstorming.* (Gower: Westmead).

Roskin, Rick (1975). "Decision Style Inventory", in Pfeiffer, William and Jones, John, *Annual Handbook for Group Facilitators,* 1975. (University Associates: La Jolla, Calif.)

Sagan, Carl (1979). *The Dragons of Eden.* (Book Club Associates: London).

Schulman, Paul (1980). *Large-scale Policy-making.* (Elsevier: New York).

Simon, Herbert A. (1961). *Administrative Behaviour.* (Macmillan: New York).

Stoner, James A.F. (1980). *Management.* (Prentice-Hall: New Jersey).

Stoner, James A.F., Collins, Roger R. and Yetton, Phillips W. (1985). *Management in Australia.* (Prentice-Hall of Australia Pty Ltd: Sydney).

Strenio, Anthony J. (1981). *The Testing Trap.* (Rawson Wade: New York).

Suojanen, Waino W. (1980). "Creativity, Management and the Minds of Man", in *Human Resource Management Australia,* Winter.

Toffler, Alvin (1985). *The Adaptive Corporation.* (McGraw-Hill: New York).

Van Gundy, Arthur B. (1981). *Techniques of Structured Problem-Solving.* (Van Nostrand Reinhold: New York).

Waddington, C.H. (1977). *Tools for Thought.* (Paladin: London).

Wallechinsky, David and Wallace, Irving (1978). *The People's Almanac #2.* (Bantam: New York).

Whimby, Arthur (1975). *Intelligence Can Be Taught.* (Dutton: New York).

Wilson, Glen (1974). *Improve Your I.Q.* (Futura: London).

Zoll, Allan A. (1974). *Explorations in Managing.* (Addison-Wesley: Mass.).

Films/videos

How to Avoid Decisions (Seven Dimensions).
Creative Problem-Solving: How to get Better Ideas (Video Channel).
Decisions (Video Channel).
Decision, Decisions (John Cleese) (Video Channel).
Problem-Solving: A Case Study (Rank).
Problem-Solving: Some Basic Principles (Rank).
The Peter Principle (Power Human Resources).

Part E

Behaviour: The individual and group levels

How do things get done in the workplace? Who is more effective in making decisions and solving problems: individuals, such as leaders? or groups, such as followers? or a combination of both?

Does shared decision-making and problem-solving motivate and increase productivity? Does sharing of such tasks mean a more equitable balance of power in the workplace, or does it dilute power, for example of leaders, so much that paralysis and collapse must follow?

All these issues are explored in this section and the next. This section, focusing as it does upon the interpersonal level of behaviour, begins with leadership, power and micropolitics (Chapter 10). Attention is paid to the nature of leadership, such as possible traits or characteristics of leadership, as well as styles of leadership. Power within organisations is also examined.

Leaders lead (or perhaps are controlled by) groups, and in Chapter 11 (Group dynamics) we look at how groups do and don't work, in terms of roles, norms, cohesiveness, group versus individual decision-making and problem-solving, and meetings.

How do leaders and groups interact at the workface to bring about maximum productivity and maximum satisfaction for all? Some answers to this question are contained in Chapter 12 (Job design).

Most approaches to enriching or enlarging jobs considered here involve non-management people participating more in decision-making and problem-solving. Differing national cultures need to be taken into account when looking at attempts at job design and redesign. New types of workplaces and new technology are also having dramatic impacts upon the nature of work.

10

Leadership, power and micropolitics

Men are of no importance. What counts is who commands.

Charles de Gaulle

If, in order to succeed in an enterprise, I were obliged to choose between fifty deer commanded by a lion, and fifty lions commanded by a deer, I should consider myself more certain of success with the first group than the second.

St Vincent de Paul

Leadership is nothing more than a twenty-four hour wank. Self-control is the modern way.

Ian Dury

> BRIAN: Look, you've got it all wrong. You don't need to follow me. You don't need to follow anybody. You've got to think for yourselves. You're all individuals.
> CROWD: Yes, we're all individuals.
> BRIAN: You're all different.
> CROWD: Yes, we *are* all different.
> DENNIS: I'm not.
> CROWD: Shh!
> BRIAN: Well, that's it. You've all got to work it out for yourselves.
> CROWD: Yes, yes!! We've got it work it out for ourselves.

Monty Python, Life of Brian

LEADERSHIP occurs today in a wide variety of situations. Leaders are present in sporting teams, business organisations, families, charity committees, political parties, artistic groups such as symphony orchestras and rock bands, bands or tribes of animals, and so on. Are leaders necessary? To a considerable extent, this is the same question as "are hierarchical organisations necessary?" Thus, any discussion of leadership will overlap considerations of organisational design, job design, group dynamics, and decision-making and problem-solving.

Decline in leadership?

Whether or not leaders are necessary, many observers have seen a decline in leadership in recent times in the political arena (e.g. Johnson 1980), while others have seen this decline in leadership and power as a general trend that is hitting institutions in the private and public sectors.[1] Is there a decline in leadership? And if there is, is that such a bad thing? To a considerable extent, today's leaders have to cope with a variety of factors which their predecessors did not, such as the electronic media, universal education, and the information explosion.

---

[1] What sets the future executive off from all previous generations is that he (and she) will be living in a society of which nobody can effectively be in charge. (HARLAND CLEVELEND, QUOTED IN LEE (1980))

Impact of media

It is a commonplace to hear laments for the leaders of yesterday, those colossi who seem to tower over puny mortals—Churchill, Lincoln, Bismarck, Rockefeller, J.P. Morgan, Henry Ford, and so on. But people who romanticise these leaders forget that the stature of these great men (and it is mainly *men* we are talking about here) was only partly due to their own intrinsic merit. The rest of it was stature gained from distance—distance from countervailing pressure groups and television cameras stuck up their nostrils. The media, television in particular, are great levellers. Movie superstars, royalty, politicians, tycoons, are all there on the evening news. They're not picking their noses or sitting on the toilet, but they are demystified for all that. Familiarity breeds, if not contempt, then certainly (in most cases) more critical responses. Shulman (1982) sees television as a catalyst in the "cauldron of unpopularity in which democratic politicians now stew", and considers that the very long reigns of earlier prime ministers and presidents—14 to 25 years—are simply unsustainable in the era of television. Executives in the public and private sector dread the arrival of the TV news crew intent on airing the organisation's dirty linen; the same executives take lessons in how to be interviewed, hire expensive public relations officers to keep the media at arm's length, and so on. Much of this accountability is quite unfair—trial by media, in fact—and some leaders have been quite successful in manipulating the media, but on balance, media has done much to drag leaders down from their pedestals.

Impact of education

Education has also narrowed the gap between leaders and led. The social distance between a mediaeval king and his people or a nineteenth-century industrial tycoon and his workers was not merely a function of military or coercive power, it was a function of differential access to information and knowledge (see the discussion on bases of power, in particular, expert power, p.324). This gap has been diminishing throughout history. Thus, in modern industrial countries, the recession of the 1970s and 1980s has accelerated the process of educational credentialism (demanding increasingly higher qualifications for the same job). This "paper-chase" occurs as often as not as a rationing device for scarce resources, for example jobs, desired by increasing numbers. Thus we have a better educated workforce, some would say an over-educated workforce (if such a thing is possible). A supervisor may find that university graduates on the assembly line are too much trouble, or know the job better than she does. The same might apply to the managing director, who might find that her power is not automatically unquestioned as it hitherto was. An army sergeant might find that recruits with advanced high school qualifications might want a reason for action rather than orders to be obeyed simply because they are orders. Old parish pump politicians on a local council might be perplexed by an influx of "trendy" young professionals (accountants, lawyers, economists, psychologists) into the council chambers, ignoring the old politics machine channels.

The information explosion and role overload

Finally, the contemporary explosion of information in all walks of life has meant that it is becoming increasingly difficult for single individuals to handle a particular job-role (if in fact it ever was possible). Thus political scientists have begun to argue that presidents, prime ministers and ministers of state are overstressed by current job and organisational designs, and substantial redesign is necessary if the job of politics and government is to continue. The usual solution advanced is to shift decision-making powers to other individuals and groups (Weller and Grattan 1981). Similar tendencies can be detected in the public and private sector where job redesign is shifting emphasis away from "great men" who sit at the remote apexes of hierarchies. Thus, it may not only be lonely at the top, but inefficient as well.[2]

Leadership as micropolitics

The question of leadership is also complicated by the question of power. We automatically presume that leadership behaviour among politicians is understood in terms of power, but we do not normally associate power with leadership of a teenage gang or charity committee or a work group. Yet power-oriented behaviour, political behaviour, occurs in these areas as well: you don't have to be a politician to be political. Economists make the distinction between *macroeconomics* (study of economic patterns on a large scale, e.g. a nation-state) and *microeconomics* (study of economic patterns on a small scale, e.g. an industry or firm). Let us distinguish then between *macropolitics* (study of politics on a large scale, e.g. among elected politicians), and *micropolitics* (study of politics on a small scale, e.g. within an organisation).

Viewing patterns of leadership and power within organisations as micropolitics can be a very illuminating approach. The traditional view of organisations was to see them as being *unitary*: everyone shares the goals of the organisation (the organisation is one big happy family), conflict is abnormal, and formal leadership's authority is unchallenged.

The micropolitical view is *pluralistic*: the organisation is an unruly coalition of forces, conflict is normal, and formal leadership's authority and legitimacy is continually challenged by organised labour, the informal organisation, government, consumers, etc. The notion that conflict can be engineered, managed away by "team-building" and "conflict resolution" techniques is often a dubious one in pluralistic organisations, in much the same way as it is unrealistic to expect macropoliticians to bury their differences and work together (except in times of extreme emergency where all factions, groups and parties are threatened mutally). This adversary relationship that is present in macro- and micropolitics, as well as in our industrial relations and legal systems, strikes some as being unhealthy, but it would be even more unhealthy to deny its existence.

Is it possible to be *non*-political? This is a difficult question. Some political scientists and analysts of organisations believe that there is no such thing as "non-political behaviour", because if people try to opt out of political processes, either because they feel it is ethically beneath them or simply because they are apathetic, then they are in fact being political by default: other, slicker operators will inherit the vacuum left behind and make decisions and allocate resources that will crucially affect the opters-out.

In this chapter, we will begin to examine leadership and power—micropolitics—by looking at what leaders do, ascertaining whether there are traits or characteristics of leaders which mark them off from non-leaders, studying

---

[2]   Our managerial elites are staggering under an impossible decision load. That will force the elites to allow more people to participate—to help carry the decision load. That's why we hear more and more about participatory management—more and more about involving the workers. Not because of altruism, but because the old decision system doesn't work. (ALVIN TOFFLER, 1984, P83)

various styles of leadership, and finally examining bases, styles and tactics of power, and barriers to power. Following from this, we will attempt to determine whether leaders are an endangered species, and whether or not this is a bad thing.

What do leaders do?

What is it that leaders do? What is the essence of the job of leading? A useful definition was given by Gulick and Urwick (1937) in their analysis of the job of business executive. The job could be summed up with the acronym POSDCORB:

*P*lanning
*O*rganising
*S*taffing
*D*irecting
*C*oordinating
*R*eporting
*B*udgeting

Various other functions could be generated; for example, communication, motivation, training and counselling.[3]

Leadership involves working with others to get things done. Thus a person operating alone could not be a leader (except if that person was, say, a role-model for others). Managing, as the old definition goes, is getting things done through other people. A manager/leader does this by ordering the led or subordinates to do things, or else by delegating to the led or subordinates. Ordering someone to do something implies an autocratic style of leadership, where no independence of thought or action is granted to the subordinate. Delegating a task to someone implies a less autocratic style; to a lesser or greater extent, independence of thought and action is granted to the subordinates. It is an ancient maxim of management technique that *responsibility* is matched by an equal degree of *power* or *authority*. This symmetry of responsibility and power should be present in the delegator's job role as well as the delegatee's. A lack of such symmetry is a common cause of organisational ineffectiveness. Other "classical" features of leadership concern the concepts of chain of command, unity of command, and span of control (Fayol 1949; see also Chapter 13). *Chain of command* is most obvious in military hierarchies, where differentiation is by rank, but similar patterns occur in most work organisations: roles in the hierarchy are clearly spelt out, with each person having a clear power relationship with those above and below in the hierarchy. *Unity of command* means that an employee usually receives orders from and is responsible to only one leader/manager/supervisor. *Span of control* means that each leader should have a limited number of people reporting to her, according to the nature of the task and the abilities of the supervised and the supervisor.

The gap between theory and practice

The reality of leadership and followership does not always correspond to such tidy definitions, however. Span of control, for instance, is very hard to determine. Wide span means a "flat" organisation, while a narrow span

---

[3] Cf. the model used in Box 8.A (Time-Wasters) in Chapter 8: Planning, Organising, Directing, Controlling, Communicating, Decision-Making.

means a "tall" organisation; who can say which organisational design is the more efficient or desirable?

Similarly, chain of command and unity of command are violated when formal leaders, running the formal organisation, find that they are in competition with informal leaders running the informal organisation.

These latter two principles are also violated when organisations adopt fashionable designs such as matrix or project design, wherein subordinates report to two or more bosses—the permanent, hierarchical boss, and the temporary, project boss (see Chapter 13).

Delegation

Similar confusion surrounds the concept of delegation. Given the democratic values of many modern industrial countries, organisational leaders tend to emphasise delegation rather than give orders. Delegation is meant to free leaders to concentrate on other work, while at the same time training subordinates in problem-solving. Yet delegation is often misunderstood, and often badly done. There is not much consensus on *what* should be delegated, for example. Moore (1982) suggests that the following work *should* be delegated: duties related to the making of higher level decisions; duties of group responsibility; matters which a manager would like to have her subordinate consider and decide what should be done, but to check with her before doing it; matters of lesser importance in which the superior would want her subordinate to decide what to do and then go ahead and do it but to tell her what has been done; and finally, still lesser matters which the subordinate is to perform or redelegate to *her* subordinates to do.

Moore suggests that the following *should not* be delegated: ability to decide what subordinates' jobs are to be; power to set objectives, budgets; ability to make decisions which could cause large losses; matters which imply authority over people who do not work for the delegator/delegatee; responsibilities and authority without accountability; and, finally, ability to judge work and set pay rates (Table 10.1). An autocratic leader might disagree with Moore's model, and delegate nothing at all, believing her subordinates to be dangerously incompetent. A less autocratic leader might disagree for different reasons, allowing subordinates to set objectives, budgets and even pay scales. There is a strong argument for saying that once an organisation exceeds a certain size, delegation is no longer a luxury but a necessity. Thus, if leaders do not delegate downwards, then subordinates will delegate upwards. This paradox occurs when subordinates have not been trained to do tasks, are in fact kept in a state of child-like dependency. The type of leader who allows this to happen usually has an unrealistic view of subordinates' alleged incompetence, not to mention an unrealistic view of her own competence (and indeed, her indispensability). Leaders who play such psychological games are usually not very efficient, causing bottlenecks in decision-making. When they move on or die, their successors are not ready, and often do much damage (see Chapter 8).

It is difficult to determine the quantitative threshold beyond which reverse delegation becomes inevitable. Further, it is as difficult to determine *what* should be delegated as it is to determine how much should be delegated (to a considerable extent, these two problems are merely two sides of the one coin). To use Gulick and Urwick's model, how much of POSDCORB can or should be delegated? And at what point does delegation cease to be a distinction of degree and become a distinction of kind, that is, at what point

Table 10.1 What should and should not be delegated

Duties which superiors should delegate	Duties which superiors should not delegate
Work which *should* be delegated can be classified by the degree of supervision needed.	Normally, most of the delegated authority and the obligation to work toward end accomplishments received by middle-level managers is redelegated to their subordinates. But there is always a fraction of the incoming delegation which ought not to be redelegated downward. Every middle-level manager should always retain certain responsibilities. Managers *should not*:
1. *Duties related to the making of higher-level decisions.* These are participative kinds of duties (fact collection, expert advising, idea-interchange, etc.) which help the superior make better decisions and which build up subordinate empathy and morale.	1. *Let subordinates decide what their overall jobs are to be.* A subordinate's overall job is his mission and this he should accept as it is delegated to him. Usually a subordinate cannot know enough about the whole organisation's work to know just what he should do except as his superior tells him while at the same time calling his attention to the constraints within which he must operate.
2. *Duties of the group responsibility kind.* In a manufacturing company, these could include activities such as product-design decisions, where representatives from several departments get together and make decisions concerning matters in which their several departments have a common interest.	2. *Let subordinates have full power to set their own objectives nor their own budgets.* Their objectives need to contribute to organisational objectives and thus should be determined by higher level managers. Similarly, budgets allocate money which is part of the whole organisation's resource base.
3. *Matters which a manager would like to have his subordinate consider and to decide what he thinks should be done, but to check with him before doing it.* In a retail store, a special discount sale to move certain slow-moving items would be in this category. In a factory a decision by the superintendent to have the plant work ten-hour days during the next month would be in this category.	3. *Let subordinates make decisions which could cause large losses.* A common limit even for major department heads is that all projects requiring over $50 000 of the organisation's capital will have to be approved by the central office.
4. *Matters of lesser importance in which the superior would want his subordinate to decide what to do and then go ahead and do it but tell him what he has done.* Disciplinary actions when employees violate the organisation's rules would be in this category.	4. *Delegate matters which imply authority over people who do not work for him.* Subordinates in one chain of authority should not be put in the position of giving directions to people in chains of authority which do not belong to their superior.

Table 10.1 What should and should not be delegated (*continued*)

Duties which superiors should delegate	Duties which superiors should not delegate
5. *Still lesser matters which the subordinate is to perform himself or redelegate to his subordinates to do.* Such duties would include establishing priorities among work orders, deciding whether to give a customer credit for goods returned claimed to be defective, etc. Occasional summary reports to superiors will suffice for these duties.	5. *Delegate responsibilities and authority without holding the subordinate accountable.* He should not delegate and then fail to check up; he should not abdicate. Furthermore, every subordinate should have a superior who holds him accountable.
	6. *Let subordinates be the* final *judges of their own work, nor should they decide their own pay rates.* Probably everyone should judge his own accomplishments from time to time, but no one person's self-evaluation should be the final and total appraisal.

Source: Moore (1982), pp.338–40. Reproduced with permission.

does delegation become a transfer of total decision-making power, turning industrial autocracy into industrial democracy?

Before we can answer such questions, we need to know whether there are actual differences between leaders and led. Such differences, if they exist at all, will provide a legitimising basis for elite groups to POSDCORB the affairs of larger groups.

Trait theories of leadership

Throughout history, the trait or characteristics approach to identifying leaders has been the most popular. It is also called the "recipe", "shopping list" or "identikit" approach. Think of some leaders you know, or know of, in a variety of fields (sporting, political, business, etc.). What traits do they have? What is their physical appearance like, their social background, their intelligence, their personality? Are there any patterns of traits among some or all leaders? Table 10.2 lists some of the traits of leadership that social scientists have attempted to identify and correlate.

There is no unanimity on the value of the trait approach. Psychological social scientists have largely rejected this approach to leadership,[4] while sociologists remain committed to it. Sociologists have noted that socio-economic class can be crucial predictors of whether a person will be a leader, particularly in work situations. Hirszowicz (1981) has shown that, while it is easier to become a working-class manager in the United States than it is in Europe, there are still formidable obstacles. Democracies such as America and

---

[4] Of course, there may be *negative* traits. L'etaing (1980), in analysing neuroses and psychoses of various political and business leaders, has detected traits of authoritarianism and self-destructive workaholism among many successful and not-so-successful leaders.

Table 10.2 Some possible leadership traits

Physical fitness	Extroversion
Active, energetic approach	Assertiveness
Age	Self-confidence
Physical attractiveness	Tact, diplomacy
Tallness	Aggressiveness
Weight/muscle-fat distribution	Achievement drive
Socio-economic class	Drive for responsibility
Socio-economic mobility	Tolerance of stress
Intelligence quotient (IQ)	Ability to enlist cooperation
Creativity	Persistence
Decisiveness	
Verbal fluency	
Ethical conduct	

Source: Adapted from Albanese (1983), Hellriegel, Slocum and Woodman (1983), Szilagyi and Wallace (1983).

Australia sometimes seem to be places where class factors are non-existent, or at least if they are present, they are weak, and mobility between classes is so high it doesn't matter anyway. This impression, however, does not correspond with the facts. Edgar (1980) notes that class mobility in contemporary Australia is not high, and thus it is a mistake to think that status can be achieved by sheer individual effort or unique behavioural traits. This mistaken impression has arisen, Edgar suggests, because some researchers have presumed that a free market of opportunities prevailed (i.e. that mobility was high), and hence concentrated on attempting to measure individual characteristics of people in the workforce. Sociologists have also noted that sexual and ethnic factors are also important in predicting leadership behaviour. Thus, the majority of persons in management positions in countries such as Australia, America and Great Britain would be white, Anglo-Saxon middle-class males. While for some people this is a trivial observation, for others it is most interesting, if not a matter for concern. Mukhi (1982) studied 420 chief executives in the private and public sectors in Australia. He found that the person most likely to make it to the top of the corporate ladder had the following characteristics:

- male
- attended a so-called GPS (Greater Public School)
- completed a university degree in finance/accounting subjects
- gained most experience in finance/accounting areas
- was given responsibility early in career
- worked for 3.5 organisations on average
- held 8.7 jobs on average
- was in a senior management position by age of 33
- was in top job by age 40
- possessed key personal characteristics.

These key personal characteristics included such things as technical competence, training, experience, hard work, dedication, luck/being in the right place at the right time, having imagination and a vision of the future, and being able to get on with people. There are a number of problems associated with such characteristics. First, they are self-attributed, that is, the managers surveyed believed they had them, and, second, they believed they were significant in getting them into their current positions. Neither of these sets of beliefs is self-evidently correct. Such traits may be useful, even necessary, but there are no guarantees that they will be sufficient for success.

Problems of causality, method

These problems are typical of psychological trait theories of leadership. One may or may not have a set of traits, and these traits may or may not be useful in gaining a particular end. Two people with widely different sets of traits may perform equally well in the same job. A person may be a leader in one set of circumstances, but not in another. Ribeaux and Poppleton (1978) rightly point out that the leadership prospects of an unintelligent, working-class unreliable recluse are slim, whereas those of an intelligent, reliable, socially adept member of the middle class are much better. Yet, throughout history, working-class recluses have made fine religious leaders, inventors, entre- preneurs, artists, musicians, sportsmen and heroes. Even apparently negative traits can be a recipe for success and leadership: a politician may be inarticulate, physically unattractive, and not intelligent, or at least not intellectually so, yet may be followed by many people, not because she is so *unlike* them, but because she is so *like* them.

Also, what of the problem of luck, or being in the right place at the right time? Is luck a trait? Can it be measured? Can it be acquired? Such things seem unlikely, yet luck is an important fact for all that. As Talleyrand remarked, "In a novel, the author gives the leading character intelligence and distinction. Fate goes to less trouble: mediocrities play a part in great events simply from happening to be there".[5]

Such problems with trait theory are often aggravated by serious methodo- logical weaknesses in the approaches used by social scientists. Thus, researchers have presumed that traits which they have had some success in measuring (stability, anxiety, achievement, dependency, etc.) are valid indicators of leadership ability; this remains a hope, not a fact (Hellriegel, Slocum and Woodman 1983). Also, social science studies are sometimes biased because social scientists, many of whom are academics, often study the behaviour of the most convenient group of people to hand, tertiary students. Given that Psychology I or MBA students may not be a typical sample of the entire population of a nation, the results are accordingly biased. Other biases are sometimes introduced by the values of the social scientists sampling the student group. Such biases are apparent in leadership research: because of the students' characteristics and/or because of the researchers' values, intellectual and social traits are often given emphasis, while "undesirable" power-orientation or Machiavellian traits are not given enough emphasis (Lee 1980). Mention has already been made of more psychologically inclined social scientists who discount the effect of socio- economic traits upon leadership, choosing instead to concentrate on positive behavioural traits.

Trait theory also revives and perhaps distorts the heredity/environment controversy. Are leaders born or made? Adair (1983) suggests that trait theory pre-empts the discussion by strongly suggesting that leaders are born; consequently emphasis is placed on selection of leaders, rather than training of leaders. Yet, Adair notes, even those who give lip service to the "born leader" syndrome get muddled, as with the British manager who observed that "Smith is not a born leader yet".

Because of such weaknesses, trait theories of leadership have largely been abandoned by psychologists and management theorists, who have developed

[5] Shakespeare was more charitable on the question of luck and success: "Be not afraid of greatness: some are born great, some achieve greatness, and some have greatness thrust upon them." Interestingly, Mukhi (1982) found that public sector managers rated luck significantly higher than private sector managers as a factor of success.

other models of leadership which we will now consider. Nevertheless, as Byrt notes (1980), trait theory, while being dead, refuses to lie down: it is still held in good regard by "so-called practical men" in management, politics, the public service and the military.

Styles of leadership

Faced with the fact that analysis of behavioural traits could not predict leadership behaviour, some social scientists began to consider differing *styles* of leadership. Generally speaking, two major schools of thought began to emerge: those who believed that there is one best style of leadership, and those who believed that the "best" style of leadership varies with the unique factors, or contingencies, of each situation. Those in the "one best style" camp include Douglas McGregor, Rensis Likert, Robert Blake and Jane Srygley Mouton. Those belonging to the "situationalist" or "contingency" camp include Fred Fiedler, Paul Hersey, Kenneth Blanchard, Robert Tannenbaum and Warren Schmidt. It should be noted that most of these post-traitists argue that leaders can be made, and that they are not necessarily born.[6] Leaders can be trained to achieve a particular style, or styles, just as they can be trained in the various POSDCORB skills enumerated by Gulick and Urwick. The questions that therefore logically emerge from such developments are:

1. what is it that distinguishes leaders from led, managers from managed? and
2. if there are no differences, why should some people be trained to lead but not others?

Throughout most contemporary leadership studies, there is a deafening silence on these questions.

McGregor's theory X and theory Y

Douglas McGregor's concept of theory X and theory Y (McGregor 1960) has been a seminal one in analysis of leadership styles, as well as patterns of motivation and organisational design (see Chapters 2, 13 and 14).

A person holding a theory X view of human nature believes that people do not really like to work, cannot be trusted, are motivated only by money, do not want to participate in decision-making, and need to be told what to do. A person believing in the theory Y view of human nature, by contrast, believes that people can get genuine enjoyment from working, can be trusted, are motivated more by the intrinsic satisfactions of a job, do want to participate in decision-making, and can operate autonomously to effectively achieve the goals of their organisation, that is, they do not have to be ordered about. A theory Y leader will involve subordinates as much as possible in decision-making. Her style will be participative, rather than authoritarian.

---

[6] Cf. Martin's sardonic view:

... in recent years there have been very few enthusiastic supporters of the "superior traits" school. For one thing, the correlation of specific personality traits with managerial success has been tested, and no consistent correlation has been found. A generally accepted view is that, regardless of personal characteristics, managers' chances for success will be enhanced by periodic education or training in some specific or technical aspects of managerial work, or by an updated overview of the field of management. Typically, those who are instructing or consulting emphasize a number of contingency or situational factors, only one of which might be the individual manager's personal characteristics. (With this perspective in mind, the belief that managers must possess certain innate qualities was very likely doomed to early extinction, not only because of lack of evidence to support such a belief, but also because of its potential for diminishing the need for schools of management, for management training, and for the services of management consultants. (MARTIN 1983, PP25-6)

As Byrt (1980) observes, theory X and theory Y are basically pessimistic and optimistic views about human nature. Thus, one's philosophy will determine one's leadership style. Using Maslow's concept of the hierarchy of needs (see Chapter 2), McGregor argued that theory X was an inferior management philosophy because it depended upon a crude reward–punishment psychology and kept workers trapped at the lower levels of the hierarchy, that is, physiological and safety needs. Deprived of any fulfilment of higher social and egoistic needs, workers would then become sullen and withdrawn, making insistent demands for more money (if only to buy material goods and services which can provide limited satisfaction of the thwarted upper needs). Thus theory X was in fact counter-productive because it resulted in lower productivity and greater demands for wage increases. McGregor's concepts have been central to the growth of the "human relations" school of management. Together with other members of that school, he has been criticised by the left for implying that legitimate wage demands were signs of psychological illness among workers,[7] and by the right for seeming to imply that money motivation and competitiveness were not important (and indeed, natural) human values.[8]

Likert's system 4

Rensis Likert (1961, 1967, 1976) has attempted to isolate four basic styles of leadership, the difference being primarily the degree of participation the leader seeks from subordinates (Table 10.3). The four styles are exploitive–authoritative, benevolent–authoritative, consultative and participative, which Likert also terms system 1, system 2, system 3 and system 4, respectively. Likert claims that extensive research has demonstrated that system 4 is the one best style in terms of achieving certain organisational outputs, such as maximisation of productivity, minimisation of scrap loss, minimisation of labour turnover and maximisation of product quality.

Likert stresses that leadership style and organisational design do not *directly* cause these outputs to occur. He distinguishes between *causal variables* (capital, investments, leadership behaviour, organisational structures, etc.), *intervening variables* (personalities, perceptions, attitudes, motivational forces and behaviour) and *end-result variables* (production, cost, waste, industrial relations, profit, etc.). Thus, a system 1 style (exploitive–authoritative) may, in the short run, achieve positive outputs, or end-use variables, but great damage will be done to the intervening variables, which, with various time-lags, will begin to cause damage to the organisation.

The system 4 manager, by contrast, says Likert, eventually produces the right outputs because she does not have to appeal to raw authority in telling people what to do, but instead enlists the aid of all individuals and groups (including informal groups) in making good, broad-based decisions.

---

[7] For example, see Carey (1980). Carey notes that the idea of psychological needs well pre-dates Maslow and McGregor, going back to the work of Mayo in the 1930s; thus Carey quotes the editor of the US magazine *Fortune* writing in 1950:

> What does the worker really want? . . . More than anything else, Elton Mayo and those who have followed him, have pointed out, he wants . . . the psychological security that comes from good work, the recognition of it and the esprit de corps of the group about him . . . Is the top executive the same man? . . . (H)e has different motivations . . . more than the worker he thinks in terms . . . of economic incentives . . . He is, in short, a different man.

[8] For example, Machovec and Smith (1982) argue that authoritarianism and a preference for hierarchical and territorial behaviour, not to mention selfishness and aggression, are biologically rooted traits in all of us; thus Theory Y type cooperativeness would be "unnatural".

Table 10.3 Organisational and performance characteristics of different management systems

	System of organisation			
Operating characteristics	Authoritative		Participative	
	Exploitive–authoritative	Benevolent–authoritative	Consultative	Participative group
Organisation variable	System 1	System 2	System 3	System 4
Leadership processes used Extent to which superiors have confidence and trust in subordinates	Have no confidence and trust in subordinates	Have condescending confidence and trust such as master has to servant	Substantial but not complete confidence and trust, still wishes to keep control of decisions	Complete confidence and trust in all matters
Extent to which superiors behave so that subordinates feel free to discuss important things about their jobs with their immediate superior	Fear, threats, punishment, and occasional rewards	Rewards and some actual or potential punishment	Rewards, occasional punishment and some involvement	Economic rewards based on compensation system developed through participation, group participation and involvement in setting goals, improving methods appraising progress towards goals, etc.
Extent to which immediate superior in solving job problems generally tries to get subordinates' ideas and opinions and make constructive use of them	Little interaction and always with fear and distrust	Little interaction and usually with some condescension by superiors; fear and caution by subordinates	Moderate interaction often with fair amount of confidence and trust	Extensive, friendly interaction with high degree of confidence and trust

Source: Likert (1967), p.4. Reproduced with permission.

Obviously, Likert's system 1 and system 4 bear a close resemblance to McGregor's theory X and theory Y.

Likert has suggested that leaders are also followers at other levels of the hierarchy. Thus the leader or manager should be seen as a person having at least two roles, as being in fact a *linking pin* between two work groups. Likert has gone on to suggest that work groups should overlap not only vertically, but horizontally as well. This leads him to advocate more flexible organisational designs such as matrix or project designs, where it is not uncommon for subordinates to have more than one boss. In fact leadership behaviour may well become so generalised in system 4 that the phenomenon of "peer leadership" emerges, where people lead or influence others in the same horizontal stratum of the organisation. Likert has also posited a system 5, where hierarchical relations will virtually disappear, and the organisation will be a fluid constellation of interlocking groups.

The best style of leadership?

Does it work? Likert has suggested that any organisation adopting a system 4 approach can look forward to a 20–40 per cent increase in its final outputs. Miner (1982) argues that the evidence does not support this assertion. Much of the research data is self-referenced (i.e. members of an organisation undergoing an attempted shift to system 4 fill out questionnaires based on system 1 to system 4 continuums). Miner suggests that such data is problematic. It would be better to have outside observers diagnose the organisation's ills, concentrating specifically on quantified outputs. Miner also suggests that there can be no guarantee that informal groups can be harnessed to achieve the organisation's objectives, or that new and potentially deviant informal groups will not spring up in the new participative atmosphere. He also points out that, paradoxically, increased participation can open up the "fast track" to expert and competent individuals from the lower levels of the hierarchy, who then receive greater training and information; the hierarchical structure is thus strengthened, not weakened.

Blake and Mouton's managerial grid®

Blake and Mouton (1982, 1985) have analysed leadership style in terms of two variables: concern for production and concern for people. These variables become axes on a grid, with each axis having nine points; the grid is thus composed of $9 \times 9 = 81$ different sections (Fig. 10.1). Blake and Mouton distinguish five major styles of management, designated by their coordinates:

- 1,1 impoverished management
- 1,9 country club management
- 5,5 organisation man management
- 9,1 authority–obedience type management
- 9,9 team management

The first four styles presuppose a fundamental conflict between having concern for people and having concern for production; the final style, 9,9 does not presume such a conflict.

The 1,1 manager is virtually retired on the job. If the organisation were a military unit, she would be a deserter. The 1,1 manager exerts herself only to the extent that she avoids being fired. She tells subordinates "don't come to me with your problems"; in response to questions about policy or

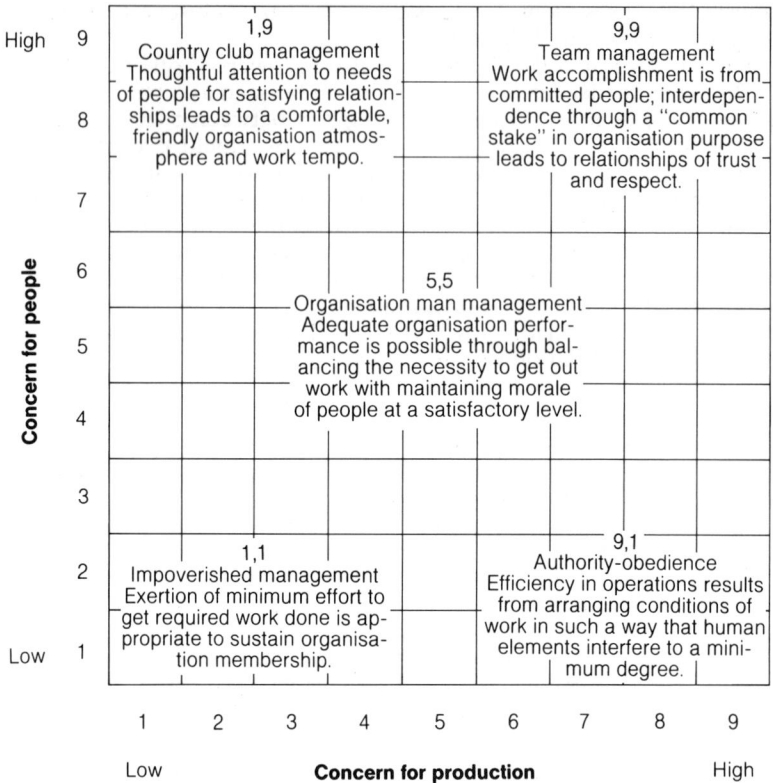

Fig 10.1 *The managerial grid* ® (BLAKE AND MOUTON 1985, P.12. REPRODUCED WITH PERMISSION)

decision-making, she will reply, "don't ask me, I only work here"; she avoids conflict by telling herself and others, "don't get involved".

The 1,9 manager has much more concern for people, but precious little concern for production: the organisation is run like a country club, run for the benefit of its employees/club managers, rather than customers, clientele, shareholders and owners. Her attitude to production and people is "laissez-faire"—let things work out for themselves. The 1,9 manager may not be very successful because subordinates may see her as "soft" and hence her caring attitudes can be exploited. If productivity declines, other managers may deduce that "that's what you get for trying to understand people with a human relations approach".

The 5,5 manager is the organisation man/woman: dedicated to the organisation's goals, but often very timid about reconciling what seems to be the conflicting demands of concern for production and concern for people. The name of the game for this manager is "compromise", so that a safe, middle-of-the-road existence can be pursued.

The 9,1 manager seeks the task as being all-important; people are just like machines, except they have soft skins, don't work 24 hours a day and talk back when they should shut up and get on with the job. The authority–

Table 10.4 "One best style" approaches to leadership compared

Analyst(s)	High concern for production, low concern for people (low emphasis on participation)	High concern for production, high concern for people (high emphasis on participation)
McGregor	Theory X	Theory Y
Likert	System 1	System 4
Blake and Mouton	9,1	9,9

obedience manager will take any suggestions from subordinates as personal criticism and will attempt to suppress (not solve) conflict by coercion. Such a person believes that people are to be controlled, and control is simply a matter of applying the requisite carrots (rewards) and sticks (punishments) in the right places.

The 9,9 manager operates as leader of a team. She enlists the aid of subordinates in fulfilling the objectives of the organisation; goals are mutually set. Subordinates participate intimately in the decision-making process. No real conflict is perceived by a 9,9 manager between concern for people and concern for production—it is not a case of "either-or" but "both-and". When interpersonal conflicts arise, they are treated openly and with sympathy.

These five styles are "ideal types", that is, they are rarely seen in reality. Instead, it is more likely that someone will have a 7,3 style or 5,7 style, and so on. Blake and Mouton have also found that managers tend to have a main style, and a second or backup style. Sometimes this backup style is their actual style, while their "main" style is in fact how they would like to be.

The grid approach to leadership is an extremely popular one. It is a simple concept, very visual, and provides a handy shorthand for analysing leadership and organisational problems. To a certain extent, however, its strength is its weakness, and the approach has been criticised for over-simplifying complex problems.[9] This approach has fundamental similarities to the other "one best style" approaches to leadership. The three approaches use different language to describe similar phenomena. The correspondences are noted in Table 10.4.

"It all depends": The contingency view

The "one best style" approaches to leadership have been criticised on the grounds that they oversimplify the situation. Some writers have argued that leader behaviour is only one variable to be considered, there being at least two others: follower or non-leader behaviour, and the situation in which leaders and followers find themselves. The unique properties, or contingencies, of the situation, need particular emphasis. This is not to presume that the contingency theories of leadership are therefore more advanced and sophisticated than the "one best style" theories. Likert and Blake and

---

[9] Thus Anthony (1977), after giving an exposition of the grid's approach, concludes:

> The reader might well have concluded by now that managers would be better (and more cheaply) employed studying the entrails of chickens and he might also have entertained the passing thought that we were all wasting our time on such ponderous nonsense... It would take a considerable programme of research to validate the hypothesis that all "behavioural science" management teaching is rubbish, so we shall have to content ourselves with the unproved assertion that most of it seems to be so. (p44)

Mouton, for example, have staged a counterattack, arguing that the contingency theories are over-complex and not very useful. Let us have a look at some of these contingency theories, keeping in mind that a contingency theorist, asked about the "best" leadership style or organisational design, may well respond by saying "it all depends. . ."

Tannenbaum and Schmidt: A continuum of leadership

Tannenbaum and Schmidt (1958, 1973) developed a continuum of leadership behaviour (Fig. 10.2). The continuum ranges from an authoritarian style to a participatory style: the upper triangle indicates the area of freedom for the leader or manager, while the lower triangle indicates the area of freedom for the followers or non-managers. The optimal mix of decision-making depends upon three factors: leader behaviour, follower behaviour and the situation.

The leader's behaviour depends upon a number of factors, such as her personal value system, her confidence in her subordinates, and ability to take risks and tolerate ambiguity. A leader might have, for example, a theory X or theory Y value system, and this will determine the extent to which participation will be allowed. The extent to which a leader does or does not have confidence in the ability and/or training of her subordinates will determine the extent to which she is willing to delegate. This may be further modified by her willingness to risk giving autonomy by relinquishing control. By doing this, she of course increases the level of ambiguity in the situation, and she may or may not be able to tolerate this.

The followers' behaviour is also critical. Thus, if a leader wishes to increase participation, it will probably only work if the followers also desire such an outcome. This will depend upon such factors as the willingness of followers to make decisions, the ability to make decisions, a commitment to the goals of the organisation, and a tolerance for the ambiguity of a participative situation.

The situation is the final factor to be taken into account. Job design and organisational design may inhibit or permit less or more participative leadership. Thus, an organisation may exhibit a theory X or theory Y value system, may be more or less organic or mechanistic (see Chapters 12 and 13).

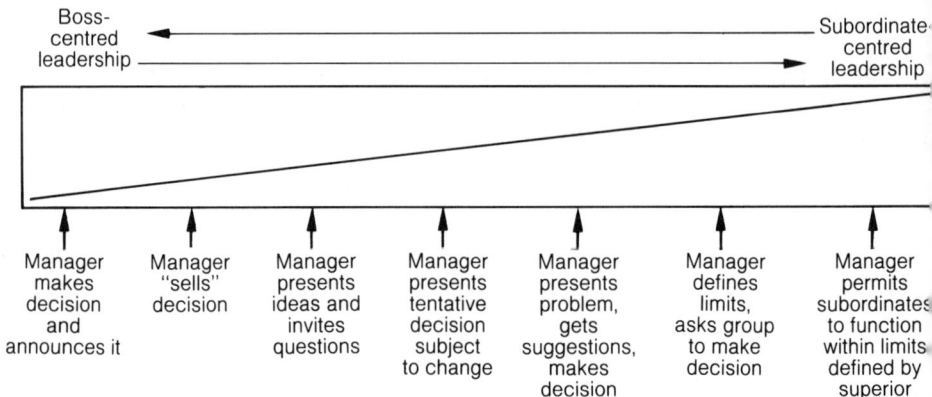

Boss-centred leadership						Subordinate-centred leadership
Manager makes decision and announces it	Manager "sells" decision	Manager presents ideas and invites questions	Manager presents tentative decision subject to change	Manager presents problem, gets suggestions, makes decision	Manager defines limits, asks group to make decision	Manager permits subordinates to function within limits defined by superior

Fig 10.2 *A continuum of leadership behaviour* (TANNENBAUM, WECHSLER AND MASSARIK 1961, P.69. REPRODUCED WITH PERMISSION)

Factors such as a need to maintain confidentiality on certain matters may inhibit a leader's ability to make decision-making (and hence information) accessible to more people. As the world gets more complex, the environment in which the organisation operates may become less predictable or placid, and may become more unpredictable or turbulent. This may lead to more crisis decision-making, where time for consultation and shared decision-making may not be available.[10]

Tannenbaum and Schmidt suggest that only when these three factors are taken into account is it possible to understand the range of leadership behaviour possible. Thus, even though a leader may wish to be more or less participative, follower behaviour and the structures of the organisation may not allow it. Followers may wish to see a more or less participative style from their leader, but her behaviour may not permit this, and the structure may also be against it (or for it). Top management may wish to see more or less participative management at middle levels, but middle manager behaviour and subordinate behaviour may or may not make it possible.

Tannenbaum and Schmidt thus suggest that there is no "right" or "wrong" leadership style—it all depends. They have acknowledged, however, that the contingency approach has a number of weaknesses. For example, some managers have used the continuum model to justify the status quo of their own and others' styles, so that nothing needs to change. Also, Tannenbaum and Schmidt acknowledge that their analysis is weak on the question of power, particularly countervailing power of trade unions and various individuals and groups who can inhibit the leader's use of power (Tannenbaum and Schmidt 1973; O'Shaughnessey 1979).

Fiedler's model of leadership

Fiedler's contingency model of leadership is still more complex. It considers concepts such as task-oriented and relationship-oriented styles of leadership, as well as leader–group relationships, but it also considers power and the structure of the task to be performed. Fiedler attempts to define leadership task–relationship style using a questionnaire which measures the LPC (least preferred co-worker) score. If you were doing this questionnaire, you would be required to think of all the people with whom you had ever worked, and then think of the person with whom you could work *least well*. (This does not necessarily mean the person whom you *liked least*.) The questionnaire is structured along various continuums: rejecting/accepting, tense/relaxed, insincere/sincere. If you think very badly of the person you have in mind, you will end up with a low LPC score and, accordingly to Fiedler, will tend to be task-motivated. If you don't think very badly of the person, you will end up with a high LPC score, and will be classified as a relationship-motivated person (Fiedler *et al.* 1977).

Three other variables or contingencies need to be measured: leader–member relations, task structure and leader position power. *Leader–member relations* are measured when the work-group is asked to express whether they accept or endorse their leader. Relations are then defined simply as being "bad" or "good". *Task structure* is determined by ascertaining whether goals are clear, whether there is only one way to accomplish the task, whether there is only one correct solution to the problem being worked at, and whether it is easy to check on whether the job has been done correctly.

---

[10] Or perceived to be not available: see Chapter 8.

If the answers to these questions is "yes", then the task is presumed to be structured, rather than unstructured. Thus, putting fruit in cans on an assembly line is very structured, while working in a research laboratory with only a vague deadline on the immediate task is very unstructured. Finally, *leader position power* is ascertained by checking to see whether the leader can evaluate or appraise the performance of subordinates, whether the leader can directly administer rewards and punishments, and so on. If these things can be done, the leader is presumed to have strong position power. If the leader cannot do such things, the leader is presumed to have weak position power.

Fiedler conducted research on these four variables—LPC, leader–group relations, task structure and leader position power—and detected relationships that suggest which leadership style is appropriate in which situation (Fig. 10.3). Thus, in octants 1, 2, 3 and 8, task-oriented leadership is appropriate, but in octants 4, 5, 6 and 7, relationship-oriented leadership is appropriate. Hersey and Blanchard (1977) have noted that the best possible situation for a leader would be that of a well-liked general inspecting an army camp (good leader–member relations, high position power, and high task structure), whereas the worst possible situation would be that of an unpopular chairman of a voluntary hospital fund-raising committee (poor leader–member relations, weak position power, and low task structure).

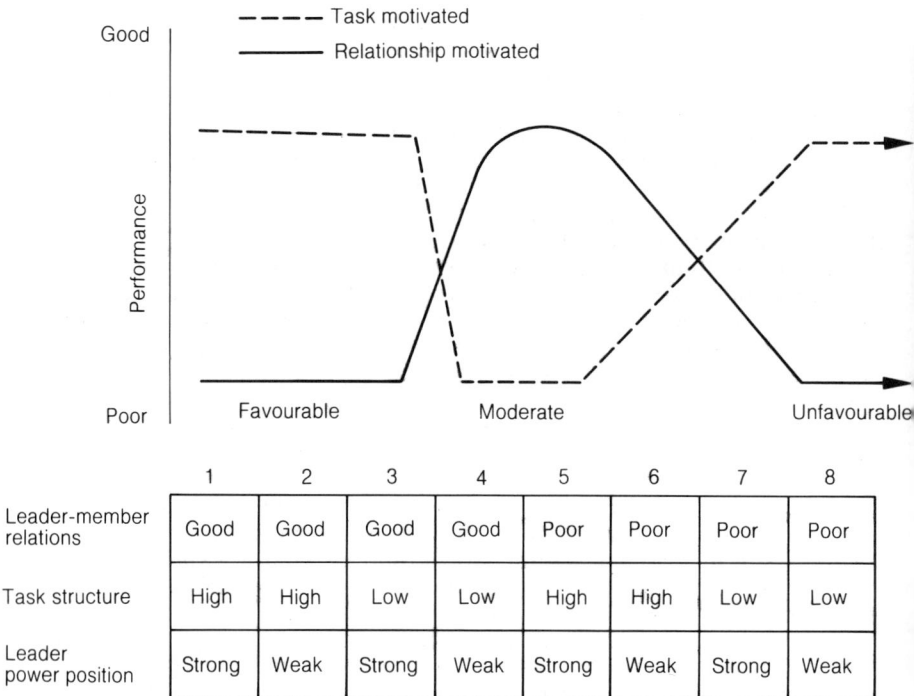

	1	2	3	4	5	6	7	8
Leader-member relations	Good	Good	Good	Good	Poor	Poor	Poor	Poor
Task structure	High	High	Low	Low	High	High	Low	Low
Leader power position	Strong	Weak	Strong	Weak	Strong	Weak	Strong	Weak

Fig 10.3 *Fiedler's model of leadership* (FIEDLER 1976, P.11. REPRINTED BY PERMISSION OF THE PUBLISHER. ALL RIGHTS RESERVED.)

Fiedler believes that leadership style is largely innate, but that virtually anyone can become a leader if that person chooses the situation carefully. Similarly, a successful leader in one situation may be quite unsuccessful in another situation. It all depends. . .

How good is Fiedler's theory? Sadly, although it has been well researched, and *seems* to be a flexible and predictive model, it has a number of critical weaknesses. Some of these are:

1. The LPC score does not always predict task/relationship orientation (Singh 1983). There are significant statistical weaknesses in the scoring (Lee 1980). Also, a person may have a real sociopath in mind when thinking about their least preferred co-worker, and otherwise be a highly relationship-oriented leader. Lee scathingly notes that while Fiedler's model is the most researched of all, it is about as useful as correlations between heights and weights of many samples of people (where a rubber ruler was used to measure the heights) (Lee 1980).
2. It is impossible to compare group/task situations in order to discover precisely where on the continuum each new situation lies. Thus a leader entering a new situation is unable to know in advance which style of leadership is most suitable (Ribeaux and Poppleton 1978).
3. Groups are commonly involved in tasks of varying degree of structure at any one time.

Hersey and Blanchard's situational leadership model

Hersey and Blanchard have developed a model of leadership that superficially appears to be quite similar to Blake and Mouton's managerial grid. Thus, the Hersey and Blanchard model features a matrix or grid of four quadrants, whose axes are "relationship behaviour" and "task behaviour" (Fig. 10.4). The difference is that Hersey and Blanchard see leadership effectiveness increasing along a bell-shaped curve which proceeds in a counter-clockwise fashion. The practical outcome of this is that they see the low-relationship/ low-task style as being *most* desirable, while for Blake and Mouton, this is a 1,1 style, or the *least* desirable style. This is because Hersey and Blanchard add to their quadrant model a continuum of follower behaviour, measuring follower "maturity". As the followers become more mature or competent, there is less need for a leader to be around, and greater opportunity for the leader to delegate and encourage participation. Hersey and Blanchard identify the four styles of leadership thus:

Style 1 (S1): Telling (high task, low relationship)
Style 2 (S2): Selling (high task, high relationship)
Style 3 (S3): Participating (low task, high relationship)
Style 4 (S4): Delegating (low task, low relationship)

Maturity is defined as being the capacity to set high but attainable goals, willingness and ability to take responsibility, and the education and/or experience of an individual or a group.

It should be noted that while S4 (low task, low relationship) is most desirable in the long run, each style is "right", according to the appropriate maturity levels of employees. Hersey and Blanchard suggest that increasing education and affluence is moving the maturity levels of employees to the left all the time, and that therefore there may be a need to move away from S1 and S2. They also point out that in training any person new on the job, S1 is the most appropriate style to start with, only moving on to other styles as the competence of the new employee increases. They recommend that

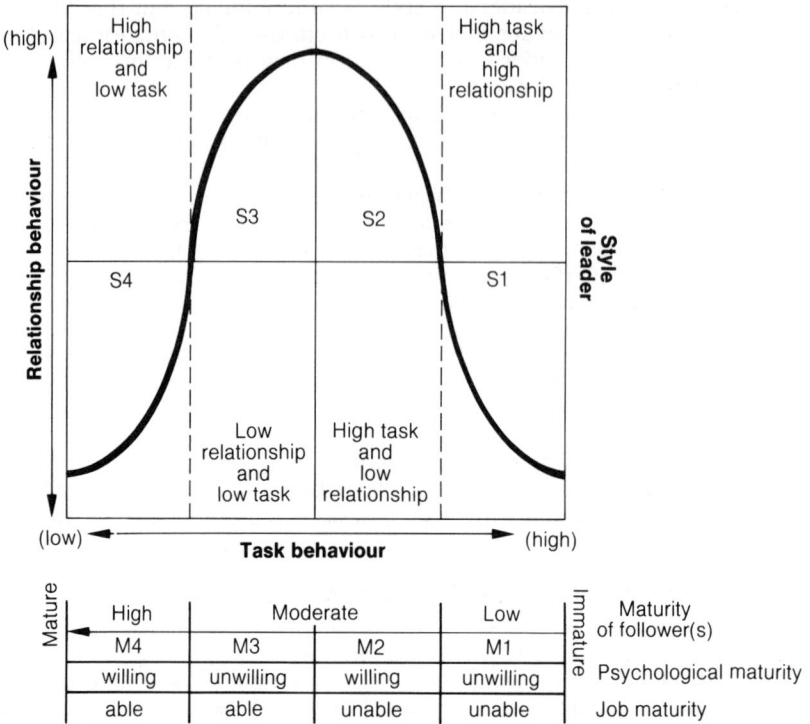

(high)

High relationship and low task		High task and high relationship

Relationship behaviour

S3   S2

S4   S1

Style of leader

| | Low relationship and low task | High task and low relationship | |

(low) ◄─────── **Task behaviour** ───────► (high)

Mature				Immature	
	High	Moderate		Low		Maturity of follower(s)
	M4	M3	M2	M1		
	willing	unwilling	willing	unwilling		Psychological maturity
	able	able	unable	unable		Job maturity

Fig 10.4 *Hersey and Blanchard's situational leadership model* (HERSEY, BLANCHARD AND HAMBLETON 1978, P.102. REPRODUCED WITH PERMISSION.)

leaders or managers can accelerate the maturity levels of followers or employees by using behaviour modification techniques such as positive reinforcement (see Chapter 3).

The Hersey and Blanchard model has been criticised by Blake and Mouton (1982) and Beck (1982) for representing a mechanistic and manipulative approach to leadership, particularly in its use of behaviour modification. Thus, Blake and Mouton suggest that a leader who uses an S1 style with an M1 employee (e.g. a trainee) will simply and impersonally tell the employee what, when, where and how, using behaviour modification techniques to control the employee. Blake and Mouton argue that this is manipulative and counter-productive; they suggest that a 9,9 manager would train an employee by using a warm, patient, question-and-answer technique which lets the employee solve problems herself, irrespective of maturity level. There is also a problem with the concept of "maturity". If it is simply a matter of familiarity with techniques, then defining maturity is no problem. Yet it is obvious that Hersey and Blanchard define it differently and more broadly. That may be the concept's simultaneous strength and weakness.

The problem of participation

Which approach to leadership is better, the contingency approach or the "one best style" approach? Hersey and Blanchard (1982) have suggested that there is a clear distinction between their situational leadership model and models such as the managerial grid. They suggest that the grid measures attitudes only, but what really counts is not words but deeds, or behaviour, and that is what their model measures. Blake and Mouton (1982) rebut this by saying that a person's behaviour can be predicted by what a person thinks, and hence there is no real conflict between attitudes and behaviour.

The great weakness of the "one best style" approach seems to be that it cannot cope with the widely different range of variables that occur in various organisations. These can be variables of leader–group relationships, task structure, power, follower behaviour, job design and organisational design.

The great weakness of contingency theory seems to be, not that it is too simple, but that it is too complex. Thus, the leader trying to behave contingently within the work situation may be faced with problems similar to those experienced by a teacher trying to teach "differentially" in the classroom, that is, behave according to the needs of the clients. The clients, whether employees or students, may perceive variations in approach not as an indication of subtlety, sensitivity and flexibility, but inconsistency, unpredictability and favouritism/victimisation.

Both schools of thought heavily emphasise "participation". Yet there are many problems with the way they treat this concept. For participation in any decision-making process is basically about the sharing of *power*. Fiedler, as we have seen, is the only researcher among those we have considered who incorporates the notion of power into his analysis of leadership (although Tannenbaum and Schmidt came to realise that their analysis was lacking because it did not consider the power of the leader vis-à-vis the power of unions and individuals and groups). The authors of *Work in America*, an influential study of participative management techniques and job redesign experiments, expressed the worry that workers will feel that participative management is merely a "refined Tayloristic technique for improving productivity at their expense" (Kerr and Rosow 1973). Grzyb (1981) suggests that Kerr and Rosow *should* worry, because, as he sees it, participative management and job redesign *are* manipulative, never really delivering what they seem to promise, power-sharing. Even one of the main apostles of job enrichment, Herzberg, has said that "the authoritarian character of American industry will continue despite the propaganda for a more democratic way of life" and has warned against participation, because there is no telling where it will lead (Nichols 1980).[11]

Leadership and culture

It is notable that all the theories of leadership we have been considering are American in origin. Might it be that some of the problems intrinsic to leadership theory, particularly relating to the concepts of participation and power, flow from American culture? Is it an accident that when participation theories are considered (see Chapter 14), American management theorists seem to stress participative *management* (i.e. a top–down flow of power)

---

[11] Lansbury and Spillane note that management training in Australia has been dominated by ideas about leadership style for two decades, in spite of the fact that research has not been able to demonstrate strong relations between management style, organisational effectiveness and employee satisfaction. They suggest that the popularity of such "fads and fashions" such as leadership style packages is partly attributable to "the fact that attention is directed towards a human relations view of organisational life rather than towards the need to change production methods, redistribute power and devolve authority" (Lansbury and Spillane, 1983, p.70). For Australian data on leadership styles, see Barry and Dowling (1984), and Messinesi (1983).

while European and Australian theorists give more attention (or at least relatively more attention) to *worker* participation (i.e. a bottom–up flow of power)? It is terribly difficult (not to say dangerous) to generalise about cultures, but given that the vast majority of theories we are considering in this book are American, perhaps it is more dangerous not to at least try (see Chapter 2).

Table 10.5 shows an approach to understanding the cultural contexts of leadership styles. The Australian context obviously shares characteristics of both European and American contexts. The political tradition of leadership in European countries is bound up with hierarchical systems such as monarchies. Although such systems are thin on the ground today, stratification by socio-economic class is still quite visible in most countries. America, by contrast, emerged as an independent nation in opposition to authoritarian government, developing a democratic form of government, in which legislative checks and balances were built in to ensure a pluralistic balance of socio-economic interests (although the Presidency was designed as a type of republican monarchy; see Zinn 1980).

These historical differences bred fundamentally different attitudes to power. The European class system, together with the rise of workers' movements and the doctrine of socialism, meant that Europeans had a clear and open debate about who was going to get what power. Americans, by contrast, says McClelland (1970, 1976), because of their traditional suspicion of authoritarian leadership, have an "anti-leadership vaccine" running in their veins, the practical upshots of which are that Americans are suspicious of politicians and are ambivalent about exercising power in organisational settings because socio-political values emphasise democracy and equality, whereas hierarchical organisations by definition depend upon unequal relationships. Thus it sometimes occurs in countries with traditions of egalitarian rhetoric (such as the US and Australia) that workers are ambivalent about being promoted up hierarchies, because it will mean leaving buddies and mates behind (see Chapter 2).

The role of the individual in America, or at least the rhetoric surrounding the role of the individual in America, has been that the individual is not

Table 10.5 Cultural contexts of leadership styles

	American system	*European system*
Political tradition of leadership	democratic checks and balances	class/hierarchical
Attitudes towards wielding of power	ambivalent	open conflict
Role of individual	individualist ("classless")	individualist within class
Economic tradition	open-market capitalism	mercantilist, mixed economy
Industrial relations environment	low union membership collective bargaining	high union membership arbitration/conciliation mechanisms government presence
Myth of leadership	emphasis on democratic, participative management	emphasis on more autocratic management
Contradictory reality	silent on sharing of power/money	sharing of power/money openly considered

fettered by class constraints as in Europe: America is the "land of opportunity", where individuals are "free to choose" either to make a million or make a mess (Friedman 1978).

The economic traditions in Europe have always involved a large degree of government intervention, from the mercantilist governments of the sixteenth century to the welfare state mixed economies of today. The United States, by contrast, has always extolled the rhetoric of free market capitalism, unconstrained by strong centralist government control. The industrial relations environment of the United States has been characterised by low union membership in the workforce, while conflicts between capital and labour are usually solved by collective bargaining. In Europe, by contrast, membership of unions is considerably higher, and governments usually play a more dominant role in the reconciliation of conflicts between labour and capital (e.g. by establishing conciliation and arbitration mechanisms, and industrial relations legislation; Lansbury 1980).[12]

It is with these factors in mind that myths of leadership (at least as they pertain to organisational micropolitics, rather than governmental macropolitics) can be considered. American management theorists, as we have seen, continuously espouse the virtues of participative or democratic management. A number of European countries seem more at home with an authoritarian myth of leadership, emphasising the prerogatives of management (Byrt 1980; Marchington and Loveridge 1979). Yet, the reality seems to contradict the myth. The lack of serious discussion of worker participation in much American managerial literature seems to confirm Herzberg's view of American organisational life. The hope expressed in *Work in America*—that participative management would "resolve a contradiction in our Nation, between democracy in society and authoritarianism in the workplace"—does not seem to be being fulfilled. Yet, within Europe, which has a longer tradition of authoritarian values, the more evenly balanced forces of labour and capital seems to have produced a more substantial debate about power-sharing, about just what is meant by "participation".

Much of this analysis, of course, verges on caricature, yet it is nonetheless important to tackle the question of "American exceptionalism" (Shalev and Korpi 1980) if we are to understand the cultural determinants of organisations and such phenomena as job design, motivation and leadership.

Obviously, the question of power needs further clarification. Let us attempt to do just that, looking now at four aspects of power: bases, styles, tactics and barriers to exercise of power.

Power
Bases

There are many definitions of power, all more or less satisfactory. Power is a relationship between two or more people whereby one person influences another person or persons. The wielder of power may even be able to make another person do something against his/her will. Nord defines power as "the ability to influence flows of the available energy and resources towards certain goals as opposed to other goals. Power is assumed to be exercised only when these goals are at least partially in conflict with each other" (Nord

---

[12] Cf. 1977 figures of union strength in various countries: Belgium/Luxembourg, 70 per cent; Italy, 53 per cent; Britain, 50 per cent; Holland, 43 per cent; Germany, 42 per cent; France, 23 per cent; USA, 27 per cent (Hirszowicz, 1981, p.188).

1978). Raven and French (1960) have attempted to classify five types or bases of power. These types or bases are legitimate power, reward power, coercive power, referent power and expert power. Possession of one or more of these power bases allows an influential person or power-wielder to exert some measure of control over a person or persons who do not possess one or more of these power bases.

Legitimate power is the power that comes from being in an authoritative position. This is the power wielded by village elders, police officers, military officers and elected officials, but it is also present in the micropolitics of organisations, when the boss is the boss *because* she is the boss. Obviously, the more hierarchical is the organisation, the more overt will be the legitimate power wielded by the boss. Barnard (1938) spoke of organisational managers operating within a *zone of indifference*, but not being able to operate outside it. Within that zone, the manager may ask a subordinate to do "normal" tasks, such as process forms or construct an appliance; within that zone, the subordinate accepts the legitimacy of the manager's power, and is indifferent to the exercise of that power. The subordinate understands what has to be done, she believes that the task is consistent with the purpose of the organisation. She believes that it is compatible with her own interests, and she is mentally and physically able to do the task. However, if the manager proceeds beyond that zone, asking the employee to do extra-ordinary things such as work late without pay, lie for the organisation, or grant sexual favours, then the employee will no longer be indifferent—the manager will have exceeded her legitimate power of authority. The reciprocal nature of power is evident here.

Reward power is fairly self-evident. A person has reward power if she is able to grant pay increases, improvements in conditions, give more responsibility and assign more interesting work. The other side of this coin is *coercive power*. A person has coercive power if she is able to punish, to instil fear. A manager may be able to dismiss, demote, cut salary, forcibly transfer, or recommend that one of these outcomes occurs.

Referent power flows from the intrinsic qualities of an individual. The wielder of referent power may have "charisma", or may simply be so stylish, handsome or knowledgeable that people wish to emulate her. A typical instance of referent power is when a sports or movie star endorses a product (which as often as not has nothing to do with sport or acting).

Expert power is wielded by people who seem to have access to special information, skill, experience or training. Even though societies, particularly societies with strong anti-intellectual values, sometimes denigrate the value of "expert opinion", within organisations it is probably unwise to ignore the opinions of the tax specialist, the lawyer, the personnel manager, the data processing manager, and so on.

Generally speaking, legitimate power, reward power and coercive power are derived from the organisational context, while referent power and expert power tend to be more personal in nature (Patchen 1974).

Shifting bases of power

Which is the most effective power base? This is quite difficult to answer. We can, however, observe various recent trends. Legitimate power seems to have declined throughout society of late. Compared to 100 or even 20 years ago, figures exuding legitimate power—politicians, judges, lawyers, doctors, priests—seem to command less respect. On either side of the so-called generation gap, people criticise the other side for indiscipline, sloppiness, rudeness and disrespect, or else for arrogance, pompousness and establishment hypocrisy. Within schools, the military, private and public enterprise, higher ranks do not seem to command the automatic obeisance from lower ranks that they once did. To some this is a bad thing, while to others it is a long-overdue change.

In organisations, coercive and reward power are usually associated with legitimate power. To that extent, they too have suffered a decline. Managers rarely have the power to grant salary increases or dismiss people, certainly not directly. Much of the power of line managers has been hived off to staff managers in personnel and industrial relations. Uniform salary provisions, union intervention, and so on, severely limit the power of a manager to reward and punish. When economic times are good, the power of a manager to reward is better than average, while the power to punish does not impress: subordinates know that they can simply go elsewhere if they lose their job. When economic times are bad, the power to reward can be strengthened, while the power to punish is also strengthened. The negotiating position of labour vis-à-vis management is not as strong, and subordinates have fewer options if they are dismissed or disciplined.

In the wider cultural context, referent power has probably increased. This has largely been due to the electronic media. Thus we are continually bombarded with images of "celebrities" (who have been cynically described as being famous for being famous), and politicians are marketed with emphasis on "image" more than on substantial policy issues. Within organisations, however, referent power has not altered dramatically as a force for decades. Expert power has probably been the most rapidly growing base in organisations. Chatterjee and McDonald (1981) point out that experts are to be found at all levels of organisations—not only in finance and marketing, but in maintenance as well. A skilled electrician is as much an expert as a research scientist.

As society becomes more technologically complex, so too do organisations, and thus dependence on expertise from all areas becomes greater. Chatterjee and McDonald point out that coping with increased technological complexity means a more educated workforce. Might this lead to a decline in respect for legitimate power, as suggested earlier (p.302)? Yet there is a real problem with expert power. The mix of skills that a person deploys generally changes as that person moves up the hierarchy of an organisation (Fig. 10.5).

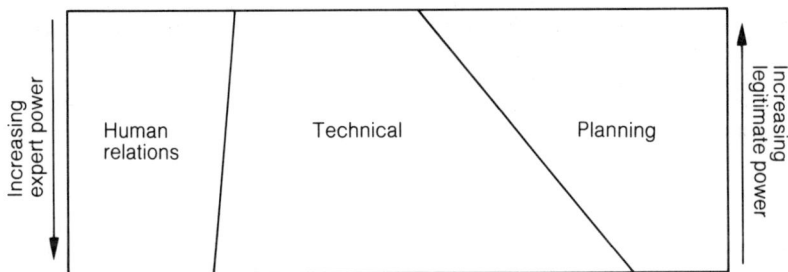

Fig 10.5 *Mix of skills at various levels of hierarchy*

At the bottom of the hierarchy, technical skills (how well you know your job) are very important, as are interpersonal or human relations skills. Planning or administrative skills—POSDCORB, if you like—are not heavily depended upon. Yet as one moves up the hierarchy, planning skills become more important, while interpersonal skills either remain constant or grow. Technical skills, however, tend to decline: a supervisor tends to oversee people from various technical areas, and the supervisor may get out of touch if she does not "keep her hand in".

Of course, the supervisor's very promotion may initially have depended upon her having technical skills, possibly in more than one area. Yet there is a danger that as the supervisor's legitimate power increases, and her expert power declines, the expert power of other people increases. Thus, the supervisor becomes more dependent upon the opinions of others. Fuelled by the information explosion, this means that managers run the risk of knowing less and less about more and more (with the *reductio ad absurdum* being that they finish up knowing nothing about everything). There are obvious similarities here with the only-half-facetious Peter Principle.[13]

No choice but to share power?

What is the solution to this dilemma? One solution seems to be to shift away from individual decision-making to group-decision-making—where experts from various fields can get together and attempt to communicate with each other, sharing the benefits of other perspectives. To the extent that this is true, then the age of individual leadership may be fast disappearing, with the age of group leadership emerging. Is group or collective leadership a contradiction in terms? We do not know that yet. Certainly, information overload is stressing leaders such as politicians, with various suggestions being made about redesigning their jobs to share the workload with others. Similar information overload is occurring in organisations.

Group decision-making, of course, has had a bad press ("a camel is a horse designed by a committee", "meetings, bloody meetings"). Yet there may be pressures at work forcing us in that direction, away from the "solitary hero" cliché of individual leadership (see Chapters 9 and 11). These pressures may not be irreversible, however (see below, p.331).

Styles of power

Christie and Geis (1970, 1978) have attempted to analyse styles of use of power. Drawing upon the theories of the Renaissance Italian writer, Niccolo Machiavelli, they have drawn a distinction between people with a more or less manipulative or political orientation. "High Machs" tend to believe that "the ends justifies the means". They tend to avoid emotional commitment to others, seeing other people more as objects to be manipulated than as empathic individuals. They tend not to be concerned with conventional morality, and ideology bores them—what counts is "getting things done".

While High Machs are examples of the "cool syndrome" (i.e. they are emotionally detached), the "Low Machs" are "soft touches" (they are more

---

[13] The Peter Principle states that "every employee tends to rise to his level of incompetence" (Peter and Hull 1969). Thus a really excellent welder on the shop floor may be promoted because of his excellence—to a desk job, where he may be quite incompetent. The corollaries of the Principle are that those at the very top are most incompetent, while the only good work in the organisation is achieved by those at the bottom—those who have not yet exceeded their level of competence.

likely to do or accept what another wants simply because that person wants it). High Machs would agree with the following statements:

- The biggest difference between most criminals and other people is that criminals are stupid enough to get caught.
- Never tell anyone the real reason you did something unless it is useful to do so.
- The best way to handle people is to tell them what they want to hear.

The Mach styles are related to another concept, that of "locus of control" (see Chapter 6). If one is an "internal", one believes that "I am the master of my fate: I am the captain of my soul". In religious matters, internals are prone to believe in free will, while externals are prone to believe in determinism or predestination. Internals are more likely to use seat belts and get preventive inoculations. Internals also believe that each individual makes and bears his own cross, and hence to be unsympathetic to appeals for sympathy or financial aid. Obviously, internals have something in common with High Machs (Baron, Byrne and Kantowitz 1980).

Does this mean that High Machs are always better operators in organisations than Low Machs? Not necessarily. Christie and Geis introduce another variable into their analysis, that of structure. This is similar to Fiedler's concept of task structure. A high structure organisation is one in which roles and rules are clearly defined, and improvisation in solving problems is neither needed nor encouraged. A low structure organisation is more wide open, a place where empires can be carved out. Indeed, an organisation may start out as being low or loosely structured and eventually change (some would say ossify) into being highly structured (see Table 10.6). The High Mach will have a happy hunting ground in a low structure organisation, while the Low Mach might be quite anxious and ineffective in such a situation.

In a highly structured situation, however, the High Mach may be thwarted by procedures and rules at every turn, eventually leaving in disgust or becoming passive and apathetic or bitter and deviant. The Low Mach, by contrast, might perform very well within the secure and predictable confines of the high structure organisation (see also Byrt 1980, Chs 7 and 8).

Table 10.6 Relationship of power drive to organisational structure

Situation	*Behaviour*	
	High Mach	*Low Mach*
Loosely structured	Tests the limits of the situation. Initiates and controls the structure. Exploits the resources available.	Implicity assumes unstated limits. Accepts the structure provided by others. Gets carried away, in interaction with others, from predefined goals.
Highly structured	Works within the given system. Gives perfunctory performance—occasional apathy.	Works within the given system. Makes a serious effort to perform well.

Source: Byrt (1980), p.106. Reproduced with permission.

Tactics

There are many tactics of power that can be deployed in organisations. Needless to say, most of the deployers tend to be more High Mach than Low Mach. Some of these tactics (of varying ethical import) are discussed below (adapted from Miles 1980; Luthans 1981; Szilyagyi and Wallace 1983; Eunson 1984).

Divide and rule

Break up existing coalitions, taking care to ensure that they do not re-form. History and military textbooks are full of examples of this tactic, but within organisations, divide and rule might mean separating individuals and departments, encouraging competition for scarce resources and positions, rumour-mongering. Adolf Hitler had a variation of this theme, that is, combine and rule: "The leader of genius must have the ability to make differing opponents appear as if they belonged to the one category."

Develop expert power

If you can't beat them, join them. Acquire formal or informal credentials in a particular area—the more arcane the better. Being known as the guru in marketing, personnel, information systems, legal matters, intuitive decision-making, can be of great value. Your mistakes may be seized upon by the envious, of course, and you may be typecast. Academic degrees, such as Master of Business Administration (MBA), may be used as a filtering device to allocate scarce resources and positions. Many of the old generalist entre-preneurs who built up Japanese empires are now abdicating to high-tech specialists. As the world becomes more complex, it will be better to be "information-rich" than "information-poor".

Manipulating classified information

This is related to the previous tactic. Control of information is vital. This means control via official channels, or via unofficial channels such as the grapevine. It may mean using correct information, to display that you are "in the know", or it may involve putting about (to borrow a term from espionage) "disinformation". Information can be creatively edited. It can take the form of research findings, which support your arguments. If you have divided and now rule, you should be the only person who has information from all areas, and hence has the big picture. Truly deviant manipulators sequester files, sit on routed documents, read other people's messages and chat up flatterable (and influential) secretaries.

Collecting and cashing in IOUs

By putting someone in your debt (e.g. by providing useful information) you place them in a position where they really should return the favour. The truly artful ingratiator "pyramids" obligations into a winning coalition.

Thin end of the wedge

A strategy of patience. Trying for everything at once may meet with disaster, but getting one foothold at a time usually meets with success. Pilot programs, progress reports with a permanent place on the agenda, creeping empire-building, are typical approaches.

Hitching your wagon to a star
Success, like guilt, can come by association. Many successful people, some altruistic, some vain, like to cultivate protégés. They, and their minders, such as secretaries, can bestow patronage and information. This tactic is sometimes successful, always highly risky. Stars can fall as well as rise, so unconditional loyalty may be short-sighted.

Mr Clean
The ethical tactic, or being nice and still winning. If all about are stabbing Judases, it may pay to be Christ-like. Don't join factions, keep your own counsel. Plod on while others' stars rise and fall. In disputes, you will be called in as an honest broker, which means that you will have maximum access to information, with all that that entails. The best way you can win is as Mr Clean. The worst way you can win is as the least objectionable candidate. Either way, you win. Not a popular strategy.

Red-tape origami
The ideal Low Mach tactic. Rather than fight bureaucracy, one goes with the flow (through official channels, of course). Learn the procedures, both official and unofficial, and learn to work through them. Above all else, exercise patience. With those who have not yet reached this nirvana-like state (e.g. customers, bosses, clientele) exert negative power—deny, delay, destroy through attrition.

Barriers
There are many barriers to the exercise of power in organisations. One may have effective power bases, styles and tactics, but if barriers are present (as they usually are, in some shape or form) then the ability to operate is limited. As has already been pointed out, many treatments of leadership and power assume that organisations are unitary in structure, that is, have a unified set of values which everyone shares. It is more accurate to see organisations as pluralistic coalitions, comprised of individuals and groups who have values and interests which often coincide, but just as often are in conflict. What are the barriers that prevent exertion of total power by managements?

Mention has already been made of how staff departments such as personnel and industrial relations often colonise parts of individual managers' empires. Of course, some functions are stripped from line managers to be given to staff managers, only to return again to line managers in some circumstances. Thus a line manager may be given back the power to make appraisals of staff (a transfer of power from the personnel department) or may be able to control data through a desk-top computer (a transfer of power from the data processing department) (see Chapter 13; see also Yuill 1983).

Organised labour presents a massive countervailing force to management, particularly when it is unionised. This balance of forces seems to vary from industry to industry, and with economic circumstances. Hard times seem to strengthen the hand of management vis-à-vis labour, in that labour has fewer options. In better times, employees, either individually or collectively in unions, exercise "affluence power"—jobs are plentiful, job mobility is high, so it doesn't matter greatly if they jump or are pushed from the organisation.

Mention has also been made of the countervailing force of expert power. Better education and higher training give subordinates bargaining chips within the current organisation and any future outside organisation. Experts in fact may see their primary loyalty not to the organisation that employs them, but to the wider group of peers outside the organisation—all other engineers, doctors, researchers, etc. Of course, if they are very highly specialised, they may not be able to take their talent elsewhere, because there are no other organisations that can give them a better deal (at least, no other organisations within the state or country). All professions, noted George Bernard Shaw, are conspiracies against the layman, and a manager of a complex organisation is a layman many times over.

Governments can constrain power within a network of legislation and regulation about health and safety, discrimination and affirmative action, normal (and not so normal) marketplace practices. Governments themselves, or at least within the public service, may find that hiring and firing and motivation is problematic, given the job security provisions of the public sector.

Discretionary powers of management are limited sometimes by the very *design of jobs*. Machine-paced and tightly scheduled jobs give little scope for change (Lee 1980). Subordinates may be dispersed geographically, and hence difficult to control within their empires. Obversely, a manager might find herself physically removed from the seat of power, where the action is, and this may inhibit rather than increase her autonomy (Hellriegel, Slocum and Woodman 1983). The manager may be confronted with an ironclad structure of rules and established procedures, and be haunted by the ghosts of predecessors—"That's not the way Ms Jenkins would have done it." Reliability and predictability might be rewarded, while innovation and unusual performance may be punished. A leader may find that her power has been usurped by her own leader: by withholding delegation, by bypassing normal channels of command and dealing directly with subordinates, by giving out too much responsibility and too little power. "Negative power" may be exercised by those who put your file at the bottom of the tray, or those who work to rules, or those who sabotage. Finally, there is the unholy trio of the electronic media, universal education and the information explosion which have challenged the legitimacy and competence of leaders in all fields.

Leadership, power and micropolitics

Are there any circumstances where micropolitics are inappropriate? One would have to look far and wide to find such circumstances. Miles (1980) has suggested that "political" rather than "rational" decision-making occurs in organisations which have the following characteristics:

* Old resources are scarce and/or new resources are opened up.
* Decision-making is more ambiguous, long-range and controversial.
* Goals are complex but unclear.
* Technology becomes more complex.
* Planned or unplanned change occurs.

In an age of "future shock", "information overload", turbulence rather than stability, complexity rather than simplicity, not to mention belt-tightening, the new austerity, and real or perceived limits to social and economic growth, it would be hard to find *any* organisation that was not political, based on these criteria.

Where to now?

What of leadership? Is it an endangered species, or is it only beginning to flourish? The four quotes at the beginning of the chapter represent two opposed attitudes to leadership: De Gaulle and Saint Vincent de Paul give expression to the traditional, "great man" theory of leadership, while Ian Dury and the Monty Python team express a more modern, cynical view of the usefulness of great men (or women). It is probably true to say that the institution of leadership is in crisis, like many of society's traditional institutions. Certainly, leadership theory gives no clear guidelines.

The demise of trait theory (as it applies to behavioural, as distinct from socio-economic traits) has left a legitimacy vacuum: we don't know which of us should be leaders and followers. This vacuum is not filled by theories of leadership styles: proponents of style theory, whether contingency or "one best style", usually presume that anyone can be trained to be a leader, but do not closely examine who is trained and who is not, or why some are trained and some are not. Style theories also largely ignore the concept of power, which involves the concept of the organisation as a pluralist coalition of unruly forces. Traditional leadership theory, whether macropolitical or micropolitical, was largely based on unequal distributions of power and resources. In both the macro- and micropolitical arenas, such distributions seem to be becoming more equal. What this means for the institution of leadership we can only wait and see.

Leadership might, for example, under the pressure of moves to democratise the workplace, shrivel up and die. People will no longer lead, manage, command and control, but coordinate, administer, chair and consult. Alternatively, the fashionableness of participation and industrial democracy might decline if people begin to perceive that industrial democracy leads to industrial anarchy, where no decisions are *ever* made, and hence that industrial autocracy—traditional, strong leadership—is preferable. In other words, people might begin trading off rights and justice (real or perceived) for efficiency and a quieter life of de-participation. Our leaders then would be the traditional management-appointed ones, or perhaps those industrial democrats who, by accident or by design, have had the stamina and a sufficiently high threshold of boredom to stick around while others vote with their feet, or perhaps an unholy alliance of both groups.

Summary

Leadership everywhere is seen by some as being under attack: the authority of leaders may have been weakened by the media, education, the information explosion and role overload.

A distinction is drawn between the macropolitics entered into by politicians and micropolitics entered into by people within organisations.

Leadership involves a number of tasks, such as planning, organising and delegating. Trait theories of leadership are used to identify unique characteristics of leaders. The use of psychological traits has fallen into disfavour, but socio-economic traits may still be useful. Styles of leadership have been identified. Theorists who subscribe to the "one best style" approach include Douglas McGregor (theory X/theory Y), Rensis Likert (system 4) and Robert Blake and Jane Srygley Mouton (managerial grid). Theorists who subscribe to the situationalist or contingency ("it all depends") approach include Fred Fielder (leadership match), Robert Tannen-baum and Warren Schmidt (leadership continuum), and Paul Hersey and Kenneth Blanchard (situational leadership).

All of these theories consider participation, but few of them consider power, which is the other side of participation. Much of this ambivalence about power can be understood by considering the American cultural matrix from which most of these theories emerge. Power can be understood more clearly by examining four aspects of power: bases, styles, tactics and barriers to its exercise.

The future of leadership in organisations, especially qua participation and power-sharing, is not at all clear.

Questions for discussion

1. Are leaders born or made?
2. What should and should not be delegated by leaders to followers?
3. What traits (if any) can be used to identify potential leaders?
4. Compare and contrast two theories of leadership style.
5. What influence does culture have upon our understanding of leadership?
6. Write a role-play in which a leader uses five differing power-bases (legitimate power, reward power, coercive power, referent power, expert power) in dealing with five differing subordinates.
7. Make a speculation about whether organisations will become more high structure or more low structure, and then speculate on whether we will see more High Machs or Low Machs as a result.
8. Write a role-play in which a person uses five power tactics at a meeting within an organisation (sporting, business, neighbourhood, etc.). Can you think of any other tactics apart from those given here?
9. Will barriers to power lessen or decrease in future?
10. What is the future of leadership?

References

Adair, John (1983). *Effective Leadership.* (Pan: London).
Albanese, Robert and Van Fleet, David D. (1983). *Organizational Behaviour: A Managerial Viewpoint.* (Dryden Press: Chicago).
Anthony, P.D. (1977). *The Ideology of Work.* (Tavistock: London).
Barnard, Chester I. (1938). *The Functions of the Executive.* (Harvard University Press: Cambridge, Mass.).
Baron, Robert A., Byrne, Donn and Kantowicz, Barry H. (1980). *Psychology: Understanding Behaviour*, 2nd edn. (Holt, Rinehart and Winston: New York).
Barry, Bernard and Dowling, Peter (1984). *An Australian Management Style?* (Australian Institute of Management: Melbourne).
Beck, Don Edward (1982). "Beyond the Grid and Situationalism: A Living Systems View", *Training and Development Journal*, August.
Blake, Robert R. and Mouton, Jane S. (1982). "A Comparative Analysis of Situationalism and 9,9 Management by Principle", *Organizational Dynamics.* Spring.
     (1985). *The Managerial Grid III.* (Gulf Publishing: Houston).
Byrt, William J. (1980). *The Human Variable: Text and Cases in Organizational Behaviour.* (McGraw-Hill: Sydney).

Carey, Alex (1980). "Worker Motivation: Social Science, Propaganda, and Democracy", in Boreham, P. and Dow, Geoff (eds), *Work and Inequality: Ideology and Control in the Capitalist Labour Process.* (Macmillan: Melbourne).
Chatterjee, S.R. and McDonald C. (1981). "Some Aspects of Expert Power in Work Organisations", *Human Resource Management Australia*, Autumn.
Christie, Richard (1978). "Mach V Attitude Inventory", in Pfeiffer, J. William and Jones, John E. (eds), *The 1978 Annual Handbook for Group Facilitators.* (University Associates: La Jolla, Calif.).
Christie, Richard and Geis, Florence L. (1970). *Studies in Machiavellianism.* (Academic Press: New York).
Edgar, Donald (1980). *Introduction to Australian Society: A Sociological Perspective.* (Prentice-Hall: Sydney).
Eunson, Baden (1984). "Power, and How to Get It", *Business Review Weekly*, 14–20 January.
Fayol, Henri (1949). *General and Industrial Management*, trans. by Constance Storrs. (Pitman: London).
Fiedler, Fred E. (1967). *A Theory of Leadership Effectiveness.* (McGraw-Hill: New York).
    (1976). "The Leadership Game: Matching the Man to the Situation", *Organizational Dynamics*, Winter. (AMACOM: New York).
Fiedler, Fred E., Chemers, Martin M. and Mahar, Linda (1977). *Improving Leadership Effectiveness: The Leader Match Concept.* (John Wiley and Sons: New York).
Friedman, Milton (1978). *Free to Choose.* (Basic Books: New York).
Gordon, Thomas (1979). *Leadership Effectiveness Training (LET): The No-Lose Way to Release the Productive Potential of People.* (Futura: London).
Grzyb, Gerard J. (1981). "Decollectivization and Recollectivization in the Workplace: The Impact of Technology on Informal Work Groups and Work Culture", *Economic and Industrial Democracy*, vol. 2, no. 4.
Gulick, L. and Urwick, L. (eds) (1937). *Papers on the Science of Administration.* (Institute of Public Administration: New York).
Hellriegel, Don, Slocum, John W. and Woodman, Richard W. (1983). *Organizational Behaviour*, 3rd edn. (West Publishing: St Paul).
Hersey, Paul and Blanchard, Kenneth H. (1977). *Management of Organizational Behaviour*, 3rd edn. (Prentice-Hall: New Jersey).
    (1982). "Leadership Styles: Attitudes and Behaviours", *Training and Development Journal*, May.
Hersey, Paul, Blanchard, Kenneth H. and Hambleton, Ronald K. (1978). "Contracting for Leadership Style: A Process and Instrumentation for Building Effective Work Relationships" in Hersey, P. and Stinson, J. (eds), *Perspectives in Leadership Effectiveness.* (Center for Leadership Studies, Ohio University Press: Ohio).
Hirszowicz, Maria (1981). *Industrial Sociology: An Introduction.* (Martin Robertson: Oxford).
Johnson, Paul (1980). "The Crisis of Leadership in the West", *The Bulletin*, 22 July.
Kerr, Clark and Rosow, Jerome M. (1973). *Work in America: The Decade Ahead.* (Van Nostrand Reinhold: New York).
Lansbury, Russell (1980). "Prospects for Industrial Democracy Under Liberal Capitalism", in Lansbury, R. (ed.), *Democracy in the Workplace.* (Longman-Cheshire: Melbourne).
Lansbury, Russell D. and Spillane, Robert (1983). *Organizational Behaviour: The Australian Context.* (Longman-Cheshire: Melbourne).
Lee, James A. (1980). *The Gold and the Garbage in Management Theories and Prescriptions.* (Ohio University Press: Athens, Ohio).
L'etaing, Hugh (1980). *Fit to Lead?* (Heinemann Medical: London).

Likert, Rensis (1961). *New Patterns of Management.* (McGraw-Hill: New York).

Likert, Rensis and Likert, Jane G. (1967). *The Human Organization: Its Management and Value.* (McGraw-Hill: New York).

———. (1976). *New Ways of Managing Conflict.* (McGraw-Hill: New York).

Luthans, Fred (1981). *Organizational Behaviour,* 3rd edn. (McGraw-Hill: New York).

McClelland, David C. (1970). "The Two Faces of Power", *Journal of International Affairs,* vol. 24, no. 1.

McClelland, David C. and Burnham, David H. (1976). "Power is the Great Motivator", *Harvard Business Review,* March–April.

McGregor, Douglas (1960). *The Human Side of Enterprise.* (McGraw-Hill: New York).

Machovec, Frank M. and Smith, Howard R. (1982). "Fear Makes the World Go 'Round: The 'Dark' Side of Management", *Management Review,* January.

Marchington, Mick and Loveridge, Ray (1979). "Non-Participation: The Management View?" *Journal of Management Studies,* May.

Martin, Shan (1983). *Managing Without Managers.* (Sage: California).

Messinesi, P.S. (1983). "Australian Managers: Descriptions and Comparisons", *Human Resource Management Australia,* May.

Miles, Robert H. (1980). *Macro-Organizational Behaviour.* (Scott Foresman: Glenview, Ill.).

Miner, John B. (1982). *Theories of Organizational Structure and Process.* (Dryden Press: Chicago).

Moore, Franklin G. (1982). *Management in Organizations.* (John Wiley and Sons: New York).

Mukhi, S.K. (1982). "Leadership Paths and Profiles: Part I: A Survey of Australian Chief Executives", *Human Resource Management Australia,* August.

Nichols, Theo (1980). "Management, Ideology and Practice", in Esland, Geoff and Salaman, Graeme (eds), *The Politics of Work and Occupations.* (Open University Press: Milton Keynes).

Nord, Walter R. (1978). "Dreams of Humanization and the Realities of Power", *Academy of Management Review,* July.

O'Shaughnessey, J. (1979). *Patterns of Business Organization.* (George Allen and Unwin: London).

Patchen, Martin (1974). "The Locus and Basis of Influence on Organizational Decisions", *Organizational Behaviour and Human Performance,* 21.

Peter, Laurence J. and Hull, Raymond (1969). *The Peter Principle.* (Pan: London).

Raven, B. and French, J.P. (1960)."The Bases of Social Power", in Cartwright, D. and Zander, A.F. (eds), *Group Dynamics,* 2nd edn. (Row, Peterson: Evanston, Ill.).

Ribeaux, Peter and Poppleton, Stephen (1978). *Psychology at Work: An Introduction.* (Macmillan: London).

Scanlon, Burt and Keys, Bernard (1983). *Management and Organizational Behaviour,* 2nd edn. (John Wiley and Sons: New York).

Shalev, Michael and Korpi, W. (1980). "Working Class Mobilization and American Exceptionalism", *Economic and Industrial Democracy,* vol. 1, no. 1.

Shulman, Marshall (1982) in Bingham, Colin (ed.), *Wit and Wisdom: A Public Affairs Miscellany.* (Melbourne University Press: Melbourne).

Singh, Ramadhar (1983). "Leadership Style and Reward Allocation: Does Least Preferred Co-Worker Scale Measure Task and Relation Orientation?", *Organizational Behaviour and Human Performance,* 32.

Szilyagyi, Andrew D., Jr. and Wallace, Marc J., Jr. (1983). *Organizational Behaviour and Human Performance,* 3rd edn. (Goodyear: Santa Monica, Calif.).

Tannenbaum, Robert and Schmidt, Warren H. (1958). "How to Choose a Leadership Pattern", *Harvard Business Review*, March–April.
(1973). "Retrospective Commentary on 'How to Choose a Leadership Pattern' ", *Harvard Business Review*, May–June.
Tannenbaum, Robert, Wechsler, T. and Massarik, J. (1961). *Leadership and Organization.* (McGraw-Hill: New York).
Toffler, Alvin (1984). *Previews and Premises.* (Pan: London).
Weller, Patrick and Grattan, Michelle (1981). *Can Ministers Cope?* (Hutchinson: Melbourne).
Yuill, B.F. (1983). "Evaluation of Departmental and Managerial Power", *Human Resource Management Australia*, August.
Zinn, Howard (1980). *A People's History of the United States.* (Longman: London).

Films/videos

Leadership and the One Minute Manager (Training Media Services).
Mates, Martyrs and Masters (Seven Dimensions).
Leadership: Style or Circumstance? (Video Channel).
The Effective Use of Power and Authority (Video Channel).
How to Manage: The Process Approach and Henri Fayol (Power Human Resources).
Situational Leadership (Power Human Resources).

11

Group dynamics

We are half-ruined by conformity, but we should be wholly ruined without it.

Charles Dudley Warner

Please accept my resignation. I don't care to belong to any club that will have me as a member.

Groucho Marx

Individually, mediocrities do not add up to much. But the essence of mediocrities is that they do not act individually, nor are they individualists. They act collectively, in groups, where they have a lot of power—not power to create, facilitate, permit, say yes, but power to destroy, obstruct, deny, say no—but power, for all that. Their use of this power, particularly against non-mediocre, individualistic individuals, is motivated by malice and envy, but also by the need for self-defence. This is the strongest power in the world.

Ian McEwan

Groups: What are they?

The group is the mechanism which links the individual to organisations and to society at large. Groups can be small or large, official or unofficial, permanent or temporary, task-oriented or relationship-oriented (or both), strongly or weakly cohesive, physically concentrated or dispersed, effective or ineffective—the list of attributes is almost endless.

Every individual is usually a member of many groups. At work, Mary is a member of at least three groups (Fig. 11.1), although she is the only person who is a member of all three groups shown.

Groups can come in all shapes and sizes, and include the following:

    committees
    families
    sporting teams
    sporting team supporters
    criminal gangs
    juries
    musicians
    fan clubs
    members of a commune
    combat units
    multidisciplinary problem-solving teams
    participants at an orgy
    construction gangs
    Porsche owners
    lynch mobs
    followers of Catholicism

Of such a list, which is by no means exhaustive, it might well be said: "If

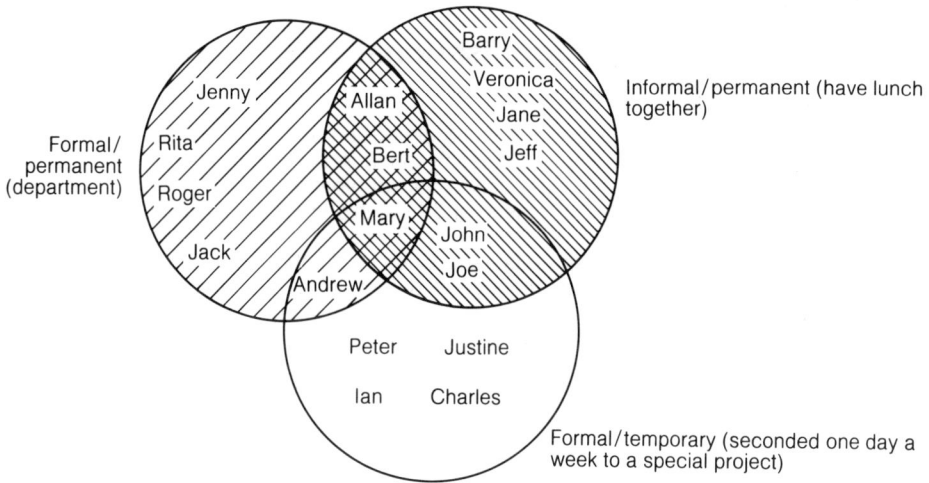

Fig 11.1 *Group membership patterns* (ADAPTED FROM HODGETTS 1980, P.111)

groups are everything, perhaps they are nothing." Is this the case? What possible connection could all these collections of people have?

A group is distinguished from a *social category* or an *aggregate*. Examples of social categories or aggregates are:

all people earning the same income

all people with the same height

all people of the same occupation.

Members of groups act together to achieve common aims or goals. For the most part, members of social categories or aggregates do not act in such a manner, although an aggregate such as people in an elevator who did not know each other might become a group if the elevator broke down and people began to talk and act together (Avery, Baker and Kane 1984). A definition of groups which comes to terms with goal-oriented or purposive behaviour is that of Newcomb (1950):

A group consists of people with shared norms and interlocking roles.

To better understand groups, let us now find out just what roles and norms are.

Roles

A role is an expected behaviour (Hodgetts 1980). Roles can have objective and static dimensions and subjective and dynamic dimensions (Box 11.A). Roles can also emerge when groups are analysed for presence or lack of cohesiveness using techniques such as sociograms (Box 11.D).

In analysing many groups—the management task force, the semi-autonomous work group, the voluntary charity committee, the weekly staff meeting, and so on—it is useful to distinguish between three types of roles usually in operation—task roles, socio-emotional roles and destructive roles.

BOX 11.A: The organisational chart and interpretive roles

Roles can have an objective and static dimension and a subjective and dynamic dimension. To know a person's place in the organisational chart, or to know a job description, is only a part of what a job role is. How people interpret the roles of others, and how this in turn shapes their own role, is important also.

Bowey studied a British restaurant, Cherry's, in 1968. The formal authority structure (a) is easy enough to detect. What is probably more interesting is how different groups and individuals interpreted the roles of others, and how their responses to others determined their roles (b).

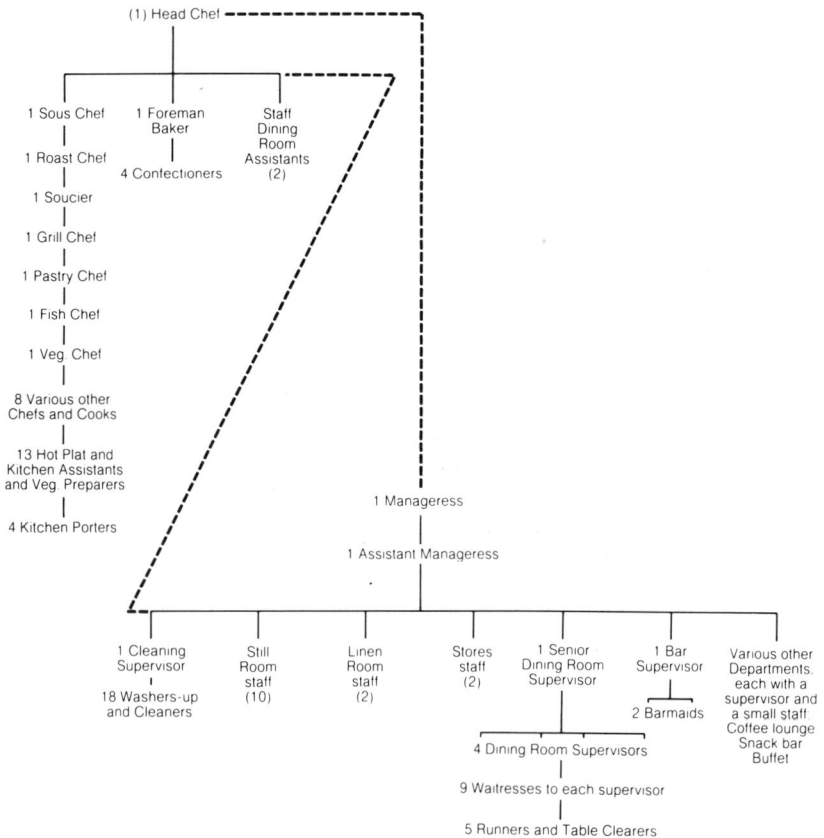

(a) The formal authority structure at Cherry's restaurant

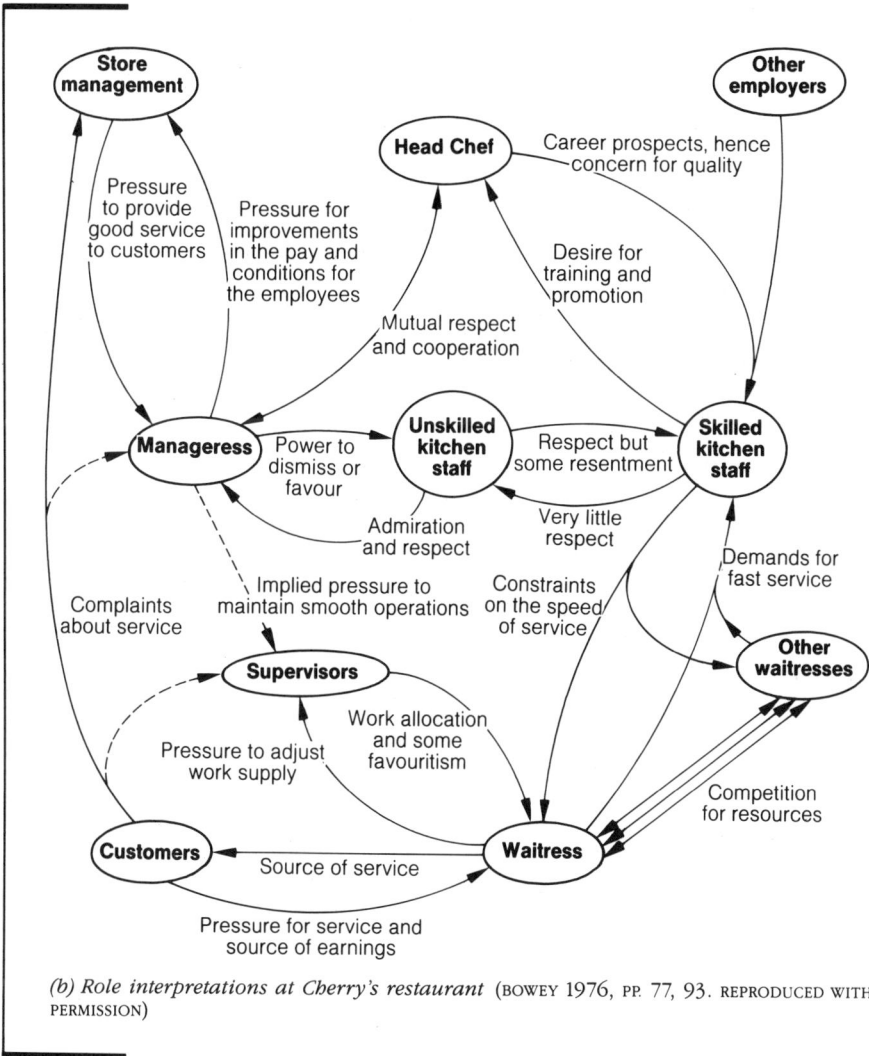

(b) Role interpretations at Cherry's restaurant (BOWEY 1976, PP. 77, 93. REPRODUCED WITH PERMISSION)

Task roles

Task roles are played by one, several or all group members to ensure that work is actually performed within the group. These are:

1. *The initiator,* who suggests new ways of perceiving or approaching the problems or goals of the group. This may entail new solutions, procedures or ways of organising the group.
2. *The information-seeker,* who asks for clarification of new ideas in terms of their factual adequacy and authoritativeness/"expertness".
3. *The information-giver,* who offers facts or generalisations which are "expert" or "authoritative" or relates her own experience pertinently to the group problem.

4. *The opinion-seeker,* who is not so much trying to find the relevant facts as the relevant values and beliefs.
5. *The opinion-giver,* who supplies values and beliefs pertinent to the problem in hand rather than facts.
6. *The evaluator,* who may develop and impose standards of "practicability", "logic", "factual validity", "correctness", etc.
7. *The implementer,* who executes the group's decisions, and is concerned with practical details, timing, methods.
8. *The procedural technician,* who may handle the technical mechanics of the group (such as distributing writing materials, setting up audio-visual equipment) or the operational mechanics (enforcing formal meeting procedures of agenda, motions, etc. and drawing the group's attention to legal, constitutional details, precedents, oversights, omissions and errors).
9. *The recorder,* who writes everything down, keeps minutes—the "group memory".

Socio-emotional roles
Socio-emotional or maintenance roles are played by one, several or all group members to ensure that constructive human relationships and communication occur and are strengthened while tasks are being performed. These are:
1. *The encourager,* who praises, rewards and supports others in the group, backing up the active contributors and drawing out the shy and reticent (and defending them against the more bumptious and impatient).
2. *The peacemaker,* who plays the diplomat and tries to build a consensus, patiently drawing out obvious and not-so-obvious similarities between the views of the opponents, trying for agreement on procedural if not substantive issues.
3. *The compromiser,* who is willing to reduce conflict by compromising with the opposition(s), by yielding status, or by admitting error, or by disciplining herself to maintain group harmony.
4. *The tension-reliever,* who can break the ice or reverse a sudden chill in the air with jokes, deflating of formality, and proposals of adjournment for drinks and/or food and/or fresh air.
5. *The confronter,* who is assertive but not aggressive, quick to challenge overly cosy and conflict-avoiding agreements within the group, ready to assume devil's advocate role when no one else will.
(ADAPTED FROM BENNE AND SHEATS (1948/1978), DUNPHY AND DICK (1981), EUNSON (1985*a*))

Destructive roles[1]
While task and socio-emotional roles are helpful and positive in group processes, destructive roles are harmful and negative. Brief descriptions of some of these roles, together with some suggestions on how to handle such role-players, are now given.
1. *The talker* Possibly the talker may not be the nuisance that some may imagine. Usually the quality of what he says is inversely proportional to the time he takes to say it. However, in saying it, he may

[1] Taken from "Making Meetings Work", *Rydge's Management Services,* November 1976. Reproduced with permission.

unwittingly spark someone off, or provoke some comment which may prove valuable. Providing he is not preventing anyone else from speaking, or drowning out someone from trying to speak, then a talker need not be a problem if properly handled.

2. *The detailer*   This type of person descends into minute detail at every opportunity, and often loses the thread of the main issue. The difficulty with this type of person is that he may confuse the primary matter to such an extent that it may fragment the meeting. The detailer has a place as he obviously does his homework, and is a worker. Consequently his talents must be channelled into a constructive area—possibly into a subcommittee to consider the matter in detail.

3. *The top-of-the-header*   There is considerable room for the person who can spontaneously come up with an idea, especially a new idea. However, there are others in this category who say the first thing that comes into their heads, and as the old saying goes, empty vessels make the most noise. In certain types of meeting, such as a think-tank, any idea is useful, but in the more orthodox meeting a top-of-the-header can be a very disruptive influence.

4. *The definer*   The definer is always seeking definitions of what is said. He cannot be happy with broadly accepted terms—he requests definitions and then argues on the definitions. This type of person can cause a meeting to bog down in trivia and get nowhere. For any meeting to cover any ground, people must be allowed some latitude with their language and terms used. When it reaches the point of a motion on a certain matter, it is then time for a closer look at the words and the phrases, and this is where this person's talents can be used.

5. *The non-decider*   There are people who are scared to make up their mind in case they are subsequently found wrong. This type of person often becomes a bandwagon-jumper, who likes to see the way everyone else is moving and then jumps on the bandwagon. If this cannot be readily determined prior to voting, he may vote both for and against or ask to change his vote on the grounds that he has misunderstood the motion. There are many people like this and they need firm but gentle handling as they are not doing it deliberately— they usually have a fear of committing themselves.

6. *The scoffer*   This person is akin to the top-of-the-header as he always has a comment to make—unsupported by facts of course—but nevertheless made to distract the attention away from the main issue. The general tone of the comment is "it will never work", "it cannot be done in time", etc. It is seldom that this person makes a constructive comment and the best way to deal with such a person is to request specific reasons for his views. After a few times of being put on the spot, he may keep quiet. While people may have genuine doubts about various issues, they should be able to express where their doubts arise and these can be debated. If a person has a gut feeling about an issue then he should vote accordingly, but all debate should proceed on a positive line.

7. *The shelver*   This person is similar to the non-decider except that he wants to put everything off until some later stage after more facts are obtained. In some cases, such a request is reasonable, but where it happens persistently, it is obvious that there will never be enough facts to satisfy this type of person.

8. *The distractor* This person is akin to the talker, but he never talks to the meeting—he talks to the people each side of him or across the table in tones loud enough to be heard and to distract the proceedings. This person must be dealt with firmly by the chairman and simple rules of debate applied.

9. *The personaliser* The personaliser always takes things personally and gets very hurt when someone disagrees with his views. Often the background of such a person is one of insecurity and he tends to feel that someone is out to get him. Such a person should be reassured that all views have value and each has a right to agree or disagree with his views. While this is obvious to all normal people, it needs saying to this person at least once per meeting.

10. *The manipulator* This person tries to manipulate people by flattery and praise, and carries out lobbying activity after the meeting with little groups to influence their thinking for the next meeting. Often such people have a desire to be chairman but do not wish to accept the responsibility or have doubts that they would be elected. Lobbying activity can achieve some crystallisation of thoughts prior to the meeting and so may facilitate the reaching of a decision, but it is better to have the things said brought out into the open where all can hear at the same time, and argument taken, than to have each person subjected to whispered or private conversations, often with facts exaggerated or suppressed. Manipulators can be counter-productive and may be best taken head-on, by asking them to nominate for chairman. This will find the real nature of their support.

11. *The dominator* In the spectrum of psychological types, there are the domineering individuals who want and expect everything their way. Often these people emerge as leaders and captains of industry, and the less strong psychological types try to placate them and fit in with their wishes. This does not mean that the group may like such an individual, or work willingly for him. They will accord him the position of leader purely because no one person is strong enough to challenge him for the position. If such a person becomes chairman then the meeting may fail to become productive because the members' views are not allowed to develop, and the meeting becomes merely a vehicle for the chairman's views. In this situation the meeting is a waste of time and the talents of the members are not being used. If anything, the procedure is counter-productive because the members either become apathetic—"who cares, it's a foregone conclusion", or obstructive—"we will show him". In either case, the commitment to the decision is lost. Where the dominator is not created chairman—such as in the case of an appointed chairman from management— the dominator will often challenge the chairman in various ways. This can lead to polarisation of the meeting and disruption of the business while the personal differences fester into a serious problem. This problem is not an easy one to solve, and may require attention under the strategy of composition of meetings.

Norms

Norms are standards of customary behaviour. If you like, "norms" can be translated as "rules". Thus a good way to define groups is

$$\text{roles} + \text{rules(norms)} = \text{groups}$$

Grasha (1976) makes a distinction between formal norms and informal norms in work groups. Formal norms are those rules which are *explicit* in the way they define the group's behaviour, while informal norms are *implicit* in the way they define the group's behaviour. Thus, if we look at a work group in a factory, we might analyse the team's norms into formal (F) and informal (I):

(F) workers show up at the factory on time
(I) workers often refer to each other by nicknames
(F) workers must observe safety regulations
(I) some workers engage in practical jokes and horseplay
(F) workers in this group have lunch in the cafeteria from 12:45 to 1:30
(I) workers in this group always sit at the one table and always drink three cups of coffee (GRASHA 1976, P.124)

Formal norms are usually laid down by management in work situations, whereas informal norms are usually laid down by the group of non-management employees. As seen earlier (Fig. 11.1), within any organisation there are official structures and groups set up and legitimised by the official leaders, but there are also unofficial structures and groups set up and legitimised by unofficial leaders. The formal organisation and the informal organisation thus co-exist, often uneasily, and sometimes in a state of open conflict. The system of communication for the unofficial organisation is known as the grapevine (see Chapter 14). As Davis (1981) points out, organisations cannot "fire" the grapevine, because they did not hire it—it is simply there, as is the entire informal group structure.

Rules, whether formal or informal, have to be enforced. Enforcement of formal norms is straightforward ("Is it legal?" "Does it violate company policy?"), while enforcement of informal norms is usually more subtle (Box 11.B).

BOX 11.B: Group pressure and the enforcement of norms

Informal, friendship groups occur most often across the hierarchy—peers, rather than bosses and subordinates, are friends. It is true that in very loose, open hierarchies, different hierarchical levels do form friendship groups, but this is still the exception rather than the rule.

The influence of the friendship group is greatest at the base of the hierarchy, where relationships between members are strongest. Conversely, members at the top of the hierarchy do have informal relationships, but there is little friendship involved; senior managers' informal relationships are based on convenience rather than love.

The power of groups to affect the behaviour of members should not be underestimated. You and I are affected by groups throughout our daily lives—in work groups, committees, families, or friendship groups. The ultimate control of the group is total rejection, a form of isolation few of us can endure for long.

This process of influencing behaviour in groups can be traced. When a deviation from the expected behaviour occurs phases of control will be seen.

Phase 1. The initial tolerance. The deviation is noted by the members of the group. They may seek an explanation ("Why are you doing that,

Harry?") or members may make excuses ("She hasn't learnt the ropes yet."). Whatever the technique (and it may be total silence), other members of the group have registered the deviation and the implied message is, "OK, we note the deviation. Now let's be sensible and not deviate."

Phase 2. Attempt to correct. The members have noted the continued deviation from group norms and deliberately attempt to correct the behaviour. "Don't keep doing that", "Put your clothes back on again", "You don't have to go home yet", "Have another beer", etc. At this stage, members of the group are still tolerant, but are signalling verbally or non-verbally that the deviation must cease.

Phase 3. Verbal aggression. Other group members are becoming more annoyed by the deviation. Verbal messages become more hostile, more aggressive, and the threat of rejection may be offered: "If you can't do it this way, don't do it at all" (fail and go elsewhere). Verbal aggression is more likely to occur than physical aggression with groups whose members come from middle or upper income families. Lower income groups use more physical aggression.

Phase 4. Physical aggression. As a control, this is limited by other group norms (e.g. no physical aggression). It is more likely to be used on the factory floor than in the boardroom (where the process is often more subtle but no less damaging).

Phase 5. Rejection. "Get out." As soon as the individual is rejected (physically or psychologically), the group members will rebalance power and roles, eliminate the deviant's contribution, and, if necessary, readjust its norms. Probably the most frequently used rejection is total silence.

In many cases, members of a group ignore all the niceties and reject immediately. Or the group may take step 2 and then go to 5. In other words, the phases are sequential but not necessarily consecutive.

The power of the peer group has been known to managers and union officials for many years, and both managers and union officials use that power to influence the behaviour of employees. What is particularly different about work groups, as opposed to others, is that the norms and standards are central to the rewards the members receive. If a deviant decides to produce more than the group norm, then all members of the group are threatened. Similarly, if the employees feel industrial action is warranted, they will not tolerate nonconformists because nonconformists weaken the group's position. Work groups are very much a case of "one in, all in".

Source: Hunt (1979), pp.61–62. Reproduced with permission.

The conflict between informal and formal group norms, and the means by which one is enforced at the expense of the other, are complex phenomena. Work groups often have clearly defined informal norms, such as: You don't dob on your mates, no matter what; a fair day's work around here is *x* amount of output. If anyone deviates from these norms, they are usually punished by various group behavioural mechanisms, such as ostracism ("sent to Coventry") or ridicule ("ratebuster!" "conch!" for over-achievers, "goldbricker!" "bludger!" for under-achievers).

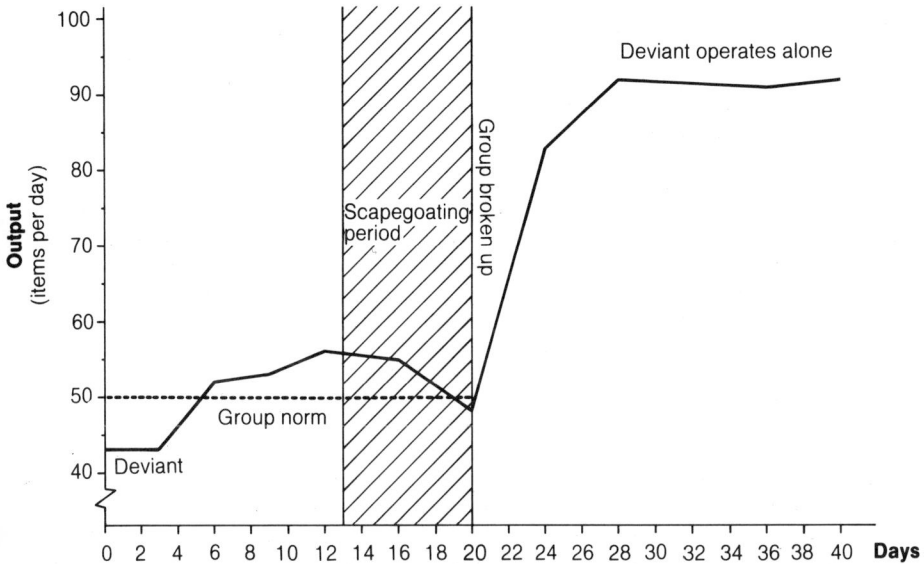

Fig 11.2 *Group norms and deviant performance in a pyjama factory* (ADAPTED FROM COCH AND FRENCH 1948)

Coch and French (1948) studied group norm behaviour in an American pyjama manufacturing plant. They observed that the informal group norm in a group of pressers was about 50 items per day. A new worker entered the group (Fig. 11.2), and after a few days' learning, began to exceed the group norm. The rest of the group began to scapegoat or punish the deviant from the norm, so that after some days the deviant conformed, and in fact over-conformed by producing slightly less than the group norm. After twenty days, the group had to be split up, and while all other workers were transferred elsewhere, the scapegoat worker remained. Her output rate increased dramatically, freed as she was from the restrictive group norm.

Such findings have fascinating implications for job design, motivation, piecework and group dynamics concepts such as conformity and cohesion. It is sometimes concluded that data like that of Coch and French prove that informal group norms are dangerous things, ruining organisational productivity. Further, it is sometimes concluded that if managements could only destroy informal groups by getting workers to participate more in the running of the organisation—for example, by setting up semi-autonomous work groups, or quality circles (see Chapter 12)—then things would be better all around, for both managment and workers.

Nevertheless, as radical and liberal critics of some job redesign and worker participation schemes (e.g. Littler and Salaman 1984; Lee 1980) have pointed out, members of informal groups are not altogether dumb, nor are they neurotic, nor just plain cranky. If a work group were to lift its production norm to the maximum, what are the guarantees that:

1. additional profits generated will be shared proportionately among management and labour, and
2. higher than normal output will not lead to staff being laid off?

If such guarantees were given, then labour and management could work in more harmonious alliance. Unfortunately, many schemes which have been dressed up in behavioural science rhetoric about "non-monetary motivation" and "job enrichment" have in fact led to staff being laid off (Kelly 1981), rather than the organisation increasing its marketing of its new high output, or re-training workers for other jobs. Equitable profit distribution has been a matter of controversy since (and well before) the first modern job redesign experiments of Frederick Taylor[2] (see Chapter 2), but workers in informal groups have often been justified in suspecting that "job enrichment equals cash impoverishment".

Managements within organisations of course also have their own informal (and formal) norms that lead to sub-maximising of output. A group of manufacturers may cause production to be artificially low because of cartelisation, administered prices, vertical and horizontal integration, lobbying for tariffs and protectionist, as opposed to free-market, conditions, and so on. Professional groups may also have norms of holding down outputs—what peer-group pressures would there be upon a doctor or lawyer if they began to cut their prices, for example?

From one point of view, then, informal groups of workers enforcing informal norms may be seen as a negative force, damaging the wider organisation; from another point of view, such groups may be seen as a positive force, acting as a countervailing force within the wider organisation to prevent exploitation. It is true to say, however, that many writers and researchers who have studied group dynamics hold to the former, rather than the latter, or both points of view (see Box 11.C).

Informal and formal norms are essential then to an understanding of formal and informal groups, together of course with roles. (Note that the Group Effectiveness Questionnaire in Box 11.E is just another way of measuring some group norms.) How and why do individuals conform to group norms, and what influence does this have on group cohesion?

Cohesiveness, conformity and deviance

Why do people conform? Do we conform more under special circumstances? Do certain people conform more than others? The following factors appear to be important in determining whether conformity takes place:

1. *Age.* Children tend to be more conforming than adults.
2. *Sex.* Women, because of traditional social conditioning, tend to be more conforming than men.
3. *Status.* Within groups, individuals with low status tend to conform to beliefs and actions of individuals with higher status.
4. *Intelligence, creativity.* People with low IQ and low creativity tend to conform more easily to group norms.
5. *Ignorance.* If a person does not understand what is going on in a group, s/he is more likely to follow the lead of someone who seems to know what is going on.
6. *Personality.* Group members with certain personality characteristics (submissiveness/passivity, low self-concept, high need for acceptance and fear of rejection) will tend to conform often.

---

[2] Taylor, a pioneer in "scientific management" at the turn of the twentieth century, developed the notion of piecework incentives so that, in a famous experiment, he got a worker to increase output by 362 per cent, for which the worker was paid an additional 62 per cent. As Dowling and Sayles (1982) remarked:

> ... scientific management saw the worker, at least the hourly employee, as essentially a passive economic man with strong muscles and a weak mind only capable of absorbing the simple routine of mass-producing technology—and, incidentally, a person willing to accept a 61 per cent increase in wages for a 362 per cent increase in productivity.

BOX 11.C: Group dynamics: The researchers and the researched—a case of bias?

A very large proportion of research and writing in group dynamics tends to be concerned with labour rather than management. Much analysis in the area seems to have a *managocratic* bias, that is, it seems to be conducted from a management viewpoint, seeing much worker behaviour which deviates from official norms as being psychologically neurotic and/or threatening industrial sabotage. Consider, for example, Hepner's remarks:

> In non-union plants the cliques are watched in order to see whether a clique is becoming the nucleus of a formal union that will spear-head group hostility to management. If such cliques are developing, it usually means that management has failed in its communication responsibilities. (HEPNER 1979, P.294)

Even within the American industrial context to which Hepner is referring (where union membership is lower than that of Europe and Australasia), it is difficult to accept this logic: the upshot seems to be that unions are unnecessary because managements are potentially more sympathetic to workers' needs—not only a manifestly untrue argument, but a perfectly reversible one.

Indeed, much research and writing on group dynamics seems to have the hidden agenda of producing behavioural science findings which can be used to weaken and perhaps destroy informal worker groups and formal groups such as unions. Research based upon the Hawthorne studies and other work was used throughout the 1940s to employ group dynamics and human relations concepts to encourage worker participation and increase worker motivation (see Chapter 2). Nevertheless, as management consultant Peter Drucker said in 1950:

> The human relations policies which American management has been buying wholesale in the past ten years have been a conspicuous waste and failure. In my opinion . . . most of us in management . . . have instituted them as a means of busting the unions. They are based on the belief that if you have good employee relations the unions will wither on the vine. (QUOTED IN CAREY 1976, P.165)

There may be so little research on informal norms within management because management doesn't want behavioural scientists being privy to its policy-making. There is a serious methodological asymmetry here: it is easy for management to pay behavioural scientists to go out into the office and on to the shop floor to peer into the psyche of the workers, but it is nigh on impossible for worker groups, formal or informal, to hire behavioural scientists to walk into the boardroom and peer into the psyche of managers.

This asymmetry gives the lie to much "behavioural science" being truly scientific and impartial, and in fact reinforces the criticism made by Baritz when he referred to many behavioural scientists as being the "servants of power" (Baritz 1965). Braverman (1974) continued this tack, castigating the community of academic researchers, human-relations-oriented management consultants and personnel/human resource managers who thought that they were overthrowing the harsh piecework strategies of Frederick Taylor and replacing it with a more compassionate workplace:

> Taylorism dominates the world of production; the practitioners of "human relations" and "industrial psychology" are the maintenance crew for the human machinery. (BRAVERMAN 1974, P.87)
>
> This criticism is true to a considerable extent today, and Drucker's words of 1950 are still relevant for the 1980s and 1990s. Behavioural scientists are sometimes expected (and indeed sometimes expect it of themselves) to use theories of group dynamics, motivation, leadership, job and organisational design and so on to engineer human beings in work groups into "teams" or pseudo-families: the "builders" of such teams often seem to believe that it is possible to engineer away
> - all real conflict
> - all individual human loneliness and desire for solitude
> - all loyalties to groups outside the workplace
> - all deep and systematic criticism of management.
>
> Such engineering, of course, is thankfully impossible outside a totalitarian system, but that impossibility doesn't stop many behavioural-science-trained servants of power still trying to perform such engineering.

7. *Crises.* Crises (particularly the appearance of a perceived common enemy) can make group members conform more often.

(ADAPTED FROM HODGETTS 1980, PP.114–15; CAPPS *ET AL.* 1981, PP.130–1)

Yet conformity is not necessarily a bad thing. Every day we trust implicitly that people will conform to traffic laws, that strangers and distant colleagues will not suddenly begin to ask us personal questions, that firemen, police officers and soldiers protecting our welfare will follow the orders of their superiors, and so on. Pure, unthinking obedience to authority, the perception that we are totally controlled by others and we have no free will or autonomy, can of course be dangerous (see the discussion of the work of Milgram and Rotter in Chapter 6).

Within groups, conformity to norms contributes to the cohesiveness of the group—the extent to which the group is united and collectively motivated to achieve the group's goals. The stronger the conformity to norms, the greater the cohesiveness, and the greater the pressure upon actual or potential deviants from the norm to conform. Being in a group with high cohesiveness can often be a pleasant and emotionally involving experience.[3] Cohesiveness creates a strong "we-feeling", accompanied as often as not as by negative feelings towards others outside the group—a "they-feeling". Cohesiveness can be measured roughly by instruments such as the group effectiveness questionnaire (Box 11.E), or sociograms (see Box 11.D).

It is often assumed that, because cohesiveness in groups—work groups, sporting teams, committees—feels so good, it must cause the group to be

---

[3] Cf. Fromm's remarks about group narcissism:

> Of particular interest is group narcissism. Group narcissism is a phenomenon of the greatest political significance. After all, the average person lives in social circumstances which restrict the development of intense narcissism. What should feed the narcissism of a poor man, who has little social prestige, whose children even tend to look down upon him? He is nothing—but if he can identify with his nation, or can transfer his personal narcissism to the nation, then he is everything. If such a person said, "I am the most wonderful man or woman in the world; I am the cleanest, cleverest, most efficient, best educated of all people; I am superior to everybody in the world," anybody who heard this would be disgusted and feel that the person was a bit crazy. But when people describe their nation in these terms, nobody takes exception. On the contrary, if a person says, "My nation is the strongest, the most cultured, the most peace-loving, the most talented of all nations," he is not looked upon as being crazy but as a very patriotic citizen. (FROMM 1982, PP.51–52)

Fromm uses the term "group" to encompass nations and religions, but the dynamics of macro-patriotism towards a nation and micro-patriotism towards a smaller group are similar.

BOX 11.D: Measuring group cohesiveness and identifying roles via sociograms

This sociogram represents a group of twelve students in a college and each circle represents an individual student. Each student was asked the following question:

> If you had to be on a committee of four members including yourself, who else (if anyone) would you choose to work with you? You may choose three people but, clearly, you don't have to nominate three, just those whom you would like most to work with. Also state those people (if any) you would dislike working with. You may identify three people you would least prefer to work with, but you don't have to.

In the sociogram the *positive choices* (most preferred) are represented by black lines, while the *negative choices* (least preferred) are represented by broken lines.

Social relationships which are typical of most groups are shown by this sociogram. Usually two personality characteristics are revealed by sociograms: popularity and isolation.

(a) Four choice patterns are associated with a popular personality:

1. *The star.* The most popular person, or the star, receives the most votes. In our sociogram, 5 is the star, because he receives six votes out of a possible eleven.
2. *Mutually attractive pair.* This refers to reciprocating friendship choices such as 7 and 8.
3. *Chain structures*, the friendship structure that links individuals in a chain form. The chain series can be either reciprocated or unreciprocated choices. The individuals 8, 7, 6, 3 and 2 form a reciprocated chain.
4. *The clique.* The trio which forms a triangle like 3, 4 and 6 forms a closed friendship group, that is, each member chooses, and is chosen by, the other two.

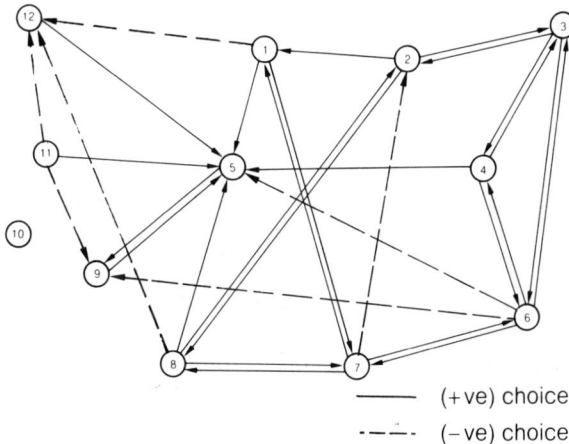

——— (+ve) choice

-·—·- (−ve) choice

Sociogram of twelve college students (TEASDALE 1976, PP. 214–16. REPRODUCED WITH PERMISSION)

(b) Three variables of isolation are often presented in the structure of a group:
 1. *The rejectee.* 12 is rejected by 1, 8 and 11, but is not chosen by anyone: in fact, he is rejected.
 2. *The neglectee.* 11 is not rejected by anyone, but is not chosen by anyone either. He is ignored and neglected.
 3. *The isolate.* The term "isolate" describes the person who neither makes a choice nor receives a choice. In our sociogram 10 is an isolate.
A final choice pattern emerges which is frequently referred to as the *power behind the throne.* Number 9 is an example of the power behind the throne for although he is chosen only once, this choice is by the star, and he can be characterised as having considerable influence within the group in an indirect way.

more effective, to make better decisions. This, however, is by no means the case. Dividing the world up into in-groups and out-groups can often lead to distorted perceptions,[4] which impair effective functioning.

Groupthink

Janis (Janis and Mann 1977) has argued that highly cohesive groups often make bad decisions because of a syndrome he called "groupthink". This syndrome has eight symptoms:

1. The group has an *illusion of invulnerability*, which leads to excessive optimism and risk-taking.
2. Group members *rationalise* away warnings or threats.
3. Group members believe in the *inherent morality* of their decisions, brushing away thoughts of unethical behaviour by saying "How could *we* do such things?"
4. Opponents of the group are *stereotyped* as being too evil, stupid or weak to take seriously.
5. Anyone foolhardy enough to question the status quo within the group has *direct pressure* applied to conform.
6. Group members with doubts *censor themselves* to preserve the appearance of consent.
7. Because silence is interpreted as consent, there is an *illusion of unanimity*.
8. Just as bodyguards protect us from physical harm, so some people set themselves up as *mind-guards* or censors or gate-keepers in order to prevent challenging or threatening information available outside the group from appearing before the group.

Janis originally applied these concepts to foreign policy decision-making under Roosevelt (Pearl Harbour), Kennedy (Bay of Pigs, Cuban Missile Crisis),

---

4 As Merton observes:
 . . . the very same behaviour undergoes a complete change of evaluation . . . in its transition from the in-group Abe Lincoln to the out-group Abe Kurosawa . . . Did Lincoln work far into the night? This testifies that he was industrious, resolute, perseverant, and eager to realise his capacities to the full. Do the out-group Jews or Japanese keep these same hours? This only bears witness to their sweatshop mentality, their ruthless undercutting of American standards, their unfair competitive practices. Is the in-group hero frugal, thrifty and sparing? Then the out-group villain is stingy, miserly, and penny-pinching. (MERTON 1975, P.342)

and Johnson (Vietnam). Raven and Rubin (1976) have applied the groupthink model to explain the Watergate crisis under Nixon,[5] while Thompson (1985) has also used the model to explain decision-making on the British and Argentinian sides in the 1982 Falklands/Malvinas war and also to speculate about the psychological mechanisms that could trigger a third world war.

The groupthink model was used in these studies in order to explain the behaviour of high-level political cabinets and ministries, but the model is just as useful in explaining the behaviour of a sporting team, a charity fund-raising committee, a teenage gang, or a work group.

How can groupthink be avoided? The syndrome is basically about decision-making that is too narrowly focused, so broadening of the focus can be brought about by wider examination of alternatives, generation of contingency plans, and setting up devil's advocates who can throw up likely criticisms without being stigmatised as being disloyal to the group.[6] Thus cohesiveness in and of itself is not an ideal quality for a group to have, although it is very useful and pleasant for a group to have it: cohesiveness is usually a necessary condition for group effectiveness but rarely a sufficient condition.

Team-building

How then can groups be made effective? Is it possible, after taking into account role-taking, norm-formation, and conformity and cohesiveness, to "build" a "team" of people? To a certain extent, yes. A good place to start with an already existing group would be to administer the group effectiveness questionnaire (Box 11.E), which will help to diagnose existing strengths and weaknesses, thus allowing consolidation of strengths and analysis and reduction of weaknesses.

Would-be team-builders have to keep certain reservations in mind, however. "Team" for many people has a sporting connotation, but the sports metaphor can be pushed too far when talking about, say, a work group. In sporting situations, the goals of a team are clear-cut, as are the rules and the roles. This is more than can be said for life off the playing fields (see Chapter 2).

One has to be careful also of using tools such as sociograms (Box 11.D) to analyse the structure of groups. It is sometimes presumed that the popularity of an individual or individuals is a mandate for leadership, while a lack of popularity implies destabilising and dysfunctional deviance. This is often the case, but it is also often not the case. A popular person may not be a good leader. People may not be clear as to whether they should use task or socio-emotional criteria in selecting others. People may choose others not because of their competence but because of their incompetence—a weak leader can be manipulated by others. An isolate may well be the expert upon whom the entire group depends.

---

[5] Although Janis believes that high esprit de corps and mutual admiration and respect are essential for groupthink, these did not exist in the Nixon group. The group was held together by mutual identification with a common leader upon whom all members were dependent. The processes of groupthink were fostered by competition between individuals and factions, and by strong runaway norms—pressures to try and at least equal, and preferably exceed, one another in taking strong, unscrupulous, and risky stands in dealing with "enemies". In trying to compare this group with other decision-making bodies, it was in many respects more like the entourage of Adolf Hitler or Joseph Stalin than that of other American presidents. The actions of Nixon's group were, of course, not so extreme, but all three groups were highly dependent upon the leader, and the members of all three groups wanted to outdo one another in taking extreme actions. (RAVEN AND RUBIN 1976, P433)

[6] Among executives of the Catholic church, the worthiness or otherwise of a person to be canonised (made a saint) is determined by a debate: one executive takes the part of God (Advocatus Dei), while one takes the role of the Devil (Advocatus Diaboli). The Devil's Advocate is not thought less Christian for this role-playing.

BOX 11.E: Group effectiveness questionnaire. How effective is your group?

1. Distribute copies of this questionnaire to all members of your group.
2. Members fill in anonymously, preferably using the same colour/type of pencils/pens.
3. Copies of the questionnaires are gathered, shuffled.
4. Copies are identified with colour pen markings (blue straight line, green dot–dash, etc.).
5. Responses are transferred to Group Effectiveness Chart (p.356), using coloured pens.
6. Group averages are calculated, transferred to Group Effectiveness Chart.
7. Analyse chart. Remarks like "Who's that idiot with the red line?" are not permitted. If the chart reveals dramatic weaknesses, then reprisals and accusations merely serve to reinforce the point that the group has problems. Work through items one by one. Try to see connections between some items and others. Note large gaps between the perceptions of some and others. Above all, remember item L, Freedom from Conformity, and try and shift the group's norm up on this.
8. Your group should clarify whether members should answer items purely from an individual, personal standpoint, or whether they should answer according to how they see others in the group, or according to how they see the whole group (themselves plus others), e.g. in a question on role clarity, do I answer it according to whether *my* role is clear, whether *other people's* roles are clear, or whether *all people's* roles are clear. If the group cannot agree on this, run the questionnaire three times (I, them, us), chart the results, and discuss the differences and similarities.

A. **GOALS**

Poor 0   1   2   3   4   5   6   7   8   9   10 Good

Confused; diverse; conflicting, indifferent; little interest

Clear to all; shared by all; all care about the goals; feel involved

---

B. **COMMUNICATION**

Poor 0   1   2   3   4   5   6   7   8   9   10 Good

Misunderstandings occur constantly

Misunderstandings occur rarely

C. TIME MANAGEMENT

Poor 0   1   2   3   4   5   6   7   8   9   10 Good

Wastes time; lurches from procrastination to crisis; obsessed with trivia; doesn't set priorities; achieves little

Uses time well; little procrastination, crisis; priorities set; achieves much

D. EXPRESSION OF FEELINGS

Poor 0   1   2   3   4   5   6   7   8   9   10 Good

Members conceal and distort real feelings

Members express real feelings naturally and honestly

E. MUTUAL SUPPORT

Poor 0   1   2   3   4   5   6   7   8   9   10 Good

Members avoid or attack others when they need support

Members provide help and support to others when they need it

F. CONFLICT MANAGEMENT

Poor 0   1   2   3   4   5   6   7   8   9   10 Good

Conflicts are avoided, suppressed, denied, distorted or smoothed over; conflict seen as abnormal, fatally divisive

Conflicts are confronted openly, constructively; conflict seen as normal, manageable

G. PARTICIPATION

Poor 0   1   2   3   4   5   6   7   8   9   10 Good

Few dominate; some passive; some not listened to; several talk at once or interrupt

All get in; all are really listened to

H. POLITICAL OPENNESS

Poor 0   1   2   3   4   5   6   7   8   9   10 Good

There always seem
to be undercurrents
in group; members
play games and
work according to
hidden agendas;
manipulators are at
work

Members are up-
front, honest about
what they want; are
game-free

I. TEAMWORK/A

Poor 0   1   2   3   4   5   6   7   8   9   10 Good

Members neither
know nor care
about skills of
others; talent is
wasted; inefficiency
results

Members know and
respect each others'
skills; talent is
harnessed;
efficiency results

J. TEAMWORK/B

Poor 0   1   2   3   4   5   6   7   8   9   10 Good

Members jealously
guard territories,
skills monopoly,
even to point of
deliberately
bamboozling others;
reject sharing of
workflow,
multiskilling

Members share
skills, territories,
workloads; accept
multiskilling because
it helps all to
understand overall
workflow, lets
members cover for
others, develops
multiple career
paths

K. ROLE CLARITY

Poor 0   1   2   3   4   5   6   7   8   9   10 Good

Members feel
confused about role
in group

Members
understand role in
group

Group dynamics   **355**

L. FREEDOM FROM CONFORMITY

Poor 0 1 2 3 4 5 6 7 8 9 10 Good

Members feel that they will be harassed, laughed at if they try new ideas out on group; feel that they cannot play devil's advocate without being victimised; sometimes go along with others to get a quick decision

Members feel that they can try out new ideas on group; feel that they can play devil's advocate without victimisation; feel confident that they can hold out against quick decisions without being pressured

M. DIAGNOSIS OF PROBLEMS

Poor 0 1 2 3 4 5 6 7 8 9 10 Good

Jump directly to remedial proposals; treat symptoms rather than basic causes

When problems arise, the situation is carefully diagnosed before action is proposed; solutions attack basic causes

N. DECISION TOUGHNESS

Poor 0 1 2 3 4 5 6 7 8 9 10 Good

Hard decisions cannot be made, especially when vested interests (inside and outside group) are threatened; integrity hopelessly compromised from outset

Hard decisions can be made, even when vested interests (inside and outside group) are threatened

O. LEADERSHIP

Poor 0 1 2 3 4 5 6 7 8 9 10 Good

Group needs for leadership not met; group depends too much on a single person or a few persons

As needs for leadership arise various members meet them ("distributed leadership"); anyone feels free to volunteer as he sees a group need

P. TAKING RESPONSIBILITY

Poor 0   1   2   3   4   5   6   7   8   9   10 Good

Members avoid or
reject responsibility

Members accept
responsibility where
appropriate

Q. SKILLS LEVEL

Poor 0   1   2   3   4   5   6   7   8   9   10 Good

Members lack the
skills needed to
contribute effectively

Members have the
skills needed to
contribute effectively

R. PROGRESS MEASUREMENT/FEEDBACK

Poor 0   1   2   3   4   5   6   7   8   9   10 Good

Members don't
know how to
measure progress
on group task

Members know how
to measure progress
of group task

(Adapted from Schein 1969; Mangham 1979; Dunphy and Dick 1981)

Group effectiveness chart

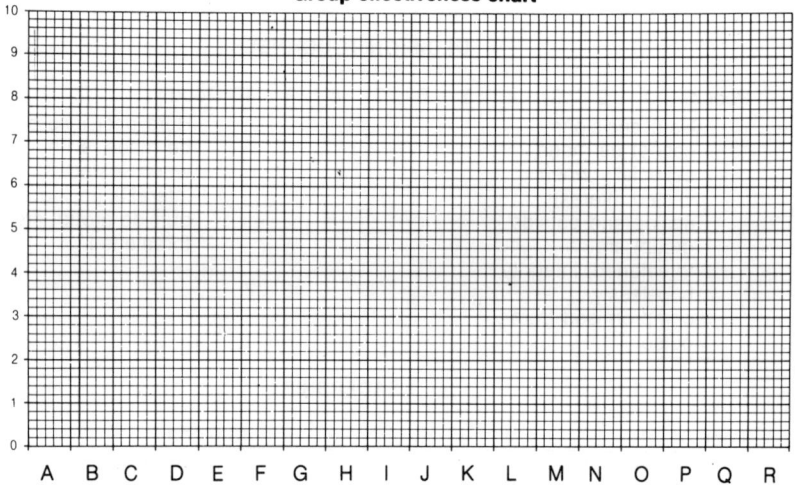

A   B   C   D   E   F   G   H   I   J   K   L   M   N   O   P   Q   R

A. Goals	G. Participation	M. Diagnosis of problems
B. Communication	H. Political openness	N. Decision toughness
C. Time management	I. Teamwork/A	O. Leadership
D. Expression of feelings	J. Teamwork/B	P. Taking responsibility
E. Mutual support	K. Role clarity	Q. Skills level
F. Conflict management	L. Freedom from conformity	R. Progress measurement/feedback

Conflict: Manageable and unmanageable

Also, within groups, it is often presumed that conflict is always a bad thing, while cohesiveness and conformity are always good things. While we may disagree with this with our heads, we may agree with it with our hearts— most of us prefer the warm inner glow of agreement to the stress of disagreement. It is sometimes presumed that conflict can be engineered away by using such methods as consensus (see below). But conflict cannot always be engineered away. A group comprised of pro- and anti-abortion campaigners may be able to agree on procedural issues such as when they want lunch, but not on substantive items like whether or not abortion is a good thing. Some problems have no solution.

It is often false and dangerous to imply that everything is fine within a group. Judges often deliver minority verdicts or opinions on panels such as higher courts. The dynamics of groups such as juries change quite dramatically according to what methods of decision-making are applied: simple majority, "strong" majority (e.g. two-thirds), unanimity. What happens when groups cannot agree? Sometimes the strongest minority prevails. Sometimes the decision is transferred elsewhere. Sometimes differences can be engineered away by team-building. Sometimes groups self-destruct, violently, through yelling and shoving, or quietly, through people becoming apathetic and voting with their feet. Fragments of the group may form coalitions with other fragments or other groups, or they may simply dissolve.

Sometimes people just take their ball and go home. Many groups contain members who cordially loathe other group members, yet the group's tasks get done. In other groups, even that minimum level of interpersonal chemistry, or at least stolid persistence in achieving goals, is not there. That's tough, but that's life.

Methods of group decision-making

How do groups make decisions? There are many methods, all of which have fallen in and out of fashion, all of which vary according to the culture and values of the individuals in the group. It is useful to try and plot some of these methods on a rough continuum (Fig. 11.3). Note that such a continuum is, to a large extent, the mirror image of various models of leadership considered in Chapter 10 (e.g. Tannenbaum and Schmidt, Likert).

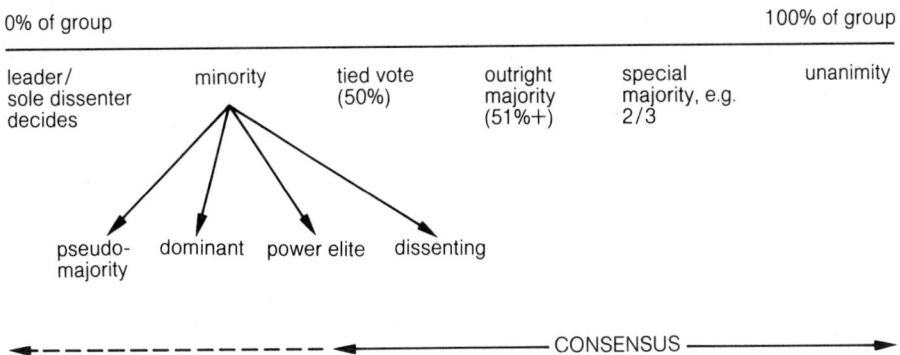

Fig 11.3 *Some methods of making decisions in groups*

In many groups, the group does not decide at all; one person, the *leader,* decides, and the others are there either to consult, advise, witness or rubber-stamp the leader's decision. The leader's real or perceived power needs to be high in such situations, and the leader needs to have a keen appreciation of the passive and active resistance and acceptance her decisions will meet with.[7] Power of veto is relevant here, of course.

Minorities can operate in a number of ways in groups. A *pseudo-majority* can exist when a minority exercises power via inequalities in votes. A political party exercising a gerrymander, or stockholders in a company having different classes of stocks and voting rights, or a minority using proxy votes of people outside the group currently meeting—all use this approach. A *dominant* minority is one which rules when its opponents cannot agree enough to form a majority, for example, if group A with 30 per cent of power and group B with 30 per cent of power loathe each other so much that they cannot form a coalition, then group C, with 40 per cent, effectively controls the wider group.

A *power elite* may control the group in much the same way as a strong individual leader does, either officially or unofficially. An elite may make decisions and not be challenged by others, or the elite may control or influence the votes of others. A *dissenting* minority occurs in many groups, for example a panel or bench of judges: the majority may give a verdict or decision, but a minority of one or several judges may, rather than remain silent or give the impression of unanimity, issue a statement of dissent. *Tied votes* occur when two sub-groups have each 50 per cent of power (of course, tied votes could just as well be three sub-groups with 33⅓ per cent, etc.). Groups sometimes have mechanisms for resolving such ties, for example, the chairperson has the casting vote, or tied votes on a motion means that the motion is lost, or the casting vote is drawn from a hat, etc. *Straight majorities* are usually anything over 50 per cent.[8] In the democratic tradition, the majority is always right, although there are many who doubt this, arguing that quantity cannot substitute for quality.[9] *Special majorities* are often required on extremely important decisions, for example, two-thirds majority rather than 50 per cent. *Unanimity* or 100 per cent agreement is unusual, but sometimes it is required for some decisions. In some parts of the world, a unanimous verdict is required of juries in trials for crimes such as murder, while in other parts of the world a straight or special majority is required. *Consensus* is basically an attempt to reach a majority or unanimous decision, usually without taking a vote. The pros and cons of issues are thrashed out at length, with someone such as the chairperson trying to find common areas of agreement between disputing parties. Elimination of dissent may not be the aim of consensus: a consensus decision is reached when a dissenting group member can say:

> I understand what most of you would like to do. I personally would not do that, but I feel that you understand what my alternative would be. I have had sufficient opportunity to sway you to my point of view but clearly have not been able to

[7] For the heroic, and possibly for the paranoid, there is the comfort of the maxim "one man in the right is a majority".

[8] Some straight majorities are in fact pseudo-unanimous: government ministries or cabinets usually operate on the principle of cabinet solidarity, i.e. decisions made by straight majority (or perhaps by a powerful leader or power elite) are defended by all ministers in public, with (officially) no breaches such as dissenting minorities or "leakers".

[9] For example, in Hendrik Ibsen's play *An Enemy of the People,* the hero Stockmann argues that the majority is always wrong: majorities by definition, says Stockmann, are mediocre and conservative, and cannot discern current realities and future trends as well as perceptive individuals and elites.

do so. Therefore, I will gladly go along with what most of you wish to do. (SCHEIN 1969, P.56)

Consensus has become fashionable as a method of making decisions within groups. Consensus decision-making in Japanese quality circles, for example, has been cited by some observers as a sure-fire method of ensuring group task commitment and lifting group motivation (and thus ensuring high overall productivity) (see Chapters 12 and 14). Some have criticised such examples of consensus, suggesting that cultures such as Japan are very group- and cooperation-oriented, whereas Western cultures are more individual- and competition-oriented, and that Japanese "cooperation" may in fact be simply conformism and manipulation of the group by paternalistic managements (Ferris and Wagner 1985). This is not to say that Westerners cannot learn to be more cooperative: it may be, however, that cooperation and agreement for their own sake, and the attempt to avoid the divisiveness of a vote, are not necessarily the best bases for making decisions.

Further points against making unanimous decisions by consensus are made by Davis (1981):

1. it may become the paramount goal, causing people to suppress their opposition or to tell the group they agree when honestly they do not;
2. it is frustrating to all members to have to keep discussing a subject long after their minds are made up, simply because they are hoping to convince honest dissenters (a waste of time and an embarrassment to the dissenters);
3. it can cause great delays;
4. it permits one dissenter to make the decision for the whole group, which destroys the basic purpose for which the group was convened. (P.62)

Methods of reaching voting decisions

Voting can be either private (e.g. secret ballot) or public (e.g. show of hands). Groups choose one of these methods because they value public demonstration of belief over privacy, or privacy over public demonstration of belief, or because they simply haven't thought about the pros and cons of the method they use. Public voting can be quick, it can be convenient in small groups, and it forces people to commit themselves publicly to a decision. It can however force people to conform to the pressure coming from articulate and assertive individuals who dismiss attempts to have secret ballots with remarks like "what have you got to hide?", "All right-thinking people know there's only one way to vote on this one." Secret ballots have the virtue of protecting privacy and preventing pressure to conform in public settings, but it can be inconvenient in small groups, and it may allow people to vote in a particular way without demonstrating overt commitment to a belief, which may lead to hypocrisy (saying one thing, and voting for another). Electronic voting systems are now available for small groups, although some people still retain suspicions about the fool- and knave-proofness of electronic voting.

Group decision-making and problem-solving: Pro and con[10]

Are groups effective or ineffective at making decisions and solving problems? Do too many cooks spoil the broth, or do many hands make light work? Is it true that a camel is a horse designed by a committee? We hear many complaints about the groups that we meet—committees, sub-committees, advisory groups, conferences, task forces, panels, or even the carload of friends deliberating on what kind of pizza to buy—but the fact remains that

---

[10] Cf. the discussions of participation in Chapters 10 and 14.

groups are part and parcel of living, and that they can be more or less effective according to our understanding or lack of understanding of group processes. What then are the strengths and weaknesses of group decision-making and problem-solving, or, to put it another way, the weaknesses and strengths of individual decision-making and problem-solving?

Pro: Many hands make light work

Groups are good at generating many new ideas (Table 11.1). They are also good at recalling information accurately. They can make a wide range of skills, contributions and experiences available. They can present a wide range of approaches or styles of problem-solving and decision-making (see Chapter 9), thus ensuring that blind spots, such as those an individual might have, do not distort perceptions. Of course, groups can have blind spots too, particularly if the group is over-homogeneous and lacking in alternative points of view. Related to this multiplicity of styles is multiplicity of roles (task, socio-emotional and, of course, destructive), which individuals would be hard put to emulate. Motivation can be increased through participation. No matter how high the quality of a decision, it has to be accepted by those who are going to implement that decision. If people have not been consulted or involved in the decision-making process, there is no mandate for change, and people may either implement the decision in an apathetic fashion or may actively work against it. Group involvement means group commitment. Such involvement of the group may mean a dilution of power for a leader or individual. This damping down of autocratic decision-making, a setting up of checks and balances through committees, may be an intended or unintended consequence of working through groups.

Wider communication through group structures will probably enhance greater coordination of departments, plans and policies. Greater risk-taking is sometimes seen as a weakness of group operations (see below). Yet a high risk decision for an individual can often be a moderate risk decision for a group because risk is a function of knowledge, and group deliberations may increase knowledge about a particular situation. Thus risks can be managed more competently.

Groups are also criticised because they may cause unplanned delays, but what if delays are planned? What if, for example, someone or some group decides that a problem could benefit from some benign neglect or, even better, suffer the death of a thousand sub-committees and attempts to gain more data? This is not very honest, but such things do happen. This "strength" of group decision-making and problem-solving could just as well appear as a "weakness", but, as in many such things, it really depends upon your point of view (and your vested interest).

Con: Too many cooks spoil the broth

When are groups not as good as individuals in making decisions and solving problems? Groups are not needed for routine decisions of most types: there is no need to agonise over which option to use when there is a standard operating procedure laid down and accepted by all. Similarly, a group of non-specialists is not necessarily better than one specialist. Groups are not very good at solving problems which require long chains of decisions and solutions. Groups are great at playing concertos, but not at composing them; or solving crossword puzzles but not writing them; or making films but not novels.

Table 11.1 Pros and cons of group decision-making and
problem-solving

Pro	Con
• Can generate many new ideas.	• Not needed for routine decisions.
• Can recall information accurately.	• Not good at solving problems which
• Can make a wide range of skills,	require long chains of decisions and
contributions and experiences	solutions.
available.	• Often slow and costly.
• Can present wide range of styles of	• Members' personal needs may be
decision-making and	given priority over group's needs
problem-solving.	(hidden agendas).
• Can present multiplicity of roles	• Minority tyranny can occur (cliques,
(task, socio-emotional or destructive).	factions, consensus holdouts).
• Motivation can increase through	• Majority tyranny can occur—
participation (quality/acceptance,	enforcement of conformity may stifle
mandate).	creative individuals, produce faulty
• Authoritarian power can be checked.	decisions.
• Makes coordination easier.	• Conservative, lowest-common-
• More competent risk management.	denominator decisions may occur.
• Can bring about useful delays.	• Risky decisions may occur (risky
	shift, dilution of responsibility).
	• Group inertia may develop.

Source: Adapted from Koontz, O'Donnell and Weihrich (1980), Lee (1980), Hodgetts (1980), Stoner, Collins and Yetton (1985), Byrt (1980).

Groups can be slow and costly. Slowness is often related to group size: if group size increases arithmetically, then interactions between group members increase geometrically, and for everyone to talk to everyone else in a large group is time- and cash-consuming (avoidance or delay of action may of course be a deliberate strategy).

Group members' personal needs for power and influence may overwhelm the collective good of the group. In addition to the formal agenda of a group, there may be one or several hidden agendas in operation with which individuals or sub-groups may try to manipulate others. Cliques or factions may dominate the group, and such cliques or factions may choose to paralyse and perhaps destroy the group rather than see their opponents win. Minority tyranny may occur where the group seeks consensus, and those who hold out from unanimity can block (horse-trade, compromise) with a power of leverage way beyond what their numbers would suggest.

Majority tyranny can occur when sheer force of numbers swamps individuals or minorities. Such individuals may or may not be wrong, but unless other mechanisms operate (e.g. minority verdicts being published, or minorities avoiding group solidarity and leaking information to outsiders), we will never know. This enforcement of conformity can lead to groupthink situations.

Such majority tyranny can often lead to stodginess and conservatism, with groups producing lowest-common-denominator decisions, which usually please no one and often aggravate many.

Alternatively, groups sometimes produce, not conservative decisions, but radical decisions. Group decision-making and problem-solving is sometimes characterised by the *risky shift*, whereby groups make decisions that are riskier than any of the group's members would have made individually. While this is not always a bad thing, it can be bad and indeed disastrous if group members feel that group membership entails dilution of responsibility (what belongs to everyone belongs to no one) and hence that normal procedures of risk evaluation are not relevant.

Following such behaviour, is the emergence of group inertia, wherein group members come to rely upon others to think and act for them. In such cases, an individual leader or an elite may emerge as the real force within the group, with the rest of the group merely a rubber-stamp, and thus unnecessary ("when two people agree all the time, one of them is unnecessary").

These remarks apply primarily to conventional, "interacting" or "normal" groups, meetings run according to standard procedures, for example. Three methods of group decision-making and problem-solving which have been designed to circumvent problems associated with the conventional model are brainstorming, Delphi and nominal group technique.

Brainstorming

Brainstorming is a way of trying to break the dynamics (or more accurately the statics) of groups that are conformist and that have become stuck in a rut of logical, analytical, linear, convergent thinking and cannot, as a matter of routine, make the leap to imaginative, creative, non-linear, divergent thinking (see the discussion of styles of thinking in Chapter 9). Creativity, getting new perspectives on things, cannot be programmed or commanded: it usually happens only when group members can step outside their task roles and relax and have fun. This does not normally happen in work or task-oriented situations. So much of what we do is concerned with making sure that existing processes are operating and that like things and ideas are tidily pigeon-holed together; yet as Rawlinson (1981) points out, so much creativity is about the relating of things or ideas which were previously unrelated.

Brainstorming as a process depends on two principles: *defer judgment* and *quantity breeds quality*. Normally we judge our own and others' ideas immediately they see the light of day. This, suggested brainstorming's inventor, Alex Osborn, is often a bad thing, in that many good ideas strike people as being too way-out or impractical, when in fact they may simply be ahead of their time. How "practical" would aeroplanes or automobiles have been to a citizen of the eighteenth, or even very early twentieth, century? Quantity can breed quality, Osborn argued, if an enormous amount of dud ideas nevertheless contained one good idea.

Thus, the purpose of the brainstorming process is to generate as many ideas as possible, without judging such ideas prematurely. Brainstorming is normally conducted in a group of six to twelve people, preferably of equal status (the presence of both superiors and subordinates tends to freeze up creativity). The group has usually been informed of the problem to be brainstormed several days before. The group has a leader, and a secretary who records all suggestions. Participants are exhorted to come up with as many far-out solutions as possible. Building on other people's ideas ("hitchhiking", "piggybacking", "cross-fertilising") is encouraged. After 30 to 45 minutes, the group ceases brainstorming. An evaluation group, usually of five people (so that there will be no tied votes) begins to evaluate the accumulated solutions. It is a matter of controversy as to whether the evaluation group should be the same as or different from the brainstorming group. Solutions are organised into categories, and assigned priorities as to their practicality.

Solutions emerging from brainstorming are often zany and impractical, but occasionally illuminating—and after all, that is what the process is meant to achieve.[11] Brainstorming, however, should be applied only where problems can be stated specifically, where there is a possibility of multiple solutions, and where the solution or concept or thing being sought is genuinely new (inventing a new product rather than developing a marketing strategy for an existing product, for example; see Table 11.2).

Group cohesiveness can be built into brainstorming, especially when extroverts can give full play to their sense of play and desire to outdazzle peers with ideas which are more and more way out (De Bono 1971). Brainstorming has been criticised, however, because of a number of apparent weaknesses: its usefulness is limited to relatively simple problems; creativity can collapse into anarchy; dominant individuals can have too much influence; and, most seriously, it is often inferior to nominal groups (see below) or individuals working alone in terms of output of creative ideas (Van Gundy 1981; Ferris and Wagner 1985).

Delphi

Delphi is a town in Greece where, in ancient times, priests and priestesses called upon the god Apollo to give them insight into the future. Delphi, the group decision-making technique, was first used in America in the 1950s to predict the impacts of Russian atomic bomb attacks on US industry. The technique basically consists of administering a series of questionnaires to experts in a given field. The experts are usually geographically distant from one another, do not meet, and have no direct or written communication with one another. They are asked to make a series of predictions in a particular area. Their responses are gathered and analysed for trends, convergences and similarities. These patterns form the basis of the next round of questionnaires which are sent out, the experts this time being asked to be more specific in their responses. This process can occur several times, until the analysts running the Delphi process decide that enough significant trends have emerged to base forecasts upon. Delphi has been used in various areas, such as military, educational, marketing and local government planning. Delphi can remove the potentially harmful group pressure to conform that is present in brainstorming and conventional decision-making groups. Anonymous experts are free to make up their own minds in a quiet, reflective environment, and each participant has an equal opportunity to contribute, with all ideas being given equal consideration. A large quantity of ideas can be generated, and some precision can be given ("What is the probability of *x* happening in the next six years?").

Delphi is also useful when it is impractical to bring together people who are widely separated by geography (Delbecq, Van de Ven and Gustafson 1975). However, Delphi can lead to perhaps too much detachment on the part of the participants. Because others are not close at hand to clarify their ideas or terms, confusion can arise. Any conflicts in predictions of the future are "solved" by simple majority vote, which may mean that the correct prediction will be swamped. Related to this, Delphi panels are usually made up of experts in a given field, who may be too close to the problem, or more

---

[11] For example, some brainstorming groups run by Van Gundy came up with the following possible uses for a wire coat-hanger: fish-hook, cooking grill, car muffler repair, toilet unplugger, pants suspenders, toothpick, tip for an arrow, heavy picture hanger (Van Gundy 1981).

bluntly, just plain wrong.[12] The apparent precision of the "predictions" ("54 per cent of the panel think that this has an 86 per cent chance of happening") may trick people into half-believing that the future can be predicted scientifically. Finally, Delphi can be very time-consuming: a three-round process may take over 45 days to complete, which presupposes very high levels of organisation on the part of the organisers and very high levels of motivation on the part of the participants (although some of the time and motivation problems are solved in real-time Delphi, using computer networking (Davis 1981; Van Gundy 1981)).

Nominal group technique (NGT)

Like Delphi, NGT can be used when normal group dynamics of conformity and pressure might possibly distort decision-making and problem-solving in groups. As with Delphi, NGT involves individuals making written responses to problems, but like brainstorming and interacting or nominal groups there is some group discussion.

A group of from five to nine people meets in a normal meeting venue. A leader poses a problem, and group members then begin, silently and individually, to write out possible solutions to the problem. After about 10 to 20 minutes, the group moves to the idea-recording phase. The leader asks each member in turn to give an idea, recording these on a chart or board (round-robin recording). There is no discussion at this stage. All ideas are numbered.

The group then moves to the discussion phase. All ideas are clarified and discussed, but not to the stage where passionate differences are allowed to emerge. The group then moves to the voting stage. Each individual member selects a number (e.g. 5–9) of ideas as being better than the rest, ranking each idea according to a weighting system (e.g. 5 = excellent, 1 = just all right). These votes are written on cards, with idea number at top right and ranking number at bottom right (usually underlined, or circled, or with "R" beside it to ensure no confusion with idea number occurs). The leader collects these cards, shuffles them (to preserve anonymity), and then records the votes for the various ideas.

If no clear pattern of preferences emerges, it is sometimes useful to analyse the voting for unusual patterns; for example, if one proposal receives three 1's and four 5's, there may be differing perceptions about the nature of the idea. Further discussion could take place, followed by a second ballot. Nominal group technique relieves individuals of pressures to conform, allowing individuality to flourish irrespective of individual personality or status differences such as extroversion and introversion, articulateness and inarticulateness, high status and low status: everyone's ideas are treated equally. Yet because idea authors are not known, and do not need to be

---

[12]   ... the specialist is not necessarily the best forecaster. He focuses on a subsystem and frequently takes no account of the larger system. Reciprocating engine experts in the 1930s forecast that propellor aircraft would be standard up to 1980. Military aircraft experts forecast a succession of manned bombers beyond the B-52 as primary weapons systems and for many years did not consider the replacement of manned bombers by missiles. These experts concentrate on a single logistic curve rather than on the envelope of a series of such curves... A dogmatic drive for conformity, the "tyranny of the majority", sometimes threatens to swamp the single maverick who may actually have better insight than the rest of the "experts" who all agree with each other. This is not unknown in science; it is, in fact, a normal situation in the arduous process of creating new paradigms, i.e. scientific revolutions. In short, a consensus of experts does not assure good judgment or superior estimates. (LINSTONE 1975, PP.581–82).

Cf. the discussion of paradigms in Chapter 9.

known if authors decide not to defend ideas strenuously in public, then attention switches away from personalities to the ideas themselves. This is not to say that the group is exclusively task-role-oriented, as often happens in Delphi, for example: the discussion period or periods allows socio-emotional-role-orientation as well. NGT groups often produce a lot of ideas, and the outcome of the group—expressed as quantified priorities—is often much clearer than interacting groups.

NGT of course has drawbacks: it can only be used to solve one problem at a time, it can inhibit spontaneity and freewheeling enthusiasm, it requires a skilled leader, and it sometimes makes people uncomfortable because of its controlled or ritualistic sequencing.

Table 11.2 Pros and cons of brainstorming, Delphi, and nominal group technique

Pro	Con
Brainstorming	
• Many ideas generated—often quantity does mean quality.	• Usefulness limited to relatively simple problems.
• Group cohesiveness can be built.	• Creativity can collapse into anarchy.
• Extroverts' energy can be harnessed to group's purpose.	• Dominant individuals can have too much influence.
• Premature judging avoided.	• Often inferior to NGT or individuals working alone in producing solutions.
• Fun, zaniness, creativity given legitimate role (socio-emotional needs satisfied).	
Delphi	
• Removes group pressures to conform.	• Participants can become overly detached—"too much" task orientation.
• All ideas given equal consideration.	
• Anonymity allows group to focus on issues rather than personalities.	• Confusion can arise because clarification is difficult (less so in real-time Delphi).
• Large quantity of ideas generated.	• Conflicts are "solved" by brute force of majority vote.
• Ideas can be quantified easily.	• Experts are not always right.
• Useful even when/especially if group is geographically dispersed.	• Apparent precision of predictions may be spurious.
• Task needs satisfied.	• Time-consuming (less so with real-time Delphi).
	• Requires lot of organisation.
	• Requires high levels of motivation of participants.
Nominal group technique	
• Removes group pressure to conform.	• Can only be used for one problem at a time.
• All ideas given equal consideration.	
• Anonymity allows group to focus on issues rather than on personalities.	• Can inhibit spontaneity, freewheeling, enthusiasm.
• Task- and socio-emotional needs satisfied.	• Can make people uncomfortable because of degree of control required.
• Many ideas generated.	• Requires a skilled leader.
• Voting, priorities give precise basis for decision-making.	

Source: Adapted from Delbecq, Van de Ven and Gustafson (1975), Davis (1981), Van Gundy (1981).

BOX 11.F: Individual versus group problem-solving questionnaire

Think of a problem. Should you try and solve it yourself, or should you call in others to solve it within a group? This questionnaire may help you solve your problem-solving problem.

Instructions: Read each question carefully and place an X above the one response to each question that best describes your general reaction. Do not spend too much time on any one question; your first reaction is to be the most accurate one.

1. How much time do you have to solve this problem?

Very little	Some	Just enough	More than needed	Much more than needed

2. How likely is it that you could obtain more time to solve this problem?

Unlikely	Somewhat unlikely	About 50/50	Somewhat likely	Likely

3. How likely is it that your subordinates will accept the solution if you try to solve this problem by yourself?

Unlikely	Somewhat unlikely	About 50/50	Somewhat likely	Likely

4. How important to your subordinates is acceptance of the solution to this problem?

Unimportant	Somewhat unimportant	Hard to tell	Somewhat important	Important

5. How reluctant would your subordinates be to implement a solution to this problem if they did not participate in solving it?

Completely	Somewhat	Hard to tell	A little	Not at all

6. How much do the advantages of solving the problem by yourself outweigh the need to obtain acceptance of the solution by your subordinates?

Completely	Somewhat	Hard to tell	A little	Not at all

7. How likely is it that solution uniqueness and originality would be decreased if you tried to solve this problem by yourself?

| Unlikely | Somewhat unlikely | About 50/50 | Somewhat likely | Likely |

8. How much do the advantages of solving the problem by yourself outweigh the need for unique and original solutions?

| Completely | Somewhat | Hard to tell | A little | Not at all |

9. How important is it for your subordinates to interact with one another while solving this problem?

| Unimportant | Somewhat unimportant | Hard to tell | Somewhat important | Important |

10. How much do the advantages of solving this problem by yourself outweigh your subordinates' need to interact with one another in solving this problem?

| Completely | Somewhat | Hard to tell | A little | Not at all |

11. How much information do you have about this problem?

| Very little | Some | A moderate amount | Quite a bit | A lot |

12. How useful is the information you have about this problem (with respect to its ability to help you solve this problem alone)?

| Not very useful | Slightly useful | Moderately useful | Useful | Very useful |

13. How important is it that your subordinates become more cohesive?

| Unimportant | Somewhat unimportant | Hard to tell | Somewhat important | Important |

14. How much do the advantages of solving this problem by yourself outweigh the need for your subordinates to become more cohesive?

| Completely | Somewhat | Hard to tell | A little | Not at all |

15. How important is it for your subordinates to develop their creative problem-solving skills?

| Unimportant | Somewhat unimportant | Hard to tell | Somewhat important | Important |

16. How much do the advantages of solving this problem by yourself outweigh the need for your subordinates to develop their creative problem-solving skills?

| Completely | Somewhat | Hard to tell | A little | Not at all |

17. How likely is it that interpersonal conflict will develop among your subordinates if you attempt to solve this problem as a group?

| Unlikely | Somewhat unlikely | About 50/50 | Somewhat likely | Likely |

18. How much do the advantages of solving the problem by yourself outweigh taking a chance on interpersonal conflict developing among your subordinates?

| Completely | Somewhat | Hard to tell | A little | Not at all |

Scoring and Interpretation: Change each of your responses for questions 1, 2, 4, 6–10, 13–16, and 18 to a numerical score between 1 and 5, going from left to right. For example, if you placed an X over the response "more than needed" for question 1, you would score it as a 4. For questions 3, 5, 11, 12, and 17, assign a "reverse" score to each of your responses. That is, score these questions by going from right to left. Thus, if you placed an X over the response "somewhat likely" for question 3, it would be scored as a 2. Once you have scored all 18 questions, add up the scores to determine your total score.

As a rough guide to interpreting your total score, you probably should involve your subordinates if your score is between 70 and 90. If your score is between 40 and 69, give serious consideration to using group problem solving. Your ratings on the time factor (questions 1 and 2) may help you to make this decision. For example, if you have little time and are unlikely to be able to obtain additional time, you probably will want to attempt to solve the problem by yourself. In this situation, time constraints will outweigh most of the other factors. If your score is between 18 and 39, however, you will be better off solving the problem yourself, regardless of your ratings on the time factor.

Meetings: Tactics nice and nasty

The type of group many people find themselves in most often is that of the meeting. Meetings can be long or short, big or small, effective or ineffective, fair or unfair. The outcomes of meetings are often determined by what tactics are being used by meeting attenders. What follows are lists of some instructive and amusing, and not-so-amusing, tactics, some of which are nasty, and some of which are nice.[13]

Nasty tactics

Stack the meeting. Beloved of political parties, but becoming more important in organisations which pay increasing lip service to participation in decision-making, that is, are publicly politicised rather than privately politicised within the boardroom and executive suite. Only invite your people, or consign notice of the meeting to the void of official channels, or hold the meeting at inconvenient times and places. Announce after the meeting has started that proxies, promised in writing, are acceptable (guess who's got some?).

Disinformation. Use the grapevine to broadcast scurrilous information about your opponents, and yourself. Have proof of your own innocence at hand and play it for the self-righteous vote; have proof (or at least some accidentally disclosed circumstantial evidence) of your opponents' guilt.

Fake fight. Caucus with allies before the meeting and script a fight. Do the fight in the meeting, then get cosy as strange bedfellows at the critical moment: when the decision is nigh and your opponents have dropped their guard.

Write the minutes. Everybody loves a volunteer, but your interest in this is not altruistic. Your selective recall, if buried in enough verbiage, will not be challenged at the next meeting. History is written by victorious powers, not defeated ones, and as the late A. Hitler remarked, "Posterity will not ask if the victor was wrong."

When losing, defer. Pursue red herrings over hill and dale to waste time, thus causing time to run out for your opponents. Run away and fight another day. Your opponents may be dead, on vacation, ill, out of it, less organised, and even if they are still organised and hot, you will at least have had time to re-group and dig up new counter-arguments.

When losing, ask for a budget. This gives you the appearance of fiscal responsibility rather than a worm twisting on a hook. Budgets, particularly the really detailed ones you want, take time, and what with inflation the way it is, by the time it is presented, the figures will be obsolete, and you, more in sorrow than in anger, will just have to move that the whole thing be cancelled because of dangerously escalating costs (Baker 1983).

Interrogation. Fletcher (1983) suggests some delightfully malicious questioning techniques to confound your enemies, such as delaying ("Hadn't we better consider all the consequences in depth before finally...?"), inciting ("How can we rely on that in the light of your past...?"), inciting via transferred questions ("Surely what Charles is trying to say, isn't he, John, is that your report is complete and utter...?"), covertly transferring responsibility and blame ("How many times have you forgotten that?" "Why

---

[13] Note also the discussion on meetings in Chapter 8.

is it there's nearly always a mistake in the plans?''), and, of course, smearing (''I don't suppose there's any chance that you or one of your team is getting a kickback from X in return for this contract, is there?'').

Dobbing. Some people appear not to want a quiet life, and keep on getting ideas. Make sure that any such person is immediately punished by being given total responsibility to flesh it out in minute detail, and give faint praise if it succeeds and crushing damnation if it fails (which you should be able to arrange). This will stamp out this type of thing.

Meet with the boss before the meeting. Arrange to see the power-figure on quite another matter before a meeting on a hot issue. Be seen going in and out. Let on cryptically that you are now privy to great truths, and that the meeting was a caucus rather than a consultation (Snell 1979). It's worked well enough for prime ministers, so why shouldn't you use it?

The numbers racket. Produce a calculator to blind people with figures. Unfortunately, many former dupes are on to this themselves now, so the current price of getting the numbers via the numbers is a portable computer, preferably with printout with cute little graphics (you, of course, cannot go past the sheer biblical authority of real full-size printout, preferably by the kilo).

Use acronyms (BHP, ACTU, SPQR, ROI, CEO, JITPARV, MITI, etc.). If challenged on a six-letter acronym, roll your eyes in contempt of such ignorance and toss off a throw-away line about it being related to two or three other (equally mythical) three-letter acronyms, then continue talking to others (Baker 1983).

Use jargon. Be careful of using jargon in front of people who understand it. Instead, use marketing jargon with legal people, use computer jargon with marketing people, and so on. If trapped in a room with all departments, create havoc quickly, preferably by using interrogation techniques mentioned above. If they're not fighting each other, they'll be fighting you. Kill or be killed (Baker 1983).

Use catch-phrases (''What's the bottom line?'' ''At the end of the day...'' ''You've got to look at the big picture...'' ''Fresh facts have been uncovered...''). You, too, can speak banalities. Journalists on TV do, and they get paid more than you; why shouldn't you?

Ways to run good meetings (nice tactics)

Pick a good chairperson. Remember, a good chairperson is someone who is happy to know where she is, is happy to feel significant, and is happy to be in a position where she does not need strong convictions.

Start on time. Don't punish the virtuous and reward the sinful by delaying.

Finish on time. Meetings usually drag on because of the ''death of the meeting'' phase—people get comfy, and don't want to go home.

Be aware of and respect motives, irrational or a-rational, of people for attending meetings. As Fletcher (1983) remarks, people go to meetings because

- we feel lonely working on our own
- we are scared of decisions being taken in our absence
- it makes us feel important
- we want a rest from our real work

- we want to offload the responsibility for a difficult decision
- we particularly like the sound of our own voices
- simply because the meeting happens to be happening.

Oh yes, of course—and to work.

Don't avoid conflict inside the meeting because you won't be able to avoid it outside if you do—and it won't be on your terms or ground. Conflict is normal.

Are the appropriate people present? As a test of this, try to minimise the "nobody told us" effect.

Agendas should be clear, giving headline and background information. If participants are required to bring materials, stipulate or attach to agenda. Proposers of items might be requested to append outlines of two solutions to the problem. This discourages frivolity and encourages pre-digestion of facts and values.

Remember the Rule of Halves. Get all items to be discussed to the agenda maker half the time between the meetings (e.g. in the second week of a four-week cycle) (Tropman 1980).

Remember the Rule of Three-Quarters. At the three-quarter point between meetings, all relevant material is sent to group members (Tropman 1980).

Remember the Rule of Thirds. Schedule the heavy items for the middle third of the meeting: this is when people are most fresh and concentrated, and latecomers are present and so are early-goers (most meetings usually end up considering the most important items last, with maximum time pressure and maximum aggravation, with people voting more with their feet than with their hands) (Tropman 1980).

Limit time on agenda items (spike Parkinson's Fifth Law: The amount of time spent on any agenda item is in inverse proportion to its importance).

Control speakers by nominating five or six at a time, in sequence: minimises ego-tripping and top-of-the-heading (if that is your aim), maximises succinctness because of speakers' guilt about others in the queue.

Use gimmicks to motivate people to finish quickly and work efficiently (e.g. hold stand-up meetings, schedule meetings immediately prior to lunch or knock-off time).

Protect the weak. Make sure everyone is heard from: some may be useless people, but some may have the secret of the meaning of life.

Respect people's individual differences. As each person walks into the room, imagine that they are coming up the ramp of the Ark. They are different more in ideas than form. Remember, it's easier to persuade each person in a group than it is to persuade the group *in situ*; and if you get the individuals, you get the group eventually (Snell 1979).

Avoid groupthink. Set at least one person up as a devil's advocate, free to put the most wrong-headed, bloody-minded, nit-picking alternative viewpoints without pressure to conform from the group.

Keep a record of who agreed to do what, where, when, how, and with or on whom; reproduce and distribute.

Ask yourself: is this meeting really necessary? If there's nothing to discuss at the daily/weekly/monthly meeting, don't discuss it. Meetings are tools, not sacraments. Rather trying for those who live by the dictum, *comito, ergo sum* (I attend committees, therefore I exist), but then a little Darwinian stress never hurt anyone.

Summary

A group consists of people with shared norms and interlocking roles. Three types of roles are considered: task, socio-emotional and destructive. Norms can be formal or informal. There is often conflict between formal and informal norms, and this usually reflects conflict between the informal and formal group or organisation structure.

Conformity to norms can produce cohesiveness in groups. Cohesiveness can be beneficial to groups, but only so long as it does not lead to behaviour such as the groupthink phenomenon.

Groups can be structured using team-building tools such as sociograms and diagnostic questionnaires, but irreconcilable conflicts need to be recognised and respected. Different methods of group decision-making can sometimes affect the nature of the decision reached.

Decision-making and problem-solving in conventional or interacting groups has various strengths and weaknesses. Three alternative techniques —brainstorming, Delphi and nominal group technique— have been designed to avoid the weaknesses of conventional group processes, but such alternative techniques have some problems of their own.

A common type of group, the meeting, can be partly understood in terms of the tactics—both nice and nasty—deployed there.

Questions for discussion

1. Explain the different types of task, socio-emotional and destructive roles which are played in groups. Can you think of any such roles not described here?
2. What is the relationship of formal and informal norms?
3. Observe a group and attempt to describe the role and norm behaviour occurring.
4. Compare two or three differing groups (e.g. department in a workplace, friendship group in a workplace, sporting team, volunteer committee) and compare and contrast role and norm behaviour in such groups.
5. Write two role-plays/scripts of the same meeting—one in which groupthink occurs, one in which groupthink is prevented.
6. Can teams be built?
7. How might the methods of decision-making operating in a group affect the decisions made by that group?
8. What are the advantages and disadvantages of group decision-making and problem-solving? Compare conventional groups with brainstorming, Delphi and nominal group technique groups.
8. What tactics might be used in meetings? Can you think of any other tactics not described here?

References

Avery, Gayle, Baker, Ellen and Kane, Bob (1984). *Psychology at Work: Fundamentals and Applications.* (Prentice-Hall: Sydney).

Baker, Stephen (1983). *I Hate Meetings.* (William Collins: Sydney).

Baritz, Loren (1965). *The Servants of Power.* (John Wiley and Sons: New York).

Benne, Kenneth D. and Sheats, Paul (1948/75). "Functional Roles of Group Members", *Journal of Social Issues*, 1948, 4(2), reprinted in Bradford, Leland P. (ed.), *Group Development*, 2nd edn. (University Associates: San Diego).

Bowey, Angela M. (1976). *The Sociology of Organizations.* (Hodder and Stoughton Educational: London).

Braverman, H. (1974). *Labour and Monopoly Capital.* (Monthly Review Press: New York).

Byrt, William J. (1980). *The Human Variable: Text and Cases in Organizational Behaviour.* (McGraw-Hill: Sydney).

Capps, Randall *et al.* (1981). *Communication for the Business and Professional Speaker.* (Macmillan: New York).

Carey, Alex (1976). "Industrial Psychology and Sociology in Australia", in Boreham, P. *et al.* (eds), *The Professions in Australia: A Critical Appraisal.* (University of Queensland Press: St Lucia).

Coch, Lester and French, John R.P. (1948). "Overcoming Resistance to Change", *Human Relations*, vol. 2, no. 4.

Davis, Keith (1981). *Human Behaviour at Work: Organizational Behaviour.* (McGraw-Hill: New York).

DeBono, Edward (1971). *Lateral Thinking for Management.* (McGraw-Hill: London).

Delbecq, Andre L., Van de Ven, Andrew H. and Gustafson, David H. (1975). *Group Techniques for Program Planning: A Guide to Nominal Group and Delphi Processes.* (Scott Foresmen: Glenview, Ill.).

Dowling, William F. and Sayles, Leonard R. (1978). *How Managers Motivate: The Imperatives of Supervision.* (McGraw-Hill: New York).

Dunphy, Dexter C. and Dick, Robert (1981). *Organizational Change by Choice.* (McGraw-Hill: Sydney).

Eunson, Baden (1985a). "Why Groupthink Will Never Beat the Protestant Ethic", *Business Review Weekly*, 2 August.

(1985b). "War and Peace in the Meeting Room", *Business Review Weekly*, 4 October.

Ferris, Gerald R. and Wagner, John A. (1985). "Quality Circles in the United States: A Conceptual Reevaluation", *The Journal of Applied Behavioural Science*, vol. 21, no. 2.

Fletcher, Winston (1983). *Meetings, Meetings: How to Manipulate Them and Make Them More Fun.* (Michael Joseph: London).

Fromm, Erich (1982). *Greatness and Limitations of Freud's Thought.* (Abacus: London).

Grasha, Anthony (1976). *Practical Applications of Psychology.* (Prentice-Hall: New Jersey).

Hepner, Harry Walker (1979). *Psychology Applied to Life and Work*, 6th edn. (Prentice-Hall: New Jersey).

Hodgetts, Richard M. (1980). *Modern Human Relations.* (Dryden Press: Hinsdale, Ill.).

Hunt, John (1979). *Managing People at Work.* (McGraw-Hill: London).

Janis, Irving and Mann, Leon (1977). *Decision-Making: A Psychological Analysis of Conflict, Choice and Commitment.* (Free Press: New York).

Kelly, John E. (1981). *Scientific Management, Job Redesign, and Work Performance.* (Academic Press: New York).

Koontz, Harold, O'Donnell, Cyril and Weihrich, Heinz (1980). *Management*, 7th edn. (McGraw-Hill: New York).

Lee, James A. (1980). *The Gold and the Garbage in Management Theories and Prescriptions*. (Ohio University Press: Athens, Ohio).

Linstone, Harold A. (1975). "Eight Basic Pitfalls: A Checklist", in Linstone, Harold A. and Turoff, Murray (eds), *The Delphi Method: Techniques and Applications*. (Addison-Wesley: Reading, Mass.).

Littler, Craig R. and Salaman, Graeme (1984). *Class at Work: The Design, Allocation and Control of Jobs*. (Batsford Academic and Educational: London).

Mangham, Iain (1979). *The Politics of Organizational Change*. (Greenwood Press: Massachusetts).

Merton, Robert K. (1975) quoted in Hall, E. (ed.), *Psychology Today*. (Random House/CRM: New York), p.342.

Newcomb, T.M. (1950). *Social Psychology*. (Dryden Press: New York).

Raven, Bertram and Rubin, Jeffrey (1976). *Social Psychology: People in Groups*. (John Wiley and Sons: New York).

Rawlinson, J. Geoffrey (1981). *Creative Thinking and Brainstorming*. (Gower, Wetmead, Farnborough, Hants).

Schein, Edgar H. (1969). *Process Consultation*. (Addison-Wesley: Reading, Mass.).

Snell, Frank (1979). *How to Win the Meeting*. (Hawthorn Books: New York).

Stoner, James A., Collins, Roger R. and Yetton, Phillip W. (1985). *Management in Australia*. (Prentice-Hall: Sydney).

Teasedale, T.C. (1976). *Social Psychology: A Two Year Course*. (Lloyd O'Neil: Windsor, Vic.).

Thompson, James (1985). *Psychological Aspects of Nuclear War*. (British Psychological Society/John Wiley: Chichester).

Tropman, John E. (1980). *Effective Meetings: Improving Group Decision-Making*. (Sage: Beverly Hills).

Van Gundy, Arthur B. (1981). *Techniques of Structured Problem Solving*. (Van Nostrand Reinhold: New York).

(1984). *Managing Group Creativity*. (Amacon: New York).

Films/video

Team Building (Video Channel).
Group Dynamics: Groupthink (Video Channel).
Meetings, Bloody Meetings (John Cleese) (Video Channel).
More Bloody Meetings (Video Channel).
The Art of Team Building (Rank).
Communicating with a Group (Rank).
Roles People Play in Groups (Box Hill College of TAFE).

12

Job design

Job enrichment has been around for sixty years. It's been successful every time it has been tried, but industry is not interested.

Peter Drucker

You move from one boring, dirty monotonous job to another boring, dirty monotonous job. And somehow you're supposed to come out of it all "enriched". But I never feel "enriched". I just feel knackered.

British chemical worker

Modern industry . . . necessitates variation of labour, fluency of function, universal mobility of the labourer . . . consequently the greatest possible development of his aptitudes. . . Modern industry, indeed, compels society, under penalty of death, to replace the detail-worker of today, crippled by life-long repetition of one and the same trivial operation and thus reduced to the mere fragment of a man, by the fully developed individual, fit for a variety of labours, ready to face any change of production and to whom the different social functions he performs are but so many modes of giving free scope to his own natural and acquired powers.

Karl Marx

THAT jobs, like organisations, should have a "design" seems peculiar to many people. Jobs are just "there"—they are not consciously designed, like buildings or paintings. Yet jobs do have a design, whether that design is conscious or unconscious, good or bad. One becomes aware of such design when one is taught a job, or teaches a job, or reads a job profile, or reads an advertisement description of a job. Jobs interact with each other, and with the organisation that contains them, not to mention the environment external to the organisation, such as the socio-economic environment. This chapter, focusing as it does upon the design of jobs, will take a "micro" view of work. Chapters 13 and 14, by contrast, take a "macro" view, a bigger picture. You will notice also a considerable overlap between these chapters and the chapters on leadership, group dynamics, motivation, and decision-making and problem solving.

Job design
The classic approach
The classic approach to job design was first developed in the "job engineering" or "scientific management" concepts of Frederick W. Taylor. Taylor's main contribution was to increase efficiency in various work situations by isolating the parts of a job sequence, and then getting workers to concentrate upon that part, that is, to specialise. Taylor removed much inefficiency in this way, but he also removed much variety, not to mention the scope to make decisions

about work flow and techniques, which were now removed and given to a specialised managerial, executive section of the work organisation (although Taylor was not necessarily the dehumanising villain as his opponents often portray him; see Chapter 2).

The classic approach is still seen today in most organisations, both blue-collar and white-collar. Job engineering is still seen in time-and-motion studies, which attempt to use the Taylor model of analysis-specialisation to improve efficiency (Cooley 1980). It is also seen in the use of such approaches as *ergonomics*, which considers the total psychomotor environment of the worker: ventilation, illumination, control of noise and atmospheric pollution, visibility of task, hand and limb movements, and so on. Ergonomics is becoming a crucial tool in the emerging area of occupational safety and health, where the range of work technologies—from assembly lines to visual display units—is examined for possible injurious outcomes, such as back injury, deafness, tenosynovitis, and other preventable diseases (Ferguson 1979).

Yet there has been much criticism of the classic approach to job design. For each of the alleged advantages of scientific or technocratic work design, there are marked disadvantages (Table 12.1). Some critics argue that scientific management, by treating human beings like machines, misunderstood the true needs of workers, and thus was in effect more, not less, inefficient as a model of job and organisational design[1] (Littler 1985).

Various approaches have been advocated to overcome the shortcomings of classic job design principles. Let us examine some of these approaches now.

Job rotation

Job rotation occurs when workers are shifted from one job to another to minimise boredom. Workers' motivation, interest and performance in a particular job will often decline if there is no variety. If, however, members of one department exchange or rotate the tasks within the department on an hourly, daily or weekly basis, such negative trends might be reversed. Ford (1983) notes that job rotation in Western countries tends to be a "managerial Band-aid or gimmick", whereas in Japan it leads to genuine multiskilling (thus ensuring that no worker is over-specialised) and to an overview of just what the entire work process is about.

Job enlargement

Job enlargement is sometimes referred to as "horizontally loading" a task, that is, if the worker is seen as having a position in a hierarchy with vertical and horizontal dimensions, then job enlargement helps that worker to participate more in the horizontal dimension. Basically, job enlargement means that a worker completes several stages of a process rather than only one. Thus, a worker may assemble a complete machine or process an entire

---

[1] Thus even newer, more humane job engineering approaches such as ergonomics are sometimes used to avoid, rather than confront, issues of job and organisational design. A purely technical, solely ergonomic approach to repetition strain injury (RSI) in word processor typists may be to reposition the keyboard; a more comprehensive approach may be to redefine a typist's job as only partly typing, the rest of the time being allocated to higher grade decision-making normally reserved for supervisory and managerial personnel. This, of course, not only challenges power relationships on the job, but also sex-role relationships (the majority of typists are women; many male executives still cannot bring themselves to work with desk-top computers because they define any work involving a keyboard as being "woman's work").

Table 12.1 Traditional technocratic work design principles and (negative) effects

Traditional technocratic work design principles	*Negative effects*
External design control Use engineering experts and line managers to carry out the work design or redesign.	Reduces participation and creates alienation. ("They are doing this to us. This is their idea, not ours.") Reduces commitment; reduces self-esteem. ("They don't think our ideas are worth anything.") If successfully implemented, creates a sense of dependency.
Specialisation Break the total workflow into minimal discrete tasks and assign a minimal number of tasks (one or more) to each job.	Except in extremely varied professional jobs, creates boredom and apathy by reducing the variety of work.
Technological dominance Centre job design around the demands of technology and physical workflow.	By ignoring or downgrading human capabilities, creates alienation and reduces self-esteem ("I'm just an extension of this machine").
Repetition Make the activities involved in each job as simple and repetitive as possible; closely prescribe the most efficient sequence of activities.	Reduces creativity and creates boredom and apathy.
Deskilling Reduce cost requirements and hence training costs.	Stifles learning, contributing to boredom and hopelessness.
Equalised, "distributed" workloads Adjust the allocation of tasks between jobs so that individuals holding different jobs have similar workloads ("balancing the line").	Destroys a sense of responsibility for the whole task ("That's not my job. Why should I help him?").
Work measurement Set uniform output standards for all those in the same job and measure individual performance against those standards.	Places artificial limits on performance and increases alienation ("Those management blokes are gonna tell me what to do again").
Individual financial incentives Reward with financial incentives, paid for individual effort.	Creates competitiveness and reduces social support, increasing alienation.
Minimal social interaction Minimise opportunities for social interaction and communication on the job and use supervision to support this aspect of design.	Reduces social support, increasing alienation.
Close supervision Coordinate and control through close supervision.	Creates dependency and lowers self-respect or, alternatively, creates resentment and rebellion.

Source: Adapted from Dunphy and Dick (1981), pp.148–9. Adapted with permission.

form. Job satisfaction may increase, and time may be saved by not having to pass the item of work from one specialised individual to another (although the classical work design model would predict that time would be lost because a group of workers performing specialised tasks repetitively will always be more efficient).

Job enrichment

Job enrichment is usually associated with Herzberg's two-factor theory of motivation (see Chapter 2). Herzberg argued that, in seeking to find out just what really motivates people, we should not look to money or working conditions or style of supervision or organisational policy, but rather to factors such as a sense of achievement, recognition, responsibility, advancement, and the work itself (Herzberg 1968, 1976, 1979). The first group of factors Herzberg called "hygiene factors": like physical hygiene measures, these will prevent disease but will not necessarily improve health; in organisations, these factors will prevent discontent but will not motivate people. The second set of factors, according to Herzberg, are the motivating factors, the one that will really change people's work behaviour in a positive way.

Job enrichment does not "horizontally load" jobs, but "vertically loads" them: it does not necessarily mean more tasks, but rather gives more autonomy and responsibility to a worker in a particular area. Examples of job enrichment might be:

- clerks sign letters with their own names and develop personal contacts with particular clients;
- a typist in a word-processing pool establishes personal contacts with clients and schedules workload according to her own priorities;
- an assembly-line worker builds an entire bicycle, making decisions about workflow and quality control hitherto made by a supervisor.

Practitioners of job enrichment argue that satisfaction intrinsic to the job itself will improve productivity, as well as overcoming the alienation of a workforce suffering from the "blue collar blues" or the "white collar woes". Job enrichment is superior to job rotation or job enlargement, says Herzberg, because it injects meaning into work; rotation and enlargement of fundamentally meaningless jobs is ultimately futile (Herzberg 1968).

There have been many attempts at job enrichment as enunciated by Herzberg. Two of the most famous attempts in the United States have been the job enrichment programs at Texas Instruments and Bell Systems (Luthans 1981). Yet job enrichment, at least as understood in Herzbergian terms, is not always successful, as attractive as it might initially appear. Some of the reasons for this failure are:

1. Many workers and unions see the emphasis of "psychological growth on the job" and the de-emphasis upon money as being a con; they would prefer "cash enrichment", that is, some type of productivity increase sharing (O'Shaughnessey 1979). It is notable that Herzberg himself has apparently expressed a personal preference for "hygiene factors", that is, money (Carey 1980).
2. Job enrichment programs may lead to redundancies, and redundant workers may be laid off without chance of retraining, relocation, etc. A study of 60 job redesign programs showed that for every 100 jobs redesigned, 25 were lost (Kelly 1982). This may be a deliberate tactic

on the part of managements to cause speed-ups, redundancies and heightened exploitation (Ducker 1975).

3. Many workers and union officials question why workers should seek psychological growth or self-actualisation on the job, when the job is just a meal-ticket for their "real" life with their family and friends (Dabschek and Niland 1981; Goldthorpe *et al.* 1968). In fact, some American union officials have argued that jobs should be more, not less repetitive, so that workers can take their minds off their jobs and think about their hobbies (Lee 1980).

4. Many workers are made quite anxious by the thought of more responsibility, opportunities for autonomy, and so on. In other words, a distinction is not drawn between employees with high growth needs and those with low growth needs (Luthans 1981).

5. Supervisors may be stressed unduly by having some decision-making power devolved on to workers; what then does the supervisor do? (One person's job enrichment may be another person's job impoverishment.)

6. Management may see job enrichment as the thin end of the wedge of industrial democracy, with decision-making power shifting from executives to the rank and file workers on the shop floor. Consequently they may not introduce it, or if they do, consciously hamstring it (Hellriegel, Slocum and Woodman 1983).

7. Management philosophy may be seriously at variance with the job enrichment approach, thus jeopardising the whole venture. A bureaucratic announcement out of the blue that some or all jobs will now be enriched, and workers will enjoy assuming responsibility and autonomy, is obviously doomed to failure (*Rydges'*, March 1978; Luthans 1981).

8. Many job enrichment programs fail to take account of the values and strategies of unions. While many European unions have in fact initiated some job enrichment programs (Hodgetts 1980), the response has been more lukewarm, and often hostile, in the United States, United Kingdom and Australia. While most of this hostility has been over wholly commendable concerns (see points 1–4), union officials may see their vested interests threatened by job enrichment. Union officials are management managers by trade, and they act to influence workflow and conditions, defend demarcation lines, and so on. They may see job enrichment as the thin end of the industrial democracy wedge (see point 6), which might shift decision-making power to the rank and file, render the concept of demarcation obsolete as jobs are radically redesigned, etc. (Yerbury 1980).

9. Technological constraints, for example, machine-paced work flow, often mean that job enrichment is a waste of time. While it is too easy to say that job enrichment is too hard a concept to implement, there are a core of jobs that will resist enrichment.

10. On the other hand, technology may be the critical factor of job enrichment. In fact, Lee (1980) argues that most of the job enrichment which has taken place over the last century is not due to job redesign so much as engineering and capital investment: automation has relieved millions of workers from endless, muscle-powered drudgery.

11. Job enrichment is often expensive. Retraining, repositioning and redesign of capital equipment, all cost money. Do the benefits of job enrichment, in terms of productivity gains, outweigh such costs? Lee

suggests that the evidence is either ambivalent or discouraging (Lee 1980).

12. Job enrichment, at least as Herzberg saw it, over-emphasised individual workflow and did not sufficiently heed work groups. Also it was basically non-participative—job redesign was left up to managers and experts, not workers (Dunphy and Dick 1981).[2]

13. Following from point 3, many workers do not want to be freed from the alienation of jobs so much as freed from the alienation of the middle-class concept of job enrichment. Many see nothing wrong with boring work. Lee, in fact, suggests that middle-class social scientists have projected on to workers their own, inappropriate, middle-class needs and values, for example, the belief that all institutions should be democratised; the belief that high autonomy needs are paramount; the emotions of hostility in response to any body of authority, such as corporate management (Lee 1980; Luthans 1981).

Others working in the field of job design have developed models which are purported to be superior to Herzbergian or "orthodox" job enrichment models. Let us examine the strengths (and weaknesses) of these models.

The job diagnostic survey: Enrichment plus growth needs

The job diagnostic survey approach is an attempt at a model of job enrichment which takes into account the differing "psychological growth needs"[3] of different individuals. As developed by Hackman and Oldham (1976), the model posits that five core job characteristics are critical in job design (Fig. 12.1). These are:

1. *skill variety*—the extent to which a worker has a variety of tasks to perform that extend her talents and skills;
2. *task identity*—the extent to which a job role entails a worker completing a whole task, and not just a specialised aspect of it;
3. *task significance*—the extent to which the individual worker's input to the whole enterprise is significant, and is perceived to be so by the worker;
4. *autonomy*—the extent to which a worker has discretion and independence on task factors such as scheduling and quality control;
5. *feedback*—the extent to which the worker gets clear information about her work output and her performance.

These five core job characteristics can lead to three critical psychological states: experienced meaningfulness of the work; experienced responsibility for work outcomes; and knowledge of results from work activities. This can in turn lead to such personal and work outcomes as high motivation, high quality work performance, high job satisfaction, and low turnover and absenteeism.

So far the Hackman–Oldham model does not appear dramatically different from Herzberg's model. Hackman and Oldham add other variables,

---

[2] Thus Herzberg and his followers have dismissed participation in job re-design because "it contaminates the process with human relations hygiene". Herzberg has also dismissed industry democracy as "an equality of ignorance" (quoted in Kelly, 1982, p.175).

[3] Some psychologists have suggested that humans have certain innate needs, the satisfaction of which will enhance a process of psychological development or "growth". See Chapter 2.

Core job characteristics	Critical psychological states	Personal and work outcomes

Variety of skill
Identity of the task
Significance of the task ⟶ Experienced meaningfulness of the work

Autonomy ⟶ Experienced responsibility for work outcomes

Feedback ⟶ Knowledge of results from work activities

High internal work motivation

High quality work performance

High satisfaction with the work

Low turnover and absenteeism

Moderated by employee growth need strength

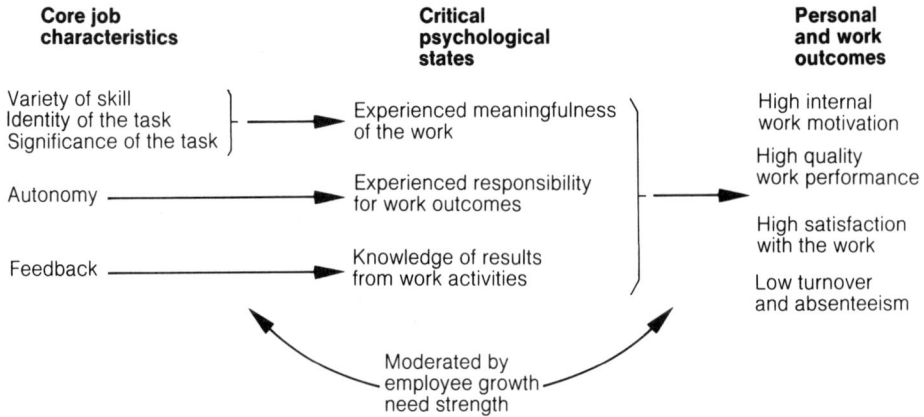

Fig 12.1 *The job characteristics model of work design* (HACKMAN AND OLDHAM 1976, P.256. REPRODUCED WITH PERMISSION)

however: the objective variable is the actual potential of any job to motivate, expressed as a numerical score; the subjective factor is the growth needs strength of the worker.

The core job characteristics can be quantified, using the job diagnostic survey (JDS). Questions adapted from the survey are shown in Table 12.2. After ascribing scores to questions on the table, it is possible to calculate the motivating potential score (MPS) of a job thus:

$$\text{MPS} = \frac{\text{skill variety} + \text{task identity} + \text{task significance}}{3} \times \text{autonomy} \times \text{feedback}$$

Various assumptions are made in this equation. It is assumed that skill variety, task identity and task significance as a combined factor equal autonomy and feedback in importance. Autonomy and feedback are still of greater importance in the big picture, however: if a job lacks task significance (score = 0) and skill variety (score = 0) but nevertheless has task identity, for example, then the MPS will be a number greater than 0. But if there is no autonomy (score = 0) and/or feedback (score = 0), then the MPS will be 0, no matter what the scores for skill variety, task identity, and task significance.

Let us consider two jobs: an engineer at an automobile company and an assembly line worker at the same company. The engineer designs engine components, the assembler assembles those components. The engineer has a creative job, with a lot of variety; initiates projects, and sees them through the entire design process to the point where they begin to be manufactured; perceives her creativity to be critical to the welfare of the organisation; has a lot of independence in setting her own goals for designing components; and is continually informed of whether her designs are successful or not. The assembler, by comparison, has a monotonous job, lacking in variety; it is highly specialised, and she does not see how it relates to the whole operation; the work appears to be trivial, and she sees herself as being all-too-quickly replaceable by any semi-skilled person; she is totally dominated by the machine-pacing of the assembly-line, so that even going to the toilet or having a meal is a major operation; she receives very little feedback at all on her performance, apart from a few negative remarks from quality-control checkers and supervisors.

The engineer's motivating potential score might look like this:

$$MPS = \frac{(6 + 5 + 6)}{3} \times 5.5 \times 5 = 155.83$$

The assembler's MPS might look like this:

$$MPS = \frac{(1 + 1 + 1.5)}{3} \times 1 \times 1.5 = 1.75$$

Does this mean that the engineer is almost 90 times as motivated as the assembler? Even if we could measure such things, it seems unlikely. What it does mean is that the engineer's *job* has much higher potential to motivate than the assembler's *job*. All other things being equal, we could then presume that the engineer was a "good deal more" motivated than the assembler. Also, the MPS score categories, that is, the core job characteristics, would give us a useful model to analyse the assembler's job and to determine whether these job characteristics could be enriched in some way.

But of course, all other things are rarely equal in human affairs, and Hackman and Oldham have argued that the objective motivating potential of a job has to be reconciled with the growth needs strength of an individual doing that job. "Growth needs" are here understood as Maslow's upper needs and Herzberg's motivators (advancement, recognition, self-actualisation, etc; see Chapter 2). People who have high growth need strength will respond more positively to high MPS jobs, the theory runs.

There are a few problems with the Hackman/Oldham model. First, how "objective" is the motivating potential score of a job? Two people doing the same job (people with differing growth needs, perhaps) might allocate different figures to the same variable—although such disagreements could be a fruitful basis for analysing the job itself and people's perceptions of it.

Also, some research indicates that when this model of job redesign is applied, all workers, irrespective of the growth needs strength scores, demonstrate improved performance (although to a differing degree; Blunt 1983).

Finally, just how valid is the notion of "growth needs"? As is pointed out in Chapter 2, it is by no means clear that such needs can be measured precisely, let alone arranged in a hierarchy of "higher" and "lower" needs. To the extent that theories such as those of Maslow and Herzberg are not proved, it is inaccurate, not to mention patronising and insulting, to say that one individual's growth needs are "lower" than another individual's (indeed, the word "growth" is charged with value). It is obvious that people are *different* in what they want out of a job: it is another thing to say that our engineer is necessarily "happier" than our assembler, or that our assembler is "alienated", "suffering from the blue collar blues", and so on, when she may be quite happy with her lot, switching her mind off the job and day-dreaming about her family, her upcoming holiday and her other job.

Job design matched to organisational design

If one still accepts the notion of higher and lower growth needs, or if one prefers to simply use these terms as code terms for different needs, it is useful to see how the smaller-scale concept of job design can be integrated with the larger-scale concept of organisational design by using the human needs concept. Organisations, for example, are sometimes classified as to whether they are more or less "mechanistic" or more or less "organic" (see Chapter 13). Mechanistic organisations tend to be rigid hierarchies with authoritiarian value systems and clear-cut, specialised roles. Organic organisations tend to be networks of equals rather than hierarchies of unequals, with democratic value systems and overlapping, amorphous roles. This is not to say, however, that high-growth need workers and enriched jobs are *only* to be found in organic organisations, while low-growth need workers and routine jobs are *only* to be found in mechanistic organisations. A mechanistic organisation may introduce a job enrichment program as a pilot or, indeed, the managers of such an organisation might have jobs which are already enriched according to the criteria of Herzberg and Hackman and Oldham. An organic organisation might contain a few jobs which resist attempts to enrich them (e.g. security guard, window washer). A high-growth need worker may survive in a mechanistic organisation, perhaps even flourish under certain circumstances; while a low-growth need worker might do likewise in an organic organisation.

Nevertheless, a matching of growth needs, job design, and organisational design is probably a desirable outcome. Figure 12.2 is a model of these three factors. There are eight triangles or cells which correspond to differing

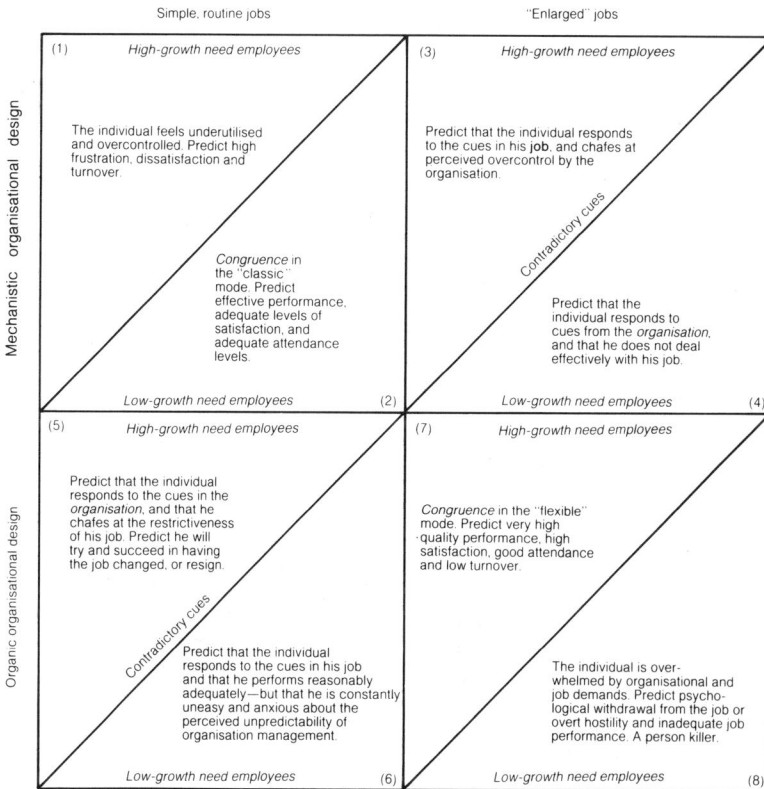

Fig. 12.2 *Contingency model of job design* (PORTER, LAWLER AND HACKMAN 1975, P.309. REPRODUCED WITH PERMISSION)

Table 12.2 Sample questions from the job diagnostic survey

Please describe your job as objectively as you can.

1. How much *variety* is there in your job? That is, to what extent does the job require you to do many different things at work, using a variety of your skills and talents?

1 ——— 2 ——— 3 ——— 4 ——— 5 ——— 6 ——— 7

Very little; the job requires me to do the same routine things over and over again.

Moderate variety.

Very much; the job requires me to do many different things, using a number of different skills and talents.

2. To what extent does your job involve doing a *"whole" and identifiable piece of work?* That is, is the job a complete piece of work that has an obvious beginning and end? Or is it only a part of the overall piece of work, which is finished by other people or by automatic machines?

1 ——— 2 ——— 3 ——— 4 ——— 5 ——— 6 ——— 7

My job is only a tiny part of the overall piece of work; the results of my activities cannot be seen in the final product or service.

My job is a moderate-sized "chunk" of the overall piece of work; my own contribution can be seen in the final outcome.

My job involves doing the whole piece of work, from start to finish; the results of my activities are easily seen in the final product or service.

Table 12.2 Sample questions from the job diagnostic survey (*continued*)

3. In general, how *significant or important* is your job? That is, are the results of your work likely to significantly affect the lives or well-being of other people?

1 ———— 2 ———— 3 ———— 4 ———— 5 ———— 6 ———— 7

Not very significant; the outcomes of my work are *not* likely to have important effects on other people.	Moderately significant.	Highly significant; the outcomes of my work can affect other people in very important ways.

4. How much *autonomy* is there in your job? That is, to what extent does your job permit you to decide *on your own* how to go about doing the work?

1 ———— 2 ———— 3 ———— 4 ———— 5 ———— 6 ———— 7

Very little; the job gives me almost no personal "say" about how and when the work is done.	Moderate autonomy; many things are standardised and not under my control, but I can make some decisions about the work.	Very much; the job gives me almost complete responsibility for deciding how and when the work is done.

5. To what extent does *doing the job itself* provide you with information about your work performance? That is, does the actual *work itself* provide clues about how well you are doing—aside from any "feedback" co-workers or supervisors may provide?

1 ———— 2 ———— 3 ———— 4 ———— 5 ———— 6 ———— 7

Very little; the job itself is set up so I could work forever without finding out how well I am doing.	Moderately; sometimes doing the job provides "feedback" to me, sometimes it does not.	Very much; the job is set up so that I get almost constant "feedback" as I work about how well I am doing.

Source: Adapted from Hackman, J.R. and Oldham, G.R. "Development of the Job Diagnostic Survey", *Journal of Applied Psychology*, vol. 60, 1975, pp.159–70.

combinations of growth needs, job design and organisational design. Cells 2 and 7 provide the best match or "congruence": low-growth needs, routine jobs, mechanistic organisation (2), and high-growth needs, enriched jobs and organic organisation (7). Individuals located in other cells of the model will cope with conflicting demands with varying degrees of success.

Sociotechnical approaches

Another approach to redesigning or enriching jobs is the sociotechnical systems approach. This approach, first developed at the Tavistock Institute in London, attempts to come to grips with another weakness of Herzbergian or orthodox job enrichment—its overemphasis of individual job design and underemphasis of group job design.

Sociotechnical approaches to job design begin with the notion that technology is relatively inflexible, although not as inflexible as the classical scientific management approach would have us believe. Acting within those constraints, it is possible to develop the potential of the social or human aspects of work, although not in such a naive and idealistic way as envisaged by such "human relations" writers as Mayo (see Chapter 2), and indeed, Herzberg. The sociotechnical approach emphasises "joint optimisation" of social and technical factors. It also emphasises the fact that people usually work in groups, and emphasises the potential of group processes of communication and problem-solving (see Chapter 11). Sociotechnical job design attempts to replace the classical hierarchical model of manager–supervisor–assembly line with the more participative structure of "semi-autonomous work groups"—teams or groups of workers which have a fair amount of autonomy or independence from management in making decisions about workflow scheduling, quality control, problem-solving, and so on.

Early sociotechnical approaches looked at work group job design in Indian textile mills, British coal mines and Norwegian factories. There has been criticism of these experiments on the grounds that the role of money as a motivator was not adequately considered (Carey 1980). Later approaches to sociotechnical design usually attempt to at least come to grips with the problem (or solution) of money as a motivator. Thus, a comparison of sociotechnical principles of job design with those of classical job design shows that individual financial incentives are replaced either by group bonuses or individual increments for skill over and above the basic wage for group members (Table 12.3; compare also Table 12.1).

Perhaps the most famous example of this approach is that of the Volvo automobile factory at Kalmar in Sweden. Saab-Scania, another Swedish car manufacturer, has also been prominent in the field. Prominent American examples have been those of General Foods and Non-Linear Systems (Davis 1981). Australian examples have been at Philips telecommunications and ICI petrochemicals, both in Melbourne.

The Volvo experiment

The Volvo experiment with redesigning jobs began in the 1960s. Job rotation was introduced at plants with conventional assembly lines. Yet high turnover rates and other indicators convinced Volvo management that something was missing: workers were less accepting of traditional job design, and changing social values meant that the quality of worklife was becoming a crucial concern. Espousing a "small-is-beautiful" philosophy, Volvo management

Table 12.3 Sociotechnical job design and traditional job design compared

Traditional principles	Sociotechnical principles
1. External design control	Participative design with external support
2. Specialisation	Task variety and identity
3. Technological dominance	Optimisation of technological and human requirements
4. Repetition	Challenge and significance
5. Deskilling	Multiskilling
6. Equalised workloads	Group work with flexible workloads
7. Work measurement	Negotiated output standards with feedback on results
8. Individual financial incentives	Standard wage, with increments for skill level. Group bonus if incentive system is used
9. Minimal social interaction	Social interaction around task-related activity
10. Close supervision	Autonomy and participation in decision making

Source: Dunphy and Dick (1981), p.163. Reproduced with permission.

(and workers, represented by unions) began in 1970 to plan a new plant in Kalmar which was opened in 1974. *Technically*, it is a radical departure: rather than a rectangular shed housing an assembly line, Kalmar is an array of four two-storey, hexagonal structures with car bodies moved about on electronically controlled trollies. *Socially* the plant was also a breakthrough. About twenty-five work groups of about twenty members handle different aspects of construction (electrical, upholstery, welding, etc.). These groups negotiate with management about schedules, deadlines, raw materials and quality control. Quality control is rechecked centrally, and feedback is given to work groups via television monitors. Groups elect supervisors. Groups are paid according to a group piece rate, with the supervisor making more (Gunzberg 1980; Emery 1980). Volvo claims that the experiment has been a success, with turnover and absenteeism markedly reduced, and improved quality—there are no, or at least fewer, "Monday" or "Friday" cars. Opinions differ as to the cost of the project. Volvo claims that Kalmar is only 10 per cent more expensive than a normal plant, but executives from Peugeot and BMW have estimated that the true margin must be in the 30–100 per cent range (Haganaes and Hales 1983). Systematic data on productivity and job satisfaction are not available. It is interesting to note that only half of Volvo's sociotechnical approach has been copied by some other car manufacturers— the technical half. The more flexible trolley system has supplanted the assembly line in some plants (e.g. Fiat), but this has facilitated much more automation, that is, has reduced "human" employment.[4]

---

[4] Lansbury and Spillane suggest that the Volvo and Saab production methods are nothing new: they were in fact pioneered at American manufacturers such as General Motors in World War II, when changes had to be made in production and management methods when skilled labour (engineers, supervisors, etc.) were scarce. When the war ended, however, the companies reverted to traditional methods (Lansbury and Spillane 1983, p.242).

Other sociotechnical experiments

The position is unclear or only negative in relation to some other socio-technical projects. The American General Foods pet food plant in Kansas, when opened in 1971, was built around semi-autonomous work groups. Quality of product and productivity was high—so high, in fact, that 35 per cent of employees were no longer needed to run the plant. However, problems began to emerge. Managers and supervisors were often not happy about their traditional decision-making powers devolving on to workers. Some workers objected to others being paid extra for mastering additional skills. Some people were simply "loners" by temperament, desiring only a quiet life; these qualities did not prepare them for a more participative, group-centred mode of production (Luthans 1981; Davis 1981).

The American digital electronics firm, Non-Linear Systems, introduced a pioneering sociotechnical approach in the early 1960s. By 1965, however, the company had reverted to a traditional, hierarchical mode of production. While job satisfaction rose for workers in teams, it apparently declined for managers and technical specialists. The technical specialists, in particular, seemed to become less productive under the new scheme, which proved critical in an innovation-dependent industry (Davis 1981; Lee 1980).

The Australian experience is also unclear or problematic. The ICI Welvic plant was well planned along sociotechnical lines (Robinson and McCarroll 1981; Andreatta 1981). While apparently successful, it is notable that ICI has not replicated the experiment at plants since constructed, and has tended to concentrate on more low-profile workplace changes such as eliminating differences in pay and conditions between staff and line personnel (McIver 1983).

Quality circles

Another approach to job design that depends heavily upon group processes is that of quality circles. Usually thought of as a Japanese invention, quality circles, as Visser (1982) points out, were developed by Japan in the 1960s and 1970s using many American theories of human relations, job design and statistical quality control. J.M. Juran predicted in 1966 that Japan would become the world leader in industrial quality control, largely through the use of quality circles (Dewar 1980), and proponents of quality circles, such as Ingle (1982) argue that they are *the* key to much-envied Japanese productivity levels (see also Sprouster 1984).

What are quality circles? Depending upon the organisation and, indeed, the country, quality circles are usually small groups of workers who voluntarily meet to discuss and analyse methods of improving work quality. Meetings are with the group's supervisor, although the supervisor is not necessarily always the leader. Meetings are held regularly, for example, once a week. Quality circles (QCs) usually require a fair amount of training in problem-solving methods, and human relations and communications skills, and this can consume a fair amount of time and money. Specialists in developing QCs argue that these outlays are repaid many times over by dramatic increases in productivity and quality (Briscomb 1983). QCs originally began in industrial situations, with meetings on factory floors, but are now being developed in white-collar environments in the private and public sectors.

Quality circles are thus yet another manifestation of job redesign where groups of workers participate in decision-making. QCs are becoming increasingly fashionable in the Western nations, due to the increasing prominence of Japanese theories and practices of management, such as "theory Z" organisational structure and leadership (see Chapter 14). Nevertheless, in grafting ideas such as quality circles on to other cultures, several points should be borne in mind:

1. It is by no means clear that group processes of decision-making and problem-solving used in QCs are always better than traditional individual processes. Indeed, it has been argued that "American research appears to suggest that intellectual, novel, brainstorming-type tasks, such as the tasks undertaken by QCs, can be better performed by individuals than by groups" (Ferris and Wagner 1985, p.175; see also Chapter 11).

2. Related to the technical aspects of problem-solving referred to in (1), and possibly indistinguishable from it, is the matter of cultural differences in attitudes towards group versus individual behaviour: Japanese culture strongly supports group action and management by consensus. Western culture tends to be more strongly individualistic, and labour–management relations are usually adversary rather than cooperative. These cultural differences should be kept in mind if QCs are regarded by Westerners as a quick technological fix for problems (Ingle 1982).

3. In group problem-solving, Japanese workers are more adept at interchanging roles—a direct extension of such practices as job rotation. Western managers, supervisors and workers often experience role conflict when confronted with demands for flexibility in leadership and decision-making (Maruyama 1983; Davis 1981).

4. Japan is a "learning society", committed to extensive and ongoing training and education, even if it is expensive. Japan is a culture poor in physical resources, yet rich in human resources; consequently it has maximised investment in human resources. Western countries have maximised investment in physical resources, which has not only led to an underuse of human resources, but is a strategy no longer tenable in a world with scarce energy and scarce capital (Ford 1983; Visser 1982).

5. Following from the previous point, Japan's workforce is usually better educated than Western workforces. In particular, the workers are more numerate, mathematically skilled, and this is crucial if QC techniques such as Pareto diagrams, Ishikawa diagrams, control sheets and other statistical tools are to be used to best advantage. Many Western QCs fall down badly here (Visser 1982).

6. It should not be presumed that QCs will automatically lead to humanisation and democratisation of the workplace. Critics of "the Japanese Miracle", such as Kamata (1983), argue that Japanese industry is basically authoritarian in approach, exploiting workers as "human robots". Kamata's view of exploitive management and subservient workers is a view not often publicised in the West (see Chapter 14).

7. Incentives, productivity sharing and money must inevitably raise their ugly (or attractive) heads. Visser points out that most Japanese incentives for participation in QCs are largely "intrinsic motivators"—praise, recognition, opportunities to speak at meetings and conferences—but this must be seen in the context of the extensive compensation system already in place. In the West, if QCs *do* produce major savings and breakthroughs in innovation, and those gains are not shared, then QCs will be seen as just another gimmick, another management "motivation" rip-off.

Perhaps the most notable feature about quality circles is the way in which they represent the love–hate relationship Western economies have with Japan: Japanophobia (expressed in the 1950s as "how do they make such *bad* goods?", and since the 1960s as "how do they make such *good* goods?") alternates with Japanophilia ("quality circles and theory Z are the only answer!"). It will indeed prove ironic if, to use the language of Chapter 2, theory X managers in the West rejected theory Y participative techniques in the 1950s and 1960s, whereupon such techniques were (partly) adopted by the Japanese, whose rise to economic dominance in the 1970s and 1980s thus forced Western managers to become more theory Y in self-defence.

Goal-setting and management by objectives

Perhaps the most widely practised, or at least most widely publicised, technique of redesign jobs and organisations in the past several decades has been management by objectives (MBO). MBO is closely related to cognitive theories of motivation such as expectancy theory (see Chapter 2) and goal-setting.

Locke's work on goal-setting has been of considerable value here (Locke 1980). Performance in organisations will tend to be high, says Locke, when goals are set participatively rather than arbitrarily handed down from on high. If one sees one's own goals as being congruent with the goals of the organisation, one has a vested interest in trying to achieve those goals. Performance will also be high when goals are specific and programmatic rather than vague or general. More controversially, Locke argues that performance tends to be higher when goals are difficult rather than easy. Goals which are too difficult will, of course, demotivate, but goals which are too easy will have the same effect.

Myers (1970) has used a problem-solving goal-setting approach to produce some impressive producitivity gains at places such as Texas Instruments. The goal-setting procedure involved giving management information to workers, who then set visible, challenging and attainable goals of cost reduction. There was continuous feedback on their performance, and work was conducted in teams. Myers, in modifying Herzberg's theory of motivation and job enrichment, saw, at least in theory, that merit pay was a motivator, rather than a hygiene or maintenance factor. Whether this was the way it panned out in actual work settings is either not clear or, as Ducker suggests, all too clear (Box 12.A).

Management by objectives is a process which attempts to put such principles into practice. MBO works basically like this: A subordinate and a superior negotiate a set of specified objectives to be achieved by the subordinate. The objectives should be few in number (five or six), should be quantitatively measurable, and should have a specific time frame. Such goals might be: reduce scrap (metal, paper) by 3 per cent over a six-month period; increase the ratio of sales telephone calls to firm orders to 30 per cent in five months. The superior and the subordinate meet at regular intervals (three months, twelve months) to evaluate progress on specific goals. This evaluation forms the basis of staff appraisal, which is, of course, critical to promotion, demotion, transfer and dismissal. Feedback on specific performance is usually given at more frequent intervals.

BOX 12.A: Job design, real and phoney

If we glance at the successful experiments in job redesign in the United States and Europe they seem to be based on the following:

1. Workers operate in self-managed teams with responsibility for a large segment of the production process.
2. They have responsibility for activities formerly carried out by maintenance, quality control, industrial engineering and personnel units.
3. In reallocating job assignments, every worker is given a task that contains at least some degree of challenge.
4. Supervisors are substituted by team leaders.
5. Management refrains from laying down plant-rules—the plant community is self-governing.
6. The workplace is stripped of status symbols so that, for example, the parking-lot becomes open to all and there is a single office–plant entrance.

Participative management, in a setting of redesigned or enriched jobs, does not give workers effective representation at the upper level. To its critics, especially its radical critics, this is the major drawback of participation at the workshop level. Workers are guaranteed no voice in major financial decisions of the company, for example. They have no say in the planning of a company's international activities, either. There is no shift in power at the highest level.

Here lies a real challenge—how to combine plans to overcome the alienation of workers on the factory floor with plans for a shift in power at the board level. The answer is, I believe, to combine these three elements of industrial democracy—job redesign, participative management and effective representation of workers at the board level. I believe that this should be a rough model for Australian experiments in this field.

Unions and enrichment

Many unions are going to be perplexed and disturbed by some of the schemes for job redesign or enrichment that will be sprung on them in the future. They will want certain conditions applied. First, I think it reasonable that unions and the workers affected must be fully consulted about plans for job redesign. In fact, the redesign should be directed by the workers themselves. The scheme must not be a front for speed-ups or redundancies, for heightened exploitation. The employees, of course, will rightly expect a share in the productivity gains that will almost certainly take place.

By these tests, of course, a lot of gimmicky schemes on the fringes of job enrichment would have to be dismissed as mere psychological manipulation. According to an article by Geoff Cleghorn, an American management consultant, Dr Scott Myers, visited Australia to push his methods of motivating workers without money rewards. At a Texas instrument factory Dr Myers was able to involve workers, through a series of "goal-setting sessions", in reducing man-hours per unit from 138 to 41 over a nine-month period. But was this handsome productivity gain shared around? "Yes," says Dr Myers, "but not with money. Satisfaction and involvement are sufficiently rewarding." Well, no trade unions are going to endorse that kind of phoney job enrichment. Significantly, Dr Myers was waging his little experiments in a non-union shop.

Source: Ducker (1975), pp.18–20. Reproduced with permission.

Advantages

Thus summarised, MBO seems crashingly obvious, and this is one of its strengths as a technique of organisational change—it is easily understood by all (Table 12.4). It also helps to improve communication and feedback within organisations. From the top down, it often encourages more delegation of time-consuming activities, thus leaving managers to concentrate on broader policy issues. From the bottom up, it encourages participative decision-making and, by having more work delegated to them, gives subordinates a broader picture of the organisation and improves their self-esteem. MBO can make life easier for subordinates and superiors by forcing a statement of clear goals, which can be measured and which have to be reached by a certain deadline. Job profiles and role statements are thus clearly spelt out, and everyone (theoretically) knows what they are doing. This concentration upon objectives means that organisations do not get hung up on rules and procedures, and personnel evaluation and appraisal become more concerned with tangible achievements rather than personality traits.

Disadvantages

The system is not perfect of course—it has disadvantages as well as advantages (Table 12.4). Many of its strengths are, from another standpoint, weaknesses. Thus the concentration upon specific measurable objectives achieved within a specific time frame can lead to an overemphasis on that which is quantifiable, and leave more amorphous, qualitative factors out of the reckoning. To take one example, the US Government used MBO approaches in the Vietnam war, developing such "management tools" as body counts. This emphasis led to an obsession with military tactics which

Table 12.4 Strengths and weaknesses of management by objectives

Advantages	Disadvantages
Easy to understand Increases participation in decision-making Increases delegation of tasks Improves communication and feedback, especially vertical communication Spells out concrete goals: measurable objectives in discrete time frame Concentrates on objectives rather than rules, procedures, activities, personality traits	Can lead to "activity trap"—everyone becomes obsessed with achieving piecemeal tasks Overemphasises quantifiable factors Paperwork and red tape may increase May lead to more written communication, less face-to-face communication; possible increases in conflict as result Too much emphasis on individual goals, rather than group goals. Stresses benefits to organisation, not to individual; may demotivate as a result Managers may not be trained in participative management techniques (e.g. negotiation, counselling), or may be uncomfortable with such techniques Can lead to relationships becoming zero-sum games (win/lose) May lead to reward/punishment mentality May be imposed from top, i.e. not truly participatory but manipulative

Source: Luthans (1981), Lee (1980), Coombes (1979), Hellriegel, Slocum, Woodman (1983).

ignored wider strategic and political factors, with results known only too well. The *reductio ad absurdum* of such an approach is: total success = total depopulation. This concentration upon quantitative factors to the detriment of other factors is a critical weakness of other approaches to organisational change, such as organisational behaviour modification (see Chapter 3). The two techniques in fact have a lot in common.

Related to this weakness is the notion of "the activity trap". In some organisations, because objectives become spelt out, many people suddenly become obsessed with not only "doing things", but "being seen to be doing things". Objectives are seen in piecemeal fashion, as a shopping list which must be achieved at all costs. Related in turn to this point is that individual goals are often concentrated upon to the detriment of group goals. Work roles overlap and are interdependent—they are not in a vacuum.

MBO can also lead to a rise, rather than a reduction in paperwork and red tape. While it is a useful exercise for individuals to detail their goals and sub-goals on paper, if these pieces of paper become holy writ, then inflexibility becomes the order of the day, and the spirit is ignored while the letter becomes supreme. This tendency will become more pronounced the more infrequently evaluation sessions occur. Ongoing evaluation and feedback can help surmount this. Communication within organisations can often shift away from face-to-face communication to written communication. While this superficially may appear tidier, it may be more bureaucratic, and may in fact increase interpersonal conflict, because there is more scope for communication breakdown. Also written objectives may become a stick to beat people over the head with. Some managers do not really like participative management, see it in fact as a contradiction in terms, and thus see their relationships with their subordinates as a zero-sum game—someone has to win, someone has to lose. MBO thus allows a mechanistic reward–punishment mentality to become part of standard procedure. This tendency is amplified if management does not actually negotiate objectives with workers, if the process is not truly participatory. The accusation "Why haven't *you* achieved *our* objectives?" takes on a hollow ring in such circumstances, and MBO appears as a sinister manipulative ploy which makes traditional authoritarian and bureaucratic practices seem honest by comparison.

Job design in the future
The electronic cottage/teleworking scenario

Technology, as we have seen, can have a critical impact upon job and organisational design. Automation, for example, has by turns reduced the levels of human employment in the primary, secondary and, increasingly, the tertiary sectors of industry (Jones 1983). New technology may be able to improve the quality of worklife, as well as reduce it, however. Futurologists such as Toffler (1980) and Martin (1981) have speculated on dramatic changes in job and organisational design being caused by the advent of technologies such as word processors and computer terminals. Such workstations do not necessarily have to be located *in* centralised offices and factories—they can be located anywhere, so long as communicating telephone lines or video cables can be connected, linking them to centralised workplaces. This may mean that people can, for example, "telework" partly or totally from home, or in decentralised "half-way houses" in suburbs outside a city's central business district. Toffler has called such a social innovation "the electronic cottage",

394 Behaviour: The individual and group levels

referring to the way most labour was done prior to the advent of the industrial revolution in the eighteenth and nineteenth centuries—in cottages, with the entire family working together in a variety of industries (see Chapter 1).

Advantages

The optimistic view of the electronic cottage concept is that it will restore intimate and supportive emotional relationships to the family, in contrast to the alleged alienation and poor communication in the nuclear family of today, where one or more breadwinners are absent for much of the time (Table 12.5). The alienation of our dormitory suburbs, where it is rare to speak to your neighbour, will diminish, as people will be home throughout the daylight hours and will be able to establish the community spirit of pre-industrial times.

Workers will be able to schedule their workload with great flexibility—one can work for a few hours in the morning, go to the beach in the afternoon, and turn the terminal on after dinner, and "converse" with the central computers which never sleep. Women will not have to give up working in order to raise a family. The disabled and ill will be able to perform meaningful work with a minimum of inconvenience. Society will save enormous amounts of energy as commuting diminishes in importance. Decentralised energy systems such as solar and wind power can provide the minimal energy requirements of computer terminals and word processors.

Disadvantages

There may be disadvantages, however (Renfro 1982; Eunson 1983) (Table 12.5). The electronic cottage doesn't apply to all jobs, only those in the tertiary sector (insurance, banking, clerical, computing, secretarial, etc.) where people produce or process services or information rather than tangible goods such as automobiles or sheep fleeces. People may become more, not less lonely, as they miss the daily rituals of interacting with their colleagues at a central workplace. Many people dread retirement for precisely this reason. Also, many may find it difficult to leave their work behind them,

Table 12.5 Pros and cons of the electronic cottage

Pro	Con
Workers' autonomy with regard to work scheduling will increase	Doesn't apply to all jobs—mainly tertiary/service sector, white-collar, middle-class jobs
Child-rearers and disabled will be able to participate in workforce	People will not be able to escape from work
Family and community communication will improve	Human contact/rapport with co-workers will decline; isolation and alienation will increase, rather than decrease
Energy consumption will decrease as commuting becomes unnecessary	Electronic communication limits non-verbal communication, humour, spontaneity
Decentralised energy systems (e.g. solar) will become more cost-effective	The disabled may be more, not less ignored by community
	Overheads (heating, cooling, insurance) may be fobbed off on to individuals by organisations

Source: Adapted from Toffler (1980), Martin (1981), Renfro (1982), Eunson (1983).

and may resent their boss electronically invading their home/castle via a computer terminal—Big Brother may be tolerable at work, but not at home.

Communication with others through electronic devices is limited and alienating. Computer terminals do not convey the non-verbal communication, the humour and spontaneity of face-to-face interaction. The disabled may find that they are even more isolated than they were before. Energy consumption may not necessarily decline if organisations merely fob off or externalise overheads such as heating and cooling (not to mention insurance, air-conditioning and other maintenance costs of high technology equipment). People may feel so alienated out in the suburbs that they might begin to commute more, not less, merely to maintain human contact with others.

At this stage, then, most of the costs and the benefits of the electronic cottage seem clear, although the weightings of those costs and benefits are not. Even if only 20–30 per cent of workers are employed in electronic cottages, however, such a situation will constitute a dramatic change in job and organisational design.[5]

Job design and technology

In the discussion of sociotechnical approaches to job design, it was noted that, while the sociotechnical ideal was *joint* optimisation of social (i.e. human) and technical (i.e. machine) factors, there did seem to be a tendency to favour technical over social systems. At the wider level, this tendency can lead us on to "the robots-are-taking our jobs" scenarios (see Chapter 1). Butera and Thurman (1984), while arguing that many of the early predictions of machines taking people's jobs have proved to be wrong, point out that much or indeed most job design is driven by "technological determinism"— that is, it is too easily presumed that the needs and behaviour of humans cannot be taken into account when designing new, and increasingly automated, work systems. Wall (1984) notes that many new technologies, such as computer numerically controlled (CNC) machine tools have led, not to job enrichment, but rather to deskilling and job impoverishment: workers become little better than machine-minders, while decision-making (e.g. machine programming) shifts back up the organisational hierarchy to supervisors and managers.

Wall asserts that this does not have to be so—technology can be designed so that programming tasks can be delegated back down the hierarchy (compare, for example, the shift in power that takes place when an organisation shifts computer power away from monolithic mainframe to desktop mini- and microcomputers). Proper approaches to technical as well as social systems, Wall argues, can not only roll back job impoverishment but lead to new levels of job enrichment:

> . . . the advent of new technology provides an unprecedented opportunity to redesign jobs. In the past, many have decided against such change because of its wider implications, for demarcation lines, industrial relations, managerial structure, and so on. They have "let well alone". The challenge of new technology, however, cannot be ignored, and will necessarily require rethinking in those sensitive areas. Since the issues are to be opened up in any case, the pursuit of job design is less threatening. (WALL 1984, P.28)

---

[5] Cetron and Appel (1984) note that IBM expects to have one-third of its workforce working from home by 1990.

In other words, change is inevitable: it only remains to be seen on whose terms change is instituted. This leads us on to the issue of control of jobs and organisations.

Job design and control

The extent to which one controls one's work environment is important, not least from the viewpoint of occupational stress (see the discussion of Karasek's model in Chapter 7). Individuals, for a variety of psychological and sociological reasons, have different needs concerning control over their environment (see discussion of locus of control in Chapter 6).

In the job design debate, much controversy occurs around the issue of control: does, for example, increasing workers' autonomy on the job, increasing the power to make decisions, take away autonomy from managers and supervisors? To many this is a foolishly naive question—of course power and control must be transferred. Kelly (1982) suggests that this may not necessarily be so: control may not be a zero-sum concept (i.e. when I win you must lose), but a non-zero-sum concept, wherein workers might gain increased control (e.g. over work pace and methods), and managers might *also* gain increased control (as a result of individualisation of workflow and roles).

Irrespective of who controls whom, the question of job design opens up the can of worms that is the control–power–participation–industrial democracy issue (see Box 12.B). This issue is perhaps now best left to more detailed discussion in Chapter 14.

Summary

Job design takes the "micro" view of work while organisational design takes the "macro" view. The classical scientific management or job engineering approach to job design is still dominant today, but because of the alleged weaknesses of this approach, alternatives have been proposed, such as job rotation, job enlargement and job enrichment.

Herzberg's approach to job enrichment can help to make jobs more meaningful, but it neglects certain key problems (e.g. money payment for higher productivity, group- or team-based workflow, etc.). Hackman and Oldham's approach is to consider the motivating potential of jobs, and also to take into account the psychological growth needs of differing individuals. Growth needs or individual differences can also be taken into account when trying to match job design with organisational design.

The sociotechnical approach to job design gives much greater weight to the fact that many people work in groups or teams. An example is the Volvo experiment. Quality circles is another group-based method of job design. Some of the uniquely Japanese features of this system will transfer to the West, some will not.

Goal-setting and management by objectives are participatory methods of selecting clear work targets (although sometimes participation can be more apparent than real). New work technologies, such as the electronic cottage, have vast potential to transform (for good or evil) people's working and personal lives. New technologies can lead to job enrichment or job impoverishment, depending on whether human factors are given (at least) equal weight with technical factors. Such decisions will be made according to the balance of power and control within organisations.

BOX 12.B: Job design and control of the workplace

Designing and redesigning jobs (and organisations) goes to the very heart of the question: who is in control? There is often conflict, in big and small organisations, about who is to make decisions—management or labour? The 1975–78 Volkswagen experiment in participative job redesign is instructive here.

Group technology

Group technology represents a realisation by some employers of the value of workgroups as a basis for work organisation, because it enables them to move beyond the cash nexus and tap the artesian sources of team-work, group problem-solving and mutual social control. These groups have been tried in mass production industries such as car manufacture in Sweden and Germany; for example, Volkswagen started experimenting with them at its new Salzgitter engine plant in 1975. Normally car engines are built on a conventional fixed speed assembly line with task cycles of about one or two minutes. Instead, Volkswagen began a small scale experiment with four groups of seven workers (two teams on each shift). Within the groups four men worked on assembly, two did testing and one man was in charge of materials. The entire group was de-coupled from the machine-paced line but had to meet a quota of seven engines per team per day. The workers received special training so that they could do all the team jobs and were free to rotate job assignments as they wished. Each group had a team leader (*Gruppensprecher*) who was responsible for liaison with management, and foremen were eliminated.

The results of the Volkswagen experiment highlighted two overlapping problems of such workgroups, which have recurred in different situations and economies. First, semi-autonomous workgroups ran up against the existing power-balance between labour and capital. Employers see such job redesign as an opportunity to undercut the union in the workplace, while the unions tend to be opposed to informally elected workgroup leaders as potential usurpers of union influence. This conflict of interests occurred at the Salzgitter plant with the eventual outcome that the team leaders were converted into shop stewards, and foremen were brought back to oversee the groups as Volkswagen wanted to prevent the erosion of management power.

Apart from the issue of autonomous groups as a threat to the existing structures of shopfloor power, there was the question of how the specially trained team workers fitted into the skill and wage hierarchy. The enlarged jobs caused a union/management dispute over wage levels. The unions demanded that the workers should be paid at a skilled rate which Volkswagen resisted. In effect, this re-combination of tasks across Taylorian boundaries disrupted the Babbage Principle of labour cheapening which, as we have said, involves stripping a skilled job to an essential core and paying less for all ancillary and servicing tasks performed by unskilled workers. Volkswagen concluded that they did not want masses of re-skilled workers on the basis that they had no jobs for them—they did not fit into the normal structure.

In 1978 the experiment was ended. Volkswagen management considered the system too costly and that it was not possible to fill the factory with the "dreams of another world".

Lessons from the Volkswagen experiment

The Volkswagen case is important. It exemplifies . . . the inherent instability of any particular management strategy as an effort to resolve the basic tension between the need for control and the need for participation as played out against a backdrop of competitive market pressures, technological developments and management/workers (i.e. class) relations. The Volkswagen experiment failed, partly at least, for the sorts of reasons given by General Motors' Director of Employee Research and Training at its Chevrolet division. He remarked that, ". . . the subjects of participation are not necessarily restricted to those few matters that management considers to be of direct, personal interest to employees. . . (A plan cannot) be maintained for long without (a) being recognised by employees as manipulative or (b) leading to expectations for wider and more significant involvement—'Why do they only ask us about plans for painting the office and not about replacing this old equipment and rearranging the layout?' Once competence is shown (or believed to have been shown) in say, rearranging the work area, and after participation has become a conscious, officially sponsored activity, participators may very well want to go on to topics of job assignment, the allocation of rewards, or even the selection of leadership. In other words, management's present monopoly of control can in itself easily become a source of contention." (quoted in Edwards 1979, p.156).

Source: Littler and Salaman (1984), pp.82–84. Reproduced with permission.

Questions for discussion

1. What are the advantages and disadvantages of the classical model of job design?
2. What is the difference between job rotation, job enlargement and job enrichment?
3. How valid are the criticisms made of job enrichment?
4. Evaluate Hackman and Oldham's model of job design.
5. What factors should be taken into account in attempting to match job design with organisational design?
6. "Group-based methods of job design, such as sociotechnical systems and quality circles, only work well in societies with strong socialist and/or group-based value systems, such as Sweden or Japan. They will not work in societies with stronger traditions of capitalism and/or individually-based value systems, such as America and Australia." Discuss.
7. In what ways are goal-setting and management by objectives different from and similar to other methods of job design?
8. Would you like to work in an electronic cottage? Why/why not?
9. Is technology a positive or negative force in job design?
10. In what ways does job design affect the balance of control and power in the workplace?

References

Ainsworth, W.M. and Willis, Q.F. (eds) (1981). *Australian Organizational Behaviour: Readings.* (Macmillan: Melbourne).

Andreatta, A.J. (1981). "Organizational Effectiveness through Semi-Autonomous Groups", in Ainsworth and Willis (1981).

Blunt, Peter (1983). "Motivation Through Job Design and Orientations to Work: A Theoretical Reconstruction and Synthesis", *Australian Psychologist*, vol. 18, no. 3, July.

Briscomb, Tony (1983). "Quality Circles: The Rieker View", *Work and People*, vol. 9, no. 1.

Butera, Federico and Thurman, Joseph E. (eds) (1984). *Automation and Work Design.* (North Holland: Amsterdam).

Carey, Alex (1976). "Industrial Psychology and Sociology in Australia", in Boreham, P. *et al.* (eds), *The Professions of Australia: A Critical Appraisal.* (University of Queensland Press: St Lucia).

— (1980). "Worker Motivation: Social Science, Propaganda and Democracy", in Boreham, P. and Dow, Geoff (eds), *Work and Inequality: Ideology and Control in the Capitalist Labour Process.* (Macmillan: Melbourne).

Cetron, Marvin J. and Appel, Marcia (1984). *Jobs of the Future.* (McGraw-Hill: New York).

Cooley, Mike (1980). "Computerization—Taylor's Latest Disguise", *Economic and Industrial Democracy*, vol. 1, pp.523–39.

Coombes, Paul (1979). "MBO Running into Heavy Flak", *Rydge's*, January.

Dabscheck, Braham and Niland, John (1981). *Industrial Relations in Australia.* (George Allen and Unwin: Sydney).

Davis, Keith (1981). *Human Behaviour at Work: Organizational Behaviour*, 6th edn. (McGraw-Hill: New York).

Dewar, Donald L. (1980). *The Quality Circle Guide to Participation Management.* (Prentice-Hall: New Jersey).

Ducker, J.P. (1975). "Industrial Democracy: Utopian Vision or Living Reality?" in Gunzberg, Doron, *Bringing Work to Life: The Australian Experience.* (Cheshire/Productivity Promotion Council of Australia: Melbourne).

Dunphy, Dexter, Andreatta, Helen and Timms, Lynne (1981). "Redesigning the Work Organization at Phillips", in Ainsworth and Williams (1981).

Dunphy, Dexter C. and Dick, Robert (1981). *Organizational Change by Choice.* (McGraw-Hill: Sydney).

Edwards, Richard (1979). *Contested Terrain: The Transformation of the Workplace in the Twentieth Century.* (Heinemann: London).

Emery, F.E. (1980). "The Assembly Line: Its Logic and our Future", in Lansbury (1980).

Eunson, Baden (1983). "Electronic Cottage: A Way Station to Fun?", *Sydney Morning Herald*, 3 October; "Electronic Cottage", *Hobart Mercury*, 3 October.

Ferguson, D.A. (ed.) (1979). "The Optimum Use of Human Resources", in Ferguson, D.A. (ed.), *Ergonomics in the Australian Workplace.* (Productivity Promotion Council of Australia: Melbourne).

Ferris, Gerald R. and Wagner, John A. III (1985). "Quality Circles in the United States: A Conceptual Reevaluation", *Journal of Applied Behavioural Science*, vol. 21, no. 2, pp.155–67.

Ford, G.W. (1983). "Japan as a Learning Society", *Work and People*, vol. 9, no. 1.

Goldthorpe, J.H., Lockwood, D., Bechhofer, F. and Platt, J. (1968). *The Affluent Worker: Industrial Attitudes and Behaviour.* (Cambridge University Press: London).

Gunzberg, Doron (1980). "Swedish Approaches to Democracy in the Workplace", in Lansbury (1980).

Hackman, J.R. and Oldham, G.R. (1976). "Motivation through the Design of Work: Test of a Theory", *Organizational Behaviour and Human Performance*, vol. 16.

Haganaes, Knut and Hales, Lee (1983). "Scandinavian Models of Employee Participation", *Advanced Management Journal*, Winter.

Hellriegel, Don, Slocum, John W. and Woodman, Richard W. (1983). *Organizational Behaviour*, 3rd edn. (West: St Paul, Minn.).

Herzberg, Frederick (1968). "One More Time: How do you Motivate Employees?", *Harvard Business Review*, Jan.–Feb.

 (1976). *The Managerial Choice.* (Richard D. Irwin: Illinois).

 (1979). "Orthodox Job Enrichment', in Davis, Louis E. and Taylor, James C., *Design of Jobs*, 2nd edn. (Goodyear: California).

Hodgetts, Richard M. (1980). *Modern Human Relations.* (Dryden Press: Illinois).

Ingle, Sud (1982). *Quality Circle Master Guide: Increasing Productivity with People Power.* (Prentice-Hall: New Jersey).

Jones, Barry (1983). *Sleepers, Wake! Technology and the Future of Work*, rev. edn. (Oxford University Press: Melbourne).

Kamata, Satoshi (1983). *Japan in the Passing Lane.* (George Allen and Unwin: London).

Kelly, John E. (1982). *Scientific Management, Job Redesign, and Work Performance.* (Academic Press: New York).

Lansbury, Russell D. (ed.) (1980). *Democracy in the Workplace.* (Longman Cheshire: Melbourne).

Lansbury, Russell D. and Prideaux, Geoffrey J. (1978). *Improving the Quality of Work Life.* (Longman Cheshire: Melbourne).

Lansbury, Russell D. and Spillane, Robert (1983). *Organizational Behaviour: the Australian Context.* (Longman Cheshire: Melbourne).

Lee, James A. (1980). *The Gold and the Garbage in Management Theories and Prescriptions.* (Ohio University Press: Athens, Ohio).

Lindsay, Don (1982). "QCs at Reckitt and Colman", *Work and People*, vol. 8, no. 3.

Littler, C. (1985). "Taylorism, Fordism and Job Design", in Knights, David, Wilmott, Hugh and Collinson, David (eds), *Job Redesign: Critical Perspectives on the Labour Process.* (Gower: Aldershot).

Littler, Craig R. and Salaman, Graeme (1984). *Class at Work: The Design, Allocation and Control of Jobs.* (Batsford: London).

Locke, Edwin A. (1978). "The Ubiquity of the Technique of Goal Setting in Theories of and Approaches to Employee Motivation", *Academy of Management Review*, July.

 (1980). "Motivation", in Karmel, Barbara (ed.), *Point and Counterpoint in Organizational Behaviour.* (Dryden Press: Illinois).

Luthans, Fred (1981). *Organizational Behaviour*, 3rd edn. (McGraw-Hill: New York).

McIver, Rhonda (1983). "Human Resource Planning for a Major New Project—A Case Study", *Work and People*, vol. 9, no. 1.

Martin, James (1981). *Telematic Society: A Challenge for Tomorrow.* (Prentice-Hall: New Jersey).

Maruyama, Magoroh (1983). "Japanese Management Theories", *Futures*, July.

Myers, M. Scott (1970). *Every Employee a Manager: More Meaningful Work through Job Enrichment.* (McGraw-Hill: New York).

O'Brien, Gordon E. (1982). "Evaluation of the Job Characteristics Theory of Work Attitudes and Performance", *Australian Journal of Psychology*, vol. 34, no. 3, pp.383–401.

O'Shaughnessey, John (1979). *Patterns of Business Organization.* (George Allen and Unwin: London).

Porter, Lyman W., Lawler, Edward E. and Hackman, Richard (1975). *Behaviour in Organizations.* (McGraw-Hill: New York).
Renfro, William (1982). "Second Thoughts on Moving the Office Home", *The Futurist*, June.
Robinson, Ann and McCarroll, Geraldine (1981). "A Work Group Approach at Welvic", in Ainsworth and Willis (1981).
Rydge's (1978). "Job Enrichment—What Can Go Wrong", March.
Savall, Henri (1981). *Work and People: An Economic Evaluation of Job Enrichment.* (Oxford University Press: Oxford).
Schermerhorn, John R., Jr., Hunt, James G. and Osborn, Richard M. (1982). *Managing Organizational Behaviour.* (John Wiley and Sons: New York).
Sprouster, John (1984). *Total Quality Control: The Australian Experience.* (Horwitz Grahame: Sydney).
Toffler, Alvin (1980). *The Third Wave.* (Pan: London).
Visser, Carla (1982). "What We Can Learn from the Japanese about QCs?", *Advanced Management Journal*, Summer.
Wall, Toby (1984). "What's New in . . . Job Design", *Personnel Management*, April.
Wood, S. (ed.) (1981). *The Degradation of Work?: Skill, Deskilling and the Braverman Debate.* (Hutchinson: London).
Wells, Claudette (1982). "Quality Circles—Features of an Australian Program", *Work and People*, vol. 8, no. 3.
Yerbury, Diane (1980). "Participation and Apathy in Trade Unions", in Lansbury (1980).

Films/videos

For My Own Cause: Quality Circles (Brittanica Video).
Smarter Together: Autonomous Working Groups (Brittanica Video).
Responsibility Shared: Autonomous Production Groups (Brittanica Video).
At Home, At Work: Alternate Work Sites (Brittanica Video).
Not Just a Number, Part 1 (Amalgamated Metals Foundry and Shipwrights Union).
Management by Objectives, Parts 1, 2 and 3 (Video Channel, Power Human Resources).
Quality Circles (Training Media Services).

Part F

Behaviour: The organisational level

How can an organisation best meet the needs of those inside and outside such an organisation? Humans make organisations, and those organisations in turn make, or break, their makers. To understand the flow of behaviour within organisations, we have to understand the structural aspects of organisations.

In Chapter 13 we consider classic organisational principles, such as bureaucracy, size, departmentation, centralisation, span of control, and so on.

In Chapter 14, other aspects of organisations, such as the grapevine or informal organisation, technology and its influence on organisational structure, participation and industrial democracy, and Japanese models of organisation, are considered.

13

Organisational design 1

ORGANISATIONS, like jobs, have a design or structure, whether that design be conscious or unconscious, good or bad. An organisation might be a private manufacturing company, or it might be a public service department, a trade union, a sporting club, a hospital, a school, a parliament, a ship, a crime syndicate, a prison, or any one of the many groupings of people in our society. We might learn much about an organisation by looking at the official organisation chart, but such charts, like job profiles, conceal as well as reveal the true structure and function of the organisation and its constituent parts.

In this chapter, we will consider the more traditional concepts of organisational analysis—centralisation, staff and line, and so on—and we shall see how such concepts have stood the test of time and how they have changed. In Chapter 14 we shall consider issues which either were missed by traditional analysts or which have only recently begun to emerge—the informal organisation, the role of technology in organisations, participation and industrial democracy, and the Japanese model of organisation.

You will notice that these organisational design chapters overlap to a substantial degree with Chapter 12. To a considerable extent, this is inevitable. All three chapters consider a similar series of concepts, with Chapter 12 taking a "micro" view, and Chapters 13 and 14 taking a "macro" view. There is also a partial overlap with the content of Chapters 2, 9, 10 and 11.

406

Bureaucracy

"Bureaucracy" nowadays is often used as a term of contempt, as in the quote above from a former US president. Ask a person what the word means to them, and they will probably answer that it means officious bumbling, red tape, inefficiency, faceless and uncaring institutions remote from human needs, and so on. Yet "bureaucracy" was once a "hurrah" word rather than a "boo" word. Max Weber, a German sociologist writing in the 1920s, saw bureaucracy as a form of organisation that was distinctly superior to organisations found in earlier societies where monarchical and/or religious authority prevailed. In such earlier societies, authority was either *traditional* (based upon custom) or *charismatic* (based upon perceived qualities of a religious or political leader). Such authority was often arbitrary and unpredictable. A bureaucracy, by contrast, possessed *rational–legal* authority—bureaucratic officials observed consistent rules and procedures and operated within a specific legal jurisdiction. Other differences were notable between bureaucratic and pre-bureaucratic forms of organisation (Table 13.1).

Decision-making was no longer the whim of one person, but systematic and routinised. A rational hierarchy encouraged specialisation of work. Rules (statutes, laws, regulations), and indeed, the organisation itself, became more predictable. Careers were no longer dependent upon the favour of the chief decision-maker, but were dependent upon one's intrinsic ability, that is, promotion through the hierarchy depended upon merit (although Weber changed his position slightly on this latter point, allowing the process of seniority more weight).

This was Weber's *ideal* bureaucracy; it didn't necessarily exist in the real world, but it was the model on which all bureaucracies were patterned. To the extent that bureaucracies do fall short of that ideal, to that same extent do the weaknesses of bureaucracy become apparent. Then again, perhaps even an ideal bureaucracy would not be quite so ideal for those inside it. We will consider the criticisms of bureaucracy shortly.

Table 13.1 Pre-bureaucratic vs. bureaucratic management

	Pre-bureaucratic	*Bureaucratic*
Purpose	Ad hoc, reflecting personal goals of political or business leader	Definite and public; normally set by law or charter
Hierarchy	Weak and fluid; lower positions held at pleasure of chief; jurisdictions not definite	Clear jurisdictions; clear channels of communication and chains of command
Rules	Unsystematic, not always enforced, not binding on rule makers	Dependable, systematic
Authority	Traditional, charismatic	Rational–legal
Careers	Unstable, non-professional; positions for sale or granted as rewards for loyalty	Official is a full-time professional, no personal following; appointment based on merit
Decision-making	Ad hoc, subject to whims of one person	Systematic, routinised

Source: Broom, Selznick and Darroch (1981), p.164. Reproduced with permission.

Classic management theory

Contemporary with Weber were management theorists who were more concerned with the day-to-day running of organisations. Prominent among these were the Frenchman Henri Fayol (1949) and the American Frederick Taylor (1947). Taylor is also discussed in Chapters 2 and 12, particularly because of his contribution to what Dunphy and Dick (1981) have called "traditional technocratic work design principles", that is,

external design control
specialisation
technological dominance
repetition
deskilling
equalised, "distributed" workloads
work measurement
individual financial incentives
minimal social interaction
close supervision.

Drucker (1981) however has argued that Taylor cannot be simply dismissed as the villainous mastermind behind allegedly dehumanising work practices of the early twentieth century (see Chapter 2).

Fayol, Taylor and others worked along lines similar to Weber's, developing various principles of organisational design. In brief, these were:

1. *Specialisation and division of labour.* Labour should be specialised, so that personnel could master one skill area and perform well. This will facilitate economies of scale.
2. *Economies of scale.* Large-scale organisation of specialised workers (e.g. assembly lines) can result in high-volume output.
3. *Departmentation.* Hierarchies are organised horizontally into departments, according to purpose, process, persons or things, and place.
4. *Staff and line.* Distinctions are drawn between line units and personnel who perform the "substantive" functions of the organisation (e.g. manufacturing), and staff units and personnel, who act in a support capacity (e.g. personnel department, accounting, public relations).
5. *Centralisation.* An optimal balance between centralisation and decentralisation of facilities should be achieved. Decentralisation usually means less power at the top of the hierarchy, and hence may be less prominent than centralisation.
6. *Unity of command.* An employee should receive orders from and be responsible to one supervisor only.
7. *Chain of command.* Roles in the hierarchy should be clearly spelt out, with each person having a clear power relationship with those above and below in the hierarchy.
8. *Span of control.* Each supervisor should have a limited amount of people reporting to her, according to the nature of the task and the abilities of supervisor and supervised.
9. *Equal power and responsibility.* A supervisor should have the power commensurate with the responsibility given her.
10. *A "theory X" value system.* A less objective, more problematic factor than the preceding nine principles of classic organisational design. McGregor (1960) argues that the traditional value system of

management can be characterised by theory X, wherein it is believed that people

- avoid work and responsibility as much as possible
- need to and prefer to be controlled by others
- are motivated only by money and concrete gains
- cannot be trusted
- do not wish to achieve anything in their job roles.

In contrast, a "theory Y" value system sees human nature being diametrically different on these points.

Evaluation of bureaucratic and classic models

There has been considerable criticism of the bureaucratic and classic models of organisation. Some of this criticism is mild and reformist, suggesting that minor modifications are needed to make these models more appropriate to realistic and modern conditions. Some criticisms are more far-reaching, going far beyond reform, and suggesting that bureaucracies need to be done away with totally, and replaced by revolutionary new forms of organisational design. Let us examine some of these criticisms now.

One of the foremost critics of bureaucratic/classic organisations is Warren Bennis, perhaps most famous for his 1966 article, "The Coming Death of Bureaucracy". Bennis argued that bureaucracy had reached its pinnacle of efficiency some time in the Victorian era, but had since then become progressively inefficient, and was in fact now directly counter-productive to its avowed goals. He saw some of its weaknesses as being:

1. It does not adequately allow for personal growth and the development of mature personalities.
2. It develops conformity and "group-think".
3. It does not take into account the "informal organisation" and the emergent and unanticipated problems.
4. Its systems of control and authority are hopelessly outdated.
5. It has no adequate judicial process.
6. It does not possess adequate means for resolving differences and conflicts among ranks and, most particularly, among functional groups.
7. Communication (and innovative ideas) are thwarted or distorted because of hierarchical divisions.
8. The full human resources of bureaucracy are not being utilised because of mistrust, fear of reprisals, etc.
9. It cannot assimilate the influx of new technology or scientists entering the organisation.
10. It will modify the personality structure such that man will become and reflect the dull, grey conditioned "organisation man". (BENNIS 1965).

Du Brin (1981), Schermerhorn (1986) and others have observed similar weaknesses in bureaucracy:

1. The bureaucratic system's outputs—decisions, goods and services—are often of mediocre quality. The customer is rarely satisfied ("Oh, it's only a customer. . .").
2. While jurisdictions and areas of responsibility are meant to be clearly delimited in a bureaucracy, often rules are used to avoid responsibility. Thus many people's experience of such organisations is the telephone runaround that even US presidents complain of, buck-passing, tales of "that's not our department", and fob-offs such as "it's being processed in official channels" and "that's classified/confidential information".

3. Related to the previous point is delay of decisions. Delay in getting decisions out of bureaucracies is unaccountable and usually non-accountable, that is, nobody is held responsible. Delay is the deadliest form of denial, as C. Northcote Parkinson remarks (Parkinson 1957). The ultimate weapon of "bureaucrats" is to put your file at the bottom of their tray.
4. Observation of rules becomes an end in itself rather than simply a means to an end; the letter, rather than the spirit, is observed. "Impersonal" administration of such rules, which for Weber meant impartial, without favouritism, becomes impersonal in the sense of lacking flexibility, compassion and civility.
5. Specialisation of work roles can lead to groups placing sectional interests above the collective good of the organisation, for example interdepartmental rivalries.
6. The establishment of a professional class of bureaucrats may mean that the class becomes a self-serving elite.
7. Adoption of seniority practices can lead to organisations becoming conservative gerontocracies, unable to accept and implement new ideas.
8. The Peter Principle: in a hierarchy, every employee tends to rise to his/her level of incompetence. Thus, an excellent tradesperson may be rewarded for her excellence by being promoted to an executive position, where she may no longer excel. Status, pride and Parkinson's Second Law (Expenditure rises to meet income) ensure that the incompetent executive will not return to her maximum level of competence and thus maximise the total performance of the organis-ation (Peter and Hull 1969). Peter and Parkinson are often dismissed as mere jokesters by organisational behaviour theorists, but their satirical approach often carries more weight than the most august analyses.

Bureaucracy, Bennis says, is incapable of meeting a number of threats, two of which are rapid and unexpected change, and change in managerial behaviour. The second factor is basically related to a humanisation of values in the workplace as management began to realise that the economistic view of man held by classic theory (more output can be guaranteed by paying more money) was naive, and ignored a complex of social and psychological factors. The "push-button worker" was mythical, the reality being human beings who were much more complex, and who wanted to share decision-making power rather than be coerced and threatened (Bennis 1966a). This value shift envisaged by Bennis is similar to McGregor's notion of theory X values being overtaken by theory Y values. Theory Y values would be:

- people are motivated not so much by money as by interesting and challenging tasks
- they relish interesting work, and will assume responsibility for such work
- they can make their own decisions about work and want to make such decisions
- they can be trusted (MCGREGOR 1960)

Bennis's first factor—rapid and unexpected change—is a threat to bureaucracy because bureaucracy is so well adapted to static, unchanging situations. In such situations, rules, regulations and rigidities make sense, but in a world reeling from future shock, where the world is a turbulent rather than a placid place, bureaucracies are seen to be organisational dinosaurs, unable to adapt.

Future shock is not simply the changes caused by technical invention and innovation. Toffler (1970, 1980, 1985) has argued that modern organisations are finding that they increasingly have to concentrate on "trans-economic objectives", objectives wider than the single "bottom line" objective of profit maximisation. Now there are multiple bottom lines, among which are:

1. *Social.* The organisation can no longer regard its actions as being separate from the "socio-sphere" or network of other private and public organisations in the community. The community disapproves of "social pollution" in the form of unemployment, community disruption, forced mobility, and so on.

2. *Environmental.* Organisations are increasingly being held accountable for whatever environmental impacts they make upon the biosphere, such as industrial and agricultural pollution, excess energy use, and so on.

3. *Informational.* The "info-sphere" is growing. Organisations increasingly find information to be a key factor in day-to-day operations. This is both a cause and an effect of the growth of computer systems. Demands are growing for greater accountability of private organisations (disclosure of profits of oil companies, "truth in advertising") and of public organisations (freedom of information legislation). Organisations are critical to widening or healing the gap between the "information rich" and the "information poor" (Jones 1983*a*).

4. *Political.* The power sphere is becoming more complex. Organisations have to cope with a wide range of government departments and quangos (quasi-autonomous non-government organisations) both at home and abroad.

5. *Ethical.* Organisational behaviour once accepted as normal is now perceived as corrupt, immoral or scandalous, or hitherto "virtuous" organisations are now seen to be not so virtuous. Public outrage greets such "robber baron" behaviour as an industrialist dismissing asbestosis in miners as a necessary cost of civilisation, or a drug company refusing to pay damages to those who took thalidomide, or a government seen to be accepting bribes from private vested interests, or a transnational corporation moving its operations from one country to another purely on economic grounds.

Given such factors, the world is a much more complicated place than when Weber first enunciated the principles of his ideal bureaucracy. Society is no longer a static, placid environment: it is a dynamic, turbulent environment. Burns and Stalker (1961) argue that conventional organisations or bureaucracies are too conventional and rigid to deal with such turbulence. Bureaucracies, or *mechanistic* organisations, cannot cope, but post-bureaucratic or *organic* organisations can. Whereas the mechanistic organisation depends upon classic design principles such as strict hierarchy (vertical communication, all power held by superiors) and rigid specialisation of work roles, the organic organisation is a network of equals rather than a hierarchy of powerful and powerless, with communications being lateral or horizontal rather than vertical, and work roles overlapping rather than been compartmented. Legitimate power (deference paid to those officially at the top of the hierarchy) and coercive power are little in evidence, while expert power (deference paid to those who are expert in their field) is the dominant mode of control or influence (see Chapter 10).

Dessler's interpretation of the organic/mechanistic distinction, using the classic management functions of planning, organising, staffing, leading and controlling, is shown in Table 13.2.

Table 13.2 Differences between organic and mechanistic organisations

	Mechanistic (Classic orientation)	Organic (Behavioural orientation)
Plan		
Goals—how specific?	Specific	General
Standards	Rigid	Flexible
Rules and procedures	Many; specified	Few; broad
Plan—how detailed?	Detailed; inflexible	Broad; flexible
Forecasts	Use historical trend	Qualitative; future projection
Decision-making	Management science techniques	Creativity—intuition
Organise		
Who reports to whom	Clear—no deviations	Broad—permit deviations
Line and staff	Clear distinction	Little distinction
Departmentation	By function or process	By product
Specialisation	Very specialised units	Broader, more "enlarged" units
Delegation	Little	Much
Span of control	Narrow	Wide
Coordination	Use chain of command	Special coordinators
Staff		
Job descriptions	Clear—limited scope	Broad—"open-ended"
Job specification	Stress skills	Stress potential
Selection methods	Specific performance tests—reference checks	General aptitude and interest tests
Performance criteria	Specific; output-oriented	General; development-oriented
Performance evaluation	Graphic rating scale	Critical incidents
Training and development	Skills training	Organisational development
Lead		
Leadership style	More autocratic	More democratic
Source of motivation	Extrinsic (money, promotion)	Intrinsic (the job itself)
Psychological climate	Structured, performance-oriented	Supportive, development-oriented
Control		
Standards	Specific, efficiency-oriented	General; "milestones"
Control	Imposed	Self control
Checks on performance	Frequent	Infrequent
Emphasis	How work performed	The final product

Source: Dessler (1982), p.19. Reprinted with permission of Reston Publishing Company, a Prentice-Hall Company, 11480 Sunset Hills Road, Reston, VA 22090, USA.

Bennis' view of an organic organisational design was what he called an *organic-adaptive* organisation or *adhocracy*. The model for an adhocracy is the research and development team:

1. the team is comprised of relative strangers who have respect for each others' skills in a variety of areas;
2. the team is temporary, existing only so long as the problem under review exists;

3. the group is comprised of professionals, whose primary loyalties may be to their professional peer group (all the world's doctors, all the world's computer software designers, etc.) rather than to whichever organisation happens to be paying their rent at the moment; and

4. the group is led by a project leader, who coordinates rather than commands.

An attempt at this type of organisational flexibility is the *matrix* organisation, where a worker might report to several coordinators in different areas (sales, quality control, research) rather than to a single supervisor immediately above her in the hierarchy (we shall examine the matrix form in greater detail soon). Such organic designs are increasingly seen in some high technology industries such as computers, or, to be more accurate, are seen in the early stages of growth when the organisation is small. Whether it is possible to have a large *and* organic organisation remains to be seen.

Handy (1984) has also sung the praises of the adhocratic or "contractual" organisation, which has staff moving flexibly in and out of the organisation as need dictates, with only a small permanent core of staff enduring in the long term (see Box 13.A).

Bureaucracy—dead, but refusing to lie down

How valid are these criticisms of bureaucratic/classic organisations? Bennis himself has switched positions somewhat. In 1969, he expressed second thoughts about his original "temporary-systems, democracy-is-inevitable" hypotheses in a piece entitled "A Funny Thing Happened on the Way to the Future". He later spoke of how "bureaucracy is the inevitable—and therefore necessary—form for governing large and complex organisations" and "there will always be a bureaucracy; the sun will never set on bureaucracies" (Bennis 1973, 1974). Miner believes that this change of heart was due to Bennis getting more experience in the actual running of organisations (a change of heart similar to McGregor's, who began to see good points in theory X after being a university administrator; Miner 1982). By 1975, however, Bennis had switched back to the "end of bureaucracy" formulation, believing that his 1965 prediction was being proved.

Organisational forms *are* changing, of that there is no doubt. Yet bureaucracy, expressed either as a boo word or a hurrah word, is still very much with us. Among the reasons for its survival are the following.

1. The "turbulence" thesis is not proved. The industries which are turned upside down are the exception, rather than the rule. "Future shock" is an unhelpful, "gee-whiz" concept that oversimplifies reality. As the French put it, *plus ça change, plus c'est la même chose* (the more it changes, the more it stays the same) (O'Shaughnessey 1979).

2. "Mechanistic" organisations may adapt quite well to such change as there is, for example, IBM. Also, organic organisations may be so vague and undisciplined that mechanistic organisations will surpass them in normal operations (O'Shaughnessey 1979; Lee 1980).

3. The adhocracy model is predominantly a middle-class, professional concept. It takes the professional model (marketable skills underwriting high job mobility, good communication and group interaction skills, high psychological needs for autonomy) and projects them on to all jobs. This is probably unrealistic, as the job enrichment

debate reveals (see Chapter 12). Bennis himself spoke of a near-future society of adhocracies wherein a hard core of 20 per cent "to my despair, will do the remaining unprogrammed, low-level jobs of society . . . perhaps there are enough people with physical or mental handicaps, or people with low aspirations, to do them. It's difficult to think about" (Bennis 1979).

4. Many of the advantages Weber saw in bureaucracies, compared with pre-bureaucratic organisations, still hold, for example, doing away with favouritism, corruption, arbitrariness (Robbins 1979).

5. The job role uncertainty of organic organisations/adhocracies causes anxiety among many employees who prefer clearly defined roles with minimum decision-making involved (see Chapter 12).

6. Personnel practices such as promotion by seniority may induce long-term stability; conversely, even where it causes stagnation, all personnel have a vested interest in it the longer they stay on. Promotion by seniority also lets management leave the issue of appraisal of employee performance in the "too hard" basket: rewards are allocated to those who are next in the queue, irrespective of their ability.

7. The lack of responsiveness to other parts of the organisation and to clienteles outside the organisation, that is, the lack of efficiency and accountability, may be the ideal pre-conditions for a quiet life for personnel—vested interests ensure inefficiency because inefficiency is very efficient for the inefficient (a popular view in monopolies, where clienteles have no choice). To employ the language of behaviourism, there is no real feedback from the environment to the system (see Chapter 3). Thus there are no consequences for either excellence or failure, and because, by definition, excellence is more difficult to achieve than failure, excellence is extinguished and failure is reinforced. Those who try to change the organisation's system from within—the cage-rattlers, the boat-rockers, the critics, the stirrers, the deviants, the whistle-blowers—can follow one of five courses:
(a) they can prevail;
(b) they can give up, go elsewhere to succeed or fail, thus allowing the system to prevail;
(c) they can self-destruct, destroyed by frustration;
(d) they can stay in the system and join them because they can't beat them—total capitulation;
(e) they can stay in the system, but remain deviant by subverting, vandalising, sabotaging, deliberately fouling up—partial capitulation.
(a) is less common than the other points. (c) is obviously a stressful outcome, but the other four are also quite stressful.

8. Management may explicitly or implicitly subscribe to a radical welfarist personnel policy, that is, even the inefficient and incompetent need to eat/there but for the grace of God go I/the organisation as sheltered workshop, etc.

9. Customers, clienteles—those that constitute part of the environment of the organisation—may not be assertive enough, or may not be sufficiently familiar with their legal rights, to give the organisation a hard time, that is, provide feedback. They may also have learned to become apathetic and cynical.

10. Theory X values are alive and well. Byrt (1980), for example, notes that authoritarian leadership tends to become prevalent in hard economic times. The 1970s and 1980s have been tougher than the 1960s, when Bennis and Burns and Stalker first developed their ideas about "post-bureaucratic" organisations. Consequently, management is more likely to see theory Y principles such as participation and consultation as expendable "frills". The countervailing power of labour is less, given more insecurity of jobs. Machovec and Smith (1982) argue that theory X never went away. Using arguments from the emerging field of sociobiology, they attempt to make the following points about human nature and organisations:
    (a) Man by nature is selfish and aggressive.
    (b) Man will only strive for (i.e. be motivated by) scarce commodities, such as money and power; these desires are insatiable.
    (c) because resources are scarce, and because desires are insatiable, there must always be winners and losers.
    (d) Destructive competition is held in check by natural biological mechanisms such as territorial behaviour and hierarchical behaviour. In organisations, this means that jobs and departments are territories, which everyone has a vested interest in maintaining, and hierarchies mean chains of command.
    (e) Managements should acknowledge these "biological truths" by practices such as big pay differentials between winners and losers (although not so big as to demotivate today's losers from becoming tomorrow's winners).

Social Darwinism arguments ("the survival of the fittest") have always been popular, especially in hard times. How true do you think they are here?

The picture on organisational design is thus seen to be a complicated one. In an attempt to get an overview, let us turn again to some of the key classic organisational principles to see to what extent they can be wholeheartedly accepted, modified, or rejected and replaced.

Economies of scale, specialisation and division of labour

The classic principles of specialisation and division of labour made economies of scale possible, thus allowing the most dramatic increase in productivity seen in history. Markets where small production runs are the only ones available, such as in Australia, do not compare well with competitors. Nevertheless there are many *dis*economies involved in large-scale production. There are the obvious factors of workers, performing the one small task all day long, becoming bored, disaffected and alienated. Such attitudes often transfer into poor quality output ("Monday"/"Friday" cars, etc.), and sometimes into deviant behaviour such as sabotage of products and harassment of clients. Schumacher (1973) and others have pointed out that industrial modes of production imposed on agriculture have resulted in monoculture, or cultivating vast areas of a single crop irrespective of the ecological variations in soil, a technique that requires increasing inputs of fertilisers, pesticides, genetic engineering and other artificialities. The increasing cost of these inputs, plus the alleged decrease in quality of food, timber, etc., are diseconomies of scale. Illich (1971, 1977) argues that the industrial mentality has also been imposed upon education and medicine. Education systems are like assembly lines, and produce similar alienation, while medicine is being plagued with a rise in iatrogenic, or doctor-induced, disease, an outcome of accumulating side-effects of drugs. Diseconomies of scale are evident here also.

Reich (1983) argues that the classic model of high-volume, standardised output which created the manufacturing wealth of the advanced industrial countries (America, Europe, Australia, etc.) in the 1920–1970 period is now in fact contributing to these countries' decline. There is nothing in the classic model that developing countries such as Korea, Taiwan, Singapore, Brazil and Mexico (and, insofar as it is still a developing country, Japan) cannot repeat, exploiting much lower wage structures and in some cases richer resource bases. The solution? Move out of mass-production items—steel, automobiles, pharmaceuticals, textiles—into precision-manufactured, custom-tailored, and technology-driven items in the same industrial areas—precision castings, speciality steels, special chemicals and drugs, custom-made synthetics, as well as fibre-optic cables, ceramics, lasers, computer hardware and software, and other "sunrise industries" (Jones 1983*b*). Because many of these products require custom designing and ongoing servicing, the distinction between goods and services blurs. Reich notes, however, that the organisational design best suited to *flexible-system production*, as opposed to standardised production, is, in Burns and Stalker's terminology, more organic than mechanistic. Network, not hierarchical, systems are needed. Customised products mean that salespeople must have a close knowledge of the production system's capability, while production people must be aware of customer's needs. Semi-permanent teams (i.e. a low staff turnover) operate to solve problems as they arise, and this is best enhanced if vertical differentiation of salary, status and power is minimal, that is, if the organisation is "flat" rather than "tall" (see "Span of control", p.425). Rather than fearing turbulence, flexible organisations relish it: their structure is ideally suited to rapid response, and that, to be brutally frank, is the only advantage flexible-system economies have over the standardised production economies of the developing world.

Reich warns, however, that slavish imitation of the most successful flexible system economy—Japan—will not work. Many industrialists and politicians, particularly in the United States, wax lyrical over Japanese management practices such as quality circles (see Chapter 12) and so-called theory Z philosophies of management and participation (see Chapter 14). Many Westerners are loath to break up mechanistic hierarchies to achieve the participative/team approach of Japanese organisations, but even when they become committed to this, they think they can successfully graft these approaches on to classic, standardised production methods of work. This, Reich says, is doomed to failure. If Reich's analysis is correct, it is the most damning critique of the economies of scale principle yet enunciated (see also Box 13.A).

Departmentation

Organisations are usually structured into sub-organisations or departments. Traditionally, *functional* departmentation was used in most situations, although *divisional* and *matrix* organisation have become popular in more recent times.

Functional departments

The *functional* method of departmentation simply means that all personnel performing common functions are grouped together. Figure 13.1 shows a manufacturing organisation and a school organised according to the different skills or processes to be found in specific departments. Separation like this encourages specialisation of skills, and job-roles are clear and unambiguous (see Table 13.3).

There are problems associated with the functional form, however. Precisely because functional areas are so clearly delimited, there is often competition between departments, with managers unable or unwilling to see the point of view of others (and thus to see that everyone is working for the same organisation and theoretically sharing the same goals). Communication between departments is often difficult, and overall accountability within the organisation—who *is* finally responsible?—is often difficult to pin down. An overemphasis upon routine tasks and short time-horizons means that functional organisations are often inflexible and unresponsive to change.

Divisional departments

Organisations can also be structured on a *divisional* basis. These divisions may be geographical, product-based, services-based, client-based, or may be to meet legal requirements of governments at home and abroad. Figure 13.2 shows a manufacturing organisation broken up into product divisions and a school broken up into mini-school divisions. The divisional form has a number of advantages. It can better cater to specific clienteles and regional

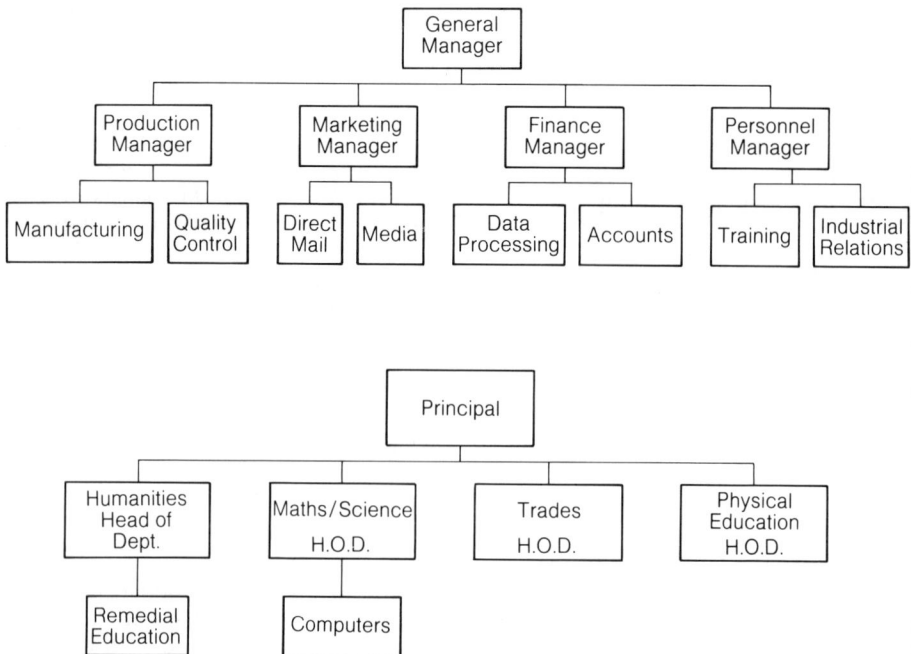

Fig. 13.1 *Departmentation by function in a manufacturing organisation and a school*

Table 13.3 Pros and cons of functional, divisional and matrix forms of departmentation

	Functional	Divisional	Matrix
PRO	• Most widely used • Best when competitive advantage is along single parameter—technology, price, performance or delivery • Promotes skill specialisation • Yields clear, unambiguous job roles • Reduces duplication of scarce resources • Best when markets are relatively stable and predictable • Easy to explain • Specialists, both superior and subordinates, have common language, and this helps problem-solving	• Can better cater to special regional needs, clients • Can allow highly specialised capital equipment to be used most efficiently • Performance of autonomous units is easier to monitor—accountability more clear-cut • Autonomous units can be pitted against one another in "friendly" rivalry • Units can be added or dropped without major disruption—flexibility enhances responses to changing circumstances • Most popular form among large, multinational conglomerates	• Increases job variety • Lends itself to job redesign, e.g. semi-autonomous work-groups • Combines strengths of functional and divisional forms • Can quickly create new products • Breaks down rigid hierarchical communication—communication is not so much vertical as horizontal, diagonal • Breaks down empire-building by legitimately cutting across formal boundaries and roles • Teaches people to handle complexity and ambiguity • Teaches management skills (trading off, negotiating) to all people • Limited time frame means that work is done quickly, not "padded out"
CON	• Emphasises routine tasks, which encourages short time horizons • Encourages empire-building by area managers, often to detriment of overall goals • Difficult to coordinate—conflicts arise between different areas • Communication hierarchical, inefficient • Slow response to change • Obscures accountability for overall outcomes	• Loss of economies of scale—duplication of effort as each division attempts to solve similar problems (financial, technical, personnel, etc.) • Difficult to coordinate for overall response to environment, e.g. new legislation • Encourages empire-building • Isolates specialists from peers in other divisions	• Combines weaknesses of functional and divisional forms • Installation can be expensive, time-consuming • Violates stability caused by classic principles of hierarchy, unity of command, staff and line • Increases role ambiguity, stress by assigning people to more than one department • Because a person is responsible to more than one boss, responsibility exceeds power, accountability unclear • May reward political skills as opposed to technical skills • Difficult to explain • Projects may not be temporary—vested interests may not want to disband

Source: Adapted from McCann and Galbraith (1981), Luthans (1981), Dunphy and Dick (1981), Schermerhorn, Hunt and Osborn (1982), Kerzner and Cleland (1985).

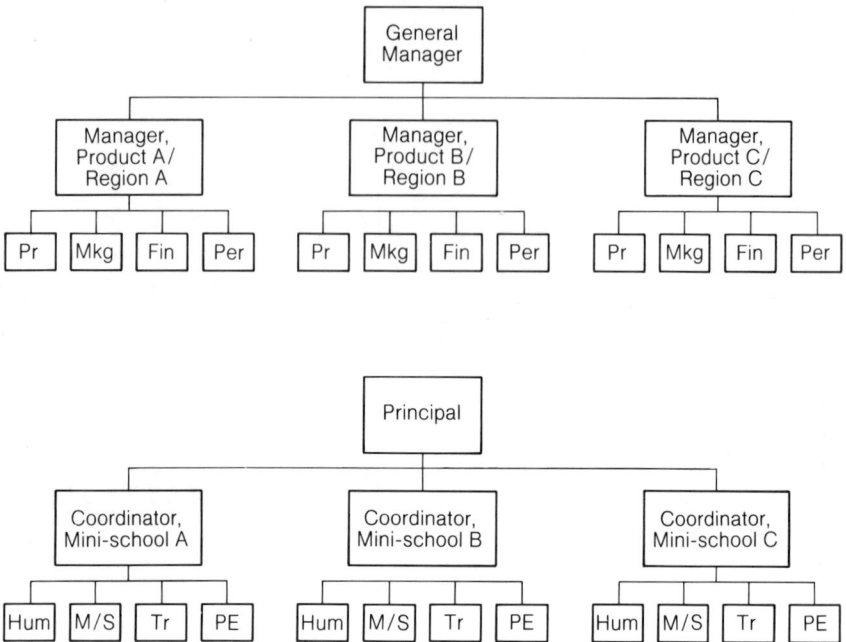

Fig. 13.2 *Departmentation by division in a manufacturing organisation and a school*

needs. Quantity and quality of specific outputs can be monitored easily, that is, accountability is not diffused and confused. If a large organisation decides to organise on the divisional model, making different product groups semi-autonomous, it can reap the benefits of both centralisation and decentralisation (see below). Divisions can be added or dropped without the whole organisation being drastically affected. Specialised capital equipment can be exploited in the most efficient manner. The divisional form in its most extreme form is the conglomerate—an organisation whose various divisions have nothing in common with each other at all, except specific goals such as making profits.

The divisional form has its drawbacks, of course. If personnel and facilities need to be duplicated within each division, then economies of scale are lost. The engineer or mathematics teacher within each division may suffer from lack of contact with other engineers and mathematics teachers in other divisions. As with the functional form of organisation, empire-building may be rife. The various divisions may also be difficult to coordinate, especially in response to rapidly emerging threats from the external environment.

Matrix departments

In recent years, a new organisational design, departmentation by *matrix*, has emerged. In mathematics, a matrix is a rectangular array of figures in columns and rows, and operations such as multiplication can take place horizontally and vertically. A matrix organisation is basically a functional organisation viewed vertically, and a project organisation viewed horizontally. Matrix organisation was originally developed in United States aerospace industries, where specific projects, temporary in duration but large in scale, were undertaken. A matrix approach to a manufacturing organisation and a school can be seen in Figure 13.3. Matrix organisations can respond rapidly and flexibly to changing circumstances. Bureaucratic features such as rigid communication channels and inflexible job roles are broken down. Parkinson's first law—work expands to fill the amount of time available—is repealed, due to the specific time constraints of the project to hand: when the project is over, that matrix disbands, personnel returning to home functional areas. This temporary project team approach lends itself to such job enrichment/job redesign strategies as semi-autonomous work groups (see Chapter 12). Personnel also learn skills such as negotiating as their time is bid for by two bosses—the functional boss, and the project boss.

This latter feature is one of the weaknesses of matrix departmentation. The classic management principle of unity of command is violated—people reporting to multiple bosses may be confused and over-stressed, and accountability may become muddled. The organisation may become over-politicised as project managers war with functional managers, and some employees may play off managers against each other. Matrix management can also be expensive and time-consuming when being put in place. Project managers are only human, and may not be interested in only a temporary position; as in the functional and divisional forms, matrix may thus encourage empire-building. The less temporary and more permanent the project, the more likely project personnel are to become staff, as opposed to line personnel (see below).

Matrix organisations have been quite fashionable since the late 1960s, and in many ways show the strengths and weaknesses of flexible and organic rather than mechanistic organisations. Of course, aspects of the three forms here discussed—functional, divisional and matrix—can be combined in most organisations.

Staff and line

Personnel in organisations are often divided into staff and line personnel. Line personnel perform "substantive" functions, such as manufacturing, clerical work, teaching, engineering, sales, and so on, depending upon the nature of the organisation. Staff personnel act in a support capacity to line personnel, so that staff personnel might be in specialised departments or units, such as legal, planning, auditing, personnel/industrial relations/human resources development/organisational development/training, finance, budgeting, accounting, purchasing, data processing, and occupational safety and health.

Line managers give orders, while staff managers (in theory) only advise. Generally, the bigger an organisation is, the more staff personnel are retained. In a small organisation, workers and supervisors can perform most staff functions, but as the organisation grows, this is no longer feasible. Sometimes the growth of staff in relation to line (or even at the expense of line) is seen as a bad thing, as an index of bureaucracy (in its pejorative sense). Thus, Parkinson facetiously noted that the British Departments of the Admiralty and the Colonial Office underwent annual 5–6 per cent staff increases in the postwar period, a period when British colonies were disappearing and there were no major wars to fight (and there were fewer ships, too; Parkinson

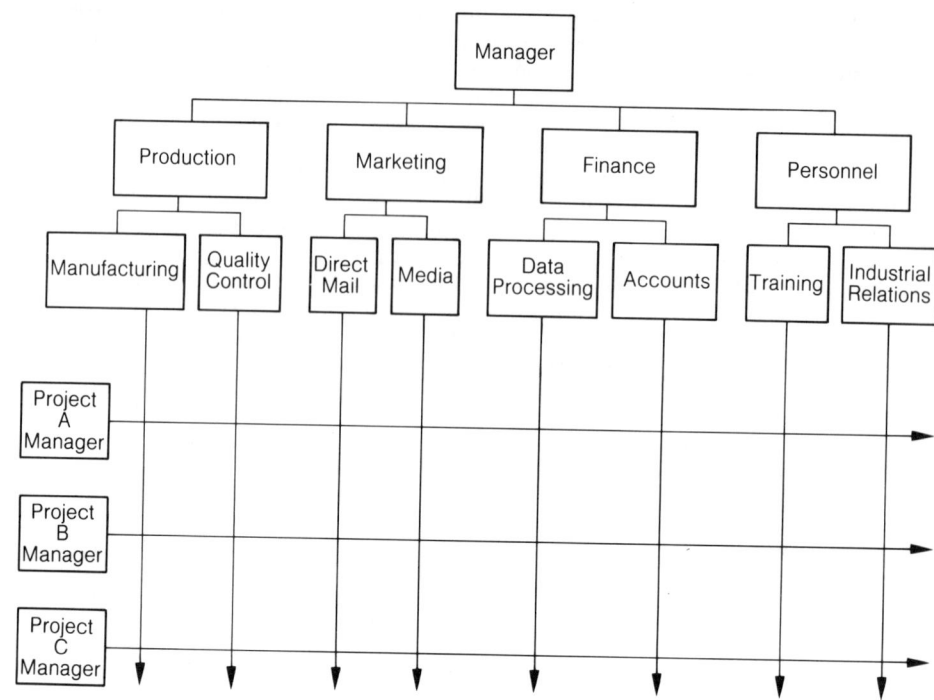

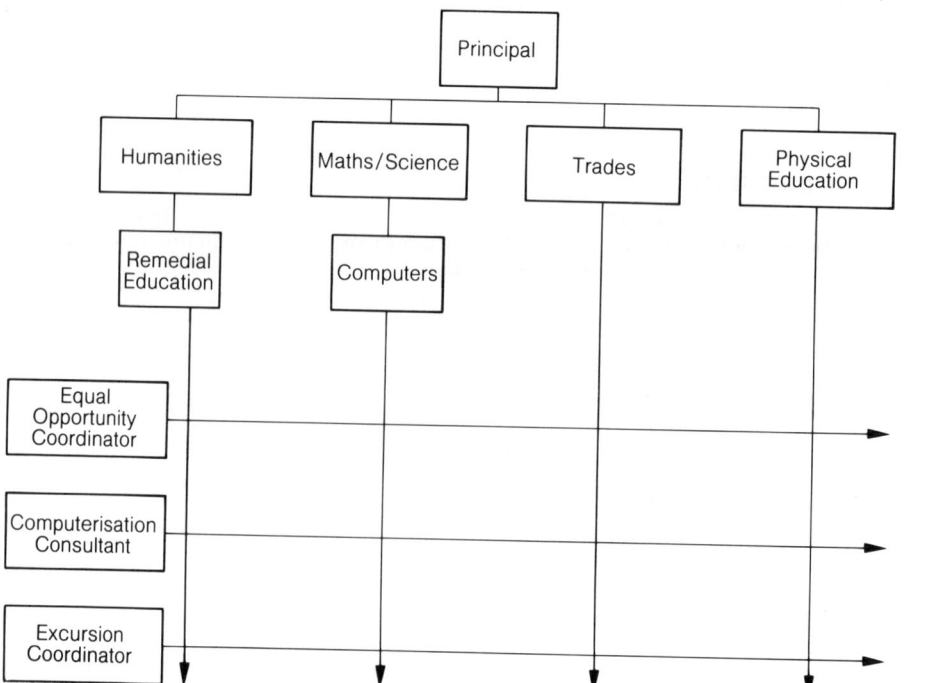

Fig. 13.3 *Departmentation by matrix in a manufacturing organisation and a school*

1957). Reich notes that the ratio of staff to line in United States manufacturing companies rose from 35 per hundred to 41 per hundred in the period 1965–1975. He unfavourably compares this trend with Japanese industry, where staff:line ratios are much lower (Reich 1983). The implication is, of course, that staff personnel are not productive, or at least are less productive than line personnel.

Conflict and interchange

Conflict can often arise between staff and line personnel. Generally speaking, staff personnel are often younger and have a better formal education than line personnel. Staff are also likely to perceive problems within a longer time frame, and in a more abstract way (Table 13.4). These differing perceptions, together with the implication that line personnel are the "real" workers, can lead to a fair amount of conflict between staff and line. Staff personnel generally need to be skilled communicators, making up for such authority they might lack with credible and creative ideas.

Of course, sometimes the distinction between staff and line is not as clear as first impressions might suggest. Some people in organisations are not clear on whether they are staff *or* line, while some managers are line qua their own departments and staff qua other departments (Luthans 1981). Also, there is no guarantee that staff departments will stay that way forever. Staff functions evolve from line inadequacies, but such functions may return to the line eventually. Thus, responsibility for appraisal of subordinates may devolve from the personnel department to the subordinate's actual supervisors. A staff unit may be created for a specific purpose and given the "protection" of a chief executive (e.g. an equal opportunity unit, a management-by-objectives implementation team), but later dispersed to line personnel when the new concepts become widely accepted and routine. This devolution can sometimes be caused by technology: thus, separate data processing units, which evolved only in the past few decades, are now threatened in some organisations by the proliferation of small, powerful personal computers among workers and managers who are newly computer-literate. A shift from functional departmentation to divisional departmentation may also cause a

Table 13.4 Staff–line conflict

Line managers	Staff specialists
Are interested in what is going to happen in the short run.	Are interested in what is going to happen in the long run.
Want simple, easy-to-use solutions.	Like to provide sophisticated difficult-to-implement solutions.
Are action-oriented; they want to solve the problem *now*.	Are thought-oriented, they want to examine the problem in depth and solve it *later*.
Do not always know the right questions to ask in obtaining help.	Have a lot of answers, so they spend their time looking for questions.
Like to solve problems on the basis of experience, intuition and "gut feeling"; quantitative, theoretical, or complex recommendations make them nervous.	Like to solve problems using the latest and most sophisticated techniques, regard solutions made "off the top of the head" as inferior.

Source: Hodgetts, Richard M. (1980), p.170. Copyright © 1980 by The Dryden Press. Reprinted with permission of The Dryden Press, CBS College Publishing.

splitting up or devolution of staff functions—the duplication of legal, personnel and other staff functions will, for most organisations, be prohibitively expensive.

Centralisation and decentralisation

Centralisation of organisational operations has been a critical part in the growth of modern industry and commerce. Apart from the fact that economies of scale can be reaped if operations are centralised, there is also the fact that greater control over operations can be achieved from a narrow apex at the top of a hierarchy. While classic organisational writers such as Fayol saw a need for a balance of centralised and decentralised operations, Toffler (1980) points out that for most of the industrial era, centralisation rather than decentralisation was the dominant trend. Toffler claims to see significant shifts away from this trend, and not only within the organisational sphere. He notes a resurgence of localised politics in various nation-states of the world, with regions, states and neighbourhoods arguing for localisation of decision-making and devolution of power from centralised governments. He sees this as being part of one of the fiercest controversies of our time: what is the most efficient scale for human institutions to operate on? Organisations and nation-states have, in modern times, believed that diseconomies of scale were virtually non-existent, that "big is better" in all things. The title of E.F. Schumacher's book, *Small is Beautiful* (1973), encapsulated the opposing view, the view that diseconomies of scale usually outweighed economies of scale in a wide variety of fields.

The battle between the proponents of "big is better" and "small is beautiful" goes on, although, as Toffler notes, big is good for some things, small is good for others, and the critical question is that of identifying the *appropriate scale* for various enterprises. Schumacher himself once remarked that if he had lived in a world of small organisations, he would have written a book entitled *Big is Beautiful* (Toffler 1980; see Box 13.A).

Decentralisation: Far out is in?

Certainly, decentralisation has become a fashionable issue in modern organisations. Many managers are deciding that many of their problems are due to the scale of operations being too big, and hence too unmanageable. The panacea is, or seems to be, to decentralise: to break up large structures, to establish decentralised profit centres to restore accountability and motivation and esprit de corps, to franchise out, to delegate decision-making to the lowest possible level of the hierarchy, to move top managers out of the remote glass boxes in the cities and into the grass roots, to the neighbourhood offices where the real people live. Much of this debate overlaps discussion of other classic organisational principles—departmentation by function versus division, staff versus line, narrow spans of control versus wide spans of control (and hence "tall" or "flat" organisations). Is decentralisation a solution to many of the problems of modern organisations, or is it just much ado about nothing? The answer is a not very helpful "yes and no; it all depends"—depends, that is, on the scale appropriate to the problem. Identifying that appropriate scale is easier said than done, and depends upon clearly perceiving the advantages and disadvantages of both centralisation and decentralisation.

Centralisation: Pro

If we examine the "pro" arguments for centralisation (see Table 13.5), we note the obvious points. Centralisation maximises economies of scale, and it produces uniformity in matters of policy and standards (such uniformity becoming more important as the scale of operations grows). As was noted in the divisional-versus-functional form of departmentation debate, centralised control better exploits scarce staff resources, such as financial and legal operations (which would otherwise have to be inefficiently duplicated at non-central points). Delegation, while attractive in theory, may lead to decision-making being undertaken by subordinates who lack information and/or skill.

Centralisation: Con

Nevertheless, diseconomies of scale might set in. Mighty political or military empires have declined even as they expanded because of the insoluble communication and control problems that sprang up. C. Northcote Parkinson has (of course) a law to describe this phenomenon: "Expansion means complexity, and complexity, decay." Success, expressed as growth for growth's sake, can be too expensive if this happens. Top management may simply be stretched too thin. Sometimes a job can become too big for one person, even for a person of exceptional ability. Political scientists are beginning to think that presidential and prime ministerial and ministerial job designs are simply too stressful for single individuals, primarily because the world is an increasingly turbulent place with an increasing degree of information overload. This overload at the top may be mirrored in underload at the bottom: workers in the lower reaches of the hierarchies of organisations may feel that they are powerless, that they are just cogs in a machine that is too big to understand. Perhaps some sharing of tasks between the upper and lower echelons, that is, delegation of authority and decision-making, would be the ideal solution. If so, then some measure of decentralisation would help.

The centralised rulers may also be insensitive to local conditions. The bank manager in Melbourne may not understand the problems of farmers in Wodonga. The manager of a transnational corporation (TNC) in New York may not understand the local industrial and political climate in Melbourne: liberal critics such as Toffler would say that this misperception is typical of the lack of awareness of "multiple bottom lines" for modern organisations, while radical critics such as Crough and Wheelwright (1982) see TNC managers as latter-day barbarians smashing the economic, social, political and cultural fabric of host countries (or "client states") in the name of corporate profit. The consequences of this insensitivity could be quite serious for the organisation, the outlying or host area, or both.

A final weakness of centralisation deals with improbable but dangerous events. Such events might be a computer memory spill, fire, sabotage, and so on. If all the organisation's eggs are in one basket, then such events can wipe it out. Some type of duplication or "protective redundancy", such as occurs automatically in decentralised systems, can help here. Such vulnerability is sometimes referred to sardonically as "the one bomb effect".

Decentralisation: Pro

Decentralisation of operations can have a series of beneficial effects, overcoming the weaknesses of over-centralisation. Lines of communication

Table 13.5 Pros and cons of centralisation and decentralisation

	Centralisation	Decentralisation
PRO	• Produces uniformity of policy, action and standards • Enables closer control and coordination • Maximises economies of scale; eliminates duplication • Some functions, e.g. financial, legal, labour/management negotiations on wages/conditions, etc., better handled from central point • Lessens risks of errors by subordinates who lack either information or skill • Best when "big picture" is needed	• Shortens lines of intra-unit communication • Increases participation in decision-making, delegation • Increases morale—no feeling of "we're just cogs in the machine" • Increases opportunities for on-the-job training for subordinates • Allows top management to concentrate on policy issues • Allows flexible, quick response to local conditions • Suited to fast change, dynamic growth • Accountability clear • May promote healthy competition among units • eggs in many baskets—creative redundancy built in
CON	• May over-stress top management • Central elite may be insensitive to local conditions e.g. TNCs • Diseconomies of scale may set in, e.g. communication breakdown, loss of control • May increase alienation, sense of "we're just cogs in machine" among non-elite • "One bomb effect"—all eggs in one basket, system vulnerable to improbable but dangerous events	• Lengthens lines of inter-unit communication • May cause problems of coordination and quick response • May result in lack of uniformity of policies, actions, standards • Jurisdictional and priority conflicts may arise • Economies of scale may be lost, e.g. access to computer, lab • Innovation and growth may be limited to existing projects or functional areas • Competition between decentralised areas may be harmful • Not good when decentralised workers are not self-motivated, self-directing, self-controlling

Source: Adapted from Hodgetts (1980), Luthans (1981), O'Shaughnessey (1979), Toffler (1980), Robbins (1979), Peters and Waterman (1983), Ginzberg and Vojta (1985).

within operating units become shortened, so fewer misunderstandings arise and decisions can be made more rapidly. Decentralisation often means an increase in delegation of authority, with a rise in participation in decision-making. Consequently, it would appear, morale and motivation will improve as "the troops" feel that they can contribute skills and perceptions. This is due to the fact that the scale of operations can be seen and understood. This same factor means that accountability is much easier to see—knaves and fools can hide in an enormous bureaucratic hive but it is much harder to hide in more transparent local cells. At local level, in fact, people may well be proud of their efforts and want to be seen as responsible for their output.

Delegation can mean that lower-echelon people get experience in making decisions, while upper-echelon people can clear their desks and do what they should be doing—planning, brainstorming, lateral thinking. Locally based operations can respond more sympathetically and rapidly to local cultures and conditions.

New technology can dramatically increase decentralisation (or centralisation, depending upon your point of view). Telematic/telecommunication systems mean that people can work from home or work stations/halfway houses in suburbs, using computers that interface with the main organisation via telephone lines (Eunson 1986). This "electronic cottage" concept was discussed in Chapter 12.

Decentralisation: Con

Yet some of the strengths of decentralisation are also weaknesses. For example, to the extent that *intra*-unit communication lines shorten, to the same extent might *inter*-unit communication lines lengthen. Thus, people may get along famously with each other within various far-flung pockets of an empire, but not coordinate or communicate with other pockets of the empire. This may lead to a lack of uniformity on policy and standards—the beginnings of chaos. As with divisional departmentation, economies of scale might be lost, with access to specialised facilities and equipment becoming the more limited the greater the decentralisation. Also, many people do not want and/or do not adapt to having decision-making delegated to them. They may feel out of their depth, and long to be "where the action is", that is, back at the central command structure.

Span of control

One of the most deceptively simple tenets of organisational design is span of control. This refers to the number of subordinates each supervisor controls. As most supervisors or bosses are in turn subordinates at a different level of the hierarchy, span of control is one of the crucial building blocks of any organisation. An organisation with a narrow span of control is going to be a "tall" organisation, that is, it will be a relatively narrow triangle, while an organisation with a wide span of control will be a "flat" organisation, that is, it will be a relatively broad triangle (Fig. 13.4). Organisation A, we see, operates a span of control of three: the supreme boss has three subordinates, they in turn have three subordinates each, and so on. Organisation B operates on a span of control of nine. Obviously, organisation A has more layers of supervisors than organisation B: in fact, given that both organisations have a lowest echelon of 729 subordinates, simple arithmetic will show that organisation A has 364 more supervisors than organisation B. If each supervisor makes, say, $18 000 to $30 000 per year, there will obviously be a dramatic difference between the two organisations in terms of salary bill alone.

Which is the better organisational structure, then? Is salary bill the sole criterion? Traditional, mechanistic bureaucracies tended to be (and perhaps still are) tall organisations. They tended to be run on the theory X assumption that people needed close supervision, and the best way to do this was with a narrow span of control. Some of the more "human relations" oriented organisational theorists have argued that the tall organisation is in fact the classic, dehumanising bureaucracy—a giant, impersonal honeycomb of blocked and distorted communication channels, a pyramidal monolith consecrated to the secular religion of officious inefficiency. Flat organisations, by contrast (the human relations argument runs) are less mechanistic, more organic: communication doesn't get clogged, people are trusted to work more on their own, more flexible responses can be given to changing environments. Some human relations oriented writers have tended to believe that, just as adhocracies will succeed bureaucracies and organic organisations will succeed mechanistic ones, so too will flat organisations succeed tall organisations—it's just a matter of natural evolution. To a considerable extent, these concepts overlap each other, of course. But are these "evolutionary" trends really inevitable? We have seen earlier (p.414) that other organisational analysts believe that evolution is on the side of theory X rather than theory Y. The truth is a bit more complicated than either school of biological determinism is willing to allow.

Organisational level	Organisation A: Span of control = 3	Number of personnel at each level	Organisation B: Span of control = 9	Number of personnel at each level
1		1		1
2		3		9
3		9		81
4		27		729
5		81		
6		243		
7		729		

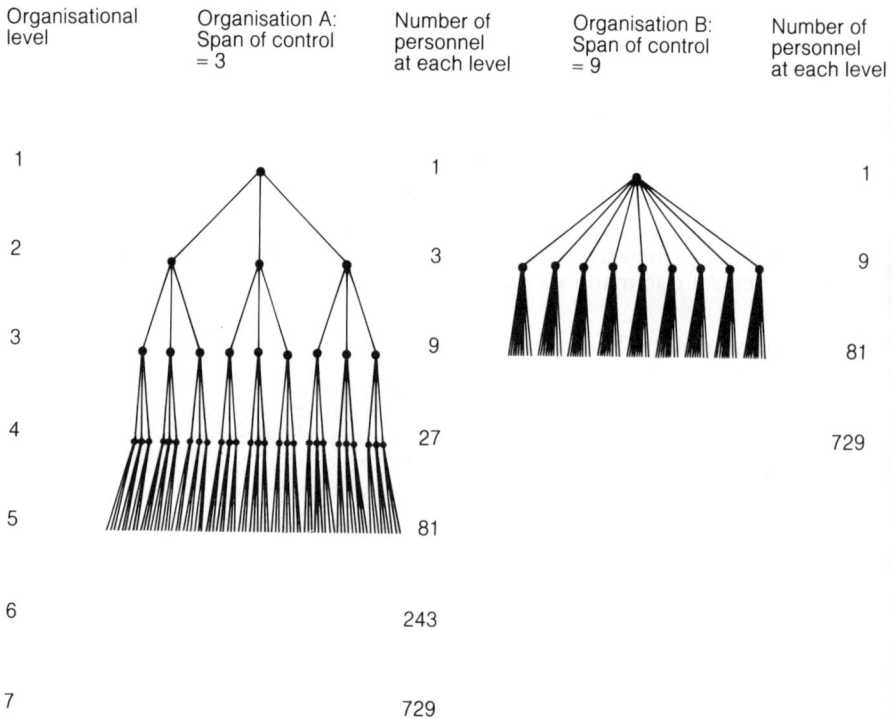

Fig. 13.4 *Tall and flat organisations*

BOX 13.A: Small is beautiful? Small-within-big is beautiful?

Scale of operations and centralisation of operations are crucial to understanding organisational design of medium-to-large organisations. But the advantages and disadvantages of scale and centralisation are crucial to understanding the biggest business in Australia (and many other countries), that is, small business. Concepts of scale and centralisation are also crucial to understanding compromises or hybrids of small and big organisations, such as franchising, the contractual organisation, and intrapreneuring.

Small business

Small businesses (those defined as having less than 10 employees) comprise 93 per cent of Australian private enterprises in primary, secondary and tertiary industries (English 1983). Drucker (1974) suggests that even though predictions have been made for the last century that small business will be swallowed up by bigger business, such predictions have proved inaccurate. Drucker has set a simple set of tests for determining whether a business is small, fair-sized, or big. These are:
1. in a genuinely small business, the person at the top knows who the few people are in the organisation in whom responsibility for key results rests without having to consult the records or any of his/her associates. The key group cannot exceed 12–15, which is about the largest number one person can really know and be familiar with.
2. in a fair-sized business ("the next and in some ways the most important category of business") the one person at the top can no longer identify and really know every one of the truly important people in the organisation. A group of 3 or 4 is essential for this, and the key group might run to 40 or 50.
3. a big business is one in which even a small group at the top no longer knows, without consultation with others or without consulting charts or records, who the crucial people are. (DRUCKER 1974, PP.647–8)

Thus Drucker's definition of small business differs from English's, and it is often a matter of opinion just what *is* the scale of a particular operation. Which is better, small business, fair-sized or big business? Drucker suggests that they are not alternatives, but complements, e.g. big automobile companies, such as General Motors, Volkswagen and Toyota, and big retailers, such as Sears and Roebuck and Marks and Spencer, all depend upon networks of smaller manufacturers, who in turn depend upon the big organisations for access to markets (Drucker 1974, pp.648–9).

Meredith (1977) suggests that small businesses have the following characteristics:
1. technological requirements are easily met
2. managerial experience requirements are low
3. funding or capital requirements are relatively low
4. the market for goods produced or resold is local
5. management by its owners or part-owners is in a personalised way and not through the medium of a formalised management structure
6. having separable manufacturing operations
7. associated with craft or precision handiwork

Table 13.6 Pros and cons of small business

Pro	Con
• adaptable, flexible	• role overload on manager, who must be jack-of-all-trades
• presents opportunities for innovation	• high stress—long hours, no overtime, sick leave
• high motivation for owners, because of feelings of freedom, independence, control, self-worth	• capital, cash-flow problems
• rewards for owner's skill and efforts	• operator usually has to rely on professionals outside the business
• close owner–employee relationships	• isolation from information on market trends
• a sense of belonging for employees	• difficult to tap into supplies at short notice
• high motivation for all may lead to efficiencies greater than those of big business	• labour-intensive—difficulty taking advantage of technological improvements
• cooperative groups of small businesses may be able to reap economies of scale, e.g. bulk-buying, group advertising, etc.	• may not have diverse product range —thus vulnerable to market fluctuations
• employees, e.g. family, may be able to accept varying payment according to circumstances	• products more susceptible to obsolescence, technological change, consumer preference shift, seasonal, cyclical (boom/bust) variations
	• very little forward planning—day-to-day survival absorbs manager's energies
	• personal factors may be put above business considerations, e.g. hiring family, lending/borrowing money for household budgets
	• employees, e.g. family, may be exploited, unprotected by existing labour agreements

Source: Adapted from Meredith (1977), English (1983), Drucker (1974), Woods (1981).

8. producing specialist services and products, independent of economies of scale.

The pros and cons of small business are set out in Table 13.6. Drucker feels that the greatest con or disadvantage of small business is that it is not "opportunistic" but "problematical", that is, it lives from problem to problem, devoid of any long-term strategy. "But the typical small business is, also, as a result, not a successful business": the failure rate of small businesses is often very high.

Spillane (1985) suggests that entrepreneurs and managers are different types of people. Entrepreneurs often lack diplomacy, they dislike red tape, they have a lot of energy and are a source of dramatic change. Managers, by contrast, tend to more introverted, more diplomatic, more conforming and sensitive to status. Entrepreneurs are more to be found in small, rather than big organisations, and appear deviant within big organisations (but see Intrapreneuring section, below).

Franchising

Franchising means that small operators can be part of a bigger operation, and thus successfully compete with bigger competitors.

Franchising accounts for about 20 per cent of retail sales in Australia today, and the figure seems to be rising to the US figure of 33 per cent. Franchising can be in fast foods, petrol, groceries/convenience stores, but also in hairdressing, hotels and an enormous variety of other lines. Franchisees can benefit from the experience of the franchiser: franchisers often run training courses and provide ongoing information on management of resources. Franchisees benefit also from the bulk-buying power of the larger organisation, the large marketing campaigns undertaken, and on-line stock control means that franchisees do not have to stock wide ranges of products in order to be able to offer such range to customers.

There are disadvantages, of course: the central franchiser may take a large (in some cases an unconscionably large) percentage of the profits, and may demand that the franchisee do a large amount of paperwork. The franchiser may be unhappy about the franchisee trying to vary procedures or alter marketing to suit local conditions (Woods 1981).

The contractual organisation
Handy (1984) sees that many people in large organisations will undergo a role shift in the next few decades, choosing (or perhaps being forced) to become subcontractors (i.e. small business people) working symbiotically with big organisations, rather than being merely employees. New automated processes increasingly mean that production units are less tightly coupled to production lines, and thus production units are in effect mini-businesses. If more employees choose to work from home via computers—the "electronic cottage" scenario in Chapter 12—they may choose to take on their own overheads of power, insurance, superannuation, etc., in exchange for the profits of a small business. As organisations begin to "outsource" labour and processing of goods and services, organisational structures will change to a shrinking core of administrators, surrounded by a ring of mini-businesses, contractors, consultants and jobbers.

Big will remain beautiful in the core organisation, where economies of scale can still be reaped (in purchasing, marketing, accounting, etc.). Handy's contractual or federal organisation has much in common with Bennis and Toffler's adhocracy, but the adhocracy has been criticised for being a middle-class white-collar creature, which leaves many out in the cold: the contractual organisation or adhocracy is fine if you are a professional with saleable skills, and thus have high mobility to move from one core organisation to another. If one has fewer skills, or has no skills at all, then the situation might be grimmer—there might be wandering bands of gypsy temps, nomadically tracking scarce part-time work (and putting part-time food into full-time stomachs; Eunson 1985).

"Intrapreneuring"
The mythology of how big organisations crush creativity, and how it is necessary for entrepreneurial people to leave in order to implement their ideas, has much truth in it. Pinchot (1985) points out that organisations usually demand conformity rather than creativity from employees, yet often the essential temperament of the entrepreneur is that of the deviant, the maverick, the non-conformist (cf. Spillane's findings, above). Many people who leave big organisations, Pinchot suggests, do this not

necessarily because they can get more money outside, but because they feel frustrated inside.

Once outside the big organisation, safely ensconced in his or her own small organisation, the entrepreneur often presents tough competition to the former employer. Thus, the founders of Apple computers, Steve Jobs and Steve Wozniac, left their former employers (Atari computers and Digitial computers, respectively) to set up Apple, which then created hot competition for the former employers.

Pinchot and others have suggested that this process does not have to occur if only the entrepreneur is allowed to flourish *inside* the large bureaucracies, that is, become *intrapreneurs*. Intrapreneurs usually operate between the fields of technical innovation and marketing implementation. They are given a lot of autonomy to take risks and fail, and be fired if necessary, but if they succeed, they reap the benefits, and even apply "intracapital" to further bright ideas.

This type of rethinking of organisational structure is currently taking place at the giant US General Electric company, whose chairman announced in 1982 that he was ". . . trying to reshape GE . . . as a band of small businesses . . . to take the strength of a large company and act with the agility of a small company" (quoted in Pinchot 1985).

Tall structure/narrow span of control: Pro

Thus for example, the "nasty theory X" notion of close supervision may in fact have a light side (see Table 13.6). One man's intrusive control can be another man's supportive consideration—both of these supervisory styles flowing from a narrow span of control. Narrow span is of particular use, for example, when people are being trained in a job, or where they are inexperienced, or where mistakes will be costly. Hodgetts (1980) observes that narrow span is of particular use if the organisation exploits high levels or low levels of technology. High technology work may mean that people work in small highly skilled groups, with a supervisor ensuring that expensive mistakes don't occur. Low technology work may be conducive to high staff turnover rates (inexperienced staff) and lower quality output due to boredom and low job satisfaction. Narrow span is useful when the organisation's environment is placid, that is, there is little product innovation and markets are predictable. In such situations, task roles can be clearly delineated and specialisation of those roles is an efficient managerial strategy. In a turbulent environment, by contrast, product innovation is high, and markets are unpredictable. Consequently, it would seem that organisations with a wide span of control would be consistently preferable in such situations. Yet, narrow span of control is preferable where jobs are non-routine—precisely what one would expect in a turbulent, not a placid environment.

Tall structure/narrow span of control: Con

Viewed from another angle, a particular strength of a system can be a weakness. Thus, as we have seen, supervision in a tall organisation can be intrusive or supportive, depending upon the values and personalities of the particular organisation's superiors and subordinates. Similarly, while tall organisations can have clearly identified communication channels, with formal procedures for that communication, communication can also become more distorted according to the number of levels it has to proceed through. In looking at the informal organisation, it will be noted that informal networks of communication (the grapevine) can spread rumour and distort truth dramatically, and the distortion is usually greater according to how many mouths the rumour has been through. Yet, the same distortion occurs through formal channels. Similarly, even though decision-making channels are clearly marked in tall organisations, distortions similar to communication patterning occur with decision-making. Thus, as O'Shaughnessey (1979) remarks, every level of decision-making can mean a veto on decisions; the more levels, the more potential vetos. Narrow span can also encourage centralisation: this, as we have seen earlier, can be an advantage or a disadvantage.

Finally, prospects for promotion can be limited within a tall organisation. For example, if we presume it takes five to seven years to be promoted from one level to another in organisation A in Figure 13.4, how long will it take an individual to be promoted from the bottom of the organisation to the top? Probably at least one individual in 729 will be patient enough to wait around that long, but not many more (and patience is perhaps not the first quality of a top manager).

Flat structure/wide span of control: Pro and con

Flat organisations exhibit paradoxical behaviour similar to that of tall organisations. Thus, flat organisations lead to decentralisation, which as we have seen can be good or bad. Flat organisations can encourage workers to exercise more self-control, to operate with less supervision, but these working conditions are not ideal for all. Taking pressure off vertical communication and depending more upon horizontal communication seems initially to be a good thing, and often is: distortion can be eliminated from vertical channels, and peers within the one level can learn to depend more upon one another and work in teams. Yet horizontal communication, precisely because it is less structured than vertical communication, can place great demands upon the interpersonal skills of the group, and these pressures are greater the larger the group, that is, the wider the span of control.

Further, it is often said that flat organisations are more informal in communication and decision-making patterns than tall organisations. This is often true: if there are only three layers of red tape to get through rather than ten, then people might not become so discouraged when offering new ideas. But does the apparent lack of hierarchy always make for flexible and informal relationships between supervisors and subordinates, for a more democratic atmosphere? Not necessarily. A supervisor who says "my door is always open" may function well when the span of control is three or eight, but might buckle if the span is thirty or fifty. In such circumstances, it might be necessary for the supervisor to resort to such controls as appointments and paperwork to ration access to herself. If unable to cope, then a "flat" supervisor might be more of a bottleneck than a "tall" boss (as the old saying goes, the bottleneck is at the top of the bottle). At least if the span of control was narrower, the supervisor could delegate more.

Wide span of control seems to work well where subordinates are more experienced (and hence can be left alone to do the job). For similar reasons, it is useful when the work is routine and/or a medium level of technology is being deployed. It is also good in turbulent environments, where task roles

Table 13.7 Pros and cons of tall organisations (narrow span of control) and flat organisations (wide span of control)

	Pro	Con
Tall organisations (narrow span of control)	• Close supervision can be supportive—more intimate communication • Encourages centralisation • Establishes clear lines of communications, especially vertical communication • Decision-making channels clearly understood • Useful where work is non-routine • Useful where subordinates are inexperienced, or in training • Useful where mistakes will be costly • Easier in organisations with high levels or low levels of technology • Good in placid environments: clear task roles, specialisation works well	• Close supervision can be intrusive—claustrophobic communication, supervision can dampen initative, autonomy • Encourages centralisation • Vertical communication can be distorted • Decision-making can be clogged—every level a veto • Promotion can be slow
Flat organisations (wide span of control)	• Encourages decentralisation • Encourages self-control, autonomy • Simplifies vertical communication, allows greater horizontal communication • Useful where work is routine • Useful where subordinates are experienced, can be minimally supervised • Useful in organisations with medium level of technology • Good in turbulent environments: unclear task roles, specialisation does not work well	• Encourages decentralisation • Difficult where people want/need control from above • Horizontal communication is often more inefficient than vertical communication • Greater demands placed upon supervisors as more people report to one boss—possibility of greater bottlenecks • Reduced promotion opportunities (less levels)

Source: Adapted from O'Shaughnessey (1979), Robbins (1979), Luthans (1981), Miner (1982), Hodgetts (1980).

are unclear, and role specialisation would be ill-advised in trying to meet rapidly changing market and production needs (but remember the reservations expressed immediately above on this point).

Finally, flat organisations may be just as difficult to get promotions in as tall organisations. Whereas with tall organisations, the promotion problem is basically one of a few rivals at your level but many levels to get through, with flat organisations, the problem is one of many rivals at your level and fewer levels to get through (meaning possibly less turnover in upper positions, possibly greater penalties for making mistakes on the way up).

Flat is beautiful?

Thus, the classical model of narrow span of control is seen to have significant flaws, as well as strengths. The alleged panacea of more modern, humanistic analysts—wide span of control, or the flat organisation—is also seen to have significant flaws, as well as strengths. Perhaps the critical weakness of the "flat is beautiful" hypothesis is that it concentrates on shortening the vertical dimension of organisations, but neglects the fact that you cannot make only one change—the horizontal dimension is pushed out in direct proportion.

BOX 13.B: Collapsing organisational pyramids to crush middle managers?

The second major research study commissioned by the Australian Institute of Management has now been published, and should provoke considerable interest and controversy. The study, entitled "New Directions in Middle Management—a Dilemma?" is by Dr John Miller and Robert Longair, of Pannell Kerr Forster. It shows that many of the 600 000 Australians who fall into the category of "middle managers" are standing at the crossroads in terms of their future careers. Dr Miller stated at the launch that as many as 50 per cent of Australia's present middle managers were at risk because of job redefinition, elimination of positions or the unsuitability of the existing job holders.

The study is based on research carried out with the cooperation of organisations of all sizes, and including companies engaged in manufacturing, retailing, finance and transport. Among the principal conclusions are:

- There is a marked tendency towards "flattening" of corporate organisational structures. Many of the traditional executive layers are being stripped away, and the middle manager of today and tomorrow will have to develop broader skills, show a greater awareness of the demands of the "bottom line", make decisions previously passed on to another layer of management, and in general display more of the characteristics of the entrepreneur. This will demand a radical change in actions and attitudes: in the past middle managers have spent up to 80 per cent of their time deferring decisions to others.
- The trend can be attributed to several major factors: the growth of computer technology, competitive pressures, cost control and the continuing spate of mergers and take-overs. Computer technology now allows top management to have direct access to information previously filtered through various reporting layers of the classic pyramid staff structure.

- Middle management will have to accept that both job redesign and redundancy are continuing threats. The flexible and adaptable will survive, and in particular those capable of making the quick decisions demanded not only by leaner companies themselves, but by their customers. A new breed of "mini general manager" will emerge, skilled particularly in marketing, people management, and the interpretation of financial and accounting data.
- Because of flatter corporate structures, there will be fewer direct opportunities for promotion, and middle management will have to be prepared for a succession of lateral moves within their companies to broaden their experience. There will also be greater mobility between companies, and loyalty to employers is likely to be a less important factor than it has been in the past.
- It will be necessary to re-examine the educational processes previously found appropriate for the training of middle management. The researchers point out that one of the greatest problems facing management development is whether and how companies and educational institutions teach innovation, decision making and leadership.

Implications for top management

Various implications for top management are underlined by the study:

- Careful control of a redundancy program is necessary from the point of view of humane management. Equally, it is necessary in order to avoid the possible loss of key executives who might otherwise leave under an ill-defined redundancy threat.
- Flatter management structures will inevitably bring top management closer to the shop floor and the customer, making it possible for corrective intervention to take place more quickly.
- Significant changes affecting middle management are taking place, and top decision makers have an obligation to manage the change.

Source: AIM News, November 1985. Reproduced with permission.

Other classic organisational principles

There are other classic principles of design of organisations that are possibly as important as the ones discussed above, although these latter principles do not need to be discussed in as much depth. These principles are unity of command, chain of command and equal power and responsibility.

Unity of command

Unity of command means that an employee should only be responsible to one supervisor, thus minimising any conflicting commands in a "too many chiefs, not enough Indians" situation. Obviously, this lack of ambiguity of command has much to recommend it. Yet we have seen that modern organisational designs, such as the matrix forms, violate this principle of having, if not too many chiefs, at least more than one chief for each Indian. It is interesting to note that Taylor was advocating a similar system at the turn of the century: he felt that "functional foremen" could be specialised supervisors working with the one individual subordinate in different phases of the subordinate's tasks. Unity of command is also sometimes violated by the staff/line system, particularly where staff and line managers tend to have competitive, rather than cooperative relationships. Properly handled, multiplicity of command can be a useful organisational strategy, ensuring flexibility and maximum exploitation of diverse people's talents. Badly handled, multiplicity of command can lead to chaotic planning and over-political behaviour on the part of superiors and subordinates—just as the logic of the classic principle would suggest.

Chain of command

Chain of command is closely related to unity of command, span of control, specialisation and division of labour, and departmentation. Chain of command basically means that roles in any hierarchy should be clearly spelt out, with each person having a clear power relationship with those above and below in the hierarchy. This principle can be undercut by multiplicity of command, lack of specificity of job roles (which depending on the circumstances, can be a good factor or a bad one), and any attempt to break down hierarchical structures, such as strategies of participation and/or industrial democracy (see Chapter 14).

Equal authority and responsibility

The final principle of equal authority and responsibility means that any supervisor should be given power commensurate with the responsibility of the job. People usually complain of too little power rather than too much power, so the responsibility/power equation usually boils down to an analysis of who has power, who hasn't, and why (see Chapter 10). The pristine integrity of this principle has also been eroded by multiplicity of command (matrix structures, line/staff rivalries) and the increased use of group, as opposed to individual decision-making (management by committee). As with the classic principles of organisational design already discussed, it is apparent here that "classic" is not a code-word for "outdated" or "irrelevant".

Summary

Bureaucracy is a term that can be applied to all large organisations, private as well as public. Although originally seen as a positive concept at the beginning of this century, many now think of bureaucracies as large, inflexible, uncreative and counter-productive organisations. Bureaucracies are sometimes referred to as having mechanistic design, whereas more flexible organisations, such as the adhocracy, are said to have a more organic design, and are said to be able to cope with rapidly changing social circumstances and also to better satisfy human needs of its employees. It is not at all clear, however, that mechanistic or bureaucratic organisations are always less efficient or worse places to work in than adhocratic or organic organisations.

It is useful to attempt to understand organisations in terms of classic management concepts. Economies of scale and division of labour made much economic growth possible, but critics have argued that diseconomies of scale have not been given enough consideration.

Organisations normally have activities divided up into departments, and such departments can be organised along three sets of principles—functional, divisional and matrix principles.

Centralisation and decentralisation of an organisation's activities occur according to whichever philosophy of concentration or dispersion is dominant. Centralisation/decentralisation and economies/diseconomies of scale help us to understand organisational phenomena that exploit small scale or small-within-big scale operations: small business, franchising, the contractual organisation and intrapreneuring.

Span of control, or narrowness or width of area of supervision, can determine whether organisations will be tall or flat pyramids.

Unity of command, chain of command, and equal authority and responsibility critically affect the ways in which power and decision-making are distributed vertically throughout the organisation.

Questions for discussion

1. Why did "bureaucracy" go from being a "hoorah" word to a "boo" word?
2. Analyse an organisation you are familiar with and determine how far it adheres to and how far it departs from classic organisational design principles.
3. How accurate are the criticisms made of bureaucracy?
4. Is the adhocracy inevitable?
5. What are the major differences between mechanistic and organic organisations? Is it possible for an organisation to combine aspects of both?
6. Would you prefer to work in a purely organic or a purely mechanistic organisation? Why?
7. Is bureaucracy inevitable?
8. Think of an organisation you are familiar with (a workplace, a department store, a supermarket, a school, the army, etc.) and list the economies and diseconomies of scale you detect there.
9. What form of department (functional, divisional, matrix) would you prefer to work in? Why?
10. Are staff personnel less productive than line personnel?
11. Which is more beautiful—big or small organisations?
12. "Tall organisations are theory X organisations, while flat organisations are theory Y organisations." Is this correct?
13. Will there be more or less unity of command in tomorrow's organisations?
14. What is the relationship between chain of command and equality of authority and responsibility?

References

Albanese, Robert and Van Fleet, David D. (1983). *Organizational Behaviour: A Managerial Viewpoint.* (Dryden Press: New York).

Baritz, L. (1960). *Servants of Power.* (Wesleyan University Press: Middletown, Conn.)

Bennis, Warren (1965). "Beyond Bureaucracy", *Trans-Action,* July–August.

(1966a). "Organizational Developments and the Fate of Bureaucracy", *Industrial Management Review,* 7.

(1966b). "Changing Organizations", *Journal of Applied Behavioural Science,* vol. 2, no. 3.

(1970). "A Funny Thing Happened on the Way to the Future", *American Psychologist,* 25.

(1973). *The Leaning Ivory Tower.* (Jossey-Bass: San Francisco).

(1974). "Conversation with Warren Bennis", *Organizational Dynamics,* vol. 2, no. 3.

(1975). "The Problem: Integrating the Organization and the Individual", in William G. Monahan (ed.)., *Theoretical Dimensions of Educational Administration.* (Macmillan: New York).

Broom, Leonard, Selznick, Phillip and Darroch, Dorothy Broom (1981). *Sociology: A Text with Adapted Readings*, 7th edn. (Harper and Row: New York).

Burns, Tom and Stalker, G.M. (1961). *The Management of Innovation.* (Tavistock Press: London).

Byrt, William J. (1980). *The Human Variable: Text and Cases in Organizational Behaviour.* (McGraw-Hill: Sydney).

Carey, Alex (1976). "Industrial Psychology and Sociology in Australia", in Boreham, P. *et al.* (eds), *The Professions in Australia: A Critical Appraisal.* (University of Queensland Press: St Lucia, Qld).

(1980). "Worker Motivation: Social Science, Propaganda and Democracy", in Boreham, P. and Dow, Geoff (eds), *Work and Inequality: Ideology and Control in the Capitalist Labour Process.* (Macmillan: Melbourne).

Crough, Greg and Wheelwright, Ted (1982). *Australia: A Client State.* (Penguin Books: Ringwood).

Davis, Keith (1981). *Human Behaviour at Work: Organizational Behaviour*, 6th edn. (McGraw-Hill: New York).

Dessler, Gary (1982). *Management Fundamentals: Modern Principles and Practices*, 3rd edn. (Reston Publishing Co.: Reston).

Drucker, Peter F. (1974). *Management: Tasks, Responsibilities, Practices.* (Heinemann: London).

(1981). "The Coming Rediscovery of Scientific Management", in *Towards the Next Economics and Other Essays.* (Harper and Row: New York).

Du Brin, Andrew J. (1981). *Human Relations: A Job-Oriented Approach*, 2nd edn. (Reston Publishing: Reston, Va).

Dunphy, Dexter C. and Dick, Robert (1981). *Organizational Change by Choice.* (McGraw-Hill: Sydney).

English, John W. (1983). *How to Organize and Operate a Small Business in Australia.* (George Allen and Unwin: Sydney).

Eunson, Baden (1985). "How to be Big and Stay Beautiful", *Business Review Weekly*, 6 December.

(1986). "A New Place for the Worker", *Business Review Weekly*, 14 February.

Fayol, Henri (1949). *General and Industrial Management* (trans. Constance Storrs). (Pitman: London).

Ginzberg, Eli and Vojta, George (1985). *Beyond Human Scale: The Large Corporation at Risk.* (Basic Books: New York).

Handy, John W. (1984). *The Future of Work.* (Blackwell: Oxford).

Herbst, Ph.G. (1976). *Alternatives to Hierarchies.* (Marinus Nijhoff Social Sciences Division: Leiden).

Hodgetts, Richard M. (1980). *Modern Human Relations.* (Dryden Press: Hinsdale, Ill.).

Illich, Ivan (1971). *Deschooling Society.* (Calder and Boyars: London).

(1977). *Limits to Medicine. Medical Nemesis: The Expropriation of Health.* (Penguin Books: Harmondsworth).

Jones, Barry (1983*a*). *Sleepers Wake! Technology and the Future of Work*, rev. edn. (Oxford University Press: Melbourne).

(1983*b*). "Sunrise Industries", *Human Resources Management Australia*, August.

Katz, Daniel and Kahn, Robert L. (1978). *The Social Psychology of Organizations*, 2nd edn. (John Wiley and Sons: New York).

Kelly, John E. (1982). *Scientific Management, Job Redesign and Work Performance.* (Academic Press: London/New York).

Kerzner, Harold and Cleland, David I. (1985). *Project/Matrix Management: Policy and Strategy, Cases and Situations.* (Van Nostrand Reinhold: New York).

Lee, James A. (1980). *The Gold and the Garbage in Management Theories and Prescriptions.* (Ohio University Press: Athens, Ohio).

Likert, Rensis (1967). *The Human Organization: Its Management and Value.* (McGraw-Hill: New York).

Luthans, Fred (1981). *Organizational Behaviour*, 3rd edn. (McGraw-Hill: New York).

McCann, J. and Galbraith,J.R. (1981). "Interdepartmental Relations", in Nystrom, P.C. and Starbuck, W.H. (eds), *Handbook of Organizational Design, Vol. 2, Remodelling Organizations and their Environments.* (Oxford University Press: New York).

McGregor, Douglas (1960). *The Human Side of Enterprise.* (McGraw-Hill: New York).

Machovec, Frank M. and Smith, Howard R. (1982). "Fear Makes the World Go 'Round: The 'Dark' Side of Management", *Management Review*, January.

Meredith, G.G. (1977). *Small Business Management in Australia.* (McGraw-Hill: Sydney).

Miner, John B. (1982). *Theories of Organizational Structure and Process.* (Dryden Press: New York).

O'Shaughnessey, John (1979). *Patterns of Business Organization.* (George Allen and Unwin: London).

Parkinson, C. Northcote (1957). *Parkinson's Law.* (Houghton Mifflin: Boston).

Peter, Lawrence J. and Hull, Raymond (1969). *The Peter Principle.* (Pan: London).

Peters, Thomas J. and Waterman, Robert H., Jr. (1983). *In Search of Excellence: Lessons from America's Best-Run Companies.* (Harper and Row: Sydney).

Pinchot, Gifford III (1985). *Intrapreneuring.* (Harper and Row: New York).

Reich, Robert B. (1983). *The Next American Frontier.* (Times Books: New York).

Robbins, Stephen P. (1979). *Organizational Behaviour: Concepts and Controversies.* (Prentice-Hall: New Jersey).

Schermerhorn, John R. (1986). *Managing for Productivity*, 2nd edn. (John Wiley and Sons: New York).

Schumacher, E.F. (1973). *Small is Beautiful: A Study of Economics as if People Mattered.* (Harper and Row: New York).

Spillane, R. (1985). "Personality and Occupation: Implications for Human Resources Management", *Human Resource Management Australia*, February.

Szilyagi, Andrew D. and Wallace, Marc J., Jr. (1983). *Organizational Behaviour and Perfomrance*, 3rd edn. (Goodyear: Santa Monica, Calif.).

Taylor, Frederick (1947). *The Principles of Scientific Management.* (Harper: New York).

Toffler, Alvin (1970). *Future Shock.* (Pan: London).
    (1980). *The Third Wave.* (Pan: London).
    (1984). *Previews and Premises.* (Pan: London).
    (1985). *The Adaptive Organization.* (Pan: London).

Vidmer, Richard (1979). "The Emergence of Administrative Science in the USSR: Towards a Theory of Organizational Emulation", *Policy Sciences*, 11.

Vroom, Victor (1979). "A Theory of Leadership", in Kolb, David *et al.* (eds), *Organizational Psychology: A Book of Readings.* (Prentice-Hall: New Jersey).

Weber, Max (1947). *Theory of Social and Economic Organization.* (Free Press: New York).

Woods, Mike (1981). *Starting and Operating a Small Business.* (Angus and Robertson: Sydney).

Films/videos

Clockwork (Educational Media Australia).

Modern Times Revisited—Alternatives to Assembly Lines (Brittanica Video).

How to Manage: The Process Approach and Henri Fayol (Power Human Resources).

14

Organisational design 2

Our managerial elites are staggering under an impossible decision load. That will force the elites to allow more people to participate—to help carry the decision load. That's why we hear more and more about participatory management—more and more about involving the workers. Not because of altruism, but because the old decision system doesn't work.

Alvin Toffler

Under any social order from now to Utopia, management is indispensable and all-enduring. The question is not "Will there be a management elite?" but "What sort of elite will it be?"

Sydney Webb

The vertical to horizontal power shift that networks bring about will be enormously liberating for individuals. Hierarchies promote moving up and getting ahead, producing stress, tension and anxiety. Networking empowers the individual, and people in networks tend to nurture one another.

John Naisbett

IN the preceding chapter, we looked at the more traditional concepts used in analysing and understanding organisations, such as bureaucracy, economies of scale, staff and line, and so on. It is apparent in that chapter, and it needs to be re-emphasised here, that merely because such concepts are "traditional" does not mean that they are obsolete—quite the contrary, in fact. Nevertheless, traditional organisational analysis contains some blind spots, and is not always useful for understanding concepts which have only recently emerged.

In this chapter, accordingly, we will consider the informal organisation, more colloquially known as the grapevine, the role of technology in determining the structure of organisations, the moves to increase worker participation and industrial democracy in organisations and, finally, the Japanese model of organisation, which so many countries outside Japan are studying and in some cases imitating.

The informal organisation

The informal organisation co-exists with the formal or "official" organisation. An organisation chart of the kind used to show factors such as span of control is obviously hierarchical. We presume that power and access to information are most concentrated at the top, and we often presume that people communicate most with those immediately above and below them in the hierarchy. This, however, is not always the case. The most powerful, or influential, or knowledgeable, person may not be the general manager but someone else—the manager's secretary, the union shop steward, the messenger boy, the tea lady. People on the same level of the hierarchy may be given access to important information, while others may be deliberately excluded from the information-rich group. It may take three weeks for information about a pay rise or cut to go through the official channels, whereas it might take three hours to go through informal networks of the organisation. Such informal networks are often known as "the grapevine" (a term derived from the United States Civil War, where communication on the battlefield took place via telegraph wires often simply strung from trees, and thus resembled grapevines; the system was not always efficient, and messages were often garbled). The grapevine, or rumour-mill, may run through a whole series of individuals and groups:

- old friends, now in different parts of the organisation, who meet for lunch
- telephonists
- cleaners
- people from the same or similar socio-economic class, ethnic group, religion, sporting, service, or other club, school or university, family, army unit, hobby group (e.g. CB radio)
- transient groups chatting idly in the toilets, at the photocopier, by the coffee machine
- the office jogging or bowling squad
- people who write graffiti and anonymous messages
- corridor politicians spreading the good or bad word about others or themselves
- people who enjoy being "in the know" and enjoy being known as "in the know"—that is, everyone.

An informal or unofficial organisational chart, showing relationships of power, influence and information, might thus be substantially different from a formal or official chart. This informal organisation can be very powerful. We saw in Chapter 2 how the presence of such groups, not predicted by classic organisational theory, was first officially discovered by Mayo and his associates in their investigations for the Hawthorne studies. Despite the methodological weaknesses of these studies, they did reveal useful information about how informal group norms can often be in conflict with official organisational norms, and about how often the group norms prevailed. Thus, the organisational norm or goal might be maximum output, to be stimulated by an individual piece rate wage, and the group norm might be less than maximum output for whatever reason (e.g. concern for health and safety, laziness, dislike of supervisor, working to rule, protection of an incompetent group member, dislike of a super-competent member, fear of unemployment if five employees can be shown to do the work of six, etc.). In such cases, the informal group or organisation might well prevail over the formal group or organisation, depending upon which was more powerful in controlling behaviour (see Chapters 2 and 11).

The unkillable grapevine

Are informal organisations good or bad? It probably depends upon your point of view. Certainly, informal organisations are not going to go away. As Davis (1981) has pointed out, organisations cannot fire the grapevine because they did not hire it—it is just there. Obviously the informal organisation fulfils a number of human needs. It is probable that the less those needs are fulfilled by the formal organisation, the more they will be fulfilled by the informal organisation. The strength of the informal organisation is linked to its longevity: in a very real sense, it is the same organisation as the pre-bureaucratic organisation (see Fig. 13.1). Given the managocratic or pro-management bias that prevails in most organisational research, the disadvantages of the informal organisation are usually stressed rather than the advantages. Let us consider these disadvantages (see Table 14.1).

Disadvantages

The informal organisation can work against the objectives of the formal organisation. To a considerable extent, this can be due to conflict between official leaders, who have authority or legitimate power, and informal leaders, who may exploit one or several or all of the other bases of power—expert power, referent power, reward power and coercive power (see Chapter 10). A non-management leader, such as a union official, leads a formally constituted group, and hence also has legitimate power. Informal leaders may influence opinion quite strongly, and if they perceive formal leadership to be inadequate, can influence others not to cooperate in the furthering of the formal organisation's goals. This non-cooperation can take numerous forms: go-slows, working to rule, withholding of resources, information and work-flow, vandalism, sabotage, and so on. The informal organisation can unduly pressure individuals to conform to group norms, such as reduced productivity. This conformity can be enforced by group sanctions, such as ostracising and harassing non-conformers. Related to this type of behaviour is the tendency of the informal organisation to resist change. The rumour mills trade in good and bad news, but bad news tends to travel faster and wider. Consequently, the world-view of the informal organisation is often more pessimistic and cynical than optimistic and idealist. This is particularly true when the formal management structure is non-communicative and/or incompetent, and thus allows the formation of an information vacuum and a policy vacuum. Nature (and the informal organisation) abhors a vacuum, and such vacuums are quickly filled. The informal organisation thus always

Table 14.1 Pros and cons of the informal organisation

Pro	Con
Can work with formal organisation to achieve congruent goals.	Can work against objectives of formal organisation.
Gives satisfaction and stability to work group.	Can induce conformity to group norms.
Can act as safety valve for frustrations.	Can present resistance to change.
Useful channel of communication.	Grapevine often distorts truth—
Faster channel of communication than formal networks.	amplifies rumour-mongering.
Information and work can be processed quicker than going through official channels.	Encourages bypassing of official channels—encourages queue-jumping for resources.
Lightens the workload of managers— fills in gaps in their abilities.	
Encourages managers to plan more carefully than they otherwise might.	

Source: Adapted from Davis (1981), Hodgetts (1980), Payne (1983).

expects the worst, and acts with not inconsiderable rationality in opposing changes. This opposition is, of course, misplaced when the changes are in fact for the better.

The grapevine can often distort truth, although some grapevines are remarkably effective. A useful definition of rumour (Hodgetts 1980) is

$$rumour = interest \times ambiguity$$

To start a rumour, or participate in the relaying of that rumour, you must have some interest in it. If all the facts are known, then by definition there is no ambiguity. However, if only some of the information is present, then ambiguity increases. Thus, the higher the interest of members of the grapevine, and the higher the ambiguity of the information, then the greater will be the virulence (and falsity) of the rumour. While it is true that management cannot fire the grapevine, they can drop massive amounts of fertiliser on it by not communicating properly in the first place. If there is an information vacuum, then the grapevine inherits that vacuum. The informal organisation can often achieve things quickly by bypassing the dreaded "official channels". This is a reasonably efficient strategy, so long as only a few people are jumping the queue for resources. As soon as a significant minority begin to do this, however, then the whole show collapses. Special consideration, favouritism, "jobbing" it, and black marketeering, all these processes start out by efficiently exploiting inefficiencies in the official system, and all end up by inefficiently collapsing under a surfeit of free riders, or else by surviving at the expense of corrupting everyone in the system. Rather than bypass official channels, then, it might be more efficient to examine those channels and find out just why they are not working.

Advantages

The informal organisation also has considerable advantages. Rather than compete with the formal organisation, it can, in certain circumstances, complement the activities of the formal organisation.[1] Specifically, it can support particular managers, providing expertise where that manager is not strong. Thus, an informal group, with its "collective memory" of procedures, techniques and short-cuts, can prove invaluable to a manager when she is just learning the job and, indeed, for a good time after that.

The informal group can also provide a sense of cohesion, satisfaction and stability to a group that might be lacking, for example, in a large, impersonal bureaucracy. It can act as a safety valve for frustrations that do not seem to be listened to by the official hierarchy. The informal organisation often gets rumours right and, where official channels of communication are notoriously undependable, then the grapevine becomes indispensable.

The informal organisation can often get things done more quickly than is possible through official channels. This is not always a good thing, as discussed above. Sometimes the margin of efficiency over the official system is due to deliberate sub-maximising behaviour by the informal group (e.g. to ensure preservation of existing, albeit inefficient, staffing levels), but as often as not it is simply a case of the grass roots of the organisation knowing best how to get a job done—it's just that no one in management ever officially asked for their advice.

---

[1] The informal organisation might die, or at least begin to wither away, says Likert, if a truly participatory decision-making structure exists in an organisation. See the discussion of Likert's system 4 theory in Chapter 10.

Finally, the informal organisation is a powerful countervailing force in a political sense, similar to unionism. Management knows that the informal organisation has enormous inertia and rat cunning (and perhaps plain common sense), so that any planning for change should take into account the needs, values and opinions of the informal organisation. This means that managers have to plan more carefully than they might otherwise have done, which is always a bonus.

Kouzmins (1983) points out that most management literature and research starts from a unitary notion of the organisation: everyone pursues official goals, conflict is abnormal, and hence informal groups are deviant. Yet if a pluralist view is adopted—conflict is normal, the organisation is a loose federation of forces—then informal groups are seen to be quite normal and rational.

The understanding of the informal organisation, then, complements our understanding of organisations gained through such classic concepts as economies of scale, and staff and line. Another concept which eluded the classic analysts of organisations was that of the role of technology in determining the structure of organisations.

The technological imperative

Some of the classic analysts of organisations, such as Taylor, were engineers by trade, and hence saw organisational structure as being substantially determined by technology—the optimal layout of machinery, facilitating maximum throughput of workflow, was the central principle of planning. It is a paradox, then, that Taylor and others did not pursue this technological determinism further, inquiring, for example, whether different types of technology determined different types of management style, personnel and communication. Indeed, the human relations oriented writers who came after the classic organisational experts went to the other extreme, de-emphasising technological factors and emphasising, perhaps overemphasising, the human side of the enterprise. Recent work has begun to reverse this trend, shifting the attention back to technology, although not neglecting "soft" human variables. Probably the most important work done in this area is that of Woodward (1965), although significant work since has been done by Thompson (1967), Perrow (1970), Lawrence and Lorsch (1967), Pugh *et al.* (1976), Blau *et al.* (1976) and Child (1984).

Woodward and her associates studied almost 100 British manufacturing firms in the 1950s and 1960s. In analysing these firms, they used various models of organisational design, such as Burns and Stalker's organic–mechanistic distinction (see Chapter 13). There did not seem to be any correlation of design with performance, however; whether firms were organic or mechanistic did not seem to have any bearing upon their success or failure. Woodward and her associates began to develop their own model of design, based upon the different types of technology used. They divided firms into three categories:

1. *Unit and small batch production:* these made custom-made products, prototypes, and one-off items—custom-built cars, engineering templates, etc.
2. *Mass and large-batch production:* these produced large numbers of items, usually on assembly lines—mass-produced cars, appliances, etc.
3. *Process and continuous flow production:* these produced goods in a continuous flow—petroleum products, chemicals, paper, etc.

Table 14.2 Woodward's analysis of British manufacturing organisations

	Small-batch	*Large-batch*	*Process*
Span of control	narrow	wide	narrow
Departmentation	functional	divisional	functional
Conflict/stress	low	high	low
Organisational design	organic	mechanistic	organic

Source: Adapted from Woodward (1965).

Significant differences seemed to emerge when these three types of organisation were compared on criteria such as span of control, departmentation, conflict/stress, and mechanistic/organic features (Table 14.2). Thus, spans of control were narrow in small-batch production, became wide in mass-production, and narrowed again for process production. Departmentation was more functional for small-batch and process, more divisional for mass-production. The mass-production organisations tended to have bad industrial relations, and interpersonal conflict seemed more common than at the other two types of organisations. Finally, the mass-production organisations tended to be more mechanistic than organic, while the other two were more organic than mechanistic (see Table 14.2). The technology seemed to be the prime determining factor in all of these phenomena. Thus, small-batch organisations were small in scale, employees tended to be highly skilled, and worked in small groups with good communication and high morale. The span of control was narrow, but this was more a function of the size of the groups than a punitive management philosophy. Process industry workers also tended to be highly skilled, and the continual arising of non-routine problems led to narrower spans of control but greater variety in work tasks. The routine nature of the work in mass-production organisations led to wider spans of control and such mechanistic features as clear-cut job duties.[2]

Later work, such as Pugh *et al.* (1976) and Child (1984), has modified the thrust of Woodward's work. It appears, for example, that the Woodward model may only apply to relatively small organisations. Once organisations get really large, technology may cease to be the critical factor in organisational design, and the bigger an organisation becomes, the more mechanistic it will be also (Miles 1980). Also, Woodward's study pertained only to manufacturing organisations, and hence was limited in this regard. Nevertheless, the study emphasised that in studying the variables or contingencies or organisational design, it was necessary to consider technical as well as social or psychological factors (see discussion of sociotechnical systems in Chapter 12).

Lee has suggested a third variable: the self-selection of employees in particular industries. Speaking in the United States context, he notes that one finds many Anglo rural westerners and southerners in a field like mining engineering, but few orthodox Jews. This situation is partially reversed in fields such as electronics engineering. Thus the populations of different

---

[2] Hampton (1981) has noted the paradox that the more an industry lays out workflow on a mass-batch basis, the lower the job satisfaction of workers and the greater the vulnerability of that industry to disruption by disgruntled workers (the longer the chain, the more vulnerable it is at various weak links). How vulnerable might small-batch and process industries be to such behaviour? Cf. also Reich's advocacy of small-batch production—on a mass scale—as the solution to the productivity crisis in advanced Western industrial nations (Chapter 13).

industrial workforces may not be randomly distributed, but may be pre-determined by factors such as culture, socio-economic class, personal style of decision-making and problem-solving (see Chapter 9) and so on. This would mean that different sets of values and world-views prevailed in differing organisations and industries, predetermining, or at least strongly influencing, the normal or ideal organisational design (Lee 1980).

Participation, industrial democracy, self-management

The classic or bureaucratic view of organisations held that all power rested naturally at the apex of the hierarchy. Management and labour were presumed to have diametrically opposite and contradictory interests, with management firmly in control of labour. Labour has tended to operate as a countervailing force, sometimes weaker than management, sometimes stronger, but basically operating reactively to management. Labour, like management, is by no means a monolithic force: some areas of the non-managerial workforce have the explicit aim of achieving worker control through politically installed socialism, while other areas have been content to allow managerial power to flourish, preferring to negotiate with management for piecemeal reforms and satisfactory resolution of "bread and butter" issues—wages, health and safety conditions, and so on.

Management power has come under challenge not only from politically radical unionists, however. Social scientists investigating motivation, decision-making, leadership, group dynamics and the design of jobs and organisations have often concluded that greater participation by workers in the hitherto sacred realms of managerial decision-making can have positive payoffs for organisations in terms of such things as job satisfaction, efficiency, productivity, and reduction of feelings of alienation and patterns of conflict.

Such changes are due partly to changing perceptions about the role of organisations. The Australian industrialist, Rod Carnegie, has noted that the traditional idea of private enterprise organisations considering only the interests of investors and shareholders is now outdated. Carnegie sees the organisation not operating in a vacuum, but intimately related to its environment; as such, there are not one, but six stakeholders to be considered:
1. the people who work in the enterprise;
2. the people who manage it;
3. the people who invest in it;
4. the people who supply it;
5. the people who buy from it;
6. the people who live near it. (QUOTED IN LANSBURY 1980)

Toffler reaches similar conclusions, in talking about the "trans-economic objectives" of the new organistion (see Chapters 1 and 13).

Industrial democracy: An inevitable revolution?

Consideration of such objectives, such diverse stakeholders, means that the contemporary organisation may well be undergoing changes similar to those undergone by political states in the past few centuries. Only a few centuries ago, virtually all states were ruled by autocratic, monarchical systems of government. Monarchy in many countries has been replaced by other systems of government, most of which claim to be democratic systems representing the will of the people. In many Western democracies, there has even been considerable discontent with such representative systems in the past decade or so; perceiving the limitations of politicians acting on behalf of electors, many have been demanding a more "participatory democracy", which can mean many things, but usually means more direct involvement in government decision-making by individuals and groups in the community. Commentators such as Haire (1962) have claimed that this model of political evolution is relevant to organisations. Thus, Haire sees power in organisations shifting inevitably from autocratic control to democratic control. Organisations in the future will not adhere to the classic model of the authoritarian pyramid, with managers with pharaoh-like powers seated at the top; power will be democratically shared by all: "The final control will be self-control."

The unionist, Ducker, has noted that there is a fundamental conflict between political democracy—which everyone shares through the ballot box—and industrial autocracy—where democracy ends at the factory gate. This conflict must reach a crisis, Ducker believes, so that by the end of the twentieth century, capitalism as we know it will have encountered its demise, management will have been transformed, and industrial democracy will prevail in the workplace (Ducker 1975).

But in fact is there a clear and unstoppable trend towards industrial democracy, towards total participation in organisational decision-making by non-managerial personnel? This is by no means clear. There is a wide variety of experience with systems of participation and industrial democracy, some positive and some negative. Indeed, whether the experience is positive or negative usually depends upon your point of view and your vested interests. Experiences vary enormously from country to country, as well: a successful participation scheme evolved in one country may or may not be directly transferable to another country, for a variety of reasons. The success or failure of a participation scheme may depend upon global or local economic conditions. Is it true, as Byrt (1980) and Ramsay (1980) assert, that worker participation schemes and participative management styles are fashions that quickly become unfashionable in hard economic times such as the 1970s have been, the 1980s are, and the 1990s may be? Let us examine these issues in greater detail.

Participation, industrial democracy and power

First, what do we mean by "participation" and "industrial democracy"? What is the difference between the two terms? Management theorists such as Likert (1967), Tannenbaum and Schmidt (1958) and Vroom and Jago (1979) have approached participation from the point of view of leadership. These analysts argue that leadership styles can vary considerably, from autocratic, or at least individual, decision-making, to participatory or group-oriented decision-making, where the leader or superior accepts, to a greater or lesser extent, decision-making input from followers or subordinates (see Chapters 9, 10 and 11). The view adopted by Likert and others is that participation is a top–down process, introduced and controlled by management. Thus, the balance of power between leader and led remains fundamentally unchanged, and any differences between experiments labelled "participatory" and "industrial democratic" are differences of degree, not kind.

Likert and others are sometimes classified as belonging to the "human relations" and/or "organisational development (OD)" schools of thought. Cole *et al.* (1983) argue that the limitation of this approach is that it ignores the question of power, trivialising the issue as one of neutral organisational "style". Cole *et al.* see the differences between participation and industrial democracy as differences of kind, rather than degree. To this end, they develop a model of organisations which distinguishes between *management*

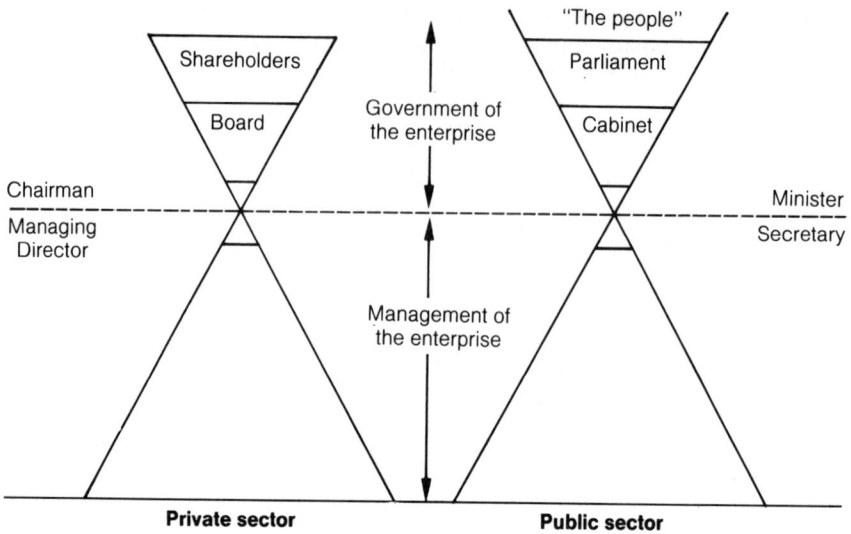

Fig. 14.1 *A model of organisation* (COLE, CROMBIE, DAVIES AND DAVIS 1983, P.4, REPRODUCED WITH PERMISSION)

of organisations or enterprises and *government* of organisations or enterprises (Fig. 14.1). This "hour-glass" model is used to show that control of organisations is a larger matter than the blanket term "management" implies. The government level of the "enterprise" (a term describing private and public sector organisations) determines what the organisation is going to do, and the management system does it. There are obvious and interesting exceptions to this model, but these can be ignored for the moment. The distinction between participation in management and industrial democratic control of government of the (private) enterprise becomes dramatically clear when takeovers and mergers occur, as they have been doing with great rapidity in the past five or so years. In such circumstances, it does not matter how much participation in decision-making has been enjoyed by workers: control has changed hands, and they are totally unable to do anything about it. Similar considerations prevail in the public sector when there is a change of (political) government.[3] Thus the factor which separates participation from industrial democracy is *power*: participation usually does not entail a shift in the balance of power within the organisation, whereas industrial democracy does. Indeed, many representatives of organised labour would argue, without the question of power being tackled, many "participation" schemes are worse than useless: they are in fact more subtle means of extending management control and manipulation. Thus, the Australian Council of Trade Unions Congress of 1980 decided that many organisational change techniques currently being experimented with were not so much concerned with increasing the discretionary decision-making power of workers as they were concerned with consolidating the power of managerial elites, and

---

[3] This raises the thorny issue of industrial democracy, and even participation, in the public sector: unelected people sharing power with elected people has perhaps even more problems associated with it than private enterprise employees sharing power with private enterprise employers.

increasing (but not sharing) organisational profits. The ACTU saw these techniques as including most approaches to

* organisation development
* management by objectives
* employee shareholding schemes
* "improved" communication systems
* so-called information sharing systems
* management "open door" policies
* suggestion box schemes
* profit sharing schemes (ACTU 1982)

Motivations of participators and democrats

Differences of definition over just what is "participation" and "industrial democracy" arise partly because different definers have different motivations. Cole *et al.* suggest that there are four main movers in the field of participation and industrial democracy—management, unions, participation professionals and government. In Australia, at least, government has been the least important or rather the least prominent of these four groups. The other three have overlapping interests but, because they have differing motivations, they also have conflicting interests (Fig. 14.2). Thus, the participation professionals—academics, consultants, personnel managers, government officials, and others—espouse a human relations ideology, working towards the liberal, reformist aim of "improving the quality of worklife". This group began to become a force in Australia in the 1960s and 1970s. They saw scientific management practices leading to dehumanisation of the workforce, and consequently low morale and job satisfaction. This in turn led to low productivity, they argued; it was simply bad human resources policy to lock workers out of the decision-making process if their inclusion in the process would lead to greater happiness on the job and also higher productivity.

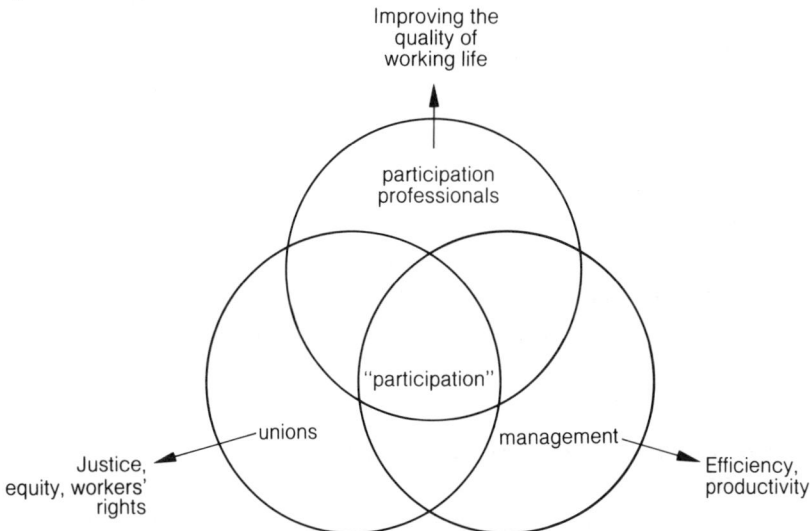

Fig. 14.2 *Motivations of "participators": Differing perspectives* (COLE, CROMBIE, DAVIES AND DAVIS 1983, P.11. REPRODUCED WITH PERMISSION)

Management had different preoccupations. Job satisfaction as an end in itself was not so important to management as job satisfaction as a means to an end—higher productivity. Thus, management has been willing to experiment with participation, but usually only in terms of changes in "managerial style" or "leadership style", that is, no real transfer of power is involved. Management has been the main patron of the participation professionals. While this has ensured the nurturing of many fertile ideas on participation and industrial democracy, it has also led critics such as Baritz and Carey to accuse the professionals of being the "servants of power", that is, intellectual scabs who have produced unscientific and biased models of motivation, leadership, group dynamics and decision-making that serve the interests of management but are inimical to the interests of labour (Baritz 1960; Carey 1976, 1980; see also Chapters 2, 10 and 11).

Trade unions have a still different motivation. Historically, they have been concerned with the issues of justice, equity, workers' rights, health and safety, and so on. They have seen, more than the participation professionals, that participation and industrial democracy are industrial relations problems, and thus are concerned with the clear-cut issue of power rather than the amorphous issues of "managerial style", "organisational climate", and so on.

Cole *et al.* note that most experiments with participation in the 1960s and 1970s were at the behest of private sector management, operating through the participation professionals. Firms such as ICI, Shell, Alcan, Alcoa, Philips, Leyland and ACI experimented with job and organisational design. This willingness to experiment was partly due to the fact that most organisations involved were not indigenously Australian but were transnational corporations, and job and organisational redesign undertaken in Australia were part of the global commitment of such TNCs to the humanisation of the workplace (cynics suggested that TNCs were in fact merely more skilled manipulators of the workforce than Australian organisations). In the 1980s, the initiative seems to have shifted to unions, particularly public sector unions, such as the Australian Telecommunications Employees Association, Australian Railways Union (Victoria), Public Servants' Association (South Australia), etc. These organisations sometimes deliberately eschew terms like participation and industrial democracy, preferring instead to concentrate on substantive workplace issues such as

- health and safety
- disclosure of information
- equal opportunities
- new technology
- participation in enterprise level planning
- reorganisation
- shop stewards' rights (COLE ET AL. 1983)

These issues are of course so far-reaching that they are more properly the domain of government of enterprises rather than management of enterprises (Fig. 14.1).

Participation in industrial democracy in four countries

Differences in definitions of participation and industrial democracy are not always due to different motivations retained by different actors. Larger factors, such as culture and political traditions, can also be crucial. The experiences of participation and industrial democracy can be quite different in different countries. This is shown by a comparison of "alternative organisations" in Sweden, Yugoslavia, Israel and the United States, four nations that could be classified under the heading of "Western culture". The organisational designs of a non-Western culture—Japan—are considered later in this chapter.

Miles (1980), drawing upon Tannenbaum *et al.* (1974) and other sources, has developed a comparison of "shop-floor democracy" in Sweden, "worker self-management" in Yugoslavia, the kibbutz program in Israel, and job design experiments in the United States (Table 14.3). The Australian context shares features of the Swedish and United States systems.

Sweden

The shop-floor democracy experiments of Sweden are most obvious to the world at large in the famous experiments at Volvo and Saab, two automobile manufacturers (see Chapter 12). Miles stresses that Sweden's experience, like that of any country, is best understood in terms of the pervasive socio-economic ideology of that country. This point is worth bearing in mind, particularly when one considers that the vast majority of research and literature on management and organisations is of United States origin, and hence may be of little use (or worse than useless) in understanding other cultures. Thus, in Sweden, the semi-autonomous work group concept at the factory floor level is supported by an industrial relations tradition of a cooperative, rather than an adversary relationship between labour and capital, and a sociopolitical tradition of strong government intervention in the economy to effect redistributions of resources and power. This power may shift still further in the near future, much further than was the case with simple job redesign. Sweden has been suffering from the world recession like other nations, and has to handle the problems of shrinking profits, inflation and wage demands. The Swedish trade unions, which traditionally have had close links with the ruling Social Democratic Party, have proposed a program of wage restraint in return for legislation that facilitates workers buying partial ownership of industry. Within a generation, worker ownership may be a quite substantial if not the predominant mode of organisational design[4] (Kuttner 1983; Albrech and Deutsch 1983).

Yugoslavia

Yugoslavia, like Sweden, has a mixed economy—partly capitalistic, partly socialistic. Whereas Sweden approached socialistic and government controls from a capitalist base, Yugoslavia has become more capitalistic after experimenting with Soviet-style socialism. Yugoslavia's leader during and after World War II, Marshal Tito, originally was committed to installing a central-ised command economy on the Russian model. Tito perceived, however, that socialism did not necessarily mean a permanent abolition of capitalist-type elites and hierarchies, wherein a small ruling group had access to a dis-proportionately large fraction of wealth and resources; indeed, Tito saw the same type of elites emerging in socialist Russia. Risking Russian wrath (and indeed invasion), Tito shifted the Yugoslavian economy in the 1950s to a more decentralised system, wherein worker-controlled collectives sold goods and services through a semi-capitalist market economy (Miles 1980).

---

[4] Thus stock ownership facilitates worker control—a form of socialism. US President Ronald Reagan, however, feels that employees owning stock is the essence of capitalism (see Chapter 2).

Table 14.3 The context of alternative organisations in four countries

Host country "innovation"	Pervasive ideology	Role of unions	Labour–management relations	Nature of workforce	Economic system	Existence of managerial elite	Legal bases
Sweden "Shop-floor democracy"	"Welfare socialism" Heavily taxed and regulated private sector; income redistribution policy	Highly organised for employers and major working groups	Centralised, national-level negotiations; stable and collaborative coexistence	Homogeneous, secure, educated, with high expectations of work	Mixed; private ownership under heavy government regulations and taxes; developed	Yes—separate unions and distinction on basis of education	Laws regulating negotiations between labour and management, but not to support "shop-floor" experiments
Yugoslavia "Worker self-management"	"Titoism" Social ownership and worker self-management	Party affiliated with emergent role to protect society's interests	"Labour manages"; most disputes handled within the organisation by elected worker representatives	Heterogeneous and transitional	Market socialism: social ownership and planning with price system for distributing goods; developing	Some evidence that one is emerging	Social ownership and worker self-management is constitutionally mandated
Israel "The kibbutz"	"Zionism" Communal living and self-management	None	Shared values and social control to deal with most situations; otherwise referred to general assembly	Heterogeneous in origin, homogeneous in values; secure, educated, with high expectations	Mixed; government ownership of core industries; transitional	No—manager jobs are rotated	None; but role of kibbutz in Israeli life is widely recognised
United States "Voluntary and experimental work redesign programs"	"Capitalism" Private ownership; individualism is highly valued	Minority of workers are unionised; emphasis on "bread-and-butter" issues	Collective bargaining between union and management at organisational level	Educated; high living standard; mixed expectations of work	Free enterprise based on price system of resource allocation with selected government regulations	Strong—based on professional management training and expertise; management on behalf of owners	Minimal; laws sanctioning unions; innovations in organisation design at discretion of local management

From: Macro Organizational Behaviour, Table 14·1, pp.442—443, by Robert H. Miles. Copyright © 1980 by Scott, Foresman and Company. Reprinted by permission.

Thus Tito, like another socialist reformer, Mao Tse Tung, tried to forestall the growth of bureaucratic hierarchies and elite, centralised control.

Workers elect their representatives to serve on self-management councils. These worker-managers serve for only two years, when they must stand down and allow others to take their place. In spite of this strategy to prevent the emergence of a self-serving managerial elite, Mintzberg and others have detected the rise of such an elite, although it is obviously not as entrenched as it is in capitalist economies. The elites in particular are government officials ("apparatchiks") who coordinate the decentralised collectives (Mintzberg 1983). Goods and services are sold for money prices through a market system. Profits are allocated to provide base salaries, and then consideration is given to bonuses or margins for individuals, work groups and companies. This can sometimes lead to a worker making two or three times the salary of a neighbour who works at a less successful enterprise.

The role of unions is most interesting: while theoretically unions would have no role in a worker self-managed state, the Yugoslavian union structure is closely linked to the ruling political party, and, being thus aware of large-scale or macro-economic imperatives, often acts as a restraint upon worker-managers who wish to channel profits into salaries rather than investments.

Israel

The kibbutzes of Israel are perhaps the most advanced forms of industrial democracy in the world. They are interesting not only in their own right, but because the Federal Labor government installed in Australia in 1983 has toyed with the idea of introducing kibbutz-style farming and industrial ventures to cope with youth unemployment.[5]

Kibbutzes in Israel are communal agricultural or industrial enterprises. There are about 250 of them, with the average size being around 300–400 people. Historically, they derive from the ideology of Zionism, which emphasised agricultural land ownership, so often denied to Jews in Europe, and self-sufficiency (Miles 1980; Stryjan 1983). They are often quite productive, producing one-third of Israel's agricultural produce and one-twelfth of its industrial produce. They are run on explicitly anti-hierarchical lines: both managerial jobs and boring and unsatisfying jobs are rotated regularly. Thus, managerial elites do not often form, mainly for the reason that many people have managerial expertise due to rotation. Collective decision-making is thus often of a high calibre. All income from the kibbutz enterprise goes into a common fund. Workers draw personal expenses, but not salary as such. Motivation to work is more of the intrinsic kind (job satisfaction) rather than of the extrinsic kind (money incentives); see Chapters 2 and 12. Most kibbutzniks are aware or at least believe that increasing the scale of an enterprise can only lead to bureaucratisation. Consequently, there is a preference for capital-intensive rather than labour-intensive industry, and a distinct dislike for organisations that exceed the Parkinsonian threshold of 1000 people.[6] Small is thus perceived to be not only beautiful, but efficient.

United States of America

American experiments with alternative organisations have not been as far-reaching as the Swedish, Yugoslav and Israeli ventures. They tend to be micro

---

[5] See *Age* and *Sydney Morning Herald*, 14 June and 21 July 1983.
[6] Once an organisation exceeds 1000 people, it becomes large enough to transact only with itself, and thus ignore the outside world (Parkinson, 1980, p.2).

rather than macro in approach, in two ways: they have been job redesign experiments run by individual corporations rather than part of a government-sponsored program of social redesign; and they tend to focus on individuals and small groups, rather than large groups, industries and industrial sectors. Miles attributes this latter emphasis to the fact that United States ventures tend to be controlled by psychologists, whereas sociologists tend to be more active in other countries (Miles 1980).

American cultural and political factors, like such factors in other countries, have largely predetermined these outcomes. Thus, the United States has strongly entrenched values of capitalism and individualism; there is widespread suspicion of government intervention in the open market; levels of unionisation are quite low compared to other countries; and there is a strong separation between management and labour, reinforced by such factors as line-staff rivalries and expensive and thoroughgoing management education programs.

Nevertheless, there have been extensive experiments with job enrichment, job redesign, and semi-autonomous work groups. Several of these are mentioned in Chapter 12, such as the General Foods pet food plant in Topeka. This venture featured the development of semi-autonomous work groups, which assumed responsibility for planning, scheduling, maintenance, as well as drudgeries such as cleaning. Pay increases were linked to the number of skills mastered, which led to multiskilling of the group members and undercut any emergent demarcation disputes. Nevertheless, the experiment met with mixed success. It was also carried out in a non-union situation, with no profit-sharing, and with supervisors appointed by management rather than elected by workgroups.

Other alternative organisations in the United States have emerged outside the structure of management-initiated job redesign. Rothschild-Whitt has studied a number of "collectivist–democratic" organisations such as alternative newspapers, free clinics and food cooperatives and noted their explicitly anti-bureaucratic structure (Rothschild-Whitt 1979). Such collectives often draw upon the counter-culture values that emerged in the United States in the 1960s, when many agricultural and urban communes were established as alternatives to conventional work organisations and the nuclear family. Zwerdling (1980) and Tannenbaum (1983) have studied such organisations, as well as a range of worker cooperatives that are often the product of workers buying out enterprises either bankrupted or weakened by the recession which began in the mid-1970s. Mintzberg (1983) notes that United States "corporate democracy" has been more characterised by representation of *external* interest groups (e.g. "public interest" directors, community representatives on decision-making panels) than of *internal* employees.

Participation: Pros and cons

We have considered the distinction between management and government of enterprises, plus the cultural contexts and group value orientations of the participation question. All the information is, however, not in yet. Let us consider the pros and cons of participation listed in Table 14.4. The cons seem to outweigh the pros, but it is worth bearing in mind that quantity does not equal quality in this or any other argument. Also it should be noted that various degrees and kinds of participation and control are considered in this table.

Table 14.4 Participation, pro and con

Pro	Con
• Increases job satisfaction • Increases efficiency • Increases commitment to decision-making • Decreases alienation • Decreases conflict • Trains people in democratic processes • Solves conflict between political democracy and industrial autocracy • Makes organisation more socially responsive • Makes organisation more legitimate by exercising "mandate of the governed" • May increase management control • May increase labour control • May allow labour and management to see~~other~~ point of view • Removes obnoxious master–servant relationship of workplace	• Alleged effects on satisfaction, efficiency, conflict, decision-making, alienation, not proven • Increases time for decision-making • Blurs responsibility, accountability • May increase bureaucratisation, centralisation • Possiblity of de-participation, industrial anarchy, and a new tyranny • May substitute peer group pressure for management control • May be expensive • Might make organisation less socially responsive • May kill entrepreneurial drive • May be limited by workflow technology • May increase management control • May increase labour control • May politicise technical questions • May jeopardise security of information, e.g. re new product • Worker representatives may be socialised into management viewpoint, i.e. neglect their constituency, not report information • Ignores property rights—illegitimate transfer of power from rightful owners • Difficult legal problems re control, responsibility • Loss-sharing, dismissal, etc., may be fudged • Unless labour is democratised, may lead to simple replacement of malign management elite by malign labour elite • May ignore needs and motivations of special groups, e.g. migrants, women, part-time workers, unemployed, religious groups

Source: Adapted from O'Shaughnessey (1979), Lansbury (1980), Ford (1980), Byrt (1980), Cole *et al.* (1983), ACTU (1982), Lee (1980), Mintzberg (1983).

Satisfaction, involvement, control versus pacification

The most obvious advantages of participation are that, by involving the maximum number of people in decision-making, it increases job satisfaction, efficiency and commitment to such decisions, while reducing the conflict and feelings of alienation so common in more classic organisational designs. The difference is, if you like, between the way a worker drives a company car and the way she drives her own; if the company car *is* her own in some way, her behaviour changes.

Workers can also learn to be better citizens by understanding and participating in democratic decision-making. By becoming aware of the "multiple bottom lines" that Toffler and Carnegie have referred to, the organisation may become more responsive to its social responsibilities. By simply involving employees in decision-making, the organisation may be like a political government that claims legitimacy because it has a mandate from its constituents; this may remove the adversary relationships many organisations have with their workforce, customers and community.

Depending upon your point of view, participation is a good thing because it increases labour control of management and/or management control of labour. Labour control of management occurs in some participation programs, particularly if those programs involve government rather than just management of the enterprise, to use Cole *et al.*'s language. Representatives of labour might see this as a good thing, insofar as labour would not make as many arbitrary and unjust decisions as management, and indeed, given that workers are so close to their jobs, labour might well make more technically competent decisions than management.

Management control of labour might occur where "worker pacification" rather than worker participation occurs (O'Shaughnessey 1979). As the ACTU has noted, many attempts at job redesign and participation have increased, rather than decreased, management control over labour. Many in management might see this as a good thing—giving the illusion of decision-making power to the incompetent, while retaining real power for the competent. One of the key tests to see if this factor is operating is to see whether participation has increased productivity and, if so, how have the gains from that productivity increase been distributed?

Breaking down barriers

Finally, participation is a good thing in that it helps break down the adversary relationship of the traditional labour/management, working class/ruling class social model; the other side is seen to be quite human, and everything can be solved by intelligent negotiation predicated upon shared, rather than conflicting interests. The legal anomaly of two people having equal rights outside the workplace but unequal rights within the workplace—the master–servant relationship enshrined in employment laws—is removed.

Do people really want participation?

The arguments *against* participation are numerous, but as has already been suggested, numbers do not necessarily equal weight. The alleged effects on satisfaction, efficiency, conflict, decision-making and alienation are not necessarily proved. It is not apparent that all workers want to participate in decision-making—some want a pay-cheque at the end of the week, a quiet life, and not much else. Even if workers did participate in making decisions, there is no guarantee that they will abide by them (the same of course applies to management). Decision-making takes longer as more people are involved, so participatory decision-making may be more time-consuming (Marchington and Loveridge 1979). Time is money, so it may be more expensive.

Bureaucracy, industrial anarchy, and . . . a new tyranny?

Because decision-making may lose flexibility (or adhocery, depending upon your point of view), formalisation may occur; if this happens, as Mintzberg points out, participatory decision-making may in fact end up being *more* bureaucratic and centralised than managocratic decision-making, not less (Mintzberg 1983).

A worse-case scenario for industrial democracy would be that decisions would become not only expensive, long-winded, bureaucratic and centralised, but impossible. An organisation could go broke if it spent too much time in deciding and not enough in doing. The rank and file might become exhausted with endless meetings, and instead of voting with their hands, vote with their feet. This de-participation could lead to industrial anarchy, or even worse, to a new type of authoritarianism, where industrial democrats with strong power drives and cast-iron backsides are the only workers left in the smoke-filled rooms of power, and thus become the new masters (either alone, or in concert with the old management-appointed masters). The spectacle of revolutionary democrats becoming reactionary authoritarians is not without precedent in history (see also p.458).

Evasion of responsibilities?

Responsibility may become blurred: incompetent managers will have a ready-made scapegoat to hand to evade responsibility for hard decisions (O'Shaughnessey 1979). The hard decisions may also be baulked at because of the group dynamics of conformity, timidity and the hidden agendas of various vested interests.

Mintzberg notes that survey data on worker-directors in Yugoslavia and Peru reveals that social impacts of production was ranked far below profitability in both countries—much the same as it might be with managocratic capitalist directors. Mintzberg suggests that it is plausible that an all-worker board controlling a monopoly could well give customers a hard time, just as an all-customer board could give workers a hard time. The critical thing is then, as always, to establish a balance of interests—but in whose interests would that balance of interests be established? (Mintzberg 1983).

Is technology intrinsically authoritarian?

Mintzberg has also offered one of the most powerful arguments against participation—that of the very technology of workflow. He notes that "machine bureaucracies" or mechanistic/large-batch organisations are extremely structured in their workflow. The technological imperatives, in other words, give very little latitude for discretionary decision-making by workers or individuals in groups. Technology is intrinsically autocratic: we are tools of our tools, no more. How true is this?

The sociotechnical theorists, such as Emery, would argue that this thinking is linked to the assembly-line, be it in the factory or office; remove the too-linear line, replace it with semi-autonomous work groups, and that rigidity is removed (Emery 1980). But, says Mintzberg, the worker at the Volvo plant in Kaalmo is constrained by design parameters of where the fender should go on the car, and those parameters are imposed by a management hierarchy beyond the worker's control.

Of course, it all depends what you mean by freedom and autonomy. Workers have tactical or micro autonomy at the job design level, but they may lack it at the strategic or macro level of organisational design. Yet does an elector in a democracy feel less free because she can only vote in an electorate, and not the entire nation? Also, there are degrees of autonomy, at both job design and organisational design levels. Thus, the Volvo worker has more autonomy than the United States General Foods worker, the Yugoslav worker-director has more autonomy than the Volvo worker, and the Israeli kibbutznik has more autonomy than the Yugoslav. Also, the long-term viability and efficiency of the machine bureaucracy assembly-line is called into question by critics such as Reich, who relate the assembly-line technology to the economic decline of nations such as the United States, suggesting smaller scale, more flexible systems of production, which in turn would lend themselves to more flexible, less autocratic modes of decision-making (cf Reich in Chapter 13, p.415).

Too much worker/labour power?

Further weaknesses of participation relate to the questions of worker control over management, and vice versa; this is a double-entry item, having already appeared on the "pro" side of the ledger. Entrepreneurial drive—the motivation to get up and go with an idea—may be inhibited. Simple technical questions may become politicised, becoming the bones of contention, thus further slowing down decision-making. This of course depends upon what meanings are given to "technical" and "political" matters. Security of information, for example regarding a new product, may be jeopardised if more people are involved (particularly if the loyalty of those people is somewhat ambivalent). Management's prerogatives may be violated in that participation is a challenge to property rights, that is, who owns the show, runs the show. This question, of course, is at the very heart of the political debate between capitalism and socialism. Related to such legal matters are existing laws pertaining to control and responsibility of companies which do not encompass the role of worker-directors sitting on boards and not being directly responsible to shareholders (Byrt 1980).

On the labour side, other problems arise. Will worker-directors become so used to the perks of office that they will not want to retire in favour of others? Will they lose their loyalty to their constituents on the work-floor and identify more with "the bosses"? Also, while representatives of labour sometimes see participation as the easy answer to profit-sharing, job security and the like, there do not appear to be easy answers on the opposing but linked issues of *loss*-sharing, dismissal of truly incompetent employees, and so on. Further, as Cole *et al.* (1983) and others have noted, some sections of organised labour need to put their own house in order on the question of organisational democracy. Some unions are run by elites who defend their privileges as savagely as some management elites. Michels observed in 1915 that an iron law of oligarchy seemed to prevail in many organisations such as private companies and labour unions. This law meant that, irrespective of circumstances, oligarchies or elites seemed to seize control of organisations, manipulating the apathy and/or ignorance of the majority of people in that organisation (Michels 1949). This iron law will have to be repealed if true participation is to work, in labour as well as management.

Needs and motives of special groups ignored

Finally, as Ford (1980) has pointed out, discussions of industrial democracy often ignore a number of specific groups within society, yet these groups should be ignored only at society's peril.

Migrant groups comprise large, sometimes very large, segments of the workforce of various countries. Their weakness in manipulating the language of their host country is often only one of their worries. They may not understand the legislative and statutory environment, for example, arbitration courts, collective bargaining, etc. They may come from authoritarian cultures, which makes it very difficult for them to reach the level of social assertiveness whereby they feel that it is right for them to participate in important job-related decisions.

Married women have begun to participate in the workforce in recent decades, and this rate of participation is usually higher for migrant women. Married women, due to functionally sexist behaviour at the family and social levels, usually have to cope with two jobs—the paying job and housework. This inhibits their ability to join in meetings after normal work hours, for example. The lack of social assertiveness is most apparent in migrant women workers. Ford mentions the example of Turkish women who are conditioned within their native culture not to be assertive and certainly not to converse with males other than their husbands; such women would have much difficulty with the negotiation and interaction of the processes of industrial democracy.

Another group often ignored is the growing group of *people who work part-time, shift work, evening and night work, casual work, contract work and shared work*. These people are very difficult to organise when participation schemes are proposed. Indeed, Ford suggests that management's demand for contract, subcontract and casual labour has grown partially to avoid labour legislation, and thus perhaps to avoid any type of industrial democracy.

The *unemployed* may also be disadvantaged by certain types of industrial democracy which limits rather than expands access to the workforce, for example, employment security agreements, tenured appointments. Finally, *religious organisations* may present barriers to industrial democracy, even within substantially atheistic/agnostic countries such as Australia. Ford notes that such religious or para-religious groups as the Freemasons and the (Catholic) Knights of the Southern Cross still wield a fair amount of influence in some organisations, such as state public service departments. As Ford notes, well-established power groups, formal and informal, rarely relinquish their power without a struggle (cf. section on the informal organisation, above).

Participation: The Japanese model

The Japanese "economic miracle" of the 1960s and 1970s has focused attention upon Japanese organisations and the methods used to run them. The attention given has become all the more intense as traditional Western economies, such as the United States, Britain and Australia, have witnessed declines in productivity at the same time as Japan has been in the ascendancy. The notion of "Made in Japan" connoting derivative, inferior-quality merchandise, so common in the 1950s and into the 1960s, now seems to be hopelessly wrong: Japanese merchandise in a wider range of consumer goods is often considered to be the market leader in terms of cost, design, quality and reliability. Some analysts believe that in the 1945–2000 period, the Japanese economy might well proceed from being a bombed-out hulk to being the biggest and most dynamic in the world (Kahn 1979). Consequently, there has been much talk in Western countries of how Japanese management practices and organisational designs might well be a panacea for ageing and frail occidental economies. There are, of course, obvious and substantial cultural differences between Japan and Western countries. To what extent, then, can Japanese organisational designs be transplanted to societies such as Australia?

Iida (1983) has compared Australian companies with Japanese companies in Japan and Japanese subsidiaries in Australia (Table 14.5). To effect this comparison, Iida isolated a number of characteristics of Japanese organisations, and then analysed Australian organisations and Japanese subsidiaries for the presence or absence of the same characteristics. These characteristics were:

1. *Employment system.* Many Japanese organisations have lifetime employment systems, that is, there is very low job mobility. An employee joins an organisation soon after graduating from an educational institution, and usually stays with that organisation until retirement.

2. *Seniority by length of service.* Seniority is a prime, if not *the* prime, criterion for promotion in many Japanese organisations.

3. *Number of layers to the non-supervisory white-collar employees.* As can be seen from the table, Japanese organisations in Japan are "taller" than Australian companies (although Australian companies are "taller" than Japanese subsidiaries in Australia).

4. *Job rotation.* Japanese employees, including many executives, are often rotated to other jobs in their own area or a dissimilar area. This ensures multiskilling, and a broader picture of the way segmented job roles interlock.

5. *Job task assignment.* Japanese organisations tend to assign tasks to groups of workers rather than to individuals.

6. *Managerial philosophy.* Japanese organisations usually have a coherent and explicit philosophy of what they are trying to achieve. In contrast to Western organisations, this philosophy is often quite ethical in approach. Thus, every Matsushita employee not only knows the company song, but knows that the organisation's basic business principles are "to recognise our responsibilities as industrialists, to foster progress, to promote the general welfare of society, and to devote ourselves to the further development of world culture" (Pascale and Athos 1983).

7. *Periodical recruitment.* Japanese organisations usually have long-range goals of recruiting personnel at regular intervals. To a large extent, such programs are insensitive to short-term market fluctuations.

8. *Type of intake.* Japanese organisations have specific quotas of recruitment.

9. *Importance of educational institution as a part of recruitment.* Differential status is ascribed to different educational institutions. The more prestigious the institution, the more desirable does the graduate seem to the organisation.

10. *Connections with educational institutions for recruitment.* Close and ongoing liaison is maintained between Japanese educational institutions and organisations.

11. *University qualification.* A degree is an important prerequisite for obtaining a job in Japan. It is notable that even though in Japan there are many more graduates in science and engineering than comparable Western countries, the subject area of the degree is often not considered to be crucial for management positions: greater stress is laid upon on-the-job training (Pascale and Athos 1983; Ouichi 1981).

12. *Mid-career recruits.* Due to the lifetime employment system, changing jobs in mid-career is not often seen.

13. *Decision-making.* Whereas most decision-making in Western firms is made at the top (i.e. is non-participatory), decision-making in Japanese organisations tends to be top-down *and* bottom-up (i.e. participatory). The *Ringi* system of bottom-up decision-making means that a fair amount of power is devolved to the lower echelons. While Western notions of "power" and "participation" might seem alien to some Japanese minds, it is perhaps enough to say that the opinions of people at the bottom of the hierarchy are actively solicited, listened to and acted upon: Pascale and Athos note that, in 1979, every employee of Matsushita averaged about 25 suggestions to management; most of these suggestions were rewarded with praise and financial payment, according to value (Pascale and Athos 1983).

14. *"Nemawashi" (informal and multi-cross organisational arrangements prior to the formal decision-making).* Lateral and informal communication, as well as vertical and formal communication, is an integral and legitimate process in Japanese organisational decision-making.

15. *Leadership.* The top echelons of many Japanese organisations contain managers who see their leadership role as coordinating rather than commanding. Middle management tends to be more autocratic, although this style of behaviour is not so much aggressive as paternalistic (indeed, the Japanese organisation has often been compared to a large extended family presided over by benevolent but firm "father figures"). Despite this middle management pattern, authority is more diffuse and ambiguous than in comparable Western organisations: the structure of controls is more implicit than explicit (Ouichi 1981). Similarly, job roles and hence responsibilities are not as clear-cut as in Western organisations, and this is not simply because jobs are assigned more often to groups than individuals.

16. *Company house.* Many Japanese organisations provide partly or totally subsidised housing and housing finance.

17. *Recreational facilities.* Many Japanese organisations provide recreational facilities for employees. These facilities are not simply physical facilities that may provide exercise on site during work hours, but may be social clubs and networks that structure recreation outside work sites and work hours.

18. *Company unions.* Many Japanese unions are symbiotically linked with Japanese organisations, as opposed to the adversary relationship unions and managements have in most Western countries.

19. *Company training facilities.* Japanese organisations tend to see training as an intensive and extensive activity that all must undergo on an ongoing basis. By contrast, training in Western countries is usually either episodic, irregular, under-funded, under-equipped, presumed to have taken place in educational institutions, or reserved for the top echelons of the organisation.

20. *Ratio of internal company training.* Consistent with the approach outlined above, systematic training programs are conducted almost totally in-house by full-time training professionals.

Iida notes that many of the features of Japanese organisations in Japan have not been successfully transferred to Japanese subsidiaries in Australia. Thus Australian employees seem to be uncomfortable with explicitly ethical statements of company philosophy of the Matsushita kind. Lifetime employment and seniority practices are also problematic in the Australian context

Table 14.5 The average profiles and management systems and practices of Australian companies, Japanese subsidiaries, and their parent companies

Item	Australian companies	Japanese subsidiaries	Parent companies
Employment system	Permanent/Casual/Part-time	Permanent/Casual/Part-time	Lifetime employment/Casual/Part-time
Seniority by length of service	None	None	Dominantly
The number of layers to the non-supervisory white-collar employees	4–5	3–4	6–8
Job rotation	Sometimes	Sometimes	Frequently
Job task assignment	Individual-unit	Individual-unit	Group or section-unit
Management philosophy	Seldom established	Moderately established	Highly established
Type of philosophy	Policy-oriented	Ethic-oriented	Ethic-oriented
Periodical recruitment	None	None	Highly established
The type of intake	Position-based	Position-based	Yearly quota-based
The importance of educational institution as a part of recruitment	Moderate	Low	Very high
Connections with educational institutions for recruitment	Moderately exists	None	Highly exists
University qualification	Getting important	Not important	Important

Table 14.5 The average profiles and management systems and practices of Australian companies, Japanese subsidiaries, and their parent companies (*continued*)

Item	Australian companies	Japanese subsidiaries	Parent companies
Mid-career recruits	Dominantly and majority	Dominantly and majority	Discriminary and minority
Decision-making (incl. the Ringi system)	Top down	Top down and bottom up	Top down and bottom up
Newawashi (informal and multi-cross organisational arrangements prior to the formal decision-making)	Hardly	Moderately	Frequently
Leadership pattern:			
Top management	Autocratic	Relatively autocratic	Coordinative
Middle management	Coordinative and democratic	Coordinative	Autocratic and paternalistic
Authority	Clear	Clear	Unclear and ambiguous
Responsibility	Individual and clear	Individual and clear	Individual or section-unit but unclear
Company house	Almost none	None	Highly developed
Recreational facilities	Rare	Very rare	Developed
Company union	None	None	Highly established
Company training facilities	Moderately developed	Hardly developed	Highly developed
The ratio of internal company training	Approximately half or less	One-third or less	Almost internal

Source: Iida (1983). Reproduced with permission.

(although some companies, such as Mitsubishi in South Australia and NEC in Melbourne, have negotiated productivity agreements with unions in return for "recession-proof" long-term job security; Cole *et al.* 1983). "Company unions" are contradictions in terms in the Australian experience, and other extensions of the company into the individual worker's life—company houses, recreational facilities, and so on—seem inimical to Australian values also. Iida notes, however, that the "Ringi" and "Nemawashi" systems of decision-making find favour with Australian employees. Both these practices promise substantial modification of the traditional Australian hierarchical, top-down, autocratic and vertical channels of communication and decision-making (see Chapter 12). Other observers have noted substantial differences between Western and Japanese organisational designs. Ouichi (1981) notes that career paths of Japanese employees are much less specialised than those of their Western counterparts. This practice is reinforced by the practice of job rotation. Ouichi also notes that evaluation and promotion is a slow and gradual process in Japan, whereas in the West things happen much quicker (although not necessarily for the better). Maruyama (1983) notes that employees are often evaluated on their *potential* ability rather than their demonstrated ability (a risky practice only if a thorough training program is not in place). Ouichi (1981) and Hall and Leidecker (1981) refer to *"management by walking around"*, that is, many Japanese managers are often out of the secure confines of their office and down where the action is, talking to the "real" workers who know how well or how badly things are operating. If necessary, a manager will move his desk down to a crisis area in order to better respond to situations and personalities. Managers/ executives are often rotated in jobs as well, not simply operatives at the lowest level of the hierarchy.

These practices point towards a substantial difference in the way Japanese and Western managers perceive time-frames for decision-making. Most Japanese organisations—often in concert with the Japanese government— plan and control their operations with long time-horizons, sometimes planning decades ahead. Western organisations, by contrast, often plan by the financial year, half-year or quarter, concentrating on quick payoffs and ignoring less obvious, but more important, long-term patterns of development (Reich 1983). Most decisions in Japanese organisations are reached by processes of consensus that would seem long-winded and wasteful to Western eyes, but consensus thus reached means stronger motivation to achieve the goals of the workgroup and organisation (Hall and Leidecker 1981).

Japan and the West: Cultural differences

These differences are rooted deep in the cultures of Japan and the West. Kahn (1979) notes that the "Protestant ethic" which has driven some Western countries to historically high levels of socio-economic achievement is now being surpassed on the historical stage by the "Confucian ethic" of Japan, South Korea, Taiwan, Singapore and, eventually, China. The Confucian ethic is much more group-centred than the Protestant ethic (where the focus is on individual achievement); drawing on the hierarchical discipline of Confucian norms, "neo-Confucian societies" such as Japan emphasise cooperation among complementary elements, as in an extended family, whereas Western societies are more characterised by competition among individuals (see Chapters 1 and 2).

This distinction has a lot in common with Hall's notion of "high context" and "low context" cultures (see Chapter 4). For Hall, a high context culture is one which conveys meaning not so much through spoken and written language as through the context of that language—what is not said (because "everyone" understands tacitly). High context cultures tend to be more group-centred than individual-centred, tend to have high sensory involvement (e.g. non-verbal communication patterns such as short interpersonal distance and much touching), and tend to be "polychronic" (i.e. such cultures are not obsessed with punctuality and the constraints of time, they have multiple senses of time). Low context cultures, by contrast, tend to place great emphasis on spoken and written communication, tend to be more individualistic, tend to have low sensory involvement, and are "monochronic". Low context cultures would be Switzerland, Germany, Britain, America and Australia; high context cultures would be Italy, Greece, Lebanon, Israel, Saudi Arabia, China and Japan. Country towns tend to be higher context than cities, even in low context countries. Japan does not snugly fit into the high context model. The Japanese, at least in the popular Western view, are not known for their high sensory involvement, nor are they known for a "sloppy" (from a low context viewpoint) approach towards appointments and having the trains run on time. Nevertheless, there may be more than superficial differences between Japanese and American or Australian managers in the way they structure time in planning and decision-making. There is definitely a much greater commitment to a group ethos in Japanese culture. Hall also notes that low-context Americans often complain that high-context Japanese "never seem to get to the point", for example, in business negotiations. Hall ascribes this to the rules of high context culture, which dictate that one does not spell out the obvious because this would be vulgar and patronising (Hall 1976*a*, 1976*b*).

The Japanese organisational model: Not for export?

Maruyama (1983) suggests that cultural differences are precisely why Japanese management practices and organisational designs cannot be imported into Western countries. Practices such as job rotation, collective responsibility and selection by potential ability are products of a culture that defines identity collectively rather than individually. To try uncritically to plunder Japanese experience may be also to overlook weaknesses in Japanese organisations. Maruyama notes that job security is something of a myth in some industries: Japanese blue-collar workers in large firms have less security than European white-collar workers. Tsuneo Iida (1983) notes that current "hoorah" concepts, such as job security and automatic increase of salary with length of employment, were "boo" concepts not so long ago, being considered the cause of Japanese *in*efficiency rather than efficiency.

Kamata (1983), drawing on his experience on the Toyota assembly line, argues that Japanese industry is efficient only because it has turned its workers into "human robots". Kamata paints a picture of organisations which are so paternalistic they are almost totalitarian in their control of workers' work and leisure time. Hall notes that the dark side of low-context life is obsessive individualism, characterised by alienation and loneliness; the dark side of high-context life is obsessive group-centredness, where identity is resolved only by total identification with class, family, organisation or group, or not at all (Hall 1976*a*). Kamata does not use the same anthropological terminology, but he seems to be talking about the same phenomena.

BOX 14.A: Of Japanese teams and Western individualists. . .

In recent years, Australian management has become obsessed with the success of the Japanese economy and many of us are led to believe its success is a product of the cohesiveness of Japanese society.

One manifestation of that cohesiveness is the strong bond between employees and the employer. The Japanese cult of subjecting individual interest to the common good produces a loyal, hard-working workforce.

The Japanese seem to believe that, ultimately, if the organisation benefits, so does the individual.

In Western societies, geographical mobility, economic independence, the demise of organised religions and the cult of the individual have weakened group formations and collective activity. A team in Australia is a group of individuals, not a cohesive unit.

Individualism requires different management to that needed for loyal, cohesive groups. Individualistic employees are not motivated by the well-being of their employers; they tend to be motivated by personal rewards, such as pay, status, power and responsibility.

Perhaps the greatest failing of Western management has been to manage, inappropriately, individuals who see themselves contracting to the organisation and not necessarily as an integral, loyal part of the organisation.

Motivation

Individuals use organisations for self-gratification and self-aggrandisement. Maybe Australian managers manage employees when they should be motivating individuals.

Western managers have continued to be driven by a misplaced urge to control and circumscribe each employee's contribution. One stultifying document which has come out of this tradition is the job specification or job description.

Another circumscribing management control device is predetermination of objectives for managers, many of whom operate in complex businesses subject to rapid change. Opportunism and entrepreneurship — the great benefits of individualism — are written out of too many Australian jobs.

If people have to be supervised closely, given tight job descriptions and told precisely what to achieve, then they are not worth employing.

Why employ someone you do not trust? Why employ someone who will not do what needs to be done? Far better to employ someone who out-performs you and opens up the horizons of your own business. Of course they're hard to find.

But, if you manage individuals properly and create a collaborative and supportive environment — and not police everything they do — then you may nurture your own entrepreneurs who will return to you the maximum contribution for the minimum supervision.

One consequence of the mismanagement of individuals is the undue emphasis which Western executives place on short-term performance. Short-term performance yields the greatest benefit to the individual manager, but it may not be in the long-term interest of the employer.

We are going to see significant changes to the way in which we manage individuals. Increasingly, we shall see performance-based remuneration packages.

In the United States only 38 per cent of award is comprised of salary, whereas a recent article in the Australian Accountant estimated that salary constitutes 75 per cent of Australian executives' remuneration. Employment consultants Cullen Egan Dell estimate that Australian salary will drop to 70 per cent of total remuneration by 1990.

Already, we see firms deliberately spawning enterprising break-away groups and fostering within their organisations intrapreneurship (rather like growing corporate reproductive cells). The danger, of course, is that the corporate culture of some Australian firms may reject these reproductive cells as foreign bodies.

My criticism of Western-style management is based on a belief that management has failed to tap the potential energy and creativity which individuals possess.

There is too much evidence of mismanagement, which stifles energy, kills commitment and leads to the perverse use of creativity, sometimes against the organisation's interest.

Management must learn how to activate the creative energy which is latent in most individuals.

Rigid, tightly controlled organisations are vulnerable in this age of rapid change. The order we see in the world today is orderly fluctuation. Organisations need to respond creatively to these fluctuations.

Freer

Young people in the Western world have come from freer, more liberal environments than the environments which the older generations knew.

These younger people expect to work in relatively democratic systems. They expect to be treated with respect, to be treated as equals, to be given responsibility and to work with dignity and on the basis of trust.

The key to good management is devising means of making people feel part of the organisation, that is, allowing people to identify with their employers' organisations.

In our increasingly complex and rapidly changing world, organisations, to survive and prosper, will need talent and not just people. The challenge to management is not to control independent, transient employees, but to find talent, to nurture it and to stimulate that creative energy which most of us have, but usually in suppressed form.

Source: "Old Habits Hamper Managers", James Hearn (Principal Lecturer, Faculty of Business, Royal Melbourne Institute of Technology), *The Herald*, 22 April 1986, p.20. Reproduced with permission.

Theory Z: A compromise between East and West?

Ouichi (1981) has proposed that it might be possible to combine the best features of Japanese organisations and Western organisations. American organisations, he says, are characterised by short-term employment, rapid evaluation and promotion, specialised career paths, and individual responsibility and decision-making. Japanese firms, by contrast, stress lifetime employment, slow evaluation and promotion, non-specialised career paths, and collective responsibility and decision-making. Ouichi suggests that the type Z organisation, incorporating features of American and Japanese models, is the way to go. The type Z organisation has many features, some of which are:

- development of interpersonal skills which can then be focused in decision-making and problem-solving groups, teams, committees;
- development of cohesiveness and teamwork via matrix organisation, elimination of status barriers where feasible, company uniforms, etc;
- seeking out of areas to implement participation;
- movement towards lifetime employment for certain employees;
- flattening of the organisation, away from hierarchies to "clans".

The theory Z model (Ouichi is obviously referring archly to McGregor's theory X/theory Y distinction) is a model based upon consensus and trust. Does it work? As we have just seen, the stereotyped view of Japanese organisational structure ("everyone is guaranteed a job", "there is no conflict", "workers are happy") is just that, stereotyped, with some but not a total basis in fact.

Lansbury and Spillane (1983) have suggested that theory Z won't work in America or Australia because the cultural barriers are still too great even after the "Western" aspects of theory Z are taken into account:

Appeals to workers to develop more trust and team spirit have always been popular in American (and Australian) management circles. Such appeals have been the basis of the influential human relations tradition in organisational theory. And this tradition has passed into history precisely because its advocates turn a blind eye to issues of profits and their distribution, employees' demands for more power over relevant decision-making, industrial conflict, managerial prerogatives and the deficiencies of traditional, hierarchical structures.

Theory Z offers benevolent paternalism at a time when we may be seeing the beginning of the end of "organisation man". It promotes trust and consensus at a time of bitter factional fighting, dissensus and industrial conflict. It advocates lifetime employment at a time of massive industry and job restructuring. It appeals for harmony, yet offers no suggestions as to how this might be achieved in countries (like Australia) with strong traditions of individualism, competitiveness and confrontation (LANSBURY AND SPILLANE 1983, P.246)

Summary

The classical concepts of organisational design considered in Chapter 13 (economies of scale, span of control, etc.) are quite powerful tools in the understanding of organisations, but they are not useful for understanding certain traditional and new organisational phenomena.

The informal organisation, or grapevine, for example, is often a crucial part of any organisation, operating separately from and sometimes in opposition to the structures and goals of the official organisation. Technology is a critical factor in determining whether organic or mechanistic, large-scale or small-scale organisations will flourish or perish. Participation by non-managerial staff in decision-making, and the wider concept of industrial democracy, are becoming controversial issues in private and public organisations. Such changes need to be seen against the background of power-sharing, vested interests, and cultural/national differences and similarities.

The Japanese model of organisation has become the focus of attention for many in Western countries. Japanese productivity does seem to depend upon certain organisational features such as participative decision-making, but it may not be possible to transplant such features to a different cultural matrix.

Questions for discussion

1. Under what circumstances (if any) might it be possible for the formal and informal organisation to merge?
2. Do the limitations of technology means that all large organisations must inevitably be mechanistic rather than organic?
3. What is the difference between the *management* of an organisation and the *government* of an organisation?
4. Is industrial democracy possible, or will decision-making always be the province of an individual or small group in an organisation? Is this such a bad thing?
5. How do cultural factors help us to understand participation in organisations?
6. What are the strengths and weaknesses of the Japanese model of organisation?

References

Australian Council of Trade Unions (ACTU) (1982). *Consolidation of the ACTU Policy Decisions, 1951–1982.* (ACTU: Melbourne).

Albrecht, Sandra L. and Deutsch, Steven (1983). "The Challenge of Economic Democracy: The Case of Sweden", *Economic and Industrial Democracy*, vol. 4, pp.287–320.

Baritz, L. (1960). *Servants of Power.* (Wesleyan University Press: Middletown, Conn.).

Blau, Peter, Falbe, Cecelia, McKinley, William and Phelps, Tracy (1976). "Technology and Organization in Manufacturing", *Administrative Science Quarterly*, March.

Byrt, William F. (1980). *The Human Variable: Text and Cases in Organizational Behaviour.* (McGraw-Hill: Sydney).

Carey, Alex (1976). "Industrial Psychology and Sociology in Australia", in Boreham, P. *et al.* (eds), *The Professionals in Australia: A Critical Appraisal.* (University of Queensland Press: St Lucia, Qld).

(1980). "Worker Motivation: Social Science, Propaganda and Democracy", in Boreham, P. and Dow, Geoff (eds), *Worker and Inequality: Ideology and Control in the Capitalist Labour Process.* (Macmillan: Melbourne).

Child, John (1984). *Organizations: A Guide to Problems and Practices*, 2nd edn. (Harper and Row: London).

Clegg, Stewart (1981). "Organization and Control", *Administrative Science Quarterly*, 26.

Cole, Reg, Crombie, Alastair, Davies, Alan and Davis, Ed (1983). *Industrial Democracy in Australia 1972–1992: Profiting from our Experience.* (Working Paper No. 2: A Green Paper: The Democratization of Work in Australia, Centre for Continuing Education: Australian National University, Canberra), August.

Crough, Greg and Wheelwright, Ted (1982). *Australia: A Client State.* (Penguin Books: Ringwood, Melbourne).

Davis, Keith (1981). *Human Behaviour at Work: Organizational Behaviour*, 6th edn. (McGraw-Hill: New York).

Dickson, John W. (1981). "Participation as a Means of Organizational Control", *Journal of Management Studies*, 18, 2.

Ducker, J.P. (1975). "Industrial Democracy: Utopian Vision or Living Reality?" in Gunzberg, D. (ed.), *Bringing Work to Life.* (Longman Cheshire: Melbourne).

Dunkerley, David and Salaman, Graeme (eds) (1981). *The International Yearbook of Organization Studies, 1981.* (Routledge and Kegan Paul: London).

Emery, Fred (1980). "The Assembly Line: Its Logic and our Future", in Lansbury R. (ed.) (1980).

Ford, G.W. (1980). "Industrial Democracy: Some Neglected Issues", in Lansbury, R. (ed.) (1980).

Haire, Mason (1962). "The Concept of Power and the Concept of Man", in Strother, G. (ed.), *Social Science Approaches to Business Behaviour.* (Tavistock: London).

Hall, Edward T. (1976*a*). *Beyond Culture.* (William Morrow: New York).

(1976*b*). "Interview", *Psychology Today*, July.

Hall, James L. and Leidecker, Joel K. (1981). "Is Japanese-Style Management Anything New? A Comparison of Japanese-Style Management with US Participative Models", *Human Resource Management*, Winter.

Hampton, David R. (1981). *Contemporary Management*, 2nd edn. (McGraw-Hill: New York).

Hodgetts, Richard M. (1980). *Modern Human Relations.* (Dryden Press: Hinsdale, Ill.).

Iida, Takeo (1983). "Transferability of Japanese Management Systems and Practices into Australian Companies", *Human Resource Management Australia*, August.

Iida, Tsuneo, quoted in Maruyama (1983).

Kahn, Herman (1979). *World Economic Development*. (Croom Helm: London).

Kamata, Satoshi (1983). *Japan in the Passing Lane*. (George Allen and Unwin: London).

Kouzmins, Alexander (1983). "Centrifugal Organizations: Technology and 'Voice' in Organizational Analysis", in Kouzmins, Alexander (ed.), *Public Sector Administration: New Perspectives*. (Longman Cheshire: Melbourne).

Kuttner, Bob (1983). "Making the Welfare State Work", *National Times*, 11–17 November.

Lansbury, Russell (ed.) (1980). *Democracy in the Workplace*. (Longman Cheshire: Melbourne).

Lansbury, Russell and Prideaux, Geoffrey (1978). *Improving the Quality of Work Life*. (Longman Cheshire: Melbourne).

Lansbury, Russell and Spillane, Robert (1983). *Organizational Behaviour: An Australian Perspective*. (Longman Cheshire: Melbourne).

Lawrence, Paul R. and Lorsch, Jay W. (1967). *Organization and Environment*. (Harvard Business School: Boston).

Lee, James A. (1980). *The Gold and the Garbage in Management Theories and Prescriptions*. (Ohio University Press: Athens, Ohio).

Likert, Rensis (1967). *The Human Organization: Its Management and Value*. (McGraw-Hill: New York).

Luthans, Fred (1981). *Organizational Behaviour*, 3rd edn. (McGraw-Hill: New York).

McCann, J. and Galbraith, J.R. (1981). "Interdepartmental Relations", in Nystrom, P.C. and Starbuck, W.H. (eds), *Handbook of Organizational Design, vol. 2, Remodelling Organizations and their Environments*. (Oxford University Press: New York).

Marchington, Mick and Loveridge, Ray (1979). "Non-Participation: The Management View?" *The Journal of Management Studies*, May.

Maruyama, Magoroh (1983). "Japanese Management Theories", *Futures*, July.

Michels, Robert (1949). *Political Parties: A Sociological Study of the Oligarchic Tendencies of Modern Democracy*. (Free Press: New York).

Miles, Robert H. (1980). *Macro Organizational Behaviour*. (Scott, Foresman: Glenview, Ill.).

Mintzberg, Henry (1983). "Why America Needs, But Cannot Have, Corporate Democracy", *Organizational Dynamics*, Spring.

O'Shaughnessey, John (1979). *Patterns of Business Organization*. (George Allen and Unwin: London).

Ouichi, William (1981). *Theory Z: How American Business Can Meet the Japanese Challenge*. (Addison-Wesley: Reading, Mass.).

Parkinson, C. Northcote (1980). *The Law*. (Houghton Mifflin: London).
      (1981). "Laws", in Dickson, Paul, *The Official Explanations*. (Arrow Books: London).

Pascale, Richard Tanner and Athos, Anthony G. (1983). *The Art of Japanese Management*. (Penguin Books: Ringwood, Melbourne).

Payne, R. (1983). "Organizational Behaviour", in Cooper, Cary L. (ed.), *Psychology and Management: A Textbook for Managers and Trade Unionists*. (Macmillan: London).

Perrow, Charles (1970). *Organizational Analysis*. (Wadsworth: Belmont, Calif.).

Peters, Thomas J. and Waterman, Robert H. Jr. (1983). *In Search of Excellence: Lessons from America's Best-Run Companies*. (Harper and Row: Sydney).

Pugh, D.S. and Hickson, David J. (1976). *Organizational Structure in its Context: The Aston Program I*. (D.C. Heath: Lexington, Mass.).

Ramsay, Harvey (1980). "Cycles of Control: Worker Participation in Sociological and Historical Perspective", in Boreham, Paul and Dow, Geoff (eds), *Work and Inequality: Ideology and Control in the Capitalist Labour Process.* (Macmillan: Melbourne).

Reich, Robert A. (1983). *The Next American Frontier.* (Times Books: New York).

Rothschild-Whitt, Joyce (1979). "The Collectivist Organization: An Alternative to Rational–Bureaucratic Models", *American Sociological Review,* August.

Rubenowitz, Sigvard, Norrgren, Flemming and Tannenbaum, Arnold S. (1983). "Some Social Psychological Effects of Direct and Indirect Participation in Ten Swedish Companies", *Organization Studies,* 4/3.

Stryjan, Yohanan (1983). "Self-Management: The Case of the Kibbutz", *Economic and Industrial Democracy,* vol. 4, no. 1.

Tannenbaum, Arnold S. (1983). "Employee-Owned Companies", in *Research in Organizational Behaviour,* vol. 5.

Tannenbaum, Arnold S., Kavcic, Bogdan, Rosner, Menachem, Vianello, Mino and Wieser George (1974). *Hierarchy in Organizations.* (Jossey-Bass: San Francisco).

Tannenbaum, Robert and Schmidt, Warren H. (1958). "How to Choose a Leadership Pattern", *Harvard Business Review,* March–April.

Thompson, James (1967). *Organization in Action.* (McGraw-Hill: New York).

Vroom, Victor H. and Jago, Arthur G. (1979). 'Decision-Making as a Social Process: Normative and Discriptive Models of Leader Behaviour", in Kolb, D.A, Rubin, I.M. and McIntyre J.M. (eds), *Organizational Psychology: A Book of Readings,* 3rd edn. (Prentice-Hall: Englewood Cliffs, NJ).

Woodward, Joan (1965). *Industrial Organization: Theory and Practice.* (Oxford University Press: Oxford).

Zwerdling, Daniel (1980). *Workplace Democracy: A Guide to Workplace Ownership, Participation and Self-Management Experiments in the United States and Europe.* (Harper and Row: New York).

Films/videos

The Grapevine (Video Channel).

Participative Management: We Learn from the Japanese (Brittanica Video).

Not Just a Number (Industrial Democracy), Parts 1, 2 and 3 (Amalgamated Metals Foundry and Shipwrights Union).

Consultation: It's Got to be Better (Department of Employment and Industrial Relations).

Theory Z (Training Media Services).

Part G

Conclusion: Future trends in organisational behaviour

It is of course impossible to predict the future: if, for example, we look at the scenarios of future work and society in Chapter 1, we see that they are equally plausible, even though their outcomes are wildly different. Nevertheless, it is fruitful to speculate upon changes in work and society, and how this might affect human experiences within organisations. Automation of jobs continues apace, but it is not yet clear whether automation creates or destroys jobs, and thus whether it degrades or enriches our experience of work. The question still remains unanswered as to who benefits from automation, both in the short and the long term. If automation merely throws people out of jobs and onto a minimal wage, then it is self-defeating, in that people will not have the effective purchasing power to ensure that there is an effective demand for what is supplied.

Allied to this question is that of compulsory and voluntary leisure, and the shifting of lines between the work and non-work parts of our lives. New alternatives of time and space for our work are emerging: flexitime, flexiweek, fleximonth, flexiyear, part-time work, job-sharing, sabbaticals, the electronic cottage or electronically decentralised organisation (telecommuting to your local city or one on the other side of the planet), the contractual organisation, the temporary or project organisation, the multi-job/permanent retraining career, and so on. Will we be able to choose among these options, or will the choice be made for us? Will the new work forms be less stressful and more enriching, or will they be more stressful and impoverishing? What impact will these changes have upon sex roles? Upon leisure? Upon the balance of power between new and old nations?

Emerging scarcities of resources may mean that humans will find themselves working in strange, glamorous and dangerous environments—space, underwater, in marginal land areas.

There appears to be a growth in market economics in socialist countries; will the capitalist ethic of individual money-based motivation radically change those societies?

Meanwhile, in Western capitalist countries, there are strong tendencies towards industrial democracy, and this, combined with the West's abiding infatuation with Japanese organisational forms (which involve, at the macro-economic level, greater integration of private organisations with government policy) and the increasing commitment to long-term high technology industrial planning (which also involves greater integration of private organisations with government policy), seems to indicate changes diametrically opposed to those in socialist countries.

The scale of future enterprises is by no means clear: will tomorrow's typical organisation be a small business or a global (or multi-global) corporation? Strong tendencies today towards either extreme are clearly obvious.

For so long as people choose to prevent machines mutating beyond their makers, the future is then still about people, and about how organisations can best serve the needs of people inside and outside such organisations.

New information and new models and theories will emerge to cope with these changes. Much of this will be under the convenient headings of the chapters in this book: stress management, motivation, group dynamics, organisational design, and so on. Information, models and theories will however also emerge in newer areas, or older areas taking on new leases of life, such as negotiation skills, neuro-linguistic programming, appraisal, career management, change management, and solid new disciplines (and trendy but empty fashions) we cannot even envisage yet.

If we survive, it's certainly going to be an interesting journey.

Subject index

A

Adam, 7
addictivities, 240
adhocracy, 408–14
Adult (ego state), 135–8
Aesop, 8
agentic personality, 171
aggression, 167–71
aggressive style, 179–85
agricultural revolution, 4, 12
Ain't it Awful (game), 149
alcohol, 222
Alcoholic/Addict (game), 146
Alderfer's model of motivation, 46n
America, participation in, 453–4
American exceptionalism, 323
Americentric view, x, 63–4
anal stage of personality, 132
ant and grasshopper, 8
anti-leadership vaccine, 322
Arabs, non-verbal communication of, 126–7
Aristotle, 8
assertion self-assessment matrix, 174–8
assertive style, 189–91
assertiveness, 167–99
  exercises in, 196
  limitations of, 196–8
Australia, motivation in, 64–5
automatic teller machines, 11
automation, 11, 18, 395–6
autonomous personality, 171
Avis car rentals, 49

B

baby boom, 11
barrier cross, 108
barter, 17
Bay of Pigs, 350

behaviour
  Freud's model of, 131–5
  modification of, 73–94, 320
  Skinner's model of, 75–7
behaviour modification, 73–94, 320
behaviourism, 141, 169, 225, 413
  and ethics, 90–1
Bennis' critique of bureaucracy, 408–14
bias, methodological, 35n, 40, 48, 50, 60, 347–8
biofeedback, 74, 225
biots, 19
black economy, 60–1, 65n
Blake and Mouton's model of leadership, 313–15, 320–1
Blemish (game), 144
body language, 99–100, 125n
body shape and personality, 102–03
body structure, 101–03
brain physiology, 274–6
brainstorming, 362–3
British chemical worker, 375
broken record (skill), 191
bureaucracy, 406–14, 456–7

C

CQ (creativity quotient), 276
caffeine, 222
cage-rattlers, 413
cancer and stress, 211
castration complex, 132
catastrophe theory, 292n
Catch-22, 239
centralisation, 13, 422–5
chain of command, 304, 435
chicken entrails, 315n
Child (ego state), 135–8
Chinese proverb, 99
classical conditioning, 74–6
clothing and adornment, 116–20

Index of names

A

ACTU, 455
Adair, John, 309
Adams, Kathleen, 180–3, 196, 197
Agor, Weston, 275, 276
Albanese, Robert, 308
Alberti, R., 180–3, 197
Albrecht, Sandra, 224, 451
Alderfer, Clayton, P., 46n
Allen, Woody, 31
Andre, Rae, 91, 91n
Andreatta, A.J., 388
Anschauung, Karl, 167
Appel, Marcia, 395
Ardrey, Robert, 123, 168
Argyle, Michael, 104, 105, 123, 126–7
Austin, Nancy, 180–3, 185, 188
Avery, Gayle, 337

B

Bacon, Francis, 73
Baker, Ellen, 337
Baker, Stephen, 369, 370
Bandura, Albert, 80–1
Baritz, Loren, 347, 450
Barker, Larry, 103, 106
Barnard, Chester I., 324
Baron, Robert A., 171, 327
Barrassi, Ron, 62
Barry, Bernard, 321n
Batterbury, Ariane, 118
Batterbury, Michael, 118
Bavin, Ronald A., 48
Beck, D.E., 320
Beck, Kate, 180–3
Beck, Ken, 180–3
Becker, H., 66n
Benne, Kenneth D., 340
Bennett, Dudley, 136, 144n
Bennett, John, 197n

Bennis, Warren, 408–12, 413, 414
Berne, Eric, 31n, 113, 131–65
Bhagavad-Gita, 203
Blake, Robert R., 310, 313–15, 320, 321
Blake, William, 5
Blanchard, Kenneth, 77, 88, 310, 319–21
Blau, Peter, 444
Bliss, Edwin C., 241, 252, 257, 258
Bloch, Arthur, 289–90
Bloom, Lynn, 180–3
Boenisch, E.W., 223
Bowey, Angela, 338–9
Bramson, R.M., 281n
Braude, W., 268
Braverman, H., 37, 347, 348
Briscomb, Tony, 388
Broom, Leonard, 215, 406
Brown, Barbara, 225
Brown, Paul L., 76, 88
Brown, Wilfred, 59
Burgoon, J.K., 105, 121n
Burley-Allen, Madelyn, 180–3
Burnham, David, 52
Burns, Tom, 410–11, 414, 444
Burrell, Gibson, 56
Busch, Douglas, 73
Butera, Federico, 395
Byrne, Donn, 171, 327
Byrt, William, 310, 311, 323, 327, 361, 414, 447, 455, 458

C

Cain, W.S., 106
Caldwell, Geoffrey, 64n, 65
Calero, H.H., 107, 109, 111, 114–15
Campbell, Annejet, 235
Campbell, Frank, 109
Canetti, Elias, 116
Capps, Randell, 348
Carey, Alex, 38, 40, 48, 311n, 347, 378, 386, 450